Student Solutions Manual

Laurel Technical Services

Introductory Mathematical Analysis

for Business, Economics, and the Life and Social Sciences

TENTH EDITION

Ernest F. Haeussler, Jr.
Richard S. Paul

Acquisitions Editor: *Quincy McDonald*
Supplements Editor: *Joanne Wendelken*
Assistant Managing Editor: *John Matthews*
Production Editor: *Donna Crilly*
Manufacturing Manager: *Trudy Pisciotti*
Manufacturing Buyer: *Trudy Pisciotti*
Supplement Cover Designer: *Blake Cooper*

Printed in the United States of America

10 9 8 7 6 5 4 3 2 1

ISBN 0-13-034022-7

Prentice-Hall International (UK) Limited, *London*
Prentice-Hall of Australia Pty. Limited, *Sydney*
Prentice-Hall Canada, Inc., *Toronto*
Prentice-Hall Hispanoamericana, S.A., *Mexico*
Prentice-Hall of India Private Limited, *New Delhi*
Pearson Education Asia Pte. Ltd., Singapore
Prentice-Hall of Japan, Inc., *Tokyo*
Editora Prentice-Hall do Brasil, Ltda., *Rio de Janeiro*

Table of Contents

Chapter 0

Exercise 0.2

1. True; –7 is a negative integer.

3. False, because the natural numbers are 1, 2, 3, and so on.

5. True, because $5 = \dfrac{5}{1}$.

7. False, because $\sqrt{25} = 5$, which is a positive integer.

9. True, because 0 and 6 are integers and $6 \neq 0$. *Note:* $\dfrac{0}{6} = 0$.

11. True

Exercise 0.3

1. False, because 0 does not have a reciprocal.

3. False; the additive inverse of 5 is –5 because $5 + (-5) = 0$.

5. False; $-x + y = y + (-x) = y - x$.

7. True; $\dfrac{x+2}{2} = \dfrac{x}{2} + \dfrac{2}{2} = \dfrac{x}{2} + 1$.

9. False; the left side is $x + y + 5$, but the right side is $x + y + x + 5$.

11. distributive

13. associative

15. commutative

17. definition of subtraction

19. distributive

21. $5a(x + 3) = (5a)x + (5a)(3)$
$= 5ax + (3)(5a)$
$= 5ax + (3 \cdot 5)(a) = 5ax + 15a$

23. $(x + y)(2) = 2(x + y) = 2x + 2y$

25. $x[(2y + 1) + 3] = x[2y + (1 + 3)] = x[2y + 4]$
$= x(2y) + x(4) = (x \cdot 2)y + 4x = (2x)y + 4x$
$= 2xy + 4x$

27. $a(b + c + d) = a[(b + c) + d]$
$= a(b + c) + a(d)$
$= ab + ac + ad$

Exercise 0.4

1. $-2 + (-4) = -6$

3. $6 + (-4) = 2$

5. $7 - (-4) = 7 + 4 = 11$

7. $-8 - (-6) = -8 + 6 = -2$

9. $7(-9) = -(7 \cdot 9) = -63$

11. $(-1)6 = -(1 \cdot 6) = -6$

13. $-(-6 + x) = -(-6) - x = 6 - x$

15. $-12(x - y) = (-12)x - (-12)(y)$
$= -12x + 12y$ (or $12y - 12x$)

17. $-3 \div 15 = \dfrac{-3}{15} = -\dfrac{3}{15} = -\dfrac{1 \cdot 3}{5 \cdot 3} = -\dfrac{1}{5}$

19. $4 \div (-2) = \dfrac{4}{-2} = -\dfrac{4}{2} = -2$

21. $3[-2(3) + 6(2)] = 3[-6 + 12] = 3[6] = 18$

23. $(-8)(-8) = (8)(8) = 64$

25. $3(x - 4) = 3(x) - 3(4) = 3x - 12$

27. $-(x - 2) = -x + 2$

29. $8\left(\dfrac{1}{11}\right) = \dfrac{8 \cdot 1}{11} = \dfrac{8}{11}$

31. $\dfrac{-5x}{7y} = \dfrac{-(5x)}{7y} = -\dfrac{5x}{7y}$

33. $\dfrac{2}{3} \cdot \dfrac{1}{x} = \dfrac{2 \cdot 1}{3 \cdot x} = \dfrac{2}{3x}$

35. $(2x)\left(\dfrac{3}{2x}\right) = 3$

37. $\dfrac{7}{y} \cdot \dfrac{1}{x} = \dfrac{7 \cdot 1}{y \cdot x} = \dfrac{7}{xy}$

39. $\dfrac{1}{2} + \dfrac{1}{3} = \dfrac{3}{6} + \dfrac{2}{6} = \dfrac{3+2}{6} = \dfrac{5}{6}$

41. $\dfrac{3}{10} - \dfrac{7}{15} = \dfrac{9}{30} - \dfrac{14}{30} = \dfrac{9-14}{30} = \dfrac{-5}{30}$

$= -\dfrac{5 \cdot 1}{5 \cdot 6} = -\dfrac{1}{6}$

43. $\dfrac{x}{9} - \dfrac{y}{9} = \dfrac{x-y}{9}$

45. $\dfrac{2}{5} - \dfrac{3}{8} = \dfrac{16}{40} - \dfrac{15}{40} = \dfrac{16-15}{40} = \dfrac{1}{40}$

47. $\dfrac{\frac{k}{9}}{n} = \dfrac{k}{9} \div \dfrac{n}{1} = \dfrac{k}{9} \cdot \dfrac{1}{n} = \dfrac{k}{9n}$

49. $\dfrac{7}{0}$ is not defined (we cannot divide by 0).

51. $\dfrac{0}{0}$ is not defined (we cannot divide by 0).

Exercise 0.5

1. $(2^3)(2^2) = 2^{3+2} = 2^5 (= 32)$

3. $w^4 w^8 = w^{4+8} = w^{12}$

5. $\dfrac{x^2 x^6}{y^7 y^{10}} = \dfrac{x^{2+6}}{y^{7+10}} = \dfrac{x^8}{y^{17}}$

7. $\dfrac{(a^3)^7}{(b^4)^5} = \dfrac{a^{3 \cdot 7}}{b^{4 \cdot 5}} = \dfrac{a^{21}}{b^{20}}$

9. $(2x^2 y^3)^3 = 2^3 (x^2)^3 (y^3)^3 = 8x^{2 \cdot 3} y^{3 \cdot 3}$

$= 8x^6 y^9$

11. $\dfrac{x^8}{x^2} = x^{8-2} = x^6$

13. $\dfrac{(x^3)^6}{x(x^3)} = \dfrac{x^{3 \cdot 6}}{x^{1+3}} = \dfrac{x^{18}}{x^4} = x^{18-4} = x^{14}$

15. $\sqrt{25} = 5$

17. $\sqrt[5]{-32} = -2$

19. $\sqrt[4]{\dfrac{1}{16}} = \dfrac{\sqrt[4]{1}}{\sqrt[4]{16}} = \dfrac{1}{2}$

21. $(49)^{1/2} = \sqrt{49} = 7$

23. $4^{3/2} = \left(\sqrt{4}\right)^3 = (2)^3 = 8$

25. $(32)^{-2/5} = \dfrac{1}{(32)^{2/5}} = \dfrac{1}{\left(\sqrt[5]{32}\right)^2} = \dfrac{1}{(2)^2} = \dfrac{1}{4}$

27. $\left(\dfrac{1}{32}\right)^{4/5} = \left(\sqrt[5]{\dfrac{1}{32}}\right)^4 = \left(\dfrac{1}{2}\right)^4 = \dfrac{1}{16}$

29. $\sqrt{32} = \sqrt{16 \cdot 2} = \sqrt{16}\sqrt{2} = 4\sqrt{2}$

31. $\sqrt[3]{2x^3} = \sqrt[3]{2}\ \sqrt[3]{x^3} = x\sqrt[3]{2}$

33. $\sqrt{16x^4} = \sqrt{16}\sqrt{x^4} = 4x^2$

35. $2\sqrt{75} - 4\sqrt{27} + \sqrt[3]{128}$

$= 2\sqrt{25 \cdot 3} - 4\sqrt{9 \cdot 3} + \sqrt[3]{64 \cdot 2}$

$= 2 \cdot 5\sqrt{3} - 4 \cdot 3\sqrt{3} + 4\sqrt[3]{2}$

$= 10\sqrt{3} - 12\sqrt{3} + 4\sqrt[3]{2}$

$= -2\sqrt{3} + 4\sqrt[3]{2}$

37. $(9z^4)^{1/2} = \sqrt{9z^4} = \sqrt{3^2(z^2)^2} = \sqrt{3^2}\sqrt{(z^2)^2}$

$= 3z^2$

39. $\left(\dfrac{27t^3}{8}\right)^{2/3} = \left(\left[\dfrac{3t}{2}\right]^3\right)^{2/3} = \left[\dfrac{3t}{2}\right]^2 = \dfrac{9t^2}{4}$

41. $\dfrac{x^3 y^{-2}}{z^2} = x^3 \cdot y^{-2} \cdot \dfrac{1}{z^2} = x^3 \cdot \dfrac{1}{y^2} \cdot \dfrac{1}{z^2} = \dfrac{x^3}{y^2 z^2}$

43. $5m^{-2} m^{-7} = 5m^{-2+(-7)} = 5m^{-9} = \dfrac{5}{m^9}$

45. $(3t)^{-2} = \dfrac{1}{(3t)^2} = \dfrac{1}{9t^2}$

47. $\sqrt[3]{7s^2} = (7s^2)^{1/3} = 7^{1/3}(s^2)^{1/3} = 7^{1/3} s^{2/3}$

49. $\sqrt{x} - \sqrt{y} = x^{1/2} - y^{1/2}$

51. $x^2 \sqrt[4]{xy^{-2}z^3} = x^2 (xy^{-2}z^3)^{1/4}$

$= x^2 x^{1/4} y^{-2/4} z^{3/4} = \dfrac{x^{9/4} z^{3/4}}{y^{1/2}}$

53. $(8x-y)^{4/5} = \sqrt[5]{(8x-y)^4}$

55. $x^{-4/5} = \dfrac{1}{x^{4/5}} = \dfrac{1}{\sqrt[5]{x^4}}$

57. $3w^{-3/5} - (3w)^{-3/5} = \dfrac{3}{w^{3/5}} - \dfrac{1}{(3w)^{3/5}}$

$= \dfrac{3}{\sqrt[5]{w^3}} - \dfrac{1}{\sqrt[5]{(3w)^3}} = \dfrac{3}{\sqrt[5]{w^3}} - \dfrac{1}{\sqrt[5]{27w^3}}$

59. $\dfrac{3}{\sqrt{7}} = \dfrac{3}{7^{1/2}} = \dfrac{3 \cdot 7^{1/2}}{7^{1/2} \cdot 7^{1/2}} = \dfrac{3\sqrt{7}}{7}$

61. $\dfrac{4}{\sqrt{2x}} = \dfrac{4}{(2x)^{1/2}} = \dfrac{4(2x)^{1/2}}{(2x)^{1/2}(2x)^{1/2}} = \dfrac{4\sqrt{2x}}{2x}$

$= \dfrac{2\sqrt{2x}}{x}$

63. $\dfrac{1}{\sqrt[3]{3x}} = \dfrac{1}{(3x)^{1/3}} = \dfrac{1(3x)^{2/3}}{(3x)^{1/3}(3x)^{2/3}} = \dfrac{\sqrt[3]{(3x)^2}}{3x}$

$= \dfrac{\sqrt[3]{9x^2}}{3x}$

65. $\dfrac{\sqrt{32}}{\sqrt{2}} = \sqrt{\dfrac{32}{2}} = \sqrt{16} = 4$

67. $\dfrac{\sqrt[5]{2}}{\sqrt[4]{a^2 b}} = \dfrac{\sqrt[5]{2}}{a^{2/4} b^{1/4}} = \dfrac{\sqrt[5]{2} \cdot a^{1/2} b^{3/4}}{a^{1/2} b^{1/4} \cdot a^{1/2} b^{3/4}}$

$= \dfrac{2^{1/5} a^{1/2} b^{3/4}}{ab} = \dfrac{2^{4/20} a^{10/20} b^{15/20}}{ab}$

$= \dfrac{(2^4 a^{10} b^{15})^{1/20}}{ab} = \dfrac{\sqrt[20]{16a^{10} b^{15}}}{ab}$

69. $2x^2 y^{-3} x^4 = 2x^6 y^{-3} = \dfrac{2x^6}{y^3}$

71. $\sqrt{\sqrt[3]{t^4}} = \sqrt{t^{4/3}} = (t^{4/3})^{1/2} = t^{4/6} = t^{2/3}$

73. $\dfrac{2^0}{(2^{-2} x^{1/2} y^{-2})^3} = \dfrac{1}{2^{-6} x^{3/2} y^{-6}} = \dfrac{2^6 y^6}{x^{3/2}}$

$= \dfrac{64 y^6 \cdot x^{1/2}}{x^{3/2} \cdot x^{1/2}} = \dfrac{64 y^6 x^{1/2}}{x^2}$

75. $\sqrt[3]{x^2 yz^3} \sqrt[3]{xy^2} = \sqrt[3]{(x^2 yz^3)(xy^2)} = \sqrt[3]{x^3 y^3 z^3}$
$= xyz$

77. $3^2 (81)^{-3/4} = 3^2 (3^4)^{-3/4} = 3^2 (3^{-3}) = 3^{-1}$
$= \dfrac{1}{3}$

79. $(2x^{-1} y^2)^2 = 2^2 x^{-2} y^4 = \dfrac{4y^4}{x^2}$

81. $\sqrt{x}\sqrt{x^2 y^3}\sqrt{xy^2} = x^{1/2}(x^2 y^3)^{1/2}(xy^2)^{1/2}$
$= x^{1/2}(xy^{3/2})(x^{1/2} y) = x^2 y^{5/2}$

83. $\dfrac{(x^2y^{-1}z)^{-2}}{(xy^2)^{-4}} = \dfrac{x^{-4}y^2z^{-2}}{x^{-4}y^{-8}} = \dfrac{y^{10}}{z^2}$

85. $\dfrac{(x^2)^3}{x^4} \div \left[\dfrac{x^3}{(x^3)^2}\right]^2 = \dfrac{x^6}{x^4} \div \dfrac{(x^3)^2}{(x^6)^2}$

$= x^2 \div \dfrac{x^6}{x^{12}} = x^2 \div x^{6-12} = x^2 \div x^{-6}$

$= x^2 \div \dfrac{1}{x^6} = x^2 \cdot x^6 = x^8$

87. $-\dfrac{8s^{-2}}{2s^3} = -\dfrac{4}{s^3s^2} = -\dfrac{4}{s^5}$

89. $\left(\dfrac{2x^2y}{3y^3z^{-2}}\right)^2 = \left(\dfrac{2x^2z^2}{3y^2}\right)^2 = \dfrac{2^2(x^2)^2(z^2)^2}{3^2(y^2)^2}$

$= \dfrac{4x^4z^4}{9y^4}$

Exercise 0.6

1. $8x - 4y + 2 + 3x + 2y - 5 = 11x - 2y - 3$

3. $8t^2 - 6s^2 + 4s^2 - 2t^2 + 6 = 6t^2 - 2s^2 + 6$

5. $\sqrt{x} + \sqrt{2y} + \sqrt{x} + \sqrt{3z} = 2\sqrt{x} + \sqrt{2y} + \sqrt{3z}$

7. $6x^2 - 10xy + \sqrt{2} - 2z + xy - 4$
$= 6x^2 - 9xy - 2z + \sqrt{2} - 4$

9. $\sqrt{x} + \sqrt{2y} - \sqrt{x} - \sqrt{3z} = \sqrt{2y} - \sqrt{3z}$

11. $9x + 9y - 21 - 24x + 6y - 6$
$= -15x + 15y - 27$

13. $3(x^2 + y^2) - x(y + 2x) + 2y(x + 3y)$
$= 3x^2 + 3y^2 - xy - 2x^2 + 2xy + 6y^2$
$= x^2 + 9y^2 + xy$

15. $2\{3[3x^2 + 6 - 2x^2 + 10]\} = 2\{3[x^2 + 16]\}$
$= 2\{3x^2 + 48\} = 6x^2 + 96$

17. $-3\{4x(x + 2) - 2[x^2 - (3 - x)]\}$
$= -3\{4x^2 + 8x - 2[x^2 - 3 + x]\}$
$= -3\{4x^2 + 8x - 2x^2 + 6 - 2x\}$
$= -3\{2x^2 + 6x + 6\}$
$= -6x^2 - 18x - 18$

19. $x^2 + (4 + 5)x + 4(5) = x^2 + 9x + 20$

21. $(w + 2)(w - 5) = w^2 + (-5 + 2)x + 2(-5)$
$= w^2 - 3w - 10$

23. $(2x)(5x) + [(2)(2) + (3)(5)]x + 3(2)$
$= 10x^2 + 19x + 6$

25. $(x + 3)^2 = x^2 + 2(3)(x) + 3^2 = x^2 + 6x + 9$

27. $x^2 - 2(5)x + 5^2 = x^2 - 10x + 25$

29. $\left(\sqrt{2y} + 3\right)^2 = \left(\sqrt{2y}\right)^2 + 2\left(\sqrt{2y}\right)(3) + 3^2$
$= 2y + 6\sqrt{2y} + 9$

31. $(2s)^2 - 1^2 = 4s^2 - 1$

33. $(x^2 - 3)(x + 4) = x^2(x + 4) - 3(x + 4)$
$= x^3 + 4x^2 - 3x - 12$

35. $x^2(3x^2 + 2x - 1) - 4(3x^2 + 2x - 1)$
$= 3x^4 + 2x^3 - x^2 - 12x^2 - 8\bar{x} + 4$
$= 3x^4 + 2x^3 - 13x^2 - 8x + 4$

37. $x\{3(x - 1)(x - 2) + 2[x(x + 7)]\}$
$= x\{3(x^2 - 3x + 2) + 2[x^2 + 7x]\}$
$= x\{3x^2 - 9x + 6 + 2x^2 + 14x\}$
$= x\{5x^2 + 5x + 6\}$
$= 5x^3 + 5x^2 + 6x$

39. $x(3x + 2y - 4) + y(3x + 2y - 4)$
$\quad + 2(3x + 2y - 4)$
$= 3x^2 + 2xy - 4x + 3xy + 2y^2 - 4y + 6x$
$\quad + 4y - 8$
$= 3x^2 + 2y^2 + 5xy + 2x - 8$

41. $(x+5)^3 = x^3 + 3x^2(5) + 3x(5)^2 + 5^3$
$= x^3 + 15x^2 + 75x + 125$

43. $(2x)^3 - 3(2x)^2(3) + 3(2x)(3)^2 - 3^3$
$= 8x^3 - 36x^2 + 54x - 27$

45. $\dfrac{z^2 - 18z}{z} = \dfrac{z^2}{z} - \dfrac{18z}{z} = z - 18$

47. $\dfrac{6x^5}{2x^2} + \dfrac{4x^3}{2x^2} - \dfrac{1}{2x^2} = 3x^3 + 2x - \dfrac{1}{2x^2}$

49.

$$x+3 \overline{)x^2 + 3x - 1}$$
$$\underline{x^2 + 3x}$$
$$-1$$

Answer: $x + \dfrac{-1}{x+3}$

51.

$$x+2 \overline{)3x^3 - 2x^2 + x - 3}$$
quotient: $3x^2 - 8x + 17$
$$\underline{3x^3 + 6x^2}$$
$$-8x^2 + x$$
$$\underline{-8x^2 - 16x}$$
$$17x - 3$$
$$\underline{17x + 34}$$
$$-37$$

Answer: $3x^2 - 8x + 17 + \dfrac{-37}{x+2}$

53.

$$t-8 \overline{)t^2 + 0t + 0}$$
quotient: $t + 8$
$$\underline{t^2 - 8t}$$
$$8t + 0$$
$$\underline{8t - 64}$$
$$64$$

Answer: $t + 8 + \dfrac{64}{t-8}$

55.

$$3x+2 \overline{)3x^2 - 4x + 3}$$
quotient: $x - 2$
$$\underline{3x^2 + 2x}$$
$$-6x + 3$$
$$\underline{-6x - 4}$$
$$7$$

Answer: $x - 2 + \dfrac{7}{3x+2}$

Exercise 0.7

1. $6x + 4 = 2(3x + 2)$

3. $5x(2y + z)$

5. $8a^3bc - 12ab^3cd + 4b^4c^2d^2$
$= 4bc(2a^3 - 3ab^2d + b^3cd^2)$

7. $z^2 - 7^2 = (z + 7)(z - 7)$

9. $p^2 + 4p + 3 = (p + 3)(p + 1)$

11. $(4x)^2 - 3^2 = (4x + 3)(4x - 3)$

13. $z^2 + 6z + 8 = (z + 4)(z + 2)$

15. $x^2 + 2(3)(x) + 3^2 = (x + 3)^2$

17. $5x^2 + 25x + 30 = 5(x^2 + 5x + 6)$
$= 5(x + 3)(x + 2)$

19. $3(x^2 - 1^2) = 3(x + 1)(x - 1)$

21. $6y^2 + 13y + 2 = (6y + 1)(y + 2)$

23. $2s(6s^2 + 5s - 4) = 2s(3s + 4)(2s - 1)$

25. $x^{2/3}y - 4x^{8/3}y^2 = x^{2/3}y(1 - 4x^2y)$
$= x^{2/3}y[1^2 - (2xy)^2]$
$= x^{2/3}y(1 + 2xy)(1 - 2xy)$

27. $2x(x^2 + x - 6) = 2x(x + 3)(x - 2)$

29. $(4x+2)^2 = [2(2x+1)]^2 = 2^2(2x+1)^2$
$= 4(2x+1)^2$

31. $x(x^2y^2 - 14xy + 49)$
$= x[(xy)^2 - 2(xy)(7) + 7^2]$
$= x(xy - 7)^2$

33. $(x^3 - 4x) + (8 - 2x^2)$
$= x(x^2 - 4) + 2(4 - x^2)$
$= x(x^2 - 4) - 2(x^2 - 4)$
$= (x^2 - 4)(x - 2)$
$= (x + 2)(x - 2)(x - 2)$
$= (x - 2)^2(x + 2)$

35. $y^2(y^2 + 8y + 16) - (y^2 + 8y + 16)$
$= (y^2 + 8y + 16)(y^2 - 1)$
$= (y + 4)^2(y + 1)(y - 1)$

37. $x^3 + 8 = x^3 + 2^3 = (x + 2)(x^2 - 2x + 4)$

39. $(x^3)^2 - 1^2 = (x^3 + 1)(x^3 - 1)$
$= (x + 1)(x^2 - x + 1)(x - 1)(x^2 + x + 1)$

41. $(x + 3)^3(x - 1) + (x + 3)^2(x - 1)^2$
$= (x + 3)^2(x - 1)[(x + 3) + (x - 1)]$
$= (x + 3)^2(x - 1)[2x + 2]$
$= (x + 3)^2(x - 1)[2(x + 1)]$
$= 2(x + 3)^2(x - 1)(x + 1)$

43. $[P(1 + r)] + [P(1 + r)]r = [P(1 + r)](1 + r)$
$= P(1 + r)^2$

45. $x^4 - 16 = (x^2)^2 - 4^2 = (x^2 + 4)(x^2 - 4)$
$= (x^2 + 4)(x + 2)(x - 2)$

47. $(y^4)^2 - 1^2 = (y^4 + 1)(y^4 - 1)$
$= (y^4 + 1)(y^2 + 1)(y^2 - 1)$
$= (y^4 + 1)(y^2 + 1)(y + 1)(y - 1)$

49. $x^4 + x^2 - 2 = (x^2 + 2)(x^2 - 1)$
$= (x^2 + 2)(x + 1)(x - 1)$

51. $y(x^4 - 2x^2 + 1) = y(x^2 - 1)^2$
$= y[(x + 1)(x - 1)]^2 = y(x + 1)^2(x - 1)^2$

Exercise 0.8

1. $\dfrac{x^2 - 4}{x^2 - 2x} = \dfrac{(x + 2)(x - 2)}{x(x - 2)} = \dfrac{x + 2}{x}$

3. $\dfrac{x^2 - 9x + 20}{x^2 + x - 20} = \dfrac{(x - 5)(x - 4)}{(x + 5)(x - 4)} = \dfrac{x - 5}{x + 5}$

5. $\dfrac{6x^2 + x - 2}{2x^2 + 3x - 2} = \dfrac{(3x + 2)(2x - 1)}{(x + 2)(2x - 1)} = \dfrac{3x + 2}{x + 2}$

7. $\dfrac{y^2(-1)}{(y - 3)(y + 2)} = -\dfrac{y^2}{(y - 3)(y + 2)}$

9. $\dfrac{(2x - 3)(2 - x)}{(x - 2)(2x + 3)} = \dfrac{(2x - 3)(-1)(x - 2)}{(x - 2)(2x + 3)}$
$= \dfrac{(2x - 3)(-1)}{2x + 3} = \dfrac{3 - 2x}{2x + 3}$

11. $\dfrac{2(x - 1)}{(x - 4)(x + 2)} \cdot \dfrac{(x + 4)(x + 1)}{(x + 1)(x - 1)}$
$= \dfrac{2(x - 1)(x + 4)(x + 1)}{(x - 4)(x + 2)(x + 1)(x - 1)}$
$= \dfrac{2(x + 4)}{(x - 4)(x + 2)}$

13. $\dfrac{x^2}{6} \div \dfrac{x}{3} = \dfrac{x^2}{6} \cdot \dfrac{3}{x} = \dfrac{3x^2}{6x} = \dfrac{x}{2}$

15. $\dfrac{2m}{n^2} \cdot \dfrac{n^3}{6m} = \dfrac{2mn^3}{6mn^2} = \dfrac{n}{3}$

17. $\dfrac{4x}{3} \div 2x = \dfrac{4x}{3} \cdot \dfrac{1}{2x} = \dfrac{4x}{6x} = \dfrac{2}{3}$

19. $\dfrac{-9x^3}{1} \cdot \dfrac{3}{x} = \dfrac{-27x^3}{x} = -27x^2$

21. $\dfrac{x-5}{\frac{x^2-7x+10}{x-2}} = (x-5) \cdot \dfrac{x-2}{x^2-7x+10}$

$= (x-5) \cdot \dfrac{x-2}{(x-5)(x-2)} = (x-5) \cdot \dfrac{1}{x-5} = 1$

23. $\dfrac{10x^3}{(x+1)(x-1)} \cdot \dfrac{x+1}{5x} = \dfrac{10x^3(x+1)}{5x(x+1)(x-1)}$

$= \dfrac{2x^2}{x-1}$

25. $\dfrac{x^2+7x+10}{x^2-2x-8} \div \dfrac{x^2+6x+5}{x^2-3x-4}$

$= \dfrac{x^2+7x+10}{x^2-2x-8} \cdot \dfrac{x^2-3x-4}{x^2+6x+5}$

$= \dfrac{(x+5)(x+2)}{(x-4)(x+2)} \cdot \dfrac{(x-4)(x+1)}{(x+5)(x+1)} = 1$

27. $\dfrac{(2x+3)(2x-3)}{(x+4)(x-1)} \cdot \dfrac{(1+x)(1-x)}{2x-3}$

$= \dfrac{(2x+3)(1+x)(1-x)}{(x+4)(x-1)}$

$= \dfrac{(2x+3)(1+x)(-1)(x-1)}{(x+4)(x-1)}$

$= -\dfrac{(2x+3)(1+x)}{x+4}$

29. $\dfrac{x^2}{x+3} + \dfrac{5x+6}{x+3} = \dfrac{x^2+(5x+6)}{x+3}$

$= \dfrac{(x+3)(x+2)}{x+3} = x+2$

31. LCD $= 3t$, so $\dfrac{2}{t} + \dfrac{1}{3t} = \dfrac{6}{3t} + \dfrac{1}{3t} = \dfrac{6+1}{3t} = \dfrac{7}{3t}$.

33. LCD $= p^2-1$

$1 - \dfrac{p^2}{p^2-1} = \dfrac{p^2-1}{p^2-1} - \dfrac{p^2}{p^2-1}$

$= \dfrac{p^2-1-p^2}{p^2-1} = \dfrac{-1}{p^2-1} = \dfrac{1}{1-p^2}$

35. LCD $= (2x-1)(x+3)$

$\dfrac{4(x+3)}{(2x-1)(x+3)} + \dfrac{x(2x-1)}{(x+3)(2x-1)}$

$= \dfrac{4(x+3)+x(2x-1)}{(2x-1)(x+3)} = \dfrac{2x^2+3x+12}{(2x-1)(x+3)}$

37. $x^2-x-2 = (x-2)(x+1)$ and
$x^2-1 = (x+1)(x-1)$, so
LCD $= (x-2)(x+1)(x-1)$.

$\dfrac{1}{(x-2)(x+1)} + \dfrac{1}{(x+1)(x-1)}$

$= \dfrac{x-1}{(x-2)(x+1)(x-1)} + \dfrac{x-2}{(x+1)(x-1)(x-2)}$

$= \dfrac{(x-1)+(x-2)}{(x-2)(x+1)(x-1)}$

$= \dfrac{2x-3}{(x-2)(x+1)(x-1)}$

39. LCD $= (x-1)(x+5)$

$\dfrac{4(x+5)}{(x-1)(x+5)} - \dfrac{3(x-1)(x+5)}{(x-1)(x+5)}$

$+ \dfrac{3x^2}{(x-1)(x+5)}$

$= \dfrac{4x+20-3(x^2+4x-5)+3x^2}{(x-1)(x+5)}$

$= \dfrac{35-8x}{(x-1)(x+5)}$

41. $(1+x^{-1})^2 = \left(1+\dfrac{1}{x}\right)^2 = \left(\dfrac{x}{x}+\dfrac{1}{x}\right)^2$

$= \left(\dfrac{x+1}{x}\right)^2 = \dfrac{(x+1)^2}{x^2} = \dfrac{x^2+2x+1}{x^2}$

43. $\left(\dfrac{1}{x}-y\right)^{-1} = \left(\dfrac{1}{x}-\dfrac{xy}{x}\right)^{-1} = \left(\dfrac{1-xy}{x}\right)^{-1}$

$= \dfrac{x}{1-xy}$

45. Multiplying the numerator and denominator of the given fraction by x gives

$\dfrac{4+\frac{1}{x}}{3} = \dfrac{\left(4+\frac{1}{x}\right)x}{3x} = \dfrac{4x+1}{3x}$.

47. Multiplying numerator and denominator by $2x(x+2)$ gives

$$\frac{3(2x)(x+2)-1(x+2)}{x(2x)(x+2)+x(2x)} = \frac{(x+2)[3(2x)-1]}{2x^2[(x+2)+1]}$$

$$= \frac{(x+2)(6x-1)}{2x^2(x+3)}$$

49. $\text{LCD} = \sqrt{x+h} \cdot \sqrt{x}$

$$\frac{2}{\sqrt{x+h}} - \frac{2}{\sqrt{x}} = \frac{2\sqrt{x}}{\sqrt{x+h}\sqrt{x}} - \frac{2\sqrt{x+h}}{\sqrt{x}\sqrt{x+h}}$$

$$= \frac{2\sqrt{x} - 2\sqrt{x+h}}{\sqrt{x}\sqrt{x+h}}$$

51. $\dfrac{1}{2+\sqrt{3}} \cdot \dfrac{2-\sqrt{3}}{2-\sqrt{3}} = \dfrac{2-\sqrt{3}}{4-3} = 2-\sqrt{3}$

53. $\dfrac{\sqrt{2}}{\sqrt{3}-\sqrt{6}} = \dfrac{\sqrt{2}}{\sqrt{3}-\sqrt{6}} \cdot \dfrac{\sqrt{3}+\sqrt{6}}{\sqrt{3}+\sqrt{6}}$

$$= \frac{\sqrt{2}\left(\sqrt{3}+\sqrt{6}\right)}{3-6} = \frac{\sqrt{6}+\sqrt{12}}{-3} = -\frac{\sqrt{6}+2\sqrt{3}}{3}$$

55. $\dfrac{2\sqrt{2}}{\sqrt{2}-\sqrt{3}} \cdot \dfrac{\sqrt{2}+\sqrt{3}}{\sqrt{2}+\sqrt{3}} = \dfrac{2\sqrt{2}\left(\sqrt{2}+\sqrt{3}\right)}{2-3}$

$$= \frac{4+2\sqrt{6}}{-1} = -4-2\sqrt{6}$$

57. $\dfrac{1}{x+\sqrt{5}} = \dfrac{1}{x+\sqrt{5}} \cdot \dfrac{x-\sqrt{5}}{x-\sqrt{5}} = \dfrac{x-\sqrt{5}}{x^2-5}$

59. $\dfrac{5\left(2-\sqrt{3}\right)}{\left(2+\sqrt{3}\right)\left(2-\sqrt{3}\right)} - \dfrac{4\left(1+\sqrt{2}\right)}{\left(1-\sqrt{2}\right)\left(1+\sqrt{2}\right)}$

$$= \frac{5\left(2-\sqrt{3}\right)}{4-3} - \frac{4\left(1+\sqrt{2}\right)}{1-2}$$

$$= \frac{5\left(2-\sqrt{3}\right)}{1} - \frac{4\left(1+\sqrt{2}\right)}{-1}$$

$$= 5\left(2-\sqrt{3}\right) + 4\left(1+\sqrt{2}\right) = 4\sqrt{2} - 5\sqrt{3} + 14$$

Mathematical Snapshot Chapter 0

1.

```
LinReg
 y=ax+b
 a=7.221004E-4
 b=.0060813684
 r²=.999988045
 r=.9999940225
■
```

The results agree.

3.

```
QuadReg
 y=ax²+bx+c
 a=-3.226931E-9
 b=7.3226523E-4
 c=4.9071053E-4
 R²=.9999999072
■
```

The results agree.

Chapter 1

Principles in Practice 1.1

1. The amount of fencing material needed is the same as the perimeter of the rectangular garden, P.
   Let w = the width of the garden. Then $w + 2$ = the length, l, of the garden.
   $P = 2l + 2w$
   $P = 2(w + 2) + 2w$
   $P = 2w + 4 + 2w$
   $P = 4w + 4$
   $(4w + 4)$ feet of fencing are needed.

2. Revenues equal costs when
   $2.25x = 0.75x + 300$.
   $2.25x = 0.75x + 300$
   $1.5x = 300$
   $x = 200$
   The coffee house needs to sell 200 specialty coffees each day.

3. Let x = the number of weeks. After x weeks, Monica will have saved $40x - 125$. Pedro has already saved $3(\$35) = \$105$. After x weeks, Pedro will have saved $35x + 105$.
   $40x - 125 = 35x + 105$
   $5x = 230$
   $x = 46$
   $40(46) - 125 = 1840 - 125 = 1715$
   Monica and Pedro will pool their savings in 46 weeks. Each will have saved $1715.

4. $d = rt$
   $\dfrac{d}{t} = r$
   The rate is $r = \dfrac{d}{t}$.

5. The box must have sides of length equal to the diameter of the sphere.
   $$4\pi\left(\frac{d}{2}\right)^2 = S$$
   $$\left(\frac{d}{2}\right)^2 = \frac{S}{4\pi}$$
   $$\frac{d}{2} = \sqrt{\frac{S}{4\pi}} = \frac{1}{2}\sqrt{\frac{S}{\pi}}$$
   $$d = \sqrt{\frac{S}{\pi}}$$

   The box must have sides of length $\sqrt{\dfrac{S}{\pi}}$.

Exercise 1.1

1. $9x - x^2 = 0$
   Set $x = 1$:
   $9(1) - (1)^2 \overset{?}{=} 0$
   $9 - 1 \overset{?}{=} 0$
   $8 \neq 0$
   Set $x = 0$:
   $9(0) - (0)^2 \overset{?}{=} 0$
   $0 - 0 \overset{?}{=} 0$
   $0 = 0$
   Thus, 0 satisfies the equation, but 1 does not.

3. $y + 2(y - 3) = 4$
   Set $x = \dfrac{10}{3}$:
   $\dfrac{10}{3} + 2\left(\dfrac{10}{3} - 3\right) \overset{?}{=} 4$
   $\dfrac{10}{3} + \dfrac{20}{3} - 6 \overset{?}{=} 4$
   $4 = 4$
   Set $x = 1$:
   $1 + 2(1 - 3) \overset{?}{=} 4$
   $1 - 4 \overset{?}{=} 4$
   $-3 \neq 4$
   Thus, $\dfrac{10}{3}$ satisfies the equation but 1 does not.

5. $x(6 + x) - 2(x + 1) - 5x = 4$
Set $x = -2$:
$(-2)(6 - 2) - 2(-2 + 1) - 5(-2) \stackrel{?}{=} 4$
$-2(4) - 2(-1) + 10 \stackrel{?}{=} 4$
$-8 + 2 + 10 \stackrel{?}{=} 4$
$4 = 4$
Set $x = 0$:
$0(6) - 2(1) - 5(0) \stackrel{?}{=} 4$
$-2 \neq 4$
Thus, -2 satisfies the equation but 0 does not.

7. Adding 5 to both sides; equivalence guaranteed

9. Raising both sides to the fourth power; equivalence not guaranteed

11. Dividing both sides by x; equivalence not guaranteed

13. Multiplying both sides by $x - 1$; equivalence not guaranteed

15. Multiplying both sides by $\dfrac{x - 5}{x}$;
equivalence not guaranteed

17. $4x = 10$
Dividing both sides by 4 gives $x = \dfrac{10}{4} = \dfrac{5}{2}$.

19. $3y = 0$
Dividing both sides by 3 gives $y = \dfrac{0}{3} = 0$.

21. $-5x = 10 - 15$
$-5x = -5$
Dividing both sides by -5 gives $x = \dfrac{-5}{-5} = 1$.

23. $5x - 3 = 9$
$5x = 12$
$x = \dfrac{12}{5}$

25. $7x + 7 = 2(x + 1)$
$7x + 7 = 2x + 2$
$5x + 7 = 2$
$5x = -5$
$x = \dfrac{-5}{5} = -1$

27. $2(p - 1) - 3(p - 4) = 4p$
$2p - 2 - 3p + 12 = 4p$
$-p + 10 = 4p$
$10 = 5p$
$p = 2$

29. $\dfrac{x}{5} = 2x - 6$
$x = 5(2x - 6)$
$x = 10x - 30$
$30 = 9x$
$x = \dfrac{30}{9} = \dfrac{10}{3}$

31. $7 + \dfrac{4x}{9} = \dfrac{x}{2}$
Multiplying both sides by $9 \cdot 2$ gives
$9 \cdot 2 \cdot 7 + 2(4x) = 9(x)$
$126 + 8x = 9x$
$x = 126$

33. $q = \dfrac{3}{2}q - 4$
Multiplying both sides by 2 gives
$2q = 3q - 8$
$-q = -8$
$q = 8$

35. $3x + \dfrac{x}{5} - 5 = \dfrac{1}{5} + 5x$
Multiplying both sides by 5 gives
$15x + x - 25 = 1 + 25x$
$16x - 25 = 1 + 25x$
$-9x = 26$
$x = -\dfrac{26}{9}$

37. $\dfrac{2y-3}{4} = \dfrac{6y+7}{3}$

Multiplying both sides by 12 gives
$3(2y - 3) = 4(6y + 7)$
$6y - 9 = 24y + 28$
$-18y = 37$
$y = -\dfrac{37}{18}$

39. $w + \dfrac{w}{2} - \dfrac{w}{3} + \dfrac{w}{4} = 5$

Multiplying both sides by 12 gives
$12w + 6w - 4w + 3w = 60$
$17w = 60$
$w = \dfrac{60}{17}$

41. $\dfrac{x+2}{3} - \dfrac{2-x}{6} = x - 2$

Multiplying both sides by 6 gives
$2(x + 2) - (2 - x) = 6(x - 2)$
$2x + 4 - 2 + x = 6x - 12$
$3x + 2 = 6x - 12$
$2 = 3x - 12$
$14 = 3x$
$x = \dfrac{14}{3}$

43. $\dfrac{9}{5}(3 - x) = \dfrac{3}{4}(x - 3)$

Multiplying both sides by 20 gives
$36(3 - x) = 15(x - 3)$
$108 - 36x = 15x - 45$
$153 = 51x$
$x = 3$

45. $\dfrac{3}{2}(4x - 3) = 2[x - (4x - 3)]$

$3(4x - 3) = 4[x - 4x + 3]$
$12x - 9 = -12x + 12$
$24x = 21$
$x = \dfrac{21}{24} = \dfrac{7}{8}$

47. $I = Prt$
$I = P(rt)$
$P = \dfrac{I}{rt}$

49. $p = 8q - 1$
$p + 1 = 8q$
$q = \dfrac{p+1}{8}$

51. $S = P(1 + rt)$
$S = P + Prt$
$S - P = r(Pt)$
$r = \dfrac{S-P}{Pt}$

53. $S = \dfrac{n}{2}(a_1 + a_n)$
$2S = n(a_1 + a_n)$
$2S = na_1 + na_n$
$2S - na_n = na_1$
$a_1 = \dfrac{2S - na_n}{n}$

55. $P = 2l + 2w$
$960 = 2(360) + 2w$
$960 = 720 + 2w$
$240 = 2w$
$w = 120$ m

57. $c = x + 0.0825x = 1.0825x$

59. $V = C\left(1 - \dfrac{n}{N}\right)$

$2000 = 3200\left(1 - \dfrac{n}{8}\right)$
$2000 = 3200 - 400n$
$400n = 1200$
$n = 3$
The furniture will have a value of \$2000 after 3 years.

61. Paula's weekly salary for working h hours is $24h + 8$. Sam's weekly salary for working h hours is $28h$.

$\dfrac{1}{4}(24h + 8 + 28h) = 405$
$52h + 8 = 1620$
$52h = 1612$
$h = 31$
They must each work 31 hours each week.

63. $I = I_0[1 + \alpha(T - T_0)]$
$1.001 = 1[1 + \alpha(100 - 0)]$
$1.001 = 1 + 100\alpha$
$0.001 = 100\alpha$
$\alpha = \dfrac{0.001}{100} = 0.00001$

65. $\dfrac{1}{8}, -\dfrac{1}{14}$

67. $\dfrac{14}{61}$

Principles in Practice 1.2

1. $d = rt$ where d = distance, r = rate, and
t = time. The times for the two boats are the
same. For the first boat, $d = 10$ and the rate
is $r + 2$. For the second boat, $d = 6$ and the
rate is $r - 2$.
$t = \dfrac{d}{r}$
$\dfrac{10}{r + 2} = \dfrac{6}{r - 2}$
$(r + 2)(r - 2)\dfrac{10}{r + 2} = (r + 2)(r - 2)\dfrac{6}{r - 2}$
$10r - 20 = 6r + 12$
$4r = 32$
$r = 8$
The boats are going 8 miles per hour.

2. $t = \dfrac{d}{r + w}$
$t(r + w) = d$
$tr + tw = d$
$tw = d - tr$
$w = \dfrac{d - tr}{t} = \dfrac{d}{t} - r$

3. Let x = the horizontal distance that the ramp
covers. By the Pythagorean theorem, the
length of the ramp is $\sqrt{x^2 + v^2}$ where v is
the vertical distance the ramp covers.
$\sqrt{x^2 + v^2} - x = 2$
$\sqrt{x^2 + 16} - x = 2$
$\sqrt{x^2 + 16} = x + 2$
$x^2 + 16 = (x + 2)^2$
$x^2 + 16 = x^2 + 4x + 4$
$12 = 4x$
$3 = x$
$\sqrt{x^2 + v^2} = \sqrt{3^2 + 16} = \sqrt{9 + 16} = \sqrt{25} = 5$
The length of the ramp is 5 feet.

Exercise 1.2

1. $\dfrac{5}{x} = 25$
Multiplying both sides by x gives
$5 = 25x$
$x = \dfrac{5}{25}$
$x = \dfrac{1}{5}$

3. Multiplying both sides by $3 - x$ gives $7 = 0$,
which is false. Thus there is no solution, so
the solution set is $\varnothing$.

5. $\dfrac{4}{8 - x} = \dfrac{3}{4}$
$4(4) = 3(8 - x)$
$16 = 24 - 3x$
$3x = 8$
$x = \dfrac{8}{3}$

7. $\dfrac{q}{5q - 4} = \dfrac{1}{3}$
$3q = 5q - 4$
$-2q = -4$
$q = 2$

9. $\dfrac{1}{p-1} = \dfrac{2}{p-2}$

$p - 2 = 2(p - 1)$

$p - 2 = 2p - 2$

$p = 0$

11. $\dfrac{1}{x} + \dfrac{1}{5} = \dfrac{4}{5}$

$\dfrac{1}{x} = \dfrac{3}{5}$

$5x\left(\dfrac{1}{x}\right) = 5x\left(\dfrac{3}{5}\right)$

$5 = 3x$

$x = \dfrac{5}{3}$

13. $\dfrac{3x-2}{2x+3} = \dfrac{3x-1}{2x+1}$

$(3x - 2)(2x + 1) = (3x - 1)(2x + 3)$

$6x^2 - x - 2 = 6x^2 + 7x - 3$

$1 = 8x$

$x = \dfrac{1}{8}$

15. $\dfrac{y-6}{y} - \dfrac{6}{y} = \dfrac{y+6}{y-6}$

$y(y-6)\left[\dfrac{y-6}{y} - \dfrac{6}{y}\right] = y(y-6)\left[\dfrac{y+6}{y-6}\right]$

$(y-6)^2 - 6(y-6) = y(y+6)$

$y^2 - 12y + 36 - 6y + 36 = y^2 + 6y$

$y^2 - 18y + 72 = y^2 + 6y$

$72 = 24y$

$y = 3$

17. $\dfrac{-4}{x-1} = \dfrac{7}{2-x} + \dfrac{3}{x+1}$

Multiplying both sides by
$(x - 1)(2 - x)(x + 1)$ gives

$-4(2 - x)(x + 1)$

$= 7(x - 1)(x + 1) + 3(x - 1)(2 - x)$

$-4(-x^2 + x + 2)$

$= 7(x^2 - 1) + 3(-x^2 + 3x - 2)$

$4x^2 - 4x - 8 = 4x^2 + 9x - 13$

$-13x = -5$

$x = \dfrac{5}{13}$

19. $\dfrac{9}{x-3} = \dfrac{3x}{x-3}$

$9 = 3x$

$x = 3$

But the given equation is not defined for
$x = 3$, so there is no solution. The solution
set is $\varnothing$.

21. $\sqrt{x+5} = 4$

$\left(\sqrt{x+5}\right)^2 = 4^2$

$x + 5 = 16$

$x = 11$

23. $\sqrt{5x-6} - 16 = 0$

$\sqrt{5x-6} = 16$

$\left(\sqrt{5x-6}\right)^2 = 16^2$

$5x - 6 = 256$

$5x = 262$

$x = \dfrac{262}{5}$

25. $\sqrt{\dfrac{x}{2}+1} = \dfrac{2}{3}$

Squaring both sides:

$\dfrac{x}{2} + 1 = \dfrac{4}{9}$

$\dfrac{x}{2} = -\dfrac{5}{9}$

$x = 2\left(-\dfrac{5}{9}\right) = -\dfrac{10}{9}$

27. $\sqrt{4x - 6} = \sqrt{x}$

$\left(\sqrt{4x - 6}\right)^2 = \left(\sqrt{x}\right)^2$

$4x - 6 = x$

$3x = 6$

$x = 2$

29. $(x - 3)^{3/2} = 8$

$[(x - 3)^{3/2}]^{2/3} = 8^{2/3}$

$x - 3 = 4$

$x = 7$

31. $\sqrt{y} + \sqrt{y + 2} = 3$

$\sqrt{y + 2} = 3 - \sqrt{y}$

$\left(\sqrt{y + 2}\right)^2 = \left(3 - \sqrt{y}\right)^2$

$y + 2 = 9 - 6\sqrt{y} + y$

$6\sqrt{y} = 7$

$\left(6\sqrt{y}\right)^2 = 7^2$

$36y = 49$

$y = \dfrac{49}{36}$

33. $\sqrt{z^2 + 2z} = 3 + z$

Squaring both sides gives

$z^2 + 2z = (3 + z)^2$

$z^2 + 2z = 9 + 6z + z^2$

$-9 = 4z$

$z = -\dfrac{9}{4}$

35. $r = \dfrac{d}{1 - dt}$

$r(1 - dt) = d$

$r - rdt = d$

$-rdt = -r + d$

$t = -\dfrac{d - r}{rd} = \dfrac{r - d}{rd}$

37. $r = \dfrac{2mI}{B(n + 1)}$

Multiplying both sides by $n + 1$ gives

$r(n + 1) = \dfrac{2mI}{B}$

$n + 1 = \dfrac{2mI}{rB}$

$n = \dfrac{2mI}{rB} - 1$

39. $y = \dfrac{1.4x}{1 + 0.09x}$

With $y = 10$ the equation is $10 = \dfrac{1.4x}{1 + 0.09x}$.

Multiplying both sides by $1 + 0.09x$ gives

$10(1 + 0.09x) = 1.4x$

$10 + 0.9x = 1.4x$

$10 = 0.5x$

$x = 20$

The prey density should be 20.

41. $t = \dfrac{d}{r - c}$

$t(r - c) = d$

$tr - tc = d$

$tr = d + tc$

$r = \dfrac{d + tc}{t} = \dfrac{d}{t} + c$

43. Let x = antenna B's height above the ground. Antenna B can broadcast $4.1\sqrt{x}$ kilometers. Antenna A's height above the ground is $x + 8.25$, and it can broadcast $4.1\sqrt{x + 8.25}$ kilometers.

$4.1\sqrt{x + 8.25} = 4.1\sqrt{x} + 6.15$

$\sqrt{x + 8.25} = \sqrt{x} + 1.5$

$x + 8.25 = \left(\sqrt{x} + 1.5\right)^2$

$x + 8.25 = x + 3\sqrt{x} + 2.25$

$6 = 3\sqrt{x}$

$2 = \sqrt{x}$

$4 = x$

Antenna B is 4 meters above the ground. Antenna A is $4 + 8.25 = 12.25$ meters above the ground.

Principles in Practice 1.3

1. Let x = the number.
$$x^2 = x + 30$$
$$x^2 - x - 30 = 0$$
$$(x - 6)(x + 5) = 0$$

$x - 6 = 0$	or	$x + 5$
$x = 6$	or	$x = -5$

The number is -5 or 6.

2. Let l = the length of the mural.
The width is $l - 10$.
$$l(l - 10) = 3000$$
$$l^2 - 10l = 3000$$
$$l^2 - 10l - 3000 = 0$$
$$(l - 60)(l + 50) = 0$$

$l - 60 = 0$	or	$l + 50 = 0$
$l = 60$	or	$l = -50$

Since a length cannot be negative, $l = 60$ and the width is $60 - 10 = 50$.
The dimensions are 50 feet by 60 feet.

3. Let w = the width of the prism. Then the height is $5w$ and its volume is
$$w \cdot w(5w) = 5w^3.$$
$$5w^3 = 5w$$
$$w^3 = w$$
$$w^3 - w = 0$$
$$w(w^2 - 1) = 0$$
$$w(w + 1)(w - 1) = 0$$

$w = 0$	or	$w + 1 = 0$	or	$w - 1 = 0$
$w = 0$	or	$w = -1$	or	$w = 1$

Since the width must be positive, $w = 1$.
The dimensions are 1 by 1 by 5.

4. $x^2 = 225$
$$x^2 - 225 = 0$$
$$(x - 15)(x + 15) = 0$$

$x - 15 = 0$	or	$x + 15 = 0$
$x = 15$	or	$x = -15$

Since you cannot sell a negative number of items, $x = 15$. You sold 15 items for $15 each.

5. $h = 160t - 16t^2$
$$300 = 160t - 16t^2$$
$$16t^2 - 160t + 300 = 0$$
$$4t^2 - 40t + 75 = 0$$
$$t = \frac{40 \pm \sqrt{(-40)^2 - 4(4)(75)}}{2(4)}$$
$$= \frac{40 \pm \sqrt{1600 - 1200}}{8}$$
$$= \frac{40 \pm \sqrt{400}}{8}$$
$$= \frac{40 \pm 20}{8}$$
$$t = \frac{40 + 20}{8} = \frac{15}{2} \quad \text{or} \quad t = \frac{40 - 20}{8} = \frac{5}{2}$$

The fireworks will be 300 feet off the ground when $t = \frac{5}{2}$ s and when $t = \frac{15}{2}$ s.

6. $20,000 = -2p^2 + 400p$
$$2p^2 - 400p + 20,000 = 0$$
$$p^2 - 200p + 10,000 = 0$$
$$p = \frac{200 \pm \sqrt{(-200)^2 - 4(1)(10,000)}}{2(1)}$$
$$= \frac{200 \pm \sqrt{0}}{2}$$
$$= 100$$
The price is $100.

7. $500 = 160t - 16t^2$
$$16t^2 - 160t + 500 = 0$$
$$4t^2 - 40t + 125 = 0$$
$$t = \frac{40 \pm \sqrt{(-40)^2 - 4(4)(125)}}{2(4)}$$
$$= \frac{40 \pm \sqrt{-400}}{8}$$
Since no real number exists whose square is -400, the equation has no real roots.
The fireworks are never 500 feet off the ground.

Exercise 1.3

1. $x^2 - 4x + 4 = 0$
$(x - 2)^2 = 0$
$x - 2 = 0$
$x = 2$

3. $(y - 4)(y - 3) = 0$
$y - 4 = 0$ or $y - 3 = 0$
$y = 4$ or $y = 3$

5. $(x - 3)(x + 1) = 0$
$x - 3 = 0$ or $x + 1 = 0$
$x = 3$ or $x = -1$

7. $u^2 - 13u + 36 = 0$
$(u - 4)(u - 9) = 0$
$u - 4 = 0$ or $u - 9 = 0$
$u = 4$ or $u = 9$

9. $(x - 2)(x + 2) = 0$
$x - 2 = 0$ or $x + 2 = 0$
$x = 2$ or $x = -2$

11. $z^2 - 8z = 0$
$z(z - 8) = 0$
$z = 0$ or $z - 8 = 0$
$z = 0$ or $z = 8$

13. $4x^2 + 1 = 4x$
$4x^2 - 4x + 1 = 0$
$(2x - 1)^2 = 0$
$2x - 1 = 0$
$2x = 1$
$x = \dfrac{1}{2}$

15. $y(2y + 3) = 5$
$2y^2 + 3y - 5 = 0$
$(y - 1)(2y + 5) = 0$
$y - 1 = 0$ or $2y + 5 = 0$
$y = 1$ or $y = -\dfrac{5}{2}$

17. $-x^2 + 3x + 10 = 0$
$x^2 - 3x - 10 = 0$
$(x - 5)(x + 2) = 0$
$x - 5 = 0$ or $x + 2 = 0$
$x = 5$ or $x = -2$

19. $2p^2 - 3p = 0$
$p(2p - 3) = 0$
$p = 0$ or $2p - 3 = 0$
$p = 0$ or $p = \dfrac{3}{2}$

21. $x(x + 4)(x - 1) = 0$
$x = 0$ or $x + 4 = 0$ or $x - 1 = 0$
$x = 0$ or $x = -4$ or $x = 1$

23. $x(x^2 - 64) = 0$
$x(x - 8)(x + 8) = 0$
$x = 0$ or $x - 8 = 0$ or $x + 8 = 0$
$x = 0$ or $x = 8$ or $x = -8$

25. $6x^3 + 5x^2 - 4x = 0$
$x(6x^2 + 5x - 4) = 0$
$x(2x - 1)(3x + 4) = 0$
$x = 0$ or $2x - 1 = 0$ or $3x + 4 = 0$
$x = 0$ or $x = \dfrac{1}{2}$ or $x = -\dfrac{4}{3}$

27. $(x + 3)(x + 1)(x - 2) = 0$
$x + 3 = 0$ or $x + 1 = 0$ or $x - 2 = 0$
$x = -3$ or $x = -1$ or $x = 2$

29. $p(p - 3)^2 - 4(p - 3)^3 = 0$
Factoring out $(p - 3)^2$ gives
$(p - 3)^2[p - 4(p - 3)] = 0$
$(p - 3)^2(12 - 3p) = 0$
$3(p - 3)^2(4 - p) = 0$
$p - 3 = 0$ or $4 - p = 0$
$p = 3$ or $p = 4$

31. $x^2 + 2x - 24 = 0$

$a = 1, b = 2, c = -24$

$x = \dfrac{-b \pm \sqrt{b^2 - 4ac}}{2a}$

$= \dfrac{-2 \pm \sqrt{4 - 4(1)(-24)}}{2(1)}$

$= \dfrac{-2 \pm \sqrt{100}}{2}$

$= \dfrac{-2 \pm 10}{2}$

$x = \dfrac{-2 + 10}{2} = 4$ or $x = \dfrac{-2 - 10}{2} = -6$

33. $4x^2 - 12x + 9 = 0$

$a = 4, b = -12, c = 9$

$x = \dfrac{-b \pm \sqrt{b^2 - 4ac}}{2a}$

$= \dfrac{-(-12) \pm \sqrt{144 - 4(4)(9)}}{2(4)}$

$= \dfrac{12 \pm \sqrt{0}}{8}$

$= \dfrac{12 \pm 0}{8}$

$= \dfrac{3}{2}$

35. $p^2 - 7p + 3 = 0$

$a = 1, b = -7, c = 3$

$p = \dfrac{-b \pm \sqrt{b^2 - 4ac}}{2a}$

$= \dfrac{-(-7) \pm \sqrt{49 - 4(1)(3)}}{2(1)}$

$= \dfrac{7 \pm \sqrt{37}}{2}$

$p = \dfrac{7 + \sqrt{37}}{2}$ or $p = \dfrac{7 - \sqrt{37}}{2}$

37. $4 - 2n + n^2 = 0$

$n^2 - 2n + 4 = 0$

$a = 1, b = -2, c = 4$

$n = \dfrac{-b \pm \sqrt{b^2 - 4ac}}{2a}$

$= \dfrac{-(-2) \pm \sqrt{4 - 4(1)(4)}}{2(1)}$

$= \dfrac{2 \pm \sqrt{-12}}{2}$

no real roots

39. $6x^2 + 7x - 5 = 0$

$a = 6, b = 7, c = -5$

$x = \dfrac{-b \pm \sqrt{b^2 - 4ac}}{2a}$

$= \dfrac{-7 \pm \sqrt{49 - 4(6)(-5)}}{2(6)}$

$= \dfrac{-7 \pm \sqrt{169}}{12}$

$= \dfrac{-7 \pm 13}{12}$

$x = \dfrac{-7 + 13}{12} = \dfrac{1}{2}$ or $x = \dfrac{-7 - 13}{12} = -\dfrac{5}{3}$

41. $0.02w^2 - 0.3w = 20$

$0.02w^2 - 0.3w - 20 = 0$

$a = 0.02, b = -0.3, c = -20$

$w = \dfrac{-b \pm \sqrt{b^2 - 4ac}}{2a}$

$= \dfrac{-(-0.3) \pm \sqrt{0.09 - 4(0.02)(-20)}}{2(0.02)}$

$= \dfrac{0.3 \pm \sqrt{1.69}}{0.04}$

$= \dfrac{0.3 \pm 1.3}{0.04}$

$w = \dfrac{0.3 + 1.3}{0.04} = \dfrac{1.6}{0.04} = 40$ or

$w = \dfrac{0.3 - 1.3}{0.04} = \dfrac{-1.0}{0.04} = -25$

43. $2x^2 + 4x - 5 = 0$

$a = 2, b = 4, c = -5$

$$x = \frac{-b \pm \sqrt{b^2 - 4ac}}{2a}$$

$$= \frac{-4 \pm \sqrt{16 - 4(2)(-5)}}{2(2)}$$

$$= \frac{-4 \pm \sqrt{56}}{4}$$

$$= \frac{-4 \pm 2\sqrt{14}}{4}$$

$$= \frac{-2 \pm \sqrt{14}}{2}$$

$$x = \frac{-2 + \sqrt{14}}{2} \text{ or } x = \frac{-2 - \sqrt{14}}{2}$$

45. $(x^2)^2 - 5(x^2) + 6 = 0$

Let $w = x^2$. Then

$w^2 - 5w + 6 = 0$

$(w - 3)(w - 2) = 0$

Thus, $w = 3, 2$.

Hence $x^2 = 3$ or $x^2 = 2$, so

$x = \pm\sqrt{3}, \pm\sqrt{2}$.

47. $2\left(\frac{1}{x}\right)^2 + 3\left(\frac{1}{x}\right) - 2 = 0$

Let $w = \frac{1}{x}$. Then

$2w^2 + 3w - 2 = 0$

$(2w - 1)(w + 2) = 0,$

so $w = \frac{1}{2}, -2$. Thus, $x = 2, -\frac{1}{2}$.

49. $(x^{-2})^2 - 9(x^{-2}) + 20 = 0$

Set $w = x^{-2}$.

$w^2 - 9w + 20 = 0$

$(w - 5)(w - 4) = 0,$

$w = 5, 4$

Thus, $\frac{1}{x^2} = 5$ or $\frac{1}{x^2} = 4$, so $x^2 = \frac{1}{5}$ or

$x^2 = \frac{1}{4}$. $x = \pm\frac{\sqrt{5}}{5}, \pm\frac{1}{2}$.

51. $(x - 3)^2 + 9(x - 3) + 14 = 0$

Let $w = x - 3$. Then

$w^2 + 9w + 14 = 0$

$(w + 7)(w + 2) = 0$

$w = -7, -2$

If $x - 3 = -7$, then $x = -4$, and if $x - 3 = -2$,

then $x = 1$. Thus, $x = -4, 1$.

53. If $w = \frac{1}{x - 2}$, then

$w^2 - 12w + 35 = 0$

$(w - 7)(w - 5) = 0$

$w = 7, 5$

Thus, $\frac{1}{x - 2} = 7$ or $\frac{1}{x - 2} = 5$.

$x = \frac{15}{7}, \frac{11}{5}$.

55. $x^2 = \frac{x + 3}{2}$

$2x^2 = x + 3$

$2x^2 - x - 3 = 0$

$(2x - 3)(x + 1) = 0$

$2x - 3 = 0$ or $x + 1 = 0$

$x = \frac{3}{2}$ or $x = -1$

57. $\frac{3}{x - 4} + \frac{x - 3}{x} = 2$

Multiplying both sides by the LCD, $x(x - 4)$,

gives $3x + (x - 3)(x - 4) = 2x(x - 4)$

$3x + x^2 - 7x + 12 = 2x^2 - 8x$

$x^2 - 4x + 12 = 2x^2 - 8x$

$0 = x^2 - 4x - 12$

$0 = (x - 6)(x + 2)$

Thus, $x = 6, -2$.

59. $\dfrac{6x+7}{2x+1} - \dfrac{6x+1}{2x} = 1$

Multiplying both sides by the LCD, $2x(2x+1)$, gives

$2x(6x+7) - (2x+1)(6x+1) = 1(2x)(2x+1)$

$12x^2 + 14x - (12x^2 + 8x + 1) = 4x^2 + 2x$

$6x - 1 = 4x^2 + 2x$

$0 = 4x^2 - 4x + 1$

$0 = (2x-1)^2$

$2x - 1 = 0$

$2x = 1$

$x = \dfrac{1}{2}$

61. $\dfrac{2}{r-2} - \dfrac{r+1}{r+4} = 0$

Multiplying both sides by the LCD, $(r-2)(r+4)$, gives

$2(r+4) - (r-2)(r+1) = 0$

$2r + 8 - (r^2 - r - 2) = 0$

$-r^2 + 3r + 10 = 0$

$r^2 - 3r - 10 = 0$

$(r-5)(r+2) = 0$

Thus, $r = 5, -2$.

63. $\dfrac{y+1}{y+3} + \dfrac{y+5}{y-2} = \dfrac{14y+7}{(y+3)(y-2)}$

Multiplying both sides by the LCD, $(y+3)(y-2)$, gives

$(y+1)(y-2) + (y+5)(y+3) = 14y + 7$

$y^2 - y - 2 + y^2 + 8y + 15 = 14y + 7$

$2y^2 + 7y + 13 = 14y + 7$

$2y^2 - 7y + 6 = 0$

$(2y-3)(y-2) = 0$

$y = \dfrac{3}{2}$ or $y = 2$

But $y = 2$ does not check. The solution is $y = \dfrac{3}{2}$.

65. $\dfrac{2}{x^2-1} - \dfrac{1}{x(x-1)} = \dfrac{2}{x^2}$

Multiplying both sides by the LCD, $x^2(x+1)(x-1)$, gives

$2x^2 - x(x+1) = 2(x+1)(x-1)$

$2x^2 - x^2 - x = 2x^2 - 2$

$x^2 - x = 2x^2 - 2$

$0 = x^2 + x - 2 = (x+2)(x-1)$

$x = -2$ or $x = 1$

But $x = 1$ does not check. The solution is -2.

67. $\left(\sqrt{2x-3}\right)^2 = (x-3)^2$

$2x - 3 = x^2 - 6x + 9$

$0 = x^2 - 8x + 12$

$0 = (x-6)(x-2)$

$x = 6$ or $x = 2$

Only $x = 6$ checks.

69. $(q+2)^2 = \left(2\sqrt{4q-7}\right)^2$

$q^2 + 4q + 4 = 16q - 28$

$q^2 - 12q + 32 = 0$

$(q-4)(q-8) = 0$

Thus, $q = 4, 8$.

71. $\sqrt{x+7} = 1 + \sqrt{2x}$

$\left(\sqrt{x+7}\right)^2 = \left(1+\sqrt{2x}\right)^2$

$x + 7 = 1 + 2\sqrt{2x} + 2x$

$6 - x = 2\sqrt{2x}$

Squaring both sides again gives

$(6-x)^2 = 4(2x)$

$36 - 12x + x^2 = 8x$

$x^2 - 20x + 36 = 0$

$(x-18)(x-2) = 0$

$x = 18$ or $x = 2$

Only $x = 2$ checks.

73. $\sqrt{x}+1=\sqrt{2x+1}$

$\left(\sqrt{x}+1\right)^2=\left(\sqrt{2x+1}\right)^2$

$x+2\sqrt{x}+1=2x+1$

$2\sqrt{x}=x$

$\left(2\sqrt{x}\right)^2=x^2$

$4x=x^2$

$0=x^2-4x$

$0=x(x-4)$

Thus, $x=0,\ 4$.

75. $\sqrt{x+5}+1=2\sqrt{x}$

$\left(\sqrt{x+5}+1\right)^2=\left(2\sqrt{x}\right)^2$

$x+5+2\sqrt{x+5}+1=4x$

$2\sqrt{x+5}=3x-6$

$\left(2\sqrt{x+5}\right)^2=(3x-6)^2$

$4(x+5)=9x^2-36x+36$

$0=9x^2-40x+16$

$0=(9x-4)(x-4)$

$x=\dfrac{4}{9}$ or $x=4$

Only $x=4$ checks.

77. $x=\dfrac{-(-2.7)\pm\sqrt{(-2.7)^2-4(0.04)(8.6)}}{2(0.04)}$

≈ 64.15 or 3.35

79. Let l = the length of the picture, then its width is $l-2$.

$l(l-2)=48$

$l^2-2l-48=0$

$(l-8)(l+6)=0$

$l-8=0\qquad$ or $\quad l+6=0$

$l=8\qquad\quad$ or $\quad l=-6$

Since length cannot be negative, $l=8$. The width of the picture is $l-2=8-2$ $=6$ inches.

The dimensions of the picture are 6 inches by 8 inches.

81. $\overline{M}=\dfrac{Q(Q+10)}{44}$

$44\overline{M}=Q^2+10Q$

$0=Q^2+10Q-44\overline{M}$

From the quadratic formula with $a=1$, $b=10,\ c=-44\overline{M}$,

$Q=\dfrac{-10\pm\sqrt{100-4(1)(-44\overline{M})}}{2(1)}$

$=\dfrac{-10+2\sqrt{25+44\overline{M}}}{2}$

$=-5\pm\sqrt{25+44\overline{M}}$

Thus, $-5+\sqrt{25+44\overline{M}}$ is a root.

83. $\dfrac{A}{A+12}d=\dfrac{A+1}{24}d$.

Dividing both sides by d and then multiplying both sides by $24(A+12)$ gives

$24A=(A+12)(A+1)$

$24A=A^2+13A+12$

$0=A^2-11A+12$

From the quadratic formula,

$A=\dfrac{11\pm\sqrt{121-48}}{2}=\dfrac{11\pm\sqrt{73}}{2}$.

$A=\dfrac{11+\sqrt{73}}{2}\approx 10$ or $A=\dfrac{11-\sqrt{73}}{2}\approx 1$.

The doses are the same at 1 year and 10 years.

85. $\dfrac{1}{p}+\dfrac{1}{120-p}=\dfrac{1}{24}$

Multiplying both sides by $24p(120-p)$ gives

$24(120-p)+24p=p(120-p)$

$2880-24p+24p=120p-p^2$

$p^2-120p+2880=0$

By the quadratic formula,

$p=\dfrac{-(-120)\pm\sqrt{(-120)^2-4(1)(2880)}}{2}$

$=\dfrac{120\pm\sqrt{2880}}{2}$

≈ 86.8 cm or 33.2 cm

87. a. When the object strikes the ground, h must be 0, so

$$0 = 44.1t - 4.9t^2 = t(44.1 - 4.9t)$$

$t = 0$ or $t = 9$

The object will strike the ground 9 s after being thrown.

b. Setting $h = 88.2$ gives

$$88.2 = 44.1t - 4.9t^2$$

$$4.9t^2 - 44.1t + 88.2 = 0$$

$$t = \frac{44.1 \pm \sqrt{(-44.1)^2 - 4(4.9)(88.2)}}{2(4.9)}$$

$$= \frac{44.1 \pm 14.7}{9.8}$$

$t = 3$ s or $t = 6$ s

89. By a program, roots are 1.5 and 0.75. Algebraically:

$$8x^2 - 18x + 9 = 0$$

$$(2x - 3)(4x - 3) = 0$$

Thus, $2x - 3 = 0$ or $4x - 3 = 0$.

So $x = \frac{3}{2} = 1.5$ or $x = \frac{3}{4} = 0.75$.

91. No real root

93. $(\pi t - 4)^2 = 4.1t - 3$

$$\pi^2 t^2 - 8\pi t + 16 = 4.1t - 3$$

$$\pi^2 t^2 + (-8\pi - 4.1)t + 19 = 0$$

Roots: 1.999, 0.963

Chapter 1 Review Problems

1. $4 - 3x = 2 + 5x$

$2 = 8x$

$x = \dfrac{2}{8} = \dfrac{1}{4}$

3. $3[2 - 4(1 + x)] = 5 - 3(3 - x)$

$3[2 - 4 - 4x] = 5 - 9 + 3x$

$-6 - 12x = -4 + 3x$

$-2 = 15x$

$x = -\dfrac{2}{15}$

5. $2 - w = 3 + w$

$-2w = 1$

$w = -\dfrac{1}{2}$

7. $x = 3x - (17 + 2x)$

$x = x - 17$

$0 = -17$

There is no solution. The solution set is $\varnothing$.

9. $2\left(4 - \dfrac{3}{5}p\right) = 5$

$8 - \dfrac{6}{5}p = 5$

$-\dfrac{6}{5}p = -3$

$-6p = -15$

$p = \dfrac{5}{2}$

11. $\dfrac{3x - 1}{x + 4} = 0$

$3x - 1 = 0$

$3x = 1$

$x = \dfrac{1}{3}$

13. $\dfrac{2x}{x - 3} - \dfrac{x + 1}{x + 2} = 1$

Multiplying both sides by the LCD, $(x - 3)(x + 2)$, gives

$$(x - 3)(x + 2)\left[\frac{2x}{x - 3} - \frac{x + 1}{x + 2}\right]$$
$$= (x - 3)(x + 2)[1]$$

$2x(x + 2) - (x - 3)(x + 1) = (x - 3)(x + 2)$

$2x^2 + 4x - (x^2 - 2x - 3) = x^2 - x - 6$

$2x^2 + 4x - x^2 + 2x + 3 = x^2 - x - 6$

$x^2 + 6x + 3 = x^2 - x - 6$

$7x = -9$

$x = -\dfrac{9}{7}$

15. $(3x + 5)(x - 1) = 0$

$3x + 5 = 0$ or $x - 1 = 0$

$x = -\dfrac{5}{3}$ or $x = 1$

17. $5q^2 = 7q$

$5q^2 - 7q = 0$

$q(5q - 7) = 0$

$q = 0$ or $5q - 7 = 0$

$q = 0$ or $q = \dfrac{7}{5}$

19. $(x - 5)^2 = 0$

$x - 5 = 0$

$x = 5$

21. $3x^2 - 7 = 1$

$3x^2 = 8$

$x^2 = \dfrac{8}{3}$

$x = \pm\sqrt{\dfrac{8}{3}} = \pm\dfrac{\sqrt{24}}{3} = \pm\dfrac{2\sqrt{6}}{3}$

23. $(8t - 5)(2t + 6) = 0$

$8t - 5 = 0$ or $2t + 6 = 0$

$t = \dfrac{5}{8}$ or $t = -3$

25. $-3x^2 + 5x - 1 = 0$

$3x^2 - 5x + 1 = 0$

Using the quadratic formula with $a = 3$, $b = -5$ and $c = 1$ gives

$x = \dfrac{-b \pm \sqrt{b^2 - 4ac}}{2a}$

$= \dfrac{-(-5) \pm \sqrt{25 - 4(3)(1)}}{2(3)}$

$= \dfrac{5 \pm \sqrt{13}}{6}$

27. $x^2(x^2 - 9) - 4(x^2 - 9) = 0$

$(x^2 - 9)(x^2 - 4) = 0$

$(x + 3)(x - 3)(x + 2)(x - 2) = 0$

Setting each factor equal to 0 gives $x = \pm 3$, ± 2.

29. $\dfrac{6w + 7}{2w + 1} - \dfrac{6w + 1}{2w} = 1$

Multiplying both sides by the LCD, $(2w + 1)(2w)$, gives

$2w(6w + 7) - (2w + 1)(6w + 1)$
$= (2w + 1)(2w)$

$12w^2 + 14w - (12w^2 + 8w + 1) = 4w^2 + 2w$

$6w - 1 = 4w^2 + 2w$

$0 = 4w^2 - 4w + 1$

$0 = (2w - 1)^2$

$2w - 1 = 0$

$2w = 1$

$w = \dfrac{1}{2}$

31. Multiplying both sides by the LCD, $(x + 3)(x - 3)$, gives

$2 - 3x(x - 3) = 1(x + 3)$

$2 - 3x^2 + 9x = x + 3$

$0 = 3x^2 - 8x + 1$

$x = \dfrac{-b \pm \sqrt{b^2 - 4ac}}{2a}$

$= \dfrac{-(-8) \pm \sqrt{64 - 4(3)(1)}}{2(3)}$

$= \dfrac{8 \pm \sqrt{52}}{6} = \dfrac{8 \pm 2\sqrt{13}}{6} = \dfrac{4 \pm \sqrt{13}}{3}$

33. $\sqrt{2x + 7} = 5$

$\left(\sqrt{2x + 7}\right)^2 = 5^2$

$2x + 7 = 25$

$2x = 18$

$x = 9$

35. $\left(\sqrt[3]{11x + 9}\right)^3 = 4^3$

$11x + 9 = 64$

$11x = 55$

$x = 5$

37. $\sqrt{y} + 6 = 5$

$\sqrt{y} = -1$, which has no solution because the square root of a real number cannot be negative.

39. $\left(\sqrt{x-1}\right)^2 = \left(7 - \sqrt{x+6}\right)^2$

$x - 1 = 49 - 14\sqrt{x+6} + x + 6$

$14\sqrt{x+6} = 56$

$\sqrt{x+6} = 4$

$x + 6 = 16$

$x = 10$

41. $x + 2 = 2\sqrt{4x-7}$

$(x+2)^2 = \left(2\sqrt{4x-7}\right)^2$

$x^2 + 4x + 4 = 4(4x-7)$

$x^2 + 4x + 4 = 16x - 28$

$x^2 - 12x + 32 = 0$

$(x-4)(x-8) = 0$

$x = 4 \text{ or } x = 8$

43. Set $w = y^{1/3}$.

$w^2 + w - 2 = 0$

$(w+2)(w-1) = 0$

$w = -2 \text{ or } w = 1$

Thus, $y^{1/3} = -2 \text{ or } y^{1/3} = 1$

$y = -8 \quad \text{ or } \quad y = 1$

45. $E = \dfrac{4\pi k Q}{A}$

$EA = (4\pi k)Q$

$Q = \dfrac{EA}{4\pi k}$

47. $n - 1 = C + \dfrac{C'}{\lambda^2}$

$n - 1 - C = \dfrac{C'}{\lambda^2}$

$C' = \lambda^2(n - 1 - C)$

49. $T^2 = 4\pi^2\left(\dfrac{L}{g}\right)$

$T = \pm\sqrt{4\pi^2\left(\dfrac{L}{g}\right)} = \pm 2\pi\sqrt{\dfrac{L}{g}}$

51. $mgh = \dfrac{1}{2}mv^2 + \dfrac{1}{2}I\omega^2$

$2mgh = mv^2 + I\omega^2$

$mgh - mv^2 = I\omega^2$

$\omega^2 = \dfrac{2mgh - mv^2}{I}$

$\omega = \pm\sqrt{\dfrac{2mgh - mv^2}{I}}$

53. $S^2 + \dfrac{R}{L}S + \dfrac{1}{LC} = 0$

By the quadratic formula,

$S = \dfrac{-\left(\frac{R}{L}\right) \pm \sqrt{\left(\frac{R}{L}\right)^2 - 4(1)\left[\frac{1}{(LC)}\right]}}{2(1)}$

$= -\dfrac{R}{2L} \pm \dfrac{\sqrt{\left(\frac{R}{L}\right)^2 - \frac{4}{LC}}}{2}$

Introducing the denominator 2 into the radical gives

$S = -\dfrac{R}{2L} \pm \sqrt{\dfrac{\left(\frac{R}{L}\right)^2 - \frac{4}{LC}}{4}}$

$= -\dfrac{R}{2L} \pm \sqrt{\left(\dfrac{R}{2L}\right)^2 - \dfrac{1}{LC}}.$

55. $6, \dfrac{5}{4}$

57. $5.6 - 7.2x - 19.3x^2 = 0$

$a = -19.3, b = -7.2, c = 5.6$

Roots: $-0.757, 0.384$

Mathematical Snapshot Chapter 1

1. **a.** $\$100 + \$100(0.0715) = \$107.15$

     b. $\$10 + \$10(0.026) = \$10.26$

     c. $\$100 \cdot \dfrac{1\text{ lb}}{\$10} = 10\text{ lb}$

     d. $\$107.15 \cdot \dfrac{1\text{ lb}}{\$10.26} \approx 10.44\text{ lb}$

e. $g = \dfrac{10.44 - 10}{10} = 0.044 = 4.4\%$

(a gain of 4.4%)

f. $g = \dfrac{y - i}{1 + i} = \dfrac{0.0715 - 0.026}{1 + 0.026} \approx 0.044 = 4.4\%$

3. $g = \dfrac{y - i}{1 + i} = \dfrac{0.01 - 0.03}{1 + 0.03} \approx -0.019 = -1.9\%$

This means a loss of 1.9%, which makes sense because the inflation rate is greater than the interest rate (the money is losing value faster than it is growing).

Chapter 2

Exercise 2.1

1. Let w be the width and $2w$ be the length of the plot.

Then area = 800.
$(2w)w = 800$
$2w^2 = 800$
$w^2 = 400$
$w = 20$ ft
Thus the length is 40 ft, so the amount of fencing needed is $2(40) + 2(20) = 120$ ft.

3. Let n = number of ounces in each part. Then we have
$3n + 5n = 128$
$8n = 128$
$n = 16$
Thus there should be $3(16) = 48$ ounces of A and $5(16) = 80$ ounces of B.

5. Let n = number of ounces in each part. Then we have
$2n + 1n = 16$
$3n = 16$
$n = \dfrac{16}{3}$
Thus the turpentine needed is
$(1)n = \dfrac{16}{3} = 5\dfrac{1}{3}$ ounces.

7. Let w = width (in meters) of pavement. The remaining plot for flowers has dimensions $8 - 2w$ by $4 - 2w$.

Thus
$(8 - 2w)(4 - 2w) = 12$
$32 - 24w + 4w^2 = 12$
$4w^2 - 24w + 20 = 0$
$w^2 - 6w + 5 = 0$
$(w - 1)(w - 5) = 0$
Hence $w = 1, 5$. But $w = 5$ is impossible since one dimension of the original plot is 4 m. Thus the width of the pavement should be 1 m.

9. Let q = number of tons for \$540,000 profit. Profit = Total Revenue − Total Cost
$540,000 = 126q - (76q + 110,000)$
$540,000 = 50q - 110,000$
$650,000 = 50q$
$\dfrac{650,000}{50} = q$
$q = 13,000$ tons

11. Let x = amount at 6% and
$20,000 - x$ = amount at $7\dfrac{1}{2}\%$.
$x(0.06) + (20,000 - x)(0.075) = 1440$
$-0.015x + 1500 = 1440$
$-0.015x = -60$
$x = 4000$, so $20,000 - x = 16,000$. Thus the investment consisted of \$4000 at 6% and
\$16,000 at $7\dfrac{1}{2}\%$.

13. Let p = selling price. Then profit = $0.2p$. selling price = cost + profit
$p = 3.40 + 0.2p$
$0.8p = 3.40$
$p = \dfrac{3.40}{0.8} = \$4.25$

15. Following the procedure in Example 6 we obtain

$$2,000,000(1 + r)^2 = 2,163,200$$

$$(1 + r)^2 = \frac{676}{625}$$

$$(1 + r) = \pm\frac{26}{25}$$

$$r = -1 \pm \frac{26}{25}$$

We choose $r = \dfrac{1}{25} = 0.04 = 4\%$.

17. Let n = number of room applications sent out.

$$0.95n = 76$$

$$n = \frac{76}{0.95} = 80$$

19. Let s = monthly salary of deputy sheriff.

$$0.30s = 200$$

$$s = \frac{200}{0.30}$$

Yearly salary $= 12s = 12\left(\dfrac{200}{0.30}\right) = \$8000$

21. Let q = number of cartridges sold to break even.

total revenue = total cost

$$19.95q = 12.92q + 8000$$

$$7.03q = 8000$$

$$q \approx 1137.98$$

1138 cartridges must be sold.

23. Let v = total annual vision-care expenses (in dollars) covered by program. Then

$$35 + 0.80(v - 35) = 100$$

$$0.80v + 7 = 100$$

$$0.80v = 93$$

$$v = \$116.25$$

25. Revenue = (number of units sold) (price per unit)

Thus

$$400 = q\left[\frac{80 - q}{4}\right]$$

$$1600 = 80q - q^2$$

$$q^2 - 80q + 1600 = 0$$

$$(q - 40)^2 = 0$$

$$q = 40 \text{ units}$$

27. Let q = required number of units. We equate incomes under both proposals.

$$2000 + 0.50q = 25,000$$

$$0.50q = 23,000$$

$$q = 46,000 \text{ units}$$

29. Let n = number of \$20 increases. Then at the rental charge of $400 + 20n$ dollars per unit, the number of units that can be rented is $50 - 2n$. The total of all monthly rents is $(400 + 20n)(50 - 2n)$, which must equal 20,240.

$$20,240 = (400 + 20n)(50 - 2n)$$

$$20,240 = 20,000 + 200n - 40n^2$$

$$40n^2 - 200n + 240 = 0$$

$$n^2 - 5n + 6 = 0$$

$$(n - 2)(n - 3) = 0$$

$$n = 2, 3$$

Thus the rent should be either
\$400 + 2(\$20) = \$440 or
\$400 + 3(\$20) = \$460.

31.
$$10,000 = 800p - 7p^2$$

$$7p^2 - 800p + 10,000 = 0$$

$$p = \frac{800 \pm \sqrt{640,000 - 280,000}}{14}$$

$$= \frac{800 \pm \sqrt{360,000}}{14} = \frac{800 \pm 600}{14}$$

For $p > 50$ we choose

$$p = \frac{(800 + 600)}{14} = \$100.$$

33. To have supply = demand,

$$2p - 8 = 300 - 2p$$

$$4p = 308$$

$$p = 77$$

35. Let w = width (in ft) of enclosed area. Then length of enclosed area is $300 - w - w = 300 - 2w$.

Thus
$w(300 - 2w) = 11,200$
$2w(150 - w) = 11,200$
$w(150 - w) = 5600$
$0 = w^2 - 150w + 5600$
$0 = (w - 80)(w - 70)$
Hence $w = 80, 70$. If $w = 70$, then length is $300 - 2w = 300 - 2(70) = 160$. Since building has length of only 150 ft, we reject $w = 70$. If $w = 80$, then length is $300 - 2w = 300 - 2(80) = 140$. Thus the dimensions are 80 ft by 140 ft.

37. Original volume = $(10)(5)(2) = 100$ cm^3
Volume cut from bar = $0.28(100) = 28$ cm^3
Volume of new bar = $100 - 28 = 72$ cm^3
Let x = number of centimeters that the length and width are each reduced. Then
$(10 - x)(5 - x)2 = 72$
$(10 - x)(5 - x) = 36$
$x^2 - 15x + 50 = 36$
$x^2 - 15x + 14 = 0$
$(x - 1)(x - 14) = 0$
$x = 1$ or 14
Because of the length and width of the original bar, we reject $x = 14$ and choose $x = 1$. The new bar has length $10 - x = 10 - 1 = 9$ cm and width is $5 - x = 5 - 1 = 4$ cm.

39. Let x = amount of loan. Then the funds actually received are $x - 0.15x$. Hence,
$x - 0.15x = 95,000$
$0.85x = 95,000$
$x = \$112,000$ (to the nearest thousand)

41. Let n = number of acres sold. Then $n + 20$ acres were originally purchased at a cost of $\dfrac{7200}{n + 20}$ each. The price of each acre sold was $30 + \left[\dfrac{7200}{n + 20} \right]$. Since the revenue from selling n acres is \$7200 (the original cost of the parcel), we have

$$n\left[30 + \frac{7200}{n + 20} \right] = 7200$$
$$n\left[\frac{30n + 600 + 7200}{n + 20} \right] = 7200$$
$$n(30n + 600 + 7200) = 7200(n + 20)$$
$$30n^2 + 7800n = 7200n + 144,000$$
$$n^2 + 20n - 4800 = 0$$
$$(n + 80)(n - 60) = 0$$
$$n = 60 \text{ acres (since } n > 0)$$

43. Let q = number of units of B and $q + 25$ = number of units of A.
Each unit of B costs $\dfrac{1000}{q}$, and each unit of A costs $\dfrac{1500}{q + 25}$. Therefore,

$$\frac{1500}{q + 25} = \frac{1000}{q} + 2$$
$$1500q = 1000(q + 25) + 2(q)(q + 25)$$
$$0 = 2q^2 - 450q + 25,000$$
$$0 = q^2 - 225q + 12,500$$
$$0 = (q - 100)(q - 125)$$
$$q = 100 \text{ or } q = 125$$

If $q = 100$, then $q + 25 = 125$; if $q = 125$, $q + 25 = 150$. Thus the company produces either 125 units of A and 100 units of B, or 150 units of A and 125 units of B.

Principles in Practice 2.2

1. $200 + 0.8S \geq 4500$
$0.8S \geq 4300$
$S \geq 5375$
He must sell at least 5375 products per month.

2. Since $x_1 \geq 0$, $x_2 \geq 0$, $x_3 \geq 0$, and $x_4 \geq 0$,
we have the inequalities
$$150 - x_4 \geq 0$$
$$3x_4 - 210 \geq 0$$
$$x_4 + 60 \geq 0$$
$$x_4 \geq 0$$

Exercise 2.2

1. $3x > 12$
$$x > \frac{12}{3}$$
$$x > 4$$
$(4, \infty)$

3. $4x - 13 \leq 7$
$$4x \leq 20$$
$$x \leq 5$$
$(-\infty, 5]$

5. $-4x \geq 2$
$$x \leq \frac{2}{-4}$$
$$x \leq -\frac{1}{2}$$
$$\left(-\infty, -\frac{1}{2}\right]$$

7. $5 - 7s > 3$
$$-7s > -2$$
$$s < \frac{2}{7}$$
$$\left(-\infty, \frac{2}{7}\right)$$

9. $3 < 2y + 3$
$$0 < 2y$$
$$0 < y$$
$$y > 0$$
$(0, \infty)$

11. $2x - 3 \leq 4 + 7x$
$$-5x \leq 7$$
$$x \geq -\frac{7}{5}$$
$$\left[-\frac{7}{5}, \infty\right)$$

13. $3(2 - 3x) > 4(1 - 4x)$
$$6 - 9x > 4 - 16x$$
$$7x > -2$$
$$x > -\frac{2}{7}$$
$$\left(-\frac{2}{7}, \infty\right)$$

15. $2(3x - 2) > 3(2x - 1)$
$$6x - 4 > 6x - 3$$
$0 > 1$, which is false for all x. Thus the
solution set is $\varnothing$.

17. $x + 2 < \sqrt{3} - x$
$$2x < \sqrt{3} - 2$$
$$x < \frac{\sqrt{3} - 2}{2}$$
$$\left(-\infty, \frac{\sqrt{3} - 2}{2}\right)$$

19. $\dfrac{5}{6}x < 40$

$5x < 240$

$x < 48$

$(-\infty, 48)$

21. $\dfrac{9y+1}{4} \le 2y - 1$

$9y + 1 \le 8y - 4$

$y \le -5$

$(-\infty, -5]$

23. $4x - 1 \ge 4(x-2) + 7$

$4x - 1 \ge 4x - 1$

$0 \ge 0$, which is true for all x. The solution is

$-\infty < x < \infty$.

$(-\infty, \infty)$

25. $\dfrac{1-t}{2} < \dfrac{3t-7}{3}$

$3 - 3t < 6t - 14$

$-9t < -17$

$t > \dfrac{17}{9}$

$\left(\dfrac{17}{9}, \infty\right)$

27. $2x + 13 \ge \dfrac{1}{2}x - 4$

$4x + 26 \ge x - 8$

$3x \ge -34$

$x \ge -\dfrac{34}{3}$

$\left[-\dfrac{34}{3}, \infty\right)$

29. $\dfrac{2}{3}r < \dfrac{5}{6}r$

$4r < 5r$

$0 < r$

$r > 0$

$(0, \infty)$

31. $\dfrac{y}{2} + \dfrac{y}{3} > y + \dfrac{y}{5}$

$15y + 10y > 30y + 6y$

$25y > 36y$

$0 > 11y$

$0 > y$

$y < 0$

$(-\infty, 0)$

33. $0.1(0.03x + 4) \ge 0.02x + 0.434$

$0.003x + 0.4 \ge 0.02x + 0.434$

$-0.017x \ge 0.034$

$x \le -2$

$(-\infty, -2]$

35. $12(37,000) < S < 12(53,000)$

$444,000 < S < 636,000$

37. The measures of the acute angles of a right triangle sum to 90°. If x is the measure of one acute angle, the other angle has measure $90 - x$.

$x < 3(90 - x) + 10$

$x < 270 - 3x + 10$

$4x < 280$

$x < 70$

The measure of the angle is less than 70°.

Exercise 2.3

1. Let q = number of units sold.

Profit > 0

Total revenue – Total cost > 0

$20q - (15q + 600,000) > 0$

$5q - 600,000 > 0$

$5q > 600,000$

$q > 120,000$

Thus at least 120,001 units must be sold.

3. Let x = number of miles driven per year.
If the auto is leased, the annual cost is
$12(420) + 0.06x$.
If the auto is purchased, the annual cost is
$4700 + 0.08x$.
We want Rental cost $\leq$ Purchase cost.
$12(420) + 0.06x \leq 4700 + 0.08x$
$5040 + 0.06x \leq 4700 + 0.08x$
$340 \leq 0.02x$
$17,000 \leq x$
The number of miles driven per year must be at least 17,000.

5. Let q be the required number of magazines.
Then cost of publication is $q(0.65)$. Revenue from dealers is $0.60q$ and from advertising is $0.10(q - 10,000)(0.60)$. Thus
Profit ≥ 0
Total Revenue − Total Cost ≥ 0
$0.60q + 0.10(q - 10,000)(0.60) - 0.65q \geq 0$
$0.01q - 600 \geq 0$
$0.01q \geq 600$
$q \geq 60,000$
At least 60,000 magazines are required.

7. Let x = amount at $6\frac{3}{4}\%$ and
$30,000 - x$ = amount at 5%. Then
interest at $6\frac{3}{4}\%$ + interest at 5%
$\geq$ interest at $6\frac{1}{2}\%$
$x(0.0675) + (30,000 - x)(0.05) \geq$
$(0.065)(30,000)$
$0.0175x + 1500 \geq 1950$
$0.0175x \geq 450$
$x \geq 25,714.29$
Thus at least \$25,714.29 must be invested at
$6\frac{3}{4}\%$.

9. Let q be the number of units sold this month at \$4.00 each. Then $2500 - q$ will be sold at \$4.50 each. Then
Total revenue $\geq 10,750$
$4q + 4.5(2500 - q) \geq 10,750$
$-0.5q + 11,250 \geq 10,750$
$500 \geq 0.5q$
$1000 \geq q$
The maximum number of units that can be sold this month is 1000.

11. For $t < 40$, we want
income on hourly basis
> income on per-job basis
$8.50t > 300 + 3(40 - t)$
$8.50t > 420 - 3t$
$11.50t > 420$
$t > 36.5$ hr

13. Let x = accounts receivable. Then
Acid test ratio $= \dfrac{450,000 + x}{398,000}$

$1.3 \leq \dfrac{450,000 + x}{398,000}$

$517,400 \leq 450,000 + x$
$x \geq 67,400$
The company must have at least \$67,400 in accounts receivable.

Principles in Practice 2.4

1. $|w - 22| \leq 0.3$

Exercise 2.4

1. $|-13| = 13$

3. $|8 - 2| = |6| = 6$

5. $\left|3\left(-\dfrac{5}{3}\right)\right| = |-5| = 5$

7. $|x| < 4, -4 < x < 4$

9. Because $2 - \sqrt{5} < 0$,
$\left|2 - \sqrt{5}\right| = -\left(2 - \sqrt{5}\right) = \sqrt{5} - 2$.

11. a. $|x - 7| < 3$

   b. $|x - 2| < 3$

   c. $|x - 7| \le 5$

   d. $|x - 7| = 4$

   e. $|x + 4| < 2$

   f. $|x| < 3$

   g. $|x| > 6$

   h. $|x - 6| > 4$

   i. $|x - 105| < 3$

   j. $|x - 850| < 100$

13. $|p_1 - p_2| \le 8$

15. $|x| = 7$
$x = \pm 7$

17. $\left|\dfrac{x}{3}\right| = 2$

$\dfrac{x}{3} = \pm 2$

$x = \pm 6$

19. $|x - 5| = 8$
$x - 5 = \pm 8$
$x = 5 \pm 8$
$x = 13 \text{ or } x = -3$

21. $|5x - 2| = 0$
$5x - 2 = 0$
$x = \dfrac{2}{5}$

23. $|7 - 4x| = 5$
$7 - 4x = \pm 5$
$-4x = -7 \pm 5$
$-4x = -2 \text{ or } -12$
$x = \dfrac{1}{2} \text{ or } x = 3$

25. $|x| < 4$
$-4 < x < 4$
$(-4, 4)$

27. $\left|\dfrac{x}{4}\right| > 2$

$\dfrac{x}{4} < -2$ or $\dfrac{x}{4} > 2$

$x < -8$ or $x > 8$, so the
solution is $(-\infty, -8) \cup (8, \infty)$.

29. $|x + 7| < 2$
$-2 < x + 7 < 2$
$-9 < x < -5$
$(-9, -5)$

31. $\left|x - \dfrac{1}{2}\right| > \dfrac{1}{2}$

$x - \dfrac{1}{2} < -\dfrac{1}{2}$ or $x - \dfrac{1}{2} > \dfrac{1}{2}$

$x < 0$ or $x > 1$
$(-\infty, 0) \cup (1, \infty)$

33. $|5 - 8x| \le 1$
$-1 \le 5 - 8x \le 1$
$-6 \le -8x \le -4$
$\dfrac{3}{4} \ge x \ge \dfrac{1}{2}$, which may be rewritten as

$\dfrac{1}{2} \le x \le \dfrac{3}{4}$.

The solution is $\left[\dfrac{1}{2}, \dfrac{3}{4}\right]$.

35. $\left|\dfrac{3x - 8}{2}\right| \ge 4$

$\dfrac{3x - 8}{2} \le -4$ or $\dfrac{3x - 8}{2} \ge 4$

$3x - 8 \le -8$ or $3x - 8 \ge 8$
$3x \le 0$ or $3x \ge 16$

$x \le 0$ or $x \ge \dfrac{16}{3}$

The solution is $(-\infty, 0] \cup \left[\dfrac{16}{3}, \infty\right)$.

37. $|d - 17.2 \text{ m}| \le 30 \text{ cm or } |d - 17.2| \le 0.030 \text{ m}$.

39. $|x - \mu| > h\sigma$

Either $x - \mu < -h\sigma$, or $x - \mu > h\sigma$.
Thus either
$x < \mu - h\sigma$ or $x > \mu + h\sigma$, so the solution is
$(-\infty, \mu - h\sigma) \cup (\mu + h\sigma, \infty)$.

Chapter 2 Review Problems

1. $3x - 8 \geq 4(x - 2)$
$3x - 8 \geq 4x - 8$
$-x \geq 0$
$x \leq 0$
$(-\infty, 0]$

3. $-(5x + 2) < -(2x + 4)$
$-5x - 2 < -2x - 4$
$-3x < -2$
$x > \dfrac{2}{3}$, or $\left(\dfrac{2}{3}, \infty \right)$

5. $3p(1 - p) > 3(2 + p) - 3p^2$
$3p - 3p^2 > 6 + 3p - 3p^2$
$0 > 6$, which is false for all x. The solution set is $\varnothing$.

7. Multiplying both sides by 6 gives
$2(x + 5) - 3(1) \leq 6(2)$
$2x + 10 - 3 \leq 12$
$2x \leq 5$
$x \leq \dfrac{5}{2}$
$\left(-\infty, \dfrac{5}{2} \right]$

9. Multiplying both sides by 8 gives
$2s - 24 \leq 3 + 2s$
$0 \leq 27$, which is true for all s. Thus
$-\infty < s < \infty$, or $(-\infty, \infty)$.

11. $|3 - 2x| = 7$

$3 - 2x = 7$	or $3 - 2x = -7$
$-2x = 4$	or $-2x = -10$
$x = -2$	or $x = 5$

13. $|4t - 1| < 1$
$-1 < 4t - 1 < 1$
$0 < 4t < 2$
$0 < t < \dfrac{1}{2}$
$\left(0, \dfrac{1}{2} \right)$

15. $|3 - 2x| \geq 4$

$3 - 2x \geq 4$	or $3 - 2x \leq -4$
$-2x \geq 1$	or $-2x \leq -7$
$x \leq -\dfrac{1}{2}$	or $x \geq \dfrac{7}{2}$

The solution is $\left(-\infty, -\dfrac{1}{2} \right] \cup \left[\dfrac{7}{2}, \infty \right)$.

17. Let x be the number of issues with decline, and $x + 48$ be the number of issues with increase. Then
$x + (x + 48) = 1132$
$2x = 1084$
$x = 542$

19. Let q units be produced at A and $10,000 - q$ at B.
Cost at A + Cost at B $\leq 117,000$
$[5q + 30,000] + [5.50(10,000 - q) + 35,000]$
$\leq 117,000$
$-0.5q + 120,000 \leq 117,000$
$-0.5q \leq -3000$
$q \geq 6000$
Thus at least 6000 units must be produced at plant A.

21. Let $c = $ operating costs
$\dfrac{c}{236,460} < 0.90$
$c < \$212,814$

Mathematical Snapshot Chapter 2

1. $t = 2l - 4 = 2\left(2\dfrac{1}{2} \right) - 4 = 1$ hour

3. $l = 2\dfrac{2}{3}$ hours. Thus

$$t = \frac{3}{2}l - 3 = \frac{3}{2}\left(2\frac{2}{3}\right) - 3 = 1 \text{ hour.}$$

5.
```
solve(X/12+(1080
-X)/20-74,X,450)
■              600
```

$x = 600$

```
solve(X/15+(1590
-X)/24-74,X,450)
               310
```

$x = 310$

Chapter 3

Principles in Practice 3.1

1. a. The formula for the area of a circle is πr^2, where r is the radius.
$$a(r) = \pi r^2$$

b. The domain of $a(r)$ is all real numbers.

c. Since a radius cannot be negative or zero, the domain for the function, in context, is $r > 0$.

2. a. The formula relating distance, time, and speed is $d = rt$ where d is the distance, r is the speed, and t is the time. This can also be written as $t = \dfrac{d}{r}$. When $d = 300$, we have $t(r) = \dfrac{300}{r}$.

b. The domain of $t(r)$ is all real numbers except 0.

c. Since speed is not negative, the domain for the function, in context, is $r > 0$.

d. Replacing r by x: $t(x) = \dfrac{300}{x}$.

Replacing r by $\dfrac{x}{2}$: $t\left(\dfrac{x}{2}\right) = \dfrac{300}{\frac{x}{2}} = \dfrac{600}{x}$.

Replacing r by $\dfrac{x}{4}$:
$$t\left(\dfrac{x}{4}\right) = \dfrac{300}{\frac{x}{4}} = \dfrac{1200}{x}.$$

e. When the speed is reduced (divided) by a constant, the time is scaled (multiplied) by the same constant;
$$t\left(\dfrac{r}{c}\right) = \dfrac{300c}{r}.$$

3. a. If the price is \$18.50 per large pizza, $p = 18.5$.
$$18.5 = 26 - \dfrac{q}{40}$$
$$-7.5 = -\dfrac{q}{40}$$
$$300 = q$$
At a price of \$18.50 per large pizza, 300 pizzas are sold each week.

b. If 200 large pizzas are being sold each week, $q = 200$.
$$p = 26 - \dfrac{200}{40}$$
$$p = 26 - 5$$
$$p = 21$$
The price is \$21 per pizza if 200 large pizzas are being sold each week.

c. To double the number of large pizzas sold, use $q = 400$.
$$p = 26 - \dfrac{400}{40}$$
$$p = 26 - 10$$
$$p = 16$$
To sell 400 large pizzas each week, the price should be \$16 per pizza.

Exercise 3.1

1. The denominator is zero when $x = 0$. Any other real number can be used for x.
Answer: all real numbers except 0

3. For $\sqrt{x - 3}$ to be real, $x - 3 \geq 0$, so $x \geq 3$.
Answer: all real numbers ≥ 3

5. Any real number can be used for t.
Answer: all real numbers

7. We exclude values of x where
$$2x + 7 = 0$$
$$2x = -7$$
$$x = -\frac{7}{2}$$

Answer: all real numbers except $-\dfrac{7}{2}$

9. We exclude values of y for which
$$y^2 - y = 0$$
$$y(y - 1) = 0$$
$$y = 0 \text{ or } 1$$
Answer: all real numbers except 0 and 1

11. We exclude all values of s for which
$$2s^2 - 7s - 4 = 0$$
$$(s - 4)(2s + 1) = 0$$
$$s = 4, -\frac{1}{2}$$

Answer: all real numbers except 4 and $-\dfrac{1}{2}$

13. $f(x) = 2x + 1$
$$f(0) = 2(0) + 1 = 1$$
$$f(3) = 2(3) + 1 = 7$$
$$f(-4) = 2(-4) + 1 = -7$$

15. $G(x) = 2 - x^2$
$$G(-8) = 2 - (-8)^2 = 2 - 64 = -62$$
$$G(u) = 2 - u^2$$
$$G(u^2) = 2 - (u^2)^2 = 2 - u^4$$

17. $g(u) = u^2 + u$
$$g(-2) = (-2)^2 + (-2) = 4 - 2 = 2$$
$$g(2v) = (2v)^2 + (2v) = 4v^2 + 2v$$
$$g(-x^2) = (-x^2)^2 + (-x^2) = x^4 - x^2$$

19. $f(x) = x^2 + 2x + 1$
$$f(1) = 1^2 + 2(1) + 1 = 1 + 2 + 1 = 4$$
$$f(-1) = (-1)^2 + 2(-1) + 1 = 1 - 2 + 1 = 0$$
$$f(x + h) = (x + h)^2 + 2(x + h) + 1$$
$$= x^2 + 2xh + h^2 + 2x + 2h + 1$$

21. $g(x) = \dfrac{x - 4}{x^2 + 5}$
$$g(5) = \frac{5 - 4}{5^2 + 5} = \frac{1}{30}$$
$$g(3x) = \frac{3x - 4}{(3x)^2 + 5} = \frac{3x - 4}{9x^2 + 5}$$
$$g(x + h) = \frac{(x + h) - 4}{(x + h)^2 + 5} = \frac{x + h - 4}{x^2 + 2xh + h^2 + 5}$$

23. $f(x) = x^{4/3}$
$$f(0) = 0^{4/3} = 0$$
$$f(64) = 64^{4/3} = \left(\sqrt[3]{64}\right)^4 = (4)^4 = 256$$
$$f\left(\frac{1}{8}\right) = \left(\frac{1}{8}\right)^{4/3} = \left(\sqrt[3]{\frac{1}{8}}\right)^4 = \left(\frac{1}{2}\right)^4 = \frac{1}{16}$$

25. $f(x) = 4x - 5$

  a. $f(x + h) = 4(x + h) - 5 = 4x + 4h - 5$

  b. $\dfrac{f(x + h) - f(x)}{h}$
$$= \frac{(4x + 4h - 5) - (4x - 5)}{h}$$
$$= \frac{4h}{h} = 4$$

27. $f(x) = x^2 + 2x$

  a. $f(x + h) = (x + h)^2 + 2(x + h)$
$$= x^2 + 2xh + h^2 + 2x + 2h$$

  b. $\dfrac{f(x + h) - f(x)}{h}$
$$= \frac{(x^2 + 2xh + h^2 + 2x + 2h) - (x^2 + 2x)}{h}$$
$$= \frac{2xh + h^2 + 2h}{h} = 2x + h + 2$$

29. $f(x) = 2 - 4x - 3x^2$

    a. $f(x + h) = 2 - 4(x + h) - 3(x + h)^2 = 2 - 4x - 4h - 3(x^2 + 2xh + h^2) = 2 - 4x - 4h - 3x^2 - 6xh - 3h^2$

    b. $\dfrac{f(x + h) - f(x)}{h} = \dfrac{2 - 4x - 4h - 3x^2 - 6xh - 3h^2 - (2 - 4x - 3x^2)}{h}$

             $= \dfrac{-4h - 6xh - 3h^2}{h} = \dfrac{h(-4 - 6x - 3h)}{h} = -4 - 6x - 3h$

31. $f(x) = \dfrac{1}{x}$

    a. $f(x + h) = \dfrac{1}{x + h}$

    b. $\dfrac{f(x + h) - f(x)}{h} = \dfrac{\frac{1}{x+h} - \frac{1}{x}}{h} = \dfrac{\frac{x - (x+h)}{x(x+h)}}{h} = \dfrac{-h}{x(x + h)h} = -\dfrac{1}{x(x + h)}$

33. $f(x) = 9x + 7$

     $\dfrac{f(2 + h) - f(2)}{h} = \dfrac{9(2 + h) + 7 - [9(2) + 7]}{h} = \dfrac{25 + 9h - [25]}{h} = \dfrac{9h}{h} = 9$

35. $9y - 3x - 4 = 0$

     The equivalent form $y = \dfrac{3x + 4}{9}$ shows that for each input x there is exactly one output, $\dfrac{3x + 4}{9}$.

     Thus y is a function of x. Solving for x gives $x = \dfrac{9y - 4}{3}$. This shows that for each input y there is

     exactly one output, $\dfrac{9y - 4}{3}$. Thus x is a function of y.

37. $y = 7x^2$

     For each input x, there is exactly one output $7x^2$. Thus y is a function of x. Solving for x gives $x = \pm\sqrt{\dfrac{y}{7}}$.

     If, for example, $y = 7$, then $x = \pm1$, so x is not a function of y.

39. Yes, because corresponding to each input r there is exactly one output, πr^2.

41. Weekly excess of income over expenses is $4000 - 3200 = 800$. After t weeks the excess accumulates to $800t$. Thus the value of V of the business at the end of t weeks is given by $V = f(t) = 20{,}000 + 800t$.

43. Yes; for each input q there corresponds exactly one output, $1.25q$, so P is a function of q.
The dependent variable is P and the independent variable is q.

45. The function can be written as $q = 50p$. At \$8.00 per pound, the coffee house will supply $q = 50(8) = 400$ pounds per week. At \$20.00 per pound, the coffee house will supply $q = 50(20) = 1000$ pounds per week. The amount the coffee house supplies increases as the price increases.

47. a. $f(1000) = \dfrac{\left(\sqrt[3]{1000}\right)^4}{2500} = \dfrac{10^4}{2500}$

$= \dfrac{10,000}{2500} = 4$

b. $f(2000) = \dfrac{\left[\sqrt[3]{1000(2)}\right]^4}{2500} = \dfrac{\left(10\sqrt[3]{2}\right)^4}{2500}$

$= \dfrac{10,000\sqrt[3]{2^4}}{2500} = 4\sqrt[3]{2^3 \cdot 2} = 8\sqrt[3]{2}$

c. $f(2I_0) = \dfrac{(2I_0)^{4/3}}{2500} = \dfrac{2^{4/3}I_0^{4/3}}{2500}$

$= 2\sqrt[3]{2}\left[\dfrac{I_0^{4/3}}{2500}\right] = 2\sqrt[3]{2}f(I_0)$

Thus $f(2I_0) = 2\sqrt[3]{2}f(I_0)$, which means that doubling the intensity increases the response by a factor of $2\sqrt[3]{2}$.

49. a. Domain: 3000, 2900, 2300, 2000
$f(2900) = 12, f(3000) = 10$

b. Domain: 10, 12, 17, 20
$g(10) = 3000, g(17) = 2300$

51. a. −5.13

b. 2.64

c. −17.43

53. a. 11.33

b. 50.62

c. 2.29

Principles in Practice 3.2

1. a. Let n = the number of visits and $p(n)$ be the premium amount.
$p(n) = 125$

b. The premiums do not change regardless of the number of doctor visits.

c. This is a constant function.

2. a. $d(t) = 3t^2$ is a quadratic function.

b. The degree of $d(t) = 3t^2$ is 2.

c. The leading coefficient of $d(t) = 3t^2$ is 3.

3. The price for n pairs of socks is given by
$c(n) = \begin{cases} 3.5n & 0 \le n \le 5 \\ 3n & 5 < n \le 10 \\ 2.75n & 10 < n \end{cases}$

4. Think of the bookshelf having 7 slots, from left to right. You have a choice of 7 books for the first slot. Once a book has been put in the first slot, you have 6 choices for which book to put in the second slot, etc. The number of arrangements is $7 \cdot 6 \cdot 5 \cdot 4 \cdot 3 \cdot 2 \cdot 1 = 7! = 5040$.

Exercise 3.2

1. yes

3. no

5. yes

7. no

9. all real numbers

11. all real numbers

13. a. 3

b. 7

15. a. 4

   b. −3

17. $f(x) = 8$
$f(2) = 8$
$f(t + 8) = 8$
$f\left(-\sqrt{17}\right) = 8$

19. $F(10) = 1$
$F\left(-\sqrt{3}\right) = -1$
$F(0) = 0$
$F\left(-\dfrac{18}{5}\right) = -1$

21. $G(8) = 8$
$G(3) = 3$
$G(-1) = 2 - (-1)^2 = 1$
$G(1) = 2 - (1)^2 = 1$

23. $6! = 6 \cdot 5 \cdot 4 \cdot 3 \cdot 2 \cdot 1 = 720$

25. $(4 - 2)! = 2! = 2 \cdot 1 = 2$

27. $\dfrac{5!}{4!} = \dfrac{5 \cdot 4 \cdot 3 \cdot 2 \cdot 1}{4 \cdot 3 \cdot 2 \cdot 1} = 5$

29. Let i = the passenger's income and
$c(i)$ = the cost for the ticket.
$c(i) = 4.5$
This is a constant function.

31. a. $C = 850 + 3q$

   b. $1600 = 850 + 3q$
$750 = 3q$
$q = 250$

33. The cost for buying n tickets is
$c(n) = \begin{cases} 8.5n & 0 \le n < 10 \\ 8n & 10 \le n \end{cases}$

35. $P(2) = \dfrac{3!\left(\frac{1}{4}\right)^2\left(\frac{3}{4}\right)^1}{2!(1!)} = \dfrac{6\left(\frac{1}{16}\right)\left(\frac{3}{4}\right)}{2(1)} = \dfrac{9}{64}$

37. a. all T such that $30 \le T \le 39$

   b. $f(30) = \dfrac{1}{24}(30) + \dfrac{11}{4} = \dfrac{5}{4} + \dfrac{11}{4} = \dfrac{16}{4} = 4$

      $f(36) = \dfrac{1}{24}(36) + \dfrac{11}{4} = \dfrac{6}{4} + \dfrac{11}{4} = \dfrac{17}{4}$

      $f(39) = \dfrac{4}{3}(39) - \dfrac{175}{4} = 52 - \dfrac{175}{4} = \dfrac{33}{4}$

39. a. 237,077.34

   b. −434.97

   c. 52.19

41. a. 2.21

   b. 9.98

   c. −14.52

Principles in Practice 3.3

1. The customer's price is
$(c \circ s)(x) = c(s(x)) = c(x + 3) = 2(x + 3)$
$= 2x + 6$

2. $g(x) = (x + 3)^2$ can be written as
$g(x) = a(l(x)) = (a \circ l)(x)$ where $a(x) = x^2$
and $l(x) = x + 3$. Then $l(x)$ represents the
length of the sides of the square, while $a(x)$
is the area of a square with side of length x.

Exercise 3.3

1. $f(x) = x + 3, \ g(x) = x + 5$

   a. $(f + g)(x) = f(x) + g(x) = (x + 3) + (x + 5)$
$= 2x + 8$

   b. $(f + g)(0) = 2(0) + 8 = 8$

   c. $(f - g)(x) = f(x) - g(x) = (x + 3) - (x + 5)$
$= -2$

   d. $(fg)(x) = f(x)g(x) = (x + 3)(x + 5)$
$= x^2 + 8x + 15$

   e. $(fg)(-2) = (-2)^2 + 8(-2) + 15 = 3$

f. $\dfrac{f}{g}(x) = \dfrac{f(x)}{g(x)} = \dfrac{x+3}{x+5}$

g. $(f \circ g)(x) = f(g(x)) = f(x+5)$
$= (x+5) + 3 = x + 8$

h. $(f \circ g)(3) = 3 + 8 = 11$

i. $(g \circ f)(x) = g(f(x)) = g(x+3)$
$= (x+3) + 5 = x + 8$

3. $f(x) = x^2$, $g(x) = x^2 + x$

a. $(f+g)(x) = f(x) + g(x)$
$= x^2 + (x^2 + x) = 2x^2 + x$

b. $(f-g)(x) = f(x) - g(x) = x^2 - (x^2 + x)$
$= -x$

c. $(f-g)\left(-\dfrac{1}{2}\right) = -\left(-\dfrac{1}{2}\right) = \dfrac{1}{2}$

d. $(fg)(x) = f(x)g(x)$
$= x^2(x^2 + x) = x^4 + x^3$

e. $\dfrac{f}{g}(x) = \dfrac{f(x)}{g(x)} = \dfrac{x^2}{x^2 + x}$
$= \dfrac{x}{x+1}$ (for $x \neq 0$)

f. $\dfrac{f}{g}\left(-\dfrac{1}{2}\right) = \dfrac{-\frac{1}{2}}{\left(-\frac{1}{2}\right)+1} = \dfrac{-\frac{1}{2}}{\frac{1}{2}} = -1$

g. $(f \circ g)(x) = f(g(x)) = f(x^2 + x)$
$= (x^2 + x)^2 = x^4 + 2x^3 + x^2$

h. $(g \circ f)(x) = g(f(x)) = g(x^2)$
$= (x^2)^2 + x^2 = x^4 + x^2$

i. $(g \circ f)(-3) = (-3)^4 + (-3)^2 = 81 + 9$
$= 90$

5. $f(g(2)) = f(4-4) = f(0) = 0 + 6 = 6$
$g(f(2)) = g(12+6) = g(18) = 4 - 36 = -32$

7. $(F \circ G)(t) = F(G(t)) = F\left(\dfrac{2}{t-1}\right)$

$= \left(\dfrac{2}{t-1}\right)^2 + 7\left(\dfrac{2}{t-1}\right) + 1$

$= \dfrac{4}{(t-1)^2} + \dfrac{14}{t-1} + 1$

$(G \circ F)(t) = G(F(t)) = G(t^2 + 7t + 1)$

$= \dfrac{2}{(t^2 + 7t + 1) - 1} = \dfrac{2}{t^2 + 7t}$

9. $(f \circ g)(v) = f(g(v)) = f\left(\sqrt{v+2}\right)$

$= \dfrac{2}{\left(\sqrt{v+2}\right)^2 + 1} = \dfrac{1}{v+2+1} = \dfrac{1}{v+3}$

$(g \circ f)(w) = g(f(w)) = g\left(\dfrac{1}{w^2 + 1}\right)$

$= \sqrt{\dfrac{1}{w^2 + 1} + 2} = \sqrt{\dfrac{1 + 2(w^2 + 1)}{w^2 + 1}}$

$= \sqrt{\dfrac{2w^2 + 3}{w^2 + 1}}$

11. Let $g(x) = 4x - 3$ and $f(x) = x^5$. Then
$h(x) = (4x - 3)^5 = [g(x)]^5 = f(g(x))$

13. Let $g(x) = x^2 - 2$ and $f(x) = \dfrac{1}{x}$. Then

$h(x) = \dfrac{1}{x^2 - 2} = \dfrac{1}{g(x)} = f(g(x))$

15. Let $g(x) = \dfrac{x+1}{3}$ and $f(x) = \sqrt[5]{x}$. Then

$h(x) = \sqrt[5]{g(x)} = f(g(x))$

17. a. The revenue is $9.75 per pound of coffee sold, so $r(x) = 9.75x$.

 b. The expenses are $e(x) = 4500 + 4.25x$.

 c. Profit = revenue − expenses.
$(r-e)(x) = 9.75x - (4500 + 4.25x)$
$= 5.5x - 4500$.

19. $(g \circ f)(m) = g(f(m)) = g\left(\dfrac{40m - m^2}{4}\right)$

$= 40\left(\dfrac{40m - m^2}{4}\right) = 10(40m - m^2)$

$= 400m - 10m^2$.

This represents the total revenue received when the total output of m employees is sold.

21. a. 14.05

  b. 1169.64

23. a. 345.03

  b. −1.94

Principles in Practice 3.4

1. Let y = the amount of money in the account. Then, after one month,
$y = 7250 - (1 \cdot 600) = \$6650$,
and after two months
$y = 7250 - (2 \cdot 600) = \$6050$.
Thus, in general, if we let x = the number of months during which Rachel spends from this account, $y = 7250 - 600x$.
To identify the x-intercept, we set $y = 0$ and solve for x.
$y = 7250 - 600x$
$0 = 7250 - 600x$
$600x = 7250$
$x = 12\dfrac{1}{12}$
The x-intercept is $\left(12\dfrac{1}{12}, 0\right)$.
Therefore, after 12 months and approximately 2.5 days Rachel will deplete her savings. To identify the y-intercept, we set $x = 0$ and solve for y.
$y = 7250 - 600x$
$y = 7250 - 600(0)$
$y = 7250$
The y-intercept is (0, 7250).
Therefore, before any months have gone by, Rachel has $7250 in her account.

2. Let y = the cost to the customer and let x = the number of rides he or she takes. Since the cost does not change, regardless of the number of rides taken, the equation $y = 24.95$ represents this situation. The graph of $y = 24.95$ is a horizontal line whose y-intercept is (0, 24.95). Since the line parallels the x-axis, there is no x-intercept.

3. The formula relating distance, time, and speed is $d = rt$, where d is the distance, r is the speed, and t is the time. Let x = the time spent biking (in hours). Then, $12x$ = the distance traveled. Brett bikes $12 \cdot 2.5 = 30$ miles and then turns around and bikes the same distance back to the rental shop. Therefore, we can represent the distance from the turn-around point at any time x as $|30 - 12x|$. Similarly, the distance from the rental shop at any time x can be represented by the function $y = 30 - |30 - 12x|$.

x	0	1	2	2.5	3	4	5
y	0	12	24	30	24	12	0

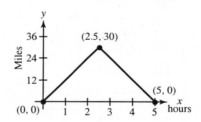

4. The monthly cost of x therms of gas is

$$y = \begin{cases} 0.53x, & \text{if } 0 \le x \le 70 \\ 0.53(70) + 0.74(x - 70), & \text{if } x > 70 \end{cases}$$

or

$$y = \begin{cases} 0.53x, & \text{if } 0 \le x \le 70 \\ 0.74x - 14.7, & \text{if } x > 70. \end{cases}$$

x	0	10	30	50	70	80	90	100
y	0	5.3	15.9	26.5	37.1	44.5	51.9	59.3

Exercise 3.4

1.

3. a. $f(0) = 1$
$f(2) = 2$
$f(4) = 3$
$f(-2) = 0$

b. Domain: all real numbers

c. Range: all real numbers

d. $f(x) = 0$ for $x = -2$. So real zero is -2.

5. a. $f(0) = 0$
$f(1) = -1$
$f(-1) = -1$

b. Domain: all real numbers

c. Range: all nonpositive real numbers

d. $f(x) = 0$ for $x = 0$. So real zero is 0.

7. $y = 2x$
If $y = 0$, then $x = 0$. If $x = 0$, then $y = 0$.
Intercept: $(0, 0)$
y is a function of x.
Domain: all real numbers
Range: all real numbers

9. $y = 3x - 5$

If $y = 0$, then $0 = 3x - 5$, $x = \dfrac{5}{3}$.

If $x = 0$, then $y = -5$.

Intercepts: $\left(\dfrac{5}{3}, 0 \right), (0, -5)$

y is a function of x.
Domain: all real numbers
Range: all real numbers

11. $y = x^2$

If $y = 0$, then $0 = x^2$, $x = 0$. If $x = 0$,
then $y = 0$. Intercept: (0, 0)
y is a function of x.
Domain: all real numbers
Range: all real numbers ≥ 0

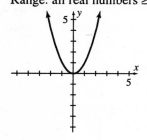

13. $x = 0$

If $y = 0$, then $x = 0$. If $x = 0$, then y can be
any real number. Intercepts: every point on
y-axis
y is not a function of x.

15. $y = x^3$

If $y = 0$, then $0 = x^3$, $x = 0$. If $x = 0$,
then $y = 0$. Intercept: (0, 0).
y is a function of x.
Domain: all real numbers
Range: all real numbers

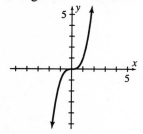

17. $x = -3y^2$

If $y = 0$, then $x = 0$. If $x = 0$, then
$0 = -3y^2$, $y = 0$. Intercept: (0, 0)
y is not a function of x.

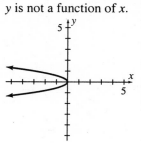

19. $2x + y - 2 = 0$

If $y = 0$, then $2x - 2 = 0$, $x = 1$. If $x = 0$, then
$y - 2 = 0$, $y = 2$. Intercepts: (1, 0), (0, 2)
Note that $y = 2 - 2x$. y is a function of x.
Domain: all real numbers
Range: all real numbers

21. $s = f(t) = 4 - t^2$

If $s = 0$, then $0 = 4 - t^2$
$0 = (2 + t)(2 - t)$
$t = \pm 2$. If $t = 0$, then $s = 4$.
Intercepts: (2, 0), (-2, 0), (0, 4)
Domain: all real numbers
Range: all real numbers ≤ 4

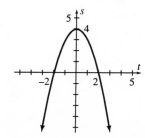

23. $y = g(x) = 2$

Because y cannot be 0, there is no
x-intercept. If $x = 0$, then $y = 2$.
Intercept: $(0, 2)$
Domain: all real numbers
Range: 2

25. $y = h(x) = x^2 - 4x + 1$

If $y = 0$, then $0 = x^2 - 4x + 1$, and by the

quadratic formula, $x = \dfrac{4 \pm \sqrt{12}}{2} = 2 \pm \sqrt{3}$.

If $x = 0$, then $y = 1$.
Intercepts: $(2 \pm \sqrt{3}, 0), (0, 1)$
Domain: all real numbers
Range: all real numbers ≥ -3

27. $f(t) = -t^3$

If $f(t) = 0$, then $0 = -t^3$, $t = 0$.
If $t = 0$, then $f(t) = 0$. Intercept: $(0, 0)$
Domain: all real numbers
Range: all real number

29. $s = F(r) = \sqrt{r - 5}$

Note that for $\sqrt{r - 5}$ to be a real number,
$r - 5 \geq 0$, or $r \geq 5$. If $s = 0$, then $0 = \sqrt{r - 5}$,
$0 = r - 5$, or $r = 5$. Because $r \geq 5$, we know
$r \neq 0$, so no s-intercept exists.
Intercept: $(5, 0)$
Domain, all real numbers ≥ 5
Range: all real numbers ≥ 0

31. $f(x) = |2x - 1|$

If $f(x) = 0$, then
$0 = |2x - 1|$
$2x - 1 = 0$
$x = \dfrac{1}{2}$

If $x = 0$, then $f(x) = |-1| = 1$.

Intercepts: $\left(\dfrac{1}{2}, 0 \right)$, $(0, 1)$

Domain: all real numbers
Range: all real numbers ≥ 0

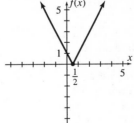

33. $F(t) = \dfrac{16}{t^2}$

If $F(t) = 0$, then $0 = \dfrac{16}{t^2}$, which has no

solution. Because $t \neq 0$, there is no vertical-axis intercept. No intercepts
Domain: all nonzero real numbers
Range: all positive real numbers

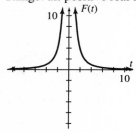

35. Domain: all real numbers ≥ 0
Range: all real c such that $0 \leq c < 6$

37. Domain: all real numbers
Range: all real numbers ≥ 0

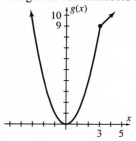

39. From the vertical-line test, the graphs that represent functions of x are (a), (b), and (d).

41. The cost of an item as a function of the time of day, x is

$$y = \begin{cases} 9, & \text{if } 10{:}30 \text{ A.M.} \leq x < 2{:}30 \text{ P.M.} \\ 8, & \text{if } 2{:}30 \text{ P.M.} \leq x < 4{:}30 \text{ P.M.} \\ 13, & \text{if } 4{:}30 \text{ P.M.} \leq x < 6{:}00 \text{ P.M.} \\ 18, & \text{if } 6{:}00 \text{ P.M.} \leq x < 8{:}00 \text{ P.M.} \\ 13, & \text{if } 8{:}00 \text{ P.M.} \leq x \leq 10{:}00 \text{ P.M.} \end{cases}$$

43. As price decreases, quantity increases; p is a function of q.

45.

47. $-1, -0.35$

49. $0.62, 1.73, 4.65$

51. $-0.84, 2.61$

53. $-0.49, 0.52, 1.25$

55.

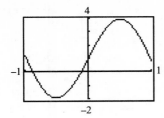

   a.   maximum value of $f(x)$: 3.94

   b.   minimum value of $f(x)$: -1.94

57.

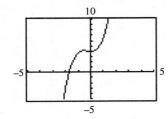

   a.   range: $(-\infty, \infty)$

   b.   intercepts: $(-1.73, 0)$, $(0, 4)$

59.

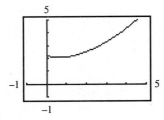

   a.   minimum value of $f(x)$: 2.07

   b.   range: $[2.07, \infty)$

   c.   intercept: $(0, 2.39)$

   d.   no real zero

Exercise 3.5

  1. $y = 5x$
     Intercepts: If $y = 0$, then $5x = 0$, or $x = 0$;
     if $x = 0$, then $y = 5 \cdot 0 = 0$. Testing for
     symmetry gives:
     x-axis: $-y = 5x$
                  $y = -5x$
     y-axis: $y = 5(-x) = -5x$
     origin: $-y = 5(-x)$
                  $y = 5x$

     Since equivalent equation is obtained in the
     third case only, the graph only has symmetry
     about the origin.
     Answer: $(0, 0)$; symmetry about origin

  3. $2x^2 + y^2 x^4 = 8 - y$
     Intercepts: If $y = 0$, then
     $2x^2 = 8$
     $x^2 = 4$
     $x = \pm 2$
     If $x = 0$, then $0 = 8 - y$, so $y = 8$. Testing for
     symmetry gives:
     x-axis: $2x^2 + (-y)^2 x^4 = 8 - (-y)$
                  $2x^2 + y^2 x^4 = 8 + y$
     y-axis: $2(-x)^2 + y^2 (-x)^4 = 8 - y$
                  $2x^2 + y^2 x^4 = 8 - y$
     origin: $2(-x)^2 + (-y)^2 (-x)^4 = 8 - (-y)$
                  $2x^2 + y^2 x^4 = 8 + y$
     Answer: $(\pm 2, 0)$, $(0, 8)$; symmetry about
     y-axis

5. $9x^2 - 4y^2 = 36$

Intercepts: If $y = 0$, then

$9x^2 = 36$

$x^2 = 4$

$x = \pm 2$

If $x = 0$, then

$-4y^2 = 36$

$y^2 = -9$, which has no real root.

Testing for symmetry gives:

x-axis: $9x^2 - 4(-y)^2 = 36$

$\qquad\qquad 9x^2 - 4y^2 = 36$

y-axis: $9(-x)^2 - 4y^2 = 36$

$\qquad\qquad 9x^2 - 4y^2 = 36$

origin: Since the graph has symmetry about x- and y-axes, there is also symmetry about origin.

Answer: $(\pm 2, 0)$; symmetry about x-axis, y-axis, origin

7. $x = -2$

Intercepts: If $y = 0$, then $x = -2$; because $x \neq 0$, there is no y-intercept. Symmetry:

x-axis: $x = -2$

y-axis: $-x = -2$

$\qquad\qquad x = 2$

origin: $-x = -2$

$\qquad\qquad x = 2$

Answer: $(-2, 0)$; symmetry about x-axis

9. $x = -y^{-4}$

Intercepts: Because $y \neq 0$, there is no x-intercept; if $x = 0$, then $0 = -\dfrac{1}{y^4}$, which has no solution. Symmetry:

x-axis: $x = -(-y)^{-4}$

$\qquad\qquad x = -y^{-4}$

y-axis: $-x = -y^{-4}$

$\qquad\qquad x = y^{-4}$

origin: $-x = -(-y)^{-4}$

$\qquad\qquad x = y^{-4}$

Answer: no intercepts; symmetry about x-axis

11. $x - 4y - y^2 + 21 = 0$

Intercepts: If $y = 0$, then

$x + 21 = 0$

$x = -21$

If $x = 0$, then

$-4y - y^2 + 21 = 0$

$y^2 + 4y - 21 = 0$

$(y + 7)(y - 3) = 0$

$y = -7$ or $y = 3$

Symmetry:

x-axis: $x - 4(-y) - (-y)^2 + 21 = 0$

$\qquad\qquad x + 4y - y^2 + 21 = 0$

y-axis: $(-x) - 4y - y^2 + 21 = 0$

$\qquad\qquad -x - 4y - y^2 + 21 = 0$

origin: $(-x) - 4(-y) - (-y)^2 + 21 = 0$

$\qquad\qquad -x + 4y - y^2 + 21 = 0.$

Answer: $(-21, 0)$, $(0, -7)$, $(0, 3)$; no symmetry of the given types

13. $y = f(x) = \dfrac{x^3}{x^2 + 5}$

Intercepts: If $y = 0$, then

$\dfrac{x^3}{x^2 + 5} = 0$

$x = 0$

If $x = 0$, then $y = 0$. Symmetry:

x-axis: Because f is not the zero function, there is no x-axis symmetry;

y-axis: $y = \dfrac{(-x)^3}{(-x)^2 + 5}$

$\qquad\qquad y = -\dfrac{x^3}{x^2 + 5}$

origin: $-y = \dfrac{(-x)^3}{(-x)^2 + 5}$

$\qquad\qquad y = \dfrac{x^3}{x^2 + 5}$

Answer: $(0, 0)$; symmetry about origin

15. $y = \dfrac{3}{x^3 + 8}$

Intercepts: If $y = 0$, then $\dfrac{3}{x^3 + 8} = 0$, which

has no solution; if $x = 0$, then $y = \dfrac{3}{8}$.

Symmetry:

x-axis: $-y = \dfrac{3}{x^3 + 8}$

             $y = -\dfrac{3}{x^3 + 8}$

y-axis: $y = \dfrac{3}{(-x)^3 + 8}$

             $y = \dfrac{3}{-x^3 + 8}$

origin: $-y = \dfrac{3}{(-x)^3 + 8}$

             $-y = \dfrac{3}{-x^3 + 8}$

             $y = \dfrac{3}{x^3 - 8}$

Answer: $\left(0, \dfrac{3}{8}\right)$; no symmetry of the given

types

17. $2x + y^2 = 4$

Intercepts: If $y = 0$, then
$2x = 4$
$x = 2$
if $x = 0$, then
$y^2 = 4$
$y = \pm 2$.
Symmetry:

x-axis: $2x + (-y)^2 = 4$

             $2x + y^2 = 4$

y-axis: $2(-x) + y^2 = 4$

             $-2x + y^2 = 4$

origin: $2(-x) + (-y)^2 = 4$

             $-2x + y^2 = 4$

Answer: $(2, 0)$, $(0, \pm 2)$; symmetry about x-axis

19. $y = f(x) = x^3 - 4x$

Intercepts: If $y = 0$, then
$x^3 - 4x = 0$
$x(x + 2)(x - 2) = 0$
$x = 0$ or $x = \pm 2$.
If $x = 0$, then $y = 0$.
Symmetry:

x-axis: Because f is not the zero
                function, there is no x-axis
                symmetry.

y-axis: $y = (-x)^3 - 4(-x)$

             $y = -x^3 + 4x$

origin: $-y = (-x)^3 - 4(-x)$

             $y = x^3 - 4x$

Answer: $(0, 0)$, $(\pm 2, 0)$; symmetry about origin.

21. $|x| - |y| = 0$

Intercepts: If $y = 0$, then
$|x| = 0$
$x = 0$
If $x = 0$, then
$-|y| = 0$
$y = 0$
Symmetry:

x-axis: $|x| - |-y| = 0$
              $|x| - |y| = 0$

y-axis: $|-x| - |y| = 0$
              $|x| - |y| = 0$

origin: Since there is symmetry about x- and y-axes, symmetry about origin exists.

Answer: $(0, 0)$; symmetry about x-axis, y-axis, origin.

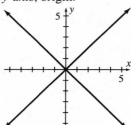

23. $4x^2 + y^2 = 16$

Intercepts: If $y = 0$, then
$4x^2 = 16$
$x^2 = 4$
$x = \pm 2$
If $x = 0$, then
$y^2 = 16$
$y = \pm 4$
Symmetry:

x-axis: $4x^2 + (-y)^2 = 16$
              $4x^2 + y^2 = 16$

y-axis: $4(-x)^2 + y^2 = 16$
              $4x^2 + y^2 = 16$

origin: Since there is symmetry about x- and y-axes, symmetry about origin exists.

Answer: $(\pm 2, 0)$, $(0, \pm 4)$; symmetry about x-axis, y-axis, origin

25.

$y = f(x) = 2 - 0.03x^2 - x^4$. Replacing x by $-x$ gives $y = 2 - 0.03(-x)^2 - (-x)^4$ or $y = 2 - 0.03x^2 - x^4$, which is equivalent to original equation. Thus the graph is symmetric about y-axis.

a. Intercepts: $(\pm 1.18, 0)$, $(0, 2)$

b. Maximum value of $f(x)$: 2

c. Range: $(-\infty, 2]$

Exercise 3.6

1.

3.

$f(x) = \frac{1}{x}$

$y = \frac{1}{x-2}$

5.

$f(x) = \frac{1}{x}$

$y = \frac{2}{3x}$

7.

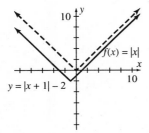

$f(x) = |x|$

$y = |x+1| - 2$

9.

$f(x) = x^2$

$y = 1 - (x-1)^2$

11.

$y = \sqrt{-x}$ $f(x) = \sqrt{x}$

13. Translate 4 units to the right and 3 units upward.

15. Reflect about the *y*-axis and translate 5 units downward.

17.

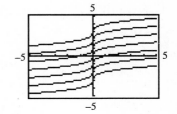

Compared to the graph for $k = 0$, the graphs for $k = 1, 2,$ and 3 are vertical shifts upward of 1, 2, and 3 units, respectively. The graphs for $k = -1, -2,$ and -3 are vertical shifts downward of 1, 2, and 3 units, respectively.

19.

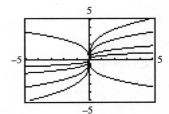

Compared to the graph for $k = 1$, the graphs for $k = 2$ and 3 are vertical stretches away from the *x*-axis by factors of 2 and 3, respectively. The graph for $k = \frac{1}{2}$ is a vertical shrinking toward the *x*-axis.

Chapter 3 Review Problems

1. Denominator is 0 when
$x^2 - 3x + 2 = 0$
$(x-1)(x-2) = 0$
$x = 1, 2$
Domain: all real numbers except 1 and 2.

3. all real numbers

5. For $\sqrt{x}$ to be real, x must be nonnegative. For the denominator $x - 1$ to be different from 0, x cannot be 1. Both conditions are satisfied by all nonnegative numbers except 1. Domain: all nonnegative real numbers except 1.

7. $f(x) = 3x^2 - 4x + 7$

   $f(0) = 3(0)^2 - 4(0) + 7 = 7$

   $f(-3) = 3(-3)^2 - 4(-3) + 7 = 27 + 12 + 7 = 46$

   $f(5) = 3(5)^2 - 4(5) + 7 = 75 - 20 + 7 = 62$

   $f(t) = 3t^2 - 4t + 7$

9. $G(x) = \sqrt{x - 1}$

   $G(1) = \sqrt{1 - 1} = \sqrt{0} = 0$

   $G(5) = \sqrt{5 - 1} = \sqrt{4} = 2$

   $G(t + 1) = \sqrt{(t + 1) - 1} = \sqrt{t}$

   $G(x^3) = \sqrt{x^3 - 1}$

11. $h(u) = \dfrac{\sqrt{u + 4}}{u}$

    $h(5) = \dfrac{\sqrt{5 + 4}}{5} = \dfrac{\sqrt{9}}{5} = \dfrac{3}{5}$

    $h(-4) = \dfrac{\sqrt{-4 + 4}}{-4} = \dfrac{0}{-4} = 0$

    $h(x) = \dfrac{\sqrt{x + 4}}{x}$

    $h(u - 4) = \dfrac{\sqrt{(u - 4) + 4}}{u - 4} = \dfrac{\sqrt{u}}{u - 4}$

13. $f(4) = 8 - 4^2 = 8 - 16 = -8$

    $f(-2) = 4$

    $f(0) = 4$

    $f(10) = 8 - 10^2 = 8 - 100 = -92$

15. **a.** $f(x + h) = 3 - 7(x + h) = 3 - 7x - 7h$

    b. $\dfrac{f(x + h) - f(x)}{h} = \dfrac{(3 - 7x - 7h) - (3 - 7x)}{h} = \dfrac{-7h}{h} = -7$

17. a. $f(x+h) = 4(x+h)^2 + 2(x+h) - 5 = 4x^2 + 8xh + 4h^2 + 2x + 2h - 5$

b. $\dfrac{f(x+h) - f(x)}{h} = \dfrac{(4x^2 + 8xh + 4h^2 + 2x + 2h - 5) - (4x^2 + 2x - 5)}{h}$

$= \dfrac{8xh + 4h^2 + 2h}{h} = \dfrac{h(8x + 4h + 2)}{h} = 8x + 4h + 2$

19. $f(x) = 3x - 1,\ g(x) = 2x + 3$

a. $(f+g)(x) = f(x) + g(x) = (3x - 1) + (2x + 3) = 5x + 2$

b. $(f+g)(4) = 5(4) + 2 = 22$

c. $(f-g)(x) = f(x) - g(x) = (3x - 1) - (2x + 3) = x - 4$

d. $(fg)(x) = f(x)g(x) = (3x - 1)(2x + 3) = 6x^2 + 7x - 3$

e. $(fg)(1) = 6(1)^2 + 7(1) - 3 = 10$

f. $\dfrac{f}{g}(x) = \dfrac{f(x)}{g(x)} = \dfrac{3x - 1}{2x + 3}$

g. $(f \circ g)(x) = f(g(x)) = f(2x + 3) = 3(2x + 3) - 1 = 6x + 8$

h. $(f \circ g)(5) = 6(5) + 8 = 38$

i. $(g \circ f)(x) = g(f(x)) = g(3x - 1) = 2(3x - 1) + 3 = 6x + 1$

21. $f(x) = \dfrac{1}{x}$

$g(x) = x - 1$

$(f \circ g)(x) = f(g(x)) = f(x - 1) = \dfrac{1}{x - 1}$

$(g \circ f)(x) = g(f(x)) = g\left(\dfrac{1}{x}\right) = \dfrac{1}{x} - 1 = \dfrac{1 - x}{x}$

23. $f(x) = \sqrt{x + 2}$

$g(x) = x^3$

$(f \circ g)(x) = f(g(x)) = f(x^3) = \sqrt{x^3 + 2}$

$(g \circ f)(x) = g(f(x)) = g\left(\sqrt{x + 2}\right) = \left(\sqrt{x + 2}\right)^3 = (x + 2)^{3/2}$

25. $y = 2x - 3x^3$

Intercepts: If $y = 0$, then

$0 = 2x - 3x^3$

$0 = 3x\left(\dfrac{2}{3} - x^2\right)$

$x = 0$ or $x = \pm\sqrt{\dfrac{2}{3}}$

If $x = 0$, then $y = 0$. Testing for symmetry gives:

x-axis: $-y = 2x - 3x^3$

$y = -2x + 3x^3$, which is not the original equation.

y-axis: $y = 2(-x) - 3(-x)^3$

$y = -2x + 3x^3$, which is not the original equation.

origin: $-y = 2(-x) - 3(-x)^3$

$y = 2x - 3x^3$, which is the original equation.

Answer: $(0, 0)$, $\left(\pm\sqrt{\dfrac{2}{3}}, 0\right)$; symmetry about origin

27. $y = 9 - x^2$

Intercepts: If $y = 0$, then

$0 = 9 - x^2 = (3 + x)(3 - x)$, or $x = \pm 3$

If $x = 0$, then $y = 9$. Testing for symmetry gives:

x-axis: $-y = 9 - x^2$

$y = -9 + x^2$, which is not the original equation.

y-axis: $y = 9 - (-x)^2$

$y = 9 - x^2$, which is the original equation.

origin: There is y-axis symmetry but there is no x-axis symmetry. So there can be no symmetry about origin.

Answer: $(0, 9)$, $(\pm 3, 0)$; symmetry about y-axis.

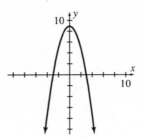

29. $G(u) = \sqrt{u + 4}$

If $G(u) = 0$, then $0 = \sqrt{u + 4}$.

$0 = u + 4$,

$u = -4$

If $u = 0$, then $G(u) = \sqrt{4} = 2$.

Intercepts: $(0, 2)$, $(-4, 0)$

Domain: all real numbers u such that $u \geq -4$

Range: all real numbers ≥ 0

31. $y = g(t) = \dfrac{2}{|t - 4|}$

If $y = 0$, then $0 = \dfrac{2}{|t - 4|}$, which has no

solution; if $t = 0$, then $y = \dfrac{2}{4} = \dfrac{1}{2}$.

Intercept: $\left(0, \dfrac{1}{2}\right)$

Domain: all real numbers t such that $t \neq 4$

Range: all real numbers > 0

33. Domain: all real numbers.
Range: all real numbers ≥ 1

35.

37. From the vertical-line test, the graphs that represent functions of x are (a) and (c).

39.

$-0.67; 0.34, 1.73$

41.

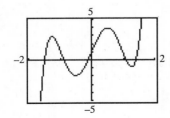

$-1.50, -0.88, -0.11, 1.09, 1.40$

43.

a. $(-\infty, \infty)$

b. $(1.92, 0), (0, 7)$

45. $k = 0, 2, 4$

$k = 1, 3$

a. none

b. $1, 3$

Mathematical Snapshot Chapter 3

1. $f(120,000)$
   $= 23,965.50 + 0.31(120,000 - 105,950)$
   $= 28,321$
   Answer: \$28,321

3. $f(290,000)$
   $= 86,854.50 + 0.396(290,000 - 288,350)$
   $= 87,507.90$
   Answer: \$87,507.90

5. Answers may vary.

Chapter 4

Principles in Practice 4.1

1. Let x = the time (in years) and let y = the selling price. Then,
   In 1991: $x_1 = 1991$ and $y_1 = 32,000$
   In 1994: $x_2 = 1994$ and $y_2 = 26,000$
   The slope is
   $$m = \frac{y_2 - y_1}{x_2 - x_1}$$
   $$= \frac{26,000 - 32,000}{1994 - 1991}$$
   $$= \frac{-6000}{3}$$
   $$= -2000$$
   The car depreciated by \$2000 per year.

2. An equation relating the growth in enrollment to the number of years can be found by using the point-slope form of an equation of a line. If S = the number of students enrolled, and T = the number of years, then the point-slope form can be written as $S - S_1 = m(T - T_1)$
   Let $m = 14$, $S_1 = 50$, and $T_1 = 3$.
   $$S - 50 = 14(T - 3)$$
   $$S - 50 = 14T - 42$$
   $$S = 14T + 8$$

3. A linear function relating Fahrenheit temperature to Celsius temperature can be found by using the point-slope form of an equation of a line.
   $$m = \frac{F_2 - F_1}{C_2 - C_1} = \frac{77 - 41}{25 - 5} = \frac{36}{20} = \frac{9}{5}$$
   $$F - F_1 = m(C - C_1)$$
   $$F - 41 = \frac{9}{5}(C - 5)$$
   $$F - 41 = \frac{9}{5}C - 9$$
   $$F = \frac{9}{5}C + 32$$

4. To find the slope and y-intercept, let $a = 1000$, then write the equation in slope-intercept form.
   $$y = \frac{1}{24}(t + 1)a$$
   $$y = \frac{1}{24}(t + 1)1000$$
   $$y = \frac{1000}{24}t + \frac{1000}{24}$$
   $$y = \frac{125}{3}t + \frac{125}{3}$$
   Thus the slope, m, is $\frac{125}{3}$ and the y-intercept, b, is $\frac{125}{3}$.

5. $F = \frac{9}{5}C + 32$
   $$5(F) = 5\left(\frac{9}{5}C + 32\right)$$
   $$5F = 9C + 160$$
   $$0 = 9C - 5F + 160$$
   Thus, $9C - 5F + 160 = 0$ is a general linear form of $F = \frac{9}{5}C + 32$.

6.

To convert Celsius to Fahrenheit, locate the Celsius temperature on the horizontal axis, move vertically to the line, then move horizontally to read the Fahrenheit temperature of the vertical axis.

7. Right angles are formed by perpendicular lines. The slopes of the sides of the triangle are:

$$\overline{AB}\left\{m = \frac{0-0}{6-0} = \frac{0}{6} = 0\right.$$

$$\overline{BC}\left\{m = \frac{7-0}{7-6} = \frac{7}{1} = 7\right.$$

$$\overline{AC}\left\{m = \frac{7-0}{7-0} = \frac{7}{7} = 1\right.$$

Since none of the slopes are negative reciprocals of each other, there are no perpendicular lines. Therefore, the points do not define a right triangle.

Exercise 4.1

1. $m = \dfrac{10-1}{7-4} = \dfrac{9}{3} = 3$

3. $m = \dfrac{3-(-2)}{-6-4} = \dfrac{5}{-10} = -\dfrac{1}{2}$

5. The difference in the x-coordinates is $5 - 5 = 0$, so the slope is undefined.

7. $m = \dfrac{-2-(-2)}{4-5} = \dfrac{0}{-1} = 0$

9. $y - 8 = 6(x - 2)$
$y - 8 = 6x - 12$
$6x - y - 4 = 0$

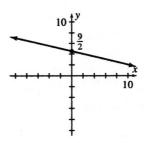

11. $y - 5 = -\dfrac{1}{4}[x - (-2)]$
$4(y - 5) = -(x + 2)$
$4y - 20 = -x - 2$
$x + 4y - 18 = 0$

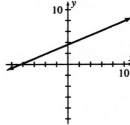

13. $m = \dfrac{4-1}{1-(-6)} = \dfrac{3}{7}$
$y - 4 = \dfrac{3}{7}(x - 1)$
$7(y - 4) = 3(x - 1)$
$7y - 28 = 3x - 3$
$3x - 7y + 25 = 0$

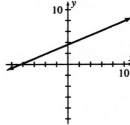

15. $m = \dfrac{-9 - (-1)}{-2 - 3} = \dfrac{-8}{-5}$

$y - (-1) = \dfrac{8}{5}(x - 3)$

$5(y + 1) = 8(x - 3)$

$5y + 5 = 8x - 24$

$8x - 5y - 29 = 0$

17. $y = 2x + 4$

$2x - y + 4 = 0$

19. $y = -\dfrac{1}{2}x - 3$

$2y = 2\left(-\dfrac{1}{2}x - 3\right)$

$2y = -x - 6$

$x + 2y + 6 = 0$

21. A horizontal line has the form $y = b$.
Thus $y = -2$, or $y + 2 = 0$.

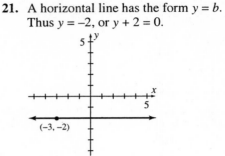

23. Line passes through $(2, -3)$ and is vertical.
Thus $x = 2$, or $x - 2 = 0$.

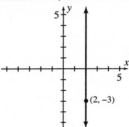

25. $y = 4x - 6$ has the form $y = mx + b$, where
$m = 4$ and $b = -6$.

27. $x + 2y - 3 = 0$

$2y = -x + 3$

$y = -\dfrac{1}{2}x + \dfrac{3}{2}$

$m = -\dfrac{1}{2}, \; b = \dfrac{3}{2}$

29. $x = -5$ is a vertical line. Thus the slope is undefined. There is no y-intercept.

31. $y = 3x$
$y = 3x + 0$
$m = 3, b = 0$

33. $y = 1$
$y = 0x + 1$
$m = 0, b = 1$

35. $2x = 5 - 3y$, or $2x + 3y - 5 = 0$
(general form)
$3y = -2x + 5$, or $y = -\frac{2}{3}x + \frac{5}{3}$
(slope-intercept form)

37. $4x + 9y - 5 = 0$ is a general form.
$9y = -4x + 5$, or $y = -\frac{4}{9}x + \frac{5}{9}$
(slope-intercept form)

39. $\frac{x}{2} - \frac{y}{3} = -4$

$6\left(\frac{x}{2} - \frac{y}{3}\right) = 6(-4)$

$3x - 2y = -24$
$3x - 2y + 24 = 0$ (general form)
$-2y = -3x - 24$
$y = \frac{3}{2}x + 12$ (slope-intercept form)

41. The lines $y = 7x + 2$ and $y = 7x - 3$ have the same slope, 7. Thus they are parallel.

43. The lines $y = 5x + 2$ and $-5x + y - 3 = 0$ (or $y = 5x + 3$) have the same slope, 5. Thus they are parallel.

45. The line $x + 2y + 1 = 0$ $\left(\text{or } y = -\frac{1}{2}x - \frac{1}{2}\right)$
has slope $m_1 = -\frac{1}{2}$ and the line $y = -2x$
has slope $m_2 = -2$. Since $m_1 \neq m_2$ and
$m_1 \neq -\frac{1}{m_2}$, the lines are neither parallel
nor perpendicular.

47. The line $y = 3$ is horizontal and the line
$x = -\frac{1}{3}$ is vertical, so the lines are
perpendicular.

49. The line $3x + y = 4$ (or $y = -3x + 4$) has slope
$m = -3$, and the line $x - 3y + 1 = 0$
$\left(\text{or } y = \frac{1}{3}x + \frac{1}{3}\right)$ has slope $m_2 = \frac{1}{3}$. Since
$m_2 = -\frac{1}{m_2}$, the lines are perpendicular.

51. The slope of $y = 4x - 5$ is 4, so the slope of a
line parallel to it must also be 4. An equation
of the desired line is $y - 2 = 4[x - (-3)]$, or
$y = 4x + 14$.

53. $y = 2$ is a horizontal line. A line parallel to it
has the form $y = b$. Since the line must pass
through $(2, 1)$ its equation is $y = 1$.

55. $y = 3x - 5$ has slope $3 \Rightarrow$ perpendicular line has slope $-\frac{1}{3}$ and its equation is

$$y - 4 = -\frac{1}{3}(x - 3)$$

$$y = -\frac{1}{3}x + 5$$

57. $y = -4$ is a horizontal line, so the perpendicular line must be vertical with equation of the form $x = a$. Since that line passes through $(7, 4)$, its equation is $x = 7$.

59. $2x + 3y + 6 = 0 \left(\text{or } y = -\frac{2}{3}x - 2 \right)$ has slope $-\frac{2}{3}$. Parallel line has $m = -\frac{2}{3}$. Equation is

$$y - (-5) = -\frac{2}{3}[x - (-7)]$$

$$y = -\frac{2}{3}x - \frac{29}{3}$$

61. $(1, 2), (-3, 8)$

$$m = \frac{8 - 2}{-3 - 1} = \frac{6}{-4} = -\frac{3}{2}$$

Point-slope form: $y - 2 = -\frac{3}{2}(x - 1)$. If first coordinate is 5, then $x = 5$ and

$$y - 2 = -\frac{3}{2}(5 - 1)$$

$$y - 2 = -\frac{3}{2}(4)$$

$$y - 2 = -6$$

$$y = -4$$

Thus the point is $(5, -4)$.

63. Let $x =$ the time (in years) and $y =$ the price per share. Then,
In 1988: $x_1 = 1988$ and $y_1 = 30$
In 1998: $x_2 = 1998$ and $y_2 = 10$
The slope is

$$m = \frac{10 - 30}{1998 - 1988} = \frac{-20}{10} = -2$$

The stock price dropped an average of $2 per year.

65. The number of home runs hit increased as a function of time (in months). The given points are $(x_1, y_1) = (3, 14)$ and $(x_2, y_2) = (5, 20)$.

$$m = \frac{y_2 - y_1}{x_2 - x_1} = \frac{20 - 14}{5 - 3} = \frac{6}{2} = 3$$

Using the point-slope form with $m = 3$ and $(x_1, y_1) = (3, 14)$ gives

$$y - y_1 = m(x - x_1)$$

$$y - 14 = 3(x - 3)$$

$$y - 14 = 3x - 9$$

$$y = 3x + 5$$

67. Solve the equation for t.

$$L = 1.53t - 6.7$$

$$L + 6.7 = 1.53t$$

$$\frac{(L + 6.7)}{1.53} = t$$

$$0.65L + 4.38 = t$$

The slope is approximately 0.65 and the y-intercept is approximately 4.38.

69. a. Using the points $(0.5, 0)$ and $(3.5, -1)$ gives a slope of $m = \frac{-1 - 0}{3.5 - 0.5} = -\frac{1}{3}$.

And an equation is

$$y - 0 = -\frac{1}{3}(x - 0.5), \text{ or } y = -\frac{1}{3}x + \frac{1}{6}.$$

b. Using the points (0.5, 0) and (−1, −4.5) gives a slope of $\frac{-4.5-0}{-1-0.5} = 3$, so an equation is

$$y - 0 = 3(x - 0.5)$$
$$y = 3x - \frac{3}{2}$$

The paths are perpendicular to each other because the slope of the line in part (a), $-\frac{1}{3}$, is the negative reciprocal of the slope in part (b), 3.

71. Let x = the distance traveled and let y = the altitude. The path of descent is a straight line with a slope of −1 and y-intercept of 3300. Therefore, using the slope-intercept form with $m = -1$ and $b = 3300$ gives

$$y = mx + b$$
$$y = (-1)x + 3300$$
$$y = -x + 3300$$

If the airport was located 4000 feet from where the plane begins its descent, the plane will crash 700 feet short of the airport.

73. The line has slope 50,000 and passes through (5, 330,000). Thus
$R - 330,000 = 50,000(T - 5)$ or
$R = 50,000T + 80,000$.

75. The lines are parallel, which is expected because they have the same slope, 1.5.

77. The slope of the first line is
$m_1 = \frac{0.1875}{0.3} = 0.625$, and the slope of the second line is $m_2 = -\frac{0.32}{0.2} = -1.6$.

Since $m_1 = -\frac{1}{m_2}$, the lines are mutually perpendicular.

Principles in Practice 4.2

1. Let x = the number of skis that are produced and let y = the number of boots that are produced. Then, the equation $8x + 14y = 1000$ describes all possible production levels of the two products.

2. The quantity and price are linearly related such that $p = 575$ when $q = 1200$, and $p = 725$ when $q = 800$. Thus
$(q_1, p_1) = (1200, 575)$ and
$(q_2, p_2) = (800, 725)$.
The slope is $m = \frac{725 - 575}{800 - 1200} = -\frac{3}{8}$.
An equation of the line is

$$p - p_1 = m(q - q_1)$$
$$p - 575 = -\frac{3}{8}(q - 1200)$$
$$p - 575 = -\frac{3}{8}q + 450$$
$$p = -\frac{3}{8}q + 1025$$

3. Answers may vary, but two possible points are (0, 60) and (2, 140).
$f(x) = 40x + 60$

x	$f(x)$
0	60
2	140

4. If t = the age of the child, then $f(t)$ = the height of the child at any age t. The height and age are linearly related such that $f(8)$ = 50.6. Since $f(t)$ is a linear function it has the form $f(t) = at + b$. Let $a = 2.3$. Then,
$$f(t) = at + b$$
$$f(8) = 2.3(8) + b$$
$$50.6 = 18.4 + b$$
$$32.2 = b$$
Thus, $f(t) = 2.3t + 32.2$ is a function that describes the height of the child at age t.

5. Let $y = f(x)$ = a linear function that describes the value of the necklace after x years. The problem states that $f(3) = 360$ and $f(7) = 640$. Thus, we set
$$(x_1,\, y_1) = (3,\, 360) = (x_2,\, y_2) = (7,\, 640).$$
The slope is
$$m = \frac{y_2 - y_1}{x_2 - x_1} = \frac{640 - 360}{7 - 3} = \frac{280}{4} = 70$$
Using the point-slope form with $m = 70$ and $(x_1,\, y_1) = (3,\, 360)$ gives
$$y - y_1 = m(x - x_1)$$
$$y - 360 = 70(x - 3)$$
$$y = f(x) = 70x + 150$$

Exercise 4.2

1. $y = f(x) = -4x = -4x + 0$ has the form $f(x) = ax + b$ with $a = -4$ and $b = 0$.
Thus the slope is -4 and the vertical-axis intercept is 0.

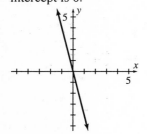

3. $g(t) = 2t - 4$ has the form $g(t) = at + b$ with $a = 2$ (the slope) and $b = -4$ (the vertical-axis intercept).

5. $h(q) = \dfrac{2 - q}{7} = \dfrac{2}{7} - \dfrac{1}{7}q$ has the form
$h(q) = aq + b$ where $a = -\dfrac{1}{7}$ (the slope) and
$b = \dfrac{2}{7}$ (the vertical-axis intercept).

7. $f(x) = ax + b = 4x + b$. Since $f(2) = 8$,
$8 = 4(2) + b$, $8 = 8 + b$, $b = 0 \Rightarrow f(x) = 4x$.

9. Let $y = f(x)$. The points $(1, 2)$ and $(-2, 8)$ lie on the graph of f. $m = \dfrac{8 - 2}{-2 - 1} = -2$. Thus
$y - 2 = -2(x - 1)$, so
$y = -2x + 4 \Rightarrow f(x) = -2x + 4$.

11. $f(x) = ax + b = -\dfrac{1}{2}x + b$. Since
$f\left(-\dfrac{1}{2}\right) = 4$, we have
$$4 = -\frac{1}{2}\left(-\frac{1}{2}\right) + b$$
$$b = 4 - \frac{1}{4} = \frac{15}{4},$$
so $f(x) = -\dfrac{1}{2}x + \dfrac{15}{4}$.

13. Let $y = f(x)$. The point $(-2, -1)$ and $(-4, -3)$ lie on the graph of f. $m = \frac{-3+1}{-4+2} = 1$. Thus $y + 1 = 1(x + 2)$, so $y = x + 1 \Rightarrow f(x) = x + 1$.

15. The points $(40, 12)$ and $(25, 18)$ lie on the graph of the equation, which is a line. $m = \frac{18-12}{25-40} = -\frac{2}{5}$. Hence an equation of the line is $p - 12 = \frac{-2}{5}(q - 40)$, which can be written $p = \frac{-2}{5}q + 28$. When $q = 30$, then $p = \frac{-2}{5}(30) + 28 = -12 + 28 = \$16$.

17. The line passes through $(3000, 940)$ and $(2200, 740)$, so $m = \frac{740 - 940}{2200 - 3000} = 0.25$.
Then
$p - 740 = 0.25(q - 2200)$ or $p = 0.25q + 190$.

19. The line passing through $(10, 40)$ and $(20, 70)$ has slope $\frac{70-40}{20-10} = 3$, so an equation for the line is
$c - 40 = 3(q - 10)$
$c = 3q + 10$
If $q = 35$, then $c = 3(35) + 10 = 105 + 10 = \$115$.

21. If $x =$ the number of kilowatt hours used in a month, then $f(x) =$ the total monthly charges for x kilowatt hours of electricity. If $f(x)$ is a linear function it has the form $f(x) = ax + b$. The problem states that $f(380) = 51.65$. Let $a = 0.125$.
$f(x) = ax + b$
$51.65 = 0.125(380) + b$
$51.65 = 47.5 + b$
$4.15 = b$
Hence, $f(x) = 0.125x + 4.15$ is a linear function that describes the total monthly charges for any number of kilowatt hours x.

23. Each year the value decreases by $0.10(8000)$. After t years the total decrease is $0.10(8000)t$. Thus
$v = 8000 - 0.10(8000)t$
$v = -800t + 8000$
The slope is -800.

25. The line has slope $45,000$ and passes through $(5, 960,000)$. Thus
$y - 960,000 = 45,000(x - 5)$ or
$y = f(x) = 45,000x + 735,000$.

27. If $x =$ the number of hours of service, then $f(x) =$ the price of x hours of service. Since $f(x)$ is a linear function, it has the form $f(x) = ax + b$. The problem states that $f(1) = 150$ and $f(3) = 280$. Thus, after 1 hour of service
$f(x) = ax + b$
$150 = a(1) + b$
$150 = a + b$
and after 3 hours of service
$f(x) = ax + b$
$280 = a(3) + b$
$280 = 3a + b$
To find the slope a and the y-intercept b we subtract
$280 = 3a + b$
$150 = a + b$
$130 = 2a$
$65 = a$
Since $a = 65$, $b = 150 - 65 = 85$. Hence, $f(x) = 65x + 85$ is a linear function that describes the price of a service call where x is the number of hours of service.

29. At $\$200$/ton, x tons cost $200x$, and at $\$2000$/acre, y acres cost $2000y$. Hence the required equation is $200x + 2000y = 20,000$, which can be written as $x + 10y = 100$.

31. **a.** $m = \dfrac{100-80}{100-56} = \dfrac{20}{44} = \dfrac{5}{11}$

$y - 100 = \dfrac{5}{11}(x - 100)$

$y = \dfrac{5}{11}x - \dfrac{500}{11} + 100$

$y = \dfrac{5}{11}x + \dfrac{600}{11}$

  b. $60 = \dfrac{5}{11}x + \dfrac{600}{11}$

$\dfrac{5}{11}x = 60 - \dfrac{600}{11} = \dfrac{660}{11} - \dfrac{600}{11} = \dfrac{60}{11}$

$x = 12$, which is the lowest passing score on original scale.

33. $p = f(t) = at + b, f(5) = 0.32,$
$a = \text{slope} = 0.059.$

  a. $p = f(t) = 0.059t + b.$ Since $f(5) = 0.32$, $0.32 = 0.059(5) + b, 0.32 = 0.295 + b,$ so $b = 0.025.$ Thus $p = 0.059t + 0.025.$

  b. When $t = 9$, then
$p = 0.059(9) + 0.025 = 0.556.$

35. **a.** $m = \dfrac{t_2 - t_1}{c_2 - c_1} = \dfrac{80 - 68}{172 - 124} = \dfrac{12}{48} = \dfrac{1}{4}.$

$t - 68 = \dfrac{1}{4}(c - 124),\ t - 68 = \dfrac{1}{4}c - 31,$

or $t = \dfrac{1}{4}c + 37.$

  b. Since c is the number of chirps per minute, then $\dfrac{1}{4}c$ is the number of chirps in $\dfrac{1}{4}$ minute or 15 seconds. Thus from part (a), to estimate temperature add 37 to the number of chirps in 15 seconds.

37. $m = \dfrac{P_2 - P_1}{T_2 - T_1} = \dfrac{100 - 90}{80 - 40} = \dfrac{1}{4}$, so an equation is given by

$P - 100 = \dfrac{1}{4}(T - 80)$

$P - 100 = \dfrac{1}{4}T - 20$

$P = \dfrac{T}{4} + 80$

39. **a.** Yes: $Q = \left(1.8704b^2\right)x + \left(3.340b^3\right),$ where b is a constant, is the equation of a straight line in slope-intercept form. The slope is $1.8704b^2$ and the Q-intercept is $3.340b^3.$

  b. If $b = 1$, the slope is
$1.8704\left(1^2\right) = 1.8704.$

Principles in Practice 4.3

1. In the quadratic function
$y = P(x) = -x^2 + 2x + 399$, $a = -1$, $b = 2$, $c = 399.$ Since $a < 0$, the parabola opens downward. The x-coordinate of the vertex is
$-\dfrac{b}{2a} = -\dfrac{2}{2(-1)} = 1.$
The y-coordinate of the vertex is
$P(1) = -\left(1^2\right) + 2(1) + 399 = 400.$ Thus, the vertex is $(1, 400)$. Since $c = 399$, the y-intercept is $(0, 399)$. To find the x-intercepts we set
$y = p(x) = 0.$
$0 = -x^2 + 2x + 399$
$0 = -\left(x^2 - 2x - 399\right)$
$0 = -(x + 19)(x - 21)$
Thus, the x-intercepts are $(-19, 0)$ and $(21, 0)$.

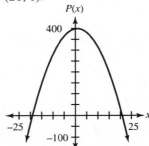

2. In the quadratic function

$h(t) = -16t^2 + 32t + 8$,

$a = -16$, $b = 32$, and $c = 8$. Since $a < 0$, the parabola opens downward. The x-coordinate of the vertex is $-\dfrac{b}{2a} = -\dfrac{32}{2(-16)} = 1$. The y-coordinate of the vertex is

$h(1) = -16\left(1^2\right) + 32(1) + 8 = 24$. Thus, the vertex is (1, 24). Since $c = 8$, the y-intercept is (0, 8). To find the x-intercepts we set $y = h(t) = 0$.

$0 = -16t^2 + 32t + 8$

$t = \dfrac{-b \pm \sqrt{b^2 - 4ac}}{2a}$

$= \dfrac{-32 \pm \sqrt{32^2 - 4(-16)(8)}}{2(-16)}$

$= \dfrac{-32 \pm \sqrt{1536}}{-32} = \dfrac{-32 \pm 16\sqrt{6}}{-32} = 1 \pm \dfrac{\sqrt{6}}{2}$

Thus, the x-intercepts are $\left(1 + \dfrac{\sqrt{6}}{2}, 0\right)$ and

$\left(1 - \dfrac{\sqrt{6}}{2}, 0\right)$.

3. If we express the revenue r as a function of the quantity produced q, we obtain

$r = pq$

$r = (6 - 0.003q)q$

$r = 6q - 0.003q^2$

We note that this is a quadratic function with $a = -0.003$, $b = 6$, and $c = 0$. Since $a < 0$, the graph of the function is a parabola that opens downward, and r is maximum at the vertex (q, r).

$q = -\dfrac{b}{2a} = -\dfrac{6}{2(-0.003)} = 1000$

$r = 6(1000) - 0.003(1000)^2 = 3000$

Thus, the maximum revenue that the manufacturer can receive is \$3000, which occurs at a production level of 1000 units.

Exercise 4.3

1. $f(x) = 5x^2$ has the form

$f(x) = ax^2 + bx + c$ where $a = 5$, $b = 0$, and $c = 0 \Rightarrow$ quadratic.

3. $g(x) = 7 - 6x$ cannot be put in the form

$g(x) = ax^2 + bx + c$ where

$a \neq 0 \Rightarrow$ not quadratic.

5. $h(q) = (q + 4)^2 = q^2 + 8q + 16$ has form

$h(q) = aq^2 + bq + c$ where $a = 1$, $b = 8$, and $c = 16 \Rightarrow$ quadratic.

7. $f(s) = \dfrac{s^2 - 9}{2} = \dfrac{1}{2}s^2 - \dfrac{9}{2}$ has the form

$f(s) = as^2 + bs + c$ where $a = \dfrac{1}{2}$, $b = 0$, and

$c = -\dfrac{9}{2} \Rightarrow$ quadratic.

9. $y = f(x) = -4x^2 + 8x + 7$

$a = -4$, $b = 8$, $c = 7$

a. Vertex occurs when

$x = -\dfrac{b}{2a} = -\dfrac{8}{2(-4)} = 1$. When $x = 1$,

then $y = f(1) = -4(1)^2 + 8(1) + 7 = 11$.

Vertex: (1, 11)

b. $a = -4 < 0$, so the vertex corresponds to the highest point.

11. $y = f(x) = x^2 + 2x - 8$

$a = 1$, $b = 2$, $c = -8$

a. $c = -8$. Thus the y-intercept is -8.

b. $x^2 + 2x - 8 = (x + 4)(x - 2) = 0$, so $x = -4, 2$. x-intercepts: $-4, 2$

c. $\dfrac{-b}{2a} = \dfrac{-2}{2 \cdot 1} = -1$

$f(-1) = (-1)^2 + 2(-1) - 8 = -9$

Vertex: $(-1, -9)$

13. $y = f(x) = x^2 - 6x + 5$

$a = 1,\ b = -6,\ c = 5$

Vertex: $-\dfrac{b}{2a} = -\dfrac{-6}{2 \cdot 1} = 3$

$f(3) = 3^2 - 6(3) + 5 = -4$

Vertex $= (3, -4)$

y-intercept: $c = 5$

x-intercepts:

$x^2 - 6x + 5 = (x - 1)(x - 5) = 0$, so $x = 1,\ 5$.

Range: all $y \geq -4$

15. $y = g(x) = -2x^2 - 6x$

$a = -2,\ b = -6,\ c = 0$

Vertex: $-\dfrac{b}{2a} = \dfrac{-(-6)}{2(-2)} = \dfrac{6}{-4} = -\dfrac{3}{2}$

$f\!\left(\dfrac{-3}{2}\right) = -2\left(\dfrac{-3}{2}\right)^2 - 6\left(\dfrac{-3}{2}\right) = \dfrac{-9}{2} + 9 = \dfrac{9}{2}$

Vertex $= \left(\dfrac{-3}{2}, \dfrac{9}{2}\right)$

y-intercept: $c = 0$

x-intercepts: $-2x^2 - 6x = -2x(x + 3) = 0$,

so $x = 0, -3$.

Range: all $y \leq \dfrac{9}{2}$

17. $s = h(t) = t^2 + 2t + 1$

$a = 1,\ b = 2,\ c = 1$

Vertex: $-\dfrac{b}{2a} = -\dfrac{2}{2 \cdot 1} = -1$

$h(-1) = (-1)^2 + 2(-1) + 1 = 0$

Vertex $= (-1, 0)$

s-intercept: $c = 1$

t-intercepts: $t^2 + 2t + 1 = (t + 1)^2 = 0$, so

$t = -1$.

Range: all $s \geq 0$

19. $y = f(x) = -9 + 8x - 2x^2$

$a = -2,\ b = 8,\ c = -9$

Vertex: $-\dfrac{b}{2a} = -\dfrac{8}{2(-2)} = 2$

$f(2) = -9 + 8(2) - 2(2)^2 = -1$

Vertex $= (2, -1)$

y-intercept: $c = -9$

x-intercepts: Because the parabola opens

downward ($a < 0$) and the vertex is below

the x-axis, there is no x-intercept.

Range: $y \leq -1$

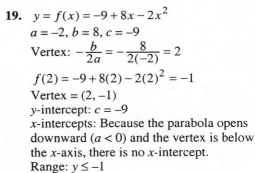

21. $t = f(s) = s^2 - 8s + 14$

$a = 1,\ b = -8,\ c = 14$

Vertex: $-\dfrac{b}{2a} = -\dfrac{-8}{2 \cdot 1} = 4$

$f(4) = 4^2 - 8(4) + 14 = -2$

Vertex $= (4,\ -2)$

t-intercept: $c = 14$

s-intercepts: Solving $s^2 - 8s + 14 = 0$ by the quadratic formula:

$$s = \frac{-(-8) \pm \sqrt{(-8)^2 - 4(1)(14)}}{2(1)}$$

$$= \frac{8 \pm \sqrt{8}}{2} = \frac{8 \pm 2\sqrt{2}}{2} = 4 \pm \sqrt{2}$$

Range: all $t \geq -2$

23. $f(x) = 100x^2 - 20x + 25$

Since $a = 100 > 0$, the parabola opens upward and $f(x)$ has a minimum value that occurs at the vertex where

$x = -\dfrac{b}{2a} = -\dfrac{-20}{2 \cdot 100} = \dfrac{1}{10}$. The minimum value is

$$f\left(\frac{1}{10}\right) = 100\left(\frac{1}{10}\right)^2 - 20\left(\frac{1}{10}\right) + 25 = 24.$$

25. $f(x) = 4x - 50 - 0.1x^2$

Since $a = -0.1 < 0$, the parabola opens downward and $f(x)$ has a maximum value that occurs when

$x = -\dfrac{b}{2a} = -\dfrac{4}{2(-0.1)} = 20$. The maximum value is

$$f(20) = 4(20) - 50 - 0.1(20)^2 = -10.$$

27. If we express the revenue r as a function of the quantity produced q, we obtain

$r = pq$

$r = (1200 - 3q)q$

$r = 1200q - 3q^2$

This is a quadratic function with $a = -3$, $b = 1200$, and $c = 0$. Since $a < 0$, the graph of the function is a parabola that opens downward, and r is maximum at the vertex $(q,\ r)$.

$$q = -\frac{b}{2a} - \frac{1200}{2(-3)} = 200$$

$$r = 1200(200) - 3(200)^2 = 120,000$$

Thus, the maximum revenue that the manufacturer can receive is \$120,000, which occurs at a production level of 200 units.

29. If we express the revenue r as a function of the quantity produced q, we obtain

$r = pq$

$r = (2400 - 6q)q$

$r = 2400q - 6q^2$

This is a quadratic function with $a = -6$, $b = 2400$, and $c = 0$. Since $a < 0$, the graph of the function is a parabola that opens downward, and r is maximum at the vertex $(q,\ r)$.

$$q = -\frac{b}{2a} = -\frac{2400}{2(-6)} = 200$$

$$r = 2400(200) - 6(200)^2 = 240,000$$

Thus, the maximum revenue that the manufacturer can receive is \$240,000, which occurs at a production level of 200 units.

31. In the quadratic function
$$P(x) = -x^2 + 18x + 144,$$
$a = -1$, $b = 18$, and $c = 144$. Since $a < 0$, the graph of the function is a parabola that opens downward. The x-coordinate of the vertex is $-\dfrac{b}{2a} = -\dfrac{18}{2(-1)} = 9$. The y-coordinate of the vertex is
$$P(9) = -\left(9^2\right) + 18(9) + 144 = 225.$$
Thus, the vertex is (9, 225). Since $c = 144$, the y-intercept is (0, 144). To find the x-intercepts, let $y = P(x) = 0$.
$$0 = -x^2 + 18x + 144$$
$$0 = -\left(x^2 - 18x - 144\right)$$
$$0 = -(x - 24)(x + 6)$$
Thus, the x-intercepts are (24, 0) and (–6, 0).

33. $f(P) = -\dfrac{1}{50}P^2 + 2P + 20$, where
$0 \le P \le 100$. Because $a = -\dfrac{1}{50} < 0$, $f(P)$ has a maximum value that occurs at the vertex.
$-\dfrac{b}{2a} = -\dfrac{2}{2\left(-\frac{1}{50}\right)} = 50$. The maximum value of $f(P)$ is
$$f(50) = \tfrac{-1}{50}(50)^2 + 2(50) + 20 = 70 \text{ grams.}$$

35. $h(t) = -16t^2 + 80t + 32$
Since $a = -16 < 0$, $h(t)$ has a maximum value that occurs at the vertex where
$$t = -\dfrac{b}{2a} = -\dfrac{80}{2(-16)} = 2.5 \text{ sec.}$$
When $t = 2.5$, then,
$$h(t) = -16(2.5)^2 + 80(2.5) + 32 = 132 \text{ feet.}$$

37. In the quadratic function
$$h(t) = -16t^2 + 80t + 16, \ a = -16, \ b = 80,$$
and $c = 16$. Since $a < 0$, the graph of the function is a parabola that opens downward. The x-coordinate of the vertex is
$$-\dfrac{b}{2a} = -\dfrac{80}{2(-16)} = \dfrac{5}{2}.$$
The y-coordinate of the vertex is
$$h\left(\tfrac{5}{2}\right) = -16\left(\tfrac{5}{2}\right)^2 + 80\left(\tfrac{5}{2}\right) + 16 = 116$$
Thus, the vertex is $\left(\tfrac{5}{2}, 116\right)$. Since $c = 16$, the y-intercept is (0, 16). To find the x-intercepts, we let $y = h(t) = 0$.
$$0 = -16t^2 + 80t + 16$$
$$t = \dfrac{-b \pm \sqrt{b^2 - 4ac}}{2a}$$
$$= \dfrac{-80 \pm \sqrt{80^2 - 4(-16)(16)}}{2(-16)}$$
$$= \dfrac{-80 \pm \sqrt{7424}}{-32} = \dfrac{5 \pm \sqrt{29}}{2}$$
Thus, the x-intercepts are $\left(\dfrac{5 + \sqrt{29}}{2}, 0\right)$ and $\left(\dfrac{5 - \sqrt{29}}{2}, 0\right)$.

39. $s = 3.2t^2 - 16t + 28.7$ (quadratic with $a = 3.2 > 0$).

a. s is minimum when
$$t = -\dfrac{b}{2a} = -\dfrac{-16}{2(3.2)} = 2.50 \text{ s}$$

b. $t = 2.50 \Rightarrow s = 3.2(2.50)^2$
$- 16(2.50) + 28.7 = 8.70 \text{ m}$

41. $M = \dfrac{w < x}{2} - \dfrac{wx^2}{2}$, which is quadratic (in x) with $a = -\dfrac{w}{2} < 0$.

  a. M is a maximum when
$$x = -\frac{b}{2a} = -\frac{\frac{w\ell}{2}}{2\left(-\frac{w}{2}\right)} = \frac{\ell}{2}$$

  b. If $x = \dfrac{\ell}{2}$, then
$$M = \frac{w\ell}{2}\left(\frac{\ell}{2}\right) - \frac{w}{2}\left(\frac{\ell}{2}\right)^2 = \frac{w\ell^2}{4} - \frac{w\ell^2}{8}$$
$$= \frac{w\ell^2}{8}$$

  c. $0 = \dfrac{w\,\ell\,x}{2} - \dfrac{wx^2}{2} = \dfrac{wx}{2}(\ell - x) \Rightarrow x = 0$
    or $x = \ell$.

43. Since the total length of fencing is 200, the side opposite the stream has length $200 - 2x$. The area A is given by
$$A = x(200 - 2x) = 200x - 2x^2,$$
which is quadratic with $a = -2 < 0$. Thus A is maximum when $x = -\dfrac{200}{2(-2)} = 50$.

Then the side opposite the stream is $200 - 2x = 200 - 2(50) = 100$. Thus the dimensions are 50 ft by 100 ft.

45. $(1.11, 2.88)$

47. a. none

  b. one

  c. two

49. 4.89

Principles in Practice 4.4

1. Let x = the number invested at 9% and let y = the amount invested at 8%. Then, the problem states
$$\begin{cases} x + y = 200,000, \\ 0.09x + 0.08y = 17,200. \end{cases}$$
We eliminate x by multiplying the first equation by -0.09 and then adding
$$\begin{cases} -0.09x - 0.09y = -18,000, \\ 0.09x + 0.08y = 17,200. \end{cases}$$
$$-0.01y = -800,$$
$$y = 80,000.$$
Therefore,
$$\begin{cases} x = 120,000, \\ y = 80,000. \end{cases}$$
Thus, \$120,000 is invested at 9% and \$80,000 is invested at 8%.

2. Let A = the number of deer of species A, and let B = the number of deer of species B. Then, the number of pounds of food pellets that will be consumed is $4A + 2B = 4000$. The number of pounds of hay that will be consumed is $5A + 7B = 9500$. Then, we have
$$\begin{cases} 4A + 2B = 4000, \\ 5A + 7B = 9500. \end{cases}$$
If we solve the first equation for B, we obtain
$$\begin{cases} B = 2000 - 2A, \\ 5A + 7B = 9500. \end{cases}$$
Substituting $2000 - 2A$ for B in the second equation gives
$$5A + 7(2000 - 2A) = 9500$$
$$A = 500$$
Thus
$$\begin{cases} B = 2000 - 2A, \\ A = 500. \end{cases}$$
and
$$\begin{cases} B = 1000, \\ A = 500. \end{cases}$$
The food will support 500 of species A and 1000 of species B.

3. Let A = the number of fish of species A, and let B = the number of fish of species B. Then, the number of milligrams of the first supplement that will be consumed is $15A + 20B = 100{,}000$. The number of milligrams of the second supplement that will be consumed is $30A + 40B = 200{,}000$.

$$\begin{cases} 15A + 20B = 100{,}000, \\ 30A + 40B = 200{,}000. \end{cases}$$

We multiply the second equation by $-\dfrac{1}{2}$ and then add.

$$\begin{cases} 15A + 20B = 100{,}000, \\ -15A - 20B = -1000, \\ 0 = 0 \end{cases}$$

Thus, there are infinitely many solutions of the form $A = \dfrac{20{,}000}{3} - \dfrac{4}{3}r$, $B = r$, where $0 \le r \le 5000$.

4. Let A = the amount of type A used, let B = the amount of type B used, and let C = the amount of type C used. If the final blend will sell for \$8.50 per pound, then $12A + 9B + 7C = 8.50$, and $A + B + C = 1$. Furthermore, since the amount of type B is to be twice the amount of type A, $B = 2A$. Thus, the system of equations is

$$\begin{cases} 12A + 9B + 7C = 8.50, \\ A + B + C = 1, \\ B = 2A. \end{cases}$$

Simplifying gives

$$\begin{cases} 30A + 7C = 8.50, \\ 3A + C = 1, \\ B = 2A. \end{cases}$$

$$\begin{cases} A = \dfrac{1}{6}, \\ C = \dfrac{1}{2}, \\ B = \dfrac{1}{3}. \end{cases}$$

Thus, the final mixture will consist of $\dfrac{1}{6}$ lb of A, $\dfrac{1}{3}$ lb of B, and $\dfrac{1}{2}$ lb of C.

Exercise 4.4

1.
$$\begin{cases} x + 4y = 3, & (1) \\ 3x - 2y = -5. & (2) \end{cases}$$

From Eq. (1), $x = 3 - 4y$. Substituting in Eq. (2) gives
$3(3 - 4y) - 2y = -5$
$9 - 12y - 2y = -5$
$-14y = -14,$
or $y = 1 \Rightarrow x = 3 - 4y = 3 - 4(1) = -1.$
Thus $x = -1$, $y = 1$.

3.
$$\begin{cases} 3x - 4y = 13, & (1) \\ 2x + 3y = 3. & (2) \end{cases}$$

Multiplying Eq. (1) by 3 and Eq. (2) by 4 gives
$$\begin{cases} 9x - 12y = 39, \\ 8x + 12y = 12. \end{cases}$$
Adding gives
$17x = 51$
$x = 3$
From Eq. (2) we have
$2(3) + 3y = 3$
$3y = -3$
$y = -1$
Thus $x = 3$, $y = -1$.

5.
$$\begin{cases} 5v + 2w = 36, & (1) \\ 8v - 3w = -54. & (2) \end{cases}$$

Multiplying Eq. (1) by 3 and Eq. (2) by 2 gives
$$\begin{cases} 15v + 6w = 108, \\ 16v - 6w = -108. \end{cases}$$
Adding gives $31v = 0 \Rightarrow v = 0$. From Eq. (1) we have
$5(0) + 2w = 36$
$w = 18$
Therefore, $v = 0$, $w = 18$.

7. $\begin{cases} x - 2y = -7, & (1) \\ 5x + 3y = -9. & (2) \end{cases}$

From Eq. (1), $x = 2y - 7$. Substituting in Eq. (2) gives
$5(2y - 7) + 3y = -9$
$13y = 26$
$y = 2 \Rightarrow x = 2y - 7 = 2(2) - 7 = -3.$
Thus $x = -3$, $y = 2$.

9. $\begin{cases} 4x - 3y - 2 = 3x - 7y, \\ x + 5y - 2 = y + 4. \end{cases}$

Simplifying, we have
$\begin{cases} x + 4y = 2, \\ x + 4y = 6. \end{cases}$
Subtracting the second equation from the first gives $0 = -4$, which is never true. Thus there is no solution.

11. $\begin{cases} \dfrac{2}{3} x + \dfrac{1}{2} y = 2, \\ \dfrac{3}{8} x + \dfrac{5}{6} y = -\dfrac{11}{2}. \end{cases}$

Clearing fractions gives the system
$\begin{cases} 4x + 3y = 12, \\ 9x + 20y = -132. \end{cases}$
Multiplying the first equation by 9 and the second equation by -4 gives
$\begin{cases} 36x + 27y = 108, \\ -36x - 80y = 528. \end{cases}$
Adding gives
$-53y = 636$
$y = -12$
From $4x + 3y = 12$, we have
$4x + 3(-12) = 12$
$4x = 48 \Rightarrow x = 12$. Thus $x = 12$, $y = -12$.

13. $\quad 4p + 12q = 6, \qquad (1)$
$\quad 2p + 6q = 3. \qquad (2)$

Multiplying Eq. (2) by -2 gives
$\begin{cases} 4p + 12q = 6, \\ -4p - 12q = -6. \end{cases}$
Adding gives $0 = 0$, which implies that both equations represent the same line,
$4p + 12q = 6$
$p = \dfrac{3}{2} - 3q$
There are infinitely many solutions, given parametrically by
$p = \dfrac{3}{2} - 3r$
$q = r,$
where r is any real number.

15. $\begin{cases} 2x + y + 6z = 3, & (1) \\ x - y + 4z = 1, & (2) \\ 3x + 2y - 2z = 2. & (3) \end{cases}$

Adding Eq. (1) and (2), and adding 2 times Eq. (2) to Eq. (3) give
$\begin{cases} 3x + 10z = 4, \\ 5x + 6z = 4. \end{cases}$
Multiplying the first equation by 5 and the second equation by -3 gives
$\begin{cases} 15x + 50z = 20, \\ -15x - 18z = -12. \end{cases}$
Adding $\Rightarrow 32z = 8$, or $z = \dfrac{1}{4}$. From
$3x + 10z = 4$, we have
$3x + 10\left(\dfrac{1}{4}\right) = 4$
$3x = \dfrac{3}{2}$
$x = \dfrac{1}{2}$
From $2x + y + 6z = 3$, we have
$2\left(\dfrac{1}{2}\right) + y + 6\left(\dfrac{1}{4}\right) = 3$
$y = \dfrac{1}{2}$
Therefore $x = \dfrac{1}{2}$, $y = \dfrac{1}{2}$, $z = \dfrac{1}{4}$.

17.
$$\begin{cases} 5x - 7y + 4z = 2, & (1) \\ 3x + 2y - 2z = 3, & (2) \\ 2x - y + 3z = 4. & (3) \end{cases}$$

From Eq. (3), $y = 2x + 3z - 4$. Substituting in Eqs. (1) and (2) gives
$$\begin{cases} 5x - 7(2x + 3z - 4) + 4z = 2, \\ 3x + 2(2x + 3z - 4) - 2z = 3, \end{cases}$$
or
$$\begin{cases} -9x - 17z = -26, \\ 7x + 4z = 11. \end{cases}$$
Multiplying the first equation by 7 and the second by 9 give
$$\begin{cases} -63x - 119z = -182, \\ 63x + 36z = 99. \end{cases}$$
By adding we have
$-83z = -83$
$z = 1$
From $7x + 4z = 11$, we have
$7x + 4(1) = 11$
$7x = 7$
$x = 1$
From $2x - y + 3z = 4$ we get
$2(1) - y + 3(1) = 4$
$-y = -1$
$y = 1$
Therefore $x = 1$, $y = 1$, $z = 1$.

19.
$$\begin{cases} x - 2z = 1, & (1) \\ y + z = 3. & (2) \end{cases}$$

From Eq. (1), $x = 1 + 2z$; from Eq. (2), $y = 3 - z$. Setting $z = r$ gives the parametric solution $x = 1 + 2r$, $y = 3 - r$, $z = r$, where r is any real number.

21.
$$\begin{cases} x - y + 2z = 0, & (1) \\ 2x + y - z = 0 & (2) \\ x + 2y - 3z = 0 & (3) \end{cases}$$

Adding Eq. (1) to Eq. (3) gives
$$\begin{cases} x - y + 2z = 0, \\ 2x + y - z = 0 \\ 2x + y - z = 0 \end{cases}$$
We can ignore the third equation because the second equation can be used to reduce it to $0 = 0$. We have
$$\begin{cases} x - y + 2z = 0, \\ 2x + y - z = 0. \end{cases}$$
Adding the first equation to the second gives
$3x + z = 0$
$x = -\dfrac{1}{3}z$
Substituting in the first equation we have
$-\dfrac{1}{3}z - y + 2z = 0$
$y = \dfrac{5}{3}z$
Letting $z = r$ gives the parametric solution $x = -\dfrac{1}{3}r$, $y = \dfrac{5}{3}r$, $z = r$, where r is any real number.

23.
$$\begin{cases} 2x + 2y - z = 3, & (1) \\ 4x + 4y - 2z = 6. & (2) \end{cases}$$

Multiplying Eq. (2) by $-\dfrac{1}{2}$ gives
$$\begin{cases} 2x + 2y - z = 3, \\ -2x - 2y + z = -3. \end{cases}$$
Adding the first equation to the second equation gives
$$\begin{cases} 2x + 2y - z = 3, \\ 0 = 0. \end{cases}$$
Solving the first equation for x, we have
$x = \dfrac{3}{2} - y + \dfrac{1}{2}z$. Letting $y = r$ and $z = s$ gives the parametric solution $x = \dfrac{3}{2} - r + \dfrac{1}{2}s$, $y = r$, $z = s$, where r and s are any real numbers.

25. Let x = number of gallons of 20% solution and y = number of gallons of 30% solution. Then
$$\begin{cases} x + y = 700, & (1) \\ 0.20x + 0.30y = 0.24(700). & (2) \end{cases}$$
From Eq. (1), $y = 700 - x$. Substituting in Eq. (2) gives
$$0.20x + 0.30(700 - x) = 0.24(700)$$
$$-0.10x + 210 = 168$$
$$-0.10x = -42$$
$$x = 420$$
$y = 700 - x = 700 - 420 = 280$. Thus 420 gal of 20% solution and 280 gal of 30% solution must be mixed.

27. Let C = the number of pounds of cotton, let P = the number of pounds of polyester, and let N = the number of pounds of nylon. If the final blend will cost \$3.25 per pound to make, then $4C + 3P + 2N = 3.25$. Furthermore, if we use the same amount of nylon as polyester to prepare, say, 1 pound of fabric, then $N = P$ and $C + P + N = 1$. Thus, the system of equations is
$$\begin{cases} 4C + 3P + 2N = 3.25, \\ C + P + N = 1, \\ N = P. \end{cases}$$
Simplifying gives
$$\begin{cases} 4C + 5N = 3.25, \\ C + 2N = 1, \\ N = P. \end{cases}$$
$$\begin{cases} N = 0.25, \\ C = 0.5, \\ P = 0.25. \end{cases}$$
Thus, the final fabric will contain 0.25 lb each of nylon and polyester, and 0.5 lb of cotton.

29. Let p = plane speed and w = wind speed. Now solve the system
$$\begin{cases} p + w = \dfrac{900}{3} \\ p - w = \dfrac{900}{3.6}, \end{cases}$$
which has solution
$$\begin{cases} p = 275, \\ w = 25. \end{cases}$$
Plane speed in still air = 275 mph and wind speed = 25 mph.

31. Let x = number of Early American units and y = number of Contemporary units. The fact that 20% more of Early American styles are sold than Contemporary styles means that
$$x = y + 0.20y$$
$$x = 1.20y$$
An analysis of profit gives
$250x + 350y = 130,000$. Thus we have the system
$$\begin{cases} x = 1.20y, & (1) \\ 250x + 350y = 130,000. & (2) \end{cases}$$
Substituting $1.20y$ for x in Eq. (2) gives
$$250(1.20y) + 350y = 130,000$$
$$300y + 350y = 130,000$$
$$650y = 130,000$$
$$y = 200$$
Thus $x = 1.20y = 1.20(200) = 240$. Therefore 240 units of Early American and 200 units of Contemporary must be sold.

33. Let x = number of calculators produced at Exton, and y = number of calculators produced at Whyton. The total cost of Exton is $7.50x + 7000$, and the total cost at Whyton is $6.00y + 8800$.

Thus $7.50x + 7000 = 6.00y + 8800$. Also, $x + y = 1500$. This gives the system
$$\begin{cases} x + y = 1500, & (1) \\ 7.50x + 7000 = 6.00y + 8800. & (2) \end{cases}$$
From Eq. (1), $y = 1500 - x$. Substituting in Eq. (2) gives
$7.50x + 7000 = 6.00(1500 - x) + 8800$
$7.50x + 7000 = 9000 - 6x + 8800$
$13.5x = 10,800$
$x = 800$
Thus $y = 1500 - x = 1500 - 800 = 700$.
Therefore 800 calculators must be made at the Exton plant and 700 calculators at the Whyton plant.

35. Let x = rate on first \$100,000 and y = rate on sales over \$100,000. Then
$$\begin{cases} 100,000x + 75,000y = 8500, & (1) \\ 100,000x + 180,000y = 14,800. & (2) \end{cases}$$
Subtracting Eq. (1) from Eq. (2) gives
$105,000y = 6300$
$y = 0.06$
Substituting in Eq. (1) gives
$100,000x + 75,000(0.06) = 8500$
$100,000x + 4500 = 8500$, $100,000x = 4000$,
or $x = 0.04$. Thus the rates are 4% on the first \$100,000 and 6% on the remainder.

37. Let x = number of units of Argon I and y = number of units of Argon II that the company can make. These require $6x + 10y$ doodles and $3x + 8y$ skeeters. Thus
$$\begin{cases} 6x + 10y = 760, & (1) \\ 3x + 8y = 500. & (2) \end{cases}$$
Multiplying Eq. (2) by -2 gives
$$\begin{cases} 6x + 10y = 760, \\ -6x - 16y = -1000. \end{cases}$$
Adding gives
$-6y = -240$
$y = 40$
From Eq. (1),
$6x + 10(40) = 760$
$6x = 360$
$x = 60$
Thus 60 units of Argon I and 40 units of Argon II can be made.

39. Let c = number of chairs company makes, r = number of rockers, and L = number of chaise lounges.
Wood used: $(1)c + (1)r + (1)L = 400$
Plastic used: $(1)c + (1)r + (2)L = 600$
Aluminum used: $(2)c + (3)r + (5)L = 1500$
Thus we have the system
$$\begin{cases} c + r + L = 400, & (1) \\ c + r + 2L = 600, & (2) \\ 2c + 3r + 5L = 1500. & (3) \end{cases}$$
Subtracting Eq. (1) from Eq. (2) gives
$L = 200$. Adding -2 times Eq. (1) to Eq. (3) gives
$r + 3L = 700$, from which
$r + 3(200) = 700$,
$r = 100$
From Eq. (1) we have $c + 100 + 200 = 400$, or $c = 100$. Thus 100 chairs, 100 rockers and 200 chaise lounges should be made.

41. Let x = number of skilled workers employed,
y = number of semiskilled workers employed,
z = number of shipping clerks employed.
Then we have the system

$$\begin{cases} \text{number of workers:} & x + y + z = 70, & (1) \\ \text{wages:} & 15x + 9y + 10z = 760, & (2) \\ \text{semiskilled:} & y = 2x. & (3) \end{cases}$$

From Eq. (3), $y = 2x$. Substituting in Eqs. (1) and (2) gives

$$\begin{cases} x + (2x) + z = 70, \\ 15x + 9(2x) + 10z = 760, \end{cases} \text{ or}$$

$$\begin{cases} 3x + z = 70, \\ 33x + 10z = 760. \end{cases}$$

Adding -10 times the first equation to the second gives
$3x = 60$
$x = 20$,
so $y = 2x = 2(20) = 40$. From
$x + y + z = 70$ we get
$20 + 40 + z = 70$
$z = 10$
The company should hire 40 semiskilled workers, 20 skilled workers, and 10 shipping clerks.

45. $x = 3, y = 2$

47. $x = 8.3, y = 14.0$

Exercise 4.5

In the following solutions, any reference to Eq. (1) or Eq. (2) refers to the first or second equation, respectively, in the given system.

1. From Eq. (2), $y = -3x$. Substituting in Eq. (1) gives

$-3x = 4 - x^2$
$x^2 - 3x - 4 = 0$
$(x - 4)(x + 1) = 0$
Thus $x = 4, -1$. From $y = -3x$, if $x = 4$, then $y = -3(4) = -12$; if $x = -1$, then $y = -3(-1) = 3$. Thus there are two solutions: $x = 4, y = -12$; $x = -1, y = 3$.

3. From Eq. (2), $q = p - 1$. Substituting in Eq. (1) gives

$p^2 = 5 - (p - 1)$
$p^2 + p - 6 = 0$
$(p + 3)(p - 2) = 0$
Thus $p = -3, 2$. From $q = p - 1$, if $p = -3$, we have $q = -3 - 1 = -4$; if $p = 2$, then $q = 2 - 1 = 1$. There are two solutions: $p = -3, q = -4$; $p = 2, q = 1$.

5. Substituting $y = x^2$ into $x = y^2$ gives

$x = x^4$, $x^4 - x = 0$
$x\left(x^3 - 1\right) = 0$
Thus $x = 0, 1$. From $y = x^2$, if $x = 0$, then $y = 0^2 = 0$; $x = 1$, then $y = 1^2 = 1$. There are two solutions: $x = 0, y = 0$; $x = 1, y = 1$.

7. Substituting $y = x^2 - 2x$ in Eq. (1) $\Rightarrow$

$x^2 - 2x = 4x - x^2 + 8$
$2x^2 - 6x - 8 = 0$
$x^2 - 3x - 4 = 0$
$(x - 4)(x + 1) = 0$
Thus $x = 4, -1$. From $y = x^2 - 2x$, if $x = 4$, then we have $y = 4^2 - 2(4) = 8$; if $x = -1$, then $y = (-1)^2 - 2(-1) = 3$. There are two solutions: $x = 4, y = 8, x = -1, y = 3$.

9. Substituting $p = \sqrt{q}$ in Eq. (2) gives

$\sqrt{q} = q^2$. Squaring both sides gives
$q = q^4$
$q^4 - q = 0$
$q\left(q^3 - 1\right) = 0$
Thus $q = 0, 1$. From $p = \sqrt{q}$, if $q = 0$, then $p = \sqrt{0} = 0$; if $q = 1$, then $p = \sqrt{1} = 1$. There are two solutions: $p = 0, q = 0$; $p = 1, q = 1$.

11. Replacing x^2 by $y^2 + 13$ in Eq. (2) gives

$$y = \left(y^2 + 13\right) - 15$$

$$y^2 - y - 2 = 0$$
$$(y - 2)(y + 1) = 0$$
Thus $y = 2, -1$. If $y = 2$, then
$$x^2 = y^2 + 13 = 2^2 + 13 = 17, \text{ so } x = \pm\sqrt{17}.$$
If $y = -1$, then
$$x^2 = y^2 + 13 = (-1)^2 + 13 = 14,$$

so $x = \pm\sqrt{14}$. Therefore, the system has four solutions: $x = \sqrt{17}, y = 2; \; x = -\sqrt{17}, y = 2;$
$x = \sqrt{14}, y = -1; \; x = -\sqrt{14}, y = -1.$

13. Substituting $x = y + 6$ in Eq. (2) gives
$$y = 3\sqrt{(y + 6) + 4} = 3\sqrt{y + 10}.$$
Squaring, we have
$$y^2 = 9(y + 10)$$
$$y^2 - 9y - 90 = 0$$
$$(y - 15)(y + 6) = 0$$
Thus $y = 15, -6$. But $y = -6$ does not satisfy Eq. (2) [a negative number does not equal a nonnegative number]. If $y = 15$, then $x = y + 6 = 15 + 6 = 21$. These values of x and y satisfy the system. Thus the only solution is $x = 21, y = 15$.

15. We can write the following system of equations.
$$\begin{cases} y = 0.01x^2 + 0.01x + 7, \\ y = 0.01x + 8.0. \end{cases}$$
By substituting $0.01x + 8.0$ for y in the first equation and simplifying, we obtain
$$0.01x + 8.0 = 0.01x^2 + 0.01x + 7$$
$$0 = 0.01x^2 - 1$$
$$0 = (0.1x + 1)(0.1x - 1)$$
$$x = -10 \quad \text{or} \quad x = 10$$
Hence, if $x = -10$ then $y = 7.9$, and if $x = 10$ then $y = 8.1$. The rope touches the streamer twice, 10 feet away from center on each side at $(-10, 7.9)$ and $(10, 8.1)$.

17. Three

19. $x = -1.3, y = 5.1$

21. $x = 1.76$

23. $x = -1.46$

Exercise 4.6

1. Equating p-values gives
$$\frac{3}{100}q + 2 = -\frac{7}{100}q + 12, \text{ from which}$$
$$\frac{1}{10}q = 10, \text{ or } q = 100. \text{ If } q = 100, \text{ then}$$
$$p = \frac{3}{100}q + 2 = \frac{3}{100}(100) + 2 = 5. \text{ The}$$
equilibrium point is $(100, 5)$.

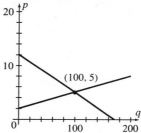

3. $\begin{cases} 35q - 2p + 250 = 0, & (1) \\ 65q + p - 537.5 = 0. & (2) \end{cases}$

Multiplying Eq. (2) by 2 and adding equations gives
$$165q - 825 = 0$$
$$q = 5$$
From Eq. (2),
$$65(5) + p - 537.5 = 0$$
$$p = 212.50$$
Thus the equilibrium point is $(5, 212.50)$.

5. Equating p-values:
$$2q + 20 = 200 - 2q^2$$
$$2q^2 + 2q - 180 = 0$$
$$q^2 + q - 90 = 0$$
$$(q + 10)(q - 9) = 0$$
Thus $q = -10, 9$. Since $q \geq 0$, choose $q = 9$.
Then $p = 2q + 20 = 2(9) + 20 = 38$. The equilibrium point is $(9, 38)$.

7. Equating p-values gives $20 - q = \sqrt{q + 10}$.
Squaring both sides gives
$$400 - 40q + q^2 = q + 10$$
$$q^2 - 41q + 390 = 0$$
$$(q - 26)(q - 15) = 0$$
Thus $q = 26, 15$. If $q = 26$, then
$p = 20 - q = 20 - 26 = -6$. But p cannot be
negative. If $q = 15$, then $p = 20 - q = 20 - 15$
$= 5$. The equilibrium point is $(15, 5)$.

9. Letting $y_{TR} = y_{TC}$ gives $3q = 2q + 4500$, or
$q = 4500$ units.

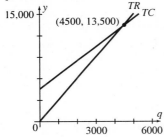

11. Letting $y_{TR} = y_{TC}$ gives
$$0.05q = 0.85q + 600$$
$$-0.80q = 600$$
$q = -750$, which is negative. Thus one cannot
break even at any level of production.

13. Letting $y_{TR} = y_{TC}$ gives
$$100 - \frac{1000}{q + 5} = q + 35.$$ Multiplying both sides
by $q + 5$ gives
$$100(q + 5) - 1000 = (q + 5)(q + 35)$$
$$q^2 - 60q + 675 = 0$$
$$(q - 15)(q - 45) = 0$$
Thus $q = 15$ or 45 units.

15.
$$\begin{cases} 3q - 200p + 1800 = 0, & (1) \\ 3q + 100p - 1800 = 0. & (2) \end{cases}$$

a. Subtracting Eq. (2) from Eq. (1) gives
$$-300p + 3600 = 0$$
$$p = \$12$$

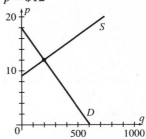

b. Before the tax the supply equation is
$$3q - 200p + 1800 = 0$$
$$-200p = -3q - 1800$$
$$p = \frac{3}{200}q + 9$$
After the tax the supply equation is
$$p = \frac{3}{200}q + 9 + 0.27$$
$$p = \frac{3}{200}q + 9.27$$
This equation can be written
$-3q + 200p - 1854 = 0$, and the new
system to solve is
$$\begin{cases} -3q + 200p - 1854 = 0, \\ 3q + 100p - 1800 = 0. \end{cases}$$
Adding gives
$$300p - 3654 = 0 \Rightarrow p = \frac{3654}{300} = \$12.18.$$

17. Since profit = total revenue − total cost, then
$4600 = 8.35q - (2116 + 7.20q)$. Solving
gives $4600 = 1.15q - 2116$
$1.15q = 6716$
$q = \frac{6716}{1.15} = 5840$ units
For a loss (negative profit) of $1150, we
solve $-1150 = 8.35q - (2116 + 7.20q)$. Thus
$-1150 = 1.15q - 2116$
$1.15q = 966$
$q = 840$ units
To break even, we have $y_{TR} = y_{TC}$, or
$8.35q = 2116 + 7.20q$
$1.15q = 2116$
$q = 1840$ units

19. Let q = break-even quantity. Since total
revenue is $5q$, we have $5q = 200,000$, which
yields
$q = 40,000$. Let c be the variable cost per
unit. Then
Tot. Rev. = Tot. Cost
= Variable Cost + Fixed Cost.
Thus
$200,000 = 40,000c + 40,000$
$160,000 = 40,000c$
$c = \$4$.

21. $y_{TC} = 2q + 1050$: $y_{TR} = 50\sqrt{q}$. Letting
$y_{TR} = y_{TC}$ gives
$50\sqrt{q} = 2q + 1050$
$25\sqrt{q} = q + 525$
Squaring gives
$625q = q^2 + 1050q + (525)^2$
$q^2 + 425q + (525)^2 = 0$
Using quad. formula,
$q = \frac{-425 \pm \sqrt{(425)^2 - 4(1)(525)^2}}{2}$, which is
not real. Thus total cost always exceeds total
revenue $\Rightarrow$ no break-even point.

23. After the subsidy the supply equation is
$p = \left[\frac{8}{100}q + 50\right] - 1.50$
$p = \frac{8}{100}q + 48.50$
The system to consider is
$$\begin{cases} p = \frac{8}{100}q + 48.50, \\ p = -\frac{7}{100}q + 65. \end{cases}$$
Equating p-values gives
$\frac{8}{100}q + 48.50 = -\frac{7}{100}q + 65$
$\frac{15}{100}q = 16.5$
$q = 110$
When $q = 110$, then
$p = \frac{8}{100}q + 48.50 = \frac{8}{100}(110) + 48.50$
$= 8.8 + 48.50 = 57.30$
Thus the original equilibrium price
decreases by $0.70.

25. Equating q_A-values gives
$8 - p_A + p_B = -2 + 5p_A - p_B$
$10 = 6p_A - 2p_B$
$5 = 3p_A - p_B$
Equating q_B-values gives
$26 + p_A - p_B = -4 - p_A + 3p_B$
$30 = -2p_A + 4p_B$
$15 = -p_A + 2p_B$.
Now we solve
$$\begin{cases} 3p_A - p_B = 5 \\ -p_A + 2p_B = 15 \end{cases}$$
Adding 2 times the first equation to the
second gives
$5p_A = 25$
$p_A = 5$
From $3p_A - p_B = 5$, $3(5) - p_B = 5$, or
$p_B = 10$. Thus $p_A = 5$ and $p_B = 10$.

27. 2.4 and 11.3

Chapter 4 Review Problems

1. Solving $\dfrac{k-5}{3-2} = 4$ gives $k - 5 = 4$, $k = 9$.

3. $(3, -2)$ and $(0, 1)$ lie on the line, so
    $m = \dfrac{1-(-2)}{0-3} = -1$. Slope-intercept form:
    $y = mx + b \Rightarrow y = -x + 1$. A general form:
    $x + y - 1 = 0$.

5. $y - 4 = \dfrac{1}{2}(x - 10)$

    $y - 4 = \dfrac{1}{2}x - 5$

    $y = \dfrac{1}{2}x - 1$, which is slope-intercept form.

    Clearing fractions, we have

    $2y = 2\left(\dfrac{1}{2}x - 1\right)$

    $2y = x - 2$
    $x - 2y - 2 = 0$, which is a general form.

7. Slope of a horizontal line is 0. Thus
    $y - 4 = 0[x - (-2)]$
    $y - 4 = 0$,
    so slope-intercept form is $y = 4$. A general
    form is $y - 4 = 0$.

9. $y + 3x = 2$ (or $y = -3x + 2$) has slope -3, so
    the line perpendicular to it has slope $\dfrac{1}{3}$.
    Since the y-intercept is 2, the equation is
    $y = \dfrac{1}{3}x + 2$. A general form is
    $x - 3y + 6 = 0$.

In Problems 11–15, m_1 = slope of first line, and
m_2 = slope of second line.

11. $x + 4y + 2 = 0$ $\left(\text{or } y = -\dfrac{1}{4}x - \dfrac{1}{2}\right)$ has slope

    $m_1 = -\dfrac{1}{4}$ and $8x - 2y - 2 = 0$ (or $y = 4x - 1$)

    has slope $m_2 = 4$. Since $m_1 = -\dfrac{1}{m_2}$, the

    lines are perpendicular to each other.

13. $x - 3 = 2(y + 4)$ $\left(\text{or } y = \dfrac{1}{2}x - \dfrac{11}{2}\right)$ has slope

    $m_1 = \dfrac{1}{2}$, and $y = 4x + 2$ has slope $m_2 = 4$.

    Since $m_1 \neq m_2$ and $m_1 \neq -\dfrac{1}{m_2}$, the lines are

    neither parallel nor perpendicular to each
    other.

15. $y = \dfrac{1}{2}x + 5$ has slope $\dfrac{1}{2}$, and $2x = 4y - 3$

    $\left(\text{or } y = \dfrac{1}{2}x + \dfrac{3}{4}\right)$ has slope $\dfrac{1}{2}$. Since

    $m_1 = m_2$, the lines are parallel.

17. $3x - 2y = 4$
    $-2y = -3x + 4$
    $y = \dfrac{3}{2}x - 2$
    $m = \dfrac{3}{2}$

19. $4 - 3y = 0$
    $-3y = -4$
    $y = \dfrac{4}{3}$
    $m = 0$

21. $y = f(x) = 4 - 2x$ has the linear form $f(x) = ax + b$, where $a = -2$ and $b = 4$. Slope $= -2$; y-intercept $(0, 4)$.

23. $y = f(x) = 9 - x^2$ has the quadratic form

$f(x) = ax^2 + bx + c$, where $a = -1$, $b = 0$ and $c = 9$.

Vertex: $-\dfrac{b}{2a} = -\dfrac{0}{2(-1)} = 0$

$f(0) = 9 - 0^2 = 9$

$\Rightarrow$ Vertex $= (0, 9)$

y-intercept: $c = 9$

x-intercepts: $9 - x^2 = (3 - x)(3 + x) = 0$, so $x = 3, -3$.

25. $y = h(t) = t^2 - 4t - 5$ has the quadratic form

$h(t) = at^2 + bt + c$, where $a = 1$, $b = -4$, and $c = -5$.

Vertex: $-\dfrac{b}{2a} = -\dfrac{-4}{2 \cdot 1} = 2$

$h(2) = 2^2 - 4(2) - 5 = -9$

$\Rightarrow$ Vertex $= (2, -9)$

y-intercept: $c = -5$

t-intercepts: $t^2 - 4t - 5 = (t - 5)(t + 1) = 0$

$\Rightarrow t = 5, -1$

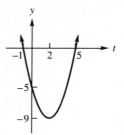

27. $p = g(t) = 3t$ has the linear form $g(t) = at + b$, where $a = 3$ and $b = 0$.

Slope $= 3$; p-intercept $(0, 0)$

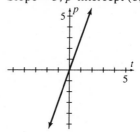

29. $y = F(x) = -\left(x^2 + 2x + 3\right) = -x^2 - 2x - 3$

has the quadratic form $F(x) = ax^2 + bx + c$, where $a = -1$, $b = -2$, and $c = -3$

Vertex: $-\dfrac{b}{2a} = -\dfrac{-2}{2(-1)} = -1$

$F(-1) = -\left[(-1)^2 + 2(-1) + 3\right] = -2$

$\Rightarrow$ Vertex $= (-1, -2)$

y-intercept: $c = -3$

x-intercepts: Because the parabola opens downward ($a < 0$) and the vertex is below the x-axis, there is no x-intercept.

31. $\begin{cases} 2x - y = 6, & (1) \\ 3x + 2y = 5. & (2) \end{cases}$

From Eq. (1), $y = 2x - 6$. Substituting in Eq. (2) gives
$3x + 2(2x - 6) = 5$
$7x - 12 = 5, 7x = 17$
$x = \frac{17}{7} \Rightarrow y = 2x - 6 = 2 \cdot \frac{17}{7} - 6 = -\frac{8}{7}.$
Thus $x = \frac{17}{7}$, $y = -\frac{8}{7}$.

33. $\begin{cases} 4x + 5y = 3, & (1) \\ 3x + 4y = 2. & (2) \end{cases}$

Multiplying Eq. (1) by 3 and Eq. (2) by -4
gives $\begin{cases} 12x + 15y = 9, \\ -12x - 16y = -8. \end{cases}$
Adding gives $-y = 1$, or $y = -1$.
From Eq. (1),
$4x + 5(-1) = 3$
$4x = 8$
$x = 2$
Thus $x = 2, y = -1$.

35. $\begin{cases} \frac{1}{4}x - \frac{3}{2}y = -4, & (1) \\ \frac{3}{4}x + \frac{1}{2}y = 8. & (2) \end{cases}$

Multiplying Eq. (2) by 3 gives
$\begin{cases} \frac{1}{4}x - \frac{3}{2}y = -4, \\ \frac{9}{4}x + \frac{3}{2}y = 24. \end{cases}$
Adding the first equation to the second gives
$\frac{5}{2}x = 20$
$x = 8$
From Eq. (1),
$\frac{1}{4}(8) - \frac{3}{2}y = -4$
$-\frac{3}{2}y = -6$
$y = 4$
Thus
$x = 8, y = 4$.

37. $\begin{cases} 3x - 2y + z = -2, & (1) \\ 2x + y + z = 1, & (2) \\ x + 3y - z = 3. & (3) \end{cases}$

Subtracting Eq. (2) from Eq. (1) and adding Eq. (2) to Eq. (3) give
$\begin{cases} x - 3y = -3, \\ 3x + 4y = 4. \end{cases}$
Multiplying the first equation by -3 gives
$\begin{cases} -3x + 9y = 9, \\ 3x + 4y = 4. \end{cases}$
Adding the first equation to the second gives
$13y = 13$
$y = 1$
From the equation $x - 3y = -3$ we get
$x - 3(1) = -3$
$x = 0$
From
$3x - 2y + z = -2$
$3(0) - 2(1) + z = -2$
$z = 0$
Thus $x = 0, y = 1, z = 0$.

39. $\begin{cases} x^2 - y + 2x = 7, & (1) \\ x^2 + y = 5. & (2) \end{cases}$

From Eq. (2), $y = 5 - x^2$. Substituting in Eq. (1) gives
$x^2 - \left(5 - x^2\right) + 2x = 7$
$2x^2 + 2x - 12 = 0$
$x^2 + x - 6 = 0$
$(x + 3)(x - 2) = 0$
Thus $x = -3, 2$. Since $y = 5 - x^2$, if $x = -3$, then $y = 5 - (-3)^2 = -4$; if $x = 2$, then $y = 5 - 2^2 = 1$. Thus the two solutions are $x = -3, y = -4$, and $x = 2, y = 1$.

41. $\begin{cases} x + 2z = -2, & (1) \\ x + y + z = 5. & (2) \end{cases}$

From Eq. (1) we have $x = -2 - 2z$.
Substituting in Eq. (2) gives
$-2 - 2z + y + z = 5$, so $y = 7 + z$.
Letting $z = r$ gives the parametric solution
$x = -2 - 2r$, $y = 7 + r$, $z = r$, where r is any real number.

43. $\begin{cases} x - y - z = 0, & (1) \\ 2x - 2y + 3z = 0. & (2) \end{cases}$

Multiplying Eq. (1) by -2 gives
$\begin{cases} -2x + 2y + 2z = 0, \\ 2x - 2y + 3z = 0. \end{cases}$
Adding Eq. (1) to Eq. (2) gives
$\begin{cases} -2x + 2y + 2z = 0, \\ 5z = 0. \end{cases}$
From the second equation, $z = 0$.
Substituting in Eq. (1) gives $x - y - 0 = 0$,
so $x = y$. Letting $y = r$ gives the parametric
solution $x = r$, $y = r$, $z = 0$, where r is any
real number.

45. $a = 1$ when $b = 2$; $a = 2$ when $b = 1$, so
$m = \dfrac{a_2 - a_1}{b_2 - b_1} = \dfrac{2 - 1}{1 - 2} = \dfrac{1}{-1} = -1$. Thus an
equation relating a and b is
$a - 1 = -1(b - 2)$
$a - 1 = -b + 2$
$a + b - 3 = 0$
When $b = 3$, then $a = -b + 3 = -(3) + 3 = 0$.

47. Slope is $\dfrac{-4}{3} \Rightarrow f(x) = ax + b = \dfrac{-4}{3}x + b$.
Since $f(1) = 5$,
$5 = -\dfrac{4}{3}(1) + b$
$b = \dfrac{19}{3}$
Thus $f(x) = -\dfrac{4}{3}x + \dfrac{19}{3}$.

49. $r = pq = (200 - 2q)q = 200q - 2q^2$, which
is a quadratic function with $a = -2$, $b = 200$,
$c = 0$. Since $a < 0$, r has a maximum value
when $q = -\dfrac{b}{2a} = -\dfrac{200}{-4} = 50$ units.
If $q = 50$, then
$r = [200 - 2(50)](50) = \$5000$.

51. $\begin{cases} 125p - q - 250 = 0, \\ 100p + q - 1100 = 0. \end{cases}$

Adding gives $225p - 1350 = 0$, or
$p = \dfrac{1350}{225} = 6$.

53. $y_{TR} = 16q$; $y_{TC} = 8q + 10,000$. Letting
$y_{TR} = y_{TC}$ gives
$16q = 8q + 10,000$
$8q = 10,000$
$q = 1250$
If $q = 1250$, then $y_{TR} = 16(1250) = 20,000$.
Thus the break-even point is (1250, 20,000).

55. Equating L-values gives
$0.0183 - \dfrac{0.0042}{p} = 0.0005 + \dfrac{0.0378}{p}$
$0.0178 = \dfrac{0.042}{p}$
$0.0178p = 0.042$
$p \approx 2.36$
The equilibrium pollution level is 2.36 tons
per square kilometer.

57. $x = 230$, $y = -130$

59. $x = 0.75$, $y = 1.43$

Mathematical Snapshot Chapter 4

1. To fill in the first blank, use the second part of the definition of $A1(t)$ and the first part of the definition of $A2(t)$, and solve the system

$$\begin{cases} A1(t) = 29.99 + 0.30(t - 120), \\ A2(t) = 39.99, \\ A1(t) = A2(t). \end{cases}$$

$$29.99 + 0.30(t - 120) = 39.99,$$
$$0.30t - 36 = 10,$$
$$0.30t = 46,$$
$$t = 153\frac{1}{3}$$

So Advantage I is the best plan for airtimes from 85 to $153\frac{1}{3}$ minutes.

To fill in the second blank, use the second part of the definition of $A2(t)$ and the first part of the definition of $A3(t)$, and solve the system

$$\begin{cases} A2(t) = 39.99 + 0.30(t - 120), \\ A3(t) = 49.99, \\ A2(t) = A3(t). \end{cases}$$

$$39.99 + 0.30(t - 200) = 49.99,$$
$$0.30t - 60 = 10,$$
$$0.30t = 70,$$
$$t = 233\frac{1}{3}.$$

So Advantage II is the best plan for airtimes from $153\frac{1}{3}$ to $233\frac{1}{3}$ minutes.

3. If the initial guess is on the horizontal portion of both graphs, the calculator may not be able to find the intersection point.

Chapter 5

1. The shapes of the graphs are the same. The value of A scales the value of any point by A.

2. If P = the amount of money invested and r = the annual rate at which P increases, then after 1 year, the investment has grown from P to $P + Pr = P(1 + r)$. Since $r = 0.10$, the factor by which P increases for the first year is $1 + r = 1 + 0.1 = 1.1$. Similarly, during the second year the investment grows from $P(1 + r)$ to $P(1+r) + r[P(1+r)]$ $= P(1+r)^2$. Again, since $r = 0.10$, the multiplicative increase for the second year is $(1 + 0.10)^2 = (1.1)^2 = 1.21$. This pattern will continue as shown in the table.

Year	Multiplicative Increase	Expression
0	1	1.1^0
1	1.1	1.1^1
2	1.21	1.1^2
3	1.33	1.1^3
4	1.46	1.1^4

Thus, the growth of the initial investment is exponential with a base of $1 + r = 1 + 0.1 = 1.1$. If we graph the multiplicative increase as a function of years we obtain the following.

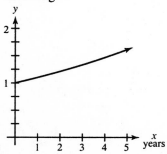

3. If V = the value of the car and r = the annual rate at which V depreciates, then after 1 year the value of the car is $V - rV = V(1 - r)$. Since $r = 0.15$, the factor by which V decreases for the first year is $1 - r = 1 - 0.15 = 0.85$. Similarly, after the second year the value of the car is $V(1 - r) - r[V(1 - r)] = V(1 - r)^2$. Again, since $r = 0.15$, the multiplicative decrease for the second year is $(1 - r)^2 = (1 - 0.15)^2 = 0.72$. This pattern will continue as shown in the table.

Year	Multiplicative Decrease	Expression
0	1	0.85^0
1	0.85	0.85^1
2	0.72	0.85^2
3	0.61	0.85^3

Thus, the depreciation is exponential with a base of $1 - r = 1 - 0.15 = 0.85$. If we graph the multiplicative decrease as a function of years, we obtain the following.

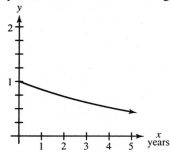

4. Let t = the time at which George's sister began saving, then since George is 3 years behind, $t - 3$ = the time when George began saving. Therefore, if $y = 1.08^t$ represents the multiplicative increase in George's sister's account $y = 1.08^{t-3}$ represents the multiplicative increase in George's account. A graph showing the projected increase in George's money will have the same shape as the graph of the projected increase in his sister's account, but will be shifted 3 units to the right.

5. $S = P(1 + r)^n$

$S = 2000(1 + 0.13)^5 = 2000(1.13)^5$
≈ 3684.87
The value of the investment after 5 years will be \$3684.87. The interest earned over the first 5 years is $3684.87 - 2000$
= \$1684.87.

6. Let $P = 2000$. With two interest periods per year, there will be a total of $n = 5(2) = 10$ interest periods. The periodic rate r is
$\dfrac{0.065}{2} = 0.0325$.

$S = P(1 + r)^n$

$S = 2000(1 + 0.0325)^{10} = 2000(1.0325)^{10}$
≈ 2753.79
The value of the investment after 5 years is \$2753.79. The interest earned over the first 5 years is $2753.79 - 2000 = \$753.79$.

7. Let $N(t)$ = the number of employees at time t, where t is in years. Then,
$N(4) = 5(1 + 1.2)^4 = 5(2.2)^4 = 117.128$
Thus, there will be 117 employees at the end of 4 years.

8. $P = e^{-0.06t} = \left(\dfrac{1}{e}\right)^{0.06t}$

Since $0 < \dfrac{1}{e} < 1$, the graph is that of an exponential function falling from left to right.

x	y
0	1
2	0.89
4	0.79
6	0.70
8	0.62
10	0.55

Exercise 5.1

1.

3.

5.

7.

9.

11.

13. For the curves, the bases involved are 0.4, 2, and 5. For base 5, the curve rises from left to right, and in the first quadrant it rises faster than the curve for base 2. Thus the graph of $y = 5^x$ is *B*.

15. For 2015 we have $t = 20$, so
$$P = 125,000(1.11)^{\frac{20}{20}} = 125,000(1.11)^1$$
$$= 138,750.$$

17. $P = 1 - \frac{1}{2}(1 - c)^0 = 1 - \frac{1}{2}(1) = \frac{1}{2}$

19. a. $4000(1.06)^7 \approx \$6014.52$

   b. $6014.52 - 4000 = \$2014.52$

21. a. $700(1.035)^{30} \approx \$1964.76$

   b. $1964.76 - 700 = \$1264.76$

23. a. $4000\left(1 + \frac{0.085}{4}\right)^{60} \approx \$14,124.86$

   b. $14,124.86 - 4000 = \$10,124.86$

25. a. $5000(1.0075)^{30} \approx \$6256.36$

   b. $6256.36 - 5000 = \$1256.36$

27. a. $8000\left(1 + \frac{0.0625}{365}\right)^{3(365)} \approx \$9649.69$

   b. $9649.69 - 8000 = \$1649.69$

29. $6000(1.02)^{28} \approx \$10,446.15$

31. a. $N = 400(1.05)^t$

   b. When $t = 1$, then
   $N = 400(1.05)^1 = 420.$

   c. When $t = 4$, then
   $N = 400(1.05)^4 \approx 486.$

33. Let P = the amount of plastic recycled and let r = the rate at which P increases each year. Then after the first year, the amount of plastic recycled, increases from P to $P + rP = P(1 + r)$, since $r = 0.3$, the factor by which P increases for the first year, is $1 + r = 1 + 0.3 = 1.3$. Similarly, during the second year, the amount of plastic recycled increases from

$P(1 + r)$ to $P(1 + r) + r[P(1 + r)] = P(1 + r)^2$.

Again, since $r = 0.3$, the multiplicative increase for the second year is

$(1 + r)^2 = (1 + 0.3)^2 = (1.3)^2 = 1.69$. This pattern will continue as shown in the table.

Year	Multiplicative Increase	Expression
0	1	1.3^0
1	1.3	1.3^1
2	1.69	1.3^2
3	2.20	1.3^3

Thus, the increase in recycling is exponential with a base $= 1 + r = 1 + 0.3 = 1.3$. If we graph the multiplicative increase as function of years, we obtaining the following.

35. $P = 100,000(1 - 0.01)^t = 100,000(0.99)^t$, where P is the population after t years. When $t = 3$, $P = 100,000(0.99)^3 \approx 97,030$.

37. 4.4817

39. 0.4966

41.

43. For $x = 3$, $P = \dfrac{e^{-3}3^3}{3!} \approx 0.2240$

45. $e^{kt} = \left(e^k\right)^t = b^t$, where $b = e^k$

47. a. When $t = 0$,
$N = 10e^{-0.028(0)} = 10 \cdot 1 = 10$.

b. When $t = 10$,
$N = 10e^{-0.028(10)} = 10e^{-0.28} \approx 7.6$.

c. When $t = 50$, $N = 10e^{-0.028(50)} \approx 2.5$.

d. After 50 hours, approximately $\frac{1}{4}$ of the initial amount remains. Because $\frac{1}{4} = \left(\frac{1}{2}\right)\left(\frac{1}{2}\right)$, 50 hours corresponds to 2 half-lives. Thus the half-life is approximately 25 hours.

49. After one half-life, $\frac{1}{2}$ gram remains. After two half-lives, $\frac{1}{2} \cdot \frac{1}{2} = \left(\frac{1}{2}\right)^2 = \frac{1}{4}$ gram remains. Continuing in this manner, after n half-lives, $\left(\frac{1}{2}\right)^n$ gram remains. Because $\frac{1}{16} = \left(\frac{1}{2}\right)^4$, after 4 half-lives, $\frac{1}{16}$ gram remains. This corresponds to $4 \cdot 8 = 32$ years.

51. $f(x) = \dfrac{e^{-4}4^x}{x!}$

$f(2) = \dfrac{e^{-4}4^2}{2!} \approx 0.1465$

53.

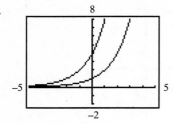

$y = 4 \cdot 2^x = 2^2 \cdot 2^x = 2^{x+2}$

If $f(x) = 2^x$, then

$y = 4 \cdot 2^x = 2^{x+2} = f(x+2)$. This implies

that the graph of $y = 4 \cdot 2^x$ is the graph of

$y = 2^x$ shifted two units to the left.

55. 3.17

57. $300\left(\dfrac{4}{3}\right)^{4.1} \approx 976$

$300\left(\dfrac{4}{3}\right)^{4.2} \approx 1004$

4.2 minutes

59. The first integer t for which the graph of
$P = 3000(1.045)^t$ lies on or above the
horizontal line $P = 2000$ is 16.

Principles in Practice 5.2

1. If $16 = 2^t$ is the exponential form then
$t = \log_2 16$ is the logarithmic form, where t
represents the number of times the bacteria
have doubled.

2. If $8.3 = \log_{10}\left(\dfrac{I}{I_0}\right)$ is the logarithmic form,

then $\dfrac{I}{I_0} = 10^{8.3}$ is the exponential form.

3. Let R = the amount of material recycled
every year. If the amount being recycled
increases by 50% every year, then the
amount recycled at the end of y years is
$R(1+r)^y = R(1+0.5)^y = R(1.5)^y$ Thus, the
multiplicative increase in recycling at the
end of y years is $(1.5)^y$. If we let
x = the multiplicative increase, then
$x = (1.5)^y$ and, in logarithmic form,
$\log_{1.5} x = y$.

4. Let V = the value of the boat. If the value
depreciates by 20% every year, then at the
end of y years the value of the boat is
$V(1-r)^y = V(1.02)^y = V(0.8)^y$. Thus, the
multiplicative decrease in value at the end of
y years is $(0.8)^y$. If we let
x = the multiplicative decrease, then
$x = (0.8)^y$ and, in logarithmic form,
$\log_{0.8} x = y$

5. The equation $t(r) = \dfrac{\ln 4}{r}$ can be rewritten as

$r = \dfrac{\ln 4}{t(r)}$. When this equation is graphed we

find that the annual rate r needed to quadruple the investment in 10 years is approximately 13.9%. Alternatively, we can solve for r by setting $t(r) = 10$.

$r = \dfrac{\ln(4)}{t(r)}$

$r = \dfrac{\ln(4)}{10} \approx 0.139 \text{ or } \approx 13.9\%$

6. Since $m = e^{rt}$, then $\ln m = rt$.

$\ln m = rt$

$\dfrac{\ln m}{t} = r$

Let $m = 3$ and $t = 12$.

$\dfrac{\ln 3}{12} = r$

$0.092 = r$

Thus, to triple your investment in 12 years, invest at an annual percentage rate of 9.2%.

Exercise 5.2

1. $\log 10{,}000 = 4$

3. $2^6 = 64$

5. $\ln 7.3891 = 2$

7. $e^{1.09861} = 3$

9.

11.

13.

15.

17. Because $6^2 = 36$, $\log_6 36 = 2$

19. Because $3^3 = 27$, $\log_3 27 = 3$

21. Because $7^1 = 7$, $\log_7 7 = 1$

23. Because $10^{-2} = 0.01$, $\log 0.01 = -2$

25. Because $5^0 = 1$, $\log_5 1 = 0$

27. Because $2^{-3} = \dfrac{1}{8}$, $\log_2 \dfrac{1}{8} = -3$

29. $3^2 = x$
$x = 9$

31. $5^3 = x$
$x = 125$

33. $10^{-1} = x$

$x = \dfrac{1}{10}$

35. $e^{-3} = x$

37. $x^3 = 8$

$x = 2$

39. $x^{-1} = \dfrac{1}{6}$

$x = 6$

41. $3^{-4} = x$

$x = \dfrac{1}{81}$

43. $x^2 = 6 - x$

$x^2 + x - 6 = 0$

$(x + 3)(x - 2) = 0$

The roots of this equation are -3 and 2.

But since $x > 0$, we choose $x = 2$.

45. $2 + \log_2 4 = 3x - 1$

$2 + 2 = 3x - 1$

$5 = 3x$

$x = \dfrac{5}{3}$

47. $x^2 = 2x + 8$

$x^2 - 2x - 8 = 0$

$(x - 4)(x + 2) = 0$

The roots of this equation are 4 and -2.

But since $x > 0$, we choose $x = 4$.

49. $e^{3x} = 2$

$3x = \ln 2$

$x = \dfrac{\ln 2}{3}$

51. $e^{2x-5} + 1 = 4$

$e^{2x-5} = 3$

$2x - 5 = \ln 3$

$x = \dfrac{5 + \ln 3}{2}$

53. 1.60944

55. 2.00013

57. If $5.5 = \log \dfrac{1}{h}$ then $10^{5.5} = \dfrac{1}{h}$.

59. $c = (12 \ln 6) + 20 \approx 41.50$

61. $1.5M = \log\left(\dfrac{E}{2.5 \times 10^{11}}\right)$

$10^{1.5M} = \dfrac{E}{2.5 \times 10^{11}}$

$E = \left(2.5 \times 10^{11}\right)\left(10^{1.5M}\right)$

$E = 2.5 \times 10^{11 + 1.5M}$

63. a. $p = 760 e^{-0.125(7.3)} \approx 305.2$ mm of mercury

b. $400 = 760 e^{-0.125h}$

$\dfrac{400}{760} = e^{-0.125h}$

$\ln \dfrac{400}{760} = -0.125h$

$h = \dfrac{\ln \frac{400}{760}}{-0.125} \approx 5.13$ km

65. $u_0 = A \ln\left(x_1\right) + \dfrac{x_2^2}{2}$

$u_0 - \dfrac{x_2^2}{2} = A \ln\left(x_1\right)$

$\ln\left(x_1\right) = \dfrac{u_0 - \frac{x_2^2}{2}}{A}$

$x_1 = e^{\frac{u_0 - \left(x_2^2/2\right)}{A}}$

67. $T = \dfrac{\ln 2}{0.03194} \approx 21.7$ years

69. $x + 2e^{3y} - 10 = 0$

$2e^{3y} = 10 - x$

$e^{3y} = \dfrac{10 - x}{2}$

$3y = \ln \dfrac{10 - x}{2}$

$y = \dfrac{1}{3} \ln \dfrac{10 - x}{2}$

71.

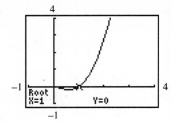

(1, 0)

73. For $y = \ln x$, when $y = 2$, then $2 = \ln x$ or $x = e^2$.

From the graph of $y = \ln x$, when $y = 2$, then $x = e^2 \approx 7.39$.

Principles in Practice 5.3

1. The magnitude (Richter Scale) of an earthquake is given by $R = \log\left(\dfrac{I}{I_0}\right)$ where I is the intensity of the earthquake and I_0 is the intensity of a zero-level reference earthquake. $\dfrac{I}{I_0} =$ how many times greater the earthquake is than a zero-level earthquake. Thus, when $\dfrac{I}{I_0} = 900,000$,

$R_1 = \log(900,000)$

When $\dfrac{I}{I_0} = 9000$

$R_2 = \log(9000)$

$R_1 - R_2 = \log(900,000) - \log 9000$

$= \log \dfrac{900,000}{9000} = \log 100 = \log 10^2$

$= 2 \log 10 = 2$

Thus, the two earthquakes differ by 2 on the Richter scale.

2. The magnitude (Richter Scale) of an earthquake is given by $R = \log\left(\dfrac{I}{I_0}\right)$ where I is the intensity of the earthquake and I_0 is the intensity of a zero-level reference earthquake. $\dfrac{I}{I_0} =$ how many times greater the earthquake is than a zero-level earthquake. Thus, if $\dfrac{I}{I_0} = 10,000$, then

$R = \log 10,000 = \log 10^4 = 4 \log 10 = 4$
The earthquake measures 4 on the Richter scale.

Exercise 5.3

1. $\log 15 = \log(3 \cdot 5) = \log 3 + \log 5 = b + c$

3. $\log \dfrac{2}{3} = \log 2 - \log 3 = a - b$

5. $\log \dfrac{8}{3} = \log 8 - \log 3 = \log 2^3 - \log 3$
$= 3 \log 2 - \log 3 = 3a - b$

7. $\log 36 = \log(2 \cdot 3)^2 = 2 \log(2 \cdot 3)$
$= 2(\log 2 + \log 3) = 2(a + b)$

9. $\log_2 3 = \dfrac{\log_{10} 3}{\log_{10} 2} = \dfrac{\log 3}{\log 2} = \dfrac{b}{a}$

11. $\log_7 7^{48} = 48$

13. $\log 0.0001 = \log 10^{-4} = -4$

15. $\ln e^{5.01} = \log_e e^{5.01} = 5.01$

17. $\ln \dfrac{1}{e^2} = -\ln e^2 = -\log_e e^2 = -2$

19. $\log \dfrac{1}{10} + \ln e^3 = \log_{10} \dfrac{1}{10} + \log_e e^3$
$= -1 + 3 = 2$

21. $\ln\left[x(x+1)^2\right] = \ln x + \ln(x+1)^2$
$= \ln x + 2 \ln(x+1)$

23. $\ln \dfrac{x^2}{(x+1)^3} = \ln x^2 - \ln(x+1)^3$

    $= 2\ln x - 3\ln(x+1)$

25. $\ln\left(\dfrac{x}{x+1}\right)^3 = 3\ln\dfrac{x}{x+1} = 3[\ln x - \ln(x+1)]$

27. $\ln \dfrac{x}{(x+1)(x+2)} = \ln x - \ln[(x+1)(x+2)]$

    $= \ln x - [\ln(x+1) + \ln(x+2)]$

    $= \ln x - \ln(x+1) - \ln(x+2)$

29. $\ln \dfrac{\sqrt{x}}{(x+1)^2(x+2)^3}$

    $= \ln x^{\frac{1}{2}} - \ln\left[(x+1)^2(x+2)^3\right]$

    $= \dfrac{1}{2}\ln x - \left[\ln(x+1)^2 + \ln(x+2)^3\right]$

    $= \dfrac{1}{2}\ln x - [2\ln(x+1) + 3\ln(x+2)]$

    $= \dfrac{1}{2}\ln x - 2\ln(x+1) - 3\ln(x+2)$

31. $\ln\left[\dfrac{1}{x+2}\sqrt[5]{\dfrac{x^2}{x+1}}\right] = \ln\left[\dfrac{1}{x+2}\left(\dfrac{x^2}{x+1}\right)^{\frac{1}{5}}\right]$

    $= \ln \dfrac{x^{\frac{2}{5}}}{(x+2)(x+1)^{\frac{1}{5}}}$

    $= \ln x^{\frac{2}{5}} - \ln\left[(x+2)(x+1)^{\frac{1}{5}}\right]$

    $= \dfrac{2}{5}\ln x - \left[\ln(x+2) + \ln(x+1)^{\frac{1}{5}}\right]$

    $= \dfrac{2}{5}\ln x - \ln(x+2) - \dfrac{1}{5}\ln(x+1)$

33. $\log(6 \cdot 4) = \log 24$

35. $\log_2 \dfrac{2x}{x+1}$

37. $\log 7^9 + \log 23^5 = \log\left[7^9(23)^5\right]$

39. $2 + 10\log(1.05) = \log 100 + \log(1.05)^{10}$

    $= \log\left[100(1.05)^{10}\right]$

41. $e^{4\ln 3 - 3\ln 4} = e^{\ln 3^4 - \ln 4^3} = e^{\ln\left(\frac{3^4}{4^3}\right)}$

    $= \dfrac{3^4}{4^3} = \dfrac{81}{64}$

43. $\log_6 54 - \log_6 9 = \log_6 \dfrac{54}{9} = \log_6 6 = 1$

45. $e^{\ln(2x)} = 5$

    $2x = 5$

    $x = \dfrac{5}{2}$

47. $10^{\log x^2} = 4$

    $x^2 = 4$

    $x = \pm 2$

49. From the change of base formula with $b = 10$, $m = x + 6$, and $a = e$, we have

    $\log(x+6) = \dfrac{\log_e(x+6)}{\log_e 10} = \dfrac{\ln(x+6)}{\ln 10}.$

51. From the change of base formula with $b = 3$, $m = x^2 + 1$, and $a = e$, we have

    $\log_3\left(x^2 + 1\right) = \dfrac{\log_e\left(x^2+1\right)}{\log_e 3} = \dfrac{\ln\left(x^2+1\right)}{\ln 3}.$

53. $e^{\ln z} = 7e^y$

    $z = 7e^y$

    $\dfrac{z}{7} = e^y$

    $y = \ln\dfrac{z}{7}$

55. $C = B + E$

    $C = B\left(1 + \dfrac{E}{B}\right)$

    $\ln C = \ln\left[B\left(1 + \dfrac{E}{B}\right)\right]$

    $\ln C = \ln B + \ln\left(1 + \dfrac{E}{B}\right)$

57. $M = \log(A) + 3$

   a. $M = \log(1) + 3 = 0 + 3 = 3$

   b. Given $M_1 = \log(A_1) + 3$, let
   $$M = \log(100A_1) + 3$$
   $$M = \log 100 + \log(A_1) + 3$$
   $$M = 2 + \left[\log(A_1) + 3\right]$$
   $$M = 2 + M_1$$

59. $\text{pH} = -\log\left(3 \times 10^{-4}\right) = -\left[\log 3 + \log 10^{-4}\right]$
   $$= -[\log(3) - 4] = 4 - \log 3 \approx 3.5229$$

61. $\left[\text{H}^+\right] \cdot \left(3 \times 10^{-2}\right) = 10^{-14}$, $\left[\text{H}^+\right] = \dfrac{1}{3} \times 10^{-12}$
   $$\text{pH} = -\log\left(\frac{1}{3} \times 10^{-12}\right)$$
   $$= -\left[\log\frac{1}{3} + \log 10^{-12}\right]$$
   $$= -[-\log(3) - 12] = 12 + \log 3 \approx 12.4771$$

63. $y = \log_4(x+2) = \dfrac{\ln(x+2)}{\ln 4}$

65.

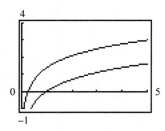

$y = \ln(4x) = \ln 4 + \ln x$. If $f(x) = \ln x$, then $y = \ln(4x) = f(x) + \ln 4$. Thus the graph of $y = \ln(4x)$ is the graph of $y = \ln x$ shifted $\ln 4$ units upward.

Principles in Practice 5.4

1. Let $x =$ the number and let $y =$ the unknown exponent. Then
   $$x \cdot 32^y = x \cdot 4^{(3y-9)}$$
   $$32^y = 4^{(3y-9)}$$
   $$\log 32^y = \log 4^{(3y-9)}$$
   $$y \log 32 = (3y - 9) \log 4$$
   $$y \log 32 = 3y \log 4 - 9 \log 4$$
   $$y(\log 32 - 3 \log 4) = -9 \log 4$$
   $$y = \frac{-9 \log 4}{\log \frac{32}{4^3}}$$
   $$y = 18$$
   Thus, Greg used 32 to the power of 18.

2. Let $S = 450$.
   $$S = 800\left(\frac{4}{3}\right)^{-0.1d}$$
   $$450 = 800\left(\frac{4}{3}\right)^{-0.1d}$$
   $$\frac{450}{800} = \left(\frac{4}{3}\right)^{-0.1d}$$
   $$\log \frac{450}{800} = -0.1d \log\left(\frac{4}{3}\right)$$
   $$\frac{\log \frac{450}{800}}{-0.1 \log\left(\frac{4}{3}\right)} = d$$
   $$20 = d$$
   Thus, he should start the new campaign 20 days after the last one ends.

3. The magnitude (Richter Scale) of an earthquake is given by $R = \log\left(\dfrac{I}{I_0}\right)$ where I is the intensity of the earthquake and I_0 is the intensity of a zero-level reference earthquake. $\dfrac{I}{I_0} =$ how many times greater the earthquake is than a zero-level earthquake.
   $$R_1 = \log(675,000)$$
   $$R_2 = \log\left(\frac{I}{I_0}\right)$$

Since $R_1 - 4 = R_2$

$$\log(675,000) - 4 = \log\left(\frac{I}{I_0}\right)$$

$$\log\left(6.75 \times 10^5\right) - 4 = \log\left(\frac{I}{I_0}\right)$$

$$\log 6.75 + 5\log 10 - 4 = \log\left(\frac{I}{I_0}\right)$$

$$1.83 = \log\left(\frac{I}{I_0}\right)$$

$$10^{1.83} = \frac{I}{I_0}$$

$$67.5 = \frac{I}{I_0}$$

Thus, the other earthquake is 67.5 times as intense as a zero-level earthquake.

Exercise 5.4

1. $\log(2x + 1) = \log(x + 6)$
   $2x + 1 = x + 6$
   $x = 5.000$

3. $\log 7 - \log(x - 1) = \log 4$
   $$\log\frac{7}{x-1} = \log 4$$
   $$\frac{7}{x-1} = 4$$
   $7 = 4x - 4$
   $4x = 11$
   $$x = \frac{11}{4} = 2.750$$

5. $\ln(-x) = \ln\left(x^2 - 6\right)$
   $-x = x^2 - 6$
   $x^2 + x - 6 = 0$
   $(x + 3)(x - 2) = 0$
   $x = -3$ or $x = 2$
   However, $x = -3$ is the only value that satisfies the original equation.
   Answer: -3.000

7. $e^{2x}e^{5x} = e^{14}$
   $e^{7x} = e^{14}$
   $7x = 14$
   $x = 2.000$

9. $(16)^{3x} = 2$
   $\left(2^4\right)^{3x} = 2$
   $2^{12x} = 2^1$
   $12x = 1$
   $$x = \frac{1}{12} \approx 0.083$$

11. $e^{2x} = 9$
    $(e^x)^2 = 3^2$
    $e^x = 3$
    $x = \ln 3 \approx 1.099$

13. $3e^{3x+1} = 15$
    $e^{3x+1} = 5$
    $3x + 1 = \ln 5$
    $$x = \frac{\ln(5) - 1}{3} \approx 0.203$$

15. $10^{\frac{4}{x}} = 6$
    $$\frac{4}{x} = \log 6$$
    $$x = \frac{4}{\log 6} \approx 5.140$$

17. $\dfrac{5}{10^{2x}} = 7$
    $$10^{2x} = \frac{5}{7}$$
    $$2x = \log\frac{5}{7}$$
    $$x = \frac{\log\left(\frac{5}{7}\right)}{2} \approx -0.073$$

19. $2^x = 5$
    $\ln 2^x = \ln 5$
    $x \ln 2 = \ln 5$
    $$x = \frac{\ln 5}{\ln 2} \approx 2.322$$

21. $5^{2x-5} = 9$

$\ln 5^{2x-5} = \ln 9$

$(2x - 5)\ln 5 = \ln 9$

$2x - 5 = \dfrac{\ln 9}{\ln 5}$

$2x = \dfrac{\ln 9}{\ln 5} + 5$

$x = \dfrac{\frac{\ln 9}{\ln 5} + 5}{2} \approx 3.183$

23. $2^{-\frac{2x}{3}} = \dfrac{4}{5}$

$\ln 2^{-\frac{2x}{3}} = \ln\dfrac{4}{5}$

$-\dfrac{2x}{3}\ln 2 = \ln\dfrac{4}{5}$

$-\dfrac{2x}{3} = \dfrac{\ln\left(\frac{4}{5}\right)}{\ln 2}$

$x = -\dfrac{3\ln\left(\frac{4}{5}\right)}{2\ln 2} \approx 0.483$

25. $(4)5^{3-x} - 7 = 2$

$5^{3-x} = \dfrac{9}{4}$

$\ln 5^{3-x} = \ln\dfrac{9}{4}$

$(3 - x)\ln 5 = \ln\dfrac{9}{4}$

$3 - x = \dfrac{\ln\left(\frac{9}{4}\right)}{\ln 5}$

$x = 3 - \dfrac{\ln\left(\frac{9}{4}\right)}{\ln 5} \approx 2.496$

27. $\log(x - 3) = 3$

$10^3 = x - 3$

$x = 10^3 + 3 = 1003.000$

29. $\log_4(9x - 4) = 2$

$4^2 = 9x - 4$

$9x = 4^2 + 4$

$x = \dfrac{4^2 + 4}{9} = \dfrac{20}{9} = 2.222$

31. $\log(3x - 1) - \log(x - 3) = 2$

$\log\dfrac{3x - 1}{x - 3} = 2$

$10^2 = \dfrac{3x - 1}{x - 3}$

$100(x - 3) = 3x - 1$

$97x = 299$

$x = \dfrac{299}{97} \approx 3.082$

33. $\log_3(2x + 3) = 4 - \log_3(x + 6)$

$\log_3(2x + 3) + \log_3(x + 6) = 4$

$\log_3[(2x + 3)(x + 6)] = 4$

$3^4 = (2x + 3)(x + 6)$

$2x^2 + 15x + 18 = 81$

$2x^2 + 15x - 63 = 0$

$(2x + 21)(x - 3) = 0$

$x = -\dfrac{21}{2}$ or $x = 3$

However, $x = 3$ is the only value that satisfies the original equation.
Answer: 3.000

35. $\log_2\left(\dfrac{2}{x}\right) = 3 + \log_2 x$

$\log_2\left(\dfrac{2}{x}\right) - \log_2 x = 3$

$\log_2\dfrac{\frac{2}{x}}{x} = 3$

$\log_2\dfrac{2}{x^2} = 3$

$2^3 = \dfrac{2}{x^2}$

$x^2 = \dfrac{1}{4}$

$x = \pm\dfrac{1}{2}$

However, $x = \dfrac{1}{2}$ is the only value that satisfies the original equation.
Answer: 0.500

37. $\log S = \log 12.4 + 0.26\log A$

$\log S = \log 12.4 + \log A^{0.26}$

$\log S = \log\left[12.4A^{0.26}\right]$

$S = 12.4A^{0.26}$

39. a. When $t = 0$,
$$Q = 100e^{-0.035(0)} = 100e^0 = 100 \cdot 1$$
$$= 100.$$

b. If $Q = 20$, then $20 = 100e^{-0.035t}$.
Solving for t gives
$$\frac{20}{100} = e^{-0.035t}$$
$$\frac{1}{5} = e^{-0.035t}$$
$$\ln\frac{1}{5} = -0.035t$$
$$-\ln 5 = -0.035t$$
$$t = \frac{\ln 5}{0.035} \approx 46$$

41. If $P = 1{,}500{,}000$, then
$1{,}500{,}000 = 1{,}000{,}000(1.02)^t$. Solving for
t gives
$$\frac{1{,}500{,}000}{1{,}000{,}000} = (1.02)^t$$
$$1.5 = (1.02)^t$$
$$\ln 1.5 = \ln(1.02)^t$$
$$\ln 1.5 = t \ln 1.02$$
$$t = \frac{\ln 1.5}{\ln 1.02} \approx 20.5.$$

43. $q = 80 - 2^P$
$$2^P = 80 - q$$
$$\log 2^P = \log(80 - q)$$
$$p \log 2 = \log(80 - q)$$
$$p = \frac{\log(80 - q)}{\log 2}$$
When $q = 60$, then $p = \dfrac{\log 20}{\log 2} \approx 4.32$.

45. Let I be the original intensity. the intensity
of light passes through 1 sheet of $0.9I$. The
intensity of light passing through 2 sheets is
$0.9[(0.9)I] = (0.9)^2 I$. Continuing in this
manner, the light passing through n sheets is
$(0.9)^n I$. The equation to solve is
$(0.9)^n I = 0.5I$ or, more simply,
$(0.9)^n = 0.5$. Solving gives
$$\ln(0.9)^n = \ln 0.5$$
$$n \ln 0.9 = \ln 0.5$$
$$n = \frac{\ln 0.5}{\ln 0.9} \approx 7$$

47. $q = 500\left(1 - e^{-0.2t}\right)$

a. If $t = 1$, then $q = 500\left(1 - e^{-0.2}\right) \approx 91$.

b. If $t = 10$, then $q = 500\left(1 - e^{-2}\right) \approx 432$.

c. We solve the equation
$$400 = 500\left(1 - e^{-0.2t}\right)$$
$$\frac{4}{5} = 1 - e^{-0.2t}$$
$$e^{-0.2t} = \frac{1}{5}$$
$$-0.2t = \ln\frac{1}{5} = -\ln 5$$
$$t = \frac{\ln 5}{0.2} \approx 8$$

49.

1.20

51. $4x + (3)4^y = 1$

$(3)4^y = 1 - 4x$

$4^y = \dfrac{1 - 4x}{3}$

$\ln 4^y = \ln\left(\dfrac{1 - 4x}{3}\right)$

$y \ln 4 = \ln\left(\dfrac{1 - 4x}{3}\right)$

$y = \dfrac{\ln\left(\frac{1-4x}{3}\right)}{\ln 4}$

Graph of the original equation is the graph

of $y = \dfrac{\ln\left(\frac{1-4x}{3}\right)}{\ln 4}$.

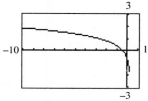

Chapter 5 Review Problems

1. $\log_3 243 = 5$

3. $16^{\frac{1}{4}} = 2$

5. $\ln 54.598 = 4$

7. Because $5^3 = 125$, $\log_5 125 = 3$

9. Because $2^{-4} = \dfrac{1}{16}$, $\log_2 \dfrac{1}{16} = -4$

11. Because $\left(\dfrac{1}{3}\right)^{-2} = 3^2 = 9$, $\log_{\frac{1}{3}} 9 = -2$

13. $5^x = 625$

$x = 4$

15. $10^{-2} = x$

$x = \dfrac{1}{10^2} = \dfrac{1}{100}$

17. $\ln(2x + 3) = 0$

$e^0 = 2x + 3$

$1 = 2x + 3$

$2x = -2$

$x = -1$

19. $\log 8000 = \log(2 \cdot 10)^3 = 3 \log(2 \cdot 10)$

$= 3(\log 2 + \log 10) = 3(a + 1)$

21. $2 \log 5 - 3 \log 3 = \log 5^2 - \log 3^3 = \log \dfrac{5^2}{3^3}$

$= \log \dfrac{25}{27}$

23. $2 \ln x + \ln y - 3 \ln z = \ln x^2 + \ln y - \ln z^3$

$= \ln x^2 y - \ln z^3 = \ln \dfrac{x^2 y}{z^3}$

25. $\dfrac{1}{2} \log_2 x + 2 \log_2 x^2 - 3 \log_2(x + 1)$

     $- 4 \log_2(x + 2)$

$= \log_2 x^{\frac{1}{2}} + \log_2\left(x^2\right)^2$

     $- \left[\log_2(x + 1)^3 + \log_2(x + 2)^4\right]$

$= \log_2\left(x^{\frac{1}{2}} x^4\right) - \log_2\left[(x + 1)^3 (x + 2)^4\right]$

$= \log_2 \dfrac{x^{\frac{9}{2}}}{(x + 1)^3 (x + 2)^4}$

27. $\ln \dfrac{x^2 y}{z^3} = \ln x^2 y - \ln z^3 = \ln x^2 + \ln y - \ln z^3$

$= 2 \ln x + \ln y - 3 \ln z$

29. $\ln \sqrt[3]{xyz} = \ln(xyz)^{\frac{1}{3}} = \dfrac{1}{3} \ln(xyz)$

$= \dfrac{1}{3}(\ln x + \ln y + \ln z)$

31. $\ln\left[\dfrac{1}{x}\sqrt{\dfrac{y}{z}}\right] = \ln \dfrac{\left(\frac{y}{z}\right)^{1/2}}{x} = \ln\left(\dfrac{y}{z}\right)^{\frac{1}{2}} - \ln x$

$= \dfrac{1}{2} \ln \dfrac{y}{z} - \ln x = \dfrac{1}{2}(\ln y - \ln z) - \ln x$

33. $\log_3(x + 5) = \dfrac{\log_e(x + 5)}{\log_e 3} = \dfrac{\ln(x + 5)}{\ln 3}$

35. $\log_5 19 = \dfrac{\log_2 19}{\log_2 5} = \dfrac{4.2479}{2.3219} \approx 1.8295$

37. $\ln\left(16\sqrt{3}\right) = \ln 4^2 + \ln\sqrt{3} = 2\ln 2 + \dfrac{1}{2}\ln 3$

$\qquad = 2y + \dfrac{1}{2}x$

39. $e^{\ln x} + \ln e^x + \ln 1 = x + x + 0 = 2x$

41. In exponential form, $y = e^{x^2 + 2}$.

43.

45. $4x + 1 = x + 2$
$3x = 1$
$x = \dfrac{1}{3}$

47. $3^{4x} = 9^{x+1}$

$3^{4x} = \left(3^2\right)^{x+1}$

$3^{4x} = 3^{2(x+1)}$
$4x = 2(x+1)$
$4x = 2x + 2$
$2x = 2$
$x = 1$

49. $\log x + \log(10x) = 3$
$\log x + \log 10 + \log x = 3$
$2\log(x) + 1 = 3$
$2\log(x) = 2$
$\log x = 1$
$x = 10^1 = 10$

51. $\ln\left(\log_x 2\right) = -1$

$\log_x 2 = e^{-1}$

$x^{e^{-1}} = 2$

$\left(x^{e^{-1}}\right)^e = 2^e$

$x^{e^{-1}e} = 2^e$

$x^1 = 2^e$

$x = 2^e$

53. $e^{3x} = 14$
$3x = \ln 14$
$x = \dfrac{\ln 14}{3} \approx 0.880$

55. $3\left(10^{x+4} - 3\right) = 9$

$10^{x+4} - 3 = 3$
$10^{x+4} = 6$
$x + 4 = \log 6$
$x = \log(6) - 4 \approx -3.222$

57. $4^{x+3} = 7$
$\ln 4^{x+3} = \ln 7$
$(x + 3)\ln 4 = \ln 7$
$x + 3 = \dfrac{\ln 7}{\ln 4}$
$x = \dfrac{\ln 7}{\ln 4} - 3 \approx -1.596$

59. Quarterly rate $= \dfrac{0.06}{4} = 0.015$

$6\dfrac{1}{2}$ yrs = 26 quarters

a. $2600(1.015)^{26} \approx \$3829.04$

b. $3829.04 - 2600 = \$1229.04$

61. $12\left(1\dfrac{1}{6}\%\right) = 14\%$

63. a. $P = 8000(1 + 0.02)^t$ or
$\qquad P = 8000(1.02)^t$

b. When $t = 2$, then
$\qquad P = 8000(1.02)^2 \approx 8323$

65. $N = 10e^{-0.41t}$

   a. When $t = 0$, then

      $N = 10e^0 = 10 \cdot 1 = 10$ mg

   b. When $t = 2$, then

      $N = 10e^{-0.82} \approx 4.4$ mg

   c. When $t = 10$, then

      $N = 10e^{-4.1} \approx 0.2$ mg

   d. $\dfrac{\ln 2}{0.41} \approx 1.7$

   e. If $N = 1$, then $1 = 10e^{-0.41t}$. Solving for t gives

      $\dfrac{1}{10} = e^{-0.41t}$

      $-0.41t = \ln \dfrac{1}{10} = -\ln 10$

      $t = \dfrac{\ln 10}{0.41} \approx 5.6$

67. $R = 10e^{-\frac{t}{40}}$

   a. If $t = 20$, $R = 10e^{-\frac{20}{40}} = 10e^{-\frac{1}{2}} \approx 6$.

   b. $5 = 10e^{-\frac{t}{40}}$, $\dfrac{1}{2} = e^{-\frac{t}{40}}$. Thus

      $-\dfrac{t}{40} = \ln \dfrac{1}{2} = -\ln 2$

      $t = 40 \ln 2 \approx 28$.

69. $T_t - T_e = (T_t - T_e)_o e^{-at}$

   $e^{-at} = \dfrac{T_t - T_e}{(T_t - T_e)_o}$

   $-at = \ln \dfrac{T_t - T_e}{(T_t - T_e)_o}$

   $a = -\dfrac{1}{t} \ln \dfrac{T_t - T_e}{(T_t - T_e)_o}$

   $a = \dfrac{1}{t} \ln \dfrac{(T_t - T_e)_o}{T_t - T_e}$

71.

$(-\infty, 0.37]$

73.

2.93

75. $y = \log_3\left(x^2 + 1\right) = \dfrac{\ln\left(x^2 + 1\right)}{\ln 3}$

77.

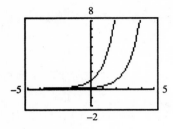

$$y = \frac{3^x}{9} = \frac{3^x}{3^2} = 3^{x-2}.$$

If $f(x) = 3^x$, then we have

$y = 3^{x-2} = f(x-2)$. Thus the graph of

$y = \dfrac{3^x}{9}$ is the graph of $y = 3^x$ shifted 2

units to the right.

Mathematical Snapshot Chapter 5

1. $T = \dfrac{P\left(1 - e^{-dkI}\right)}{e^{kI} - 1}$

   a. $T\left(e^{kI} - 1\right) = P\left(1 - e^{-dkI}\right)$

      $\dfrac{T\left(e^{kI} - 1\right)}{1 - e^{-dkI}} = P$ or $P = \dfrac{T\left(e^{kI} - 1\right)}{1 - e^{-dkI}}$

   b. $T\left(e^{kI} - 1\right) = P - Pe^{-dkI}$,

      $Pe^{-dkI} = P - T\left(e^{kI} - 1\right)$,

      $e^{-dkI} = \dfrac{P - T\left(e^{kI} - 1\right)}{P}$,

      $-dkI = \ln\left[\dfrac{P - T\left(e^{kI} - 1\right)}{P}\right]$,

      $d = -\dfrac{1}{kI} \ln\left[\dfrac{P - T\left(e^{kI} - 1\right)}{P}\right]$,

      $d = \dfrac{1}{kI} \ln\left[\dfrac{P}{P - T\left(e^{kI} - 1\right)}\right]$

3. $P = 100$, $I = 4$, $d = 3$, $H = 8$, $k = \dfrac{\ln 2}{H} = \dfrac{\ln 2}{8}$

   a. $T = \dfrac{P\left(1 - e^{-dkI}\right)}{e^{kI} - 1} = \dfrac{100\left(1 - e^{-3 \cdot \frac{\ln 2}{8} \cdot 4}\right)}{e^{\frac{\ln 2}{8} \cdot 4} - 1}$

      $= \dfrac{100\left(1 - \left[e^{\ln 2}\right]^{-\frac{3}{2}}\right)}{\left[e^{\ln 2}\right]^{\frac{1}{2}} - 1}$

      $= \dfrac{100\left(1 - 2^{-\frac{3}{2}}\right)}{2^{\frac{1}{2}} - 1} \approx 156$

   b. $R = P\left(1 - e^{-dkI}\right)$. From part (a),

      $P\left(1 - e^{-dkI}\right) = 100\left(1 - 2^{-\frac{3}{2}}\right)$.

      Thus $R = 100\left(1 - 2^{-\frac{3}{2}}\right) \approx 65$.

Chapter 6

Principles in Practice 6.1

1. There are 3 rows, one for each source. There are two columns, one for each raw material. Thus, the order of the matrix is 3×2.

2. The first column consists of 1's each representing the 1 hour needed for each phase of project 1. The second column consists of 2's for each phase of project 2 and so on. In general the nth column will consist of 2^n's, each representing the 2^n hours needed for each phase of project n. The time-analysis matrix is as follows.

$$\begin{bmatrix} 1 & 2 & 4 & 8 & 16 \\ 1 & 2 & 4 & 8 & 16 \\ 1 & 2 & 4 & 8 & 16 \end{bmatrix}$$

Exercise 6.1

1. **a.** The order is the number of rows by the columns. Thus A is 2×3, B is 3×3, C is 3×2, D is 2×2, E is 4×4, F is 1×2, G is 3×1, H is 3×3, J is 1×1.

   b. A square matrix has the same number of rows as columns. Thus the square matrices are B, D, E, H, and J.

   c. An upper triangular matrix is a square matrix where all entries below the main diagonal are zeros. Thus H and J are upper triangular. A lower triangular matrix is a square matrix where all entries above the main diagonal are zeros. Thus D and J are lower triangular.

   d. A row vector (or row matrix) has only one row. Thus F and J are row vectors.

   e. A column vector (or column matrix) has only one column. Thus G and J are column vectors.

3. a_{43} is the entry in the 4th row and 3rd column, namely 2.

5. a_{32} is the entry in the 3rd row and 2nd column, namely 4.

7. a_{44} is the entry in the 4th row and 4th column, namely 0.

9. The main diagonal entries are the entries on the diagonal extending from the upper left corner to the lower right corner. Thus the main diagonal entries are 7, 2, 1, 0.

11. $$\begin{bmatrix} 4 \cdot 1 + 2 \cdot 1 & 4 \cdot 1 + 2 \cdot 2 & 4 \cdot 1 + 2 \cdot 3 & 4 \cdot 1 + 2 \cdot 4 \\ 4 \cdot 2 + 2 \cdot 1 & 4 \cdot 2 + 2 \cdot 2 & 4 \cdot 2 + 2 \cdot 3 & 4 \cdot 2 + 2 \cdot 4 \\ 4 \cdot 3 + 2 \cdot 1 & 4 \cdot 3 + 2 \cdot 2 & 4 \cdot 3 + 2 \cdot 3 & 4 \cdot 3 + 2 \cdot 4 \end{bmatrix} = \begin{bmatrix} 6 & 8 & 10 & 12 \\ 10 & 12 & 14 & 16 \\ 14 & 16 & 18 & 20 \end{bmatrix}$$

13. $12 \cdot 10 = 120$, so A has 120 entries. For a_{33}, $i = 3 = j$, so $a_{33} = 1$. Since $5 \neq 2$, $a_{52} = 0$. For $a_{10,\,10}$, $i = 10 = j$, so $a_{10,\,10} = 1$. Since $12 \neq 10$, $a_{12,\,10} = 0$.

15. A zero matrix is a matrix in which all entries are zeros.

a. $\begin{bmatrix} 0 & 0 & 0 & 0 \\ 0 & 0 & 0 & 0 \\ 0 & 0 & 0 & 0 \\ 0 & 0 & 0 & 0 \end{bmatrix}$

b. $\begin{bmatrix} 0 & 0 & 0 & 0 & 0 & 0 \\ 0 & 0 & 0 & 0 & 0 & 0 \\ 0 & 0 & 0 & 0 & 0 & 0 \\ 0 & 0 & 0 & 0 & 0 & 0 \\ 0 & 0 & 0 & 0 & 0 & 0 \\ 0 & 0 & 0 & 0 & 0 & 0 \end{bmatrix}$

17. $\mathbf{A}^T = \begin{bmatrix} 6 & -3 \\ 2 & 4 \end{bmatrix}^T = \begin{bmatrix} 6 & 2 \\ -3 & 4 \end{bmatrix}$

19. $\mathbf{A}^T = \begin{bmatrix} 1 & 3 & 7 & 3 \\ 3 & 2 & -2 & 0 \\ -4 & 5 & 0 & 1 \end{bmatrix}^T = \begin{bmatrix} 1 & 3 & -4 \\ 3 & 2 & 5 \\ 7 & -2 & 0 \\ 3 & 0 & 1 \end{bmatrix}$

21. a. **A** and **C** are diagonal matrices.

   b. All are them are triangular matrices.

23. $\mathbf{A}^T = \begin{bmatrix} 1 & 2 & 3 \\ 4 & 5 & 6 \\ 7 & 8 & 9 \end{bmatrix}^T = \begin{bmatrix} 1 & 4 & 7 \\ 2 & 5 & 8 \\ 3 & 6 & 9 \end{bmatrix}$

$\left(\mathbf{A}^T \right)^T = \begin{bmatrix} 1 & 4 & 7 \\ 2 & 5 & 8 \\ 3 & 6 & 9 \end{bmatrix}^T = \begin{bmatrix} 1 & 2 & 3 \\ 4 & 5 & 6 \\ 7 & 8 & 9 \end{bmatrix} = \mathbf{A}$

25. Equating corresponding entries gives $6 = 6$, $2 = 2$, $x = 6$, $7 = 7$, $3y = 2$, and $2z = 7$. Thus $x = 6$, $y = \frac{2}{3}$, $z = \frac{7}{2}$.

27. Equating corresponding entries gives $2x = y$, $7 = 7$, $7 = 7$, and $2y = y$. Now $2y = y$ yields $y = 0$. Thus from $2x = y$ we get $2x = 0$, so $x = 0$. The solution is $x = 0$, $y = 0$.

29. a. From **J**, the entry in row 3 (super-duper) and column 2 (white) is 7. Thus in January, 7 white super-duper models were sold.

   b. From **F**, the entry in row 2 (deluxe) and column 3 (blue) is 3. Thus in February, 3 blue deluxe models were sold.

   c. The entries in row 1 (regular) and column 4 (purple) give the number of purple regular models sold. For **J** the entry is 2 and for **F** the entry is 4. Thus more purple regular models were sold in February.

   d. In both January and February, the deluxe blue models (row 2, column 3) sold the same number of units (3).

   e. In January a total of $0 + 1 + 3 + 5 = 9$ deluxe models were sold. In February a total of $2 + 3 + 3 + 2 = 10$ deluxe models were sold. Thus more deluxe models were sold in February.

   f. In January a total of $2 + 0 + 2 = 4$ red widgets were sold, while in February a total of $0 + 2 + 4 = 6$ red widgets were sold. Thus more red widgets were sold in February.

   g. Adding all entries in matrix **J** yields that a total of 38 widgets were sold in January.

31. By equating entries we find that x must satisfy
$x^2 + 2000x = 2001$ and $\sqrt{x^2} = -x$.
The second equation implies that $x < 0$.
From the first equation,
$x^2 + 2000x - 2001 = 0$,
$(x + 2001)(x - 1) = 0$, so $x = -2001$.

33. $\begin{bmatrix} 3 & 1 & 1 \\ 1 & 7 & 4 \\ 4 & 3 & 1 \\ 2 & 6 & 2 \end{bmatrix}$

Principles in Practice 6.2

1. $T = J + F = \begin{bmatrix} 120 & 80 \\ 105 & 130 \end{bmatrix} + \begin{bmatrix} 110 & 140 \\ 85 & 125 \end{bmatrix}$

$= \begin{bmatrix} 120 + 110 & 80 + 140 \\ 105 + 85 & 130 + 125 \end{bmatrix} = \begin{bmatrix} 230 & 220 \\ 190 & 155 \end{bmatrix}$

2. $0.8 \begin{bmatrix} x_1 \\ x_2 \\ x_3 \end{bmatrix} - \begin{bmatrix} 40 \\ 30 \\ 60 \end{bmatrix} = 2 \begin{bmatrix} 248 \\ 319 \\ 532 \end{bmatrix}$

$\begin{bmatrix} 0.8x_1 \\ 0.8x_2 \\ 0.8x_3 \end{bmatrix} - \begin{bmatrix} 40 \\ 30 \\ 60 \end{bmatrix} = \begin{bmatrix} 496 \\ 638 \\ 1064 \end{bmatrix}$

$\begin{bmatrix} 0.8x_1 - 40 \\ 0.8x_2 - 30 \\ 0.8x_3 - 60 \end{bmatrix} = \begin{bmatrix} 496 \\ 638 \\ 1064 \end{bmatrix}$

Solve $0.8x_1 - 40 = 496$ to get $x_1 = 670$.
Solve $0.8x_2 - 30 = 638$ to get $x_2 = 835$.
Solve $0.8x_3 - 60 = 1064$ to get $x_3 = 1405$.

Exercise 6.2

1. $\begin{bmatrix} 2 & 0 & -3 \\ -1 & 4 & 0 \\ 1 & -6 & 5 \end{bmatrix} + \begin{bmatrix} 2 & -3 & 4 \\ -1 & 6 & 5 \\ 9 & 11 & -2 \end{bmatrix} = \begin{bmatrix} 2+2 & 0+(-3) & -3+4 \\ -1+(-1) & 4+6 & 0+5 \\ 1+9 & -6+11 & 5+(-2) \end{bmatrix} = \begin{bmatrix} 4 & -3 & 1 \\ -2 & 10 & 5 \\ 10 & 5 & 3 \end{bmatrix}$

3. $\begin{bmatrix} 1 & 4 \\ -2 & 7 \\ 6 & 9 \end{bmatrix} - \begin{bmatrix} 6 & -1 \\ 7 & 2 \\ 1 & 0 \end{bmatrix} = \begin{bmatrix} 1-6 & 4-(-1) \\ -2-7 & 7-2 \\ 6-1 & 9-0 \end{bmatrix} = \begin{bmatrix} -5 & 5 \\ -9 & 5 \\ 5 & 9 \end{bmatrix}$

5. $3\begin{bmatrix} 1 & -3 & 1 \end{bmatrix} + 2\begin{bmatrix} -6 & 1 & 4 \end{bmatrix} - 0\begin{bmatrix} -2 & 7 & 4 \end{bmatrix}$

$= \begin{bmatrix} 3 & -9 & 3 \end{bmatrix} + \begin{bmatrix} -12 & 2 & 8 \end{bmatrix} - \begin{bmatrix} 0 & 0 & 0 \end{bmatrix}$

$= \begin{bmatrix} 3-12-0 & -9+2-0 & 3+8-0 \end{bmatrix} = \begin{bmatrix} -9 & -7 & 11 \end{bmatrix}$

7. $\begin{bmatrix} 1 & 2 \\ 3 & 4 \end{bmatrix}$ has order 2×2, and $\begin{bmatrix} 7 \\ 2 \end{bmatrix}$ has order 2×1. Thus the sum is not defined.

9. $-6 \begin{bmatrix} 2 & -6 & 7 & 1 \\ 7 & 1 & 6 & -2 \end{bmatrix} = \begin{bmatrix} -6 \cdot 2 & -6(-6) & -6 \cdot 7 & -6 \cdot 1 \\ -6 \cdot 7 & -6 \cdot 1 & -6 \cdot 6 & -6(-2) \end{bmatrix} = \begin{bmatrix} -12 & 36 & -42 & -6 \\ -42 & -6 & -36 & 12 \end{bmatrix}$

11. $\begin{bmatrix} 2 & -4 & 0 \\ 0 & 6 & -2 \\ -4 & 0 & 10 \end{bmatrix} + \frac{1}{3}\begin{bmatrix} 9 & 0 & 3 \\ 0 & 3 & 0 \\ 3 & 9 & 9 \end{bmatrix} = \begin{bmatrix} 2 & -4 & 0 \\ 0 & 6 & -2 \\ -4 & 0 & 10 \end{bmatrix} + \begin{bmatrix} 3 & 0 & 1 \\ 0 & 1 & 0 \\ 1 & 3 & 3 \end{bmatrix} = \begin{bmatrix} 5 & -4 & 1 \\ 0 & 7 & -2 \\ -3 & 3 & 13 \end{bmatrix}$

13. $-\mathbf{B} = -\begin{bmatrix} -6 & -5 \\ 2 & -3 \end{bmatrix} = (-1)\begin{bmatrix} -6 & -5 \\ 2 & -3 \end{bmatrix} = \begin{bmatrix} -1(-6) & -1(-5) \\ -1(2) & -1(-3) \end{bmatrix} = \begin{bmatrix} 6 & 5 \\ -2 & 3 \end{bmatrix}$

15. $2\mathbf{O} = 2\begin{bmatrix} 0 & 0 \\ 0 & 0 \end{bmatrix} = \begin{bmatrix} 2 \cdot 0 & 2 \cdot 0 \\ 2 \cdot 0 & 2 \cdot 0 \end{bmatrix} = \begin{bmatrix} 0 & 0 \\ 0 & 0 \end{bmatrix} = \mathbf{O}$

17. $2(\mathbf{A} - 2\mathbf{B}) = 2\left\{ \begin{bmatrix} 2 & 1 \\ 3 & -3 \end{bmatrix} - 2\begin{bmatrix} -6 & -5 \\ 2 & -3 \end{bmatrix} \right\}$

$= 2\left\{ \begin{bmatrix} 2 & 1 \\ 3 & -3 \end{bmatrix} - \begin{bmatrix} -12 & -10 \\ 4 & -6 \end{bmatrix} \right\} = 2\begin{bmatrix} 14 & 11 \\ -1 & 3 \end{bmatrix} = \begin{bmatrix} 28 & 22 \\ -2 & 6 \end{bmatrix}$

19. $3(\mathbf{A} - \mathbf{C})$ is a 2×2 matrix and 6 is a number. Therefore $3(\mathbf{A} - \mathbf{C}) + 6$ is not defined.

21. $2\mathbf{B} - 3\mathbf{A} + 2\mathbf{C} = 2\begin{bmatrix} -6 & -5 \\ 2 & -3 \end{bmatrix} - 3\begin{bmatrix} 2 & 1 \\ 3 & -3 \end{bmatrix} + 2\begin{bmatrix} -2 & -1 \\ -3 & 3 \end{bmatrix}$

$= \begin{bmatrix} -12 & -10 \\ 4 & -6 \end{bmatrix} - \begin{bmatrix} 6 & 3 \\ 9 & -9 \end{bmatrix} + \begin{bmatrix} -4 & -2 \\ -6 & 6 \end{bmatrix}$

$= \begin{bmatrix} -18 & -13 \\ -5 & 3 \end{bmatrix} + \begin{bmatrix} -4 & -2 \\ -6 & 6 \end{bmatrix} = \begin{bmatrix} -22 & -15 \\ -11 & 9 \end{bmatrix}$

23. $\frac{1}{2}\mathbf{A} - 2(\mathbf{B} + 2\mathbf{C}) = \frac{1}{2}\begin{bmatrix} 2 & 1 \\ 3 & -3 \end{bmatrix} - 2\left\{ \begin{bmatrix} -6 & -5 \\ 2 & -3 \end{bmatrix} + 2\begin{bmatrix} -2 & -1 \\ -3 & 3 \end{bmatrix} \right\}$

$= \begin{bmatrix} 1 & \frac{1}{2} \\ \frac{3}{2} & -\frac{3}{2} \end{bmatrix} - 2\left\{ \begin{bmatrix} -6 & -5 \\ 2 & -3 \end{bmatrix} + \begin{bmatrix} -4 & -2 \\ -6 & 6 \end{bmatrix} \right\}$

$= \begin{bmatrix} 1 & \frac{1}{2} \\ \frac{3}{2} & -\frac{3}{2} \end{bmatrix} - 2\begin{bmatrix} -10 & -7 \\ -4 & 3 \end{bmatrix} = \begin{bmatrix} 1 & \frac{1}{2} \\ \frac{3}{2} & -\frac{3}{2} \end{bmatrix} - \begin{bmatrix} -20 & -14 \\ -8 & 6 \end{bmatrix} = \begin{bmatrix} 21 & \frac{29}{2} \\ \frac{19}{2} & -\frac{15}{2} \end{bmatrix}$

25. $3(\mathbf{A} + \mathbf{B}) = 3\begin{bmatrix} -4 & -4 \\ 5 & -6 \end{bmatrix} = \begin{bmatrix} -12 & -12 \\ 15 & -18 \end{bmatrix}$

$3\mathbf{A} + 3\mathbf{B} = \begin{bmatrix} 6 & 3 \\ 9 & -9 \end{bmatrix} + \begin{bmatrix} -18 & -15 \\ 6 & -9 \end{bmatrix} = \begin{bmatrix} -12 & -12 \\ 15 & -18 \end{bmatrix}$

Thus $3(\mathbf{A} + \mathbf{B}) = 3\mathbf{A} + 3\mathbf{B}$.

27. $k_1(k_2\mathbf{A}) = k_1\begin{bmatrix} 2k_2 & k_2 \\ 3k_2 & -3k_2 \end{bmatrix} = \begin{bmatrix} 2k_1k_2 & k_1k_2 \\ 3k_1k_2 & -3k_1k_2 \end{bmatrix}$

$(k_1k_2)\mathbf{A} = \begin{bmatrix} 2k_1k_2 & k_1k_2 \\ 3k_1k_2 & -3k_1k_2 \end{bmatrix}$.

Thus $k_1(k_2\mathbf{A}) = (k_1k_2)\mathbf{A}$.

29. $3\mathbf{A}^{\mathsf{T}} + \mathbf{D} = 3\begin{bmatrix} 1 & 0 & 7 \\ 2 & -1 & 0 \end{bmatrix} + \begin{bmatrix} 1 & 2 & -1 \\ 1 & 0 & 2 \end{bmatrix} = \begin{bmatrix} 3 & 0 & 21 \\ 6 & -3 & 0 \end{bmatrix} + \begin{bmatrix} 1 & 2 & -1 \\ 1 & 0 & 2 \end{bmatrix} = \begin{bmatrix} 4 & 2 & 20 \\ 7 & -3 & 2 \end{bmatrix}$

31. $2\mathbf{B}^{\mathrm{T}} - 3\mathbf{C}^{\mathrm{T}} = 2\begin{bmatrix} 1 & 4 \\ 3 & -1 \end{bmatrix} - 3\begin{bmatrix} 1 & 1 \\ 0 & 2 \end{bmatrix} = \begin{bmatrix} 2 & 8 \\ 6 & -2 \end{bmatrix} - \begin{bmatrix} 3 & 3 \\ 0 & 6 \end{bmatrix} = \begin{bmatrix} -1 & 5 \\ 6 & -8 \end{bmatrix}$

33. $\mathbf{C}^{\mathrm{T}} - \mathbf{D} = \begin{bmatrix} 1 & 0 \\ 1 & 2 \end{bmatrix}^{\mathrm{T}} - \begin{bmatrix} 1 & 2 & -1 \\ 1 & 0 & 2 \end{bmatrix}$ is impossible because $\mathbf{C}^{\mathrm{T}}$ and $\mathbf{D}$ are not of the same size.

35. $x\begin{bmatrix} 2 \\ 1 \end{bmatrix} - y\begin{bmatrix} -3 \\ 5 \end{bmatrix} = 2\begin{bmatrix} 8 \\ 11 \end{bmatrix}$

$\begin{bmatrix} 2x \\ x \end{bmatrix} - \begin{bmatrix} -3y \\ 5y \end{bmatrix} = \begin{bmatrix} 16 \\ 22 \end{bmatrix}$

$\begin{bmatrix} 2x + 3y \\ x - 5y \end{bmatrix} = \begin{bmatrix} 16 \\ 22 \end{bmatrix}$

Equating corresponding entries gives

$\begin{cases} 2x + 3y = 16 \\ x - 5y = 22 \end{cases}$.

From the second equation, $x = 22 + 5y$.
Substituting in the first equation gives
$2(22 + 5y) + 3y = 16$, $13y = -28$, or

$y = -\dfrac{28}{13}$. Therefore

$x = 22 + 5y = 22 + 5\left(-\dfrac{28}{13}\right) = \dfrac{146}{13}$.

The solution is $x = \dfrac{146}{13}$, $y = -\dfrac{28}{13}$.

37. $3\begin{bmatrix} x \\ y \end{bmatrix} - 3\begin{bmatrix} -2 \\ 4 \end{bmatrix} = 4\begin{bmatrix} 6 \\ -2 \end{bmatrix}$

$\begin{bmatrix} 3x + 6 \\ 3y - 12 \end{bmatrix} = \begin{bmatrix} 24 \\ -8 \end{bmatrix}$

$3x + 6 = 24$, $3x = 18$, or $x = 6$.

$3y - 12 = -8$, $3y = 4$, or $y = \dfrac{4}{3}$.

Thus $x = 6$, $y = \dfrac{4}{3}$.

39. $\begin{bmatrix} 2 \\ 4 \\ 6 \end{bmatrix} + 2\begin{bmatrix} x \\ y \\ 4z \end{bmatrix} = \begin{bmatrix} -10 \\ -24 \\ 14 \end{bmatrix}$

$\begin{bmatrix} 2 + 2x \\ 4 + 2y \\ 6 + 8z \end{bmatrix} = \begin{bmatrix} -10 \\ -24 \\ 14 \end{bmatrix}$

$2 + 2x = -10$, $2x = -12$, or $x = -6$.
$4 + 2y = -24$, $2y = -28$, or $y = -14$.
$6 + 8z = 14$, $8z = 8$, or $z = 1$.
Thus $x = -6$, $y = -14$, $z = 1$.

41. $\mathbf{X} + \mathbf{Y} = \begin{bmatrix} 20 & 40 \\ 45 & 30 \\ 15 & 10 \end{bmatrix} + \begin{bmatrix} 15 & 25 \\ 30 & 25 \\ 10 & 5 \end{bmatrix}$

$= \begin{bmatrix} 20 + 15 & 40 + 25 \\ 45 + 30 & 30 + 25 \\ 15 + 10 & 10 + 5 \end{bmatrix}$

$= \begin{bmatrix} 35 & 65 \\ 75 & 55 \\ 25 & 15 \end{bmatrix}$

43. $P + 0.1P$
$= [p_1 \quad p_2 \quad p_3] + [0.1p_1 \quad 0.1p_2 \quad 0.1p_3]$
$= [1.1p_1 \quad 1.1p_2 \quad 1.1p_3] = 1.1\mathbf{P}$
Thus P must be multiplied by 1.1.

45. $\begin{bmatrix} 15 & -4 & 26 \\ 4 & 7 & 30 \end{bmatrix}$

47. $\begin{bmatrix} -10 & 22 & 12 \\ 24 & 36 & -44 \end{bmatrix}$

Principles in Practice 6.3

1. Represent the value of each book by $\begin{bmatrix} 28 & 22 & 16 \end{bmatrix}$ and the number of each book by $\begin{bmatrix} 100 \\ 70 \\ 90 \end{bmatrix}$.

   The total value is given by the following matrix product.

   $$\begin{bmatrix} 28 & 22 & 16 \end{bmatrix} \begin{bmatrix} 100 \\ 70 \\ 90 \end{bmatrix} = [2800 + 1540 + 1440] = [5780]$$

   The total value is $5780.

2. The total cost is given by the matrix product **PQ**.

   $$\mathbf{PQ} = \begin{bmatrix} 26.25 & 34.75 & 28.50 \end{bmatrix} \begin{bmatrix} 250 \\ 325 \\ 175 \end{bmatrix} = \begin{bmatrix} 6562.5 & 11,293.75 & 4987.5 \end{bmatrix} = 22,843.75$$

   The total cost is $22,843.75.

3. First, write the equations with the variable terms on the left-hand side.

   $$\begin{cases} y + \dfrac{8}{5}x = \dfrac{8}{5} \\ y + \dfrac{1}{3}x = \dfrac{5}{3} \end{cases}$$

   Let $\mathbf{A} = \begin{bmatrix} 1 & \frac{8}{5} \\ 1 & \frac{1}{3} \end{bmatrix}$, $\mathbf{X} = \begin{bmatrix} y \\ x \end{bmatrix}$, and $\mathbf{B} = \begin{bmatrix} \frac{8}{5} \\ \frac{5}{3} \end{bmatrix}$.

   Then the pair of lines is equivalent to the matrix equation $\mathbf{AX} = \mathbf{B}$ or $\begin{bmatrix} 1 & \frac{8}{5} \\ 1 & \frac{1}{3} \end{bmatrix} \begin{bmatrix} y \\ x \end{bmatrix} = \begin{bmatrix} \frac{8}{5} \\ \frac{5}{3} \end{bmatrix}$.

Exercise 6.3

1. $c_{11} = 1(0) + 3(-2) + (-2)(3) = -12$

3. $c_{32} = 0(-2) + 4(4) + 3(1) = 19$

5. $c_{22} = -2(-2) + 1(4) + (-1)(1) = 7$

7. **A** is 2×3 and **E** is 3×2, so **AE** is 2×2; $2 \cdot 2 = 4$ entries

9. **E** is 3×2 and **C** is 2×5, so **EC** is 3×5; $3 \cdot 5 = 15$ entries

11. **F** is 2×3 and **B** is 3×1, so **FB** is 2×1; $2 \cdot 1 = 2$ entries

13. **E** is 3×2 and **A** is 2×3, so **EA** is 3×3; $3 \cdot 3 = 9$ entries

15. **E** is 3×2. **F** is 2×3 and **B** is 3×1, so **FB** is 2×1. Thus **E(FB)** is 3×1; $3 \cdot 1 = 3$ entries.

17. An identity matrix is a square matrix (in this case 4×4) with 1's on the main diagonal and all other entries 0's.

$$T_4 = \begin{bmatrix} 1 & 0 & 0 & 0 \\ 0 & 1 & 0 & 0 \\ 0 & 0 & 1 & 0 \\ 0 & 0 & 0 & 1 \end{bmatrix}$$

19. $\begin{bmatrix} 2 & -4 \\ 3 & 2 \end{bmatrix}\begin{bmatrix} 4 & 0 \\ -1 & 3 \end{bmatrix} = \begin{bmatrix} 2(4)+(-4)(-1) & 2(0)+(-4)(3) \\ 3(4)+2(-1) & 3(0)+2(3) \end{bmatrix} = \begin{bmatrix} 12 & -12 \\ 10 & 6 \end{bmatrix}$

21. $\begin{bmatrix} 2 & 0 & 3 \\ -1 & 4 & 5 \end{bmatrix}\begin{bmatrix} 1 \\ 4 \\ 7 \end{bmatrix} = \begin{bmatrix} 2(1)+0(4)+3(7) \\ -1(1)+4(4)+5(7) \end{bmatrix} = \begin{bmatrix} 23 \\ 50 \end{bmatrix}$

23. $\begin{bmatrix} 1 & 4 & -1 \\ 0 & 0 & 2 \\ -2 & 1 & 1 \end{bmatrix}\begin{bmatrix} 2 & 1 & 0 \\ 0 & -1 & 1 \\ 1 & 1 & 2 \end{bmatrix}$

$$= \begin{bmatrix} 1(2)+4(0)+(-1)1 & 1(1)+4(-1)+(-1)(1) & 1(0)+4(1)+(-1)(2) \\ 0(2)+0(0)+2(1) & 0(1)+0(-1)+2(1) & 0(0)+0(1)+2(2) \\ -2(2)+1(0)+1(1) & -2(1)+1(-1)+1(1) & -2(0)+1(1)+1(2) \end{bmatrix} = \begin{bmatrix} 1 & -4 & 2 \\ 2 & 2 & 4 \\ -3 & -2 & 3 \end{bmatrix}$$

25. $\begin{bmatrix} -1 & 2 & 3 \end{bmatrix}\begin{bmatrix} 3 & 1 & -1 & 2 \\ 0 & 4 & 3 & 1 \\ -1 & 3 & 1 & -2 \end{bmatrix}$

$$= \begin{bmatrix} -3+0-3 & -1+8+9 & 1+6+3 & -2+2-6 \end{bmatrix} = \begin{bmatrix} -6 & 16 & 10 & -6 \end{bmatrix}$$

27. $\begin{bmatrix} 2 \\ 3 \\ -4 \\ 1 \end{bmatrix}\begin{bmatrix} 2 & 3 & -2 & 3 \end{bmatrix} = \begin{bmatrix} 2(2) & 2(3) & 2(-2) & 2(3) \\ 3(2) & 3(3) & 3(-2) & 3(3) \\ -4(2) & -4(3) & -4(-2) & -4(3) \\ 1(2) & 1(3) & 1(-2) & 1(3) \end{bmatrix} = \begin{bmatrix} 4 & 6 & -4 & 6 \\ 6 & 9 & -6 & 9 \\ -8 & -12 & 8 & -12 \\ 2 & 3 & -2 & 3 \end{bmatrix}$

29. $3\left\{\begin{bmatrix} -2 & 0 & 2 \\ 3 & -1 & 1 \end{bmatrix} + 2\begin{bmatrix} -1 & 0 & 2 \\ 1 & 1 & -2 \end{bmatrix}\right\}\begin{bmatrix} 1 & 2 \\ 3 & 4 \\ 5 & 6 \end{bmatrix}$

$= 3\left\{\begin{bmatrix} -2 & 0 & 2 \\ 3 & -1 & 1 \end{bmatrix} + \begin{bmatrix} -2 & 0 & 4 \\ 2 & 2 & -4 \end{bmatrix}\right\}\begin{bmatrix} 1 & 2 \\ 3 & 4 \\ 5 & 6 \end{bmatrix}$

$= 3\left\{\begin{bmatrix} -4 & 0 & 6 \\ 5 & 1 & -3 \end{bmatrix}\right\}\begin{bmatrix} 1 & 2 \\ 3 & 4 \\ 5 & 6 \end{bmatrix} = \begin{bmatrix} -12 & 0 & 18 \\ 15 & 3 & -9 \end{bmatrix}\begin{bmatrix} 1 & 2 \\ 3 & 4 \\ 5 & 6 \end{bmatrix}$

$= \begin{bmatrix} -12(1) + 0(3) + 18(5) & -12(2) + 0(4) + 18(6) \\ 15(1) + 3(3) + (-9)(5) & 15(2) + 3(4) + (-9)(6) \end{bmatrix} = \begin{bmatrix} 78 & 84 \\ -21 & -12 \end{bmatrix}$

31. $\begin{bmatrix} 1 & 2 \\ 3 & 4 \end{bmatrix}\left\{\begin{bmatrix} 2 & 0 & 1 \\ 1 & 0 & -2 \end{bmatrix}\begin{bmatrix} 1 & -2 \\ 2 & 1 \\ 3 & 0 \end{bmatrix}\right\} = \begin{bmatrix} 1 & 2 \\ 3 & 4 \end{bmatrix}\left\{\begin{bmatrix} 2+0+3 & -4+0+0 \\ 1+0-6 & -2+0+0 \end{bmatrix}\right\}$

$= \begin{bmatrix} 1 & 2 \\ 3 & 4 \end{bmatrix}\begin{bmatrix} 5 & -4 \\ -5 & -2 \end{bmatrix} = \begin{bmatrix} 5-10 & -4-4 \\ 15-20 & -12-8 \end{bmatrix} = \begin{bmatrix} -5 & -8 \\ -5 & -20 \end{bmatrix}$

33. $\begin{bmatrix} 0 & 0 & 1 \\ 0 & 1 & 0 \\ 1 & 0 & 0 \end{bmatrix}\begin{bmatrix} x \\ y \\ z \end{bmatrix} = \begin{bmatrix} 0 \cdot x + 0 \cdot y + 1 \cdot z \\ 0 \cdot x + 1 \cdot y + 0 \cdot z \\ 1 \cdot x + 0 \cdot y + 0 \cdot z \end{bmatrix} = \begin{bmatrix} z \\ y \\ x \end{bmatrix}$

35. $\begin{bmatrix} 2 & 1 & 3 \\ 4 & 9 & 7 \end{bmatrix}\begin{bmatrix} x_1 \\ x_2 \\ x_3 \end{bmatrix} = \begin{bmatrix} 2x_1 + x_2 + 3x_3 \\ 4x_1 + 9x_2 + 7x_3 \end{bmatrix}$

37. $\mathbf{DI} - \frac{1}{3}\mathbf{E} = \mathbf{D} - \frac{1}{3}\mathbf{E} = \begin{bmatrix} 1 & 0 & 0 \\ 0 & 1 & 1 \\ 1 & 2 & 1 \end{bmatrix} - \frac{1}{3}\begin{bmatrix} 3 & 0 & 0 \\ 0 & 6 & 0 \\ 0 & 0 & 3 \end{bmatrix}$

$= \begin{bmatrix} 1 & 0 & 0 \\ 0 & 1 & 1 \\ 1 & 2 & 1 \end{bmatrix} - \begin{bmatrix} 1 & 0 & 0 \\ 0 & 2 & 0 \\ 0 & 0 & 1 \end{bmatrix}$

$= \begin{bmatrix} 0 & 0 & 0 \\ 0 & -1 & 1 \\ 1 & 2 & 0 \end{bmatrix}$

39. $3A - 2BC = 3\begin{bmatrix} 1 & -2 \\ 0 & 3 \end{bmatrix} - 2\begin{bmatrix} -2 & 3 & 0 \\ 1 & -4 & 1 \end{bmatrix}\begin{bmatrix} -1 & 1 \\ 0 & 3 \\ 2 & 4 \end{bmatrix}$

$= \begin{bmatrix} 3 & -6 \\ 0 & 9 \end{bmatrix} - 2\begin{bmatrix} 2+0+0 & -2+9+0 \\ -1+0+2 & 1-12+4 \end{bmatrix}$

$= \begin{bmatrix} 3 & -6 \\ 0 & 9 \end{bmatrix} - \begin{bmatrix} 4 & 14 \\ 2 & -14 \end{bmatrix} = \begin{bmatrix} -1 & -20 \\ -2 & 23 \end{bmatrix}$

41. $2I - \frac{1}{2}EF = 2I - \frac{1}{2}\begin{bmatrix} 3 & 0 & 0 \\ 0 & 6 & 0 \\ 0 & 0 & 3 \end{bmatrix}\begin{bmatrix} \frac{1}{3} & 0 & 0 \\ 0 & \frac{1}{6} & 0 \\ 0 & 0 & \frac{1}{3} \end{bmatrix}$

$= 2I - \begin{bmatrix} \frac{3}{2} & 0 & 0 \\ 0 & 3 & 0 \\ 0 & 0 & \frac{3}{2} \end{bmatrix}\begin{bmatrix} \frac{1}{3} & 0 & 0 \\ 0 & \frac{1}{6} & 0 \\ 0 & 0 & \frac{1}{3} \end{bmatrix}$

$= 2I - \begin{bmatrix} \frac{1}{2}+0+0 & 0+0+0 & 0+0+0 \\ 0+0+0 & 0+\frac{1}{2}+0 & 0+0+0 \\ 0+0+0 & 0+0+0 & 0+0+\frac{1}{2} \end{bmatrix}$

$= \begin{bmatrix} 2 & 0 & 0 \\ 0 & 2 & 0 \\ 0 & 0 & 2 \end{bmatrix} - \begin{bmatrix} \frac{1}{2} & 0 & 0 \\ 0 & \frac{1}{2} & 0 \\ 0 & 0 & \frac{1}{2} \end{bmatrix} = \begin{bmatrix} \frac{3}{2} & 0 & 0 \\ 0 & \frac{3}{2} & 0 \\ 0 & 0 & \frac{3}{2} \end{bmatrix}$

43. $(DC)A = \left\{ \begin{bmatrix} 1 & 0 & 0 \\ 0 & 1 & 1 \\ 1 & 2 & 1 \end{bmatrix}\begin{bmatrix} -1 & 1 \\ 0 & 3 \\ 2 & 4 \end{bmatrix} \right\}A = \begin{bmatrix} -1+0+0 & 1+0+0 \\ 0+0+2 & 0+3+4 \\ -1+0+2 & 1+6+4 \end{bmatrix}A$

$= \begin{bmatrix} -1 & 1 \\ 2 & 7 \\ 1 & 11 \end{bmatrix}\begin{bmatrix} 1 & -2 \\ 0 & 3 \end{bmatrix} = \begin{bmatrix} -1+0 & 2+3 \\ 2+0 & -4+21 \\ 1+0 & -2+33 \end{bmatrix} = \begin{bmatrix} -1 & 5 \\ 2 & 17 \\ 1 & 31 \end{bmatrix}$

45. Impossible: **A** is not a square matrix, so A^2 is not defined.

47. $B^3 = \left(B^2\right)B = \begin{bmatrix} 0 & 0 & -1 \\ 2 & -1 & 0 \\ 0 & 0 & 2 \end{bmatrix}^2 B = \begin{bmatrix} 0 & 0 & -1 \\ 2 & -1 & 0 \\ 0 & 0 & 2 \end{bmatrix}\begin{bmatrix} 0 & 0 & -1 \\ 2 & -1 & 0 \\ 0 & 0 & 2 \end{bmatrix}B$

$= \begin{bmatrix} 0 & 0 & -2 \\ -2 & 1 & -2 \\ 0 & 0 & 4 \end{bmatrix}\begin{bmatrix} 0 & 0 & -1 \\ 2 & -1 & 0 \\ 0 & 0 & 2 \end{bmatrix} = \begin{bmatrix} 0 & 0 & -4 \\ 2 & -1 & -2 \\ 0 & 0 & 8 \end{bmatrix}$

49. $(\mathbf{AC})^2 = \left\{ \begin{bmatrix} 1 & -1 & 0 \\ 0 & 1 & 1 \end{bmatrix} \begin{bmatrix} 1 & 0 \\ 2 & -1 \\ 0 & 1 \end{bmatrix} \right\}^2 = \begin{bmatrix} -1 & 1 \\ 2 & 0 \end{bmatrix}^2 = \begin{bmatrix} -1 & 1 \\ 2 & 0 \end{bmatrix} \begin{bmatrix} -1 & 1 \\ 2 & 0 \end{bmatrix} = \begin{bmatrix} 3 & -1 \\ -2 & 2 \end{bmatrix}$

51. $\left(\mathbf{BA}^{\mathrm{T}} \right)^{\mathrm{T}} = \left\{ \begin{bmatrix} 0 & 0 & -1 \\ 2 & -1 & 0 \\ 0 & 0 & 2 \end{bmatrix} \begin{bmatrix} 1 & 0 \\ -1 & 1 \\ 0 & 1 \end{bmatrix} \right\}^{\mathrm{T}} = \begin{bmatrix} 0 & -1 \\ 3 & -1 \\ 0 & 2 \end{bmatrix}^{\mathrm{T}} = \begin{bmatrix} 0 & 3 & 0 \\ -1 & -1 & 2 \end{bmatrix}$

53. $(2\mathbf{I})^2 - 2\mathbf{I}^2 = (2\mathbf{I})^2 - 2\mathbf{I} = \begin{bmatrix} 2 & 0 & 0 \\ 0 & 2 & 0 \\ 0 & 0 & 2 \end{bmatrix}^2 - \begin{bmatrix} 2 & 0 & 0 \\ 0 & 2 & 0 \\ 0 & 0 & 2 \end{bmatrix}$

$= \begin{bmatrix} 2 & 0 & 0 \\ 0 & 2 & 0 \\ 0 & 0 & 2 \end{bmatrix} \begin{bmatrix} 2 & 0 & 0 \\ 0 & 2 & 0 \\ 0 & 0 & 2 \end{bmatrix} - \begin{bmatrix} 2 & 0 & 0 \\ 0 & 2 & 0 \\ 0 & 0 & 2 \end{bmatrix} = \begin{bmatrix} 4 & 0 & 0 \\ 0 & 4 & 0 \\ 0 & 0 & 4 \end{bmatrix} - \begin{bmatrix} 2 & 0 & 0 \\ 0 & 2 & 0 \\ 0 & 0 & 2 \end{bmatrix} = \begin{bmatrix} 2 & 0 & 0 \\ 0 & 2 & 0 \\ 0 & 0 & 2 \end{bmatrix}$

55. $\mathbf{A}(\mathbf{I} - \mathbf{O}) = \mathbf{A}(\mathbf{I}) = \mathbf{AI}$. Since $\mathbf{I}$ is 3×3 and $\mathbf{A}$ has three columns, $\mathbf{AI} = \mathbf{A}$. Thus

$\mathbf{A}(\mathbf{I} - \mathbf{O}) = \mathbf{A} = \begin{bmatrix} 1 & -1 & 0 \\ 0 & 1 & 1 \end{bmatrix}$.

57. $(\mathbf{AB})(\mathbf{AB})^{\mathrm{T}} = \begin{bmatrix} 1 & -1 & 0 \\ 0 & 1 & 1 \end{bmatrix} \begin{bmatrix} 0 & 0 & -1 \\ 2 & -1 & 0 \\ 0 & 0 & 2 \end{bmatrix} (\mathbf{AB})^{\mathrm{T}} = \begin{bmatrix} -2 & 1 & -1 \\ 2 & -1 & 2 \end{bmatrix} (\mathbf{AB})^{\mathrm{T}}$

$= \begin{bmatrix} -2 & 1 & -1 \\ 2 & -1 & 2 \end{bmatrix} \begin{bmatrix} -2 & 2 \\ 1 & -1 \\ -1 & 2 \end{bmatrix} = \begin{bmatrix} 6 & -7 \\ -7 & 9 \end{bmatrix}$

59. $\mathbf{AX} = \mathbf{B}$

$\mathbf{A} = \begin{bmatrix} 3 & 1 \\ 2 & -9 \end{bmatrix}$

$\mathbf{X} = \begin{bmatrix} x \\ y \end{bmatrix}$

$\mathbf{B} = \begin{bmatrix} 6 \\ 5 \end{bmatrix}$

The system is represented by $\begin{bmatrix} 3 & 1 \\ 2 & -9 \end{bmatrix} \begin{bmatrix} x \\ y \end{bmatrix} = \begin{bmatrix} 6 \\ 5 \end{bmatrix}$.

61. $\mathbf{AX} = \mathbf{B}$

$$\mathbf{A} = \begin{bmatrix} 4 & -1 & 3 \\ 3 & 0 & -1 \\ 0 & 3 & 2 \end{bmatrix}$$

$$\mathbf{X} = \begin{bmatrix} r \\ s \\ t \end{bmatrix}$$

$$\mathbf{B} = \begin{bmatrix} 9 \\ 7 \\ 15 \end{bmatrix}$$

The system is represented by $\begin{bmatrix} 4 & -1 & 3 \\ 3 & 0 & -1 \\ 0 & 3 & 2 \end{bmatrix}\begin{bmatrix} r \\ s \\ t \end{bmatrix} = \begin{bmatrix} 9 \\ 7 \\ 15 \end{bmatrix}$

63. $\begin{bmatrix} 6 & 10 & 7 \end{bmatrix}\begin{bmatrix} 55 \\ 150 \\ 35 \end{bmatrix} = [6 \cdot 55 + 10 \cdot 150 + 7 \cdot 35] = [\,330 + 1500 + 245] = [2075]$

The value of the inventory is $2075.

65. $\mathbf{Q} = \begin{bmatrix} 7 & 3 & 5 \end{bmatrix}$

$$\mathbf{R} = \begin{bmatrix} 5 & 20 & 16 & 7 & 17 \\ 7 & 18 & 12 & 9 & 21 \\ 6 & 25 & 8 & 5 & 13 \end{bmatrix}$$

$$\mathbf{C} = \begin{bmatrix} 2500 \\ 1200 \\ 800 \\ 150 \\ 1500 \end{bmatrix}$$

$$\mathrm{QRC} = \mathrm{Q(RC)} = \mathrm{Q}\begin{bmatrix} 5 \cdot 2500 + 20 \cdot 1200 + 16 \cdot 800 + 7 \cdot 150 + 17 \cdot 1500 \\ 7 \cdot 2500 + 18 \cdot 1200 + 12 \cdot 800 + 9 \cdot 150 + 21 \cdot 1500 \\ 6 \cdot 2500 + 25 \cdot 1200 + 8 \cdot 800 + 5 \cdot 150 + 13 \cdot 1500 \end{bmatrix}$$

$$= \begin{bmatrix} 7 & 3 & 5 \end{bmatrix}\begin{bmatrix} 75,850 \\ 81,550 \\ 71,650 \end{bmatrix} = [7 \cdot 75,850 + 3 \cdot 81,550 + 5 \cdot 71,650]$$

$$= [1,133,850]$$

The total cost of raw materials is $1,133,850.

67. a. Amount spent on goods:

coal industry: $\mathbf{D_C P} = \begin{bmatrix} 0 & 1 & 4 \end{bmatrix} \begin{bmatrix} 10,000 \\ 20,000 \\ 40,000 \end{bmatrix} = [180,000]$

elec. industry: $\mathbf{D_E P} = \begin{bmatrix} 20 & 0 & 8 \end{bmatrix} \begin{bmatrix} 10,000 \\ 20,000 \\ 40,000 \end{bmatrix} = [520,000]$

steel industry: $\mathbf{D_S P} = \begin{bmatrix} 30 & 5 & 0 \end{bmatrix} \begin{bmatrix} 10,000 \\ 20,000 \\ 40,000 \end{bmatrix} = [400,000]$

The coal industry spends \$180,000, the electric industry spends \$520,000, and the steel industry spends \$400,000.

consumer 1: $\mathbf{D_1 P} = \begin{bmatrix} 3 & 2 & 5 \end{bmatrix} \begin{bmatrix} 10,000 \\ 20,000 \\ 40,000 \end{bmatrix} = [270,000]$

consumer 2: $\mathbf{D_2 P} = \begin{bmatrix} 0 & 17 & 1 \end{bmatrix} \begin{bmatrix} 10,000 \\ 20,000 \\ 40,000 \end{bmatrix} = [380,000]$

consumer 3: $\mathbf{D_3 P} = \begin{bmatrix} 4 & 6 & 12 \end{bmatrix} \begin{bmatrix} 10,000 \\ 20,000 \\ 40,000 \end{bmatrix} = [640,000]$

Consumer 1 pays \$270,000, consumer 2 pays \$380,000 and consumer 3 pays \$640,000.

b. From Example 3 of Sec. 6.2, the number of units sold of coal, electricity, and steel are 57, 31, and 30, respectively. Thus profit for coal is $10,000(57) - 180,000 = \$390,000$, the profit for elec. is $20,000(31) - 520,000 = \$100,000$, and the profit for steel is $40,000(30) - 400,000 = \$800,000$.

c. From (a), the total amount of money that is paid by all the industries and consumers is
$180,000 + 520,000 + 400,000 + 270,000 + 380,000 + 640,000 = \$2,390,000$.

d. The proportion of the total amount in (c) paid out by the industries is
$$\frac{180,000 + 520,000 + 400,000}{2,390,000} = \frac{110}{239}$$
Proportion of total amount in (c) paid by consumers is
$$\frac{270,000 + 380,000 + 640,000}{2,390,000} = \frac{129}{239}$$

69. $\begin{bmatrix} 1 & 2 \\ 1 & 2 \end{bmatrix} \begin{bmatrix} 2 & -3 \\ -1 & \frac{3}{2} \end{bmatrix} = \begin{bmatrix} 1(2) + (2)(-1) & 1(-3) + 2\left(\frac{3}{2}\right) \\ 1(2) + 2(-1) & 1(-3) + 2\left(\frac{3}{2}\right) \end{bmatrix} = \begin{bmatrix} 0 & 0 \\ 0 & 0 \end{bmatrix}$

71. $\begin{bmatrix} 72.82 & -9.8 \\ 51.32 & -36.32 \end{bmatrix}$

73. $\begin{bmatrix} 15.606 & 64.08 \\ -739.428 & 373.056 \end{bmatrix}$

Principles in Practice 6.4

1. The corresponding system is
$$\begin{cases} 6A + B + 3C = 35, \\ 3A + 2B + 3C = 22, \\ A + 5B + 3C = 18. \end{cases}$$

Reduce the augmented coefficient matrix of the system.

$\begin{bmatrix} 6 & 1 & 3 & | & 35 \\ 3 & 2 & 3 & | & 22 \\ 1 & 5 & 3 & | & 18 \end{bmatrix}$

$\xrightarrow{R_1 \leftrightarrow R_3} \begin{bmatrix} 1 & 5 & 3 & | & 18 \\ 3 & 2 & 3 & | & 22 \\ 6 & 1 & 3 & | & 35 \end{bmatrix}$

$\xrightarrow[-6R_1 + R_3]{-3R_1 + R_2} \begin{bmatrix} 1 & 5 & 3 & | & 18 \\ 0 & -13 & -6 & | & -32 \\ 0 & -29 & -15 & | & -73 \end{bmatrix}$

$\xrightarrow{-\frac{1}{13}R_2} \begin{bmatrix} 1 & 5 & 3 & | & 18 \\ 0 & 1 & \frac{6}{13} & | & \frac{32}{13} \\ 0 & -29 & -15 & | & -73 \end{bmatrix}$

$\xrightarrow[29R_2 + R_3]{-5R_2 + R_1} \begin{bmatrix} 1 & 0 & \frac{9}{13} & | & \frac{74}{13} \\ 0 & 1 & \frac{6}{13} & | & \frac{32}{13} \\ 0 & 0 & -\frac{21}{13} & | & -\frac{21}{13} \end{bmatrix}$

$\xrightarrow{-\frac{13}{21}R_3} \begin{bmatrix} 1 & 0 & \frac{9}{13} & | & \frac{74}{13} \\ 0 & 1 & \frac{6}{13} & | & \frac{32}{13} \\ 0 & 0 & 1 & | & 1 \end{bmatrix}$

$\xrightarrow[-\frac{6}{13}R_3 + R_2]{-\frac{9}{13}R_3 + R_1} \begin{bmatrix} 1 & 0 & 0 & | & 5 \\ 0 & 1 & 0 & | & 2 \\ 0 & 0 & 1 & | & 1 \end{bmatrix}$

Thus there should be 5 blocks of A, 2 blocks of B, and 1 block of C suggested.

2. Let x be the number of tablets of X, y be the number of tablet of Y, and z be the number of tablets Z. The system is
$$40x + 10y + 10z = 180$$
$$20x + 10y + 50z = 200$$
$$10x + 30y + 20z = 190$$
Reduce the augmented coefficient matrix of the system.

$\begin{bmatrix} 40 & 10 & 10 & | & 180 \\ 20 & 10 & 50 & | & 200 \\ 10 & 30 & 20 & | & 190 \end{bmatrix}$

$\xrightarrow{R_1 \leftrightarrow R_3} \begin{bmatrix} 10 & 30 & 20 & | & 190 \\ 20 & 10 & 50 & | & 200 \\ 40 & 10 & 10 & | & 180 \end{bmatrix}$

$\xrightarrow[\frac{1}{10}R_3]{\substack{\frac{1}{10}R_1 \\ \frac{1}{10}R_2}} \begin{bmatrix} 1 & 3 & 2 & | & 19 \\ 2 & 1 & 5 & | & 20 \\ 4 & 1 & 1 & | & 18 \end{bmatrix}$

$\xrightarrow[-4R_1 + R_3]{-2R_1 + R_2} \begin{bmatrix} 1 & 3 & 2 & | & 19 \\ 0 & -5 & 1 & | & -18 \\ 0 & -11 & -7 & | & -58 \end{bmatrix}$

$\xrightarrow{-\frac{1}{5}R_2} \begin{bmatrix} 1 & 3 & 2 & | & 19 \\ 0 & 1 & -\frac{1}{5} & | & \frac{18}{5} \\ 0 & -11 & -7 & | & -58 \end{bmatrix}$

$\xrightarrow[11R_2 + R_3]{-3R_2 + R_1} \begin{bmatrix} 1 & 0 & \frac{13}{5} & | & \frac{41}{5} \\ 0 & 1 & -\frac{1}{5} & | & \frac{18}{5} \\ 0 & 0 & -\frac{46}{5} & | & -\frac{92}{5} \end{bmatrix}$

$\xrightarrow{-\frac{5}{46}R_3} \begin{bmatrix} 1 & 0 & \frac{13}{5} & | & \frac{41}{5} \\ 0 & 1 & -\frac{1}{5} & | & \frac{18}{5} \\ 0 & 0 & 1 & | & 2 \end{bmatrix}$

$\xrightarrow[\frac{1}{5}R_3 + R_2]{-\frac{13}{5}R_3 + R_1} \begin{bmatrix} 1 & 0 & 0 & | & 3 \\ 0 & 1 & 0 & | & 4 \\ 0 & 0 & 1 & | & 2 \end{bmatrix}$

She should take 3 tables of X, 4 tablets of Y, and 2 tablets of Z.

3. Let a, b, c, and d be the number of bags of foods A, B, C, and D, respectively. The corresponding system is

$$\begin{cases} 5a + 5b + 10c + 5d = 10,000, \\ 10a + 5b + 30c + 10d = 20,000, \\ 5a + 15b + 10c + 25d = 20,000. \end{cases}$$

Reduce the augmented coefficient matrix of the system.

$$\begin{bmatrix} 5 & 5 & 10 & 5 & | & 10,000 \\ 10 & 5 & 30 & 10 & | & 20,000 \\ 5 & 15 & 10 & 25 & | & 20,000 \end{bmatrix}$$

$$\xrightarrow{\frac{1}{5}R_1} \begin{bmatrix} 1 & 1 & 2 & 1 & | & 2000 \\ 10 & 5 & 30 & 10 & | & 20,000 \\ 5 & 15 & 10 & 25 & | & 20,000 \end{bmatrix}$$

$$\xrightarrow[-5R_1 + R_3]{-10R_1 + R_2} \begin{bmatrix} 1 & 1 & 2 & 1 & | & 2000 \\ 0 & -5 & 10 & 0 & | & 0 \\ 0 & 10 & 0 & 20 & | & 10,000 \end{bmatrix}$$

$$\xrightarrow{-\frac{1}{5}R_2} \begin{bmatrix} 1 & 1 & 2 & 1 & | & 2000 \\ 0 & 1 & -2 & 0 & | & 0 \\ 0 & 10 & 0 & 20 & | & 10,000 \end{bmatrix}$$

$$\xrightarrow[-10R_2 + R_3]{-R_2 + R_1} \begin{bmatrix} 1 & 0 & 4 & 1 & | & 2000 \\ 0 & 1 & -2 & 0 & | & 0 \\ 0 & 0 & 20 & 20 & | & 10,000 \end{bmatrix}$$

$$\xrightarrow{\frac{1}{20}R_3} \begin{bmatrix} 0 & 0 & 4 & 0 & | & 2000 \\ 0 & 1 & -2 & 0 & | & 0 \\ 0 & 0 & 1 & 1 & | & 500 \end{bmatrix}$$

$$\xrightarrow[2R_3 + R_2]{-4R_3 + R_1} \begin{bmatrix} 1 & 0 & 0 & -3 & | & 0 \\ 0 & 1 & 0 & 2 & | & 1000 \\ 0 & 0 & 1 & 1 & | & 500 \end{bmatrix}$$

This reduced matrix corresponds to the

system $\begin{cases} a - 3d = 0, \\ b + 2d = 1000, \\ c + d = 500. \end{cases}$

Letting $d = r$, we get the general solution of the system:
$a = 3r$,
$b = -2r + 1000$,
$c = -r + 500$.
$d = r$
Note that a, b, c, and d cannot be negative, given the context, hence $0 \le r \le 50$. One specific solution is when $r = 250$, then $a = 750$, $b = 500$, $c = 250$, and $d = 250$.

Exercise 6.4

1. The first nonzero entry in row 2 is not to the right of the first nonzero entry in row 1, hence not reduced.

3. Reduced.

5. The first row consists entirely of zeros and is not below each row containing a nonzero entry, hence not reduced.

7. $\begin{bmatrix} 1 & 3 \\ 4 & 0 \end{bmatrix} \xrightarrow{-4R_1 + R_2} \begin{bmatrix} 1 & 3 \\ 0 & -12 \end{bmatrix}$

$\xrightarrow{-\frac{1}{12}R_2} \begin{bmatrix} 1 & 3 \\ 0 & 1 \end{bmatrix}$

$\xrightarrow{-3R_2 + R_1} \begin{bmatrix} 1 & 0 \\ 0 & 1 \end{bmatrix}$

9. $\begin{bmatrix} 2 & 4 & 6 \\ 1 & 2 & 3 \\ 1 & 2 & 3 \end{bmatrix} \xrightarrow{R_1 \leftrightarrow R_3} \begin{bmatrix} 1 & 2 & 3 \\ 1 & 2 & 3 \\ 2 & 4 & 6 \end{bmatrix}$

$\xrightarrow[-2R_1 + R_3]{R_1 + R_2} \begin{bmatrix} 1 & 2 & 3 \\ 0 & 0 & 0 \\ 0 & 0 & 0 \end{bmatrix}$

11.
$$\begin{bmatrix} 2 & 0 & 3 & 1 \\ 1 & 4 & 2 & 2 \\ -1 & 3 & 1 & 4 \\ 0 & 2 & 1 & 0 \end{bmatrix} \xrightarrow{R_1 \leftrightarrow R_2} \begin{bmatrix} 1 & 4 & 2 & 2 \\ 2 & 0 & 3 & 1 \\ -1 & 3 & 1 & 4 \\ 0 & 2 & 1 & 0 \end{bmatrix}$$

$$\xrightarrow[R_1+R_3]{-2R_1+R_2} \begin{bmatrix} 1 & 4 & 2 & 2 \\ 0 & -8 & -1 & -3 \\ 0 & 7 & 3 & 6 \\ 0 & 2 & 1 & 0 \end{bmatrix} \xrightarrow{-\frac{1}{8}R_2} \begin{bmatrix} 1 & 4 & 2 & 2 \\ 0 & 1 & \frac{1}{8} & \frac{3}{8} \\ 0 & 7 & 3 & 6 \\ 0 & 2 & 1 & 0 \end{bmatrix}$$

$$\xrightarrow[\substack{-7R_2+R_3 \\ -2R_2+R_4}]{-4R_2+R_1} \begin{bmatrix} 1 & 0 & \frac{3}{2} & \frac{1}{2} \\ 0 & 1 & \frac{1}{8} & \frac{3}{8} \\ 0 & 0 & \frac{17}{8} & \frac{27}{8} \\ 0 & 0 & \frac{3}{4} & -\frac{3}{4} \end{bmatrix} \xrightarrow{\frac{8}{17}R_3} \begin{bmatrix} 1 & 0 & \frac{3}{2} & \frac{1}{2} \\ 0 & 1 & \frac{1}{8} & \frac{3}{8} \\ 0 & 0 & 1 & \frac{27}{17} \\ 0 & 0 & \frac{3}{4} & -\frac{3}{4} \end{bmatrix}$$

$$\xrightarrow[\substack{-\frac{1}{8}R_3+R_2 \\ -\frac{3}{4}R_3+R_4}]{-\frac{3}{2}R_3+R_1} \begin{bmatrix} 1 & 0 & 0 & -\frac{32}{17} \\ 0 & 1 & 0 & \frac{3}{17} \\ 0 & 0 & 1 & \frac{27}{17} \\ 0 & 0 & 0 & -\frac{33}{17} \end{bmatrix}$$

$$\xrightarrow{-\frac{17}{33}R_4} \begin{bmatrix} 1 & 0 & 0 & -\frac{32}{17} \\ 0 & 1 & 0 & \frac{3}{17} \\ 0 & 0 & 1 & \frac{27}{17} \\ 0 & 0 & 0 & 1 \end{bmatrix} \xrightarrow[\substack{-\frac{3}{17}R_4+R_2 \\ -\frac{27}{17}R_4+R_3}]{\frac{32}{17}R_4+R_1} \begin{bmatrix} 1 & 0 & 0 & 0 \\ 0 & 1 & 0 & 0 \\ 0 & 0 & 1 & 0 \\ 0 & 0 & 0 & 1 \end{bmatrix}$$

13. $\begin{bmatrix} 2 & 3 & | & 7 \\ 1 & -2 & | & 0 \end{bmatrix} \rightarrow \begin{bmatrix} 1 & -2 & | & 0 \\ 2 & 3 & | & 7 \end{bmatrix} \rightarrow \begin{bmatrix} 1 & -2 & | & 0 \\ 0 & 7 & | & 7 \end{bmatrix} \rightarrow \begin{bmatrix} 1 & -2 & | & 0 \\ 0 & 1 & | & 1 \end{bmatrix} \rightarrow \begin{bmatrix} 1 & 0 & | & 2 \\ 0 & 1 & | & 1 \end{bmatrix}$

Thus $x = 2$, $y = 1$.

15. $\begin{bmatrix} 3 & 1 & | & 4 \\ 12 & 4 & | & 2 \end{bmatrix} \rightarrow \begin{bmatrix} 3 & 1 & | & 4 \\ 0 & 0 & | & -14 \end{bmatrix} \rightarrow \begin{bmatrix} 1 & \frac{1}{3} & | & \frac{4}{3} \\ 0 & 0 & | & -14 \end{bmatrix} \rightarrow \begin{bmatrix} 1 & \frac{1}{3} & | & \frac{4}{3} \\ 0 & 0 & | & 1 \end{bmatrix} \rightarrow \begin{bmatrix} 1 & \frac{1}{3} & | & 0 \\ 0 & 0 & | & 1 \end{bmatrix}$

The last row indicates $0 = 1$, which is never true, so there is no solution.

17. $\begin{bmatrix} 1 & 2 & 1 & | & 4 \\ 3 & 0 & 2 & | & 5 \end{bmatrix} \rightarrow \begin{bmatrix} 1 & 2 & 1 & | & 4 \\ 0 & -6 & -1 & | & -7 \end{bmatrix} \rightarrow \begin{bmatrix} 1 & 2 & 1 & | & 4 \\ 0 & 1 & \frac{1}{6} & | & \frac{7}{6} \end{bmatrix} \rightarrow \begin{bmatrix} 1 & 0 & \frac{2}{3} & | & \frac{5}{3} \\ 0 & 1 & \frac{1}{6} & | & \frac{7}{6} \end{bmatrix}$,

which gives $\begin{cases} x + \frac{2}{3}z = \frac{5}{3} \\ y + \frac{1}{6}z = \frac{7}{6} \end{cases}$.

Thus, $x = -\frac{2}{3}r + \frac{5}{3}$, $y = -\frac{1}{6}r + \frac{7}{6}$, $z = r$, where r is any real number.

19. $\begin{bmatrix} 1 & -3 & | & 0 \\ 2 & 2 & | & 3 \\ 5 & -1 & | & 1 \end{bmatrix} \rightarrow \begin{bmatrix} 1 & -3 & | & 0 \\ 0 & 8 & | & 3 \\ 0 & 14 & | & 1 \end{bmatrix} \rightarrow \begin{bmatrix} 1 & -3 & | & 0 \\ 0 & 1 & | & \frac{3}{8} \\ 0 & 14 & | & 1 \end{bmatrix} \rightarrow \begin{bmatrix} 1 & 0 & | & \frac{9}{8} \\ 0 & 1 & | & \frac{3}{8} \\ 0 & 0 & | & -\frac{17}{4} \end{bmatrix}$

From third row, $0 = -\frac{17}{4}$, which is never true, so there is no solution.

21. $\begin{bmatrix} 1 & -1 & -3 & | & -5 \\ 2 & -1 & -4 & | & -8 \\ 1 & 1 & -1 & | & -1 \end{bmatrix} \rightarrow \begin{bmatrix} 1 & -1 & -3 & | & -5 \\ 0 & 1 & 2 & | & 2 \\ 0 & 2 & 2 & | & 4 \end{bmatrix} \rightarrow \begin{bmatrix} 1 & 0 & -1 & | & -3 \\ 0 & 1 & 2 & | & 2 \\ 0 & 0 & -2 & | & 0 \end{bmatrix}$

$\rightarrow \begin{bmatrix} 1 & 0 & -1 & | & -3 \\ 0 & 1 & 2 & | & 2 \\ 0 & 0 & 1 & | & 0 \end{bmatrix} \rightarrow \begin{bmatrix} 1 & 0 & 0 & | & -3 \\ 0 & 1 & 0 & | & 2 \\ 0 & 0 & 1 & | & 0 \end{bmatrix}$

Thus, $x = -3$, $y = 2$, $z = 0$.

23. $\begin{bmatrix} 2 & 0 & -4 & | & 8 \\ 1 & -2 & -2 & | & 14 \\ 1 & 1 & -2 & | & -1 \\ 3 & 1 & 1 & | & 0 \end{bmatrix} \rightarrow \begin{bmatrix} 1 & 0 & -2 & | & 4 \\ 1 & -2 & -2 & | & 14 \\ 1 & 1 & -2 & | & -1 \\ 3 & 1 & 1 & | & 0 \end{bmatrix} \rightarrow \begin{bmatrix} 1 & 0 & -2 & | & 4 \\ 0 & -2 & 0 & | & 10 \\ 0 & 1 & 0 & | & -5 \\ 0 & 1 & 7 & | & -12 \end{bmatrix}$

$\rightarrow \begin{bmatrix} 1 & 0 & -2 & | & 4 \\ 0 & 1 & 0 & | & -5 \\ 0 & -2 & 0 & | & 10 \\ 0 & 1 & 7 & | & -12 \end{bmatrix} \rightarrow \begin{bmatrix} 1 & 0 & -2 & | & 4 \\ 0 & 1 & 0 & | & -5 \\ 0 & 0 & 0 & | & 0 \\ 0 & 0 & 7 & | & -7 \end{bmatrix} \rightarrow \begin{bmatrix} 1 & 0 & -2 & | & 4 \\ 0 & 1 & 0 & | & -5 \\ 0 & 0 & 1 & | & -1 \\ 0 & 0 & 0 & | & 0 \end{bmatrix} \rightarrow \begin{bmatrix} 1 & 0 & 0 & | & 2 \\ 0 & 1 & 0 & | & -5 \\ 0 & 0 & 1 & | & -1 \\ 0 & 0 & 0 & | & 0 \end{bmatrix}$

Thus $x = 2$, $y = -5$, $z = -1$.

25. $\begin{bmatrix} 1 & 1 & -1 & 1 & 1 & | & 0 \\ 1 & 1 & 1 & -1 & 1 & | & 0 \\ 1 & -1 & -1 & 1 & -1 & | & 0 \\ 1 & 1 & -1 & -1 & -1 & | & 0 \end{bmatrix} \rightarrow \begin{bmatrix} 1 & 1 & -1 & 1 & 1 & | & 0 \\ 0 & 0 & 2 & -2 & 0 & | & 0 \\ 0 & -2 & 0 & 0 & -2 & | & 0 \\ 0 & 0 & 0 & -2 & -2 & | & 0 \end{bmatrix}$

$\rightarrow \begin{bmatrix} 1 & 1 & -1 & 1 & 1 & | & 0 \\ 0 & -2 & 0 & 0 & -2 & | & 0 \\ 0 & 0 & 2 & -2 & 0 & | & 0 \\ 0 & 0 & 0 & -2 & -2 & | & 0 \end{bmatrix} \rightarrow \begin{bmatrix} 1 & 1 & -1 & 1 & 1 & | & 0 \\ 0 & 1 & 0 & 0 & 1 & | & 0 \\ 0 & 0 & 1 & -1 & 0 & | & 0 \\ 0 & 0 & 0 & 1 & 1 & | & 0 \end{bmatrix}$

$\rightarrow \begin{bmatrix} 1 & 0 & -1 & 1 & 0 & | & 0 \\ 0 & 1 & 0 & 0 & 1 & | & 0 \\ 0 & 0 & 1 & -1 & 0 & | & 0 \\ 0 & 0 & 0 & 1 & 1 & | & 0 \end{bmatrix} \rightarrow \begin{bmatrix} 1 & 0 & 0 & 0 & 0 & | & 0 \\ 0 & 1 & 0 & 0 & 1 & | & 0 \\ 0 & 0 & 1 & -1 & 0 & | & 0 \\ 0 & 0 & 0 & 1 & 1 & | & 0 \end{bmatrix} \rightarrow \begin{bmatrix} 1 & 0 & 0 & 0 & 0 & | & 0 \\ 0 & 1 & 0 & 0 & 1 & | & 0 \\ 0 & 0 & 1 & 0 & 1 & | & 0 \\ 0 & 0 & 0 & 1 & 1 & | & 0 \end{bmatrix}$

Thus, $x_1 = 0$, $x_2 = -r$, $x_3 = -r$, $x_4 = -r$, $x_5 = r$, where r is any real number.

27. Let x = federal tax and y = state tax. Then $x = 0.25(312,000 - y)$ and $y = 0.10(312,000 - x)$. Equivalently,

$$\begin{cases} x + 0.25y = 78,000 \\ 0.10x + y = 31,200. \end{cases}$$

$$\begin{bmatrix} 1 & 0.25 & | & 78,000 \\ 0.10 & 1 & | & 31,200 \end{bmatrix} \rightarrow \begin{bmatrix} 1 & 0.25 & | & 78,000 \\ 0 & 0.975 & | & 23,400 \end{bmatrix} \rightarrow \begin{bmatrix} 1 & 0.25 & | & 78,000 \\ 0 & 1 & | & 24,000 \end{bmatrix} \rightarrow \begin{bmatrix} 1 & 0 & | & 72,000 \\ 0 & 1 & | & 24,000 \end{bmatrix}.$$

Thus $x = 72,000$ and $y = 24,000$, so the federal tax is \$72,000 and the state tax is \$24,000.

29. Let x = number of units of A produced, y = number of units of B produced, and z = number of units of C produced. Then

no. of units: $x + y + z = 11,000$

total cost: $4x + 5y + 7z + 17,000 = 80,000$

total profit: $x + 2y + 3z = 25,000$

Equivalently,

$$\begin{cases} x + y + z = 11,000 \\ 4x + 5y + 7z = 63,000 \\ x + 2y + 3z = 25,000 \end{cases}$$

$$\begin{bmatrix} 1 & 1 & 1 & | & 11,000 \\ 4 & 5 & 7 & | & 63,000 \\ 1 & 2 & 3 & | & 25,000 \end{bmatrix} \rightarrow \begin{bmatrix} 1 & 1 & 1 & | & 11,000 \\ 0 & 1 & 3 & | & 19,000 \\ 0 & 1 & 2 & | & 14,000 \end{bmatrix}$$

$$\rightarrow \begin{bmatrix} 1 & 0 & -2 & | & -8,000 \\ 0 & 1 & 3 & | & 19,000 \\ 0 & 0 & -1 & | & -5,000 \end{bmatrix} \rightarrow \begin{bmatrix} 1 & 0 & -2 & | & -8,000 \\ 0 & 1 & 3 & | & 19,000 \\ 0 & 0 & 1 & | & 5,000 \end{bmatrix} \rightarrow \begin{bmatrix} 1 & 0 & 0 & | & 2000 \\ 0 & 1 & 0 & | & 4000 \\ 0 & 0 & 1 & | & 5000 \end{bmatrix}$$

Thus $x = 2000$, $y = 4000$, and $z = 5000$, so 2000 units of A, 4000 units of B and 5000 units of C should be produced.

31. Let x = number of brand X pills, y = number of brand Y pills, and z = number of brand Z pills. Considering the unit requirements gives the system

$$\begin{cases} 2x + 1y + 1z = 10 & \text{(vitamin A)} \\ 3x + 3y + 0z = 9 & \text{(vitamin D)} \\ 5x + 4y + 1z = 19 & \text{(vitamin E)} \end{cases}$$

$$\begin{bmatrix} 2 & 1 & 1 & | & 10 \\ 3 & 3 & 0 & | & 9 \\ 5 & 4 & 1 & | & 19 \end{bmatrix} \rightarrow \begin{bmatrix} 1 & \frac{1}{2} & \frac{1}{2} & | & 5 \\ 3 & 3 & 0 & | & 9 \\ 5 & 4 & 1 & | & 19 \end{bmatrix} \rightarrow \begin{bmatrix} 1 & \frac{1}{2} & \frac{1}{2} & | & 5 \\ 0 & \frac{3}{2} & -\frac{3}{2} & | & -6 \\ 0 & \frac{3}{2} & -\frac{3}{2} & | & -6 \end{bmatrix}$$

$$\rightarrow \begin{bmatrix} 1 & \frac{1}{2} & \frac{1}{2} & | & 5 \\ 0 & 1 & -1 & | & -4 \\ 0 & 0 & 0 & | & 0 \end{bmatrix} \rightarrow \begin{bmatrix} 1 & 0 & 1 & | & 7 \\ 0 & 1 & -1 & | & -4 \\ 0 & 0 & 0 & | & 0 \end{bmatrix}$$

Thus $\begin{cases} x = 7 - r \\ y = r - 4 \text{ where } r = 4, 5, 6, 7. \\ z = r \end{cases}$

The only solutions for the problem are $z = 4$, $x = 3$, and $y = 0$; $z = 5$, $x = 2$, and $y = 1$; $z = 6$, $x = 1$, and $y = 2$; $z = 7$, $x = 0$, and $y = 3$. Their respective costs (in cents) are 15, 23, 31, and 39.

a. The possible combinations are 3 of X, 4 of Z; 2 of X, 1 of Y, 5 of Z; 1 of X, 2 of Y, 6 of Z; 3 of Y, 7 of Z.

b. The combination 3 of X, 4 of Z costs 15 cents a day.

c. The least expensive combination is 3 of X, 4 of Z; the most expensive is 3 of Y, 7 of Z.

33. a. Let s, d, and g represent the number of units of S, D, and G, respectively. Then

$$\begin{cases} 12s + 20g + 32d = 220 & \text{(stock A)} \\ 16s + 12g + 28d = 176 & \text{(stock B)} \\ 8s + 28g + 36d = 264 & \text{(stock C)} \end{cases}$$

$$\begin{bmatrix} 12 & 20 & 32 & | & 220 \\ 16 & 12 & 28 & | & 176 \\ 8 & 28 & 36 & | & 264 \end{bmatrix} \xrightarrow[\left(\frac{1}{8}\right)R_3]{\begin{subarray}{l} \left(\frac{1}{4}\right)R_1 \\ \left(\frac{1}{4}\right)R_2 \end{subarray}} \begin{bmatrix} 3 & 5 & 8 & | & 55 \\ 4 & 3 & 7 & | & 44 \\ 1 & \frac{7}{2} & \frac{9}{2} & | & 33 \end{bmatrix}$$

$$\xrightarrow{R_1 \leftrightarrow R_3} \begin{bmatrix} 1 & \frac{7}{2} & \frac{9}{2} & | & 33 \\ 4 & 3 & 7 & | & 44 \\ 3 & 5 & 8 & | & 55 \end{bmatrix}$$

$$\xrightarrow[-3R_1 + R_3]{-4R_1 + R_2} \begin{bmatrix} 1 & \frac{7}{2} & \frac{9}{2} & | & 33 \\ 0 & -11 & -11 & | & -88 \\ 0 & -\frac{11}{2} & -\frac{11}{2} & | & -44 \end{bmatrix}$$

$$\xrightarrow{-\frac{1}{11}R_2} \begin{bmatrix} 1 & \frac{7}{2} & \frac{9}{2} & | & 33 \\ 0 & 1 & 1 & | & 8 \\ 0 & -\frac{11}{2} & -\frac{11}{2} & | & -44 \end{bmatrix}$$

$$\xrightarrow[\frac{11}{2}R_2 + R_3]{-\frac{7}{2}R_2 + R_1} \begin{bmatrix} 1 & 0 & 1 & | & 5 \\ 0 & 1 & 1 & | & 8 \\ 0 & 0 & 0 & | & 0 \end{bmatrix}$$

Thus $s = 5 - r$, $d = 8 - r$, and $g = r$, where $r = 0, 1, 2, 3, 4, 5$. The six possible combinations are given by

COMBINATION

r	0	1	2	3	4	5
S	5	4	3	2	1	0
D	8	7	6	5	4	3
G	0	1	2	3	4	5

b. Computing the cost of each combination, we find that they are 4700, 4600, 4500, 4400, 4300, and 4200 dollars, respectively. Buying 3 units of Deluxe and 5 units of Gold Star ($s = 0$, $d = 3$, $g = 5$) minimizes the cost.

Principles in Practice 6.5

1. Write the coefficients matrix and reduce.

$$\begin{bmatrix} 5 & 3 & 4 \\ 6 & 8 & 7 \\ 3 & 1 & 2 \end{bmatrix} \xrightarrow{\frac{1}{5}R_1} \begin{bmatrix} 1 & \frac{3}{5} & \frac{4}{5} \\ 6 & 8 & 7 \\ 3 & 1 & 2 \end{bmatrix} \xrightarrow[-3R_1+R_3]{-6R_1+R_2} \begin{bmatrix} 1 & \frac{3}{5} & \frac{4}{5} \\ 0 & \frac{22}{5} & \frac{11}{5} \\ 0 & -\frac{4}{5} & -\frac{2}{5} \end{bmatrix}$$

$$\xrightarrow{\frac{5}{22}R_2} \begin{bmatrix} 1 & \frac{3}{5} & \frac{4}{5} \\ 0 & 1 & \frac{1}{2} \\ 0 & -\frac{4}{5} & -\frac{2}{5} \end{bmatrix} \xrightarrow[\frac{4}{5}R_2+R_3]{-\frac{3}{5}R_2+R_1} \begin{bmatrix} 1 & 0 & \frac{1}{2} \\ 0 & 1 & \frac{1}{2} \\ 0 & 0 & 0 \end{bmatrix}$$

The system has infinitely many solutions since there are two nonzero rows in the reduced coefficient matrix.

$$x + \frac{1}{2}z = 0$$

$$y + \frac{1}{2}z = 0$$

Let $z = r$, so $x = -\frac{1}{2}r$ and $y = -\frac{1}{2}r$, where r is any real number.

Exercise 6.5

1. $$\left[\begin{array}{cccc|c} 1 & -1 & -1 & 4 & 5 \\ 2 & -3 & -4 & 9 & 13 \\ 2 & 1 & 4 & 5 & 1 \end{array}\right] \rightarrow \left[\begin{array}{cccc|c} 1 & -1 & -1 & 4 & 5 \\ 0 & -1 & -2 & 1 & 3 \\ 0 & 3 & 6 & -3 & -9 \end{array}\right]$$

$$\rightarrow \left[\begin{array}{cccc|c} 1 & -1 & -1 & 4 & 5 \\ 0 & 1 & 2 & -1 & -3 \\ 0 & 3 & 6 & -3 & -9 \end{array}\right] \rightarrow \left[\begin{array}{cccc|c} 1 & 0 & 1 & 3 & 2 \\ 0 & 1 & 2 & -1 & -3 \\ 0 & 0 & 0 & 0 & 0 \end{array}\right]$$

Thus $w = -r - 3s + 2$, $x = -2r + s - 3$, $y = r$, $z = s$ (where r and s are any real numbers).

3. $$\left[\begin{array}{cccc|c} 3 & -1 & -3 & -1 & -2 \\ 2 & -2 & -6 & -6 & -4 \\ 2 & -1 & -3 & -2 & -2 \\ 3 & 1 & 3 & 7 & 2 \end{array}\right] \rightarrow \left[\begin{array}{cccc|c} 1 & -\frac{1}{3} & -1 & -\frac{1}{3} & -\frac{2}{3} \\ 2 & -2 & -6 & -6 & -4 \\ 2 & -1 & -3 & -2 & -2 \\ 3 & 1 & 3 & 7 & 2 \end{array}\right]$$

$$\rightarrow \left[\begin{array}{cccc|c} 1 & -\frac{1}{3} & -1 & -\frac{1}{3} & -\frac{2}{3} \\ 0 & -\frac{4}{3} & -4 & -\frac{16}{3} & -\frac{8}{3} \\ 0 & -\frac{1}{3} & -1 & -\frac{4}{3} & -\frac{2}{3} \\ 0 & 2 & 6 & 8 & 4 \end{array}\right] \rightarrow \left[\begin{array}{cccc|c} 1 & -\frac{1}{3} & -1 & -\frac{1}{3} & -\frac{2}{3} \\ 0 & 1 & 3 & 4 & 2 \\ 0 & -\frac{1}{3} & -1 & -\frac{4}{3} & -\frac{2}{3} \\ 0 & 2 & 6 & 8 & 4 \end{array}\right] \rightarrow \left[\begin{array}{cccc|c} 1 & 0 & 0 & 1 & 0 \\ 0 & 1 & 3 & 4 & 2 \\ 0 & 0 & 0 & 0 & 0 \\ 0 & 0 & 0 & 0 & 0 \end{array}\right]$$

Thus, $w = -s$, $x = -3r - 4s + 2$, $y = r$, $z = s$ (where r and s are any real numbers).

5. $\begin{bmatrix} 1 & 1 & 3 & -1 & | & 2 \\ 2 & 1 & 5 & -2 & | & 0 \\ 2 & -1 & 3 & -2 & | & -8 \\ 3 & 2 & 8 & -3 & | & 2 \\ 1 & 0 & 2 & -1 & | & -2 \end{bmatrix} \rightarrow \begin{bmatrix} 1 & 1 & 3 & -1 & | & 2 \\ 0 & -1 & -1 & 0 & | & -4 \\ 0 & -3 & -3 & 0 & | & -12 \\ 0 & -1 & -1 & 0 & | & -4 \\ 0 & -1 & -1 & 0 & | & -4 \end{bmatrix}$

$\rightarrow \begin{bmatrix} 1 & 1 & 3 & -1 & | & 2 \\ 0 & 1 & 1 & 0 & | & 4 \\ 0 & -3 & -3 & 0 & | & -12 \\ 0 & -1 & -1 & 0 & | & -4 \\ 0 & -1 & -1 & 0 & | & -4 \end{bmatrix} \rightarrow \begin{bmatrix} 1 & 0 & 2 & -1 & | & -2 \\ 0 & 1 & 1 & 0 & | & 4 \\ 0 & 0 & 0 & 0 & | & 0 \\ 0 & 0 & 0 & 0 & | & 0 \\ 0 & 0 & 0 & 0 & | & 0 \end{bmatrix}$

Thus, $w = -2r + s - 2$, $x = -r + 4$, $y = r$, $z = s$ (where r and s are any real numbers).

7. $\begin{bmatrix} 4 & -3 & 5 & -10 & 11 & | & -8 \\ 2 & 1 & 5 & 0 & 3 & | & 6 \end{bmatrix} \rightarrow \begin{bmatrix} 0 & -5 & -5 & -10 & 5 & | & -20 \\ 2 & 1 & 5 & 0 & 3 & | & 6 \end{bmatrix}$

$\rightarrow \begin{bmatrix} 2 & 1 & 5 & 0 & 3 & | & 6 \\ 0 & -5 & -5 & -10 & 5 & | & -20 \end{bmatrix} \rightarrow \begin{bmatrix} 2 & 1 & 5 & 0 & 3 & | & 6 \\ 0 & 1 & 1 & 2 & -1 & | & 4 \end{bmatrix}$

$\rightarrow \begin{bmatrix} 2 & 0 & 4 & -2 & 4 & | & 2 \\ 0 & 1 & 1 & 2 & -1 & | & 4 \end{bmatrix} \rightarrow \begin{bmatrix} 1 & 0 & 2 & -1 & 2 & | & 1 \\ 0 & 1 & 1 & 2 & -1 & | & 4 \end{bmatrix}$

Thus, $x_1 = -2r + s - 2t + 1$, $x_2 = -r - 2s + t + 4$, $x_3 = r$, $x_4 = s$, $x_5 = t$ (where r, s and t are any real numbers).

9. The system is homogeneous with fewer equations than unknowns $(2 < 3)$, so there are infinitely many solutions.

11. $\begin{bmatrix} 3 & -4 \\ 1 & 5 \\ 4 & -1 \end{bmatrix} \rightarrow \begin{bmatrix} 1 & 5 \\ 3 & -4 \\ 4 & -1 \end{bmatrix} \rightarrow \begin{bmatrix} 1 & 5 \\ 0 & -19 \\ 0 & -21 \end{bmatrix} \rightarrow \begin{bmatrix} 1 & 5 \\ 0 & 1 \\ 0 & -21 \end{bmatrix} \rightarrow \begin{bmatrix} 1 & 0 \\ 0 & 1 \\ 0 & 0 \end{bmatrix} = \mathbf{A}$

A has $k = 2$ nonzero rows. Number of unknowns is $n = 2$. Thus $k = n$, so the system has the trivial solution only.

13. $\begin{bmatrix} 1 & 1 & 1 \\ 1 & 0 & -1 \\ 1 & -2 & -5 \end{bmatrix} \rightarrow \begin{bmatrix} 1 & 1 & 1 \\ 0 & -1 & -2 \\ 0 & -3 & -6 \end{bmatrix} \rightarrow \begin{bmatrix} 1 & 1 & 1 \\ 0 & 1 & 2 \\ 0 & -3 & -6 \end{bmatrix} \rightarrow \begin{bmatrix} 1 & 0 & -1 \\ 0 & 1 & 2 \\ 0 & 0 & 0 \end{bmatrix} = \mathbf{A}$

A has $k = 2$ nonzero rows. Number of unknowns is $n = 3$. Thus $k < n$, so the system has infinitely many solutions.

15. $\begin{bmatrix} 1 & 1 \\ 3 & -4 \end{bmatrix} \rightarrow \begin{bmatrix} 1 & 1 \\ 0 & -7 \end{bmatrix} \rightarrow \begin{bmatrix} 1 & 1 \\ 0 & 1 \end{bmatrix} \rightarrow \begin{bmatrix} 1 & 0 \\ 0 & 1 \end{bmatrix}$

The solution is $x = 0$, $y = 0$.

17. $\begin{bmatrix} 1 & 6 & -2 \\ 2 & -3 & 4 \end{bmatrix} \rightarrow \begin{bmatrix} 1 & 6 & -2 \\ 0 & -15 & 8 \end{bmatrix} \rightarrow \begin{bmatrix} 1 & 6 & -2 \\ 0 & 1 & -\frac{8}{15} \end{bmatrix} \rightarrow \begin{bmatrix} 1 & 0 & \frac{6}{5} \\ 0 & 1 & -\frac{8}{15} \end{bmatrix}$

The solution is $x = -\frac{6}{5}r$, $y = \frac{8}{15}r$, $z = r$.

19. $\begin{bmatrix} 1 & 1 \\ 3 & -4 \\ 5 & -8 \end{bmatrix} \rightarrow \begin{bmatrix} 1 & 1 \\ 0 & -7 \\ 0 & -13 \end{bmatrix} \rightarrow \begin{bmatrix} 1 & 1 \\ 0 & 1 \\ 0 & -13 \end{bmatrix} \rightarrow \begin{bmatrix} 1 & 0 \\ 0 & 1 \\ 0 & 0 \end{bmatrix}$

The solution is $x = 0$, $y = 0$.

21. $\begin{bmatrix} 1 & 1 & 1 \\ 5 & -2 & -9 \\ 3 & 1 & -1 \\ 3 & -2 & -7 \end{bmatrix} \rightarrow \begin{bmatrix} 1 & 1 & 1 \\ 0 & -7 & -14 \\ 0 & -2 & -4 \\ 0 & -5 & -10 \end{bmatrix} \rightarrow \begin{bmatrix} 1 & 1 & 1 \\ 0 & 1 & 2 \\ 0 & -2 & -4 \\ 0 & -5 & -10 \end{bmatrix} \rightarrow \begin{bmatrix} 1 & 0 & -1 \\ 0 & 1 & 2 \\ 0 & 0 & 0 \\ 0 & 0 & 0 \end{bmatrix}$

The solution is $x = r$, $y = -2r$, $z = r$.

23. $\begin{bmatrix} 1 & 1 & 1 & 4 \\ 1 & 1 & 0 & 5 \\ 2 & 1 & 3 & 4 \\ 1 & -3 & 2 & -9 \end{bmatrix} \rightarrow \begin{bmatrix} 1 & 1 & 1 & 4 \\ 0 & 0 & -1 & 1 \\ 0 & -1 & 1 & -4 \\ 0 & -4 & 1 & -13 \end{bmatrix} \rightarrow \begin{bmatrix} 1 & 1 & 1 & 4 \\ 0 & -1 & 1 & -4 \\ 0 & 0 & -1 & 1 \\ 0 & -4 & 1 & -13 \end{bmatrix}$

$\rightarrow \begin{bmatrix} 1 & 1 & 1 & 4 \\ 0 & 1 & -1 & 4 \\ 0 & 0 & -1 & 1 \\ 0 & -4 & 1 & -13 \end{bmatrix} \rightarrow \begin{bmatrix} 1 & 0 & 2 & 0 \\ 0 & 1 & -1 & 4 \\ 0 & 0 & -1 & 1 \\ 0 & 0 & -3 & 3 \end{bmatrix} \rightarrow \begin{bmatrix} 1 & 0 & 2 & 0 \\ 0 & 1 & -1 & 4 \\ 0 & 0 & 1 & -1 \\ 0 & 0 & -3 & 3 \end{bmatrix} \rightarrow \begin{bmatrix} 1 & 0 & 0 & 2 \\ 0 & 1 & 0 & 3 \\ 0 & 0 & 1 & -1 \\ 0 & 0 & 0 & 0 \end{bmatrix}$

The solution is $w = -2r$, $x = -3r$, $y = r$, $z = r$.

Principles in Practice 6.6

1. $\begin{bmatrix} 1 & 3 \\ 2 & 4 \end{bmatrix} \begin{bmatrix} -2 & 1.5 \\ 1 & -0.5 \end{bmatrix} = \begin{bmatrix} 1 & 0 \\ 0 & 1 \end{bmatrix}$

Yes, they are inverses.

2. $\begin{bmatrix} -2 & 1.5 \\ 1 & -0.5 \end{bmatrix} \begin{bmatrix} 28 \\ 46 \end{bmatrix} = \begin{bmatrix} 13 \\ 5 \end{bmatrix} = \begin{bmatrix} M \\ E \end{bmatrix}$

$\begin{bmatrix} -2 & 1.5 \\ 1 & -0.5 \end{bmatrix} \begin{bmatrix} 65 \\ 90 \end{bmatrix} = \begin{bmatrix} 5 \\ 20 \end{bmatrix} = \begin{bmatrix} E \\ T \end{bmatrix}$

$\begin{bmatrix} -2 & 1.5 \\ 1 & -0.5 \end{bmatrix} \begin{bmatrix} 61 \\ 82 \end{bmatrix} = \begin{bmatrix} 1 \\ 20 \end{bmatrix} = \begin{bmatrix} A \\ T \end{bmatrix}$

$\begin{bmatrix} -2 & 1.5 \\ 1 & -0.5 \end{bmatrix} \begin{bmatrix} 59 \\ 88 \end{bmatrix} = \begin{bmatrix} 14 \\ 15 \end{bmatrix} = \begin{bmatrix} N \\ O \end{bmatrix}$

$\begin{bmatrix} -2 & 1.5 \\ 1 & -0.5 \end{bmatrix} \begin{bmatrix} 57 \\ 86 \end{bmatrix} = \begin{bmatrix} 15 \\ 14 \end{bmatrix} = \begin{bmatrix} O \\ N \end{bmatrix}$

$\begin{bmatrix} -2 & 1.5 \\ 1 & -0.5 \end{bmatrix} \begin{bmatrix} 60 \\ 84 \end{bmatrix} = \begin{bmatrix} 6 \\ 18 \end{bmatrix} = \begin{bmatrix} F \\ R \end{bmatrix}$

$\begin{bmatrix} -2 & 1.5 \\ 1 & -0.5 \end{bmatrix} \begin{bmatrix} 21 \\ 34 \end{bmatrix} = \begin{bmatrix} 9 \\ 4 \end{bmatrix} = \begin{bmatrix} I \\ D \end{bmatrix}$

$\begin{bmatrix} -2 & 1.5 \\ 1 & -0.5 \end{bmatrix} \begin{bmatrix} 76 \\ 102 \end{bmatrix} = \begin{bmatrix} 1 \\ 25 \end{bmatrix} = \begin{bmatrix} A \\ Y \end{bmatrix}$

The message is "MEET AT NOON FRIDAY."

3. $[\mathbf{E}\,|\,\mathbf{I}] = \begin{bmatrix} 3 & 1 & 2 & | & 1 & 0 & 0 \\ 2 & 2 & 2 & | & 0 & 1 & 0 \\ 2 & 1 & 3 & | & 0 & 0 & 1 \end{bmatrix} \xrightarrow{R_1 \leftrightarrow R_2} \begin{bmatrix} 2 & 2 & 2 & | & 0 & 1 & 0 \\ 3 & 1 & 2 & | & 1 & 0 & 0 \\ 2 & 1 & 3 & | & 0 & 0 & 1 \end{bmatrix}$

$\xrightarrow{\frac{1}{2}R_1} \begin{bmatrix} 1 & 1 & 1 & | & 0 & \frac{1}{2} & 0 \\ 3 & 1 & 2 & | & 1 & 0 & 0 \\ 2 & 1 & 3 & | & 0 & 0 & 1 \end{bmatrix} \xrightarrow[-2R_1 + R_3]{-3R_1 + R_2} \begin{bmatrix} 1 & 1 & 1 & | & 0 & \frac{1}{2} & 0 \\ 0 & -2 & -1 & | & 1 & -\frac{3}{2} & 0 \\ 0 & -1 & 1 & | & 0 & -1 & 1 \end{bmatrix}$

$\xrightarrow{R_2 \leftrightarrow R_3} \begin{bmatrix} 1 & 1 & 1 & | & 0 & \frac{1}{2} & 0 \\ 0 & -1 & 1 & | & 0 & -1 & 1 \\ 0 & -2 & -1 & | & 1 & -\frac{3}{2} & 0 \end{bmatrix} \xrightarrow{-R_2} \begin{bmatrix} 1 & 1 & 1 & | & 0 & \frac{1}{2} & 0 \\ 0 & 1 & -1 & | & 0 & 1 & -1 \\ 0 & -2 & -1 & | & 1 & -\frac{3}{2} & 0 \end{bmatrix}$

$\xrightarrow[2R_2 + R_3]{-R_2 + R_1} \begin{bmatrix} 1 & 0 & 2 & | & 0 & -\frac{1}{2} & 1 \\ 0 & 1 & -1 & | & 0 & 1 & -1 \\ 0 & 0 & -3 & | & 1 & \frac{1}{2} & -2 \end{bmatrix} \xrightarrow{-\frac{1}{3}R_3} \begin{bmatrix} 1 & 0 & 2 & | & 0 & -\frac{1}{2} & 1 \\ 0 & 1 & -1 & | & 0 & 1 & -1 \\ 0 & 0 & 1 & | & -\frac{1}{3} & -\frac{1}{6} & \frac{2}{3} \end{bmatrix}$

$\xrightarrow[R_3 + R_2]{-2R_3 + R_1} \begin{bmatrix} 1 & 0 & 0 & | & \frac{2}{3} & -\frac{1}{6} & -\frac{1}{3} \\ 0 & 1 & 0 & | & -\frac{1}{3} & \frac{5}{6} & -\frac{1}{3} \\ 0 & 0 & 1 & | & -\frac{1}{3} & -\frac{1}{6} & \frac{2}{3} \end{bmatrix}$

$[\mathbf{E}\,|\,\mathbf{I}] = \begin{bmatrix} 2 & 1 & 2 & | & 1 & 0 & 0 \\ 3 & 2 & 3 & | & 0 & 1 & 0 \\ 4 & 3 & 4 & | & 0 & 0 & 1 \end{bmatrix}$

$\xrightarrow{\frac{1}{2}R_1} \begin{bmatrix} 1 & \frac{1}{2} & 1 & | & \frac{1}{2} & 0 & 0 \\ 3 & 2 & 3 & | & 0 & 1 & 0 \\ 4 & 3 & 4 & | & 0 & 0 & 1 \end{bmatrix} \xrightarrow[-4R_1 + R_3]{-3R_1 + R_2} \begin{bmatrix} 1 & \frac{1}{2} & 1 & | & \frac{1}{2} & 0 & 0 \\ 0 & \frac{1}{2} & 0 & | & -\frac{3}{2} & 1 & 0 \\ 0 & 1 & 0 & | & -2 & 0 & 1 \end{bmatrix}$

$\xrightarrow{2R_2} \begin{bmatrix} 1 & \frac{1}{2} & 1 & | & \frac{1}{2} & 0 & 0 \\ 0 & 1 & 0 & | & -3 & 2 & 0 \\ 0 & 1 & 0 & | & -2 & 0 & 1 \end{bmatrix} \xrightarrow[-R_2 + R_3]{-\frac{1}{2}R_2 + R_1} \begin{bmatrix} 1 & 0 & 1 & | & 2 & -1 & 0 \\ 0 & 1 & 0 & | & -3 & 2 & 0 \\ 0 & 0 & 0 & | & 1 & -2 & 1 \end{bmatrix}$

F does not reduce to **I** so **F** is not invertible.

4. Let x be the number of shares of A, y be the number of shares of B, and z be the number of shares of C. We got the following equations from the given conditions.

$50x + 20y + 80z = 500{,}000$

$x = 2z$

$0.13(50x) + 0.15(20y) + 0.10(80z) = 0.12(50x + 20y + 80z)$

Simplify the first equation.

$5x + 2y + 8z = 50{,}000$

Simplify the second equation.

$x - 2z = 0$

Simplify the third equation.

$6.5x + 3y + 8z = 6x + 2.4y + 9.6z$

$0.5x + 0.6y - 1.6z = 0$

$5x + 6y - 16z = 0$

Thus, we solve the following system of equations.

$x - 2z = 0$

$5x + 6y - 16z = 0$

$5x + 2y + 8z = 50{,}000$

The coefficient matrix is $\mathbf{A} = \begin{bmatrix} 1 & 0 & -2 \\ 5 & 6 & -16 \\ 5 & 2 & 8 \end{bmatrix}$.

$$[\mathbf{A}\,|\,\mathbf{I}] = \begin{bmatrix} 1 & 0 & -2 & | & 1 & 0 & 0 \\ 5 & 6 & -16 & | & 0 & 1 & 0 \\ 5 & 2 & 8 & | & 0 & 0 & 1 \end{bmatrix} \xrightarrow[-5R_1 + R_3]{-5R_1 + R_2} \begin{bmatrix} 1 & 0 & -2 & | & 1 & 0 & 0 \\ 0 & 6 & -6 & | & -5 & 1 & 0 \\ 0 & 2 & 18 & | & -5 & 0 & 1 \end{bmatrix}$$

$$\xrightarrow{\frac{1}{6}R_2} \begin{bmatrix} 1 & 0 & -2 & | & 1 & 0 & 0 \\ 0 & 1 & -1 & | & -\frac{5}{6} & \frac{1}{6} & 0 \\ 0 & 2 & 18 & | & -5 & 0 & 1 \end{bmatrix} \xrightarrow{-2R_2 + R_3} \begin{bmatrix} 1 & 0 & -2 & | & 1 & 0 & 0 \\ 0 & 1 & -1 & | & -\frac{5}{6} & \frac{1}{6} & 0 \\ 0 & 0 & 20 & | & -\frac{10}{3} & -\frac{1}{3} & 1 \end{bmatrix}$$

$$\xrightarrow{\frac{1}{20}R_3} \begin{bmatrix} 1 & 0 & -2 & | & 1 & 0 & 0 \\ 0 & 1 & -1 & | & -\frac{5}{6} & \frac{1}{6} & 0 \\ 0 & 0 & 1 & | & -\frac{1}{6} & -\frac{1}{60} & \frac{1}{20} \end{bmatrix} \xrightarrow[R_3 + R_2]{2R_3 + R_1} \begin{bmatrix} 1 & 0 & 0 & | & \frac{2}{3} & -\frac{1}{30} & \frac{1}{10} \\ 0 & 1 & 0 & | & -1 & \frac{3}{20} & \frac{1}{20} \\ 0 & 0 & 1 & | & -\frac{1}{6} & -\frac{1}{60} & \frac{1}{20} \end{bmatrix}$$

$$\mathbf{A}^{-1} = \begin{bmatrix} \frac{2}{3} & -\frac{1}{30} & \frac{1}{10} \\ -1 & \frac{3}{20} & \frac{1}{20} \\ -\frac{1}{6} & -\frac{1}{60} & \frac{1}{20} \end{bmatrix} \begin{bmatrix} x \\ y \\ z \end{bmatrix} = \begin{bmatrix} \frac{2}{3} & -\frac{1}{30} & \frac{1}{10} \\ -1 & \frac{3}{20} & \frac{1}{20} \\ -\frac{1}{6} & -\frac{1}{60} & \frac{1}{20} \end{bmatrix} \begin{bmatrix} 0 \\ 0 \\ 50,000 \end{bmatrix} = \begin{bmatrix} 5000 \\ 2500 \\ 2500 \end{bmatrix}$$

They should buy 5000 shares of Company A, 2500 shares of Company B, and 2500 shares of Company C.

Exercise 6.6

1. $\begin{bmatrix} 6 & 1 & | & 1 & 0 \\ 7 & 1 & | & 0 & 1 \end{bmatrix} \rightarrow \begin{bmatrix} 1 & \frac{1}{6} & | & \frac{1}{6} & 0 \\ 7 & 1 & | & 0 & 1 \end{bmatrix} \rightarrow \begin{bmatrix} 1 & \frac{1}{6} & | & \frac{1}{6} & 0 \\ 0 & -\frac{1}{6} & | & -\frac{7}{6} & 1 \end{bmatrix} \rightarrow \begin{bmatrix} 1 & 0 & | & -1 & 1 \\ 0 & -\frac{1}{6} & | & -\frac{7}{6} & 1 \end{bmatrix} \rightarrow \begin{bmatrix} 1 & 0 & | & -1 & 1 \\ 0 & 1 & | & 7 & -6 \end{bmatrix}$

The inverse is $\begin{bmatrix} -1 & 1 \\ 7 & -6 \end{bmatrix}$.

3. $\begin{bmatrix} 1 & 1 & | & 1 & 0 \\ 1 & 1 & | & 0 & 1 \end{bmatrix} \rightarrow \begin{bmatrix} 1 & 1 & | & 1 & 0 \\ 0 & 0 & | & -1 & 1 \end{bmatrix}$

The given matrix is not invertible.

5. $\begin{bmatrix} 1 & 0 & 0 & | & 1 & 0 & 0 \\ 0 & -3 & 0 & | & 0 & 1 & 0 \\ 0 & 0 & 4 & | & 0 & 0 & 1 \end{bmatrix} \rightarrow \begin{bmatrix} 1 & 0 & 0 & | & 1 & 0 & 0 \\ 0 & 1 & 0 & | & 0 & -\frac{1}{3} & 0 \\ 0 & 0 & 1 & | & 0 & 0 & \frac{1}{4} \end{bmatrix}$

The inverse is $\begin{bmatrix} 1 & 0 & 0 \\ 0 & -\frac{1}{3} & 0 \\ 0 & 0 & \frac{1}{4} \end{bmatrix}$.

7.
$$\left[\begin{array}{ccc|ccc} 1 & 2 & 3 & 1 & 0 & 0 \\ 0 & 0 & 4 & 0 & 1 & 0 \\ 0 & 0 & 5 & 0 & 0 & 1 \end{array}\right] \rightarrow \left[\begin{array}{ccc|ccc} 1 & 2 & 3 & 1 & 0 & 0 \\ 0 & 0 & 1 & 0 & \frac{1}{4} & 0 \\ 0 & 0 & 5 & 0 & 0 & 1 \end{array}\right] \rightarrow \left[\begin{array}{ccc|ccc} 1 & 2 & 0 & 1 & -\frac{3}{4} & 0 \\ 0 & 0 & 1 & 0 & \frac{1}{4} & 0 \\ 0 & 0 & 0 & 0 & -\frac{5}{4} & 1 \end{array}\right]$$

The given matrix is not invertible.

9. The matrix is not square, so it is not invertible.

11.
$$\left[\begin{array}{ccc|ccc} 1 & 1 & 1 & 1 & 0 & 0 \\ 0 & 1 & 1 & 0 & 1 & 0 \\ 0 & 0 & 1 & 0 & 0 & 1 \end{array}\right] \rightarrow \left[\begin{array}{ccc|ccc} 1 & 0 & 0 & 1 & -1 & 0 \\ 0 & 1 & 1 & 0 & 1 & 0 \\ 0 & 0 & 1 & 0 & 0 & 1 \end{array}\right] \rightarrow \left[\begin{array}{ccc|ccc} 1 & 0 & 0 & 1 & -1 & 0 \\ 0 & 1 & 0 & 0 & 1 & -1 \\ 0 & 0 & 1 & 0 & 0 & 1 \end{array}\right]$$

The inverse is $\begin{bmatrix} 1 & -1 & 0 \\ 0 & 1 & -1 \\ 0 & 0 & 1 \end{bmatrix}$.

13.
$$\left[\begin{array}{ccc|ccc} 7 & 0 & -2 & 1 & 0 & 0 \\ 0 & 1 & 0 & 0 & 1 & 0 \\ -3 & 0 & 1 & 0 & 0 & 1 \end{array}\right] \rightarrow \left[\begin{array}{ccc|ccc} 1 & 0 & -\frac{2}{7} & \frac{1}{7} & 0 & 0 \\ 0 & 1 & 0 & 0 & 1 & 0 \\ -3 & 0 & 1 & 0 & 0 & 1 \end{array}\right] \rightarrow \left[\begin{array}{ccc|ccc} 1 & 0 & -\frac{2}{7} & \frac{1}{7} & 0 & 0 \\ 0 & 1 & 0 & 0 & 1 & 0 \\ 0 & 0 & \frac{1}{7} & \frac{3}{7} & 0 & 1 \end{array}\right]$$

$$\rightarrow \left[\begin{array}{ccc|ccc} 1 & 0 & 0 & 1 & 0 & 2 \\ 0 & 1 & 0 & 0 & 1 & 0 \\ 0 & 0 & \frac{1}{7} & \frac{3}{7} & 0 & 1 \end{array}\right] \rightarrow \left[\begin{array}{ccc|ccc} 1 & 0 & 0 & 1 & 0 & 2 \\ 0 & 1 & 0 & 0 & 1 & 0 \\ 0 & 0 & 1 & 3 & 0 & 7 \end{array}\right]$$

The inverse is $\begin{bmatrix} 1 & 0 & 2 \\ 0 & 1 & 0 \\ 3 & 0 & 7 \end{bmatrix}$.

15.
$$\left[\begin{array}{ccc|ccc} 2 & 1 & 0 & 1 & 0 & 0 \\ 4 & -1 & 5 & 0 & 1 & 0 \\ 1 & -1 & 2 & 0 & 0 & 1 \end{array}\right] \rightarrow \left[\begin{array}{ccc|ccc} 1 & -1 & 2 & 0 & 0 & 1 \\ 4 & -1 & 5 & 0 & 1 & 0 \\ 2 & 1 & 0 & 1 & 0 & 0 \end{array}\right] \rightarrow \left[\begin{array}{ccc|ccc} 1 & -1 & 2 & 0 & 0 & 1 \\ 0 & 3 & -3 & 0 & 1 & -4 \\ 0 & 3 & -4 & 1 & 0 & -2 \end{array}\right]$$

$$\rightarrow \left[\begin{array}{ccc|ccc} 1 & -1 & 2 & 0 & 0 & 1 \\ 0 & 1 & -1 & 0 & \frac{1}{3} & -\frac{4}{3} \\ 0 & 3 & -4 & 1 & 0 & -2 \end{array}\right] \rightarrow \left[\begin{array}{ccc|ccc} 1 & 0 & 1 & 0 & \frac{1}{3} & -\frac{1}{3} \\ 0 & 1 & -1 & 0 & \frac{1}{3} & -\frac{4}{3} \\ 0 & 0 & -1 & 1 & -1 & 2 \end{array}\right] \rightarrow \left[\begin{array}{ccc|ccc} 1 & 0 & 1 & 0 & \frac{1}{3} & -\frac{1}{3} \\ 0 & 1 & -1 & 0 & \frac{1}{3} & -\frac{4}{3} \\ 0 & 0 & 1 & -1 & 1 & -2 \end{array}\right]$$

$$\rightarrow \left[\begin{array}{ccc|ccc} 1 & 0 & 0 & 1 & -\frac{2}{3} & \frac{5}{3} \\ 0 & 1 & 0 & -1 & \frac{4}{3} & -\frac{10}{3} \\ 0 & 0 & 1 & -1 & 1 & -2 \end{array}\right].$$

The inverse is $\begin{bmatrix} 1 & -\frac{2}{3} & \frac{5}{3} \\ -1 & \frac{4}{3} & -\frac{10}{3} \\ -1 & 1 & -2 \end{bmatrix}$.

17. $\begin{bmatrix} 1 & 2 & 3 & | & 1 & 0 & 0 \\ 1 & 3 & 5 & | & 0 & 1 & 0 \\ 1 & 5 & 12 & | & 0 & 0 & 1 \end{bmatrix} \rightarrow \begin{bmatrix} 1 & 2 & 3 & | & 1 & 0 & 0 \\ 0 & 1 & 2 & | & -1 & 1 & 0 \\ 0 & 3 & 9 & | & -1 & 0 & 1 \end{bmatrix} \rightarrow \begin{bmatrix} 1 & 0 & -1 & | & 3 & -2 & 0 \\ 0 & 1 & 2 & | & -1 & 1 & 0 \\ 0 & 0 & 3 & | & 2 & -3 & 1 \end{bmatrix}$

$\rightarrow \begin{bmatrix} 1 & 0 & -1 & | & 3 & -2 & 0 \\ 0 & 1 & 2 & | & -1 & 1 & 0 \\ 0 & 0 & 1 & | & \frac{2}{3} & -1 & \frac{1}{3} \end{bmatrix} \rightarrow \begin{bmatrix} 1 & 0 & 0 & | & \frac{11}{3} & -3 & \frac{1}{3} \\ 0 & 1 & 0 & | & -\frac{7}{3} & 3 & -\frac{2}{3} \\ 0 & 0 & 1 & | & \frac{2}{3} & -1 & \frac{1}{3} \end{bmatrix}$

The inverse is $\begin{bmatrix} \frac{11}{3} & -3 & \frac{1}{3} \\ -\frac{7}{3} & 3 & -\frac{2}{3} \\ \frac{2}{3} & -1 & \frac{1}{3} \end{bmatrix}$.

19. $\mathbf{X} = \begin{bmatrix} x_1 \\ x_2 \end{bmatrix} = \mathbf{A}^{-1}\mathbf{B} = \begin{bmatrix} 1 & 2 \\ 8 & 1 \end{bmatrix}\begin{bmatrix} 2 \\ 4 \end{bmatrix} = \begin{bmatrix} 10 \\ 20 \end{bmatrix} \Rightarrow x_1 = 10,\ x_2 = 20$

21. $\begin{bmatrix} 6 & 5 & | & 1 & 0 \\ 1 & 1 & | & 0 & 1 \end{bmatrix} \rightarrow \begin{bmatrix} 1 & 1 & | & 0 & 1 \\ 6 & 5 & | & 1 & 0 \end{bmatrix} \rightarrow \begin{bmatrix} 1 & 1 & | & 0 & 1 \\ 0 & -1 & | & 1 & -6 \end{bmatrix}$

$\rightarrow \begin{bmatrix} 1 & 1 & | & 0 & 1 \\ 0 & 1 & | & -1 & 6 \end{bmatrix} \rightarrow \begin{bmatrix} 1 & 0 & | & 1 & -5 \\ 0 & 1 & | & -1 & 6 \end{bmatrix}$

$\begin{bmatrix} x \\ y \end{bmatrix} = \mathbf{A}^{-1}\mathbf{B} = \begin{bmatrix} 1 & -5 \\ -1 & 6 \end{bmatrix}\begin{bmatrix} 2 \\ -3 \end{bmatrix} = \begin{bmatrix} 17 \\ -20 \end{bmatrix} \Rightarrow x = 17,\ y = -20$

23. $\begin{bmatrix} 2 & 1 & | & 1 & 0 \\ 3 & -1 & | & 0 & 1 \end{bmatrix} \rightarrow \begin{bmatrix} 1 & \frac{1}{2} & | & \frac{1}{2} & 0 \\ 3 & -1 & | & 0 & 1 \end{bmatrix} \rightarrow \begin{bmatrix} 1 & \frac{1}{2} & | & \frac{1}{2} & 0 \\ 0 & -\frac{5}{2} & | & -\frac{3}{2} & 1 \end{bmatrix}$

$\rightarrow \begin{bmatrix} 1 & \frac{1}{2} & | & \frac{1}{2} & 0 \\ 0 & 1 & | & \frac{3}{5} & -\frac{2}{5} \end{bmatrix} \rightarrow \begin{bmatrix} 1 & 0 & | & \frac{1}{5} & \frac{1}{5} \\ 0 & 1 & | & \frac{3}{5} & -\frac{2}{5} \end{bmatrix}$

$\begin{bmatrix} x \\ y \end{bmatrix} = \mathbf{A}^{-1}\mathbf{B} = \begin{bmatrix} \frac{1}{5} & \frac{1}{5} \\ \frac{3}{5} & -\frac{2}{5} \end{bmatrix}\begin{bmatrix} 5 \\ 0 \end{bmatrix} = \begin{bmatrix} 1 \\ 3 \end{bmatrix} \Rightarrow x = 1,\ y = 3$

25. The coefficient matrix is not invertible. The method of reduction yields
$\begin{bmatrix} 2 & 6 & | & 2 \\ 3 & 9 & | & 3 \end{bmatrix} \rightarrow \begin{bmatrix} 1 & 3 & | & 1 \\ 3 & 9 & | & 3 \end{bmatrix} \rightarrow \begin{bmatrix} 1 & 3 & | & 1 \\ 0 & 0 & | & 0 \end{bmatrix}$.
Thus $x = -3r + 1,\ y = r$.

27. $\begin{bmatrix} 1 & 2 & 1 & | & 1 & 0 & 0 \\ 3 & 0 & 1 & | & 0 & 1 & 0 \\ 1 & -1 & 1 & | & 0 & 0 & 1 \end{bmatrix} \rightarrow \begin{bmatrix} 1 & 2 & 1 & | & 1 & 0 & 0 \\ 0 & -6 & -2 & | & -3 & 1 & 0 \\ 0 & -3 & 0 & | & -1 & 0 & 1 \end{bmatrix}$

$\rightarrow \begin{bmatrix} 1 & 2 & 1 & | & 1 & 0 & 0 \\ 0 & 1 & \frac{1}{3} & | & \frac{1}{2} & -\frac{1}{6} & 0 \\ 0 & -3 & 0 & | & -1 & 0 & 1 \end{bmatrix} \rightarrow \begin{bmatrix} 1 & 0 & \frac{1}{3} & | & 0 & \frac{1}{3} & 0 \\ 0 & 1 & \frac{1}{3} & | & \frac{1}{2} & -\frac{1}{6} & 0 \\ 0 & 0 & 1 & | & \frac{1}{2} & -\frac{1}{2} & 1 \end{bmatrix}$

$\rightarrow \begin{bmatrix} 1 & 0 & 0 & | & -\frac{1}{6} & \frac{1}{2} & -\frac{1}{3} \\ 0 & 1 & 0 & | & \frac{1}{3} & 0 & -\frac{1}{3} \\ 0 & 0 & 1 & | & \frac{1}{2} & -\frac{1}{2} & 1 \end{bmatrix}$

$\begin{bmatrix} x \\ y \\ z \end{bmatrix} = \mathbf{A}^{-1}\mathbf{B} = \begin{bmatrix} -\frac{1}{6} & \frac{1}{2} & -\frac{1}{3} \\ \frac{1}{3} & 0 & -\frac{1}{3} \\ \frac{1}{2} & -\frac{1}{2} & 1 \end{bmatrix} \begin{bmatrix} 4 \\ 2 \\ 1 \end{bmatrix} = \begin{bmatrix} 0 \\ 1 \\ 2 \end{bmatrix}$

Thus, $x = 0$, $y = 1$, $z = 2$.

29. $\begin{bmatrix} 1 & 1 & 1 & | & 1 & 0 & 0 \\ 1 & -1 & 1 & | & 0 & 1 & 0 \\ 1 & -1 & -1 & | & 0 & 0 & 1 \end{bmatrix} \rightarrow \begin{bmatrix} 1 & 1 & 1 & | & 1 & 0 & 0 \\ 0 & -2 & 0 & | & -1 & 1 & 0 \\ 0 & -2 & -2 & | & -1 & 0 & 1 \end{bmatrix}$

$\rightarrow \begin{bmatrix} 1 & 1 & 1 & | & 1 & 0 & 0 \\ 0 & 1 & 0 & | & \frac{1}{2} & -\frac{1}{2} & 0 \\ 0 & -2 & -2 & | & -1 & 0 & 1 \end{bmatrix} \rightarrow \begin{bmatrix} 1 & 0 & 1 & | & \frac{1}{2} & \frac{1}{2} & 0 \\ 0 & 1 & 0 & | & \frac{1}{2} & -\frac{1}{2} & 0 \\ 0 & 0 & -2 & | & 0 & -1 & 1 \end{bmatrix}$

$\rightarrow \begin{bmatrix} 1 & 0 & 1 & | & \frac{1}{2} & \frac{1}{2} & 0 \\ 0 & 1 & 0 & | & \frac{1}{2} & -\frac{1}{2} & 0 \\ 0 & 0 & 1 & | & 0 & \frac{1}{2} & -\frac{1}{2} \end{bmatrix} \rightarrow \begin{bmatrix} 1 & 0 & 0 & | & \frac{1}{2} & 0 & \frac{1}{2} \\ 0 & 1 & 0 & | & \frac{1}{2} & -\frac{1}{2} & 0 \\ 0 & 0 & 1 & | & 0 & \frac{1}{2} & -\frac{1}{2} \end{bmatrix}$

$\begin{bmatrix} x \\ y \\ z \end{bmatrix} = \mathbf{A}^{-1}\mathbf{B} = \begin{bmatrix} \frac{1}{2} & 0 & \frac{1}{2} \\ \frac{1}{2} & -\frac{1}{2} & 0 \\ 0 & \frac{1}{2} & -\frac{1}{2} \end{bmatrix} \begin{bmatrix} 2 \\ 1 \\ 0 \end{bmatrix} = \begin{bmatrix} 1 \\ \frac{1}{2} \\ \frac{1}{2} \end{bmatrix}$

Thus, $x = 1$, $y = \frac{1}{2}$, $z = \frac{1}{2}$.

31. The coefficient matrix is not invertible. The method of reduction yields
$\begin{bmatrix} 1 & 3 & 3 & | & 7 \\ 2 & 1 & 1 & | & 4 \\ 1 & 1 & 1 & | & 4 \end{bmatrix} \rightarrow \begin{bmatrix} 1 & 3 & 3 & | & 7 \\ 0 & -5 & -5 & | & -10 \\ 0 & -2 & -2 & | & -3 \end{bmatrix} \rightarrow \begin{bmatrix} 1 & 3 & 3 & | & 7 \\ 0 & 1 & 1 & | & 2 \\ 0 & -2 & -2 & | & -3 \end{bmatrix} \rightarrow \begin{bmatrix} 1 & 0 & 0 & | & 1 \\ 0 & 1 & 1 & | & 2 \\ 0 & 0 & 0 & | & 1 \end{bmatrix}$.

The third row indicates that $0 = 1$, which is never true, so there is no solution.

33.
$$\left[\begin{array}{cccc|cccc} 1 & 0 & 2 & 1 & 1 & 0 & 0 & 0 \\ 1 & -1 & 0 & 2 & 0 & 1 & 0 & 0 \\ 2 & 1 & 0 & 1 & 0 & 0 & 1 & 0 \\ 1 & 2 & 1 & 1 & 0 & 0 & 0 & 1 \end{array}\right] \rightarrow \left[\begin{array}{cccc|cccc} 1 & 0 & 2 & 1 & 1 & 0 & 0 & 0 \\ 0 & -1 & -2 & 1 & -1 & 1 & 0 & 0 \\ 0 & 1 & -4 & -1 & -2 & 0 & 1 & 0 \\ 0 & 2 & -1 & 0 & -1 & 0 & 0 & 1 \end{array}\right]$$

$$\rightarrow \left[\begin{array}{cccc|cccc} 1 & 0 & 2 & 1 & 1 & 0 & 0 & 0 \\ 0 & 1 & 2 & -1 & 1 & -1 & 0 & 0 \\ 0 & 0 & -6 & 0 & -3 & 1 & 1 & 0 \\ 0 & 0 & -5 & 2 & -3 & 2 & 0 & 1 \end{array}\right] \rightarrow \left[\begin{array}{cccc|cccc} 1 & 0 & 2 & 1 & 1 & 0 & 0 & 0 \\ 0 & 1 & 2 & -1 & 1 & -1 & 0 & 0 \\ 0 & 0 & 1 & 0 & \frac{1}{2} & -\frac{1}{6} & -\frac{1}{6} & 0 \\ 0 & 0 & -5 & 2 & -3 & 2 & 0 & 1 \end{array}\right]$$

$$\rightarrow \left[\begin{array}{cccc|cccc} 1 & 0 & 0 & 1 & 0 & \frac{1}{3} & \frac{1}{3} & 0 \\ 0 & 1 & 0 & -1 & 0 & -\frac{2}{3} & \frac{1}{3} & 0 \\ 0 & 0 & 1 & 0 & \frac{1}{2} & -\frac{1}{6} & -\frac{1}{6} & 0 \\ 0 & 0 & 0 & 2 & -\frac{1}{2} & \frac{7}{6} & -\frac{5}{6} & 1 \end{array}\right] \rightarrow \left[\begin{array}{cccc|cccc} 1 & 0 & 0 & 1 & 0 & \frac{1}{3} & \frac{1}{3} & 0 \\ 0 & 1 & 0 & -1 & 0 & -\frac{2}{3} & \frac{1}{3} & 0 \\ 0 & 0 & 1 & 0 & \frac{1}{2} & -\frac{1}{6} & -\frac{1}{6} & 0 \\ 0 & 0 & 0 & 1 & -\frac{1}{4} & \frac{7}{12} & -\frac{5}{12} & \frac{1}{2} \end{array}\right]$$

$$\rightarrow \left[\begin{array}{cccc|cccc} 1 & 0 & 0 & 0 & \frac{1}{4} & -\frac{1}{4} & \frac{3}{4} & -\frac{1}{2} \\ 0 & 1 & 0 & 0 & -\frac{1}{4} & -\frac{1}{12} & -\frac{1}{12} & \frac{1}{2} \\ 0 & 0 & 1 & 0 & \frac{1}{2} & -\frac{1}{6} & -\frac{1}{6} & 0 \\ 0 & 0 & 0 & 1 & -\frac{1}{4} & \frac{7}{12} & -\frac{5}{12} & \frac{1}{2} \end{array}\right]$$

$$\begin{bmatrix} w \\ x \\ y \\ z \end{bmatrix} = A^{-1}B = \begin{bmatrix} \frac{1}{4} & -\frac{1}{4} & \frac{3}{4} & -\frac{1}{2} \\ -\frac{1}{4} & -\frac{1}{12} & -\frac{1}{12} & \frac{1}{2} \\ \frac{1}{2} & -\frac{1}{6} & -\frac{1}{6} & 0 \\ -\frac{1}{4} & \frac{7}{12} & -\frac{5}{12} & \frac{1}{2} \end{bmatrix} \begin{bmatrix} 4 \\ 12 \\ 12 \\ 12 \end{bmatrix} = \begin{bmatrix} 1 \\ 3 \\ -2 \\ 7 \end{bmatrix}$$

Thus, $w = 1$, $x = 3$, $y = -2$, $z = 7$.

35. $I - A = \begin{bmatrix} 1 & 0 \\ 0 & 1 \end{bmatrix} - \begin{bmatrix} 2 & -1 \\ 1 & 3 \end{bmatrix} = \begin{bmatrix} -1 & 1 \\ -1 & -2 \end{bmatrix}$

$$\left[\begin{array}{cc|cc} -1 & 1 & 1 & 0 \\ -1 & -2 & 0 & 1 \end{array}\right] \rightarrow \left[\begin{array}{cc|cc} 1 & -1 & -1 & 0 \\ -1 & -2 & 0 & 1 \end{array}\right] \rightarrow \left[\begin{array}{cc|cc} 1 & -1 & -1 & 0 \\ 0 & -3 & -1 & 1 \end{array}\right]$$

$$\rightarrow \left[\begin{array}{cc|cc} 1 & -1 & -1 & 0 \\ 0 & 1 & \frac{1}{3} & -\frac{1}{3} \end{array}\right] \rightarrow \left[\begin{array}{cc|cc} 1 & 0 & -\frac{2}{3} & -\frac{1}{3} \\ 0 & 1 & \frac{1}{3} & -\frac{1}{3} \end{array}\right]$$

Thus $(I - A)^{-1} = \begin{bmatrix} -\frac{2}{3} & -\frac{1}{3} \\ \frac{1}{3} & -\frac{1}{3} \end{bmatrix}$.

37. Let x = number of model A and y = number of model B.

a. The system is
$$\begin{cases} x + y = 100 & \text{(painting)} \\ \frac{1}{2}x + y = 80 & \text{(polishing)} \end{cases}$$

Let $\mathbf{A} = \begin{bmatrix} 1 & 1 \\ \frac{1}{2} & 1 \end{bmatrix}$

$$\left[\begin{array}{cc|cc} 1 & 1 & 1 & 0 \\ \frac{1}{2} & 1 & 0 & 1 \end{array}\right] \rightarrow \left[\begin{array}{cc|cc} 1 & 1 & 1 & 0 \\ 0 & \frac{1}{2} & -\frac{1}{2} & 1 \end{array}\right] \rightarrow \left[\begin{array}{cc|cc} 1 & 1 & 1 & 0 \\ 0 & 1 & -1 & 2 \end{array}\right] \rightarrow \left[\begin{array}{cc|cc} 1 & 0 & 2 & -2 \\ 0 & 1 & -1 & 2 \end{array}\right]$$

$$\begin{bmatrix} x \\ y \end{bmatrix} = \mathbf{A}^{-1}\begin{bmatrix} 100 \\ 80 \end{bmatrix} = \begin{bmatrix} 2 & -2 \\ -1 & 2 \end{bmatrix}\begin{bmatrix} 100 \\ 80 \end{bmatrix} = \begin{bmatrix} 40 \\ 60 \end{bmatrix}$$

Thus 40 of model A and 60 of model B can be produced.

b. The system is
$$\begin{cases} 10x + 7y = 800 & \text{(widgets)} \\ 14x + 10y = 1130 & \text{(shims)} \end{cases}$$

Let $\mathbf{A} = \begin{bmatrix} 10 & 7 \\ 14 & 10 \end{bmatrix}$.

$$\left[\begin{array}{cc|cc} 10 & 7 & 1 & 0 \\ 14 & 10 & 0 & 1 \end{array}\right] \rightarrow \left[\begin{array}{cc|cc} 1 & \frac{7}{10} & \frac{1}{10} & 0 \\ 14 & 10 & 0 & 1 \end{array}\right]$$

$$\rightarrow \left[\begin{array}{cc|cc} 1 & \frac{7}{10} & \frac{1}{10} & 0 \\ 0 & \frac{1}{5} & -\frac{7}{5} & 1 \end{array}\right] \rightarrow \left[\begin{array}{cc|cc} 1 & \frac{7}{10} & \frac{1}{10} & 0 \\ 0 & 1 & -7 & 5 \end{array}\right] \rightarrow \left[\begin{array}{cc|cc} 1 & 0 & 5 & -\frac{7}{2} \\ 0 & 1 & -7 & 5 \end{array}\right]$$

$$\begin{bmatrix} x \\ y \end{bmatrix} = \mathbf{A}^{-1}\begin{bmatrix} 800 \\ 1130 \end{bmatrix} = \begin{bmatrix} 5 & -\frac{7}{2} \\ -7 & 5 \end{bmatrix}\begin{bmatrix} 800 \\ 1130 \end{bmatrix} = \begin{bmatrix} 45 \\ 50 \end{bmatrix}$$

Thus 45 of model A and 50 of model B can be produced.

39. a. $\left(\mathbf{B}^{-1}\mathbf{A}^{-1}\right)(\mathbf{AB}) = \mathbf{B}^{-1}\left(\mathbf{A}^{-1}\mathbf{A}\right)\mathbf{B} = \mathbf{B}^{-1}\mathbf{IB} = \mathbf{B}^{-1}\mathbf{B} = \mathbf{I}$

Since an invertible matrix has exactly one inverse, $\mathbf{B}^{-1}\mathbf{A}^{-1}$ is the inverse of $\mathbf{AB}$.

b. From part (a),
$$(\mathbf{AB})^{-1} = \mathbf{B}^{-1}\mathbf{A}^{-1} = \begin{bmatrix} 1 & 1 \\ 1 & 2 \end{bmatrix}\begin{bmatrix} 1 & 2 \\ 3 & 4 \end{bmatrix} = \begin{bmatrix} 4 & 6 \\ 7 & 10 \end{bmatrix}$$

41. $\mathbf{P}^{T}\mathbf{P} = \begin{bmatrix} \frac{3}{5} & \frac{4}{5} \\ -\frac{4}{5} & \frac{3}{5} \end{bmatrix}\begin{bmatrix} \frac{3}{5} & -\frac{4}{5} \\ \frac{4}{5} & \frac{3}{5} \end{bmatrix} = \begin{bmatrix} 1 & 0 \\ 0 & 1 \end{bmatrix} = \mathbf{I}$, so $\mathbf{P}^{T} = \mathbf{P}^{-1}$. Yes, $\mathbf{P}$ is orthogonal.

43. Let x be the number of shares of D, y be the number of shares of E, and z be the number of shares of F. We get the following conditions.

$60x + 80y + 30z = 500,000$

$0.16(60x) + 0.12(80y) + 0.09(30z) = 0.1368(60x + 80y + 30z)$

$z = 4y$

Simplify the first equation.

$6x + 8y + 3z = 50,000$

Simplify the second equation.

$9.6x + 9.6y + 2.7z = 8.208x + 10.944y + 4.104z$

$1.392x - 1.344y - 1.404z = 0$

$1392x - 1344y - 1404z = 0$

$116x - 112y - 117z = 0$

Simplify the third equation.

$4y - z = 0$

Thus we solve the following system of equations.

$6x + 8y + 3z = 50,000$

$116x - 112y - 117z = 0$

$4y - z = 0$

The coefficient matrix is $\mathbf{A} = \begin{bmatrix} 6 & 8 & 3 \\ 116 & -112 & -117 \\ 0 & 4 & -1 \end{bmatrix}$.

$$[\mathbf{A}\,|\,\mathbf{I}] = \begin{bmatrix} 6 & 8 & 3 & 1 & 0 & 0 \\ 116 & -112 & -117 & 0 & 1 & 0 \\ 0 & 4 & -1 & 0 & 0 & 1 \end{bmatrix}$$

$$\xrightarrow{\frac{1}{6}R_1} \begin{bmatrix} 1 & \frac{4}{3} & \frac{1}{2} & \frac{1}{6} & 0 & 0 \\ 116 & -112 & -117 & 0 & 1 & 0 \\ 0 & 4 & -1 & 0 & 0 & 1 \end{bmatrix}$$

$$\xrightarrow{-116R_1 + R_2} \begin{bmatrix} 1 & \frac{4}{3} & \frac{1}{2} & \frac{1}{6} & 0 & 0 \\ 0 & -\frac{800}{3} & -175 & -\frac{58}{3} & 1 & 0 \\ 0 & 4 & -1 & 0 & 0 & 1 \end{bmatrix}$$

$$\xrightarrow[\;-\frac{1}{4}R_3\;]{-\frac{3}{800}R_2} \begin{bmatrix} 1 & \frac{4}{3} & \frac{1}{2} & \frac{1}{6} & 0 & 0 \\ 0 & 1 & \frac{21}{32} & \frac{29}{400} & -\frac{3}{800} & 0 \\ 0 & -1 & \frac{1}{4} & 0 & 0 & -\frac{1}{4} \end{bmatrix}$$

$$\xrightarrow{R_2 + R_3} \begin{bmatrix} 1 & \frac{4}{3} & \frac{1}{2} & \frac{1}{6} & 0 & 0 \\ 0 & 1 & \frac{21}{32} & \frac{29}{400} & -\frac{3}{800} & 0 \\ 0 & 0 & \frac{29}{32} & \frac{29}{400} & -\frac{3}{800} & -\frac{1}{4} \end{bmatrix}$$

$$\xrightarrow{\frac{32}{29}R_3} \begin{bmatrix} 1 & \frac{4}{3} & \frac{1}{2} & \frac{1}{6} & 0 & 0 \\ 0 & 1 & \frac{21}{32} & \frac{29}{400} & -\frac{3}{800} & 0 \\ 0 & 0 & 1 & \frac{2}{25} & -\frac{3}{725} & -\frac{8}{29} \end{bmatrix}$$

$$\begin{matrix} -\frac{1}{2}R_3 + R_1 \\ \xrightarrow{} \\ -\frac{21}{32}R_3 + R_2 \end{matrix} \left[\begin{array}{ccc|ccc} 1 & \frac{4}{3} & 0 & \frac{19}{150} & \frac{3}{1450} & \frac{4}{29} \\ 0 & 1 & 0 & \frac{1}{50} & -\frac{3}{2900} & \frac{21}{116} \\ 0 & 0 & 1 & \frac{2}{25} & -\frac{3}{725} & -\frac{8}{29} \end{array} \right]$$

$$\xrightarrow{-\frac{4}{3}R_2 + R_1} \left[\begin{array}{ccc|ccc} 1 & 0 & 0 & \frac{1}{10} & \frac{1}{290} & -\frac{3}{29} \\ 0 & 1 & 0 & \frac{1}{50} & -\frac{3}{2900} & \frac{21}{116} \\ 0 & 0 & 1 & \frac{2}{25} & -\frac{3}{725} & -\frac{8}{29} \end{array} \right]$$

$$\begin{bmatrix} x \\ y \\ z \end{bmatrix} = \begin{bmatrix} \frac{1}{10} & \frac{1}{290} & -\frac{3}{29} \\ \frac{1}{50} & -\frac{3}{2900} & \frac{21}{116} \\ \frac{2}{25} & -\frac{3}{725} & -\frac{8}{29} \end{bmatrix} \begin{bmatrix} 50,000 \\ 0 \\ 0 \end{bmatrix} = \begin{bmatrix} 5000 \\ 1000 \\ 4000 \end{bmatrix}$$

They should buy 5000 shares of company D, 1000 shares of company E, and 4000 shares of company F.

45. a. $\begin{bmatrix} 1.46 & 0.56 \\ 0.51 & 1.35 \end{bmatrix}$

b. $\begin{bmatrix} \frac{130}{89} & \frac{50}{89} \\ \frac{45}{89} & \frac{120}{89} \end{bmatrix}$

47. $\begin{bmatrix} 1.80 & 1.10 & -0.46 \\ 0.35 & 1.31 & -0.17 \\ 0.44 & 0.42 & 0.59 \end{bmatrix}$

49. $\begin{bmatrix} w \\ x \\ y \\ z \end{bmatrix} = \begin{bmatrix} \frac{2}{5} & 4 & \frac{1}{2} & -\frac{3}{7} \\ \frac{5}{9} & -\frac{2}{3} & -4 & -1 \\ 0 & 1 & -\frac{4}{9} & \frac{5}{6} \\ \frac{1}{2} & 0 & 4 & -\frac{1}{3} \end{bmatrix}^{-1} \begin{bmatrix} \frac{14}{13} \\ \frac{7}{8} \\ 9 \\ \frac{4}{7} \end{bmatrix} = \begin{bmatrix} 14.44 \\ 0.03 \\ -0.80 \\ 10.33 \end{bmatrix}$

$w = 14.44$, $x = 0.03$, $y = -0.80$, $z = 10.33$

Principles in Practice 6.7

1. Expand along the first row.

$$\begin{vmatrix} 1 & 1 & 2 \\ 3 & 4 & 10 \\ 4 & 2 & 6 \end{vmatrix} = (1)(-1)^2 \begin{vmatrix} 4 & 10 \\ 2 & 6 \end{vmatrix} - (1)(-1)^3 \begin{vmatrix} 3 & 10 \\ 4 & 6 \end{vmatrix} + (2)(-1)^4 \begin{vmatrix} 3 & 4 \\ 4 & 2 \end{vmatrix} = (1)(4) + (-1)(-22) + 2(-10) = 6$$

Exercise 6.7

1. $2(2) - 1(3) = 4 - 3 = 1$

3. $(-2)(-6) - (-7)(-4) = 12 - 28 = -16$

5. $1(y) - x(0) = y$

7. $\dfrac{1(4) - 2(3)}{2(6) - 1(5)} = \dfrac{-2}{7} = -\dfrac{2}{7}$

9. $2(k) - 3(4) = 12$, $2k - 12 = 12$, $2k = 24$, $k = 12$

11. $\begin{vmatrix} 1 & 3 \\ 7 & 9 \end{vmatrix} = 1(9) - 3(7) = -12$

13. $(-1)^{3+2} \begin{vmatrix} 1 & 3 \\ 4 & 6 \end{vmatrix} = -[1(6) - 3(4)] = -[-6] = 6$

15. $\begin{vmatrix} a_{11} & a_{13} & a_{14} \\ a_{21} & a_{23} & a_{24} \\ a_{41} & a_{43} & a_{44} \end{vmatrix}$

17. $(-1)^{1+3} \begin{vmatrix} a_{21} & a_{22} & a_{24} \\ a_{31} & a_{32} & a_{34} \\ a_{41} & a_{42} & a_{44} \end{vmatrix} = (-1)^4 \cdot \begin{vmatrix} a_{21} & a_{22} & a_{24} \\ a_{31} & a_{32} & a_{34} \\ a_{41} & a_{42} & a_{44} \end{vmatrix}$

$= \begin{vmatrix} a_{21} & a_{22} & a_{24} \\ a_{31} & a_{32} & a_{34} \\ a_{41} & a_{42} & a_{44} \end{vmatrix}$

19. Expanding along column 2 gives

$1(-1)^3 \begin{vmatrix} 2 & 1 \\ -4 & 6 \end{vmatrix} + 0 + 0 = 1(-1)[12 - (-4)] = -16$

21. Expanding along row 1 gives

$1(-1)^2 \begin{vmatrix} 5 & 4 \\ -2 & 1 \end{vmatrix} + 2(-1)^3 \begin{vmatrix} 4 & 4 \\ 3 & 1 \end{vmatrix} - 3(-1)^4 \begin{vmatrix} 4 & 5 \\ 3 & -2 \end{vmatrix}$

$= 1(1)[5 - (-8)] + 2(-1)[4 - 12] - 3(1)[-8 - 15]$

$= 13 + 16 + 69 = 98$

23. Expanding along row 3 gives

$0 + 6(-1)^5 \begin{vmatrix} 2 & 5 \\ -3 & -1 \end{vmatrix} - 1(-1)^6 \begin{vmatrix} 2 & 1 \\ -3 & 4 \end{vmatrix}$

$= 6(-1)[-2 - (-15)] - 1(1)[8 - (-3)]$

$= -78 - 11 = -89.$

25. Expanding along row 1 gives

$2(-1)^2 \begin{vmatrix} 1 & -1 \\ 2 & -3 \end{vmatrix} - 1(-1)^3 \begin{vmatrix} 1 & -1 \\ 1 & -3 \end{vmatrix} + 3(-1)^4 \begin{vmatrix} 1 & 1 \\ 1 & 2 \end{vmatrix}$

$= 2(1)[-3 - (-2)] - 1(-1)[-3 - (-1)] + 3(1)[2 - 1]$

$= -2 - 2 + 3 = -1.$

27. Expanding along row 1 gives

$$\frac{1}{2}(-1)^2\begin{vmatrix}\frac{1}{3} & \frac{2}{3}\\ -4 & 1\end{vmatrix}+\frac{2}{3}(-1)^3\begin{vmatrix}-1 & \frac{2}{3}\\ 3 & 1\end{vmatrix}-\frac{1}{2}(-1)^4\begin{vmatrix}-1 & \frac{1}{3}\\ 3 & -4\end{vmatrix}$$

$$=\frac{1}{2}(1)\left[\frac{1}{3}-\left(-\frac{8}{3}\right)\right]+\frac{2}{3}(-1)[-1-2]-\frac{1}{2}(1)[4-1]$$

$$=\frac{3}{2}+2-\frac{3}{2}=2$$

29. Expanding along column 3 gives

$$3(-1)^4\begin{vmatrix}4 & -1 & 1\\ 2 & 1 & 3\\ -1 & 2 & -1\end{vmatrix}+0+0+3(-1)^7\begin{vmatrix}1 & 0 & 2\\ 4 & -1 & 1\\ 2 & 1 & 3\end{vmatrix}$$

$$=3\left\{4(-1)^2\begin{vmatrix}1 & 3\\ 2 & -1\end{vmatrix}-1(-1)^3\begin{vmatrix}2 & 3\\ -1 & -1\end{vmatrix}+1(-1)^4\begin{vmatrix}2 & 1\\ -1 & 2\end{vmatrix}\right\}-3\left\{1(-1)^2\begin{vmatrix}-1 & 1\\ 1 & 3\end{vmatrix}+0+2(-1)^4\begin{vmatrix}4 & -1\\ 2 & 1\end{vmatrix}\right\}$$

$$=3\{4(1)[-1-6]-1(-1)[-2-(-3)]+1(1)[4-(-1)]\}-3\{1(1)[-3-1]+2(1)[4-(-2)]\}$$

$$=3\{-28+1+5\}-3\{-4+12\}=-66-24=-90.$$

31. Since all entries below the main diagonal are zeros, the determinant is $(1)(1)(1)(1) = 1$.

33. Since all entries below (as well as above) main diagonal are zeros, the determinant is $(1)(-2)(4)(-3) = 24$.

35. $$\begin{vmatrix}1 & -1 & 2 & -1\\ 2 & 3 & -1 & 2\\ 1 & 4 & -3 & 3\\ 4 & 1 & 3 & 0\end{vmatrix}\xrightarrow{R_3+R_1}\begin{vmatrix}2 & 3 & -1 & 2\\ 2 & 3 & -1 & 2\\ 1 & 4 & -3 & 3\\ 4 & 1 & 3 & 0\end{vmatrix}=0,\text{ since row 1 and row two are identical}$$

37. Multiplying column 2 by 2 and adding the result to column 5 gives all zeros in column 5. Thus the determinant is 0.

39. $$\begin{vmatrix}x & -2\\ 7 & 7-x\end{vmatrix}=26$$

$$x(7-x)-(-2)(7)=26$$

$$7x-x^2+14=26$$

$$x^2-7x+12=0$$

$$(x-3)(x-4)=0\text{ so }x=3\text{ or }x=4$$

41. Multiplying each entry of $\mathbf{A}$ by 2 gives $2\mathbf{A}$. Since $\mathbf{A}$ has order 4, property 7 gives

$$|2\mathbf{A}|=2^4|\mathbf{A}|=16(12)=192.$$

43. a. Since $\mathbf{A}^{-1}\mathbf{A}=\mathbf{I}$, we have

$$|\mathbf{A}^{-1}\mathbf{A}|=|\mathbf{I}|\text{ so }|\mathbf{A}^{-1}||\mathbf{A}|=1.$$

Thus $|\mathbf{A}^{-1}|=\frac{1}{|\mathbf{A}|}$.

b. From part (a), if $|\mathbf{A}|=3$, then

$$|\mathbf{A}^{-1}|=\frac{1}{|\mathbf{A}|}=\frac{1}{3}.$$

45. The given system is equivalent to the system

$$\begin{cases} x + 3y + 2z = 0 \\ x + cy + 4z = 0 \\ 2y + cz = 0 \end{cases}$$

For the system to have infinitely many solutions, the coefficient matrix must not be invertible; that is, its determinant must be zero.

$$\begin{vmatrix} 1 & 3 & 2 \\ 1 & c & 4 \\ 0 & 2 & c \end{vmatrix} = 0$$

$$\left(c^2 + 4 + 0\right) - (0 + 8 + 3c) = 0$$

$$c^2 - 3c - 4 = 0$$

$$(c+1)(c-4) = 0$$

$$c = -1 \text{ or } c = 4$$

47. −1630

49. −3864

Exercise 6.8

1. $\Delta = \begin{vmatrix} 2 & -1 \\ 4 & 1 \end{vmatrix} = 6$

$$\Delta_x = \begin{vmatrix} 4 & -1 \\ 5 & 1 \end{vmatrix} = 9$$

$$\Delta_y = \begin{vmatrix} 2 & 4 \\ 4 & 5 \end{vmatrix} = -6$$

$$x = \frac{\Delta_x}{\Delta} = \frac{9}{6} = \frac{3}{2}$$

$$y = \frac{\Delta_y}{\Delta} = \frac{-6}{6} = -1$$

3. $\begin{cases} -2x = 4 - 3y \\ y = 6x - 1 \end{cases}$ is equivalent to

$$\begin{cases} -2x + 3y = 4 \\ -6x + y = -1 \end{cases}$$

$$\Delta = \begin{vmatrix} -2 & 3 \\ -6 & 1 \end{vmatrix} = 16$$

$$\Delta_x = \begin{vmatrix} 4 & 3 \\ -1 & 1 \end{vmatrix} = 7$$

$$\Delta_y = \begin{vmatrix} -2 & 4 \\ -6 & -1 \end{vmatrix} = 26$$

$$x = \frac{\Delta_x}{\Delta} = \frac{7}{16}$$

$$y = \frac{\Delta_y}{\Delta} = \frac{26}{16} = \frac{13}{8}$$

5. $\begin{cases} 3(x+2) = 5 \\ 6(x+y) = -8 \end{cases}$ is equivalent to

$$\begin{cases} 3x = -1 \\ 6x + 6y = -8 \end{cases}$$

$$\Delta = \begin{vmatrix} 3 & 0 \\ 6 & 6 \end{vmatrix} = 18$$

$$\Delta_x = \begin{vmatrix} -1 & 0 \\ -8 & 6 \end{vmatrix} = -6$$

$$\Delta_y = \begin{vmatrix} 3 & -1 \\ 6 & -8 \end{vmatrix} = -18$$

$$x = \frac{\Delta_x}{\Delta} = -\frac{6}{18} = -\frac{1}{3}$$

$$y = \frac{\Delta_y}{\Delta} = -\frac{18}{18} = -1$$

7. $\Delta = \begin{vmatrix} \frac{3}{2} & -\frac{1}{4} \\ \frac{1}{3} & \frac{1}{2} \end{vmatrix} = \frac{5}{6}$

$\Delta_x = \begin{vmatrix} 1 & -\frac{1}{4} \\ 2 & \frac{1}{2} \end{vmatrix} = 1$

$\Delta_z = \begin{vmatrix} \frac{3}{2} & 1 \\ \frac{1}{3} & 2 \end{vmatrix} = \frac{8}{3}$

$x = \frac{\Delta_x}{\Delta} = \frac{1}{\frac{5}{6}} = \frac{6}{5}$

$z = \frac{\Delta_z}{\Delta} = \frac{\frac{8}{3}}{\frac{5}{6}} = \frac{16}{5}$

9. $\Delta = \begin{vmatrix} 1 & 1 & 1 \\ 1 & -1 & 1 \\ 2 & -1 & 3 \end{vmatrix} = -2$

$\Delta_x = \begin{vmatrix} 6 & 1 & 1 \\ 2 & -1 & 1 \\ 6 & -1 & 3 \end{vmatrix} = -8$

$\Delta_y = \begin{vmatrix} 1 & 6 & 1 \\ 1 & 2 & 1 \\ 2 & 6 & 3 \end{vmatrix} = -4$

$\Delta_z = \begin{vmatrix} 1 & 1 & 6 \\ 1 & -1 & 2 \\ 2 & -1 & 6 \end{vmatrix} = 0$

$x = \frac{\Delta_x}{\Delta} = \frac{-8}{-2} = 4$

$y = \frac{\Delta_y}{\Delta} = \frac{-4}{-2} = 2$

$z = \frac{\Delta_z}{\Delta} = \frac{0}{-2} = 0$

11. $\Delta = \begin{vmatrix} 2 & -3 & 4 \\ 1 & 1 & -3 \\ 3 & 2 & -1 \end{vmatrix} = 30$

$\Delta_x = \begin{vmatrix} 0 & -3 & 4 \\ 4 & 1 & -3 \\ 0 & 2 & -1 \end{vmatrix} = 20$

$\Delta_y = \begin{vmatrix} 2 & 0 & 4 \\ 1 & 4 & -3 \\ 3 & 0 & -1 \end{vmatrix} = -56$

$\Delta_z = \begin{vmatrix} 2 & -3 & 0 \\ 1 & 1 & 4 \\ 3 & 2 & 0 \end{vmatrix} = -52$

$x = \frac{\Delta_x}{\Delta} = \frac{20}{30} = \frac{2}{3}$

$y = \frac{\Delta_y}{\Delta} = \frac{-56}{30} = -\frac{28}{15}$

$z = \frac{\Delta_z}{\Delta} = \frac{-52}{30} = -\frac{26}{15}$

13. $\Delta = \begin{vmatrix} 1 & -2 & 1 \\ 2 & 1 & 2 \\ 1 & 8 & 1 \end{vmatrix} = 0$, so Cramer's rule does not apply. We solve the system by matrix reduction.

$\begin{bmatrix} 1 & -2 & 1 & | & 3 \\ 2 & 1 & 2 & | & 6 \\ 1 & 8 & 1 & | & 3 \end{bmatrix} \rightarrow \begin{bmatrix} 1 & -2 & 1 & | & 3 \\ 0 & 5 & 0 & | & 0 \\ 0 & 10 & 0 & | & 0 \end{bmatrix} \rightarrow \begin{bmatrix} 1 & -2 & 1 & | & 3 \\ 0 & 1 & 0 & | & 0 \\ 0 & 0 & 0 & | & 0 \end{bmatrix} \rightarrow \begin{bmatrix} 1 & 0 & 1 & | & 3 \\ 0 & 1 & 0 & | & 0 \\ 0 & 0 & 0 & | & 0 \end{bmatrix}$

Thus $x = 3 - r$, $y = 0$, $z = r$.

15. $\Delta = \begin{vmatrix} 2 & -3 & 1 \\ 1 & -6 & 3 \\ 3 & 3 & -2 \end{vmatrix} = -6$

$\Delta_x = \begin{vmatrix} -2 & -3 & 1 \\ -2 & -6 & 3 \\ 2 & 3 & -2 \end{vmatrix} = -6$

$\Delta_y = \begin{vmatrix} 2 & -2 & 1 \\ 1 & -2 & 3 \\ 3 & 2 & -2 \end{vmatrix} = -18$

$\Delta_z = \begin{vmatrix} 2 & -3 & -2 \\ 1 & -6 & -2 \\ 3 & 3 & 2 \end{vmatrix} = -30$

$x = \dfrac{\Delta_x}{\Delta} = \dfrac{-6}{-6} = 1$

$y = \dfrac{\Delta_y}{\Delta} = \dfrac{-18}{-6} = 3$

$z = \dfrac{\Delta_z}{\Delta} = \dfrac{-30}{-6} = 5$

17. $\Delta = \begin{vmatrix} 1 & -1 & 3 & 1 \\ 1 & 2 & 0 & -3 \\ 2 & 3 & 6 & 1 \\ 1 & 1 & 1 & 1 \end{vmatrix}$

$= 1(-1)^3 \begin{vmatrix} -1 & 3 & 1 \\ 3 & 6 & 1 \\ 1 & 1 & 1 \end{vmatrix} + 2(-1)^4 \begin{vmatrix} 1 & 3 & 1 \\ 2 & 6 & 1 \\ 1 & 1 & 1 \end{vmatrix} + 0 - 3(-1)^6 \begin{vmatrix} 1 & -1 & 3 \\ 2 & 3 & 6 \\ 1 & 1 & 1 \end{vmatrix}$

$= 1(-1)(-14) + 2(1)(-2) - 3(1)(-10) = 14 - 4 + 30 = 40$

$\Delta_y = \begin{vmatrix} 1 & -14 & 3 & 1 \\ 1 & 12 & 0 & -3 \\ 2 & 1 & 6 & 1 \\ 1 & 6 & 1 & 1 \end{vmatrix}$

$= 3(-1)^4 \begin{vmatrix} 1 & 12 & -3 \\ 2 & 1 & 1 \\ 1 & 6 & 1 \end{vmatrix} + 0 + 6(-1)^6 \begin{vmatrix} 1 & -14 & 1 \\ 1 & 12 & -3 \\ 1 & 6 & 1 \end{vmatrix} + 1(-1)^7 \begin{vmatrix} 1 & -14 & 1 \\ 1 & 12 & -3 \\ 2 & 1 & 1 \end{vmatrix}$

$= 3(1)(-50) + 6(1)(80) + 1(-1)(90) = -150 + 480 - 90 = 240$

$$\Delta_w = \begin{vmatrix} 1 & -1 & 3 & -14 \\ 1 & 2 & 0 & 12 \\ 2 & 3 & 6 & 1 \\ 1 & 1 & 1 & 6 \end{vmatrix}$$

$$= 1(-1)^3 \begin{vmatrix} -1 & 3 & -14 \\ 3 & 6 & 1 \\ 1 & 1 & 6 \end{vmatrix} + 2(-1)^4 \begin{vmatrix} 1 & 3 & -14 \\ 2 & 6 & 1 \\ 1 & 1 & 6 \end{vmatrix} + 0 + 12(-1)^6 \begin{vmatrix} 1 & -1 & 3 \\ 2 & 3 & 6 \\ 1 & 1 & 1 \end{vmatrix}$$

$$= 1(-1)(-44) + 2(1)(58) + 12(1)(-10) = 44 + 116 - 120 = 40$$

Thus $y = \dfrac{\Delta_y}{\Delta} = \dfrac{240}{40} = 6$, $w = \dfrac{\Delta_w}{\Delta} = \dfrac{40}{40} = 1$

19. $\begin{cases} 2 - y = x \\ 3 + x = -y \end{cases}$ is equivalent to $\begin{cases} x + y = 2 \\ x + y = -3 \end{cases}$

Since $\Delta = \begin{vmatrix} 1 & 1 \\ 1 & 1 \end{vmatrix} = 0$, Cramer's rule does

not apply. However, the equations represent distinct parallel lines, so no solutions exists.

21. Let c, h, t denote the number of concerts, hockey games, and theater productions she should attend, respectively. Then we are given that

$c + h + t = 24$, $c = 2h$, and $c = \dfrac{h+t}{2}$.

Simplifying gives the system
$c + h + t = 24$
$c - 2h = 0$
$2c - h - t = 0$

$$\Delta = \begin{vmatrix} 1 & 1 & 1 \\ 1 & -2 & 0 \\ 2 & -1 & -1 \end{vmatrix} = 6$$

$$\Delta_h = \begin{vmatrix} 1 & 24 & 1 \\ 1 & 0 & 0 \\ 2 & 0 & -1 \end{vmatrix} = 24$$

$h = \dfrac{\Delta_h}{\Delta} = \dfrac{24}{6} = 4$ hockey games

23. $\Delta = \begin{vmatrix} \frac{4}{7} & -\frac{7}{3} & \frac{2}{5} \\ -8 & \frac{5}{8} & -6 \\ 2 & \frac{3}{5} & \frac{4}{3} \end{vmatrix}$

$$x = \frac{\Delta_x}{\Delta} = \frac{\begin{vmatrix} \frac{14}{9} & -\frac{7}{3} & \frac{2}{5} \\ \frac{13}{9} & \frac{5}{8} & -6 \\ \frac{10}{3} & \frac{3}{5} & \frac{4}{3} \end{vmatrix}}{\Delta} \approx 17.85$$

$$y = \frac{\Delta_y}{\Delta} = \frac{\begin{vmatrix} \frac{4}{7} & \frac{14}{9} & \frac{2}{5} \\ -8 & \frac{13}{9} & -6 \\ 2 & \frac{10}{3} & \frac{4}{3} \end{vmatrix}}{\Delta} \approx -0.42$$

$$z = \frac{\Delta_z}{\Delta} = \frac{\begin{vmatrix} \frac{4}{7} & -\frac{7}{3} & \frac{14}{9} \\ -8 & \frac{5}{8} & \frac{13}{9} \\ 2 & \frac{3}{5} & \frac{10}{3} \end{vmatrix}}{\Delta} \approx -24.09$$

Exercise 6.9

1. $A = \begin{bmatrix} \frac{200}{1200} & \frac{500}{1500} \\ \frac{400}{1200} & \frac{200}{1500} \end{bmatrix}$

$C = \begin{bmatrix} 600 \\ 805 \end{bmatrix}$

$X = (I - A)^{-1}C = \begin{bmatrix} 1290 \\ 1425 \end{bmatrix}$

The total value of other production costs is

$P_A + P_B = \frac{600}{1200}(1290) + \frac{800}{1500}(1425) = 1405$

3. $A = \begin{bmatrix} \frac{18}{108} & \frac{30}{120} & \frac{45}{180} \\ \frac{27}{108} & \frac{30}{120} & \frac{60}{180} \\ \frac{54}{108} & \frac{40}{120} & \frac{60}{180} \end{bmatrix}$

a. $C = \begin{bmatrix} 50 \\ 40 \\ 30 \end{bmatrix}$

$X = (I - A)^{-1}C = \begin{bmatrix} 297.80 \\ 349.54 \\ 443.12 \end{bmatrix}$

b. $C = \begin{bmatrix} 10 \\ 10 \\ 24 \end{bmatrix}$

$X = (I - A)^{-1}C = \begin{bmatrix} 102.17 \\ 125.28 \\ 175.27 \end{bmatrix}$

5. $A = \begin{bmatrix} \frac{400}{1000} & \frac{200}{1000} & \frac{200}{1000} \\ \frac{200}{1000} & \frac{400}{1000} & \frac{100}{1000} \\ \frac{200}{1000} & \frac{100}{1000} & \frac{300}{1000} \end{bmatrix}$

$C = \begin{bmatrix} 300 \\ 350 \\ 450 \end{bmatrix}$

$(I - A)^{-1}C = \begin{bmatrix} 1301 \\ 1215 \\ 1188 \end{bmatrix}$

7. $A = \begin{bmatrix} \frac{400}{1000} & \frac{200}{1000} & \frac{200}{1000} \\ \frac{200}{1000} & \frac{400}{1000} & \frac{100}{1000} \\ \frac{200}{1000} & \frac{100}{1000} & \frac{300}{1000} \end{bmatrix}$

$C = \begin{bmatrix} 250 \\ 300 \\ 350 \end{bmatrix}$

$(I - A)^{-1}C = \begin{bmatrix} 1073 \\ 1016 \\ 952 \end{bmatrix}$

Chapter 6 Review Problems

1. $2\begin{bmatrix} 3 & 4 \\ -5 & 1 \end{bmatrix} - 3\begin{bmatrix} 1 & 0 \\ 2 & 4 \end{bmatrix} = \begin{bmatrix} 6 & 8 \\ -10 & 2 \end{bmatrix} - \begin{bmatrix} 3 & 0 \\ 6 & 12 \end{bmatrix} = \begin{bmatrix} 3 & 8 \\ -16 & -10 \end{bmatrix}$

3. $\begin{bmatrix} 1 & 7 \\ 2 & -3 \\ 1 & 0 \end{bmatrix}\begin{bmatrix} 1 & 0 & -2 \\ 0 & 6 & 1 \end{bmatrix} = \begin{bmatrix} 1+0 & 0+42 & -2+7 \\ 2+0 & 0-18 & -4-3 \\ 1+0 & 0+0 & -2+0 \end{bmatrix} = \begin{bmatrix} 1 & 42 & 5 \\ 2 & -18 & -7 \\ 1 & 0 & -2 \end{bmatrix}$

5. $\begin{bmatrix} 1 & 0 \\ -1 & 4 \end{bmatrix} \left\{ \begin{bmatrix} 1 & 4 \\ 6 & 5 \end{bmatrix} - \begin{bmatrix} 2 & 6 \\ 5 & 0 \end{bmatrix} \right\} = \begin{bmatrix} 1 & 0 \\ -1 & 4 \end{bmatrix} \begin{bmatrix} -1 & -2 \\ 1 & 5 \end{bmatrix}$

$= \begin{bmatrix} -1+0 & -2+0 \\ 1+4 & 2+20 \end{bmatrix} = \begin{bmatrix} -1 & -2 \\ 5 & 22 \end{bmatrix}$

7. $2\begin{bmatrix} 1 & -2 \\ 3 & 1 \end{bmatrix}^2 [1 \quad -2]^T = 2\begin{bmatrix} -5 & -4 \\ 6 & -5 \end{bmatrix}\begin{bmatrix} 1 \\ -2 \end{bmatrix} = 2\begin{bmatrix} 3 \\ 16 \end{bmatrix} = \begin{bmatrix} 6 \\ 32 \end{bmatrix}$

9. $(2\mathbf{A})^T - 3\mathbf{I}^2 = 2\mathbf{A}^T - 3\mathbf{I} = 2\begin{bmatrix} 1 & -1 \\ 1 & 2 \end{bmatrix} - \begin{bmatrix} 3 & 0 \\ 0 & 3 \end{bmatrix}$

$= \begin{bmatrix} 2 & -2 \\ 2 & 4 \end{bmatrix} - \begin{bmatrix} 3 & 0 \\ 0 & 3 \end{bmatrix} = \begin{bmatrix} -1 & -2 \\ 2 & 1 \end{bmatrix}$

11. $\mathbf{B}^4 + \mathbf{I}^4 = \begin{bmatrix} 1 & 0 \\ 0 & 2 \end{bmatrix}^4 + \begin{bmatrix} 1 & 0 \\ 0 & 1 \end{bmatrix}^4 = \begin{bmatrix} 1 & 0 \\ 0 & 16 \end{bmatrix} + \begin{bmatrix} 1 & 0 \\ 0 & 1 \end{bmatrix} = \begin{bmatrix} 2 & 0 \\ 0 & 17 \end{bmatrix}$

13. $\begin{bmatrix} 5x \\ 7x \end{bmatrix} = \begin{bmatrix} 15 \\ y \end{bmatrix}$

$5x = 15$, or $x = 3$

$7x = y, 7 \cdot 3 = y$, or $y = 21$

15. $\begin{bmatrix} 1 & 4 \\ 5 & 8 \end{bmatrix} \rightarrow \begin{bmatrix} 1 & 4 \\ 0 & -12 \end{bmatrix} \rightarrow \begin{bmatrix} 1 & 4 \\ 0 & 1 \end{bmatrix} \rightarrow \begin{bmatrix} 1 & 0 \\ 0 & 1 \end{bmatrix}$

17. $\begin{bmatrix} 2 & 4 & 3 \\ 1 & 2 & 3 \\ 4 & 8 & 6 \end{bmatrix} \rightarrow \begin{bmatrix} 1 & 2 & 3 \\ 2 & 4 & 3 \\ 4 & 8 & 6 \end{bmatrix} \rightarrow \begin{bmatrix} 1 & 2 & 3 \\ 0 & 0 & -3 \\ 0 & 0 & -6 \end{bmatrix} \rightarrow \begin{bmatrix} 1 & 2 & 3 \\ 0 & 0 & 1 \\ 0 & 0 & -6 \end{bmatrix} \rightarrow \begin{bmatrix} 1 & 2 & 0 \\ 0 & 0 & 1 \\ 0 & 0 & 0 \end{bmatrix}$

19. $\begin{bmatrix} 2 & -5 & | & 0 \\ 4 & 3 & | & 0 \end{bmatrix} \rightarrow \begin{bmatrix} 2 & -5 & | & 0 \\ 0 & 13 & | & 0 \end{bmatrix} \rightarrow \begin{bmatrix} 1 & -\frac{1}{2} & | & 0 \\ 0 & 1 & | & 0 \end{bmatrix} \rightarrow \begin{bmatrix} 1 & 0 & | & 0 \\ 0 & 1 & | & 0 \end{bmatrix}$

Thus $x = 0, y = 0$.

21. $\begin{bmatrix} 1 & 1 & 2 & | & 1 \\ 3 & -2 & -4 & | & -7 \\ 2 & -1 & -2 & | & 2 \end{bmatrix} \rightarrow \begin{bmatrix} 1 & 1 & 2 & | & 1 \\ 0 & -5 & -10 & | & -10 \\ 0 & -3 & -6 & | & 0 \end{bmatrix} \rightarrow \begin{bmatrix} 1 & 1 & 2 & | & 1 \\ 0 & 1 & 2 & | & 2 \\ 0 & -3 & -6 & | & 0 \end{bmatrix} \rightarrow \begin{bmatrix} 1 & 0 & 0 & | & -1 \\ 0 & 1 & 2 & | & 2 \\ 0 & 0 & 0 & | & 6 \end{bmatrix}$

Row three indicates that $0 = 6$, which is never true, so there is no solution.

23.
$$\begin{bmatrix} 1 & 5 & | & 1 & 0 \\ 3 & 9 & | & 0 & 1 \end{bmatrix} \to \begin{bmatrix} 1 & 5 & | & 1 & 0 \\ 0 & -6 & | & -3 & 1 \end{bmatrix} \to \begin{bmatrix} 1 & 5 & | & 1 & 0 \\ 0 & 1 & | & \frac{1}{2} & -\frac{1}{6} \end{bmatrix}$$

$$\to \begin{bmatrix} 1 & 0 & | & -\frac{3}{2} & \frac{5}{6} \\ 0 & 1 & | & \frac{1}{2} & -\frac{1}{6} \end{bmatrix} \Rightarrow \mathbf{A}^{-1} = \begin{bmatrix} -\frac{3}{2} & \frac{5}{6} \\ \frac{1}{2} & -\frac{1}{6} \end{bmatrix}$$

25.
$$\begin{bmatrix} 1 & 3 & -2 & | & 1 & 0 & 0 \\ 4 & 1 & 0 & | & 0 & 1 & 0 \\ 3 & -2 & 2 & | & 0 & 0 & 1 \end{bmatrix} \to \begin{bmatrix} 1 & 3 & -2 & | & 1 & 0 & 0 \\ 0 & -11 & 8 & | & -4 & 1 & 0 \\ 0 & -11 & 8 & | & -3 & 0 & 0 \end{bmatrix}$$

$$\begin{bmatrix} 1 & 3 & -2 & | & 1 & 0 & 0 \\ 0 & -11 & 8 & | & -4 & 1 & 0 \\ 0 & 0 & 0 & | & 1 & -1 & 0 \end{bmatrix} \to \begin{bmatrix} 1 & 3 & -2 & | & 1 & 0 & 0 \\ 0 & 1 & -\frac{8}{11} & | & \frac{4}{11} & -\frac{1}{11} & 0 \\ 0 & 0 & 0 & | & 1 & -1 & 0 \end{bmatrix}$$

$$\to \begin{bmatrix} 1 & 0 & \frac{2}{11} & | & -\frac{1}{11} & \frac{3}{11} & 0 \\ 0 & 1 & -\frac{8}{11} & | & \frac{4}{11} & -\frac{1}{11} & 0 \\ 0 & 0 & 0 & | & 1 & 0 & 0 \end{bmatrix} \Rightarrow \text{no inverse exists}$$

27.
$$\begin{bmatrix} 3 & 1 & 4 & | & 1 & 0 & 0 \\ 1 & 0 & 1 & | & 0 & 1 & 0 \\ 0 & 2 & 1 & | & 0 & 0 & 1 \end{bmatrix} \to \begin{bmatrix} 1 & 0 & 1 & | & 0 & 1 & 0 \\ 3 & 1 & 4 & | & 1 & 0 & 0 \\ 0 & 2 & 1 & | & 0 & 0 & 1 \end{bmatrix}$$

$$\to \begin{bmatrix} 1 & 0 & 1 & | & 0 & 1 & 0 \\ 0 & 1 & 1 & | & 1 & -3 & 0 \\ 0 & 2 & 1 & | & 0 & 0 & 1 \end{bmatrix} \to \begin{bmatrix} 1 & 0 & 1 & | & 0 & 1 & 0 \\ 0 & 1 & 1 & | & 1 & -3 & 0 \\ 0 & 0 & -1 & | & -2 & 6 & 1 \end{bmatrix}$$

$$\to \begin{bmatrix} 1 & 0 & 1 & | & 0 & 1 & 0 \\ 0 & 1 & 1 & | & 1 & -3 & 0 \\ 0 & 0 & 1 & | & 2 & -6 & -1 \end{bmatrix} \to \begin{bmatrix} 1 & 0 & 0 & | & -2 & 7 & 1 \\ 0 & 1 & 0 & | & -1 & 3 & 1 \\ 0 & 0 & 1 & | & 2 & -6 & -1 \end{bmatrix}$$

$$\begin{bmatrix} x \\ y \\ z \end{bmatrix} = \mathbf{A}^{-1}\mathbf{B} = \begin{bmatrix} -2 & 7 & 1 \\ -1 & 3 & 1 \\ 2 & -6 & -1 \end{bmatrix}\begin{bmatrix} 1 \\ 0 \\ 2 \end{bmatrix} = \begin{bmatrix} 0 \\ 1 \\ 0 \end{bmatrix}$$

Thus $x = 0$, $y = 1$, $z = 0$.

29. $2(7) - (-1)4 = 18$

31. Expanding along row 2 gives $0 + 1(-1)^4\begin{vmatrix} 1 & -1 \\ 1 & 2 \end{vmatrix} + 4(-1)^5\begin{vmatrix} 1 & 2 \\ 1 & 2 \end{vmatrix}$

$= 1(1)[2 - (-1)] + 4(-1)[2 - 2] = 3 + 0 = 3$

33. Since all entries below the main diagonal are zeros, the determinant is $(r)(i)(c)(h) = rich$.

35. $\Delta = \begin{vmatrix} 3 & -1 \\ 2 & 3 \end{vmatrix} = 11$

$\Delta_x = \begin{vmatrix} 1 & -1 \\ 8 & 3 \end{vmatrix} = 11$

$\Delta_y = \begin{vmatrix} 3 & 1 \\ 2 & 8 \end{vmatrix} = 22$

$x = \dfrac{\Delta_x}{\Delta} = \dfrac{11}{11} = 1$

$y = \dfrac{\Delta_y}{\Delta} = \dfrac{22}{11} = 2$

37. $\left| \mathbf{A}^{-1}\mathbf{B}^{\mathrm{T}} \right| = \left| \mathbf{A}^{-1} \right|\left| \mathbf{B}^{\mathrm{T}} \right| = \dfrac{1}{|\mathbf{A}|}\cdot|\mathbf{B}| = \dfrac{1}{-2}\cdot 4 = -2$

39. $\mathbf{A}^2 = \mathbf{AA} = \begin{bmatrix} 0 & 0 & 1 \\ 0 & 1 & 0 \\ 1 & 0 & 0 \end{bmatrix}\begin{bmatrix} 0 & 0 & 1 \\ 0 & 1 & 0 \\ 1 & 0 & 0 \end{bmatrix}$

$= \begin{bmatrix} 1 & 0 & 0 \\ 0 & 1 & 0 \\ 0 & 0 & 1 \end{bmatrix} = \mathbf{I}_3$

From above, $\mathbf{AA} = \mathbf{I}$. Since $\mathbf{A}^{-1}$ is unique,
$\mathbf{A}^{-1} = \mathbf{A}$.

$\mathbf{A}^{2000} = \left(\mathbf{A}^2\right)^{1000} = \mathbf{I}^{1000} = \mathbf{I}_3$

41. $\Delta = \begin{vmatrix} a & 0 & c \\ b & b & 0 \\ a & a & c \end{vmatrix} = (abc + abc + 0) - (abc + 0 + 0) = abc$

$\Delta_x = \begin{vmatrix} a & 0 & c \\ b & b & 0 \\ c & a & c \end{vmatrix} = (abc + abc + 0) - \left(bc^2 + 0 + 0\right) = 2abc - bc^2$

$\Delta_y = \begin{vmatrix} a & a & c \\ b & b & 0 \\ a & c & c \end{vmatrix} = \left(abc + bc^2 + 0\right) - (abc + 0 + abc) = bc^2 - abc$

$\Delta_z = \begin{vmatrix} a & 0 & a \\ b & b & b \\ a & a & c \end{vmatrix} = \left(abc + a^2b + 0\right) - \left(a^2b + a^2b + 0\right) = abc - a^2b$

Thus $x = \dfrac{\Delta_x}{\Delta} = \dfrac{2abc - bc^2}{abc} = 2 - \dfrac{c}{a}$

$y = \dfrac{\Delta_y}{\Delta} = \dfrac{bc^2 - abc}{abc} = \dfrac{c}{a} - 1$

$z = \dfrac{\Delta_y}{\Delta} = \dfrac{abc - a^2b}{abc} = 1 - \dfrac{a}{c}$

43. a. Let x, y, and z represent the weekly doses of capsules of brand I, II, and III, respectively. Then

$$\begin{cases} x + y + 4z = 13 & \text{(vitamin A)} \\ x + 2y + 7z = 22 & \text{(vitamin B)} \\ x + 3y + 10z = 31 & \text{(vitamin C)} \end{cases}$$

$$\begin{bmatrix} 1 & 1 & 4 & | & 13 \\ 1 & 2 & 7 & | & 22 \\ 1 & 3 & 10 & | & 31 \end{bmatrix} \xrightarrow[{-1R_1 + R_3}]{-1R_1 + R_2} \begin{bmatrix} 1 & 1 & 4 & | & 13 \\ 0 & 1 & 3 & | & 9 \\ 0 & 2 & 6 & | & 18 \end{bmatrix}$$

$$\xrightarrow[{(-2)R_2 + R_3}]{(-1)R_2 + R_1} \begin{bmatrix} 1 & 0 & 1 & | & 4 \\ 0 & 1 & 3 & | & 9 \\ 0 & 0 & 0 & | & 0 \end{bmatrix}$$

Thus $x = 4 - r$, $y = 9 - 3r$, and $z = r$, where $r = 0, 1, 2, 3$.
The four possible combinations are

Combination	x	y	z
1	4	9	0
2	3	6	1
3	2	3	2
4	1	0	3

b. Computing the cost of each combination, we find that they are $83, 77, 71$, and 65 cents, respectively.
Thus combination 4, namely $x = 1$, $y = 0$, $z = 3$, minimizes weekly cost.

45. $\begin{bmatrix} 215 & 87 \\ 89 & 141 \end{bmatrix}$

47. $\mathbf{A} = \begin{bmatrix} \frac{10}{34} & \frac{20}{39} \\ \frac{15}{34} & \frac{14}{39} \end{bmatrix}$

$\mathbf{C} = \begin{bmatrix} 8 \\ 8 \end{bmatrix}$

$\mathbf{X} = (\mathbf{I} - \mathbf{A})^{-1}\mathbf{C} = \begin{bmatrix} 40.8 \\ 40.56 \end{bmatrix}$

Mathematical Snapshot Chapter 6

1. $A = \begin{bmatrix} 20 & 40 & 30 & 10 \\ 30 & 0 & 10 & 10 \\ 10 & 0 & 30 & 50 \end{bmatrix}$

$T = \begin{bmatrix} 7 \\ 10 \\ 7 \\ 5 \end{bmatrix}$

$C = \begin{bmatrix} 9 \\ 8 \\ 10 \end{bmatrix}$

$$C^T(AT) = C^T \left\{ \begin{bmatrix} 20 & 40 & 30 & 10 \\ 30 & 0 & 10 & 10 \\ 10 & 0 & 30 & 50 \end{bmatrix} \begin{bmatrix} 7 \\ 10 \\ 7 \\ 5 \end{bmatrix} \right\} = C^T \begin{bmatrix} 800 \\ 330 \\ 530 \end{bmatrix}$$

$$= \begin{bmatrix} 9 & 8 & 10 \end{bmatrix} \begin{bmatrix} 800 \\ 330 \\ 530 \end{bmatrix} = [15,140]$$

The cost is $151.40.
To the linear system, add $x_1 + x_2 + x_3 + x_4 = 52$.

3. It is not possible. Guest 3 and 4 each cost the lodge $70 per day in insulin. Therefore, even if the total number of days for all four guests is known, in general there will be different distributions of days for guests 3 and 4 that lead to the same total cost.

Chapter 7

Principles in Practice 7.1

1. Let x = the number of type A magnets and y = the number of type B magnets.
   The cost for producing x type A magnets and y type B magnets is $50 + 0.90x + 0.70y$. The revenue for selling x type A magnets and y type B magnets is $2.00x + 1.50y$.
   Revenue is greater than cost when
   $2x + 1.5y > 50 + 0.9x + 0.7y$.
   $0.8y > -1.1x + 50$
   $y > -1.375x + 62.5$
   Sketch the dashed line $y = -1.375x + 62.5$ and shade the half plane above the line. In order to make a profit, the number of magnets of types A and B must correspond to an ordered pair in the shaded region. Also, to take reality into account, both x and y must be positive (negative numbers of magnets are not feasible).

2. Since negative numbers of cameras cannot be sold, $x \geq 0$ and $y \geq 0$. Selling at least 50 cameras per week corresponds to $x + y \geq 50$. Selling twice as many of type I as of type II corresponds to $x \geq 2y$. The system of inequalities is
   $$\begin{cases} x + y \geq 50, \\ \quad x \geq 2y, \\ \quad x \geq 0, \\ \quad y \geq 0. \end{cases}$$
   The region consists of points on or above the x-axis and on or to the right of the y-axis. In addition, the points must be on or above the line $x + y = 50$ and on or below the line $x = 2y$.

Exercise 7.1

1.

3.

5.

7.

9.

11.

13.

15.

17.

19.

21.

23.

25. $5x + 3y \le 15$

27. Let x be the amount purchased from supplier A, and y the amount purchased from B. The system of inequalities is
$x + y \le 100,$
$x \ge 0,$
$y \ge 0.$

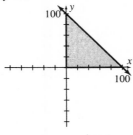

29. Since negative numbers of chairs cannot be produced, $x \ge 0$ and $y \ge 0$. The inequality for assembly time is $3x + 2y \le 240$. The inequality for painting time is $\dfrac{1}{2}x + y \le 80$.

The system of inequalities is
$$\begin{cases} 3x + 2y \le 240, \\ \dfrac{1}{2}x + y \le 80, \\ \quad x \ge 0, \\ \quad y \ge 0. \end{cases}$$
The region consists of points on or above the x-axis and on or to the right of the y-axis. In addition, the points must be on or below the line $3x + 2y = 240$ and on or below the line $\dfrac{1}{2}x + y = 80$ (or, equivalently $x + 2y = 160$).

Exercise 7.2

1. The feasible region appears below. The corner points are (0, 0), (60, 0) and (40, 20). Using the method of evaluating the objective function at each corner point, we have $P(0, 0) = 0$, $P(60, 0) = 600$, and $P(40, 20) = 640$. Thus P has a maximum value of 640 at (40, 20) That is, P has a maximum value of 640 when $x = 40$ and $y = 20$. [Alternatively, the indicated dashed line is the member of the family of lines
$$P = 10x + 12\,y \left(\text{or } y = -\frac{5}{6}x + \frac{P}{12} \right) \text{ that}$$
gives a maximum value of P and that has at

least one point in common with the feasible region. It is clear that the line contains corner point (40, 20).]

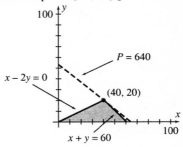

3. The feasible region appears below. The corner points are (2, 3), (0, 5), (0, 7) and $\left(\dfrac{10}{3}, 7 \right)$. Evaluating Z at each point, we find that Z has a maximum value of -10 when $x = 2$ and $y = 3$.

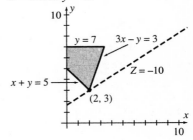

5. The feasible region is empty, so there is no optimum solution.

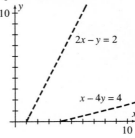

7. The feasible region is a line segment. The corner points are $(0, 1)$ and $(4, 5)$. Z has a minimum value of 3 when $x = 0$ and $y = 1$.

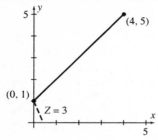

9. The feasible region is unbounded with 4 corner points. The member (see dashed line) of the family of lines $C = 2x + y$ which gives a minimum value of C, subject to the constraints, intersects the feasible region at corner point $\left(\frac{3}{5}, \frac{6}{5}\right)$ where $C = 2.4$. Thus C has a minimum value of 2.4 when $x = \frac{3}{5}$ and $y = \frac{6}{5}$. [Note: Here we chose the member of the family $y = -2x + C$ whose y-intercept was *closest* to the origin and which had at least one point in common with the feasible region.]

11. The feasible region is unbounded with 2 corner points. The family of lines given by $Z = 10x + 2y$ has members (see dashed lines for two sample members) that have arbitrarily large values of Z and that also intersect the feasible region. Thus no optimum solution exists.

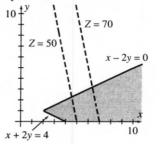

13. Let x and y be the numbers of widgets and wadgits made per week, respectively. Then we are to maximize $P = 4x + 6y$ subject to

$$\begin{cases} x \geq 0, \\ y \geq 0, \\ 2x + y \leq 70 \text{ (for machine A)}, \\ x + y \leq 40 \text{ (for machine B)}, \\ x + 3y \leq 90 \text{ (for finishing)}. \end{cases}$$

The feasible region appears below. The corner points are $(0, 0)$, $(0, 30)$, $(15, 25)$, $(30, 10)$ and $(35, 0)$. By evaluating P at each corner point, we find that P is maximized at corner point $(15, 25)$, where its value is 210. Thus 15 widgets and 25 wadgets should be made each week to give a maximum profit of \$210.

15. Let x and y be the numbers of units of Food A and Food B, respectively, that are purchased. Then we are to minimize $C = 1.20x + 0.80y$, where

$$\begin{cases} x \geq 0, \\ y \geq 0, \\ 2x + 2y \geq 16 \text{ (for carbohydrates),} \\ 4x + y \geq 20 \text{ (for protein).} \end{cases}$$

The feasible region is unbounded. The corner points are $(8, 0)$, $(4, 4)$ and $(0, 20)$. C is minimized at corner point $(4, 4)$ where $C = 8$ (see the minimum cost line). Thus 4 units of Food A and 4 units of Food B gives a minimum cost of \$8.

17. Let x and y be the numbers of tons of ores I and II, respectively, that are processed. Then we are to minimize $C = 50x + 60y$, where

$$\begin{cases} x \geq 0, \\ y \geq 0, \\ 100x + 200y \geq 3000 \text{ (for mineral A),} \\ 200x + 50y \geq 2500 \text{ (for mineral B).} \end{cases}$$

The feasible region is unbounded with 3 corner points. C is minimized at the corner point $(10, 10)$ where $C = 1100$ (see the minimum cost line). Thus 10 tons of ore I and 10 tons of ore II give a minimum cost of \$1100.

19. Let x and y be the number of chambers of type A and B, respectively. Then we are to minimize $C = 600{,}000x + 300{,}000y$, where

$$\begin{cases} x \geq 4, \\ y \geq 4, \\ 10x + 4y \geq 100 \text{ (for polymer P}_1\text{),} \\ 20x + 30y \geq 420 \text{ (for polymer P}_2\text{).} \end{cases}$$

The feasible region is unbounded with 3 corner points. Evaluating C at each corner point, we find C is minimized at corner point $(6, 10)$ where $C = 6{,}600{,}000$. Thus the solution is 6 chambers of type A and 10 chambers of type B.

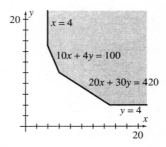

21. a. A builds x km of highway and y km of expressway, so B builds $(200 - x)$ km of highway and $(100 - y)$ km of expressway. Thus
$$D = 1x + 6y + 2(200 - x) + 5(100 - y)$$
$$= 900 - x + y.$$

b. The first constraint is company A's construction limit. The second constraint is company B's construction limit, which arises as follows:
$$\begin{aligned} (200 - x) + (100 - y) &\leq 150, \\ 300 - x - y &\leq 150, \\ -x - y &\leq -150, \\ x + y &\geq 150. \end{aligned}$$

The third constraint is the minimum contract for A. The fourth constraint is the minimum contract for B, which arises as follows:
$$\begin{aligned} 1(200 - x) + 5(100 - y) &\geq 250, \\ 700 - x - 5y &\geq 250, \\ -x - 5y &\geq -450, \\ x + 5y &\leq 450. \end{aligned}$$

c. The feasible region (see below) is
bounded. The corner points are $(75, 75)$,
$(125, 25)$, $(187.5, 12.5)$ and
$(137.5, 62.5)$. Evaluating D at each
corner point, we find that D is
maximized at point $(75, 75)$, where
$D = 900$. That is, D is maximized if
$x = y = 75$.

23. $Z = 15.54$ when $x = 2.56$, $y = 6.74$

25. $Z = -75.98$ when $x = 9.48$, $y = 16.67$

Principles in Practice 7.3

1. Using the hint, the cost of shipping the
TV sets is
$Z = 18x + 24(25 - x) + 9y + 15(30 - y)$
$= 1050 - 6x - 6y$.
Since negative numbers of TV sets cannot
be shipped, $x \geq 0$, $y \geq 0$, $25 - x \geq 0$, and
$30 - y \geq 0$. Since warehouse C has only
45 TV sets, $x + y \leq 45$. Similarly, since
warehouse D has only 40 TV sets,
$25 - x + 30 - y \leq 45$ or $x + y \geq 10$.
We need to minimize $Z = 1050 - 6x - 6y$
subject to the constraints
$x + y \leq 45$,
$x + y \geq 10$,
$x \leq 25$,
$y \leq 30$,
$x \geq 0$, $y \geq 0$.

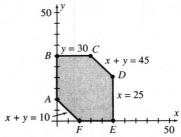

The feasible region shown has corners
$A = (0, 10)$, $B = (0, 30)$, $C = (15, 30)$,
$D = (25, 20)$, $E = (25, 0)$, and $F = (10, 0)$.
Evaluating the cost function at the corners
gives
$Z(A) = 1050 - 6(0) - 6(10) = 990$
$Z(B) = 1050 - 6(0) - 6(30) = 870$
$Z(C) = 1050 - 6(15) - 6(30) = 780$
$Z(D) = 1050 - 6(25) - 6(20) = 780$
$Z(E) = 1050 - 6(25) - 6(0) = 900$
$Z(F) = 1050 - 6(10) - 6(0) = 990$
The minimum value of Z is 780 which
occurs at all points on the line segment
joining C and D. This is
$x = (1 - t)(15) + t(25) = 15 + 10t$ and
$y = (1 - t)(30) + t(20) = 30 - 10t$ for
$0 \leq t \leq 1$. Thus, ship $10t + 15$ TV sets from
C to A, $-10t + 30$ TV sets from C to B,
$25 - (10t + 15) = -10t + 10$ TV sets from
D to A, and $30 - (-10t + 30) = 10t$ TV sets
from D to B, for $0 \leq t \leq 1$. The minimum
cost is $\$780$.

Exercise 7.3

1. The feasible region is unbounded. Z is minimized at corner points $(2, 3)$ and $(5, 2)$, where its value is 33. Z is also minimized at all points on the line segment joining $(2, 3)$ and $(5, 2)$, so the solution is $Z = 33$ when
$x = (1 - t)(2) + 5t = 2 + 3t$
$y = (1 - t)(3) + 2t = 3 - t$ and $0 \le t \le 1$.

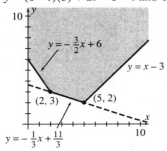

3. The feasible region appears below. The corner points are $(0, 0)$, $(0, 4)$, $(3, 2)$ and $(4, 0)$. Z is maximized at $(3, 2)$ and $(4, 0)$, where its value is 72. Thus Z is also maximized at all points on the line segment joining $(3, 2)$ and $(4, 0)$. The solution is $Z = 72$ when $x = (1 - t)(3) + 4t = 3 + t$
$y = (1 - t)(2) + 0t = 2 - 2t$ and $0 \le t \le 1$.

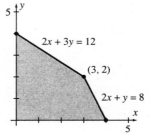

Principles in Practice 7.4

In these problems, the pivot entry is underlined.

1. Let x_1, x_2, and x_3 be the numbers of Type 1, Type 2, and Type 3 gadgets, respectively, that the company produces. The situation is to maximize the profit $P = 150x_1 + 250x_2 + 200x_3$, subject to the constraints
$300x_1 + 300x_2 + 400x_3 \le 30,000$,
$15x_1 + 15x_2 + 10x_3 \le 1200$,
$2x_1 + 2x_2 + 3x_3 \le 180$, and
x_1, x_2, $x_3 \ge 0$.
The constraint inequalities can be simplified by dividing by the greatest common factor of the numbers involved. Thus, we will use
$3x_1 + 3x_2 + 4x_3 \le 300$,
$3x_1 + 3x_2 + 2x_3 \le 240$,
$2x_1 + 2x_2 + 3x_3 \le 180$, and
x_1, x_2, $x_3 \ge 0$.

$$
\begin{array}{c}
\begin{array}{cccccccc}
& x_1 & x_2 & x_3 & s_1 & s_2 & s_3 & P & b
\end{array} \\
\begin{array}{c}
s_1 \\
s_2 \\
s_3 \\
P
\end{array}
\left[
\begin{array}{ccccccc|c}
3 & 3 & 4 & 1 & 0 & 0 & 0 & 300 \\
3 & \underline{3} & 2 & 0 & 1 & 0 & 0 & 240 \\
2 & 2 & 3 & 0 & 0 & 1 & 0 & 180 \\
\hline
-150 & -250 & -200 & 0 & 0 & 0 & 1 & 0
\end{array}
\right]
\end{array}
$$

$$\begin{array}{c} \\ s_1 \\ x_2 \\ s_3 \\ P \end{array} \begin{array}{cccccccc} x_1 & x_2 & x_3 & s_1 & s_2 & s_3 & P & b \\ \left[\begin{array}{ccccccc|c} 0 & 0 & 2 & 1 & -1 & 0 & 0 & 60 \\ 1 & 1 & \frac{2}{3} & 0 & \frac{1}{3} & 0 & 0 & 80 \\ 0 & 0 & \frac{5}{3} & 0 & -\frac{2}{3} & 1 & 0 & 20 \\ \hline 100 & 0 & -\frac{100}{3} & 0 & \frac{250}{3} & 0 & 1 & 20,000 \end{array}\right] \end{array}$$

$$\begin{array}{c} \\ s_1 \\ x_2 \\ x_3 \\ P \end{array} \begin{array}{cccccccc} x_1 & x_2 & x_3 & s_1 & s_2 & s_3 & P & b \\ \left[\begin{array}{ccccccc|c} 0 & 0 & 0 & 1 & -\frac{1}{5} & -\frac{6}{5} & 0 & 36 \\ 1 & 1 & 0 & 0 & \frac{3}{5} & -\frac{2}{5} & 0 & 72 \\ 0 & 0 & 1 & 0 & -\frac{2}{5} & \frac{3}{5} & 0 & 12 \\ \hline 100 & 0 & 0 & 0 & 70 & 20 & 1 & 20,400 \end{array}\right] \end{array}$$

The maximum value of P is 20,400 when $x_1 = 0$, $x_2 = 72$, and $x_3 = 12$. The maximum profit is $20,400 when 72 Type 2 gadgets and 12 Type 3 gadgets are produced and sold.

Exercise 7.4

In these problems, the pivot entry is underlined.

1.

$$\begin{array}{c} \\ s_1 \\ s_2 \\ Z \end{array} \begin{array}{cccccc} x_1 & x_2 & s_1 & s_2 & Z \\ \left[\begin{array}{ccccc|c} 2 & 1 & 1 & 0 & 0 & 8 \\ 2 & \underline{3} & 0 & 1 & 0 & 12 \\ \hline -1 & -2 & 0 & 0 & 1 & 0 \end{array}\right] \begin{array}{c} 8 \\ 4 \\ {} \end{array} \end{array}$$

$$\begin{array}{c} \\ s_1 \\ x_2 \\ Z \end{array} \begin{array}{cccccc} x_1 & x_2 & s_1 & s_2 & Z \\ \left[\begin{array}{ccccc|c} \frac{4}{3} & 0 & 1 & -\frac{1}{3} & 0 & 4 \\ \frac{2}{3} & 1 & 0 & \frac{1}{3} & 0 & 4 \\ \hline \frac{1}{3} & 0 & 0 & \frac{2}{3} & 1 & 8 \end{array}\right] \end{array}$$

The solution is $Z = 8$ when $x_1 = 0$, $x_2 = 4$.

3.

$$\begin{array}{c} \\ s_1 \\ s_2 \\ Z \end{array} \begin{array}{cccccc} x_1 & x_2 & s_1 & s_2 & Z \\ \left[\begin{array}{ccccc|c} 1 & 1 & 1 & 0 & 0 & 6 \\ -1 & \underline{1} & 0 & 1 & 0 & 4 \\ \hline 1 & -3 & 0 & 0 & 1 & 0 \end{array}\right] \begin{array}{c} 6 \\ 4 \\ {} \end{array} \end{array}$$

$$\begin{array}{c} \\ s_1 \\ x_2 \\ Z \end{array} \begin{array}{cccccc} x_1 & x_2 & s_1 & s_2 & Z \\ \left[\begin{array}{ccccc|c} \underline{2} & 0 & 1 & -1 & 0 & 2 \\ -1 & 1 & 0 & 1 & 0 & 4 \\ \hline -2 & 0 & 0 & 3 & 1 & 12 \end{array}\right] \begin{array}{c} 1 \\ {} \\ {} \end{array} \end{array}$$

$$\begin{array}{c} \\ x_1 \\ x_2 \\ Z \end{array} \begin{array}{cccccc} x_1 & x_2 & s_1 & s_2 & Z \\ \left[\begin{array}{ccccc|c} 1 & 0 & \frac{1}{2} & -\frac{1}{2} & 0 & 1 \\ 0 & 1 & \frac{1}{2} & \frac{1}{2} & 0 & 5 \\ \hline 0 & 0 & 1 & 2 & 1 & 14 \end{array}\right] \end{array}$$

The solution is $Z = 14$ when $x_1 = 1$, $x_2 = 5$.

5.

	x_1	x_2	s_1	s_2	s_3	Z		
s_1	1	−1	1	0	0	0	1	1
s_2	1	2	0	1	0	0	8	8
s_3	1	1	0	0	1	0	5	5
Z	−8	−2	0	0	0	1	0	

	x_1	x_2	s_1	s_2	s_3	Z		
x_1	1	−1	1	0	0	0	1	
s_2	0	3	−1	1	0	0	7	$\frac{7}{3}$
s_3	0	2	−1	0	1	0	4	2
Z	0	−10	8	0	0	1	8	

	x_1	x_2	s_1	s_2	s_3	Z	
x_1	1	0	$\frac{1}{2}$	0	$\frac{1}{2}$	0	3
s_2	0	0	$\frac{1}{2}$	1	$-\frac{3}{2}$	0	1
x_2	0	1	$-\frac{1}{2}$	0	$\frac{1}{2}$	0	2
Z	0	0	3	0	5	1	28

The solution is $Z = 28$ when $x_1 = 3$, $x_2 = 2$.

7.

	x_1	x_2	x_3	s_1	s_2	Z		
s_1	1	2	0	1	0	0	10	5
s_2	2	2	1	0	1	0	10	5
Z	−3	−4	$-\frac{3}{2}$	0	0	1	0	

choosing s_2 as departing variable

	x_1	x_2	x_3	s_1	s_2	Z	
s_1	−1	0	−1	1	0	0	4
x_2	1	1	$\frac{1}{2}$	0	$\frac{1}{2}$	0	5
Z	1	0	$\frac{1}{2}$	0	2	1	20

The solution is $Z = 20$ when
$x_1 = 0$, $x_2 = 5$, $x_3 = 0$

9. To obtain a standard linear programming problem, we write the second constraint as $-x_1 + 2x_2 + x_3 \leq 2$.

	x_1	x_2	x_3	s_1	s_2	Z		
s_1	1	1	0	1	0	0	1	1
s_2	−1	2	1	0	1	0	2	
Z	−2	−1	1	0	0	1	0	

	x_1	x_2	x_3	s_1	s_2	Z	
x_1	1	1	0	1	0	0	1
s_2	0	3	1	1	1	0	3
Z	0	1	1	2	0	1	2

The solution is $Z = 2$ when
$x_1 = 1$, $x_2 = 0$, $x_3 = 0$.

11.

	x_1	x_2	s_1	s_2	s_3	s_4	Z		
s_1	1	−1	1	0	0	0	0	4	4
s_2	−1	1	0	1	0	0	0	4	
s_3	8	5	0	0	1	0	0	40	5
s_4	2	1	0	0	0	1	0	6	3
Z	−1	−1	0	0	0	0	1	0	

choosing x_1 as departing variable

	x_1	x_2	s_1	s_2	s_3	s_4	Z		
s_1	0	$-\frac{3}{2}$	1	0	0	$-\frac{1}{2}$	0	1	
s_2	0	$\frac{3}{2}$	0	1	0	$\frac{1}{2}$	0	7	$\frac{14}{3}$
s_3	0	1	0	0	1	−4	0	16	16
x_1	1	$\frac{1}{2}$	0	0	0	$\frac{1}{2}$	0	3	6
Z	0	$-\frac{1}{2}$	0	0	0	$\frac{1}{2}$	1	3	

	x_1	x_2	s_1	s_2	s_3	s_4	Z	
s_1	0	0	1	1	0	0	0	8
x_2	0	1	0	$\frac{2}{3}$	0	$\frac{1}{3}$	0	$\frac{14}{3}$
s_3	0	0	0	$-\frac{2}{3}$	1	$-\frac{13}{3}$	0	$\frac{34}{3}$
x_1	1	0	0	$-\frac{1}{3}$	0	$\frac{1}{3}$	0	$\frac{2}{3}$
Z	0	0	0	$\frac{1}{3}$	0	$\frac{2}{3}$	1	$\frac{16}{3}$

Thus the maximum value of Z is $\dfrac{16}{3}$, when

$x_1 = \dfrac{2}{3}$, $x_2 = \dfrac{14}{3}$. If we choose x_2 as the entering variable, then we have:

	x_1	x_2	s_1	s_2	s_3	s_4	Z		
s_1	1	−1	1	0	0	0	0	4	
s_2	−1	1	0	1	0	0	0	4	4
s_3	8	5	0	0	1	0	0	40	8
s_4	2	1	0	0	0	1	0	6	6
Z	−1	−1	0	0	0	0	1	0	

	x_1	x_2	s_1	s_2	s_3	s_4	Z		
s_1	0	0	1	1	0	0	0	8	
x_2	−1	1	0	1	0	0	0	4	
s_3	13	0	0	−5	1	0	0	20	$\frac{20}{13}$
s_4	3	0	0	−1	0	1	0	2	$\frac{2}{3}$
Z	−2	0	0	1	0	0	1	4	

	x_1	x_2	s_1	s_2	s_3	s_4	Z	
s_1	0	0	1	1	0	0	0	8
x_2	0	1	0	$\frac{2}{3}$	0	$\frac{1}{3}$	0	$\frac{14}{3}$
s_3	0	0	0	$-\frac{2}{3}$	1	$-\frac{13}{3}$	0	$\frac{34}{3}$
x_1	1	0	0	$-\frac{1}{3}$	0	$\frac{1}{3}$	0	$\frac{2}{3}$
Z	0	0	0	$\frac{1}{3}$	0	$\frac{2}{3}$	1	$\frac{16}{3}$

The solution is $Z = \dfrac{16}{3}$ when

$x_1 = \dfrac{2}{3}$, $x_2 = \dfrac{14}{3}$.

15.

	x_1	x_2	x_3	x_4	s_1	s_2	s_3	s_4	Z		
s_1	1	−2	0	0	1	0	0	0	0	2	
s_2	1	1	0	0	0	1	0	0	0	5	
s_3	0	0	1	1	0	0	1	0	0	4	4
s_4	0	0	1	−2	0	0	0	1	0	7	7
Z	−60	0	−90	0	0	0	0	0	1	0	

13. To obtain a standard linear programming problem, we write the second constraint as $-x_1 - x_2 + x_3 \le 2$ and the third constraint as $x_1 - x_2 - x_3 \le 1$.

	x_1	x_2	x_3	s_1	s_2	s_3	W		
s_1	4	3	−1	1	0	0	0	1	
s_2	−1	−1	1	0	1	0	0	2	2
s_3	1	−1	−1	0	0	1	0	1	
W	−1	12	−4	0	0	0	1	0	

	x_1	x_2	x_3	s_1	s_2	s_3	W		
s_1	3	2	0	1	1	0	0	3	1
x_3	−1	−1	1	0	1	0	0	2	
s_3	0	−2	0	0	1	1	0	3	
W	−5	8	0	0	4	0	1	8	

	x_1	x_2	x_3	s_1	s_2	s_3	W	
x_1	1	$\frac{2}{3}$	0	$\frac{1}{3}$	$\frac{1}{3}$	0	0	1
x_3	0	$-\frac{1}{3}$	1	$\frac{1}{3}$	$\frac{4}{3}$	0	0	3
s_3	0	−2	0	0	1	1	0	3
W	0	$\frac{34}{3}$	0	$\frac{5}{3}$	$\frac{17}{3}$	0	1	13

The solution is $W = 13$ when $x_1 = 1$, $x_2 = 0$, $x_3 = 3$.

$$
\begin{array}{c}
\begin{array}{ccccccccc}
x_1 & x_2 & x_3 & x_4 & s_1 & s_2 & s_3 & s_4 & Z
\end{array}\\
\begin{array}{c}
s_1\\ s_2\\ x_3\\ s_4\\ Z
\end{array}
\left[
\begin{array}{ccccccccc|cc}
1 & -2 & 0 & 0 & 1 & 0 & 0 & 0 & 0 & 2 & 2\\
1 & 1 & 0 & 0 & 0 & 1 & 0 & 0 & 0 & 5 & 5\\
0 & 0 & 1 & 1 & 0 & 0 & 1 & 0 & 0 & 4 & \\
0 & 0 & 0 & -3 & 0 & 0 & -1 & 1 & 0 & 3 & \\
\hline
-60 & 0 & 0 & 90 & 0 & 0 & 90 & 0 & 1 & 360 &
\end{array}
\right]
\end{array}
$$

$$
\begin{array}{c}
\begin{array}{ccccccccc}
x_1 & x_2 & x_3 & x_4 & s_1 & s_2 & s_3 & s_4 & Z
\end{array}\\
\begin{array}{c}
x_1\\ s_2\\ x_3\\ s_4\\ Z
\end{array}
\left[
\begin{array}{ccccccccc|cc}
1 & -2 & 0 & 0 & 1 & 0 & 0 & 0 & 0 & 2 & \\
0 & 3 & 0 & 0 & -1 & 1 & 0 & 0 & 0 & 3 & 1\\
0 & 0 & 1 & 1 & 0 & 0 & 1 & 0 & 0 & 4 & \\
0 & 0 & 0 & -3 & 0 & 0 & -1 & 1 & 0 & 3 & \\
\hline
0 & -120 & 0 & 90 & 60 & 0 & 90 & 0 & 1 & 480 &
\end{array}
\right]
\end{array}
$$

$$
\begin{array}{c}
\begin{array}{ccccccccc}
x_1 & x_2 & x_3 & x_4 & s_1 & s_2 & s_3 & s_4 & Z
\end{array}\\
\begin{array}{c}
x_1\\ x_2\\ x_3\\ s_4\\ Z
\end{array}
\left[
\begin{array}{ccccccccc|c}
1 & 0 & 0 & 0 & \frac{1}{3} & \frac{2}{3} & 0 & 0 & 0 & 4\\
0 & 1 & 0 & 0 & -\frac{1}{3} & \frac{1}{3} & 0 & 0 & 0 & 1\\
0 & 0 & 1 & 1 & 0 & 0 & 1 & 0 & 0 & 4\\
0 & 0 & 0 & -3 & 0 & 0 & -1 & 1 & 0 & 3\\
\hline
0 & 0 & 0 & 90 & 20 & 40 & 90 & 0 & 1 & 600
\end{array}
\right]
\end{array}
$$

The solution is $Z = 600$ for $x_1 = 4$, $x_2 = 1$, $x_3 = 4$, $x_4 = 0$.

17. Let x_1 and x_2 denote the numbers of boxes transported from A and B, respectively. The revenue received is $R = 0.75x_1 + 0.50x_2$. We want to maximize R subject to

$2x_1 + x_2 \le 2400$ (volume),

$3x_1 + 5x_2 \le 36,800$ (weight),

$x_1, x_2 \ge 0$.

$$
\begin{array}{c}
\begin{array}{ccccc}
x_1 & x_2 & s_1 & s_2 & R
\end{array}\\
\begin{array}{c}
s_1\\ s_2\\ R
\end{array}
\left[
\begin{array}{ccccc|cc}
2 & 1 & 1 & 0 & 0 & 2400 & 1200\\
3 & 5 & 0 & 1 & 0 & 36,800 & 12,266\frac{2}{3}\\
\hline
-\frac{3}{4} & -\frac{1}{2} & 0 & 0 & 1 & 0 &
\end{array}
\right]
\end{array}
$$

$$
\begin{array}{c}
\begin{array}{ccccc}
x_1 & x_2 & s_1 & s_2 & R
\end{array}\\
\begin{array}{c}
x_1\\ s_2\\ R
\end{array}
\left[
\begin{array}{ccccc|cc}
1 & \frac{1}{2} & \frac{1}{2} & 0 & 0 & 1200 & 2400\\
0 & \frac{7}{2} & -\frac{3}{2} & 1 & 0 & 33,200 & 9485\frac{5}{7}\\
\hline
0 & -\frac{1}{8} & \frac{3}{8} & 0 & 1 & 900 &
\end{array}
\right]
\end{array}
$$

$$
\begin{array}{c}
\begin{array}{ccccc}
x_1 & x_2 & s_1 & s_2 & R
\end{array}\\
\begin{array}{c}
x_2\\ s_2\\ {}
\end{array}
\left[
\begin{array}{ccccc|c}
2 & 1 & 1 & 0 & 0 & 2400\\
-7 & 0 & -5 & 1 & 0 & 24,800\\
\hline
\frac{1}{4} & 0 & \frac{1}{2} & 0 & 1 & 1200
\end{array}
\right]
\end{array}
$$

Thus 0 boxes from A and 2400 from B give a maximum revenue of $1200.

19. Let x_1, x_2, and x_3 denote the numbers of chairs, rockers, and chaise lounges produced, respectively. We want to maximize $R = 21x_1 + 24x_2 + 36x_3$ subject to

$$x_1 + x_2 + x_3 \le 400,$$
$$x_1 + x_2 + 2x_3 \le 500,$$
$$2x_1 + 3x_2 + 5x_3 \le 1450,$$
$$x_1, \ x_2, \ x_3 \ge 0.$$

	x_1	x_2	x_3	s_1	s_2	s_3	R		
s_1	1	1	1	1	0	0	0	400	400
s_2	1	1	$\underline{2}$	0	1	0	0	500	250
s_3	2	3	5	0	0	1	0	1450	290
R	−21	−24	−36	0	0	0	1	0	

	x_1	x_2	x_3	s_1	s_2	s_3	R		
s_1	$\frac{1}{2}$	$\frac{1}{2}$	0	1	$-\frac{1}{2}$	0	0	150	300
x_3	$\frac{1}{2}$	$\frac{1}{2}$	1	0	$\frac{1}{2}$	0	0	250	500
s_3	$-\frac{1}{2}$	$\frac{1}{2}$	0	0	$-\frac{5}{2}$	1	0	200	400
R	−3	−6	0	0	18	0	1	9000	

	x_1	x_2	x_3	s_1	s_2	s_3	R	
x_2	1	1	0	2	−1	0	0	300
x_3	0	0	1	−1	1	0	0	100
s_3	−1	0	0	−1	−2	1	0	50
R	3	0	0	12	12	0	1	10,800

The production of 0 chairs, 300 rockers, and 100 chaise lounges gives the maximum revenue of $10,800.

Principles in Practice 7.5

1. Let x_1, x_2, x_3 be the numbers of device 1, device 2, and device 3, respectively, that the company produces. The situation is to maximize the profit $P = 50x_1 + 50x_2 + 50x_3$ subject to the constraints

$$5.5x_1 + 5.5x_2 + 6.5x_3 \le 190,$$
$$3.5x_1 + 6.5x_2 + 7.5x_3 \le 180,$$
$$4.5x_1 + 6.0x_2 + 6.5x_3 \le 165,$$

and x_1, x_2, $x_3 \ge 0$.

The matrices are shown rounded to 2 decimal places, although the exact values are used in the row operations.

Since the indicators are equal, we choose the first column as the pivot column.

	x_1	x_2	x_3	s_1	s_2	s_3	P	b
s_1	$\underline{5.5}$	5.5	6.5	1	0	0	0	190
s_2	3.5	6.5	7.5	0	1	0	0	180
s_3	4.5	6.0	6.5	0	0	1	0	165
P	−50	−50	−50	0	0	0	1	0

	x_1	x_2	x_2	s_1	s_2	s_3	P	b
x_1	1	1	1.18	0.18	0	0	0	34.55
s_2	0	3	3.36	−0.64	1	0	0	59.09
s_3	0	<u>1.50</u>	1.18	−0.82	0	1	0	9.55
P	0	0	9.09	9.09	0	0	1	1727.27

An optimum solution is $x_1 = 35$, $x_2 = 0$, $x_3 = 0$, and $P = 1727$. However, x_2 is a nonbasic variable and its indicator is 0, so we check for multiple solutions. Treating x_2 as an entering variable, the following tableau is obtained:

	x_1	x_2	x_3	s_1	s_2	s_3	P	b
x_1	1	0	0.39	0.73	0	−0.67	0	28.18
s_2	0	0	1.00	1.00	1	−2.00	0	40.00
x_2	0	1	0.79	−0.55	0	0.67	0	6.36
P	0	0	9.09	9.09	0	0	1	1727.27

Another optimum solution is $x_1 = 28$, $x_2 = 6$, $x_3 = 0$, and $P = 1727$. Thus, the optimum solution is for the company to produce $(1 − t)35 + 28t = 35 − 7t$ of device 1, $(1 − t)0 + 6t = 6t$ of device 2, and none of device 3, for $0 \le t \le 1$.

Exercise 7.5

1. Yes; for the tableau, x_2 is the entering variable and the quotients $\dfrac{6}{2}$ and $\dfrac{3}{1}$ tie for being the smallest.

3.

	x_1	x_2	s_1	s_2	s_3	Z	
s_1	4	−3	1	0	0	0	4
s_2	3	−1	0	1	0	0	6
s_3	5	0	0	0	1	0	8
Z	−2	−7	0	0	0	1	0

The entering variable is x_2. Since no quotients exist, the problem has an unbounded solution. Thus, no optimum solution (unbounded).

5.

	x_1	x_2	s_1	s_2	s_3	Z		
s_1	<u>1</u>	−1	1	0	0	0	4	4
s_2	−1	1	0	1	0	0	4	
s_3	1	1	0	0	1	0	6	6
Z	−3	3	0	0	0	1	0	

	x_1	x_2	s_1	s_2	s_3	Z		
x_1	1	−1	1	0	0	0	4	
s_2	0	0	1	1	0	0	8	
s_3	0	2	−1	0	1	0	2	1
Z	0	0	3	0	0	1	12	

The maximum value of Z is 12, when $x_1 = 4$, $x_2 = 0$. Since x_2 is nonbasic for the last tableau and its indicator is 0, there may be multiple optimum solutions. Treating x_2 as an entering variable and continuing, we have

	x_1	x_2	s_1	s_2	s_3	Z	
x_1	1	0	$\frac{1}{2}$	0	$\frac{1}{2}$	0	5
s_2	0	0	1	1	0	0	8
x_2	0	1	$-\frac{1}{2}$	0	$\frac{1}{2}$	0	1
Z	0	0	3	0	0	1	12

Here $Z = 12$ when $x_1 = 5$, $x_2 = 1$. Thus multiple optimum solutions exist. Hence Z is maximum when $x_1 = (1 − t)(4) + 5t = 4 + t$, $x_2 = (1 − t)(0) + (1)t = t$, and $0 \le t \le 1$. For the last tableau, s_3 is nonbasic and its indicator is 0. If we continue the process for determining other optimum solutions, we return to the second tableau.

7.

	x_1	x_2	x_3	s_1	s_2	s_3	Z		
s_1	9	3	-2	1	0	0	0	5	$\frac{5}{3}$
s_2	4	2	-1	0	1	0	0	2	1
s_3	1	-4	1	0	0	1	0	3	
Z	-5	-6	-1	0	0	0	1	0	

	x_1	x_2	x_3	s_1	s_2	s_3	Z	
s_1	3	0	$-\frac{1}{2}$	1	$-\frac{3}{2}$	0	0	2
x_2	2	1	$-\frac{1}{2}$	0	$\frac{1}{2}$	0	0	1
s_3	9	0	-1	0	2	1	0	7
Z	7	0	-4	0	3	0	1	6

For the last tableau, x_3 is the entering variable. Since no quotients exist, the problem has an unbounded solution. Thus, no optimum solution (unbounded).

9. To obtain a standard linear programming problem, we write the second constraint as $4x_1 + x_2 \le 6$.

	x_1	x_2	x_3	s_1	s_2	Z		
s_1	2	1	1	1	0	0	7	$\frac{7}{2}$
s_2	4	1	0	0	1	0	6	$\frac{3}{2}$
Z	-6	-2	-1	0	0	1	0	

	x_1	x_2	x_3	s_1	s_2	Z		
s_1	0	$\frac{1}{2}$	1	1	$-\frac{1}{2}$	0	4	4
x_1	1	$\frac{1}{4}$	0	0	$\frac{1}{4}$	0	$\frac{3}{2}$	
Z	0	$-\frac{1}{2}$	-1	0	$\frac{3}{2}$	1	9	

	x_1	x_2	x_3	s_1	s_2	Z	
x_3	0	$\frac{1}{2}$	1	1	$-\frac{1}{2}$	0	4
x_1	1	$\frac{1}{4}$	0	0	$\frac{1}{4}$	0	$\frac{3}{2}$
Z	0	0	0	1	1	1	13

Entering the column labels shown: 4 with 8, $\frac{3}{2}$ with 6.

Z has a maximum value of 13 when $x_1 = \frac{3}{2}$, $x_2 = 0$, $x_3 = 4$. Since x_2 is nonbasic for the last tableau and its indicator is 0, there may be multiple optimum solutions. Treating x_2 as an entering variable, we have

	x_1	x_2	x_3	s_1	s_2	Z	
x_3	-2	0	1	1	-1	0	1
x_2	4	1	0	0	1	0	6
Z	0	0	0	1	1	1	13

Here $Z = 13$ when $x_1 = 0$, $x_2 = 6$, $x_3 = 1$. Thus multiple optimum solutions exist. Hence Z is maximum when

$$x_1 = (1-t)\left(\frac{3}{2}\right) + 0t = \frac{3}{2} - \frac{3}{2}t,$$

$$x_2 = (1-t)(0) + 6t = 6t,$$

$x_3 = (1-t)(4) + (1)t = 4 - 3t$, and $0 \le t \le 1$. For the last tableau, x_1 is nonbasic and its indicator is 0. If we continue the process for determining other optimum solutions, we return to the third tableau.

11. Let x_1, x_2, and x_3 denote the numbers of chairs, rockers, and chaise lounges produced, respectively. We want to maximize $R = 24x_1 + 32x_2 + 48x_3$ subject to $x_1 + x_2 + x_3 \le 400$, $x_1 + x_2 + 2x_3 \le 600$, $2x_1 + 3x_2 + 5x_3 \le 1500$, x_1, x_2, $x_3 \ge 0$.

	x_1	x_2	x_3	s_1	s_2	s_3	R		
s_1	1	1	1	1	0	0	0	400	400
s_2	1	1	2	0	1	0	0	600	300
s_3	2	3	5	0	0	1	0	1500	300
R	-24	-32	-48	0	0	0	1	0	

choosing s_3 as departing variable

	x_1	x_2	x_3	s_1	s_2	s_3	R		
s_1	$\frac{3}{5}$	$\frac{2}{5}$	0	1	0	$-\frac{1}{5}$	0	100	$\frac{500}{3}$
s_2	$\frac{1}{5}$	$-\frac{1}{5}$	0	0	1	$-\frac{2}{5}$	0	0	0
x_3	$\frac{2}{5}$	$\frac{3}{5}$	1	0	0	$\frac{1}{5}$	0	300	750
R	$-\frac{24}{5}$	$-\frac{16}{5}$	0	0	0	$\frac{48}{5}$	1	14,400	

	x_1	x_2	x_3	s_1	s_2	s_3	R		
s_1	0	1	0	1	-3	1	0	100	100
x_1	1	-1	0	0	5	-2	0	0	0
x_3	0	1	1	0	-2	1	0	300	300
R	0	-8	0	0	24	0	1	14,400	

	x_1	x_2	x_3	s_1	s_2	s_3	R		
x_2	0	1	0	1	-3	1	0	100	
x_1	1	0	0	1	2	-1	0	100	50
x_3	0	0	1	-1	1	0	0	200	200
R	0	0	0	8	0	8	1	15,200	

The maximum value of R is 15,200 when $x_1 = 100$, $x_2 = 100$, $x_3 = 200$. Since s_2 is nonbasic for the last tableau and its indicator is 0, there may be multiple optimum solutions. Treating s_2 as an entering variable, we have

	x_1	x_2	x_3	s_1	s_2	s_3	R	
x_2	$\frac{3}{2}$	1	0	$\frac{5}{2}$	0	$-\frac{1}{2}$	0	250
s_2	$\frac{1}{2}$	0	0	$\frac{1}{2}$	1	$-\frac{1}{2}$	0	50
x_3	$-\frac{1}{2}$	0	1	$-\frac{3}{2}$	0	$\frac{1}{2}$	0	150
R	0	0	0	8	0	8	1	15,200

Here $R = 15{,}200$ when $x_1 = 0$, $x_2 = 250$, $x_3 = 150$. Thus multiple optimum solutions exist.

Hence R is maximum when $x_1 = (1 - t)(100) + 0t = 100 - 100t$, $x_2 = (1 - t)(100) + 250t = 100 + 150t$, $x_3 = (1 - t)(200) + 150t = 200 - 50t$, and $0 \le t \le 1$. For the last tableau, x_1 is nonbasic and its indicator is 0. If we continue the process for determining other optimum solutions, we return to the fourth tableau. If we were to initially choose s_2 as the departing variable, then

	x_1	x_2	x_3	s_1	s_2	s_3	R		
s_1	1	1	1	1	0	0	0	400	400
s_2	1	1	2	0	1	0	0	600	300
s_3	2	3	5	0	0	1	0	1500	300
R	-24	-32	-48	0	0	0	1	0	

	x_1	x_2	x_3	s_1	s_2	s_3	R		
s_1	$\frac{1}{2}$	$\frac{1}{2}$	0	1	$-\frac{1}{2}$	0	0	100	200
x_3	$\frac{1}{2}$	$\frac{1}{2}$	1	0	$\frac{1}{2}$	0	0	300	600
s_3	$-\frac{1}{2}$	$\frac{1}{2}$	0	0	$-\frac{5}{2}$	1	0	0	0
R	0	-8	0	0	24	0	1	14,400	

	x_1	x_2	x_3	s_1	s_2	s_3	R		
s_1	1	0	0	1	2	-1	0	100	50
x_3	1	0	1	0	3	-1	0	300	100
x_2	-1	1	0	0	-5	2	0	0	
R	-8	0	0	0	-16	16	1	14,400	

	x_1	x_2	x_3	s_1	s_2	s_3	R		
s_2	$\frac{1}{2}$	0	0	$\frac{1}{2}$	1	$-\frac{1}{2}$	0	50	100
x_3	$-\frac{1}{2}$	0	1	$-\frac{3}{2}$	0	$\frac{1}{2}$	0	150	
x_2	$\frac{3}{2}$	1	0	$\frac{5}{2}$	0	$-\frac{1}{2}$	0	250	$\frac{500}{3}$
R	0	0	0	8	0	8	1	15,200	

the maximum value of R is 15,200 when $x_1 = 0$, $x_2 = 250$, $x_3 = 150$. For the last tableau, x_1 is nonbasic and its indicator is 0. Treating x_1 as an entering variable, we have

$$
\begin{array}{c}
\begin{array}{cccccccc}
x_1 & x_2 & x_3 & s_1 & s_2 & s_3 & R \\
\end{array} \\
\begin{array}{c}
x_1 \\
x_3 \\
x_2 \\
R
\end{array}
\left[
\begin{array}{ccccccc|c}
1 & 0 & 0 & 1 & 2 & -1 & 0 & 100 \\
0 & 0 & 1 & -1 & 1 & 0 & 0 & 200 \\
0 & 1 & 0 & 1 & -3 & 1 & 0 & 100 \\
\hline
0 & 0 & 0 & 8 & 0 & 8 & 1 & 15,200
\end{array}
\right]
\end{array}
$$

Here $R = 15,200$ when $x_1 = 100$, $x_2 = 100$, $x_3 = 200$. For the last tableau, s_2 is nonbasic and its indicator is 0. If we continue the process of determining other optimum solutions, we return to the tableau corresponding to the solution $x_1 = 0$, $x_2 = 250$, $x_3 = 150$. Thus, the maximum revenue is $15,200 when $x_1 = 100 - 100t$, $x_2 = 100 + 150t$, $x_3 = 200 - 50t$, and $0 \le t \le 1$

Principles in Practice 7.6

1. Using the hint, $1000 - x_1$ standard and $800 - x_2$ deluxe snowboards must be manufactured at plant II. The constraints for plant I are $x_1 + x_2 \le 1200$ and $x_2 - x_1 \le 200$. The constraints for plant II are $(1000 - x_1) + (800 - x_2) \le 1000$ or $x_1 + x_2 \ge 800$. The quantity to be maximized is the profit $P = 40x_1 + 60x_2 + 45(1000 - x_1) + 50(800 - x_2) = -5x_1 + 10x_2 + 85,000$ subject to the constraints $x_1 + x_2 \le 1200$, $-x_1 + x_2 \le 200$, $x_1 + x_2 \ge 800$, and x_1, $x_2 \ge 0$. Note that maximizing $Z = -5x_1 + 10x_2$ also maximizes the profit. The corresponding equations are: $x_1 + x_2 + s_1 = 1200$, $-x_1 + x_2 + s_2 = 200$, $x_1 + x_2 - s_3 + t = 800$. The artificial objective equation is $W = -5x_1 + 10x_2 - Mt$. The augmented coefficient matrix is:

$$
\begin{array}{c}
\begin{array}{ccccccc}
x_1 & x_2 & s_1 & s_2 & s_3 & t & w \\
\end{array} \\
\left[
\begin{array}{ccccccc|c}
1 & 1 & 1 & 0 & 0 & 0 & 0 & 1200 \\
-1 & 1 & 0 & 1 & 0 & 0 & 0 & 200 \\
1 & 1 & 0 & 0 & -1 & 1 & 0 & 800 \\
\hline
5 & -10 & 0 & 0 & 0 & M & 1 & 0
\end{array}
\right]
\end{array}
$$

The simplex tableaux follow.

$$
\begin{array}{c}
\begin{array}{ccccccc}
 & x_1 & x_2 & s_1 & s_2 & t & W \\
\end{array} \\
\begin{array}{c}
s_1 \\
s_2 \\
t_1 \\
W
\end{array}
\left[
\begin{array}{cccccc|c}
1 & 1 & 1 & 0 & 0 & 0 & 1200 \\
-1 & \underline{1} & 0 & 0 & 0 & 0 & 200 \\
1 & 1 & 0 & -1 & 1 & 0 & 800 \\
\hline
5-M & -10-M & 0 & M & 0 & 1 & -800M
\end{array}
\right]
\end{array}
$$

$$
\begin{array}{c}
\begin{array}{ccccccc}
 & x_1 & x_2 & s_1 & s_2 & t & W \\
\end{array} \\
\begin{array}{c}
s_1 \\
x_2 \\
t_1 \\
W
\end{array}
\left[
\begin{array}{cccccc|c}
2 & 0 & 1 & 0 & 0 & 0 & 1000 \\
-1 & 1 & 0 & 0 & 0 & 0 & 200 \\
\underline{2} & 0 & 0 & -1 & 1 & 0 & 600 \\
\hline
-5-2M & 0 & 0 & M & 0 & 1 & 2000-600M
\end{array}
\right]
\end{array}
$$

$$
\begin{array}{c}
\begin{array}{ccccccc}
 & x_1 & x_2 & s_1 & s_2 & t & W \\
\end{array} \\
\begin{array}{c}
s_1 \\
x_2 \\
x_1 \\
W
\end{array}
\left[
\begin{array}{cccccc|c}
0 & 0 & 1 & 1 & -1 & 0 & 400 \\
0 & 1 & 0 & -\frac{1}{2} & \frac{1}{2} & 0 & 500 \\
1 & 0 & 0 & -\frac{1}{2} & \frac{1}{2} & 0 & 300 \\
\hline
0 & 0 & 0 & -\frac{5}{2} & \frac{5}{2}+M & 1 & 3500
\end{array}
\right]
\end{array}
$$

Delete the t-column since $t = 0$ and return to Z.

$$
\begin{array}{c@{}c}
& \begin{array}{cccccc} x_1 & x_2 & s_1 & s_2 & Z & \end{array} \\
\begin{array}{c} s_2 \\ x_2 \\ x_1 \\[4pt] Z \end{array} &
\left[\begin{array}{ccccc|c}
0 & 0 & 1 & 1 & 0 & 400 \\
0 & 1 & \frac{1}{2} & 0 & 0 & 700 \\
1 & 0 & \frac{1}{2} & 0 & 0 & 500 \\
\hline
0 & 0 & \frac{5}{2} & 0 & 1 & 4500
\end{array}\right]
\end{array}
$$

Thus, $x_1 = 500$, $x_2 = 700$, and $Z = 4500$. Plant I should manufacture 500 standard and 700 deluxe snowboards. Plant II should manufacture $1000 - 500 = 500$ standard and $800 - 700 = 100$ deluxe snowboards. The maximum profit is $P = -5(500) + 10(700) + 85{,}000 = \$89{,}500$.

Exercise 7.6

1.

$$
\begin{array}{c@{}c}
& \begin{array}{cccccc} x_1 & x_2 & s_1 & s_2 & t_2 & W \end{array} \\
& \left[\begin{array}{cccccc|c}
1 & 1 & 1 & 0 & 0 & 0 & 6 \\
-1 & 1 & 0 & -1 & 1 & 0 & 4 \\
\hline
-2 & -1 & 0 & 0 & M & 1 & 0
\end{array}\right]
\end{array}
$$

$$
\begin{array}{c@{}c}
& \begin{array}{cccccc} x_1 & x_2 & s_1 & s_2 & t_2 & W \end{array} \\
\begin{array}{c} s_1 \\ t_2 \\[4pt] W \end{array} &
\left[\begin{array}{cccccc|c}
1 & 1 & 1 & 0 & 0 & 0 & 6 \\
-1 & \underline{1} & 0 & -1 & 1 & 0 & 4 \\
\hline
-2+M & -1-M & 0 & M & 0 & 1 & -4M
\end{array}\right]\begin{array}{c}6\\4\\ \end{array}
\end{array}
$$

$$
\begin{array}{c@{}c}
& \begin{array}{cccccc} x_1 & x_2 & s_1 & s_2 & t_2 & W \end{array} \\
\begin{array}{c} s_1 \\ x_2 \\[4pt] W \end{array} &
\left[\begin{array}{cccccc|c}
\underline{2} & 0 & 1 & 1 & -1 & 0 & 2 \\
-1 & 1 & 0 & -1 & 1 & 0 & 4 \\
\hline
-3 & 0 & 0 & -1 & M+1 & 1 & 4
\end{array}\right]\begin{array}{c}1\\ \\ \end{array}
\end{array}
$$

$$
\begin{array}{c@{}c}
& \begin{array}{ccccc} x_1 & x_2 & s_1 & s_2 & Z \end{array} \\
\begin{array}{c} x_1 \\ x_2 \\[4pt] Z \end{array} &
\left[\begin{array}{ccccc|c}
1 & 0 & \frac{1}{2} & \frac{1}{2} & 0 & 1 \\
0 & 1 & \frac{1}{2} & -\frac{1}{2} & 0 & 5 \\
\hline
0 & 0 & \frac{3}{2} & \frac{1}{2} & 1 & 7
\end{array}\right]
\end{array}
$$

The maximum is $Z = 7$ when $x_1 = 1$, $x_2 = 5$.

3.

$$
\begin{array}{c@{}c}
& \begin{array}{ccccccc} x_1 & x_2 & x_3 & s_1 & s_2 & t_2 & W \end{array} \\
& \left[\begin{array}{ccccccc|c}
1 & 2 & 1 & 1 & 0 & 0 & 0 & 5 \\
-1 & 1 & 1 & 0 & -1 & 1 & 0 & 1 \\
\hline
-2 & -1 & 1 & 0 & 0 & M & 1 & 0
\end{array}\right]
\end{array}
$$

$$
\begin{array}{c}
\begin{array}{ccccccc} x_1 & x_2 & x_3 & s_1 & s_2 & t_2 & W \end{array} \\
\begin{array}{c} s_1 \\ t_2 \\ W \end{array}
\left[\begin{array}{ccccccc|c}
1 & 2 & 1 & 1 & 0 & 0 & 0 & 5 \\
-1 & 1 & 1 & 0 & -1 & 1 & 0 & 1 \\
\hline
-2+M & -1-M & 1-M & 0 & M & 0 & 1 & -M
\end{array}\right]
\begin{array}{c} \frac{5}{2} \\ 1 \\ \end{array}
\end{array}
$$

$$
\begin{array}{c}
\begin{array}{ccccccc} x_1 & x_2 & x_3 & s_1 & s_2 & t_2 & W \end{array} \\
\begin{array}{c} s_1 \\ x_2 \\ W \end{array}
\left[\begin{array}{ccccccc|c}
3 & 0 & -1 & 1 & 2 & -2 & 0 & 3 \\
-1 & 1 & 1 & 0 & -1 & 1 & 0 & 1 \\
\hline
-3 & 0 & 2 & 0 & -1 & 1+M & 1 & 1
\end{array}\right]
\begin{array}{c} 1 \\ \\ \end{array}
\end{array}
$$

$$
\begin{array}{c}
\begin{array}{cccccc} x_1 & x_2 & x_3 & s_1 & s_2 & Z \end{array} \\
\begin{array}{c} x_1 \\ x_2 \\ Z \end{array}
\left[\begin{array}{cccccc|c}
1 & 0 & -\frac{1}{3} & \frac{1}{3} & \frac{2}{3} & 0 & 1 \\
0 & 1 & \frac{2}{3} & \frac{1}{3} & -\frac{1}{3} & 0 & 2 \\
\hline
0 & 0 & 1 & 1 & 1 & 1 & 4
\end{array}\right]
\end{array}
$$

The maximum is $Z = 4$ when $x_1 = 1$, $x_2 = 2$, $x_3 = 0$.

5.
$$
\begin{array}{c}
\begin{array}{cccccc} x_1 & x_2 & x_3 & s_1 & t_2 & W \end{array} \\
\left[\begin{array}{cccccc|c}
2 & 1 & 3 & 1 & 0 & 0 & 10 \\
1 & -1 & 1 & 0 & 1 & 0 & 4 \\
\hline
-4 & -1 & -2 & 0 & M & 1 & 0
\end{array}\right]
\end{array}
$$

$$
\begin{array}{c}
\begin{array}{cccccc} x_1 & x_2 & x_3 & s_1 & t_2 & W \end{array} \\
\begin{array}{c} s_1 \\ t_2 \\ W \end{array}
\left[\begin{array}{cccccc|c}
2 & 1 & 3 & 1 & 0 & 0 & 10 \\
1 & -1 & 1 & 0 & 1 & 0 & 4 \\
\hline
-4-M & -1+M & -2-M & 0 & 0 & 1 & -4M
\end{array}\right]
\begin{array}{c} 5 \\ 4 \\ \end{array}
\end{array}
$$

$$
\begin{array}{c}
\begin{array}{cccccc} x_1 & x_2 & x_3 & s_1 & t_2 & W \end{array} \\
\begin{array}{c} s_1 \\ x_1 \\ W \end{array}
\left[\begin{array}{cccccc|c}
0 & 3 & 1 & 1 & -2 & 0 & 2 \\
1 & -1 & 1 & 0 & 1 & 0 & 4 \\
\hline
0 & -5 & 2 & 0 & 4+M & 1 & 16
\end{array}\right]
\begin{array}{c} \frac{2}{3} \\ \\ \end{array}
\end{array}
$$

$$
\begin{array}{c}
\begin{array}{ccccc} x_1 & x_2 & x_3 & s_1 & Z \end{array} \\
\begin{array}{c} x_2 \\ x_1 \\ Z \end{array}
\left[\begin{array}{ccccc|c}
0 & 1 & \frac{1}{3} & \frac{1}{3} & 0 & \frac{2}{3} \\
1 & 0 & \frac{4}{3} & \frac{1}{3} & 0 & \frac{14}{3} \\
\hline
0 & 0 & \frac{11}{3} & \frac{5}{3} & 1 & \frac{58}{3}
\end{array}\right]
\end{array}
$$

The maximum is $Z = \dfrac{58}{3}$ when $x_1 = \dfrac{14}{3}$, $x_2 = \dfrac{2}{3}$, $x_3 = 0$.

7.

	x_1	x_2	s_1	s_2	s_3	t_3	W	
	1	−1	1	0	0	0	0	1
	1	2	0	1	0	0	0	8
	1	1	0	0	−1	1	0	5
	−1	10	0	0	0	M	1	0

	x_1	x_2	s_1	s_2	s_3	t_3	W		
s_1	1	−1	1	0	0	0	0	1	1
s_2	1	2	0	1	0	0	0	8	8
t_3	1	1	0	0	−1	1	0	5	5
W	$-1-M$	$10-M$	0	0	M	0	1	$-5M$	

	x_1	x_2	s_1	s_2	s_3	t_3	W		
x_1	1	−1	1	0	0	0	0	1	$\frac{7}{3}$
s_2	0	3	−1	1	0	0	0	7	2
t_3	0	2	−1	0	−1	1	0	4	
W	0	$9-2M$	$1+M$	0	M	0	1	$1-4M$	

	x_1	x_2	s_1	s_2	s_3	t_3	W	
x_1	1	0	$\frac{1}{2}$	0	$-\frac{1}{2}$	$\frac{1}{2}$	0	3
s_2	0	0	$\frac{1}{2}$	1	$\frac{3}{2}$	$-\frac{3}{2}$	0	1
x_2	0	1	$-\frac{1}{2}$	0	$-\frac{1}{2}$	$\frac{1}{2}$	0	2
W	0	0	$\frac{11}{2}$	0	$\frac{9}{2}$	$-\frac{9}{2}+M$	1	−17

For the above tableau, $t_3 = 0$. Thus $W = Z$. The maximum is $Z = -17$ when $x_1 = 3$, $x_2 = 2$.

9. We first write the third constraint as $-x_1 + x_2 + x_3 \ge 6$.

	x_1	x_2	x_3	s_1	s_2	s_3	t_2	t_3	W	
	1	1	1	1	0	0	0	0	0	1
	1	−1	1	0	−1	0	1	0	0	2
	−1	1	1	0	0	−1	0	1	0	6
	−3	2	−1	0	0	0	M	M	1	0

	x_1	x_2	x_3	s_1	s_2	s_3	t_2	t_3	W		
s_1	1	1	1	1	0	0	0	0	0	1	1
t_2	1	−1	1	0	−1	0	1	0	0	2	2
t_3	−1	1	1	0	0	−1	0	1	0	6	6
W	−3	2	$-1-2M$	0	M	M	0	0	1	$-8M$	

	x_1	x_2	x_3	s_1	s_2	s_3	t_2	t_3	W	
x_3	1	1	1	1	0	0	0	0	0	1
t_2	0	-2	0	-1	-1	0	1	0	0	1
t_3	-2	0	0	-1	0	-1	0	1	0	5
W	-2+2M	3+2M	0	1+2M	M	M	0	0	1	1-6M

There is no solution (empty feasible region).

11.

	x_1	x_2	s_1	s_3	t_2	t_3	W	
	1	-1	1	0	0	0	0	4
	-1	1	0	0	1	0	0	4
	1	0	0	-1	0	1	0	6
	3	-2	0	0	M	M	1	0

	x_1	x_2	s_1	s_3	t_2	t_3	W		
s_1	1	-1	1	0	0	0	0	4	
t_2	-1	_1_	0	0	1	0	0	4	4
t_3	1	0	0	-1	0	1	0	6	
W	3	-2-M	0	M	0	0	1	-10M	

	x_1	x_2	s_1	s_2	s_3	t_2	t_3	W		
s_1	0	0	1	0	1	0	0	0	8	
x_2	-1	1	0	0	1	0	0	0	4	
t_3	_1_	0	0	-1	0	1	0	0	6	6
W	1-M	0	0	M	2+M	0	0	1	8-6M	

	x_1	x_2	s_1	s_2	s_3	t_2	t_3	W	
s_1	0	0	1	0	1	0	0	0	8
x_2	0	1	0	-1	1	1	0	0	10
x_1	1	0	0	-1	0	1	0	0	6
W	0	0	0	1	2+M	-1+M		1	2

For the above tableau, $t_2 = t_3 = 0$. Thus $W = Z$. The maximum is $Z = 2$ when $x_1 = 6$, $x_2 = 10$.

13. Let x_1 and x_2 denote the numbers of Standard and Executive bookcases produced, respectively, each week. We want to maximize the profit function $P = 30x_1 + 36x_2$ subject to $x_1 + 2x_2 \leq 400$, $2x_1 + 3x_2 \leq 510$, $2x_1 + 3x_2 \geq 240$, $x_1, \; x_2 \geq 0$. The artificial objective function is $W = P - Mt_3$.

$$
\begin{array}{ccccccc}
x_1 & x_2 & s_1 & s_2 & s_3 & t_3 & W \\
\end{array}
$$

$$
\left[\begin{array}{ccccccc|c}
1 & 2 & 1 & 0 & 0 & 0 & 0 & 400 \\
2 & 3 & 0 & 1 & 0 & 0 & 0 & 510 \\
2 & 3 & 0 & 0 & -1 & 1 & 0 & 240 \\
\hline
-30 & -36 & 0 & 0 & 0 & M & 1 & 0
\end{array} \right]
$$

$$
\begin{array}{c}
s_1 \\ s_2 \\ t_3 \\ W
\end{array}
\left[\begin{array}{ccccccc|c}
x_1 & x_2 & s_1 & s_2 & s_3 & t_3 & W & \\
1 & 2 & 1 & 0 & 0 & 0 & 0 & 400 \\
2 & 3 & 0 & 1 & 0 & 0 & 0 & 510 \\
2 & \underline{3} & 0 & 0 & -1 & 1 & 0 & 240 \\
\hline
-30-2M & -36-3M & 0 & 0 & M & 0 & 1 & -240M
\end{array} \right]
\begin{array}{c} 200 \\ 170 \\ 80 \\ \end{array}
$$

$$
\begin{array}{c}
s_1 \\ s_2 \\ x_2 \\ W
\end{array}
\left[\begin{array}{ccccccc|c}
x_1 & x_2 & s_1 & s_2 & s_3 & t_3 & W & \\
-\frac{1}{3} & 0 & 1 & 0 & \frac{2}{3} & -\frac{2}{3} & 0 & 240 \\
0 & 0 & 0 & 1 & \underline{1} & -1 & 0 & 270 \\
\frac{2}{3} & 1 & 0 & 0 & -\frac{1}{3} & \frac{1}{3} & 0 & 80 \\
\hline
-6 & 0 & 0 & 0 & -12 & 12+M & 1 & 2880
\end{array} \right]
\begin{array}{c} 360 \\ 270 \\ \end{array}
$$

$$
\begin{array}{c}
s_1 \\ s_3 \\ x_2 \\ P
\end{array}
\left[\begin{array}{cccccc|c}
x_1 & x_2 & s_1 & s_2 & s_3 & P & \\
-\frac{1}{3} & 0 & 1 & -\frac{2}{3} & 0 & 0 & 60 \\
0 & 0 & 0 & 1 & 1 & 0 & 270 \\
\frac{2}{3} & 1 & 0 & \frac{1}{3} & 0 & 0 & 170 \\
\hline
-6 & 0 & 0 & 12 & 0 & 1 & 6120
\end{array} \right]
\begin{array}{c} \\ \\ 255 \\ \end{array}
$$

$$
\begin{array}{c}
s_1 \\ s_3 \\ x_1 \\ P
\end{array}
\left[\begin{array}{cccccc|c}
x_1 & x_2 & s_1 & s_2 & s_3 & P & \\
0 & \frac{1}{2} & 1 & -\frac{1}{2} & 0 & 0 & 145 \\
0 & 0 & 0 & 1 & 1 & 0 & 270 \\
1 & \frac{3}{2} & 0 & \frac{1}{2} & 0 & 0 & 255 \\
\hline
0 & 9 & 0 & 15 & 0 & 1 & 7650
\end{array} \right]
$$

To maximize profit, the company should produce 255 Standard and 0 Executive bookcases.

15. Suppose I is the total investment. Let x_1, x_2, and x_3 be the proportions invested in A, AA, and AAA bonds, respectively. If Z is the total annual yield expressed as a proportion of I, then $ZI = 0.08x_1I + 0.07x_2I + 0.06x_3I$, or equivalently, $Z = 0.08x_1 + 0.07x_2 + 0.06x_3$. We want to maximize Z subject to $x_1 + x_2 + x_3 = 1$, $x_2 + x_3 \geq 0.50$, $x_1 + x_2 \leq 0.30$, x_1, x_2, $x_3 \geq 0$. The artificial objective function is $W = Z - Mt_1 - Mt_2$.

	x_1	x_2	x_3	s_2	s_3	t_1	t_2	W	
	1	1	1	0	0	1	0	0	1
	0	1	1	−1	0	0	1	0	0.5
	1	1	0	0	1	0	0	0	0.3
	−0.08	−0.07	−0.06	0	0	M	M	1	0

	x_1	x_2	x_3	s_2	s_3	t_1	t_2	W	
t_1	1	1	1	0	0	1	0	0	1
t_2	0	1	1	−1	0	0	1	0	0.5
s_3	1	1	0	0	1	0	0	0	0.3
W	$-0.08 - M$	$-0.07 - 2M$	$-0.06 - 2M$	M	0	0	0	1	$-1.5M$

	x_1	x_2	x_3	s_2	s_3	t_1	t_2	W	
t_1	0	0	1	0	−1	1	0	0	0.7
t_2	−1	0	1	−1	−1	0	1	0	0.2
x_2	1	1	0	0	1	0	0	0	0.3
W	$-0.01 + M$	0	$-0.06 - 2M$	M	$0.07 + 2M$	0	0	1	$0.021 - 0.9M$

	x_1	x_2	x_3	s_2	s_3	t_1	t_2	W	
t_1	1	0	0	1	0	1	−1	0	0.5
x_3	−1	0	1	−1	−1	0	1	0	0.2
x_2	1	1	0	0	1	0	0	0	0.3
W	$-0.07 - M$	0	0	$-0.06 - M$	$.01$	0	$0.06 + 2M$	1	$0.033 - 0.5M$

	x_1	x_2	x_3	s_2	s_3	t_1	t_2	W	
t_1	0	−1	0	1	−1	1	−1	0	0.2
x_3	0	1	1	−1	0	0	1	0	0.5
x_1	1	1	0	0	1	0	0	0	0.3
W	0	$0.07 + M$	0	$-0.06 - M$	$0.08 + M$	0	$0.06 + 2M$	1	$0.054 - 0.2M$

	x_1	x_2	x_3	s_2	s_3	t_1	t_2	W	
s_2	0	−1	0	1	−1	1	−1	0	0.2
x_3	0	0	1	0	−1	1	0	0	0.7
x_1	1	1	0	0	1	0	0	0	0.3
W	0	0.01	0	0	0.02	$0.06 + M$	M	1	0.066

For the above tableau, $t_1 = t_2 = 0$. Thus $W = Z$.

The fund should put 30% in A bonds, 0% in AA, and 70% in AAA for a yield of 6.6%.

Exercise 7.7

1.

$$
\begin{array}{ccccccc}
x_1 & x_2 & s_1 & s_2 & t_1 & t_2 & W
\end{array}
$$
$$
\left[\begin{array}{ccccccc|c}
-1 & 1 & -1 & 0 & 1 & 0 & 0 & 6 \\
1 & 1 & 0 & -1 & 0 & 1 & 0 & 10 \\
\hline
3 & 6 & 0 & 0 & M & M & 1 & 0
\end{array}\right]
$$

$$
\begin{array}{cccccccc}
 & x_1 & x_2 & x_3 & s_2 & s_3 & t_1 & t_2 & W
\end{array}
$$
$$
\begin{array}{c}
t_1 \\
t_2 \\
W
\end{array}
\left[\begin{array}{ccccccc|cc}
-1 & \underline{1} & -1 & 0 & 1 & 0 & 0 & 6 & 6 \\
1 & 1 & 0 & -1 & 0 & 1 & 0 & 10 & 10 \\
\hline
3 & 6-2M & M & M & 0 & 0 & 1 & -16M
\end{array}\right]
$$

$$
\begin{array}{cccccccc}
 & x_1 & x_2 & x_3 & s_2 & s_3 & t_1 & t_2 & W
\end{array}
$$
$$
\begin{array}{c}
x_2 \\
t_2 \\
W
\end{array}
\left[\begin{array}{ccccccc|c}
-1 & 1 & -1 & 0 & 1 & 0 & 0 & 6 \\
\underline{2} & 0 & 1 & -1 & -1 & 1 & 0 & 4 \\
\hline
9-2M & 0 & 6-M & M & -6+2M & 0 & 1 & -36-4M
\end{array}\right]\begin{array}{c} \\ 2\end{array}
$$

$$
\begin{array}{ccccccc}
 & x_1 & x_2 & x_3 & s_2 & s_3 & t_1 & t_2 & W
\end{array}
$$
$$
\begin{array}{c}
x_2 \\
x_1 \\
W
\end{array}
\left[\begin{array}{cccccccc|c}
0 & 1 & -\frac{1}{2} & -\frac{1}{2} & \frac{1}{2} & \frac{1}{2} & 0 & 8 \\
1 & 0 & \frac{1}{2} & -\frac{1}{2} & -\frac{1}{2} & \frac{1}{2} & 0 & 2 \\
\hline
0 & 0 & \frac{3}{2} & \frac{9}{2} & -\frac{3}{2}+M & -\frac{9}{2}+M & 1 & -54
\end{array}\right]
$$

The minimum is $Z = 54$ when $x_1 = 2$, $x_2 = 8$.

3.

$$
\begin{array}{cccccc}
x_1 & x_2 & x_3 & s & t & W
\end{array}
$$
$$
\left[\begin{array}{cccccc|c}
1 & -1 & -1 & -1 & 1 & 0 & 18 \\
\hline
12 & 6 & 3 & 0 & M & 1 & 0
\end{array}\right]
$$

$$
\begin{array}{cccccc}
 & x_1 & x_2 & x_3 & s & t & W
\end{array}
$$
$$
\begin{array}{c}
t \\
W
\end{array}
\left[\begin{array}{cccccc|c}
\underline{1} & -1 & -1 & -1 & 1 & 0 & 18 \\
\hline
12-M & 6+M & 3+M & M & 0 & 1 & -18M
\end{array}\right]\begin{array}{c}18\\ \end{array}
$$

$$
\begin{array}{cccccc}
 & x_1 & x_2 & x_3 & s & & t & W
\end{array}
$$
$$
\begin{array}{c}
x_1 \\
W
\end{array}
\left[\begin{array}{cccccc|c}
1 & -1 & -1 & -1 & 1 & 0 & 18 \\
\hline
0 & 18 & 15 & 12 & -12+M & 1 & -216
\end{array}\right]
$$

The minimum is $Z = 216$ when $x_1 = 18$, $x_2 = 0$, $x_3 = 0$.

5. We write the second constraint as $-x_1 + x_3 \geq 4$.

	x_1	x_2	x_3	s_1	s_2	s_3	t_2	W	
	1	1	1	1	0	0	0	0	6
	−1	0	1	0	−1	0	1	0	4
	0	1	1	0	0	1	0	0	5
	2	3	1	0	0	0	M	1	0

	x_1	x_2	x_3	s_1	s_2	s_3	t_2	W		
s_1	1	1	1	1	0	0	0	0	6	6
t_2	−1	0	$\underline{1}$	0	−1	0	1	0	4	4
s_3	0	1	1	0	0	1	0	0	5	5
W	$2+M$	3	$1-M$	0	M	0	0	1	$-4M$	

	x_1	x_2	x_3	s_1	s_2	s_3	t_2	W	
s_1	2	1	0	1	1	0	−1	0	2
x_3	−1	0	1	0	−1	0	1	0	4
s_3	1	1	0	0	1	1	−1	0	1
W	3	3	0	0	1	0	$-1+M$	1	−4

The minimum is $Z = 4$ when $x_1 = 0$, $x_2 = 0$, $x_3 = 4$.

7.

	x_1	x_2	x_3	s_3	t_1	t_2	W	
	1	2	1	0	1	0	0	4
	0	1	1	0	0	1	0	1
	1	1	0	1	0	0	0	6
	1	−1	−3	0	M	M	1	0

	x_1	x_2	x_3	s_3	t_1	t_2	W		
t_1	1	2	1	0	1	0	0	4	2
t_2	0	$\underline{1}$	1	0	0	1	0	1	1
s_3	1	1	0	1	0	0	0	6	6
W	$1-M$	$-1-3M$	$-3-2M$	0	0	0	1	$-5M$	

	x_1	x_2	x_3	s_3	t_1	t_2	W		
t_1	$\underline{1}$	0	−1	0	1	−2	0	2	2
x_2	0	1	1	0	0	1	0	1	
s_3	1	0	−1	1	0	−1	0	5	5
W	$1-M$	0	$-2+M$	0	0	$1+3M$	1	$1-2M$	

	x_1	x_2	x_3	s_3	t_1	t_2	W	
x_1	1	0	-1	0	1	-2	0	2
x_2	0	1	$\underline{1}$	0	0	1	0	1
s_3	0	0	0	1	-1	1	0	3
W	0	0	-1	0	$-1+M$	$3+M$	1	-1

	x_1	x_2	x_3	s_3	$-Z$	
x_1	1	1	0	0	0	3
x_3	0	1	1	0	0	1
s_3	0	0	0	1	0	3
$-Z$	0	1	0	0	1	0

The minimum is $Z = 0$ when $x_1 = 3$, $x_2 = 0$, $x_3 = 1$.

9.

x_1	x_2	x_3	s_1	s_2	t_1	t_2	W	
1	1	1	-1	0	1	0	0	8
-1	2	1	0	-1	0	1	0	2
1	8	5	0	0	M	M	1	0

	x_1	x_2	x_3	s_1	s_2	t_1	t_2	W		
t_1	1	1	1	-1	0	1	0	0	8	8
t_2	-1	$\underline{2}$	1	0	-1	0	1	0	2	1
W	1	$8-3M$	$5-2M$	M	M	0	0	1	$-10M$	

	x_1	x_2	x_3	s_1	s_2	t_1	t_2	W		
t_1	$\frac{3}{2}$	0	$\frac{1}{2}$	-1	$\frac{1}{2}$	1	$-\frac{1}{2}$	0	7	$\frac{14}{3}$
x_2	$-\frac{1}{2}$	1	$\frac{1}{2}$	0	$-\frac{1}{2}$	0	$\frac{1}{2}$	0	1	
W	$5-\frac{3}{2}M$	0	$1-\frac{1}{2}M$	M	$4-\frac{1}{2}M$	0	$-4+\frac{3}{2}M$	1	$-8-7M$	

	x_1	x_2	x_3	s_1	s_2	t_1	t_2	W		
x_1	1	0	$\frac{1}{3}$	$-\frac{2}{3}$	$\frac{1}{3}$	$\frac{2}{3}$	$-\frac{1}{3}$	0	$\frac{14}{3}$	14
x_2	0	1	$\frac{2}{3}$	$-\frac{1}{3}$	$-\frac{1}{3}$	$\frac{1}{3}$	$\frac{1}{3}$	0	$\frac{10}{3}$	5
W	0	0	$-\frac{2}{3}$	$\frac{10}{3}$	$\frac{7}{3}$	$-\frac{10}{3}+M$	$-\frac{7}{3}+M$	1	$-\frac{94}{3}$	

	x_1	x_2	x_3	s_1	s_2	t_1	t_2	W	
x_1	1	$-\frac{1}{2}$	0	$-\frac{1}{2}$	$\frac{1}{2}$	$\frac{1}{2}$	$-\frac{1}{2}$	0	3
x_3	0	$\frac{3}{2}$	1	$-\frac{1}{2}$	$-\frac{1}{2}$	$\frac{1}{2}$	$\frac{1}{2}$	0	5
W	0	1	0	3	2	$-3+M$	$-2+M$	1	-28

The minimum is $Z = 28$ when $x_1 = 3$, $x_2 = 0$, $x_3 = 5$.

11. Let x_1, x_2, and x_3 denote the annual numbers of barrels of cement produced in kilns that use device A, device B, and no device, respectively. We want to minimize the annual emission control cost C (C in dollars) where

$$C = \frac{1}{4}x_1 + \frac{2}{5}x_2 + 0x_3 \text{ subject to}$$

$$x_1 + x_2 + x_3 = 3,300,000,$$

$$\frac{1}{2}x_1 + \frac{1}{4}x_2 + 2x_3 \leq 1,000,000,$$

$$x_1, \ x_2, \ x_3 \geq 0.$$

$$
\begin{array}{cccccc}
x_1 & x_2 & x_3 & s_2 & t_1 & W \\
\end{array}
$$

$$
\left[\begin{array}{cccccc|c}
1 & 1 & 1 & 0 & 1 & 0 & 3,300,000 \\
\frac{1}{2} & \frac{1}{4} & 2 & 1 & 0 & 0 & 1,000,000 \\
\hline
\frac{1}{4} & \frac{2}{5} & 0 & 0 & M & 1 & 0 \\
\end{array}\right]
$$

$$
\begin{array}{ccccccc}
& x_1 & x_2 & x_3 & s_2 & t_1 & W \\
t_1 & 1 & 1 & 1 & 0 & 1 & 0 & 3,300,000 & 3,300,000 \\
s_2 & \frac{1}{2} & \frac{1}{4} & 2 & 1 & 0 & 0 & 1,000,000 & 500,000 \\
W & \frac{1}{4}-M & \frac{2}{5}-M & -M & 0 & 0 & 1 & -3,300,000M \\
\end{array}
$$

$$
\begin{array}{ccccccc}
& x_1 & x_2 & x_3 & s_2 & t_1 & W \\
t_1 & \frac{3}{4} & \frac{7}{8} & 0 & -\frac{1}{2} & 1 & 0 & 2,800,000 & 3,200,000 \\
x_3 & \frac{1}{4} & \frac{1}{8} & 1 & \frac{1}{2} & 0 & 0 & 500,000 & 4,000,000 \\
W & \frac{1}{4}-\frac{3}{4}M & \frac{2}{5}-\frac{7}{8}M & 0 & \frac{1}{2}M & 0 & 1 & -2,800,000M \\
\end{array}
$$

$$
\begin{array}{ccccccc}
& x_1 & x_2 & x_3 & s_2 & t_1 & W \\
x_2 & \frac{6}{7} & 1 & 0 & -\frac{4}{7} & \frac{8}{7} & 0 & 3,200,000 & \frac{11,200,000}{3} \\
x_3 & \frac{1}{7} & 0 & 1 & \frac{4}{7} & -\frac{1}{7} & 0 & 100,000 & 700,000 \\
W & -\frac{13}{140} & 0 & 0 & \frac{8}{35} & -\frac{16}{35}+M & 1 & -1,280,000 \\
\end{array}
$$

$$
\begin{array}{cccccc}
& x_1 & x_2 & x_3 & s_2 & -C \\
x_2 & 0 & 1 & -6 & -4 & 0 & 2,600,000 \\
x_1 & 1 & 0 & 7 & 4 & 0 & 700,000 \\
-C & 0 & 0 & \frac{13}{20} & \frac{3}{5} & 1 & -1,215,000 \\
\end{array}
$$

Thus the minimum value of C is $1,215,000$ when $x_1 = 700,000$, $x_2 = 2,600,000$, $x_3 = 0$.

The plant should install device A on kilns producing 700,000 barrels annually, and device B on kilns producing 2,600,000 barrels annually.

13. Let x_A = number of refrigerators shipped from A to Exton,

x_B = number of refrigerators shipped from B to Exton,

y_A = number of refrigerators shipped from A to Whyton,

y_B = number of refrigerators shipped from B to Whyton.

We want to minimize $C = 15x_A + 11x_B + 13y_A + 12y_B$ subject to

$$x_A + x_B = 15,$$
$$y_A + y_B = 15,$$
$$x_A + y_A \le 25,$$
$$x_B + y_B \le 10,$$
$$x_A, \ x_B, \ y_A, \ y_B \ge 0.$$

	x_A	x_B	y_A	y_B	s_3	s_4	t_1	t_2	W	
	1	1	0	0	0	0	1	0	0	15
	0	0	1	1	0	0	0	1	0	15
	1	0	1	0	1	0	0	0	0	25
	0	1	0	1	0	1	0	0	0	10
	15	11	13	12	0	0	M	M	1	0

	x_A	x_B	y_A	y_B	s_3	s_4	t_1	t_2	W		
t_1	1	1	0	0	0	0	1	0	0	15	15
t_2	0	0	1	1	0	0	0	1	0	15	
s_3	1	0	1	0	1	0	0	0	0	25	
s_4	0	$\underline{1}$	0	1	0	1	0	0	0	10	10
W	$15-M$	$11-M$	$13-M$	$12-M$	0	0	0	0	1	$-30M$	

	x_A	x_B	y_A	y_B	s_3	s_1	t_1	t_2	W		
t_1	1	0	0	-1	0	-1	1	0	0	5	
t_2	0	0	$\underline{1}$	1	0	0	0	1	0	15	15
s_3	1	0	1	0	1	0	0	0	0	25	25
x_B	0	1	0	1	0	1	0	0	0	10	
W	$15-M$	0	$13-M$	1	0	$-11+M$	0	0	1	$-110-20M$	

	x_A	x_B	y_A	y_B	s_3	s_4	t_1	t_2	W		
t_1	$\underline{1}$	0	0	-1	0	-1	1	0	0	5	5
y_A	0	0	1	1	0	0	0	1	0	15	
s_3	1	0	0	-1	1	0	0	-1	0	10	10
x_B	0	1	0	1	0	1	0	0	0	20	
W	$15-M$	0	0	$-12+M$	0	$-11+M$	0	$-13+M$	1	$-305-5M$	

	x_A	x_B	y_A	y_B	s_3	s_4	t_1	t_2	W	
x_A	1	0	0	-1	0	-1	1	0	0	5
y_A	0	0	1	1	0	0	0	1	0	15
s_3	0	0	0	0	1	1	-1	-1	0	5
x_B	0	1	0	1	0	1	0	0	0	10
W	0	0	0	3	0	4	$-15+M$	$-13+M$	1	-380

The retailer should ship as follows: to Exton, 5 from A and 10 from B; to Whyton, 15 from A. The transportation cost is $380

15. a. Roll width $\begin{cases} 15" \\ 10" \end{cases}$ $\begin{array}{cccc} 3 & 2 & 1 & 0 \\ 0 & 1 & \underline{3} & \underline{4} \end{array}$

Trim loss 3 8 $\underline{3}$ $\underline{8}$

b. We want to minimize L $3x_1 + 8x_2 + 3x_3 + 8x_4$ subject to

$$3x_1 + 2x_2 + x_3 \geq 50,$$
$$x_2 + 3x_3 + 4x_4 \geq 60,$$
$$x_1, \ x_2, \ x_3, \ x_4 \geq 0.$$

	x_1	x_2	x_3	x_4	s_1	s_2	t_1	t_2	W	
	3	2	1	0	−1	0	1	0	0	50
	0	1	3	4	0	−1	0	1	0	60
	3	8	3	8	0	0	M	M	1	0

	x_1	x_2	x_3	x_4	s_1	s_2	t_1	t_2	W		
t_1	3	2	1	0	−1	0	1	0	0	50	50
t_2	0	1	3	4	0	−1	0	1	0	60	20
W	$3-3M$	$8-3M$	$3-4M$	$8-4M$	M	M	0	0	1	$-110M$	

	x_1	x_2	x_3	x_4	s_1	s_2	t_1	t_2	W		
t_1	3	$\frac{5}{3}$	0	$-\frac{4}{3}$	−1	$\frac{1}{3}$	1	$-\frac{1}{3}$	0	30	10
x_3	0	$\frac{1}{3}$	1	$\frac{4}{3}$	0	$-\frac{1}{3}$	0	$\frac{1}{3}$	0	20	
W	$3-3M$	$7-\frac{5}{3}M$	0	$4+\frac{4}{3}M$	M	$1-\frac{1}{3}M$	0	$-1+\frac{4}{3}M$	1	$-60-30M$	

	x_1	x_2	x_3	x_4	s_1	s_2	t_1	t_2	W	
x_1	1	$\frac{5}{9}$	0	$-\frac{4}{9}$	$-\frac{1}{3}$	$\frac{1}{9}$	$\frac{1}{3}$	$-\frac{1}{9}$	0	10
x_3	0	$\frac{1}{3}$	1	$\frac{4}{3}$	0	$-\frac{1}{3}$	0	$\frac{1}{3}$	0	20
W	0	$\frac{16}{3}$	0	$\frac{16}{3}$	1	$\frac{2}{3}$	$-1+M$	$-\frac{2}{3}+M$	1	−90

$x_1 = 10, \ x_2 = 0, \ x_3 = 20, \ x_4 = 0.$

c. 90 in.

Principles in Practice 7.8

1. Let $x_1, \ x_2,$ and x_3 be the numbers respectively, of Type 1, Type 2, and Type 3 gadgets produced. The original problem is to maximize
$P = 300x_1 + 200x_2 + 200x_3$, subject to
$$300x_1 + 220x_2 + 180x_3 \leq 60,000,$$
$$20x_1 + 40x_2 + 20x_3 \leq 2000,$$
$$3x_1 + x_2 + 2x_3 \leq 120,$$
$$\text{and } x_1, \ x_2, \ x_3 \leq 0.$$

The dual problem is to minimize
$W = 60,000y_1 + 2000y_2 + 120y_3,$
subject to
$300y_1 + 20y_2 + 3y_3 \geq 300,$
$220y_1 + 40y_2 + y_3 \geq 200,$
$180y_1 + 20y_2 + 2y_3 \geq 200,$
and $y_1,\ y_2,\ y_3 \geq 0.$

2. Let x_1 and x_2 be the amounts, respectively of supplement 1 and supplement 2.
The original problem is to minimize $C = 6x_1 + 2x_2$, subject to

$20x_1 + 6x_2 \geq 98,$
$8x_1 + 16x_2 \geq 80,$
and $x_1,\ x_2 \geq 0.$
The dual problem is to maximize
$W = 98y_1 + 80y_2$, subject to

$20y_1 + 8y_2 \leq 6,$
$6y_1 + 16y_2 \leq 2,$
and $y_1,\ y_2 \geq 0.$

3. Let x_1, x_2, and x_3 be the numbers, respectively, of devices 1, 2, and 3 produced.
The original problem is to maximize $P = 30x_1 + 20x_2 + 20x_3$, subject to
$30x_1 + 15x_2 + 10x_3 \leq 300,\ 20x_1 + 30x_2 + 20x_3 \leq 400,\ 40x_1 + 30x_2 + 25x_3 \leq 600,$ and $x_1, x_2, x_3 \geq 0.$
The dual problem is to minimize $W = 300y_1 + 400y_2 + 600y_3$, subject to
$30y_1 + 20y_2 + 40y_3 \geq 30,\ 15y_1 + 30y_2 + 30y_3 \geq 20,$
$10y_1 + 20y_2 + 25y_3 \geq 20,$
and $y_1, y_2, y_3 \geq 0.$
The tableaux to maximize $Z = -W = -300y_1 - 400y_2 - 600y_3$ follow.

	y_1	y_2	y_3	s_1	s_2	s_3	t_1	t_2	t_3	Z	
	30	20	40	−1	0	0	1	0	0	0	30
	15	30	30	0	−1	0	0	1	0	0	20
	10	20	25	0	0	−1	0	0	1	0	20
	300	400	600	0	0	0	M	M	M	1	0

	y_1	y_2	y_3	s_1	s_2	s_3	t_1	t_2	t_3	Z	
t_1	30	20	40	−1	0	0	1	0	0	0	30
t_2	15	30	30	0	−1	0	0	1	0	0	20
t_3	10	20	25	0	0	−1	0	0	1	0	20
Z	$300 - 55M$	$400 - 70M$	$600 - 95M$	M	M	M	0	0	0	1	$-70M$

	y_1	y_2	y_3	s_1	s_2	s_3	t_1	t_2	t_3	Z	
t_1	10	−20	0	−1	$\frac{4}{3}$	0	1	$-\frac{4}{3}$	0	0	$\frac{10}{3}$
y_3	$\frac{1}{2}$	1	1	0	$-\frac{1}{30}$	0	0	$\frac{1}{30}$	0	0	$\frac{2}{3}$
t_3	$-\frac{5}{2}$	−5	0	0	$\frac{5}{6}$	−1	0	$-\frac{5}{6}$	1	0	$\frac{10}{3}$
Z	$-\frac{15}{2}M$	$-200 + 25M$	0	M	$20 - \frac{13}{6}M$	M	0	$-20 + \frac{19}{6}M$	0	1	$-400 - \frac{20}{3}M$

	y_1	y_2	y_3	s_1	s_2	s_3	t_1	t_2	t_3	Z	
y_1	1	-2	0	$-\frac{1}{10}$	$\frac{2}{15}$	0	$\frac{1}{10}$	$-\frac{2}{15}$	0	0	$\frac{1}{3}$
y_3	0	2	1	$\frac{1}{20}$	$-\frac{1}{10}$	0	$-\frac{1}{20}$	$\frac{1}{10}$	0	0	$\frac{1}{2}$
t_3	0	-10	0	$-\frac{1}{4}$	$\frac{7}{6}$	-1	$\frac{1}{4}$	$-\frac{7}{6}$	1	0	$\frac{25}{6}$
Z	0	$-200+10M$	0	$\frac{1}{4}M$	$20-\frac{7}{6}M$	M	$\frac{3}{4}M$	$-20+\frac{13}{6}M$	0	1	$-400-\frac{25}{6}M$

	y_1	y_2	y_3	s_1	s_2	s_3	t_1	t_2	t_3	Z	
s_2	$\frac{15}{2}$	-15	0	$-\frac{3}{4}$	1	0	$\frac{3}{4}$	-1	0	0	$\frac{5}{2}$
y_3	$\frac{3}{4}$	$\frac{1}{2}$	1	$-\frac{1}{40}$	0	0	$\frac{1}{40}$	0	0	0	$\frac{3}{4}$
t_3	$-\frac{35}{4}$	$\frac{15}{2}$	0	$\frac{5}{8}$	0	-1	$-\frac{5}{8}$	0	1	0	$\frac{5}{4}$
Z	$-150+\frac{35}{4}M$	$100-\frac{13}{2}M$	0	$15-\frac{5}{8}M$	0	M	$-15+\frac{13}{8}M$	M	0	1	$-450-\frac{5}{4}M$

	y_1	y_2	y_3	s_1	s_2	s_3	t_1	t_2	t_3	Z	
s_2	-10	0	0	$\frac{1}{2}$	1	-2	$-\frac{1}{2}$	-1	2	0	5
y_3	$\frac{4}{3}$	0	1	$-\frac{1}{15}$	0	$\frac{1}{15}$	$\frac{1}{15}$	0	$-\frac{1}{15}$	0	$\frac{2}{3}$
y_2	$-\frac{7}{6}$	1	0	$\frac{1}{12}$	0	$-\frac{2}{15}$	$-\frac{1}{12}$	0	$\frac{2}{15}$	0	$\frac{1}{6}$
Z	$-\frac{100}{3}$	0	0	$\frac{20}{3}$	0	$\frac{40}{3}$	$-\frac{20}{3}+M$	M	$-\frac{40}{3}+M$	1	$-\frac{1400}{3}$

The t_1, t_2, and t_3 columns are no longer needed.

	y_1	y_2	y_3	s_1	s_2	s_3	Z	
s_2	0	0	$\frac{15}{2}$	0	1	$-\frac{3}{2}$	0	10
y_1	1	0	$\frac{3}{4}$	$-\frac{1}{20}$	0	$\frac{1}{20}$	0	$\frac{1}{2}$
y_2	0	1	$\frac{7}{8}$	$\frac{1}{40}$	0	$-\frac{3}{40}$	0	$\frac{3}{4}$
Z	0	0	25	5	0	15	1	-450

From this tableau, the maximum profit of \$450 corresponds to $x_1 = 5$, $x_2 = 0$, and $x_3 = 15$.
The company should produce 5 of device 1 per hour and 15 of device 3 per hour.

Exercise 7.8

1. Minimize $W = 6y_1 + 4y_2$ subject to

$y_1 - y_2 \geq 2,$
$y_1 + y_2 \geq 3,$
$y_1,\ y_2 \geq 0.$

3. Maximize $W = 8y_1 + 2y_2$ subject to

$y_1 - y_2 \leq 1,$
$y_1 + 2y_2 \leq 8,$
$y_1 + y_2 \leq 5,$
$y_1,\ y_2 \geq 0.$

5. The second and third constraints can be written as $x_1 - x_2 \leq -3$ and $-x_1 - x_2 \leq -11$.
Minimize $W = 13y_1 - 3y_2 - 11y_3$ subject to

$-y_1 + y_2 - y_3 \geq 1,$
$2y_1 - y_2 - y_3 \geq -1,$
$y_1,\ y_2,\ y_3 \geq 0.$

7. The first constraint can be written as $-x_1 + x_2 + x_3 \geq -3$. Maximize
$W = -3y_1 + 3y_2$ subject to

$-y_1 + y_2 \leq 4,$
$y_1 - y_2 \leq 4,$
$y_1 + y_2 \leq 6,$
$y_1,\ y_2 \geq 0.$

9. The dual is: Maximize $W = y_1 + 2y_2$ subject to

$y_1 - y_2 \le 4,$
$-y_1 + y_2 \le 4,$
$y_1 + y_2 \le 6,$
$y_1, \ y_2 \ge 0.$

	y_1	y_2	s_1	s_2	s_3	W		
s_1	1	-1	1	0	0	0	4	
s_2	-1	$\underline{1}$	0	1	0	0	4	4
s_3	1	1	0	0	1	0	6	6
W	-1	-2	0	0	0	1	0	

	y_1	y_2	s_1	s_2	s_3	W		
s_1	0	0	1	1	0	0	8	
y_2	-1	1	0	1	0	0	4	
s_3	$\underline{2}$	0	0	-1	1	0	2	1
W	-3	0	0	2	0	1	8	

	y_1	y_2	s_1	s_2	s_3	W	
s_1	0	0	1	1	0	0	8
y_2	0	1	0	$\frac{1}{2}$	$\frac{1}{2}$	0	5
y_1	1	0	0	$-\frac{1}{2}$	$\frac{1}{2}$	0	1
W	0	0	0	$\frac{1}{2}$	$\frac{3}{2}$	1	11

The minimum is $Z = 11$ when $x_1 = 0, \ x_2 = \dfrac{1}{2}, \ x_3 = \dfrac{3}{2}.$

11. The dual is: Minimize $W = 8y_1 + 12y_2$ subject to

$y_1 + y_2 \ge 3,$
$2y_1 + 6y_2 \ge 8,$
$y_1, \ y_2 \ge 0.$

y_1	y_2	s_1	s_2	t_1	t_2	U	
1	1	-1	0	1	0	0	3
2	6	0	-1	0	1	0	8
8	12	0	0	M	M	1	0

	y_1	y_2	s_1	s_2	t_1	t_2	U		
t_1	1	1	-1	0	1	0	0	3	3
t_2	2	$\underline{6}$	0	-1	0	1	0	8	$\frac{4}{3}$
U	$8-3M$	$12-7M$	M	M	0	0	1	$-11M$	

	y_1	y_2	s_1	s_2	t_1	t_2	U		
t_1	$\frac{2}{3}$	0	-1	$\frac{1}{6}$	1	$-\frac{1}{6}$	0	$\frac{5}{3}$	$\frac{5}{2}$
y_2	$\frac{1}{3}$	1	0	$-\frac{1}{6}$	0	$\frac{1}{6}$	0	$\frac{4}{3}$	4
U	$4-\frac{2}{3}M$	0	M	$2-\frac{1}{6}M$	0	$-2+\frac{7}{6}M$	1	$-16-\frac{5}{3}M$	

$$
\begin{array}{c c}
 & \begin{array}{c c c c c c c}
y_1 & y_2 & s_1 & s_2 & t_1 & t_2 & U
\end{array} \\
\begin{array}{c}
y_1 \\ y_2 \\ U
\end{array} &
\left[
\begin{array}{c c c c c c c | c}
1 & 0 & -\frac{3}{2} & \frac{1}{4} & \frac{3}{2} & -\frac{1}{4} & 0 & \frac{5}{2} \\
0 & 1 & \frac{1}{2} & -\frac{1}{4} & -\frac{1}{2} & \frac{1}{4} & 0 & \frac{1}{2} \\
\hline
0 & 0 & 6 & 1 & -6+M & -1+M & 1 & -26
\end{array}
\right]
\end{array}
$$

The maximum is $Z = 26$ when $x_1 = 6$, $x_2 = 1$.

13. The first constraint can be written as $x_1 - x_2 \ge -1$. The dual is: Maximize $W = -y_1 + 3y_2$ subject to

$$y_1 + y_2 \le 6,$$
$$-y_1 + y_2 \le 4,$$
$$y_1, \ y_2 \ge 0.$$

$$
\begin{array}{c c}
 & \begin{array}{c c c c c}
y_1 & y_2 & s_1 & s_2 & W
\end{array} \\
\begin{array}{c}
s_1 \\ s_2 \\ W
\end{array} &
\left[
\begin{array}{c c c c c | c}
1 & 1 & 1 & 0 & 0 & 6 \\
-1 & 1 & 0 & 1 & 0 & 4 \\
\hline
1 & -3 & 0 & 0 & 1 & 0
\end{array}
\right]
\begin{array}{c}
6 \\ 4 \\ \\
\end{array}
\end{array}
$$

$$
\begin{array}{c c}
 & \begin{array}{c c c c c}
y_1 & y_2 & s_1 & s_2 & W
\end{array} \\
\begin{array}{c}
s_1 \\ y_2 \\ W
\end{array} &
\left[
\begin{array}{c c c c c | c}
2 & 0 & 1 & -1 & 0 & 2 \\
-1 & 1 & 0 & 1 & 0 & 4 \\
\hline
-2 & 0 & 0 & 3 & 1 & 12
\end{array}
\right]
\begin{array}{c}
1 \\ \\ \\
\end{array}
\end{array}
$$

$$
\begin{array}{c c}
 & \begin{array}{c c c c c}
y_1 & y_2 & s_1 & s_2 & W
\end{array} \\
\begin{array}{c}
y_1 \\ y_2 \\ W
\end{array} &
\left[
\begin{array}{c c c c c | c}
1 & 0 & \frac{1}{2} & -\frac{1}{2} & 0 & 1 \\
0 & 1 & \frac{1}{2} & \frac{1}{2} & 0 & 5 \\
\hline
0 & 0 & 1 & 2 & 1 & 14
\end{array}
\right]
\end{array}
$$

The minimum is $Z = 14$ when $x_1 = 1$, $x_2 = 2$.

15. Let x_1 = amount spent on newspaper advertising,

x_2 = amount spent on radio advertising.

We want to minimize $C = x_1 + x_2$ subject to

$$40x_1 + 50x_2 \ge 80,000,$$
$$100x_1 + 25x_2 \ge 60,000,$$
$$x_1, \ x_2 \ge 0.$$

The dual is: Maximize $W = 80,000y_1 + 60,000y_2$ subject to

$$40y_1 + 100y_2 \le 1,$$
$$50y_1 + 25y_2 \le 1,$$
$$y_1, \ y_2 \ge 0.$$

$$
\begin{array}{c c}
 & \begin{array}{c c c c c}
y_1 & \quad y_2 & s_1 & s_2 & W
\end{array} \\
\begin{array}{c}
s_1 \\ s_2 \\ W
\end{array} &
\left[
\begin{array}{c c c c c | c}
40 & 100 & 1 & 0 & 0 & 1 \\
50 & 25 & 0 & 1 & 0 & 1 \\
\hline
-80,000 & -60,000 & 0 & 0 & 1 & 0
\end{array}
\right]
\begin{array}{c}
\frac{1}{40} \\ \frac{1}{50} \\ \\
\end{array}
\end{array}
$$

$$\begin{array}{c}
\begin{array}{cccccc} & y_1 & y_2 & s_1 & s_2 & W \end{array}\\
\begin{array}{c} s_1 \\ y_1 \\ W \end{array}
\left[\begin{array}{ccccc|c}
0 & 80 & 1 & -\frac{4}{5} & 0 & \frac{1}{5} \\[4pt]
1 & \frac{1}{2} & 0 & \frac{1}{50} & 0 & \frac{1}{50} \\[4pt]
\hline
0 & -20{,}000 & 0 & 1600 & 1 & 1600
\end{array}\right.
\left.\begin{array}{c} \frac{1}{400} \\[4pt] \frac{1}{25} \\[4pt] \hline \\ \end{array}\right]
\end{array}$$

$$\begin{array}{c}
\begin{array}{cccccc} & y_1 & y_2 & s_1 & s_2 & W \end{array}\\
\begin{array}{c} y_2 \\ y_1 \\ W \end{array}
\left[\begin{array}{ccccc|c}
0 & 1 & \frac{1}{80} & -\frac{1}{100} & 0 & \frac{1}{400} \\[4pt]
1 & 0 & -\frac{1}{160} & \frac{1}{40} & 0 & \frac{3}{160} \\[4pt]
\hline
0 & 0 & 250 & 1400 & 1 & 1650
\end{array}\right]
\end{array}$$

The firm should spend \$250 on newspaper advertising and \$1400 on radio advertising for a cost of \$1650.

17. Let y_1 = number of shipping clerk apprentices,

    y_2 = number of shipping clerks,

    y_3 = number of semiskilled workers,

    y_4 = number of skilled workers.

We want to minimize $W = 6y_1 + 9y_2 + 8y_3 + 14y_4$ subject to

$$y_1 + y_2 \ge 60,$$
$$-2y_1 + y_2 \ge 0,$$
$$y_3 + y_4 \ge 90,$$
$$y_3 - 2y_4 \ge 0,$$
$$y_1,\ y_2,\ y_3,\ y_4 \ge 0.$$

The dual is: Maximize $Z = 60x_1 + 0x_2 + 90x_3 + 0x_4$ subject to

$$x_1 - 2x_2 \le 6,$$
$$x_1 + x_2 \le 9,$$
$$x_3 + x_4 \le 8,$$
$$x_3 - 2x_4 \le 14,$$
$$x_1,\ x_2,\ x_3,\ x_4 \ge 0.$$

$$\begin{array}{c}
\begin{array}{cccccccccc} & x_1 & x_2 & x_3 & x_4 & s_1 & s_2 & s_3 & s_4 & Z \end{array}\\
\begin{array}{c} s_1 \\ s_2 \\ s_3 \\ s_4 \\ Z \end{array}
\left[\begin{array}{ccccccccc|c}
1 & -2 & 0 & 0 & 1 & 0 & 0 & 0 & 0 & 6 \\
1 & 1 & 0 & 0 & 0 & 1 & 0 & 0 & 0 & 9 \\
0 & 0 & 1 & 1 & 0 & 0 & 1 & 0 & 0 & 8 \\
0 & 0 & 1 & -2 & 0 & 0 & 0 & 1 & 0 & 14 \\
\hline
-60 & 0 & -90 & 0 & 0 & 0 & 0 & 0 & 1 & 0
\end{array}\right.
\left.\begin{array}{c} \\ \\ 8 \\ 14 \\ \hline \\ \end{array}\right]
\end{array}$$

$$\begin{array}{c}
\begin{array}{cccccccccc} & x_1 & x_2 & x_3 & x_4 & s_1 & s_2 & s_3 & s_4 & Z \end{array}\\
\begin{array}{c} s_1 \\ s_2 \\ x_3 \\ s_4 \\ Z \end{array}
\left[\begin{array}{ccccccccc|c}
1 & -2 & 0 & 0 & 1 & 0 & 0 & 0 & 0 & 6 \\
1 & 1 & 0 & 0 & 0 & 1 & 0 & 0 & 0 & 9 \\
0 & 0 & 1 & 1 & 0 & 0 & 1 & 0 & 0 & 8 \\
0 & 0 & 0 & -3 & 0 & 0 & -1 & 1 & 0 & 6 \\
\hline
-60 & 0 & 0 & 90 & 0 & 0 & 90 & 0 & 1 & 720
\end{array}\right.
\left.\begin{array}{c} 6 \\ 9 \\ \\ \\ \hline \\ \end{array}\right]
\end{array}$$

	x_1	x_2	x_3	x_4	s_1	s_2	s_3	s_4	Z		
x_1	1	−2	0	0	1	0	0	0	0	6	
s_2	0	<u>3</u>	0	0	−1	1	0	0	0	3	1
x_3	0	0	1	1	0	0	1	0	0	8	
s_4	0	0	0	−3	0	0	−1	1	0	6	
Z	0	−120	0	90	60	0	90	0	1	1080	

	x_1	x_2	x_3	x_4	s_1	s_2	s_3	s_4	Z	
x_1	1	0	0	0	$\frac{1}{3}$	$\frac{2}{3}$	0	0	0	8
x_2	0	1	0	0	$-\frac{1}{3}$	$\frac{1}{3}$	0	0	0	1
x_3	0	0	1	1	0	0	1	0	0	8
s_4	0	0	0	−3	0	0	−1	1	0	6
Z	0	0	0	90	20	40	90	0	1	1200

The company should employ 20 shipping clerk apprentices, 40 shipping clerks, 90 semiskilled workers, and 0 skilled workers for a total hourly wage of $1200.

Chapter 7 Review Problems

1.

3.

5.

7.

9.

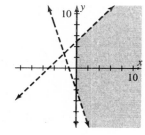

11. Feasible region follows. Corner points are $(0, 0)$, $(0, 2)$, $(1, 3)$, $(3, 1)$, $(3, 0)$. Z is maximized at $(3, 0)$ where its value is 3. Thus $Z = 3$ when $x = 3$ and $y = 0$.

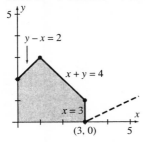

13. Feasible region is unbounded. Z is minimized at the corner point $(0, 2)$ where its value is -2. Thus $Z = -2$ when $x = 0$ and $y = 2$.

15. Feasible region is empty. Thus there is no optimum solution.

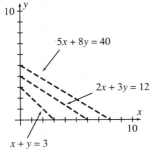

17. Feasible region follows. Corner points are $(0, 0)$, $(0, 4)$, $(2, 3)$, and $(4, 0)$. Z is maximized at $(2, 3)$ and $(4, 0)$ where its value is 36. Thus Z is maximized at all points on the line segment joining $(2, 3)$ and $(4, 0)$. The solution is $Z = 36$ when $x = (1 - t)(2) + 4t = 2 + 2t$, $y = (1 - t)(3) + 0t = 3 - 3t$, and $0 \leq t \leq 1$.

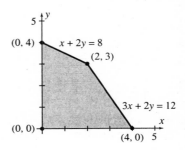

19.

$$\begin{array}{c} \\ s_1 \\ s_2 \\ Z \end{array} \begin{array}{c} x_1 \quad x_2 \quad s_1 \quad s_2 \quad Z \\ \left[\begin{array}{ccccc|c} 1 & 6 & 1 & 0 & 0 & 12 \\ 1 & 2 & 0 & 1 & 0 & 8 \\ \hline -4 & -5 & 0 & 0 & 1 & 0 \end{array}\right] \begin{array}{c} 2 \\ 4 \\ {} \end{array} \end{array}$$

$$\begin{array}{c} \\ x_2 \\ s_2 \\ Z \end{array} \begin{array}{c} x_1 \quad x_2 \quad s_1 \quad s_2 \quad Z \\ \left[\begin{array}{ccccc|c} \frac{1}{6} & 1 & \frac{1}{6} & 0 & 0 & 2 \\ \frac{2}{3} & 0 & -\frac{1}{3} & 1 & 0 & 4 \\ \hline -\frac{19}{6} & 0 & \frac{5}{6} & 0 & 1 & 10 \end{array}\right] \begin{array}{c} 12 \\ 6 \\ {} \end{array} \end{array}$$

$$\begin{array}{c} \\ x_2 \\ x_1 \\ Z \end{array} \begin{array}{c} x_1 \quad x_2 \quad s_1 \quad s_2 \quad Z \\ \left[\begin{array}{ccccc|c} 0 & 1 & \frac{1}{4} & -\frac{1}{4} & 0 & 1 \\ 1 & 0 & -\frac{1}{2} & \frac{3}{2} & 0 & 6 \\ \hline 0 & 0 & -\frac{3}{4} & \frac{19}{4} & 1 & 29 \end{array}\right] \begin{array}{c} 4 \\ {} \\ {} \end{array} \end{array}$$

$$\begin{array}{c} \\ s_1 \\ x_1 \\ Z \end{array} \begin{array}{c} x_1 \quad x_2 \quad s_1 \quad s_2 \quad Z \\ \left[\begin{array}{ccccc|c} 0 & 4 & 1 & -1 & 0 & 4 \\ 1 & 2 & 0 & 1 & 0 & 8 \\ \hline 0 & 3 & 0 & 4 & 1 & 32 \end{array}\right] \end{array}$$

Thus $Z = 32$ when $x_1 = 8$ and $x_2 = 0$.

21.

$$
\begin{array}{cccccc}
x_1 & x_2 & x_3 & s & t & W \\
\end{array}
$$

$$
\left[\begin{array}{cccccc|c}
1 & 2 & 3 & -1 & 1 & 0 & 6 \\
\hline
2 & 3 & 1 & 0 & M & 1 & 0 \\
\end{array}\right]
$$

$$
\begin{array}{ccccccc}
 & x_1 & x_2 & x_3 & s & t & W \\
\end{array}
$$

$$
\begin{array}{c}
t \\
W
\end{array}
\left[\begin{array}{cccccc|c}
1 & 2 & \underline{3} & -1 & 1 & 0 & 6 \\
\hline
2-M & 3-2M & 1-3M & M & 0 & 1 & -6M \\
\end{array}\right]2
$$

$$
\begin{array}{ccccccc}
 & x_1 & x_2 & x_3 & s & t & W \\
\end{array}
$$

$$
\begin{array}{c}
x_3 \\
W
\end{array}
\left[\begin{array}{cccccc|c}
\frac{1}{3} & \frac{2}{3} & 1 & -\frac{1}{3} & \frac{1}{3} & 0 & 2 \\
\hline
\frac{5}{3} & \frac{7}{3} & 0 & \frac{1}{3} & -\frac{1}{3}+M & 1 & -2 \\
\end{array}\right]
$$

Thus $Z = 2$ when $x_1 = 0$, $x_2 = 0$ and $x_3 = 2$.

23.

$$
\begin{array}{ccccccc}
x_1 & x_2 & s_1 & s_2 & s_3 & t_2 & W \\
\end{array}
$$

$$
\left[\begin{array}{ccccccc|c}
1 & 1 & 1 & 0 & 0 & 0 & 0 & 12 \\
1 & 1 & 0 & -1 & 0 & 1 & 0 & 5 \\
1 & 0 & 0 & 0 & 1 & 0 & 0 & 10 \\
\hline
-1 & -2 & 0 & 0 & 0 & M & 1 & 0 \\
\end{array}\right]
$$

$$
\begin{array}{cccccccc}
 & x_1 & x_2 & s_1 & s_2 & s_3 & t_2 & W \\
\end{array}
$$

$$
\begin{array}{c}
s_1 \\
t_2 \\
s_3 \\
W
\end{array}
\left[\begin{array}{ccccccc|c}
1 & 1 & 1 & 0 & 0 & 0 & 0 & 12 \\
1 & \underline{1} & 0 & -1 & 0 & 1 & 0 & 5 \\
1 & 0 & 0 & 0 & 1 & 0 & 0 & 10 \\
\hline
-1-M & -2-M & 0 & M & 0 & 0 & 1 & -5M \\
\end{array}\right]
\begin{array}{c}12\\5\\ \\ \end{array}
$$

$$
\begin{array}{cccccccc}
 & x_1 & x_2 & s_1 & s_2 & s_3 & t_2 & W \\
\end{array}
$$

$$
\begin{array}{c}
s_1 \\
x_2 \\
s_3 \\
W
\end{array}
\left[\begin{array}{ccccccc|c}
0 & 0 & 1 & \underline{1} & 0 & -1 & 0 & 7 \\
1 & 1 & 0 & -1 & 0 & 1 & 0 & 5 \\
1 & 0 & 0 & 0 & 1 & 0 & 0 & 10 \\
\hline
1 & 0 & 0 & -2 & 0 & 2+M & 1 & 10 \\
\end{array}\right]7
$$

$$
\begin{array}{cccccc}
 & x_1 & x_2 & s_1 & s_2 & s_3 & Z \\
\end{array}
$$

$$
\begin{array}{c}
s_2 \\
x_2 \\
s_3 \\
Z
\end{array}
\left[\begin{array}{cccccc|c}
0 & 0 & 1 & 1 & 0 & 0 & 7 \\
1 & 1 & 1 & 0 & 0 & 0 & 12 \\
1 & 0 & 0 & 0 & 1 & 0 & 10 \\
\hline
1 & 0 & 2 & 0 & 0 & 1 & 24 \\
\end{array}\right]
$$

Thus $Z = 24$ when $x_1 = 0$ and $x_2 = 12$.

25. We write the first constraint as $-x_1 + x_2 + x_3 \geq 1$.

$$
\begin{array}{ccccccc}
x_1 & x_2 & x_3 & s_1 & t_1 & t_2 & W \\
\end{array}
$$
$$
\left[\begin{array}{ccccccc|c}
-1 & 1 & 1 & -1 & 1 & 0 & 0 & 1 \\
6 & 3 & 2 & 0 & 0 & 1 & 0 & 12 \\
\hline
1 & 2 & 1 & 0 & M & M & 1 & 0
\end{array}\right]
$$

$$
\begin{array}{cccccccc}
 & x_1 & x_2 & x_3 & s_1 & t_1 & t_2 & W \\
t_1 & -1 & 1 & 1 & -1 & 1 & 0 & 0 & 1 \\
t_2 & 6 & 3 & 2 & 0 & 0 & 1 & 0 & 12 \\
W & 1-5M & 2-4M & 1-3M & M & 0 & 0 & 1 & -13M
\end{array}
$$

with right-side labels 2

$$
\begin{array}{ccccccc}
 & x_1 & x_2 & x_3 & s_1 & t_1 & t_2 & W \\
t_1 & 0 & \frac{3}{2} & \frac{4}{3} & -1 & 1 & \frac{1}{6} & 0 & 3 \\
x_1 & 1 & \frac{1}{2} & \frac{1}{3} & 0 & 0 & \frac{1}{6} & 0 & 2 \\
W & 0 & \frac{3}{2}-\frac{3}{2}M & \frac{2}{3}-\frac{4}{3}M & M & 0 & -\frac{1}{6}+\frac{5}{6}M & 1 & -2-3M
\end{array}
$$

with right-side labels 2, 4

$$
\begin{array}{cccccccc}
 & x_1 & x_2 & x_3 & s_1 & t_1 & t_2 & W \\
x_2 & 0 & 1 & \frac{8}{9} & -\frac{2}{3} & \frac{2}{3} & \frac{1}{9} & 0 & 2 \\
x_1 & 1 & 0 & -\frac{1}{9} & \frac{1}{3} & -\frac{1}{3} & \frac{1}{9} & 0 & 1 \\
W & 0 & 0 & -\frac{2}{3} & 1 & -1+M & -\frac{1}{3}+M & 1 & -5
\end{array}
$$

with right-side labels $\frac{9}{4}$

$$
\begin{array}{cccccc}
 & x_1 & x_2 & x_3 & s_1 & -Z \\
x_3 & 0 & \frac{9}{8} & 1 & -\frac{3}{4} & 0 & \frac{9}{4} \\
x_1 & 1 & \frac{1}{8} & 0 & \frac{1}{4} & 0 & \frac{5}{4} \\
-Z & 0 & \frac{3}{4} & 0 & \frac{1}{2} & 1 & -\frac{7}{2}
\end{array}
$$

Thus $Z = \dfrac{7}{2}$ when $x_1 = \dfrac{5}{4}$, $x_2 = 0$, and $x_3 = \dfrac{9}{4}$.

27.

$$
\begin{array}{ccccccc}
 & x_1 & x_2 & x_3 & s_1 & s_2 & Z \\
s_1 & 4 & -1 & 0 & 1 & 0 & 0 & 2 \\
s_2 & -10 & 1 & 3 & 0 & 1 & 0 & 1 \\
Z & -1 & -4 & -2 & 0 & 0 & 1 & 0
\end{array}
$$

with right-side label 1

$$
\begin{array}{ccccccc}
 & x_1 & x_2 & x_3 & s_1 & s_2 & Z \\
x_2 & -6 & 0 & 3 & 1 & 1 & 0 & 3 \\
s_2 & -10 & 1 & 3 & 0 & 1 & 0 & 1 \\
Z & -41 & 0 & 10 & 0 & 4 & 1 & 4
\end{array}
$$

For the last tableau, x_1 is the entering variable. Since no quotients exist, the problem has an unbounded solution. That is, no optimum solution (unbounded).

29. The dual is: Maximize $W = 35y_1 + 25y_2$ subject to

$$y_1 + y_2 \le 2,$$
$$2y_1 + y_2 \le 7,$$
$$3y_1 + y_2 \le 8,$$
$$y_1, \ y_2 \ge 0.$$

	y_1	y_2	s_1	s_2	s_3	W		
s_1	1	1	1	0	0	0	2	2
s_2	2	1	0	1	0	0	7	$\frac{7}{2}$
s_3	3	1	0	0	1	0	8	$\frac{8}{3}$
W	−35	−25	0	0	0	1	0	

	y_1	y_2	s_1	s_2	s_3	W	
y_1	1	1	1	0	0	0	2
s_2	0	−1	−2	1	0	0	3
s_3	0	−2	−3	0	1	0	2
W	0	10	35	0	0	1	70

Thus $Z = 70$ when $x_1 = 35$, $x_2 = 0$, and $x_3 = 0$.

31. Let x, y, and z denote the numbers of units of X, Y, and Z produced weekly, respectively. If P is the total profit obtained, we want to maximize
$P = 10x + 15y + 22z$ subject to

$$x + 2y + 2z \le 40,$$
$$x + y + 2z \le 34,$$
$$x, \ y, \ z \ge 0.$$

	x	y	z	s_1	s_2	P		
s_1	1	2	2	1	0	0	40	20
s_2	1	1	2	0	1	0	34	17
P	−10	−15	−22	0	0	1	0	

	x	y	z	s_1	s_2	P		
s_1	0	1	0	1	−1	0	6	6
z	$\frac{1}{2}$	$\frac{1}{2}$	1	0	$\frac{1}{2}$	0	17	34
P	1	−4	0	0	11	1	374	

	x	y	z	s_1	s_2	P	
y	0	1	0	1	−1	0	6
z	$\frac{1}{2}$	0	1	$-\frac{1}{2}$	1	0	14
P	1	0	0	4	7	1	398

Thus 0 units of X , 6 units of Y, and 14 units of Z give a maximum profit of $398.

33. Let x_{AC}, x_{AD}, x_{BC}, and x_{BD} denote the amounts (in hundreds of thousands of gallons) transported from A to C, A to D, B to C, and B to D, respectively. If C is the total transportation cost in thousands of dollars, we want to minimize $C = x_{AC} + 2x_{AD} + 2x_{BC} + 4x_{BD}$ subject to

$$x_{AC} + x_{AD} \leq 6,$$
$$x_{BC} + x_{BD} \leq 6,$$
$$x_{AC} + x_{BC} = 5,$$
$$x_{AD} + x_{BD} = 5,$$
$$x_{AC},\ x_{AD},\ x_{BC},\ x_{BD} \geq 0.$$

x_{AC}	x_{AD}	x_{BC}	x_{BD}	s_1	s_2	t_3	t_4	W	
1	1	0	0	1	0	0	0	0	6
0	0	1	1	0	1	0	0	0	6
1	0	1	0	0	0	1	0	0	5
0	1	0	1	0	0	0	1	0	5
1	2	2	4	0	0	M	M	1	0

	x_{AC}	x_{AD}	x_{BC}	x_{BD}	s_1	s_2	t_3	t_4	W		
s_1	1	1	0	0	1	0	0	0	0	6	6
s_2	0	0	1	1	0	1	0	0	0	6	
t_3	1	0	1	0	0	0	1	0	0	5	5
t_4	0	1	0	1	0	0	0	1	0	5	
W	$1-M$	$2-M$	$2-M$	$4-M$	0	0	0	0	1	$-10M$	

	x_{AC}	x_{AD}	x_{BC}	x_{BD}	s_1	s_2	t_3	t_4	W		
s_1	0	1	-1	0	1	0	-1	0	0	1	1
s_2	0	0	1	1	0	1	0	0	0	6	
x_{AC}	1	0	1	0	0	0	1	0	0	5	
t_4	0	1	0	1	0	0	0	1	0	5	5
W	0	$2-M$	1	$4-M$	0	0	$-1+M$	0	1	$-5-5M$	

	x_{AC}	x_{AD}	x_{BC}	x_{BD}	s_1	s_2	t_3	t_4	W		
x_{AD}	0	1	-1	0	1	0	-1	0	0	1	
s_2	0	0	1	1	0	1	0	0	0	6	6
x_{AC}	1	0	1	0	0	0	1	0	0	5	5
t_4	0	0	1	1	-1	0	1	1	0	4	4
W	0	0	$3-M$	$4-M$	$-2+M$	0	1	0	1	$-7-4M$	

	x_{AC}	x_{AD}	x_{BC}	x_{BD}	s_1	s_2	t_3	t_4	W	
x_{AD}	0	1	0	1	0	0	0	1	0	5
s_2	0	0	0	0	1	1	-1	-1	0	2
x_{AC}	1	0	0	-1	1	0	0	-1	0	1
x_{BC}	0	0	1	1	-1	0	1	1	0	4
W	0	0	0	1	1	0	$-2+M$	$-3+M$	1	-19

The minimum value of C is 19, when $x_{AC} = 1$, $x_{AD} = 5$, $x_{BC} = 4$, and $x_{BD} = 0$. Thus 100,000 gal from A to C, 500,000 gal from A to D, and 400,000 gal from B to C give a minimum cost of $19,000.

35. Let x and y represent daily consumption of foods A and B in 100-gram units. We want to minimize $C = 8x + 22y$ subject to the constraints

$$8x + 4y \geq 176,$$
$$16x + 32y \geq 1024,$$
$$2x + 5y \geq 200,$$
$$x \geq 0,$$
$$y \geq 0.$$

The feasible region is unbounded with corner points $(100, 0)$, $\left(\dfrac{5}{2}, 39\right)$ and $(0, 44)$. C has a minimum value at $(100, 0)$. Thus the animals should be fed $100 \times 100 = 10,000$ grams $= 10$ kilograms of food A each day.

37.

$Z = 117.88$ when $x = 7.23$, $y = 3.40$

Mathematical Snapshot Chapter 7

1.

	CURATIVE UNITS	TOXIC UNITS	RELATIVE DISCOMFORT
Drug (per ounce)	500	400	1
Radiation (per min)	1000	600	1
Requirement	≥ 2000	≤ 1400	

Let x_1 = number of ounces of drug and let x_2 = number of minutes of radiation. We want to minimize the discomfort D, where $D = x_1 + x_2$, subject to

$$500x_1 + 1000x_2 \geq 2000,$$
$$400x_1 + 600x_2 \leq 1400,$$

where $x_1,\ x_2 \geq 0$.

The corner points are $(0, 2)$, $\left(0, \frac{7}{3}\right)$, and $(2, 1)$.

At $(0, 2)$, $D = 0 + 2 = 2$;

at $\left(0,\ \frac{7}{3}\right)$, $D = 0 + \frac{7}{3} = \frac{7}{3}$;

at $(2, 1)$, $D = 2 + 1 = 3$.

Thus D is minimum at $(0, 2)$.

The patient should get 0 ounce of drug and 2 minutes of radiation.

3. Answers may vary.

Chapter 8

Principles in Practice 8.1

1. Let $P = 518$ and let $n = 3(365) = 1095$.

   $S = P(1+r)^n$

   $S = 518\left(1+\dfrac{r}{365}\right)^{1095}$

   By graphing S as a function of the nominal rate r, we find that when $r = 0.049$, $S = 600$. Thus, at the nominal rate of 4.9% compounded daily, the initial amount of $518 will grow to $600 after 3 years.

2. Let $P = 520$ and let $r = 0.052$.

   $S = P(1+r)^n$

   $S = 520\left(1+\dfrac{0.052}{365}\right)^n$

   $S = 520\left(\dfrac{365.052}{365}\right)^n$

   By graphing S as a function of n, we find that when $n = 2571$, $S = 750$. Thus, it will take $\dfrac{2571}{365} = 7.044$ years, or 7 years and 16 days for $520 to grow to $750 at the nominal rate of 5.2% compounded daily.

   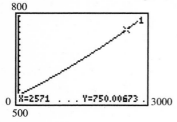

3. Let $n = 12$.

   $r_e = \left(1+\dfrac{r}{n}\right)^n - 1$

   $r_e = \left(1+\dfrac{r}{12}\right)^{12} - 1$

By graphing r_e as a function of r, we find that, when the nominal rate $r = 0.077208$ or 7.7208%, the effective rate $r_e = 0.08$ or 8%.

4. The respective effective rates of interest are found using the formula $r_e = \left(1+\dfrac{r}{n}\right)^n - 1$.

   Let $n = 12$ when $r = 0.11$:

   $r_e = \left(1+\dfrac{0.11}{12}\right)^{12} - 1 \approx 0.1157$. Hence, when the nominal rate $r = 11\%$ is compounded monthly, the effective rate $r_e = 11.57\%$.

   When $r = 0.1125$:

   $r_e = \left(1+\dfrac{0.1125}{4}\right)^4 - 1 \approx 0.1173$. Hence in the second case when the nominal rate $r = 11.25\%$ is compounded quarterly, the effective rate $r_e = 11.73\%$. This is the better effective rate of interest. To find the better investment, compare the compound amounts, S at the end of n years. With $P = 10,000$ and $r_e = 0.1157$,

   $S_1 = P(1+r)^n = 10,000(1+0.1157)^n$, and, in the second case, when $P = 9700$ and $r_e = 0.1173$

   $S_2 = P(1+r)^n = 9700(1+0.1173)^n$.

   $S_1(20) = 10,000(1.1157)^{20} \approx 89,319.99$

   $S_2(20) = 9700(1.1173)^{20} \approx 89,159.52$

   The $10,000 investment is slightly better over 20 years.

Exercise 8.1

1. a. $6000(1.08)^8 \approx \$11,105.58$

   b. $11,105.58 - 6000 = \$5105.58$

3. $\left(1 + \dfrac{0.04}{4}\right)^4 - 1 = (1.01)^4 - 1 \approx 0.04060$ or 4.060%

5. $\left(1 + \dfrac{0.04}{365}\right)^{365} - 1 \approx 0.04081$ or 4.081%

7. a. A nominal rate compounded yearly is the same as the effective rate, so the effective rate is 10%.

   b. $\left(1 + \dfrac{0.10}{2}\right)^2 - 1 = 0.1025$ or 10.25%

   c. $\left(1 + \dfrac{0.10}{4}\right)^4 - 1 \approx 0.10381$ or 10.381%

   d. $\left(1 + \dfrac{0.10}{12}\right)^{12} - 1 \approx 0.10471$ or 10.471%

   e. $\left(1 + \dfrac{0.10}{365}\right)^{365} - 1 \approx 0.10516$ or 10.516%

9. Let r_e be the effective rate. Then

$$2000(1 + r_e)^5 = 2950$$
$$(1 + r_e)^5 = \frac{2950}{2000}$$
$$1 + r_e = \sqrt[5]{\frac{2950}{2000}}$$
$$r_e = \sqrt[5]{\frac{2950}{2000}} - 1$$
$$r_e \approx 0.0808 \text{ or } 8.08\%.$$

11. From Example 6, the number of years, n, is given by $n = \dfrac{\ln 2}{\ln(1.08)} \approx 9.0$ years.

13. $6000(1.08)^7 \approx \$10,282.95$

15. $21,500(1.06)^{10} \approx \$38,503.23$

17. a. $(0.015)(12) = 0.18$ or 18%

   b. $(1.015)^{12} - 1 \approx 0.1956$ or 19.56%

19. The compound amount after the first four years is $2000(1.06)^4$. After the next four years the compound amount is $\left[2000(1.06)^4\right](1.03)^8 \approx \$3198.54$.

21. 7.8% compounded semiannually is equivalent to an effective rate of $(1.039)^2 - 1 = 0.079521$ or 7.9521%. Thus 8% compounded annually, which is the effective rate, is the better rate.

23. a. $\left(1 + \dfrac{0.0525}{360}\right)^{365} - 1 \approx 0.0547$ or 5.47%

   b. $\left(1 + \dfrac{0.0525}{365}\right)^{365} - 1 \approx 0.0539$ or 5.39%

25. Let r_e = effective rate.

$$300,000 = 100,000(1 + r_e)^{10}$$
$$(1 + r_e)^{10} = 3$$
$$1 + r_e = \sqrt[10]{3}$$
$$r_e = \sqrt[10]{3} - 1 \approx 0.1161 \text{ or } 11.61\%.$$

27. Let r = the required nominal rate.

$$420\left(1 + \frac{r}{2}\right)^{28} = 1000$$
$$\left(1 + \frac{r}{2}\right)^{28} = \frac{1000}{420} = \frac{50}{21}$$
$$1 + \frac{r}{2} = \sqrt[28]{\frac{50}{21}}$$
$$r = 2\left[\sqrt[28]{\frac{50}{21}} - 1\right] \approx 0.0629 \text{ or } 6.29\%$$

Exercise 8.2

1. $6000(1.05)^{-20} \approx \$2261.34$

3. $4000(1.035)^{-24} \approx \$1751.83$

5. $8000\left(1+\dfrac{0.06}{4}\right)^{-30} \approx \$5118.10$

7. $8000\left(1+\dfrac{0.10}{12}\right)^{-60} \approx \$4862.31$

9. $10,000\left(1+\dfrac{0.095}{365}\right)^{-4(365)} \approx \$6838.95$

11. $10,000(1+0.005)^{-12} \approx \$9419.05$

13. $27,000(1.03)^{-22} \approx \$14,091.10$

15. Let x be the payment 2 years from now. The equation of value at year 2 is
    $x = 600(1.04)^{-2} + 800(1.04)^{-4}$, from which $x \approx \$1238.58$.

17. Let x be the payment at the end of 6 years. The equation of value at year 6 is
    $2000(1.025)^{4} + 4000(1.025)^{2} + x = 5000(1.025) + 5000(1.025)^{-4}$
    $x = 5000(1.025) + 5000(1.025)^{-4} - 2000(1.025)^{4} - 4000(1.025)^{2}$
    $x \approx \$3244.63$.

19. **a.** $NPV = 8000(1.025)^{-6} + 10,000(1.025)^{-8} + 14,000(1.025)^{-12} - 25,000 \approx \$515.62$

    b. Since $NPV > 0$, the investment is profitable.

21. We consider the value of each investment at the end of eight years. The savings account has a value of
    $10,000(1.03)^{16} \approx \$16,047.06$.
    The business investment has a value of $16,000. Thus the better choice is the savings account.

23. $1000\left(1+\dfrac{0.075}{4}\right)^{-80} \approx \$226.25$

25. Let r be the nominal discount rate, compounded quarterly. Then
    $4700 = 10,000\left(1+\dfrac{r}{4}\right)^{-32}$
    $4700 = \dfrac{10,000}{\left(1+\frac{r}{4}\right)^{32}}$
    $\left(1+\dfrac{r}{4}\right)^{32} = \dfrac{10,000}{4700} = \dfrac{100}{47}$
    $1+\dfrac{r}{4} = \sqrt[32]{\dfrac{100}{47}}$
    $r = 4\left[\sqrt[32]{\dfrac{100}{47}} - 1\right] \approx 0.0955$ or 9.55%

Principles in Practice 8.3

1. Let $a = 64$ and let $r = \dfrac{3}{4}$. Then, the next five heights of the ball are $64\left(\dfrac{3}{4}\right)$, $64\left(\dfrac{3}{4}\right)^{2}$, $64\left(\dfrac{3}{4}\right)^{3}$, $64\left(\dfrac{3}{4}\right)^{4}$, $64\left(\dfrac{3}{4}\right)^{5}$, or 48 ft, 36 ft, 27 ft, $20\dfrac{1}{4}$ ft, and $15\dfrac{3}{16}$ ft.

2. Let $a = 500$ and let $r = 1.5$. Then, the number of bacteria at the end of each minute for the first six minutes is $500(1.5)$, $500(1.5)^{2}$, $500(1.5)^{3}$, $500(1.5)^{4}$, $500(1.5)^{5}$, $500(1.5)^{6}$, or 750, 1125, 1688, 2531, 3797, 5695.

3. The total vertical distance traveled in the air after n bounces is equal to 2 times the sum of heights. If $a = 6$ and $r = \frac{2}{3}$, then when the ball hits the ground for the twelfth time, $n = 12$ and the distance traveled in the air is

$$2s = 2\left[\frac{a\left(1 - r^n\right)}{1 - r}\right] = 2\left[\frac{6\left(1 - \left(\frac{2}{3}\right)^{12}\right)}{1 - \frac{2}{3}}\right]$$

$$\approx 35.72 \text{ meters}$$

4. The amount of profit earned in the first two years is the sum of the monthly profits. Let $a = 2000$, $r = 1.1$, and $n = 24$.

$$s = \frac{2000\left(1 - (1.1)^{24}\right)}{1 - 1.1} \approx 176,994.65$$

Thus, the company earned \$176,994.65 in the first two years.

5. Let $R = 500$ and let $n = 72$. Then, the present value A of the annuity is given by

$$A = R\left(\frac{1 - (1 + r)^{-n}}{r}\right) = 500\left(\frac{1 - (1 + r)^{-72}}{r}\right)$$

By graphing A as a function of r, we find that when $r \approx 0.005167$, $A = 30,000$. Thus, if the present value of the annuity is \$30,000, the monthly interest rate is 0.5167%, and the nominal rate is $12(0.005167) = 0.062$ or 6.2%.

6. Since the man pays \$2000 for 6 years and \$3500 for 8 years, we can consider the payments to be an annuity of \$3500 for 14 years minus an annuity of \$1500 for 6 years so that the first 24 payments are \$2000 each. Thus, the present value is

$$3500a_{\overline{56}|0.015} - 1500a_{\overline{24}|0.015}$$

$$\approx 3500(37.705879) - 1500(20.030405)$$

$$= 101,924.97$$

Thus, the present value of the payments is \$101,925. Since the man made an initial down payment of \$20,000, list price was $101,925 + 20,000 = \$121,925$.

7. Let $r = \frac{0.048}{4} = 0.012$, and $n = 24$.

$$A = R\left(\frac{1 - (1 + r)^{-n}}{r}\right)$$

$$A = R\left(\frac{1 - (1 + 0.012)^{-24}}{0.012}\right) = R\left(\frac{1 - (1.012)^{-24}}{0.012}\right)$$

By Graphing A as a function of R, we find that when $R = 723.03$, $A = 15,000$. Thus the monthly payment is \$723.03 if the present value of the annuity is \$15,000.

8. Find the annuity due. The man makes an initial payment of $1200 followed by an ordinary annuity of $1200 for 11 months. Thus, let $R = 1200$, $n = 11$, and $r = \dfrac{0.068}{12}$. The present value of the annuity due is

$$1200\left(1 + a_{\overline{11}|\frac{0.068}{12}}\right) = 1200(1 + 10.635005) = 13{,}962.01$$

Thus, he should pay $13,962.01.

9. Let $R = 2000$ and let $r = 0.057$. Then, the value of the IRA at the end of 15 years, when $n = 15$, is given by

$$S = R\left(\frac{(1+r)^n - 1}{r}\right)$$

$$S = 2000\left(\frac{(1+0.057)^{15} - 1}{0.057}\right) \approx 45{,}502.06$$

Thus, at the end of 15 years the IRA will be worth $45,502.06.

10. Let $R = 2000$ and let $r = 0.057$. Since the deposits are made at the beginning of each year, the value of the IRA at the end of 15 years is given by

$$S = R\left(\frac{(1+r)^{n+1} - 1}{r}\right) - R.$$

Let $n = 15$.

$$S = 2000\left(\frac{(1+0.057)^{16} - 1}{0.057}\right) - 2000 \approx 48{,}095.67$$

Thus, the IRA is worth $48,095.67 at the end of 15 years.

Exercise 8.3

1. 64

$$64\left(\frac{1}{2}\right) = 32$$

$$64\left(\frac{1}{2}\right)^2 = 16$$

$$64\left(\frac{1}{2}\right)^3 = 8$$

$$64\left(\frac{1}{2}\right)^4 = 4$$

3. 100

$$100(1.02) = 102$$

$$100(1.02)^2 = 104.04$$

5. $s = \dfrac{\frac{2}{3}\left[1 - \left(\frac{2}{3}\right)^5\right]}{1 - \frac{2}{3}} = \dfrac{\frac{2}{3}\left[\frac{211}{243}\right]}{\frac{1}{3}} = \dfrac{422}{243}$

7. $s = \dfrac{1\left[1 - (0.1)^6\right]}{1 - 0.1} = 1.11111$

9. $a_{\overline{35}|0.04} \approx 18.664613$

11. $s_{\overline{8}|0.0075} \approx 8.213180$

13. $500 a_{\overline{5}|0.07} \approx 500(4.100197) \approx \$2050.10$

15. $2000a_{\overline{18}|0.02} \approx 2000(14.992031) \approx \$29,984.06$

17. $800 + 800a_{\overline{11}|0.035} \approx 800 + 800(9.001551)$
     $\approx \$8001.24$

19. $2000s_{\overline{36}|0.0125} \approx 2000(45.115505)$
     $= \$90,231.01$

21. $5000s_{\overline{20}|0.07} \approx 5000(40.995492) = \$204,977.46$

23. $1200\left(s_{\overline{13}|0.08} - 1\right) \approx 1200(21.495297 - 1)$
     $\approx \$24,594.36$

25. $75a_{\overline{30}|0.005} - 25a_{\overline{6}|0.005}$
     $\approx 75(27.794054) - 25(5.896384)$
     $\approx \$1937.14$

27. $R = \dfrac{5000}{a_{\overline{12}|0.015}} \approx \dfrac{5000}{10.907505} \approx \$458.40$

29. a. $\left(50s_{\overline{48}|0.005}\right)(1.005)^{24}$
        $\approx 50(54.097832)(1.005)^{24}$
        $\approx \$3048.85$

    b. $3048.85 - 48(50) = \$648.85$

31. $R = \dfrac{48,000}{s_{\overline{10}|0.07}} \approx \dfrac{48,000}{13.816448} \approx \$3474.12$

33. The original annual payment is $\dfrac{25,000}{s_{\overline{10}|0.06}}$. After six years the value of the fund is

$\dfrac{25,000}{s_{\overline{10}|0.06}}s_{\overline{6}|0.06}$.

This accumulates to

$\left[\dfrac{25,000}{s_{\overline{10}|0.06}}s_{\overline{6}|0.06}\right](1.07)^{4}$.

Let x be the amount of the new payment.

$xs_{\overline{4}|0.07} = 25,000 - \left[\dfrac{25,000}{s_{\overline{10}|0.06}}s_{\overline{6}|0.06}(1.07)^{4}\right]$

$$x = \frac{25,000 - \left[\frac{25,000}{s_{\overline{10}|0.06}} s_{\overline{6}|0.06}(1.07)^4\right]}{s_{\overline{4}|0.07}}$$

$$x \approx \frac{25,000 - \left[\frac{25,000}{13.180795}(6.975319)(1.07)^4\right]}{4.439943}$$

$$x \approx \$1725$$

35. $s_{\overline{60}|0.017} = \dfrac{(1.017)^{60} - 1}{0.017} \approx 102.91305$

37. $700a_{\overline{360}|0.0125} = 700\left[\dfrac{1 - (1.0125)^{-360}}{0.0125}\right]$

$\approx 55,360.30$

39. $R = \dfrac{3000}{s_{\overline{20}|0.01375}} = \dfrac{3000(0.01375)}{(1.01375)^{20} - 1} \approx \$131.34$

41. $200,000 + 200,000a_{\overline{19}|0.10}$

$= 200,000 + 200,000\left[\dfrac{1 - (1.10)^{-19}}{0.10}\right]$

$\approx \$1,872,984.02$

43. For the first situation, the compound amount is

$$\left[2000\left(s_{\overline{11}|0.07} - 1\right)\right](1.07)^{30}$$

$$= 2000\left[\frac{(1.07)^{11} - 1}{0.07} - 1\right](1.07)^{30}$$

$\approx \$225,073,$
so the net earnings are
$225,073 - 20,000 = \$205,073.$
For the second situation, the compound amount is

$$2000\left(s_{\overline{31}|0.07} - 1\right) = 2000\left[\frac{(1.07)^{31} - 1}{0.07} - 1\right]$$

$\approx \$202,146,$
so the net earnings are $202,146 - 60,000 = \$142,146.$

Exercise 8.4

1. $R = \dfrac{2000}{a_{\overline{36}|0.0125}} \approx \dfrac{2000}{28.847267} \approx \$69.33$

3. $R = \dfrac{8000}{a_{\overline{36}|\frac{0.04}{12}}} \approx \dfrac{8000}{33.870766} \approx \$236.19$

Finance charge = $36(236.19) - 8000 = \$502.84$

5. a. $R = \dfrac{7500}{a_{\overline{36}|\frac{0.04}{12}}} \approx \dfrac{7500}{33.870766} \approx \$221.43$

b. $7500\dfrac{0.04}{12} = \$25$

c. $221.43 - 25 = \$196.43$

7. $R = \dfrac{5000}{a_{\overline{4}|0.07}} \approx \dfrac{5000}{3.387211} \approx \$1476.14$

The interest for the first period is $(0.07)(5000) = \$350$, so the principal repaid at the end of that period is $1476.14 - 350 = \$1126.14$. The principal outstanding at the beginning of period 2 is $5000 - 1126.14 = \$3873.86$. The interest for period 2 is $(0.07)(3873.86) = \$271.17$, so the principal repaid at the end of that period is $1476.14 - 271.17 = \$1204.97$. The principal outstanding at beginning of period 3 is $3873.86 - 1204.97 = \$2668.89$. Continuing in this manner, we construct the following amortization schedule.

Period	Prin. Outs. at Beginning	Int. for Period	Pmt. at End	Prin. Repaid at End
1	5000.00	350.00	1476.14	1126.14
2	3873.86	271.17	1476.14	1204.97
3	2668.89	186.82	1476.14	1289.32
4	1379.57	96.57	1476.14	1379.57
Total		904.56	5904.56	5000.00

9. $R = \dfrac{900}{a_{\overline{5}|0.025}} \approx \dfrac{900}{4.645828} \approx \$193.72$

The interest for period 1 is $(0.025)(900) = \$22.50$, so the principal repaid at the end of that period is $193.72 - 22.50 = \$171.22$. The principal outstanding at the beginning of period 2 is $900 - 171.22 = \$728.78$. The interest for that period is $(0.025)(728.78) = \$18.22$, so the principal repaid at the end of that period is $193.72 - 18.22 = \$175.50$. The principal outstanding at the beginning of period 3 is $728.78 - 175.50 = \$553.28$. Continuing in this manner, we obtain the following amortization schedule. Note the adjustment in the final payment.

Period	Prin. Outs. at Beginning	Int. for Period	Pmt. at End	Prin. Repaid at End
1	900.00	22.50	193.72	171.22
2	728.78	18.22	193.72	175.50
3	553.28	13.83	193.72	179.89
4	373.39	9.33	193.72	184.39
5	189.00	4.73	193.73	189.00
Total		68.61	968.61	900.00

11. From Eq. (1),

$$n = \dfrac{\ln\left[\dfrac{100}{100-1000(0.02)}\right]}{\ln(1.02)} \approx 11.268.$$

Thus the number of full payments is 11.

13. Each of the original payments is $\dfrac{10,000}{a_{\overline{10}|0.04}}$.

After two years the value of the remaining payments is $\left(\dfrac{10,000}{a_{\overline{10}|0.04}}\right) a_{\overline{6}|0.04}$. Thus the new annual payment is

$$\dfrac{10,000 a_{\overline{6}|0.04}}{a_{\overline{10}|0.04}} \cdot \dfrac{1}{a_{\overline{6}|0.05}}$$

$$\approx \dfrac{10,000(5.242137)}{8.110896} \cdot \dfrac{1}{5.075692} \approx \$1273.$$

15. a. Monthly interest rate is $\dfrac{0.092}{12}$.

Monthly payment is

$$\dfrac{245,000}{a_{\overline{300}|\frac{0.092}{12}}} = 245,000\left[\dfrac{\frac{23}{3000}}{1-\left(1+\frac{0.092}{12}\right)^{-300}}\right]$$

$$\approx \$2089.69$$

b. $245,000\left(\dfrac{0.092}{12}\right) = \$1878.33$

c. $2089.69 - 1878.33 = \$211.36$

d. $300(2089.69) - 245,000 = \$381,907$

17. $n = \dfrac{\ln\left[\dfrac{100}{100-2000(0.015)}\right]}{\ln 1.015} \approx 23.956$. Thus the number of full payments is 23.

19. Present value of mortgage payments is

$$600a_{\overline{360}|\frac{0.076}{12}} = 600\left[\frac{1-\left(1+\frac{0.076}{12}\right)^{-360}}{\frac{0.076}{12}}\right]$$

$\approx \$84,976.84$
This amount is 75% of the purchase price x.
$0.75x = 84,976.84$
$x = \$113,302.45$

21. $\dfrac{25,000}{a_{\overline{60}|0.0125}} - \dfrac{25,000}{a_{\overline{60}|0.01}}$

$= 25,000\left[\dfrac{1}{a_{\overline{60}|0.0125}} - \dfrac{1}{a_{\overline{60}|0.01}}\right]$

$= 25,000\left[\dfrac{0.0125}{1-(1.0125)^{-60}} - \dfrac{0.01}{1-(1.01)^{-60}}\right]$

$\approx \$38.64$

Chapter 8 Review Problems

1. $s = 2+1+\dfrac{1}{2}+\ldots+2\left(\dfrac{1}{2}\right)^5 = \dfrac{2\left[1-\left(\frac{1}{2}\right)^6\right]}{1-\frac{1}{2}}$

$= \dfrac{2\left[\frac{63}{64}\right]}{\frac{1}{2}} = \dfrac{63}{16}$

13. Let x be the first payment. The equation of value now is

$x + 2x(1.07)^{-3} = 500(1.05)^{-3} + 500(1.03)^{-8}$

$x\left[1 + 2(1.07)^{-3}\right] = 500(1.05)^{-3} + 500(1.03)^{-8}$

$x = \dfrac{500(1.05)^{-3} + 500(1.03)^{-8}}{1 + 2(1.07)^{-3}}$

$x \approx \$314.00$

3. 8.2% compounded semiannually corresponds to an effective rate of $(1.041)^2 - 1 = 0.083681$ or 8.37%. Thus the better choice is 8.5% compounded annually.

5. Let x be the payment at the end of 2 years. The equation of value at the end of year 2 is
$1000(1.04)^4 + x$
$= 1200(1.04)^{-4} + 1000(1.04)^{-8}$
x
$= 1200(1.04)^{-4} + 1000(1.04)^{-8} - 1000(1.04)^4$
$\approx \$586.60$

7. a. $A = 200a_{\overline{13}|0.04} \approx 200(9.985648)$
$\approx \$1997.13$

   b. $S = 200s_{\overline{13}|0.04} \approx 200(16.626838)$
$\approx \$3325.37$

9. $100s_{\overline{9}|0.035} - 100 \approx 100(10.368496) - 100$
$\approx \$936.85$

11. $\dfrac{5000}{s_{\overline{5}|0.06}} \approx \dfrac{5000}{5.637093} \approx \$886.98$

15. $R = \dfrac{15,000}{a_{\overline{5}|0.0075}} \approx \dfrac{15,000}{4.889440} \approx \$3067.84$

The interest for period 1 is $(0.0075)(15,000) = \$112.50$, so the principal repaid at the end of that period is $3067.84 - 112.50 = \$2955.34$. The principal outstanding at beginning of period 2 is $15,000 - 2955.34 = \$12,044.66$. The interest for period 2 is $0.0075(12,044.66) = \$90.33$, so the principal repaid at the end of that period is $3067.84 - 90.33 = \$2977.51$. Principal outstanding at the beginning of period 3 is $12,044.66 - 2977.51 = \$9067.15$. Continuing, we obtain the following amortization schedule. Note the adjustment in the final payment.

Period	Prin. Outs. at Beginning	Int. for Period	Pmt. at End	Prin. Repaid at End
1	15,000.00	112.50	3067.84	2955.34
2	12,044.66	90.33	3067.84	2977.51
3	9067.15	68.00	3067.84	2999.84
4	6067.31	45.50	3067.84	3022.34
5	3044.97	22.84	3067.81	3044.97
Total		339.17	15,339.17	15,000.00

17. The monthly payment is

$$\frac{11,000}{a_{\overline{48}|\frac{0.055}{12}}} = 11,000\left[\frac{\frac{0.055}{12}}{1 - \left(1 + \frac{0.055}{12}\right)^{-48}}\right] \approx \$255.82$$

The finance charge is $48(255.82) - 11,000 = \$1279.36$

Mathematical Snapshot Chapter 8

1. $\dfrac{0.075}{2} = 0.0375$, thus $R = 0.0375(15,000) = 562.50$.

$$P = 15,000(1.0725)^{-20} + 562.50 \cdot \frac{1 - (1.0725)^{-20}}{\sqrt{1.0725} - 1} \approx \$15,597.85$$

3. The normal yield curve assumes a stable economic climate. By contrast, if investors are expecting a drop in interest rates, and with it a drop in yields from future investments, they will gladly give up liquidity for long-term investment at current, more favorable, interest rates. T-bills, which force the investor to find a new investment in a short time, are correspondingly less attractive, and so prices drop and yields rise.

Chapter 9

1.

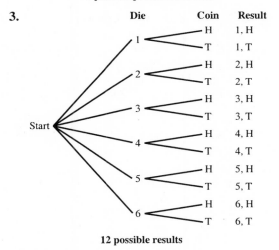

Assembly Line	Finishing Line	Production Route

6 possible production routes

3.

12 possible results

5. There are 5 science courses and 4 humanities courses. By the basic counting principle, the number of selections is $5 \cdot 4 = 20$.

7. There are 2 appetizers, 4 entrees, 4 desserts, and 3 beverages. By the basic counting principle, the number of possible complete dinners is $2 \cdot 4 \cdot 4 \cdot 3 = 96$.

9. For each of the 10 questions, there are 2 choices. By the basic counting principle, the number of ways to answer the examination is $2 \cdot 2 \cdot \cdots \cdot 2 = 2^{10} = 1024$.

11. $_5P_2 = 5 \cdot 4 = 20$

13. $_6P_6 = \dfrac{6!}{(6-6)!} = \dfrac{6!}{0!} = \dfrac{6 \cdot 5 \cdot 4 \cdot 3 \cdot 2 \cdot 1}{1} = 720$

15. $_4P_2 \cdot _5P_3 = (4 \cdot 3)(5 \cdot 4 \cdot 3) = (12)(60) = 720$

17. $\dfrac{1000!}{999!} = \dfrac{1000 \cdot 999!}{999!} = 1000$

For most calculators, attempting to evaluate $\dfrac{1000!}{999!}$ results in an error message (because of the magnitude of the numbers involved).

19. A name for the firm is an ordered arrangement of the three last names. Thus the number of possible firm names is $_3P_3 = 3! = 3 \cdot 2 \cdot 1 = 6$.

21. The number of ways of selecting 3 of 8 contestants in an order is $_8P_3 = 8 \cdot 7 \cdot 6 = 336$.

23. On each roll of a die, there are 6 possible outcomes. By the basic counting principle, on 3 rolls the number of possible results is $6 \cdot 6 \cdot 6 = 6^3 = 216$.

25. The number of ways of selecting 3 of the 12 students in an order is $_{12}P_3 = 12 \cdot 11 \cdot 10 = 1320$.

27. The number of ways an employee can choose 3 of the 8 items in an order is $_8P_3 = 8 \cdot 7 \cdot 6 = 336$.

29. The number of ways to select six of the six different letters in the word MEADOW in an order is $_6P_6 = 6! = 6 \cdot 5 \cdot 4 \cdot 3 \cdot 2 \cdot 1 = 720$.

31. For an arrangement of books, order is important. The number of ways to arrange 5 of 7 books is $_7P_5 = 7 \cdot 6 \cdot 5 \cdot 4 \cdot 3 = 2520$. All 7 books can be arranged in $_7P_7 = 7! = 5040$ ways.

33. After a "four of a kind" hand is dealt, the cards can be arranged so that the first four have the same face value, and order is not important, There are 13 possibilities for the first four cards (all 2's, all 3's, ..., all aces). The fifth card can be any one of the 48 cards that remain. By the basic counting principle, the number of "four of a kind" hands is $13 \cdot 48 = 624$.

35. The number of ways the waitress can place four of the four different sandwiches (and order is important) is
$${}_4P_4 = 4! = 4 \cdot 3 \cdot 2 \cdot 1 = 24.$$

37. a. To fill the four offices by different people, 4 of 12 members must be selected, and order is important. This can be done in
$${}_{12}P_4 = 12 \cdot 11 \cdot 10 \cdot 9 = 11,880 \text{ ways.}$$

b. If the president and vice president must be different members, then there are 12 choices for president, 11 for vice president, 12 for secretary, and 12 for treasurer. By the basic counting principle, the offices can be filled in $12 \cdot 11 \cdot 12 \cdot 12 = 19,008$ ways.

39. There are 2 choices for the center position. After that choice is made, to fill the remaining four positions (and order is important), there are ${}_4P_4$ ways. By the basic counting principle, to assign positions to the five-member team there are
$$2 \cdot {}_4P_4 = 2(4!) = 2(24) = 48 \text{ ways.}$$

41. There are ${}_4P_4$ ways to select the first four batters (order is important) and there are ${}_5P_5$ ways to select the remaining batters. By the basic counting principle, the number of possible batting orders is
$${}_4P_4 \cdot {}_5P_5 = 4! \cdot 5! = 24 \cdot 120 = 2880.$$

Exercise 9.2

1. ${}_6C_4 = \dfrac{6!}{4!(6-4)!} = \dfrac{6!}{4! \cdot 2!} = \dfrac{6 \cdot 5 \cdot 4!}{4!(2 \cdot 1)} = \dfrac{6 \cdot 5}{2 \cdot 1} = 15$

3. ${}_{100}C_{100} = \dfrac{100!}{100!(100-100)!} = \dfrac{1}{0!} = \dfrac{1}{1} = 1$

5. ${}_3P_2 \cdot {}_3C_2 = (3 \cdot 2)\dfrac{3!}{2!(3-2)!} = (3 \cdot 2)\dfrac{3 \cdot 2!}{2! \cdot 1!} = (3 \cdot 2) \cdot 3 = 18$

7. ${}_nC_r = \dfrac{n!}{r!(n-r)!}$

${}_nC_{n-r} = \dfrac{n!}{(n-r)![n-(n-r)]!} = \dfrac{n!}{(n-r)!r!}.$

Thus ${}_nC_r = {}_nC_{n-r}.$

9. The number of ways of selecting 4 of 17 people so that order is not important is

$$_{17}C_4 = \frac{17!}{4!(17-4)!} = \frac{17!}{4! \cdot 13!}$$

$$= \frac{17 \cdot 16 \cdot 15 \cdot 14 \cdot 13!}{4 \cdot 3 \cdot 2 \cdot 1(13!)} = 2380$$

11. The number of ways of selecting 10 of 12 questions (without regard to order) is

$$_{12}C_{10} = \frac{12!}{10!(12-10)!} = \frac{12!}{10! \cdot 2!} = \frac{12 \cdot 11 \cdot 10!}{10! \cdot 2 \cdot 1}$$

$$= 66.$$

13. The order of selecting 10 of the 74 dresses is of no concern. Thus the number of possible

samples $_{74}C_{10} = \dfrac{74!}{10! \cdot (74-10)!} = \dfrac{74!}{10! \cdot 64!}$.

15. To score 80, 90, or 100, exactly 8, 9, or 10 questions must be correct, respectively. The number of ways in which 8 of 10 questions can be correct is

$$_{10}C_8 = \frac{10!}{8!(10-8)!} = \frac{10!}{8! \cdot 2!} = \frac{10 \cdot 9 \cdot 8!}{8! \cdot 2 \cdot 1} = 45.$$

For 9 of 10 questions, the number of ways is

$$_{10}C_9 = \frac{10!}{9!(10-9)!} = \frac{10!}{9! \cdot 1!} = \frac{10 \cdot 9!}{9! \cdot 1} = 10,$$

and for 10 of 10 questions, it is

$$_{10}C_{10} = \frac{10!}{10!(10-10)!} = \frac{10!}{10! \cdot 0!} = 1.$$

Thus the number of ways to score 80 or better is $45 + 10 + 1 = 56$.

17. The word REMEMBER has 8 letters with repetition: two R's, three E's, two M's, and one B. Thus the number of distinguishable horizontal arrangements is

$$\frac{8!}{2! \cdot 3! \cdot 2! \cdot 1!} = \frac{8 \cdot 7 \cdot 6 \cdot 5 \cdot 4 \cdot 3!}{(2)3!(2)} = 1680.$$

19. The number of ways 4 heads and 3 tails can occur in 7 tosses of a coin is the same as the number of distinguishable permutations in the "word" HHHHTTT, which is

$$\frac{7!}{4! \cdot 3!} = \frac{7 \cdot 6 \cdot 5 \cdot 4!}{4!(6)} = 35.$$

21. Since the order in which the calls are made is important, the number of possible schedules for the 6 calls is $_6P_6 = 6! = 720$.

23. The number of ways to assign 9 scientists so 3 work on project A, 3 work on B, and

3 work on C is $\dfrac{9!}{3!3!3!} = 1680$.

25. A response to the true-false questions can be considered an ordered arrangement of 10 letters, 5 of which are T's and 5 of which are F's. The number of different responses is

$$\frac{10!}{5! \cdot 5!} = \frac{10 \cdot 9 \cdot 8 \cdot 7 \cdot 6 \cdot 5!}{5!(5 \cdot 4 \cdot 3 \cdot 2 \cdot 1)} = 252.$$

27. The number of ways to assign 15 clients to 3 caseworkers (cells) with 5 clients to each

caseworker is $\dfrac{15!}{5! \cdot 5! \cdot 5!} = 756,756$.

29. a. Six flags must be arranged: two are red (type 1), two are green (type 2), and two are yellow (type 3). Thus the number of distinguishable arrangements

(messages) is $\dfrac{6!}{2! \cdot 2! \cdot 2!} = 90$.

b. If exactly one yellow flag is used, then five flags are involved and the number

of different messages is $\dfrac{5!}{2! \cdot 2! \cdot 1!} = 30$.

If exactly two yellow flags are used, then six flags are involved and the number of different messages is

$\dfrac{6!}{2! \cdot 2! \cdot 2!} = 90$. If all three yellow flags

are used, then seven flags are involved and the number of different messages is

$\dfrac{7!}{2! \cdot 2! \cdot 3!} = 210$. Thus if at least one

yellow flag is used, the number of different messages is
$30 + 90 + 210 = 330$.

31. The order in which the securities go into the portfolio is not important. The number of ways to select 8 of 12 stocks is $_{12}C_8$. The number of ways to select 4 of 7 bonds is $_7C_4$. By the basic counting principle, the number of ways to create the portfolio is

$$_{12}C_8 \cdot {}_7C_4 = \frac{12!}{8!(12-8)!} \cdot \frac{7!}{4!(7-4)!}$$

$$= \frac{12!}{8! \cdot 4!} \cdot \frac{7!}{4! \cdot 3!} = \frac{12 \cdot 11 \cdot 10 \cdot 9 \cdot 8!}{8! \cdot 4 \cdot 3 \cdot 2 \cdot 1} \cdot \frac{7 \cdot 6 \cdot 5 \cdot 4!}{4! \cdot 3 \cdot 2 \cdot 1}$$

$$= 495 \cdot 35 = 17,325.$$

33. a. Selecting 3 of the 3 males can be done in only 1 way.

b. Selecting 4 of the 4 females can be done in only 1 way.

c. Selecting 2 males and 2 females can be considered as a two-stage process. In the first stage, 2 of the 3 males are selected (and order is not important), which can be done in $_3C_2$ ways. In the second stage, 2 of the 4 females are selected, which can be done in $_4C_2$ ways. By the basic counting principle, the ways of selecting the subcommittee is $_3C_2 \cdot {}_4C_2 = \frac{3!}{2!(3-2)!} \cdot \frac{4!}{2!(4-2)!}$

$$= \frac{3!}{2! \cdot 1!} \cdot \frac{4!}{2! \cdot 2!} = 3 \cdot 6 = 18$$

35. There are 4 cards of a given denomination and the number of ways of selecting 3 cards of that denomination is $_4C_3$.
Since there are 13 denominations, the number of ways of selecting 3 cards of one denomination is $13 \cdot {}_4C_3$. After that selection is made, the 2 other cards must be of the same denomination (of which 12 denominations remain). Thus for the remaining 2 cards there are $12 \cdot {}_4C_2$ selections. By the basic counting principle, the number of possible full-house hands is

$$13 \cdot {}_4C_3 \cdot 12 \cdot {}_4C_2 = 13 \cdot \frac{4!}{3! \cdot 1!} \cdot 12 \cdot \frac{4!}{2! \cdot 2!}$$

$$= 13 \cdot 4 \cdot 12 \cdot 6 = 3744.$$

37. This situation can be considered as placing 18 tourists into 3 cells: 7 tourist go to the 7-passenger tram, 8 go to the 8-passenger tram, and 3 tourists remain at the bottom of the mountain. This can be done in

$$\frac{18!}{7! \cdot 8! \cdot 3!} = 5,250,960 \text{ ways.}$$

Principles in Practice 9.3

1. This is a combination problem because the order in which the videos are selected is not important. The number of possible choices is the number of ways 3 videos can be selected from 400 without regard to order.

$$_{400}C_3 = \frac{400!}{3!(400-3)!} = \frac{400!}{3!397!}$$

$$= \frac{400 \cdot 399 \cdot 398 \cdot 397!}{3!397!}$$

$$= \frac{400 \cdot 399 \cdot 398}{3 \cdot 2}$$

$$= 10,586,800$$

Exercise 9.3

1. {9D, 9H, 9C, 9S}

3. {1H, 1T, 2H, 2T, 3H, 3T, 4H, 4T, 5H, 5T, 6H, 6T}

5. {mo, mu, ms, me, om, ou, os, oe, um, uo, us, ue, sm, so, su, se, em, eo, eu, es}

7. a. {RR, RW, RB, WR, WW, WB, BR, BW, BB};

b. {RW, RB, WR, WB, BR, BW}

9. Sample space consists of ordered sets of six elements and each element is H or T. Since there are two possibilities for each toss (H or T), and there are six tosses, by he basic counting principle, the number of sample points is $2 \cdot 2 \cdot 2 \cdot 2 \cdot 2 \cdot 2 = 2^6 = 64$.

11. Sample space consists of ordered pairs where the first element indicates the card drawn (52 possibilities) and the second element indicates the number on the die (6 possibilities). By the basic counting principle, the number of sample points is $52 \cdot 6 = 312$.

13. Sample space consists of combinations of 52 cards taken 13 at a time. Thus the number of sample points is $_{52}C_{13}$.

15. The sample points that are either in E, or in F, or in both E and F are 1, 3, 5, 7, and 9. Thus $E \cup F = \{1, 3, 5, 7, 9\}$.

17. The sample points in S that are not in E are 2, 4, 6, 7, 8, 9, and 10. Thus $E' = \{2, 4, 6, 7, 8, 9, 10\}$. The sample points common to both E' and F are 7 and 9. Thus $E' \cap F = \{7, 9\}$.

19. The sample points in S that are not in F are 1, 2, 4, 6, 8, and 10. Thus $F' = \{1, 2, 4, 6, 8, 10\}$.

21. $(F \cap G)' = \varnothing' = S$

23. $E_1 \cap E_2 \neq \varnothing$; $E_1 \cap E_3 \neq \varnothing$; $E_1 \cap E_4 = \varnothing$;

$E_2 \cap E_3 = \varnothing$; $E_2 \cap E_4 \neq \varnothing$; $E_3 \cap E_4 = \varnothing$. Thus E_1 and E_4, E_2 and E_3, and E_3 and E_4 are mutually exclusive.

25. $E \cap F \neq \varnothing$, $E \cap G \neq \varnothing$, $E \cap H = \varnothing$, $E \cap I \neq \varnothing$, $F \cap G \neq \varnothing$, $F \cap H \neq \varnothing$ $F \cap I \neq \varnothing$, $G \cap H = \varnothing$, $G \cap I \neq \varnothing$, $H \cap I = \varnothing$. Thus E and H, G and H, and H and I are mutually exclusive.

27. a. $S = \{$HHH, HHT, HTH, HTT, THH, THT, TTH, TTT$\}$

   b. $E_1 = \{$HHH, HHT, HTH, HTT, THH, THT, TTH$\}$

c. $E_2 = \{$HHT, HTH, HTT, THH, THT, TTH, TTT$\}$

d. $E_1 \cup E_2 = \{$HHH, HHT, HTH, HTT, THH, THT, TTH, TTT$\} = S$

e. $E_1 \cap E_2 = \{$HHT, HTH, HTT, THH, THT, TTH$\}$

f. $(E_1 \cup E_2)' = S' = \varnothing$

g. $(E_1 \cap E_2)' = \{$HHT, HTH, HTT, THH, THT, TTH$\}' = \{$HHH, TTT$\}$

29. a. $\{$ABC, ACB, BAC, BCA, CAB, CBA$\}$

   b. $\{$ABC, ACB$\}$

   c. $\{$BAC, BCA, CAB, CBA$\}$

31. Using the properties in Table 9.1, we have
$(E \cap F) \cap (E \cap F')$
$= (E \cap F \cap E) \cap F'$ [property 15]
$= (E \cap E \cap F) \cap F'$ [property 11]
$= (E \cap E) \cap (F \cap F')$ [porperty 15]
$= E \cap \varnothing$ [property 5]
$= \varnothing$ [property 9]
Thus $(E \cap F) \cap (E \cap F') = \varnothing$, so $E \cap F$ and $E \cap F'$ are mutually exclusive.

Exercise 9.4

1. $2000P(E) = 2000(0.3) = 600$

3. a. $P(E') = 1 - P(E) = 1 - 0.2 = 0.8$

   b. $P(E \cup F) = P(E) + P(F) - P(E \cap F)$
$= 0.2 + 0.3 - 0.1 = 0.4$

5. If E and F are mutually exclusive, then $E \cap F = \varnothing$.
Thus $P(E \cap F) = P(\varnothing) = 0$. Since it is given that $P(E \cap F) = 0.831 \neq 0$, E and F are not mutually exclusive.

7. a. $E_8 = \{(2, 6), (3, 5), (4, 4), (5, 3), (6, 2)\}$

$$P(E_8) = \frac{n(E_8)}{n(S)} = \frac{5}{36}$$

b. $E_{2 \text{ or } 3} = \{(1, 1), (1, 2), (2, 1)\}$

$$P(E_{2 \text{ or } 3}) = \frac{n(E_{2 \text{ or } 3})}{n(S)} = \frac{3}{36} = \frac{1}{12}$$

c. $E_{3, 4, \text{or } 5} = \{(1,2),(2,1),(1,3),(2,2),(3,1),$
$$(1,4),(2,3),(3,2),(4,1)\}$$

$$P(E_{3, 4, \text{or } 5}) = \frac{n(E_{3,4, \text{ or } 5})}{n(S)} = \frac{9}{36} = \frac{1}{4}$$

d. $E_{12 \text{ or } 13} = E_{12}$, since E_{13} is an impossible event.
$$E_{12} = \{(6,6)\}$$

$$P(E_{12 \text{ or } 13}) = \frac{n(E_{12 \text{ or } 13})}{n(S)} = \frac{1}{36}$$

e. $E_2 = \{(1,1)\}$
$E_4 = \{(1,3),(2,2),(3,1)\}$
$E_6 = \{(1,5),(2,4),(3,3,),(4,2),(5,1)\}$
$E_8 = \{(2,6),(3,5),(4,4),(5,3),(6,2)\}$
$E_{10} = \{(4,6),(5,5),(6,4)\}$
$E_{12} = \{(6,6)\}$
$P(E_{\text{even}}) = P(E_2) + P(E_4) + P(E_6) + P(E_8) + P(E_{10}) + P(E_{12})$

$$= \frac{1}{36} + \frac{3}{36} + \frac{5}{36} + \frac{5}{36} + \frac{3}{36} + \frac{1}{36} = \frac{18}{36} = \frac{1}{2}$$

f. $P(E_{\text{odd}}) = 1 - P(E_{\text{even}}) = 1 - \frac{1}{2} = \frac{1}{2}$

g. $E'_{\text{less than } 10} = E_{10} \cup E_{11} \cup E_{12}$
$= \{(4,6),(5,5),(6,4)\} \cup \{(5,6),(6,5)\} \cup \{(6,6)\} = \{(4,6),(5,5),(6,4),(5,6),(6,5),(6,6)\}.$
$P(E_{\text{less than } 10}) = 1 - P(E'_{\text{less than } 10})$

$$= 1 - \frac{6}{36} = \frac{30}{36} = \frac{5}{6}.$$

9. $n(S) = 52.$

a. $P(\text{king of hearts}) = \dfrac{n(E_{\text{king of hearts}})}{n(S)} = \dfrac{1}{52}$

b. $P(\text{diamond}) = \dfrac{n(E_{\text{ diamond}})}{n(S)} = \dfrac{13}{52} = \dfrac{1}{4}$

c. $P(\text{jack}) = \dfrac{n(E_{\text{jack}})}{n(S)} = \dfrac{4}{52} = \dfrac{1}{13}$

d $P(\text{red}) = \dfrac{n(E_{\text{red}})}{n(S)} = \dfrac{26}{52} = \dfrac{1}{2}$

e.   Because a heart is not a club,
$E_{\text{heart}} \cap E_{\text{club}} = \varnothing.$
Thus
$P(E_{\text{heart or club}}) = P(E_{\text{heart}} \cup E_{\text{club}})$
$= P(E_{\text{heart}}) + P(E_{\text{club}})$
$= \dfrac{n(E_{\text{heart}})}{n(S)} + \dfrac{n(E_{\text{club}})}{n(S)} = \dfrac{13}{52} + \dfrac{13}{52}$
$= \dfrac{26}{52} = \dfrac{1}{2}$

f. $E_{\text{club and 4}} = \{4C\}$
$P(E_{\text{club and 4}}) = \dfrac{n(E_{\text{club and 4}})}{n(S)} = \dfrac{1}{52}$

g. $P(\text{club or 4})$
$= P(\text{club}) + P(4) - P(\text{club and 4})$
$= \dfrac{13}{52} + \dfrac{4}{52} - \dfrac{1}{52} = \dfrac{16}{52} = \dfrac{4}{13}$

h. $E_{\text{red and king}} = \{KH, KD\}$
$P(\text{red and king}) = \dfrac{n(E_{\text{red and king}})}{n(S)}$
$= \dfrac{2}{52} = \dfrac{1}{26}$

i. $E_{\text{spade and heart}} = \varnothing$
Thus $P(\text{spade and heart}) = 0$

11. $n(S) = 2 \cdot 6 \cdot 52 = 624$

a. $P(\text{tail, 3, queen of hearts})$
$= \dfrac{n(E_{T,3,QH})}{n(S)} = \dfrac{1 \cdot 1 \cdot 1}{624} = \dfrac{1}{624}$

b. $P(\text{tail, 3, queen})$
$= \dfrac{n(E_{T,3,Q})}{n(S)} = \dfrac{1 \cdot 1 \cdot 4}{624} = \dfrac{1}{156}$

c. $P(\text{head, 2 or 3, queen})$
$= \dfrac{n(E_{H,2 \text{ or } 3,Q})}{n(S)} = \dfrac{1 \cdot 2 \cdot 4}{624} = \dfrac{1}{78}$

d. $P(\text{head, even, diamond})$
$= \dfrac{n(E_{H,E,D})}{n(S)} = \dfrac{1 \cdot 3 \cdot 13}{624} = \dfrac{1}{16}$

13. $n(S) = 52 \cdot 51 = 2652$

a. $P(\text{both kings}) = \dfrac{n(E_{\text{both kings}})}{n(S)} = \dfrac{4 \cdot 3}{2652}$
$= \dfrac{1}{221}$

b.   The number of ways that first card is a diamond and second card is a heart is $13 \cdot 13$; for first card a heart and second card a diamond, the number of ways is $13 \cdot 13$. Thus
$P(E_{\text{one card diamond \& other is heart}})$
$= \dfrac{13 \cdot 13 + 13 \cdot 13}{2652} = \dfrac{338}{2652} = \dfrac{13}{102}.$

15. $n(S) = 2 \cdot 2 \cdot 2 = 8$

a. $E_{3 \text{ girls}} = \{GGG\}$
$P(3 \text{ girls}) = \dfrac{n(E_{3 \text{ girls}})}{n(S)} = \dfrac{1}{8}$

b. $E_{1 \text{ boy}} = \{BGG, GBG, GGB\}$
$P(1 \text{ boy}) = \dfrac{n(E_{1 \text{ boy}})}{n(S)} = \dfrac{3}{8}$

c. $E_{\text{no girl}} = \{BBB\}$
$P(\text{no girl}) = \dfrac{n(E_{\text{no girl}})}{n(S)} = \dfrac{1}{8}$

d. $P(\text{at least 1 girl}) = 1 - P(\text{no girl})$
$= 1 - \dfrac{1}{8} = \dfrac{7}{8}$

17. The sample space consists of 60 stocks. Thus $n(S) = 60$.

a. $P(\text{6\% or more}) = \dfrac{n(E_{\text{6\% or more}})}{n(S)} = \dfrac{48}{60} = \dfrac{4}{5}$

b. $P(\text{less than 6\%}) = 1 - P(\text{6\% or more}) = 1 - \dfrac{4}{5} = \dfrac{1}{5}$

19. $n(S) = 40$
Of the 40 students, 4 received an A, 10 a B, 14 a C, 10 a D, and 2 an F.

a. $P(A) = \dfrac{n(E_A)}{n(S)} = \dfrac{4}{40} = \dfrac{1}{10} = 0.1$

b. $P(A \text{ or } B) = \dfrac{n(E_{A \text{ or } B})}{n(S)} = \dfrac{4 + 10}{40} = \dfrac{14}{40} = 0.35$

c. $P(\text{neither D nor F}) = P(A, B, \text{ or } C) = \dfrac{n(E_{A, B, \text{ or } C})}{n(S)} = \dfrac{4 + 10 + 14}{40} = \dfrac{28}{40} = 0.7$

d. $P(\text{no F}) = 1 - P(F) = 1 - \dfrac{n(E_F)}{n(S)} = 1 - \dfrac{2}{40} = \dfrac{38}{40} = 0.95$

e. Let N = number of students. Then $n(S) = N$. Of the N students, $0.10N$ received an A, $0.25N$ a B, $0.35N$ a C, $0.25N$ a D, $0.05N$ an F.
$$P(A) = \dfrac{0.10N}{N} = 0.1;$$
$$P(A \text{ or } B) = \dfrac{0.10N + 0.25N}{N} = \dfrac{0.35N}{N} = 0.35$$
$$P(\text{neither D nor F}) = P(A, B, \text{ or } C) = \dfrac{0.10N + 0.25N + 0.35N}{N} = \dfrac{0.70N}{N} = 0.7$$
$$P(\text{no F}) = 1 - P(F) = 1 - \dfrac{0.05N}{N} = 1 - 0.05 = 0.95$$

21. The sample space consists of combinations of 2 people selected from 5. Thus
$n(S) = {}_5C_2 = \dfrac{5!}{2! \cdot 3!} = \dfrac{5 \cdot 4}{2} = 10$. Because there are only 2 women in the group, the number of possible

2 women committees is 1. Thus $P(\text{2 women}) = \dfrac{n(E_{\text{2 women}})}{n(S)} = \dfrac{1}{10}$.

23. Number of ways to answer exam is
$$2^{10} = 1024 = n(S).$$

   a. There is only one way to achieve 100 points, namely to answer each question correctly. Thus
$$P(100 \text{ points}) = \frac{n(E_{100 \text{ points}})}{n(S)} = \frac{1}{1024}.$$

   b. Number of ways to score 90 points = number of ways that exactly one question is answered incorrectly = 10.
Thus
$$P(90 \text{ or more points})$$
$$= P(90 \text{ points}) + P(100 \text{ points})$$
$$= \frac{10}{1024} + \frac{1}{1024} = \frac{11}{1024}.$$

25. A poker hand is a 5 card deal from 52 cards. Thus $n(S) = {}_{52}C_5$. In 52 cards, there are 4 cards of a particular denomination. Thus, for a full house, the number of ways of selecting 3 of 4 cards of a particular denomination is ${}_4C_3$. Since there are 13 denominations, 3 cards of the same denomination can be dealt in $13 \cdot {}_4C_3$ ways. For the two remaining cards in the full house, there are 12 denominations that are possible, and for each denomination there are ${}_4C_2$ ways of dealing a pair. Thus
$P(\text{full house})$
$$= \frac{n(E_{\text{full house}})}{n(S)} = \frac{13 \cdot {}_4C_3 \cdot 12 \cdot {}_4C_2}{{}_{52}C_5}$$

27. $n(S) = {}_{100}C_3 = \dfrac{100!}{3! \cdot 97!} = 161,700$

   a. $n(E_{3 \text{ females}}) = {}_{35}C_3 = \dfrac{35!}{3! \cdot 32!} = 6545$
$$P(E_{3 \text{ females}}) = \frac{n(E_{3 \text{ females}})}{n(S)}$$
$$= \frac{6545}{161,700} \approx 0.040$$

   b. The number of ways of selecting one professor is 15; the number of ways of selecting two associate professors is ${}_{24}C_2$. Thus
$$n(E_{1 \text{ professor \& 2 associate professors}})$$
$$= 15 \cdot \frac{24!}{2! \cdot 22!} = 15 \cdot 276 = 4140.$$
Therefore,
$$P(E_{1 \text{ professor \& 2 associate professers}})$$
$$= \frac{4140}{161,700} \approx 0.026.$$

29. Let $p = P(1) = P(3) = P(5)$. Then $2p = P(2) = P(4) = P(6)$. Since $P(S) = 1$, then $3(p) + 3(2p) = 1,\ 9p = 1,\ p = p(1) = \dfrac{1}{9}$.

31. a. Of the 100 voters, 51 favor the tax increase. Thus $P(\text{favors tax increase})$
$$= \frac{51}{100} = 0.51.$$

   b. Of the 100 voters, 44 oppose the tax increase. Thus
$$P(\text{opposes tax increase}) = \frac{44}{100} = 0.44.$$

   c. Of the 100 voters, 3 are Republican with no opinion. Thus
$P(\text{is a Republican with no opinion})$
$$= \frac{3}{100} = 0.03.$$

33. $\dfrac{P(E)}{P(E')} = \dfrac{P(E)}{1 - P(E)} = \dfrac{\frac{4}{5}}{1 - \left(\frac{4}{5}\right)} = \dfrac{\frac{4}{5}}{\frac{1}{5}} = \dfrac{4}{1}$

The odds are 4:1.

35. $\dfrac{P(E)}{P(E')} = \dfrac{P(E)}{1 - P(E)} = \dfrac{0.3}{1 - 0.3} = \dfrac{0.3}{0.7} = \dfrac{3}{7}$

The odds are 3:7.

37. $P(E) = \dfrac{5}{5+4} = \dfrac{5}{9}$

39. $P(E) = \dfrac{4}{4+10} = \dfrac{4}{14} = \dfrac{2}{7}$

41. Odds that it will rain tomorrow

$$= \frac{P(\text{rain})}{P(\text{no rain})} = \frac{0.75}{1-0.75} = \frac{0.75}{0.25} = 3.$$

The odds are 3:1.

Exercise 9.5

1. a. $P(E|F) = \dfrac{n(E \cap F)}{n(F)} = \dfrac{2}{5}$

b. Using the result of part (a),

$$P(E'|F) = 1 - P(E|F) = 1 - \frac{2}{5} = \frac{3}{5}.$$

c. $F' = \{3,7,8\}$

$$P(E|F') = \frac{n(E \cap F')}{n(F')} = \frac{1}{3}$$

d. $P(F|E) = \dfrac{n(F \cap E)}{n(E)} = \dfrac{2}{3}$

e. $F \cap G = \{2,4,5\}$

$$P(E|(F \cap G)) = \frac{n(E \cap (F \cap G))}{n(F \cap G)} = \frac{1}{3}$$

3. $P(E|E) = \dfrac{P(E \cap E)}{P(E)} = \dfrac{P(E)}{P(E)} = 1$

5. $P(E'|F) = 1 - P(E|F) = 1 - 0.57 = 0.43$

7. a. $P(E|F) = \dfrac{P(E \cap F)}{P(F)} = \dfrac{1/6}{1/3} = \dfrac{1}{2}$

b. $P(F|E) = \dfrac{P(F \cap E)}{P(E)} = \dfrac{1/6}{1/4} = \dfrac{2}{3}$

9. a. $P(F|E) = \dfrac{P(F \cap E)}{P(E)} = \dfrac{1/5}{1/3} = \dfrac{3}{5}$

b. $P(E \cup F) = P(E) + P(F) - P(E \cap F)$

$$\frac{8}{15} = \frac{1}{3} + P(F) - \frac{1}{5}$$

Thus $P(F) = \dfrac{8}{15} - \dfrac{1}{3} + \dfrac{1}{5} = \dfrac{2}{5}.$

c. From part (b) $P(F) = \dfrac{2}{5}.$

Then $P(E|F) = \dfrac{P(E \cap F)}{P(F)} = \dfrac{1/5}{2/5} = \dfrac{1}{2}.$

d. $P(E) = P(E \cap F) + P(E \cap F')$

$$\frac{1}{3} = \frac{1}{5} + P(E \cap F')$$

so $P(E \cap F') = \dfrac{1}{3} - \dfrac{1}{5} = \dfrac{2}{15}.$

Then $P(E|F') = \dfrac{P(E \cap F')}{P(F')}$

$$= \frac{2/15}{1-(2/5)} = \frac{2/15}{3/5} = \frac{2}{9}.$$

11. a. $P(F) = \dfrac{125}{200} = \dfrac{5}{8}$

b. $P(F|\mathrm{II}) = \dfrac{n(F \cap \mathrm{II})}{n(\mathrm{II})} = \dfrac{35}{58}$

c. $P(O|\mathrm{I}) = \dfrac{n(O \cap \mathrm{I})}{n(\mathrm{I})} = \dfrac{22}{78} = \dfrac{11}{39}$

d. $P(\mathrm{III}) = \dfrac{64}{200} = \dfrac{8}{25}$

e. $P(\mathrm{III}|O) = \dfrac{n(\mathrm{III} \cap O)}{n(O)} = \dfrac{10}{47}$

f. $P(\mathrm{II}|N') = \dfrac{n(\mathrm{II} \cap N')}{n(N')}$

$$= \frac{35+15}{125+47} = \frac{50}{172} = \frac{25}{86}$$

13. a. $P(A|B) = \dfrac{P(A \cap B)}{P(B)} = \dfrac{0.20}{0.40} = \dfrac{1}{2}$

b. $P(B|A) = \dfrac{P(B \cap A)}{P(A)} = \dfrac{0.20}{0.45} = \dfrac{4}{9}$

15. $S = \{BB, BG, GG, GB\}$
Let $E = \{$at least one girl$\} = \{BG, GG, GB\}$,
$F = \{$at least one boy$\} = \{BB, BG, GB\}$.
Thus $P(E|F) = \dfrac{n(E \cap F)}{n(F)} = \dfrac{2}{3}$.

17. $S = \{HHH, HHT, HTH, THH, THT, TTH, TTT\}$.
Let $E = \{$exactly two tails$\} = \{HTT, THT, TTH\}$,
$F = \{$second toss is a tail$\} = \{HTH, HTT, TTH, TTT\}$,
$G = \{$second toss is a head$\} = \{HHH, HHT, THH, THT\}$.

a. $\quad P(E|F) = \dfrac{n(E \cap F)}{n(F)} = \dfrac{2}{4} = \dfrac{1}{2}$

b. $\quad P(E|G) = \dfrac{n(E \cap G)}{n(G)} = \dfrac{1}{4}$

19. $P(< 4 \,|\, \text{odd}) = \dfrac{n(< 4 \cap \text{odd})}{n(\text{odd})} = \dfrac{n(\{1,3\})}{n(\{1,3,5\})} = \dfrac{2}{3}$

21. *Method 1.* The usual sample space has 36 outcomes, where the event "two 6's" is $\{(6, 6)\}$. Note that $\{$at least one 6$\}' = \{$no 6's$\}$, and the event "no 6's" occurs in $5 \cdot 5 = 25$ ways. Thus
$P($two 6's $|$ at least one 6$)$
$= \dfrac{n(\text{two 6's} \cap \text{at least one 6})}{n(\text{at least one 6})}$
$= \dfrac{n(\{(6,6)\})}{36 - 25} = \dfrac{1}{11}$.
Method 2. From the usual sample space, we find that the reduced sample space for "at least one 6" (which has 11 outcomes) is
$\{(6, 1), (6, 2), (6, 3), (6, 4), (6, 5), (6, 6), (1, 6), (2, 6), (3, 6), (4, 6), (5, 6)\}$.
Thus $P($two 6's $|$ at least one 6$) = \dfrac{1}{11}$.

23. The usual sample space consists of ordered pairs (R, G), where $R =$ no. on red die and $G =$ no. on green die. Now, $n($green is even$) = 6 \cdot 3 = 18$, because the red die can show any of six numbers and the green any of three: 2, 4, or 6. Also, $n($total of 7 $\cap$ green even$)$
$= n(\{(5, 2), (3, 4), (1, 6)\}) = 3$.

Thus
$P($total of 7 $|$ green even$)$
$= \dfrac{n(\text{total of 7} \cap \text{green even})}{n(\text{green even})}$
$= \dfrac{3}{18} = \dfrac{1}{6}$.

25. The usual sample space consists of 36 ordered pairs.
Let $E = \{$total $> 5\}$ and $F = \{$first toss $< 4\}$.
Then $n(F) = 3 \cdot 6 = 18$, and
$n(E \cap F) = n(\{(1, 5), (1, 6), (2, 4), (2, 5), (2, 6), (3, 3), (3, 4), (3, 5), (3, 6)\}) = 9$.
Thus $P(E|F) = \dfrac{n(E \cap F)}{n(F)} = \dfrac{9}{18} = \dfrac{1}{2}$.

27. $P(K|H) = \dfrac{n(K \cap H)}{n(H)} = \dfrac{1}{13}$

29. Let $E = \{$second card is not a face card$\}$ and $F = \{$first card is a face card$\}$.
$P(E \,|\, F) = \dfrac{n(E \cap F)}{n(F)} = \dfrac{12 \cdot \frac{51-11}{51}}{12} = \dfrac{40}{51}$

31. $P(K_1 \cap Q_2 \cap J_3) = P(K_1)P(Q_2 \mid K_1)P(J_3 \mid (K_1 \cap Q_2)) = \dfrac{4}{52} \cdot \dfrac{4}{51} \cdot \dfrac{4}{50} = \dfrac{8}{16{,}575}$

33. $P(D_1 \cap D_2 \cap D_3) = P(D_1)P(D_2 \mid D_1)P(D_3 \mid (D_1 \cap D_2)) = \dfrac{13}{52} \cdot \dfrac{12}{51} \cdot \dfrac{11}{50} = \dfrac{11}{850}$

35. Let $D = \{$two diamonds$\}$ and $R = \{$first card red$\}$. We have $D \cap R = \{$two diamonds$\} = D$ and

$P(D) = \dfrac{13}{52} \cdot \dfrac{12}{51}$. Thus $P(D \mid R) = \dfrac{P(D \cap R)}{P(R)} = \dfrac{\frac{13}{52} \cdot \frac{12}{51}}{\frac{26}{52}} = \dfrac{2}{17}$.

37. a. $P(U) = P(F \cap U) + P(O \cap U) + P(N \cap U) = P(F)P(U|F) + P(O)P(U|O) + P(N)P(U|N)$

$= (0.60)(0.45) + (0.30)(0.55) + (0.10)(0.35) = 0.47 = \dfrac{47}{100}$

    b. $P(F|U) = \dfrac{P(F \cap U)}{P(U)} = \dfrac{(0.60)(0.45)}{0.47} = \dfrac{27}{47}$

39. a. After the first draw, if the marble drawn is red, then 4 marbles remain, 3 of which are yellow.

    $P(\text{second is yellow} \mid \text{first is red}) = \dfrac{3}{4}$

    b. After red marble is replaced, 5 marbles remain, 3 of which are yellow.

    $P(\text{second is yellow} \mid \text{first is red}) = \dfrac{3}{5}$

41. $P(W) = P(\text{Urn } 1 \cap W) + P(\text{Urn } 2 \cap W) = P(\text{Urn } 1)P(W \mid \text{Urn } 1) + P(\text{Urn } 2)P(W \mid \text{Urn } 2)$

$= \dfrac{1}{2} \cdot \dfrac{2}{5} + \dfrac{1}{2} \cdot \dfrac{2}{4} = \dfrac{9}{20}$

43. $P(W_3) = P(U1 \cap G_2 \cap W_3) + P(U1 \cap R_2 \cap W_3) + P(U2 \cap W_2 \cap W_3)$

$= P(U1)P(G_2|U1)P(W_3|(G_2 \cap U1)) + P(U1)P(R_2|U1)P(W_3|(R_2 \cap U1)) + P(U2)P(W_2|U2)P(W_3|(W_2 \cap U2))$

$= \dfrac{1}{2} \cdot \dfrac{1}{2} \cdot \dfrac{1}{3} + \dfrac{1}{2} \cdot \dfrac{1}{2} \cdot \dfrac{1}{3} + \dfrac{1}{2} \cdot \dfrac{1}{2} \cdot \dfrac{1}{3} = \dfrac{1}{4}$

45. $P(\text{Def}) = P(A \cap \text{Def}) + P(B \cap \text{Def}) = P(A)P(\text{Def} \mid A) + P(B)P(\text{Def} \mid B) = \dfrac{200}{600} \cdot \dfrac{2}{100} + \dfrac{400}{600} \cdot \dfrac{5}{100} = \dfrac{1}{25}$

47. $P(\text{Def}) = P(A \cap \text{Def}) + P(B \cap \text{Def}) + P(C \cap \text{Def}) = P(A)P(\text{Def} \mid A) + P(B)P(\text{Def} \mid B) + P(C)P(\text{Def} \mid C)$

$= (0.10)(0.06) + (0.20)(0.04) + (0.70)(0.05) = 0.049$

49. a. $P(D \cap V) = P(D)P(V|D) = (0.40)(0.15) = 0.06$

    b. $P(V) = P(D \cap V) + P(R \cap V) + P(I \cap V) = P(D)P(V \mid D) + P(R)P(V \mid R) + P(I)P(V \mid I)$

    $= (0.40)(0.15) + (0.35)(0.20) + (0.25)(0.10) = 0.155$

51. $P(3 \text{ Fem}|\text{at least one Fem})$

$= \dfrac{P(3 \text{ Fem} \cap \text{at least one Fem})}{P(\text{at least one Fem})}$

$= \dfrac{P(3 \text{ Fem})}{1 - P(\text{no Fem})} = \dfrac{\frac{_6C_3}{_{11}C_3}}{1 - \frac{_5C_3}{_{11}C_3}} = \dfrac{\frac{4}{33}}{1 - \frac{2}{33}} = \dfrac{4}{31}$

Exercise 9.6

1. a. $P(E \cap F) = P(E)P(F) = \dfrac{1}{3} \cdot \dfrac{3}{4} = \dfrac{1}{4}$

  b. $P(E \cup F) = P(E) + P(F) - P(E \cap F)$

     $= \dfrac{1}{3} + \dfrac{3}{4} - \dfrac{1}{4} = \dfrac{5}{6}$

  c. $P(E|F) = \dfrac{P(E \cap F)}{P(F)} = \dfrac{1/4}{3/4} = \dfrac{1}{3}$

  d. $P(E'|F) = 1 - P(E|F) = 1 - \dfrac{1}{3} = \dfrac{2}{3}$

  e. $P(E \cap F') = P(E)P(F') = \dfrac{1}{3} \cdot \dfrac{1}{4} = \dfrac{1}{12}$

  f. $P(E \cup F') = P(E) + P(F') - P(E \cap F')$

     $= \dfrac{1}{3} + \dfrac{1}{4} - \dfrac{1}{12} = \dfrac{1}{2}$

  g. $P(E|F') = \dfrac{P(E \cap F')}{P(F')} = \dfrac{1/12}{1/4} = \dfrac{1}{3}$

3. $P(E \cap F) = P(E)P(F),$

$\dfrac{1}{3} = \dfrac{2}{5} \cdot P(F)$ so $P(F) = \dfrac{1}{3} \cdot \dfrac{5}{2} = \dfrac{5}{6}$

5. $P(E)P(F) = \dfrac{3}{4} \cdot \dfrac{8}{9} = \dfrac{2}{3} = P(E \cap F)$

Since $P(E)P(F) = P(E \cap F)$, events E and F are independent.

7. Let $F = \{\text{full service}\}$ and $I = \{\text{increase in value}\}$.

$P(F) = \dfrac{400}{600} = \dfrac{2}{3}$

and $P(F|I) = \dfrac{n(F \cap I)}{n(I)} = \dfrac{320}{480} = \dfrac{2}{3}$

Since $P(F \mid I) = P(F)$, events F and I are independent.

9. Let S be the usual sample space consisting of ordered pairs of the form (R, G), where the first component of each pair represents the number showing on the red die. Then $n(S) = 6 \cdot 6 = 36$. For E, any of four numbers can occur on the red die, and any of six numbers can appear on the green die. Thus $n(E) = 4 \cdot 6 = 24$. For F we have $F = \{(1, 4), (2, 3), (3, 2), (4, 1)\}$, so $n(F) = 4$. Also, $E \cap F = \{(1,4),(2,3),(3,2)\}$ so, $n(E \cap F) = 3$. Thus

$P(E)P(F) = \dfrac{24}{36} \cdot \dfrac{4}{36} = \dfrac{2}{27}$ and

$P(E \cap F) = \dfrac{3}{36} = \dfrac{1}{12}$.

Since $P(E)P(F) \neq P(E \cap F)$, events E and F are dependent.

11. $S = \{\text{HH, HT, TH, TT}\}$,

$E = \{\text{HT, TH, TT}\}$,

$F = \{\text{HT, TH}\}$, and $E \cap F = \{\text{HT, TH}\}$.

Thus $P(E) = \dfrac{3}{4}$

$P(F) = \dfrac{2}{4} = \dfrac{1}{2}$, and

$P(E \cap F) = \dfrac{2}{4} = \dfrac{1}{2}$. We have

$P(E)P(F) = \dfrac{3}{4} \cdot \dfrac{1}{2} = \dfrac{3}{8} \neq P(E \cap F)$, so

events E and F are dependent.

13. Let S be the set of ordered pairs whose first (*second*) component represents the number on the first (*second*) chip. Then $n(S) = 7 \cdot 7 = 49$, $n(E) = 1 \cdot 7 = 7$, and $n(F) = 7 \cdot 1 = 7$. For G, if the first chip is 1, 3, 5 or 7, then the second chip must be 2, 4 or 6; if the first chip is 2, 4 or 6, the second must be 1, 3, 5 or 7. Thus $n(G) = 4 \cdot 3 + 3 \cdot 4 = 24$.

a. $E \cap F = \{(3,3)\}$, so $P(E \cap F) = \dfrac{1}{49}$.

Since
$$P(E)P(F) = \frac{7}{49} \cdot \frac{7}{49} = \frac{1}{49} = P(E \cap F),$$
events E and F are independent.

b. $E \cap G = \{(3,2),(3,4),(3,6)\}$,

so $P(E \cap G) = \dfrac{3}{49}$. Since

$$P(E)P(G) = \frac{7}{49} \cdot \frac{24}{49} = \frac{24}{343} \ne P(E \cap G),$$

events E and G are dependent.

c. $F \cap G = \{(2,3),(4,3),(6,3)\}$

so $P(F \cap G) = \dfrac{3}{49}$.

Since

$$P(F)P(G) = \frac{7}{49} \cdot \frac{24}{49} = \frac{24}{343} \ne P(F \cap G).$$
Events F and G are dependent.

d. $E \cap F \cap G = \varnothing$, so $P(E \cap F \cap G) = 0$. However,
$P(E)P(F)P(G) \ne 0 = P(E \cap F \cap G)$,
so events E, F and G are not independent.

15. $P(E \cap F) = P(E)P(F \mid E)$, thus
$$P(E) = \frac{P(E \cap F)}{P(F \mid E)} = \frac{0.28}{0.4} = 0.7$$
Since $P(E) = 0.7 \ne 0.6 = P(E \mid F)$, E and F are dependent.

17. Let $E = \{\text{red } 4\}$ and $F = \{\text{green} > 4\}$. Assume E and F are independent.
$$P(E \cap F) = P(E)P(F) = \frac{1}{6} \cdot \frac{1}{3} = \frac{1}{18}$$

19. Let $F = \{\text{first person attends regularly}\}$ and $S = \{\text{second person attends regularly}\}$.
Then $P(F \cap S) = P(F)P(S) = \dfrac{1}{5} \cdot \dfrac{1}{5} = \dfrac{1}{25}$.

21. Because of replacement, assume the cards selected on the draws are independent events.
$P(\text{ace, then face card, then spade}) = P(\text{ace}) \cdot P(\text{face card}) \cdot P(\text{spade})$
$$= \frac{4}{52} \cdot \frac{12}{52} \cdot \frac{13}{52} = \frac{3}{676}$$

23. a. $P(\text{Bill gets A} \cap \text{Jim gets A} \cap \text{Linda gets A})$
$= P(\text{Bill gets A}) \cdot P(\text{Jim gets A}) \cdot P(\text{Linda gets A})$
$$= \frac{3}{4} \cdot \frac{1}{2} \cdot \frac{4}{5} = \frac{3}{10}.$$

b. $P(\text{Bill no A} \cap \text{Jim no A} \cap \text{Linda no A})$
    $= P(\text{Bill no A}) \cdot P(\text{Jim no A}) \cdot P(\text{Linda no A})$
    $= \dfrac{1}{4} \cdot \dfrac{1}{2} \cdot \dfrac{1}{5} = \dfrac{1}{40}$

c. $P(\text{Bill no A} \cap \text{Jim no A} \cap \text{Linda gets A})$
    $= P(\text{Bill no A}) \cdot P(\text{Jim no A}) \cdot P(\text{Linda gets A})$
    $= \dfrac{1}{4} \cdot \dfrac{1}{2} \cdot \dfrac{4}{5} = \dfrac{1}{10}$

25. Let $A = \{A \text{ survives 15 more years}\}$,
     $B = \{B \text{ survives 15 more years}\}$.

   a. $P(A \cap B) = P(A)P(B) = \dfrac{2}{3} \cdot \dfrac{3}{5} = \dfrac{2}{5}$

   b. $P(A' \cap B) = P(A')P(B) = \dfrac{1}{3} \cdot \dfrac{3}{5} = \dfrac{1}{5}$

   c. $P[(A \cap B') \cup (A' \cap B)]$
      $= P(A)P(B') + P(A')P(B)$
      $(A \cap B' \text{ and } A' \cap B \text{ are mutually exclusive})$
      $= \dfrac{2}{3} \cdot \dfrac{2}{5} + \dfrac{1}{3} \cdot \dfrac{3}{5} = \dfrac{7}{15}$

   d.   From parts c and a,
      $P(\text{at least one survives})$
      $= P(\text{exactly one survives}) + P(\text{both survive})$
      $= \dfrac{7}{15} + \dfrac{2}{5} = \dfrac{13}{15}.$

   e. $P(\text{neither survives}) = 1 - P(\text{at least one survives})$
      $= 1 - \dfrac{13}{15} = \dfrac{2}{15}.$

27. Assume the colors selected on the draws are independent events.

   a. $P(W_1 \cap G_2) = P(W_1)P(G_2) = \dfrac{6}{15} \cdot \dfrac{5}{15} = \dfrac{2}{15}$

   b. $P[(W_1 \cap G_2) \cup (G_1 \cap W_2)] = P(W_1)P(G_2) + P(G_1)P(W_2)$

      $= \dfrac{6}{15} \cdot \dfrac{5}{15} + \dfrac{5}{15} \cdot \dfrac{6}{15} = \dfrac{4}{15}$

29. Assume that the selections are independent.
   $P(\text{both red} \cup \text{both white} \cup \text{both green}) = \dfrac{3}{19} \cdot \dfrac{3}{19} + \dfrac{7}{19} \cdot \dfrac{7}{19} + \dfrac{9}{19} \cdot \dfrac{9}{19} = \dfrac{139}{361}$

31. Assume that the draws are independent.
$P(\text{particular 1st ticket} \cap \text{particular 2nd ticket})$

$$= \frac{1}{20} \cdot \frac{1}{20} = \frac{1}{400}$$

$P(\text{sum is } 35) = P\{(20, 15), (19, 16), (18, 17), (17, 18), (16, 19), (15, 20)\}$

$$= 6\left(\frac{1}{400}\right) = \frac{3}{200}$$

33. a. $\dfrac{1}{12} \cdot \dfrac{1}{12} \cdot \dfrac{1}{12} = \dfrac{1}{1728}$

b. To get exactly one even, there are $_3C_1 = 3$ ways.
$P(\text{one even and two odd}) = 3[P(\text{even 1st spin}) \cdot P(\text{odd 2nd spin}) \cdot P(\text{odd 3rd spin})]$

$$= 3\left(\frac{6}{12} \cdot \frac{6}{12} \cdot \frac{6}{12}\right) = \frac{3}{8}.$$

35. a. The number of ways of getting exactly four correct answers out of five is $_5C_4 = 5$. Each of these

ways has a probability of $\dfrac{1}{4} \cdot \dfrac{1}{4} \cdot \dfrac{1}{4} \cdot \dfrac{1}{4} \cdot \dfrac{3}{4} = \dfrac{3}{1024}$. Thus

$P(\text{exactly 4 correct}) = 5 \cdot \dfrac{3}{1024} = \dfrac{15}{1024}.$

b. $P(\text{at least 4 correct}) = P(\text{exactly 4}) + P(\text{exactly 5})$

$$= \frac{15}{1024} + \frac{1}{4} \cdot \frac{1}{4} \cdot \frac{1}{4} \cdot \frac{1}{4} \cdot \frac{1}{4} = \frac{1}{64}$$

c. The number of ways of getting exactly three correct answers out of five is

$_5C_3 = 10$. Each of these ways has a probability of $\dfrac{1}{4} \cdot \dfrac{1}{4} \cdot \dfrac{1}{4} \cdot \dfrac{3}{4} \cdot \dfrac{3}{4} = \dfrac{9}{1024}$, so

$P(\text{exactly 3 correct}) = 10 \cdot \dfrac{9}{1024} = \dfrac{45}{512}$. Thus

$P(\text{3 or more correct}) = P(\text{exactly 3}) + P(\text{at least 4})$

$$= \frac{45}{512} + \frac{1}{64} = \frac{53}{512}.$$

37. A wrong majority decision can occur in one of two mutually exclusive ways: exactly two wrong recommendations, or three wrong recommendations. Exactly two wrong recommendations can occur in $_3C_2 = 3$ mutually exclusive ways. Thus
$P(\text{wrong majority decision})$
$= [(0.04)(0.05)(0.9) + (0.04)(0.95)(0.1) + (0.96)(0.05)(0.1)] + (0.04)(0.05)(0.1)$
$= 0.0106.$

Exercise 9.7

1. $P(E|D) = \dfrac{P(E)P(D|E)}{P(E)P(D|E) + P(F)P(D|F)}$

$= \dfrac{\frac{2}{5} \cdot \frac{1}{10}}{\frac{2}{5} \cdot \frac{1}{10} + \frac{3}{5} \cdot \frac{1}{5}} = \dfrac{1}{4}$

For the second part, $P(D'|F) = 1 - P(D|F) = 1 - \dfrac{1}{5} = \dfrac{4}{5}$, and

$P(D'|E) = 1 - P(D|E) = 1 - \dfrac{1}{10} = \dfrac{9}{10}$. Then

$P(F|D') = \dfrac{P(F)P(D'|F)}{P(E)P(D'|E) + P(F)P(D'|F)}$

$= \dfrac{\frac{3}{5} \cdot \frac{4}{5}}{\frac{2}{5} \cdot \frac{9}{10} + \frac{3}{5} \cdot \frac{4}{5}} = \dfrac{4}{7}.$

3. $D = \{\text{is Democrat}\},$
$R = \{\text{is Republican}\},$
$I = \{\text{is Independent}\},$
$V = \{\text{voted}\}.$

$P(D|V) = \dfrac{P(D)P(V|D)}{P(D)P(V|D) + P(R)P(V|R) + P(I)P(V|I)}$

$= \dfrac{(0.40)(0.15)}{(0.40)(0.15) + (0.35)(0.20) + (0.25)(0.10)}$

$= \dfrac{12}{31} \approx 0.387$

5. $D = \{\text{has the disease}\}$
$D' = \{\text{does not have the disease}\}$
$R = \{\text{positive reaction}\}$
$N = \{\text{negative reaction}\} = R'$

a. $P(D|R) = \dfrac{P(D)P(R|D)}{P(D)P(R|D) + P(D')P(R|D')}$

$= \dfrac{(0.03)(0.86)}{(0.03)(0.86) + (0.97)(0.07)} = \dfrac{258}{937}$

≈ 0.275

b. $P(D|N) = \dfrac{P(D)P(N|D)}{P(D)P(N|D) + P(D')P(N|D')}$

$= \dfrac{(0.03)(0.14)}{(0.03)(0.14) + (0.97)(0.93)} = \dfrac{14}{3021}$

≈ 0.005

7. $U_1 = \{$first urn selected$\}$
    $U_2 = \{$second urn selected$\}$
    $R = \{$red marble drawn$\}$
    $P(U_1) = P(U_2) = \dfrac{1}{2}$.

    $P(U_1|R) = \dfrac{P(U_1)P(R|U_1)}{P(U_1)P(R|U_1) + P(U_2)P(R|U_2)}$

    $= \dfrac{\frac{1}{2} \cdot \frac{4}{6}}{\frac{1}{2} \cdot \frac{4}{6} + \frac{1}{2} \cdot \frac{2}{5}} = \dfrac{5}{8}$.

9. $A = \{$unit from line A$\}$
    $B = \{$unit from line B$\}$
    $D = \{$defective unit$\}$.

    $P(A) = \dfrac{300}{800} = \dfrac{3}{8}$

    $P(B) = \dfrac{500}{800} = \dfrac{5}{8}$

    $P(A|D) = \dfrac{P(A)P(D|A)}{P(A)P(D|A) + P(B)P(D|B)}$

    $= \dfrac{\frac{3}{8} \cdot \frac{2}{100}}{\frac{3}{8} \cdot \frac{2}{100} + \frac{5}{8} \cdot \frac{5}{100}} = \dfrac{6}{31}$

11. $C = \{$call made$\}$
    $T = \{$on time for meeting$\}$

    $P(C|T) = \dfrac{P(C)P(T|C)}{P(C)P(T|C) + P(C')P(T|C')}$

    $= \dfrac{(0.9)(0.9)}{(0.9)(0.9) + (0.1)(0.8)} = \dfrac{81}{89} \approx 0.910$

13. $W = \{$walking reported$\}$
    $B = \{$bicycling reported$\}$
    $R = \{$running reported$\}$
    $C = \{$completed requirement$\}$

    $P(W|C) = \dfrac{P(W)P(C|W)}{P(W)P(C|W) + P(B)P(C|B) + P(R)P(C|R)}$

    $= \dfrac{\frac{1}{2} \cdot \frac{9}{10}}{\frac{1}{2} \cdot \frac{9}{10} + \frac{1}{4} \cdot \frac{4}{5} + \frac{1}{4} \cdot \frac{2}{3}} = \dfrac{27}{49} \approx 0.551$

    55.1% would be expected to report walking.

15. $J = \{$had Japanese-made car$\}$
$E = \{$had European-made car$\}$
$A = \{$had American-made car$\}$
$B = \{$buy same make again$\}$

$$P(J \mid B) = \frac{P(J)P(B \mid J)}{P(J)P(B \mid J) + P(E)P(B \mid E) + P(A)P(B \mid A)}$$

$$= \frac{\frac{3}{5} \cdot \frac{85}{100}}{\frac{3}{5} \cdot \frac{85}{100} + \frac{1}{10} \cdot \frac{50}{100} + \frac{3}{10} \cdot \frac{40}{100}} = \frac{3}{4}$$

17. $P = \{$pass the exam$\}$
$A = \{$answer every question$\}$

$$P(A \mid P) = \frac{P(A)P(P \mid A)}{P(A)P(P \mid A) + P(A')P(P \mid A')}$$

$$= \frac{(0.75)(0.8)}{(0.75)(0.8) + (0.25)(0.50)} = \frac{24}{29} \approx 0.828$$

19. $S = \{$signals sent$\}$
$D = \{$signals detected$\}$

$$P(S \mid D) = \frac{P(S)P(D \mid S)}{P(S)P(D \mid S) + P(S')P(D \mid S')}$$

$$= \frac{\frac{2}{5} \cdot \frac{3}{5}}{\frac{2}{5} \cdot \frac{3}{5} + \frac{3}{5} \cdot \frac{1}{10}} = \frac{4}{5}$$

21. $S = \{$movie is a success$\}$
$U = \{$"Two Thumbs Up"$\}$

$$P(S \mid U) = \frac{P(S)P(U \mid S)}{P(S)P(U \mid S) + P(S')P(U \mid S')}$$

$$= \frac{\frac{8}{10} \cdot \frac{70}{100}}{\frac{8}{10} \cdot \frac{70}{100} + \frac{2}{10} \cdot \frac{20}{100}} = \frac{14}{15} \approx 0.933$$

23. $S = \{$is substandard request$\}$
$C = \{$is considered substandard request by Risky$\}$

a. $P(C) = P(S)P(C \mid S) + P(S')P(C \mid S')$

$$= (0.15)(0.8) + (0.85)(0.10) = 0.205 = \frac{41}{200}$$

b. $P(S \mid C) = \dfrac{P(S)P(C \mid S)}{P(S)P(C \mid S) + P(S')P(C \mid S')}$

$$= \frac{(0.15)(0.8)}{0.205} = \frac{0.12}{0.205} = \frac{120}{205} = \frac{24}{41} \approx 0.585$$

c. $P(\text{Error}) = P(C' \cap S) + P(C \cap S')$
  $= P(S)(C' \mid S) + P(S')P(C \mid S')$

  $= (0.15)(0.2) + (0.85)(0.10) = 0.115 = \dfrac{23}{200}$

25. a. $P(L \mid E) = \dfrac{P(L)P(E \mid L)}{P(L)P(E \mid L) + P(M)P(E \mid M) + P(H)P(E \mid H)}$

  $= \dfrac{(0.25)(0.49)}{(0.25)(0.49) + (0.25)(0.64) + (0.5)(0.81)} \approx 0.18$

b. $P(M \mid E) = \dfrac{P(M)P(E \mid M)}{P(L)P(E \mid L) + P(M)P(E \mid M) + P(H)P(E \mid H)}$

  $= \dfrac{(0.25)(0.64)}{(0.25)(0.49) + (0.25)(0.64) + (0.5)(0.81)} \approx 0.23$

c. $P(H \mid E) = \dfrac{P(H)P(E \mid H)}{P(L)P(E \mid L) + P(M)P(E \mid M) + P(H)P(E \mid H)}$

  $= \dfrac{(0.5)(0.81)}{(0.25)(0.49) + (0.25)(0.64) + (0.5)(0.81)} \approx 0.59$

d. High quality

27. $F = \{\text{fair weather}\}$
  $I = \{\text{inclement weather}\}$
  $W = \{\text{predict fair weather}\}.$
  $P(F \mid W) = \dfrac{P(F)P(W \mid F)}{P(F)P(W \mid F) + P(I)P(W \mid I)}$

  $= \dfrac{(0.6)(0.7)}{(0.6)(0.7) + (0.4)(0.3)} = \dfrac{7}{9} \approx 0.78$

Chapter 9 Review Problems

1. $_8P_3 = 8 \cdot 7 \cdot 6 = 336$

3. $_9C_7 = \dfrac{9!}{7!(9-7)!} = \dfrac{9!}{7! \cdot 2!} = \dfrac{9 \cdot 8 \cdot 7!}{7! \cdot 2 \cdot 1} = \dfrac{9 \cdot 8}{2} = 36$

5. For each of the first two symbols there are 26 choices, for the third there are 9 choices, and for each of the last two symbols there are 10 choices. By the basic counting principle, the number of license plates that are possible is
$26 \cdot 26 \cdot 9 \cdot 10 \cdot 10 = 608{,}400.$

7. Each of the five switches has 2 possible positions. By the basic counting principle, the number of different codes is
$2 \cdot 2 \cdot 2 \cdot 2 \cdot 2 = 2^5 = 32.$

9. A possibility for first, second, and third place is a selection of three of the seven teams so that order is important. Thus the number of ways the season can end is $_7P_3 = 7 \cdot 6 \cdot 5 = 210$.

11. A group is any five of the nine people, and the order of the five is not important. Thus the number of groups is
$$_9C_5 = \frac{9!}{5! \cdot 4!} = \frac{9 \cdot 8 \cdot 7 \cdot 6 \cdot 5!}{5! \cdot 4 \cdot 3 \cdot 2 \cdot 1} = 126.$$

13. **a.** Three bulbs are selected from 24, and the order of selection is not important. Thus the number of possible selections is $_{24}C_3 = \dfrac{24!}{3!(24-3)!} = \dfrac{24!}{3! \cdot 21!}$
$$= \frac{24 \cdot 23 \cdot 22 \cdot 21!}{3 \cdot 2 \cdot 1 \cdot 21!} = \frac{24 \cdot 23 \cdot 22}{3 \cdot 2 \cdot 1} = 2024.$$

b. Only one bulb is defective and that bulb must be included in the selection. The other two bulbs must be selected from the 23 remaining bulbs and there are $_{23}C_2$ such selections possible. Thus the number of ways of selecting three bulbs such that one is defective is
$$1 \cdot {}_{23}C_2 = {}_{23}C_2 = \frac{23!}{2!(23-2)!} = \frac{23!}{2! \cdot 21!}$$
$$\frac{23 \cdot 22 \cdot 21!}{2 \cdot 1 \cdot 21!} = \frac{23 \cdot 22}{2 \cdot 1} = 253.$$

15. In the word MISSISSIPPI, there are 11 letters with repetition: 1 M, 4 I's, 4 S's, and 2 P's. Thus the number of distinguishable horizontal arrangements is
$$\frac{11!}{1! \cdot 4! \cdot 4! \cdot 2!} = 34,650.$$

17. Of the eight nurses, three go to hospital A (Cell A), two go to hospital B (cell B), and three are not assigned (cell C). The number of possible assignments is $\dfrac{8!}{3! \cdot 2! \cdot 3!} = 560$.

19. **a.** $\{1, 2, 3, 4, 5, 6, 7\}$

    b. $\{4, 5, 6\}$

    c. $E_1' \cup E_2 = \{7,8\} \cup \{4,5,6,7\} = \{4,5,6,7,8\}$

    d. The intersection of any event and its complement is $\varnothing$.

    e. $(E_1 \cap E_2')' = (\{1,2,3,4,5,6\} \cap \{1,2,3,8\})'$
$= \{1, 2, 3\}' = \{4, 5, 6, 7, 8\}$

    f. From (b), $E_1 \cap E_2 \neq \varnothing$, so E_1 and E_2 are not mutually exclusive.

21. **a.** $\{R_1R_2R_3, R_1R_2G_3, R_1G_2R_3, R_1G_2G_3,$
$G_1R_2R_3, G_1R_2G_3, G_1G_2R_3, G_1G_2G_3\}$

    b. $\{R_1R_2G_3, R_1G_2R_3, G_1R_2R_3\}$

    c. $\{R_1R_2R_3, G_1G_2G_3\}$

23. $n(S) = {}_{10}C_2 = \dfrac{10!}{2! \cdot 8!} = \dfrac{10 \cdot 9 \cdot 8!}{2 \cdot 1 \cdot 8!} = \dfrac{10 \cdot 9}{2 \cdot 1} = 45$

Let E be the event that box is rejected. If box is rejected, the one defective chip must be in the two-chip sample and there are nine possibilities for the other chip. Thus $n(E) = 9$ and

$P(E) = \dfrac{n(E)}{n(S)} = \dfrac{9}{45} = \dfrac{1}{5} = 0.2$.

25. Number of ways to answer exam is $4^5 = 1024 = n(S)$. Let
$E = \{$exactly two questions are incorrect$\}$. The number of ways of selecting two of the five questions that

are incorrect is ${}_5C_2 = \dfrac{5!}{2! \cdot 3!} = 10$. However, there are three ways to answer a question incorrectly. Since

two questions are incorrect $n(E) = 10 \cdot 3 \cdot 3 = 90$. Thus $P(E) = \dfrac{n(E)}{n(S)} = \dfrac{90}{1024} = \dfrac{45}{512}$.

27. a. There are 10 marbles in the urn.

$n(S) = 10 \cdot 10 = 100$

$n(E_{\text{both red}}) = 4 \cdot 4 = 16$

Thus $P(E_{\text{both red}}) = \dfrac{n(E_{\text{both red}})}{n(S)} = \dfrac{16}{100} = \dfrac{4}{25}$.

b. $n(S) = 10 \cdot 9 = 90$

$n(E_{\text{both red}}) = 4 \cdot 3 = 12$

Thus $P(E_{\text{both red}}) = \dfrac{12}{90} = \dfrac{2}{15}$.

29. $n(S) = 52 \cdot 52$.

a. There are 26 red cards in a deck. Thus $n(E_{\text{both red}}) = 26 \cdot 26$ and

$P(E_{\text{both red}}) = \dfrac{26 \cdot 26}{52 \cdot 52} = \dfrac{1}{4}$.

b. There are 13 clubs in a deck, none of which are red. If $E =$ event that one card is red and the other is a club, then E occurs if the first card is red and the second is a club, or vice versa. Thus

$n(E) = 26 \cdot 13 + 13 \cdot 26 = 2 \cdot 26 \cdot 13$ and $P(E) = \dfrac{2 \cdot 26 \cdot 13}{52 \cdot 52} = \dfrac{1}{4}$.

31. $\dfrac{P(E)}{P(E')} = \dfrac{\frac{3}{8}}{1 - \left(\frac{3}{8}\right)} = \dfrac{\frac{3}{8}}{\frac{5}{8}} = \dfrac{3}{5}$ or 3:5

33. $P(E) = \dfrac{6}{6 + 1} = \dfrac{6}{7}$

35. $P(F \mid H') = \dfrac{P(F \cap H')}{P(H')} = \dfrac{\frac{9}{52}}{\frac{39}{52}} = \dfrac{3}{13}$

37. $P(S \cap M) = P(S)P(M|S) = (0.6)(0.7) = 0.42$

39. a. The reduced sample space consists of (4, 1), (4, 2), (4, 3), (4, 4), (4, 5), (4, 6), (1, 4), (2, 4), (3, 4), (5, 4), (6, 4). In two of these 11 points, the sum of the components is 7. Thus

$$P(\text{sum} = 7 \mid \text{a 4 shows}) = \frac{2}{11}.$$

b. Out of 36 sample points, the event {getting a total of 7 and having a 4 show} is {(4, 3), (3, 4)}. Thus the probability of this event is $\dfrac{2}{36} = \dfrac{1}{18}$.

41. The second number must be a 5 or 6, so the reduced sample space has $6 \cdot 2 = 12$ sample points. Of these, the event {first number $\geq$ second number} consists of (5,5), (6,5), and (6,6).

Thus the conditional probability is $\dfrac{3}{12} = \dfrac{1}{4}$.

43. a. $P(L'|F) = \dfrac{n(L' \cap F)}{n(F)} = \dfrac{160}{480} = \dfrac{1}{3}$

b. $P(L) = \dfrac{400}{600} = \dfrac{2}{3}$ and $P(L|M) = \dfrac{n(L \cap M)}{n(M)} = \dfrac{80}{120} = \dfrac{2}{3}$.

Since $P(L|M) = P(L)$, events L and M are independent.

45. $P = \{\text{attend public college}\}$
$M = \{\text{from middle-class family}\}$

$P(P) = \dfrac{125}{175} = \dfrac{5}{7}$

$P(P \mid M) = \dfrac{n(P \cap M)}{n(M)} = \dfrac{55}{80} = \dfrac{11}{16}$

Since $P(P \mid M) \neq P(P)$, events P and M are dependent.

47. a. $P(\text{none takes root}) = (0.3)(0.3)(0.3)(0.3) = 0.0081$

b. The probability that a particular two shrubs take root and the remaining two do not is $(0.7)(0.7)(0.3)(0.3)$. The number of ways the two that take root can be chosen from the four shrubs is ${}_4C_2$. Thus $P(\text{exactly two take root}) = {}_4C_2(0.7)^2(0.3)^2 = 0.2646$.

c. For at most two shrubs to take root, either none does, exactly one does, or exactly two do.
$P(\text{none}) + P(\text{exactly one}) + P(\text{exactly two})$
$= 0.0081 + {}_4C_1(0.7)(0.3)^3 + 0.2646$
$= 0.0081 + 0.0756 + 0.2646$
$= 0.3483$

49. $P(R_{\text{II}}) = P(G_{\text{I}})P(R_{\text{II}} \mid G_{\text{I}}) + P(R_{\text{I}})P(R_{\text{II}} \mid R_{\text{I}}) = \dfrac{3}{5} \cdot \dfrac{4}{9} + \dfrac{2}{5} \cdot \dfrac{5}{9} = \dfrac{22}{45}.$

51. $P(G|A) = \dfrac{P(G \cap A)}{P(A)} = \dfrac{0.1}{0.4} = \dfrac{1}{4}$

53. a. $F = \{\text{produced by first shift}\}$
$S = \{\text{produced by second shift}\}$
$D = \{\text{defective}\}$
$P(D) = P(F)P(D|F) + P(S)P(D|S)$
$= \dfrac{300}{500} \cdot (0.01) + \dfrac{200}{500} \cdot (0.02)$
$= 0.006 + 0.008 = 0.014$

b. $P(S|D) = \dfrac{P(S)P(D|S)}{P(F)P(D|F) + P(S)P(D|S)}$
$= \dfrac{0.008}{0.014} = \dfrac{4}{7} \approx 0.57$

Mathematical Snapshot Chapter 9

1. Trial and error should yield a critical value of around 0.645.

Chapter 10

Exercise 10.1

1. $\mu = \sum_x x\,f(x) = 0(0.1) + 1(0.4) + 2(0.2) + 3(0.3) = 1.7$

$Var(X) = \sum_x x^2 f(x) - \mu^2$

$\qquad = [0^2(0.1) + 1^2(0.4) + 2^2(0.2) + 3^2(0.3)] - (1.7)^2$

$\qquad = 1.01$

$\sigma = \sqrt{Var(X)} = \sqrt{1.01} \approx 1.00$

See below for histogram.

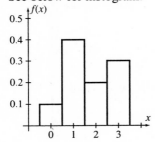

3. $\mu = \sum_x x\,f(x) = 1\left(\dfrac{1}{4}\right) + 2\left(\dfrac{1}{4}\right) + 3\left(\dfrac{1}{2}\right) = \dfrac{9}{4} = 2.25$

$Var(X) = \sum_x x^2 f(x) - \mu^2 = \left[1^2\left(\dfrac{1}{4}\right) + 2^2\left(\dfrac{1}{4}\right) + 3^2\left(\dfrac{1}{2}\right)\right] - \left(\dfrac{9}{4}\right)^2 = \dfrac{11}{16} = 0.6875$

$\sigma = \sqrt{\dfrac{11}{16}} = \dfrac{\sqrt{11}}{4} \approx 0.83$

5. a. $P(X = 2) = 1 - [P(X = 4) + P(X = 7)] = 1 - [0.5 + 0.4] = 0.1.$

b. $\mu = \sum_x x\,f(x) = 2(0.1) + 4(0.5) + 7(0.4) = 5$

c. $\sigma^2 = \sum_x x^2 f(x) - \mu^2 = [2^2(0.1) + 4^2(0.5) + 7^2(0.4)] - 5^2 = 3$

7. Distribution of X:

$$f(0) = \frac{1}{8}, \quad f(1) = \frac{3}{8}, \quad f(2) = \frac{3}{8}, \quad f(3) = \frac{1}{8}$$

$$E(X) = \sum_x x f(x) = 0\left(\frac{1}{8}\right) + 1\left(\frac{3}{8}\right) + 2\left(\frac{3}{8}\right) + 3\left(\frac{1}{8}\right) = \frac{12}{8} = \frac{3}{2} = 1.5$$

$$\sigma^2 = \text{Var}(X) = \sum_x x^2 f(x) - [E(x)]^2$$

$$= \left[0^2\left(\frac{1}{8}\right) + 1^2\left(\frac{3}{8}\right) + 2^2\left(\frac{3}{8}\right) + 3^2\left(\frac{1}{8}\right)\right] - \left(\frac{3}{2}\right)^2$$

$$= \frac{24}{8} - \frac{9}{4} = \frac{6}{8} = \frac{3}{4} = 0.75$$

$$\sigma = \sqrt{\frac{3}{4}} = \frac{\sqrt{3}}{2} \approx 0.87$$

9. The number of outcomes in the sample space is $_5C_2 = 10$.

Distribution of X:

$$f(0) = \frac{_2C_2}{10} = \frac{1}{10}, \quad f(1) = \frac{_2C_1 \cdot _3C_1}{10} = \frac{3}{5},$$

$$f(2) = \frac{_3C_2}{10} = \frac{3}{10}$$

$$E(X) = \sum_x x f(x) = 0\left(\frac{1}{10}\right) + 1\left(\frac{3}{5}\right) + 2\left(\frac{3}{10}\right)$$

$$= \frac{6}{5} = 1.2$$

$$\sigma^2 = \sum_x x^2 f(x) - [E(x)]^2$$

$$= \left[0^2\left(\frac{1}{10}\right) + 1^2\left(\frac{3}{5}\right) + 2^2\left(\frac{3}{10}\right)\right] - \left(\frac{6}{5}\right)^2$$

$$= \frac{9}{5} - \frac{36}{25} = \frac{9}{25} = 0.36$$

$$\sigma = \sqrt{\frac{9}{25}} = \frac{3}{5} = 0.6$$

11. $f(0) = P(X = 0) = \dfrac{_2C_2}{_5C_2} = \dfrac{1}{10}$

$f(1) = P(X = 1) = \dfrac{_3C_1 \cdot _2C_1}{_5C_2} = \dfrac{6}{10} = \dfrac{3}{5}$

$f(2) = P(X = 2) = \dfrac{_3C_2}{_5C_2} = \dfrac{3}{10}$

13. a. If X is the gain (in dollars), then $X = -1$ or 8499.

Distribution of X:

$$f(-1) = \frac{9999}{10,000}, \quad f(8499) = \frac{1}{10,000}$$

$$E(X) = \sum_x x f(x)$$

$$= -1 \cdot \frac{9999}{10,000} + 8499 \cdot \frac{1}{10,000}$$

$$= -\frac{1500}{10,000} = -\$0.15 \text{ (a loss)}$$

b. Here $X = -2$ or 8498. Distribution of X:

$$f(-2) = \frac{9998}{10,000}, \quad f(8499) = \frac{2}{10,000}$$

$$E(X) = \sum_x x f(x)$$

$$= -2 \cdot \frac{9998}{10,000} + 8498 \cdot \frac{2}{10,000}$$

$$= -\$0.30 \text{ (a loss)}$$

15. Let X = daily earnings (in dollars).
Distribution of X:

$$f(200) = \frac{4}{7}, \quad f(-30) = \frac{3}{7}$$

$$E(X) = \sum_x x \, f(x)$$

$$= 200 \cdot \frac{4}{7} + (-30) \cdot \frac{3}{7}$$

$$= \frac{710}{7} \approx \$101.43$$

17. The probability that a person in the group is not hospitalized is
$1 - (0.001 + 0.002 + 0.003 + 0.004 + 0.008) = 0.982$.
Let X = gain (in dollars) to the company from a policy.
Distribution of X:

$f(10) = 0.982, \quad f(-90) = 0.001, \quad f(-190) = 0.002, \quad f(-290) = 0.003,$

$f(-390) = 0.004, \quad f(-490) = 0.008$

$E(X) = 10(0.982) + (-90)(0.001) + (-190)(0.002) + (-290)(0.003) + (-390)(0.004) + (-490)(0.008)$

$= \$3.00$

19. Let p = the annual premium (in dollars) per policy. If X = gain (in dollars) to the company from a policy, then either $X = p$ or $X = -(180,000 - p)$. We set $E(X) = 50$:

$$-(180,000 - p)(0.002) + p(0.998) = 50$$
$$-360 + 0.002p + 0.998p = 50$$
$$-360 + p = 50$$
$$p = \$410$$

21. Let X = gain (in dollars) on a play.

If 0 heads show, then $X = 0 - 1.25 = -\dfrac{5}{4}$.

If exactly 1 head shows, then

$$X = 1.00 - 1.25 = -\frac{1}{4}.$$

If 2 heads show, then $X = 2.00 - 1.25 = \dfrac{3}{4}$.

Distribution of X:

$$f\left(-\frac{5}{4}\right) = \frac{1}{4}, \quad f\left(-\frac{1}{4}\right) = \frac{1}{2}, \quad f\left(\frac{3}{4}\right) = \frac{1}{4}$$

$$E(X) = \left(-\frac{5}{4}\right)\left(\frac{1}{4}\right) + \left(-\frac{1}{4}\right)\left(\frac{1}{2}\right) + \left(\frac{3}{4}\right)\left(\frac{1}{4}\right)$$

$$= -\frac{1}{4} = -0.25$$

Thus there is an expected loss of \$0.25 on each play.
For a fair game, let
p = amount (in dollars) paid to play.
Distribution of X:

$$f(-p) = \frac{1}{4}, \quad f(1-p) = \frac{1}{2}, \quad f(2-p) = \frac{1}{4}$$

We set $E(X) = 0$:

$$(-p)\frac{1}{4} + (1-p)\frac{1}{2} + (2-p)\frac{1}{4} = 0$$
$$-\frac{p}{4} + \frac{1}{2} - \frac{p}{2} + \frac{1}{2} - \frac{p}{4} = 0$$
$$1 - p = 0$$
$$p = 1$$

Thus you should pay \$1 for a fair game.

Principles in Practice 10.2

1. Here $p = 0.30$, $q = 1 - p = 0.70$, and $n = 4$.

$$P(X = x) = {}_nC_x p^x q^{n-x}, \quad x = 0, \ 1, \ 2, \ 3, \ 4$$

$$P(X = 0) = {}_4C_0 (0.3)^0 (0.7)^4 = 0.2401$$

$$= \frac{2401}{10,000}$$

$P(X = 1) = {}_4C_1(0.3)^1(0.7)^3 = 0.4116$

$= \dfrac{4116}{10,000}$

$P(X = 2) = {}_4C_2(0.3)^2(0.7)^2 = 0.2646$

$= \dfrac{2646}{10,000}$

$P(X = 3) = {}_4C_3(0.3)^3(0.7)^1 = 0.0756$

$= \dfrac{756}{10,000}$

$P(X = 4) = {}_4C_4(0.3)^4(0.7)^0 = 0.0081$

$= \dfrac{81}{10,000}$

Exercise 10.2

1. $f(0) = {}_2C_0\left(\dfrac{1}{4}\right)^0\left(\dfrac{3}{4}\right)^2 = \dfrac{2!}{0! \cdot 2!} \cdot 1 \cdot \dfrac{9}{16}$

$= 1 \cdot 1 \cdot \dfrac{9}{16} = \dfrac{9}{16}$

$f(1) = {}_2C_1\left(\dfrac{1}{4}\right)^1\left(\dfrac{3}{4}\right)^1 = \dfrac{2!}{1! \cdot 1!} \cdot \dfrac{1}{4} \cdot \dfrac{3}{4}$

$= 2 \cdot \dfrac{1}{4} \cdot \dfrac{3}{4} = \dfrac{3}{8}$

$f(2) = {}_2C_2\left(\dfrac{1}{4}\right)^2\left(\dfrac{3}{4}\right)^0 = \dfrac{2!}{2! \cdot 0!} \cdot \dfrac{1}{16} \cdot 1$

$= 1 \cdot \dfrac{1}{16} \cdot 1 = \dfrac{1}{16}.$

$\mu = np = 2 \cdot \dfrac{1}{4} = \dfrac{1}{2}; \ \sigma = \sqrt{npq} = \sqrt{2 \cdot \dfrac{1}{4} \cdot \dfrac{3}{4}}$

$= \sqrt{\dfrac{6}{16}} = \dfrac{\sqrt{6}}{4}$

3. $f(0) = {}_3C_0\left(\dfrac{2}{3}\right)^0\left(\dfrac{1}{3}\right)^3 = 1 \cdot 1 \cdot \dfrac{1}{27} = \dfrac{1}{27}$

$f(1) = {}_3C_1\left(\dfrac{2}{3}\right)^1\left(\dfrac{1}{3}\right)^2 = \dfrac{3!}{1! \cdot 2!} \cdot \dfrac{2}{3} \cdot \dfrac{1}{9}$

$= 3 \cdot \dfrac{2}{3} \cdot \dfrac{1}{9} = \dfrac{2}{9}$

$f(2) = {}_3C_2\left(\dfrac{2}{3}\right)^2\left(\dfrac{1}{3}\right)^1 = \dfrac{3!}{2! \cdot 1!} \cdot \dfrac{4}{9} \cdot \dfrac{1}{3}$

$= 3 \cdot \dfrac{4}{9} \cdot \dfrac{1}{3} = \dfrac{4}{9}$

$f(3) = {}_3C_3\left(\dfrac{2}{3}\right)^3\left(\dfrac{1}{3}\right)^0 = \dfrac{3!}{3! \cdot 0!} \cdot \dfrac{8}{27} \cdot 1$

$= 1 \cdot \dfrac{8}{27} \cdot 1 = \dfrac{8}{27}$

$\mu = np = 3 \cdot \dfrac{2}{3} = 2; \ \sigma = \sqrt{npq} = \sqrt{3 \cdot \dfrac{2}{3} \cdot \dfrac{1}{3}}$

$= \sqrt{\dfrac{2}{3}} = \dfrac{\sqrt{6}}{3}$

5. $P(X = 5) = {}_6C_5(0.2)^5(0.8)^1$

$= 6(0.00032)(0.8) = 0.001536$

7. $P(X = 2) = {}_4C_2\left(\dfrac{4}{5}\right)^2\left(\dfrac{1}{5}\right)^2 = 6 \cdot \dfrac{16}{25} \cdot \dfrac{1}{25}$

$= \dfrac{96}{625} = 0.1536$

9. $P(X < 2) = P(X = 0) + P(X = 1)$

$= {}_5C_0\left(\dfrac{1}{2}\right)^0\left(\dfrac{1}{2}\right)^5 + {}_5C_1\left(\dfrac{1}{2}\right)^1\left(\dfrac{1}{2}\right)^4$

$= 1 \cdot 1 \cdot \dfrac{1}{32} + 5 \cdot \dfrac{1}{2} \cdot \dfrac{1}{16} = \dfrac{6}{32} = \dfrac{3}{16}$

11. Let X = number of heads that occurs.

$p = \dfrac{1}{2}, \ n = 11$

$P(X = 8) = {}_{11}C_8\left(\dfrac{1}{2}\right)^8\left(\dfrac{1}{2}\right)^3$

$= 165 \cdot \dfrac{1}{256} \cdot \dfrac{1}{8}$

$= \dfrac{165}{2048} \approx 0.081$

13. Let X = number of green marbles drawn. The probability of selecting a green marble on any draw is $\dfrac{6}{10} = \dfrac{3}{5}$. $n = 4$

$$P(X = 1) = {}_4C_1\left(\frac{3}{5}\right)^1\left(\frac{2}{5}\right)^3 = 4\cdot\frac{3}{5}\cdot\frac{8}{125}$$

$$= \frac{96}{625} = 0.1536$$

15. Let X = number of defective switches selected. The probability that a switch is defective is $p = 0.02$. $n = 4$.

$$P(X = 2) = {}_4C_2(0.02)^2(0.98)^2$$
$$= 6(0.0004)(0.9604) \approx 0.002$$

17. Let X = number of heads that occurs.

$$p = \frac{1}{4},\ n = 3$$

a. $P(X = 2) = {}_3C_2\left(\dfrac{1}{4}\right)^2\left(\dfrac{3}{4}\right)^1 = 3\cdot\dfrac{1}{16}\cdot\dfrac{3}{4}$

$$= \frac{9}{64}$$

b. $P(X = 3) = {}_3C_3\left(\dfrac{1}{4}\right)^3\left(\dfrac{3}{4}\right)^0 = 1\cdot\dfrac{1}{64}\cdot 1$

$$= \frac{1}{64}$$

Thus

$$P(X = 2) + P(X = 3) = \frac{9}{64} + \frac{1}{64}$$

$$= \frac{10}{64} = \frac{5}{32}$$

19. Let X = number of defective in sample.

$$p = \frac{1}{3},\ n = 4$$

$$P(X \le 1) = P(X = 0) + P(X = 1)$$

$$= {}_4C_0\left(\frac{1}{3}\right)^0\left(\frac{2}{3}\right)^4 + {}_4C_1\left(\frac{1}{3}\right)^1\left(\frac{2}{3}\right)^3$$

$$= 1\cdot 1\cdot\frac{16}{81} + 4\cdot\frac{1}{3}\cdot\frac{8}{27} = \frac{48}{81}$$

$$= \frac{16}{27} \approx 0.593$$

21. Let X = number of hits in four bats.
$p = 0.300$, $n = 4$
$$P(X \ge 1) = 1 - P(X = 0)$$
$$= 1 - {}_4C_0(0.300)^0(0.700)^4$$
$$= 1 - 1\cdot 1\cdot (0.2401) = 0.7599$$

23. Let X = number of girls. The probability that a child is a girl is $p = \dfrac{1}{2}$. Here $n = 5$.

We must find $P(X \ge 2) = 1 - P(X < 2)$
$= 1 - [P(X = 0) + P(X = 1)]$.

$$P(X = 0) = {}_5C_0\left(\frac{1}{2}\right)^0\left(\frac{1}{2}\right)^5 = 1\cdot 1\cdot\frac{1}{32} = \frac{1}{32}$$

$$P(X = 1) = {}_5C_1\left(\frac{1}{2}\right)^1\left(\frac{1}{2}\right)^4 = 5\cdot\frac{1}{2}\cdot\frac{1}{16} = \frac{5}{32}$$

Thus,
$$P(X \ge 2) = 1 - [P(X = 0) + P(X = 1)]$$

$$= 1 - \left[\frac{1}{32} + \frac{5}{32}\right] = 1 - \frac{3}{16} = \frac{13}{16}$$

25. $\mu = 2$, $\sigma^2 = \dfrac{3}{2}$

Since $\mu = np$, then $np = 2$. Since $\sigma^2 = npq$,

then $(np)q = \dfrac{3}{2}$, or $2q = \dfrac{3}{2}$, so $q = \dfrac{3}{4}$.

Thus, $p = 1 - q = 1 - \dfrac{3}{4} = \dfrac{1}{4}$. Since $np = 2$,

then $n\cdot\dfrac{1}{4} = 2$, or $n = 8$. Thus

$$P(X = 1) = {}_8C_1\left(\frac{1}{4}\right)^1\left(\frac{3}{4}\right)^7 = 8\cdot\frac{3^7}{4^8} = \frac{2187}{8192}$$

$$\approx 0.267.$$

Exercise 10.3

1. $\begin{bmatrix} \frac{1}{2} & 0 \\ \frac{2}{3} & \frac{1}{3} \end{bmatrix}$

No, since the sum of the entries in row 1 is not 1.

3. $\begin{bmatrix} \frac{1}{2} & -\frac{1}{4} & \frac{3}{4} \\ \frac{1}{8} & \frac{5}{8} & \frac{1}{4} \\ \frac{1}{3} & \frac{1}{3} & \frac{1}{3} \end{bmatrix}$

No, since there is a negative entry.

5. $\begin{bmatrix} 0.4 & 0.2 & 0.4 \\ 0 & 0.1 & 0.9 \\ 0.5 & 0.3 & 0.2 \end{bmatrix}$

Yes, since all entries are nonnegative and the sum of the entries in each row is 1.

7. $\begin{bmatrix} \frac{2}{3} & a \\ b & \frac{1}{4} \end{bmatrix}$

$\dfrac{2}{3} + a = 1,\ \text{so } a = \dfrac{1}{3}.\quad b + \dfrac{1}{4} = 1,\ \text{so } b = \dfrac{3}{4}.$

9. $\begin{bmatrix} 0.4 & a & 0.3 \\ a & 0.1 & b \\ a & b & c \end{bmatrix}$

$0.4 + a + 0.3 = 1$, so $a = 0.3$.
$a + 0.1 + b = 1$, $0.3 + 0.1 + b = 1$, so $b = 0.6$.
$a + b + c = 1$, $0.3 + 0.6 + c = 1$, so $c = 0.1$.

11. [0.4, 0.6]

Yes, all entries are nonnegative and their sum is 1.

13. [0.2 0.7 0.5]

No, the sum of the entries is not 1.

15. $\mathbf{X_1} = \mathbf{X_0 T} = \begin{bmatrix} \frac{1}{4} & \frac{3}{4} \end{bmatrix}\begin{bmatrix} \frac{2}{3} & \frac{1}{3} \\ 1 & 0 \end{bmatrix} = \begin{bmatrix} \frac{11}{12} & \frac{1}{12} \end{bmatrix}$

$\mathbf{X_2} = \mathbf{X_1 T} = \begin{bmatrix} \frac{11}{12} & \frac{1}{12} \end{bmatrix}\begin{bmatrix} \frac{2}{3} & \frac{1}{3} \\ 1 & 0 \end{bmatrix} = \begin{bmatrix} \frac{25}{36} & \frac{11}{36} \end{bmatrix}$

$\mathbf{X_3} = \mathbf{X_2 T} = \begin{bmatrix} \frac{25}{36} & \frac{11}{36} \end{bmatrix}\begin{bmatrix} \frac{2}{3} & \frac{1}{3} \\ 1 & 0 \end{bmatrix}$

$= \begin{bmatrix} \frac{83}{108} & \frac{25}{108} \end{bmatrix}$

17. $\mathbf{X_1} = \mathbf{X_0 T} = [0.4 \quad 0.6]\begin{bmatrix} 0.3 & 0.7 \\ 0.5 & 0.5 \end{bmatrix}$

$= [0.42 \quad 0.58]$

$\mathbf{X_2} = \mathbf{X_1 T} = [0.42 \quad 0.58]\begin{bmatrix} 0.3 & 0.7 \\ 0.5 & 0.5 \end{bmatrix}$

$= [0.416 \quad 0.584]$

$\mathbf{X_3} = \mathbf{X_2 T} = [0.416 \quad 0.584]\begin{bmatrix} 0.3 & 0.7 \\ 0.5 & 0.5 \end{bmatrix}$

$= [0.4168 \quad 0.5832]$

19. $\mathbf{X_1} = \mathbf{X_0 T} = [0.2 \quad 0 \quad 0.8]\begin{bmatrix} 0.1 & 0.2 & 0.7 \\ 0 & 0.4 & 0.6 \\ 0.3 & 0.3 & 0.4 \end{bmatrix}$

$= [0.26 \quad 0.28 \quad 0.46]$

$\mathbf{X_2} = \mathbf{X_1 T}$

$= [0.26 \quad 0.28 \quad 0.46]\begin{bmatrix} 0.1 & 0.2 & 0.7 \\ 0 & 0.4 & 0.6 \\ 0.3 & 0.3 & 0.4 \end{bmatrix}$

$= [0.164 \quad 0.302 \quad 0.534];$

$\mathbf{X_3} = \mathbf{X_2 T}$

$= [0.164 \quad 0.302 \quad 0.534]\begin{bmatrix} 0.1 & 0.2 & 0.7 \\ 0 & 0.4 & 0.6 \\ 0.3 & 0.3 & 0.4 \end{bmatrix}$

$= [0.1766 \quad 0.3138 \quad 0.5096].$

21. a. $\mathbf{T}^2 = \begin{bmatrix} \frac{1}{4} & \frac{3}{4} \\ \frac{3}{4} & \frac{1}{4} \end{bmatrix}\begin{bmatrix} \frac{1}{4} & \frac{3}{4} \\ \frac{3}{4} & \frac{1}{4} \end{bmatrix} = \begin{bmatrix} \frac{5}{8} & \frac{3}{8} \\ \frac{3}{8} & \frac{5}{8} \end{bmatrix}$

$\mathbf{T}^3 = \mathbf{T}^2\mathbf{T} = \begin{bmatrix} \frac{5}{8} & \frac{3}{8} \\ \frac{3}{8} & \frac{5}{8} \end{bmatrix}\begin{bmatrix} \frac{1}{4} & \frac{3}{4} \\ \frac{3}{4} & \frac{1}{4} \end{bmatrix}$

$= \begin{bmatrix} \frac{7}{16} & \frac{9}{16} \\ \frac{9}{16} & \frac{7}{16} \end{bmatrix}.$

b. Entry in row 1, column 2, of $\mathbf{T}^2$ is $\dfrac{3}{8}$.

c. Entry in row 2, column 1 of $\mathbf{T}^3$ is $\dfrac{9}{16}$.

23. a. $\mathbf{T}^2$

$$= \begin{bmatrix} 0 & 1 & 0 \\ 0.5 & 0.4 & 0.1 \\ 0.3 & 0.3 & 0.4 \end{bmatrix} \begin{bmatrix} 0 & 1 & 0 \\ 0.5 & 0.4 & 0.1 \\ 0.3 & 0.3 & 0.4 \end{bmatrix}$$

$$= \begin{bmatrix} 0.50 & 0.40 & 0.10 \\ 0.23 & 0.69 & 0.08 \\ 0.27 & 0.54 & 0.19 \end{bmatrix}$$

$\mathbf{T}^3 = \mathbf{T}^2 \mathbf{T}$

$$= \begin{bmatrix} 0.50 & 0.40 & 0.10 \\ 0.23 & 0.69 & 0.08 \\ 0.27 & 0.54 & 0.19 \end{bmatrix} \begin{bmatrix} 0 & 1 & 0 \\ 0.5 & 0.4 & 0.1 \\ 0.3 & 0.3 & 0.4 \end{bmatrix}$$

$$= \begin{bmatrix} 0.230 & 0.690 & 0.080 \\ 0.369 & 0.530 & 0.101 \\ 0.327 & 0.543 & 0.130 \end{bmatrix}$$

b. Entry in row 1, column 2, of $\mathbf{T}^2$ is 0.40.

c. Entry in row 2, column 1 of $\mathbf{T}^3$ is 0.369.

25. $\mathbf{T}^T - \mathbf{I} = \begin{bmatrix} \frac{1}{2} & \frac{3}{4} \\ \frac{1}{2} & \frac{1}{4} \end{bmatrix} - \begin{bmatrix} 1 & 0 \\ 0 & 1 \end{bmatrix} = \begin{bmatrix} -\frac{1}{2} & \frac{3}{4} \\ \frac{1}{2} & -\frac{3}{4} \end{bmatrix}$

$$\begin{bmatrix} -\frac{1}{2} & \frac{3}{4} & | & 0 \\ \frac{1}{2} & -\frac{3}{4} & | & 0 \\ 1 & 1 & | & 1 \end{bmatrix} \rightarrow \cdots \rightarrow \begin{bmatrix} 1 & 0 & | & \frac{3}{5} \\ 0 & 1 & | & \frac{2}{5} \\ 0 & 0 & | & 0 \end{bmatrix}$$

$$\mathbf{Q} = \begin{bmatrix} \frac{3}{5} & \frac{2}{5} \end{bmatrix}$$

27. $\mathbf{T}^T - \mathbf{I} = \begin{bmatrix} \frac{1}{5} & \frac{3}{5} \\ \frac{4}{5} & \frac{2}{5} \end{bmatrix} - \begin{bmatrix} 1 & 0 \\ 0 & 1 \end{bmatrix} = \begin{bmatrix} -\frac{4}{5} & \frac{3}{5} \\ \frac{4}{5} & -\frac{3}{5} \end{bmatrix}$

$$\begin{bmatrix} -\frac{4}{5} & \frac{3}{5} & | & 0 \\ \frac{4}{5} & -\frac{3}{5} & | & 0 \\ 1 & 1 & | & 1 \end{bmatrix} \rightarrow \cdots \rightarrow \begin{bmatrix} 1 & 0 & | & \frac{3}{7} \\ 0 & 1 & | & \frac{4}{7} \\ 0 & 0 & | & 0 \end{bmatrix}$$

$$\mathbf{Q} = \begin{bmatrix} \frac{3}{7} & \frac{4}{7} \end{bmatrix}$$

29. $\mathbf{T}^T - \mathbf{I} = \begin{bmatrix} 0.4 & 0.6 & 0.6 \\ 0.3 & 0.3 & 0.1 \\ 0.3 & 0.1 & 0.3 \end{bmatrix} - \begin{bmatrix} 1 & 0 & 0 \\ 0 & 1 & 0 \\ 0 & 0 & 1 \end{bmatrix} = \begin{bmatrix} -0.6 & 0.6 & 0.6 \\ 0.3 & -0.7 & 0.1 \\ 0.3 & 0.1 & -0.7 \end{bmatrix}$

$$\begin{bmatrix} -0.6 & 0.6 & 0.6 & | & 0 \\ 0.3 & -0.7 & 0.1 & | & 0 \\ 0.3 & 0.1 & -0.7 & | & 0 \\ 1 & 1 & 1 & | & 1 \end{bmatrix} \rightarrow \cdots \rightarrow \begin{bmatrix} 1 & 0 & 0 & | & 0.5 \\ 0 & 1 & 0 & | & 0.25 \\ 0 & 0 & 1 & | & 0.25 \\ 0 & 0 & 0 & | & 0 \end{bmatrix}$$

$\mathbf{Q} = \begin{bmatrix} 0.5 & 0.25 & 0.25 \end{bmatrix}$

31. a.
$$\mathbf{T} = \begin{array}{c} \\ \text{Flu} \\ \text{No flu} \end{array} \begin{array}{c} \text{Flu} \quad \text{No flu} \\ \begin{bmatrix} 0.1 & 0.9 \\ 0.2 & 0.8 \end{bmatrix} \end{array}$$

b. $\mathbf{X_0} = \begin{bmatrix} \frac{120}{200} & \frac{80}{200} \end{bmatrix} = \begin{bmatrix} 0.6 & 0.4 \end{bmatrix}$.

If a period is 4 days, then 8 days corresponds to 2 periods, and 12 days corresponds to 3 periods. The state vector corresponding to 8 days from now is

$$\mathbf{X_2} = \mathbf{X_0} \mathbf{T}^2 = \begin{bmatrix} 0.6 & 0.4 \end{bmatrix} \begin{bmatrix} 0.19 & 0.81 \\ 0.18 & 0.82 \end{bmatrix} = \begin{bmatrix} 0.186 & 0.814 \end{bmatrix}.$$

Thus $0.186(200) \approx 37$ students can be expected to have the flu 8 days from now. The state vector corresponding to 12 days from now is

$$\mathbf{X_3} = \mathbf{X_0}\mathbf{T}^3 = [0.6 \quad 0.4]\begin{bmatrix} 0.181 & 0.819 \\ 0.182 & 0.818 \end{bmatrix} = [0.1814 \quad 0.8186].$$

Thus $0.1814(200) \approx 36$ students can be expected to have the flu 12 days from now.

33. **a.**

$$\begin{array}{cc} & \text{A} \quad \text{B} \\ \mathbf{T} = & \begin{array}{c} \text{A} \\ \text{B} \end{array}\begin{bmatrix} 0.9 & 0.1 \\ 0.2 & 0.8 \end{bmatrix} \end{array}$$

b. Thursday corresponds to step 3.

$$\mathbf{T}^2 = \begin{bmatrix} 0.83 & 0.17 \\ 0.34 & 0.66 \end{bmatrix}$$

$$\mathbf{T}^3 = \begin{bmatrix} 0.781 & 0.219 \\ 0.438 & 0.562 \end{bmatrix}.$$

The probability is 0.781.

35. **a.**

$$\begin{array}{cc} & \text{D} \quad \text{R} \quad \text{O} \\ \mathbf{T} = & \begin{array}{c} \text{D} \\ \text{R} \\ \text{O} \end{array}\begin{bmatrix} 0.8 & 0.1 & 0.1 \\ 0.1 & 0.8 & 0.1 \\ 0.3 & 0.2 & 0.5 \end{bmatrix} \end{array}$$

b.

$$\mathbf{T}^2 = \begin{bmatrix} 0.68 & 0.18 & 0.14 \\ 0.19 & 0.67 & 0.14 \\ 0.41 & 0.29 & 0.30 \end{bmatrix}$$

The probability is 0.19.

c. $\mathbf{X_1} = \mathbf{X_0}\mathbf{T}$

$$= [0.40 \quad 0.40 \quad 0.20]\begin{bmatrix} 0.8 & 0.1 & 0.1 \\ 0.1 & 0.8 & 0.1 \\ 0.3 & 0.2 & 0.5 \end{bmatrix}$$

$$= [0.42 \quad 0.40 \quad 0.18]$$

40% will be Republican.

37. **a.**

$$\begin{array}{cc} & \text{A} \quad \text{Compet.} \\ \mathbf{T} = & \begin{array}{c} \text{A} \\ \text{Compet.} \end{array}\begin{bmatrix} 0.8 & 0.2 \\ 0.3 & 0.7 \end{bmatrix} \end{array}$$

b. $\mathbf{X_1} = \mathbf{X_0}\mathbf{T} = [0.70 \quad 0.30]\begin{bmatrix} 0.8 & 0.2 \\ 0.3 & 0.7 \end{bmatrix}$

$$= [0.65 \quad 0.35]$$

A is expected to control 65% of the market.

c. $\mathbf{T}^T - \mathbf{I} = \begin{bmatrix} 0.8 & 0.3 \\ 0.2 & 0.7 \end{bmatrix} - \begin{bmatrix} 1 & 0 \\ 0 & 1 \end{bmatrix} = \begin{bmatrix} -0.2 & 0.3 \\ 0.2 & -0.3 \end{bmatrix}$

$$\begin{bmatrix} -0.2 & 0.3 & | & 0 \\ 0.2 & -0.3 & | & 0 \\ 1 & 1 & | & 1 \end{bmatrix} \rightarrow \dots \rightarrow \begin{bmatrix} 1 & 0 & | & 0.6 \\ 0 & 1 & | & 0.4 \\ 0 & 0 & | & 0 \end{bmatrix}$$

$$\mathbf{Q} = \begin{bmatrix} 0.6 & 0.4 \end{bmatrix}$$

In the long run, A can expect to control 60% of the market.

39. a. $T = \begin{array}{c} \\ 1 \\ 2 \end{array}\begin{array}{cc} 1 & 2 \\ \begin{bmatrix} \frac{5}{7} & \frac{2}{7} \\ \frac{3}{7} & \frac{4}{7} \end{bmatrix} \end{array}$

b. $X_2 = X_0 T^2 = \begin{bmatrix} \frac{1}{2} & \frac{1}{2} \end{bmatrix}\begin{bmatrix} \frac{31}{49} & \frac{18}{49} \\ \frac{27}{49} & \frac{22}{49} \end{bmatrix} = \begin{bmatrix} \frac{29}{49} & \frac{20}{49} \end{bmatrix}$

$\approx [0.5918 \quad 0.4082]$

About 59.18% in compartment 1 and 40.82% in compartment 2.

c. $T^T - I = \begin{bmatrix} \frac{5}{7} & \frac{3}{7} \\ \frac{2}{7} & \frac{4}{7} \end{bmatrix} - \begin{bmatrix} 1 & 0 \\ 0 & 1 \end{bmatrix} = \begin{bmatrix} -\frac{2}{7} & \frac{3}{7} \\ \frac{2}{7} & -\frac{3}{7} \end{bmatrix}$

$\begin{bmatrix} -\frac{2}{7} & \frac{3}{7} & 0 \\ \frac{2}{7} & -\frac{3}{7} & 0 \\ 1 & 1 & 1 \end{bmatrix} \rightarrow \dots \rightarrow \begin{bmatrix} 1 & 0 & \frac{3}{5} \\ 0 & 1 & \frac{2}{5} \\ 0 & 0 & 0 \end{bmatrix}$

$Q = \begin{bmatrix} \frac{3}{5} & \frac{2}{5} \end{bmatrix} = [0.60 \quad 0.40]$

In the long run, there will be 60% in compartment 1 and 40% in compartment 2.

41. a. $T^T - I = \begin{bmatrix} \frac{3}{4} & \frac{1}{2} \\ \frac{1}{4} & \frac{1}{2} \end{bmatrix} - \begin{bmatrix} 1 & 0 \\ 0 & 1 \end{bmatrix} = \begin{bmatrix} -\frac{1}{4} & \frac{1}{2} \\ \frac{1}{4} & -\frac{1}{2} \end{bmatrix}$

$\begin{bmatrix} -\frac{1}{4} & \frac{1}{2} & 0 \\ \frac{1}{4} & -\frac{1}{2} & 0 \\ 1 & 1 & 1 \end{bmatrix} \rightarrow \dots \rightarrow \begin{bmatrix} 1 & 0 & \frac{2}{3} \\ 0 & 1 & \frac{1}{3} \\ 0 & 0 & 0 \end{bmatrix}$

$Q = \begin{bmatrix} \frac{2}{3} & \frac{1}{3} \end{bmatrix}$

b.   Presently, A accounts for 50% of sales and in long run A will account for $\frac{2}{3}$, or $66\frac{2}{3}\%$, of sales. Thus the percentage increase in sales above the present level is

$\frac{66\frac{2}{3} - 50}{50} \cdot 100\% = \frac{16\frac{2}{3}}{50} \cdot 100\% = 33\frac{1}{3}\%.$

43. $T^2 = TT = \begin{bmatrix} \frac{1}{2} & \frac{1}{2} \\ 1 & 0 \end{bmatrix}\begin{bmatrix} \frac{1}{2} & \frac{1}{2} \\ 1 & 0 \end{bmatrix} = \begin{bmatrix} \frac{3}{4} & \frac{1}{4} \\ \frac{1}{2} & \frac{1}{2} \end{bmatrix}$

Since all entries of T^2 are positive, T is regular.

Chapter 10 Review Problems

1. $\mu = \sum_x xf(x) = 1 \cdot f(1) + 2 \cdot f(2) + 3 \cdot f(3)$

$= 1(0.7) + 2(0.1) + 3(0.2) = 1.5$

$\text{Var}(X) = \sum_x x^2 f(x) - \mu^2$

$= \left[1^2(0.7) + 2^2(0.1) + 3^2(0.2)\right] - (1.5)^2$

$= 0.65$

$\sigma = \sqrt{\text{Var}(X)} = \sqrt{0.65} \approx 0.81$

3. a. $n(S) = 2 \cdot 6 = 12$

$E_1 = \{T1\}, \quad E_2 = \{T2, H1\},$

$E_3 = \{T3, H2\}, \quad E_4 = \{T4, H3\},$

$E_5 = \{T5, H4\}, \quad E_6 = \{T6, H5\},$

$E_7 = \{H6\}$

$f(1) = P(E_1) = \dfrac{n(E_1)}{n(S)} = \dfrac{1}{12}$

$f(2) = P(E_2) = \dfrac{n(E_2)}{n(S)} = \dfrac{2}{12} = \dfrac{1}{6}$

Similarly, $f(3), f(4), f(5)$, and $f(6)$ equal $\dfrac{1}{6}$.

$f(7) = P(E_7) = \dfrac{n(E_7)}{n(S)} = \dfrac{1}{12}$

b. $E(X) = \sum_x xf(x)$

$= 1 \cdot \dfrac{1}{12} + \dfrac{2+3+4+5+6}{6} + 7 \cdot \dfrac{1}{12}$

$= \dfrac{1}{12} + \dfrac{20}{6} + \dfrac{7}{12} = \dfrac{48}{12} = 4$

5. Let X = gain (in dollars) on a play. If no 10 appears, then $X = 0 - \dfrac{1}{4} = -\dfrac{1}{4}$; if exactly one 10 appears, then $X = 1 - \dfrac{1}{4} = \dfrac{3}{4}$; if two 10's appear, then $X = 2 - \dfrac{1}{4} = \dfrac{7}{4}$.

$n(S) = 52 \cdot 52$. In a deck, there are 4 10's and 48 non 10's. Thus $n(E_{\text{no }10}) = 48 \cdot 48$. The event $E_{\text{one }10}$ occurs if the first card is a 10 and the second is a non-10, or vice versa. Thus $n(E_{\text{one }10}) = 4 \cdot 48 + 48 \cdot 4 = 2 \cdot 4 \cdot 48$.

$n(E_{\text{two }10's}) = 4 \cdot 4$.

Dist. of X:

$f\left(-\dfrac{1}{4}\right) = \dfrac{48 \cdot 48}{52 \cdot 52} = \dfrac{144}{169}$,

$f\left(\dfrac{3}{4}\right) = \dfrac{2 \cdot 4 \cdot 48}{52 \cdot 52} = \dfrac{24}{169}$,

$f\left(\dfrac{7}{4}\right) = \dfrac{4 \cdot 4}{52 \cdot 52} = \dfrac{1}{169}$.

$E(X) = -\dfrac{1}{4} \cdot \dfrac{144}{169} + \dfrac{3}{4} \cdot \dfrac{24}{169} + \dfrac{7}{4} \cdot \dfrac{1}{169}$

$= \dfrac{-144 + 72 + 7}{4 \cdot 169} = -\dfrac{65}{676} = -\dfrac{5}{52} \approx -0.10$

There is a loss of $0.10 per play.

7. a. Let X = gain (in dollars) on each unit shipped. Then $P(X = -100) = 0.08$ and $P(X = 200) = 1 - 0.08 = 0.92$.

$E(X) = -100f(-100) + 200f(200)$

$= -100(0.08) + 200(0.92)$

$= \$176$ per unit

b. Since the expected gain per unit is $176 and 4000 units are shipped per year, then expected annual profit is $4000(176) = \$704,000$.

9. $f(0) = {}_3C_0(0.1)^0(0.9)^3 = \dfrac{3!}{0! \cdot 3!} \cdot 1(0.729)$

$= 1 \cdot 1(0.729) = 0.729$

$f(1) = {}_3C_1(0.1)^1(0.9)^2 = \dfrac{3!}{1! \cdot 2!}(0.1)(0.81)$

$= 3(0.1)(0.81) = 0.243$

$f(2) = {}_3C_2(0.1)^2(0.9)^1 = \dfrac{3!}{2! \cdot 1!}(0.01)(0.9)$

$= 3(0.01)(0.9) = 0.027$

$$f(3) = {}_3C_3(0.1)^3(0.9)^0 = \frac{3!}{3! \cdot 0!}(0.001) \cdot 1$$
$$= 1 \cdot (0.001) \cdot 1 = 0.001$$
$$\mu = np = 3(0.1) = 0.3$$
$$\sigma = \sqrt{npq} = \sqrt{3(0.1)(0.9)} \approx 0.52$$

11. $P(X \le 1) = P(X = 0) + P(X = 1)$
$$= {}_5C_0\left(\frac{3}{4}\right)^0\left(\frac{1}{4}\right)^5 + {}_5C_1\left(\frac{3}{4}\right)^1\left(\frac{1}{4}\right)^4$$
$$= 1 \cdot 1 \cdot \frac{1}{1024} + 5 \cdot \frac{3}{4} \cdot \frac{1}{256} = \frac{16}{1024} = \frac{1}{64}$$

13. The probability that a 2 or 3 results on one roll is $\frac{2}{6} = \frac{1}{3}$. Let X = number of 2's or 3's that appear on 4 rolls. Then X is binomial with $p = \frac{1}{3}$ and $n = 4$.
$$P(X = 3) = {}_4C_3\left(\frac{1}{3}\right)^3\left(\frac{2}{3}\right)^1 = 4 \cdot \frac{1}{27} \cdot \frac{2}{3} = \frac{8}{81}$$

15. Let X = number of heads that occur. Then X is binomial.
$$P(X = 0) = {}_4C_0\left(\frac{1}{3}\right)^0\left(\frac{2}{3}\right)^4 = \frac{4!}{0! \cdot 4!}(1)\left(\frac{16}{81}\right)$$
$$= 1(1)\left(\frac{16}{81}\right) = \frac{16}{81}$$
$$P(X = 1) = {}_4C_1\left(\frac{1}{3}\right)^1\left(\frac{2}{3}\right)^3 = \frac{4!}{1! \cdot 3!}\left(\frac{1}{3}\right)\left(\frac{8}{27}\right)$$
$$= 4\left(\frac{1}{3}\right)\left(\frac{8}{27}\right) = \frac{32}{81}$$
$$P(X \ge 2) = 1 - [P(X = 0) + P(X = 1)]$$
$$= 1 - \left[\frac{16}{81} + \frac{32}{81}\right] = 1 - \frac{48}{81} = \frac{11}{27}$$

17. From row 1, $0.1 + a + 0.6 = 1$, so $a = 0.3$.
From row 2, $2a + b + b = 1$, so $2b = 1 - 2a$,
or $b = \dfrac{1 - 2a}{2} = \dfrac{1 - 2(0.3)}{2} = 0.2$.
From row 3, $a + b + c = 1$, so $c = 1 - a - b$,
or
$c = 1 - 0.3 - 0.2 = 0.5$.

19. $X_1 = X_0T = [0.5 \quad 0 \quad 0.5]\begin{bmatrix} 0.1 & 0.2 & 0.7 \\ 0.3 & 0.4 & 0.3 \\ 0.1 & 0.1 & 0.8 \end{bmatrix}$
$$= [0.10 \quad 0.15 \quad 0.75]$$
$$X_2 = X_1T$$
$$= [0.10 \quad 0.15 \quad 0.75]\begin{bmatrix} 0.1 & 0.2 & 0.7 \\ 0.3 & 0.4 & 0.3 \\ 0.1 & 0.1 & 0.8 \end{bmatrix}$$
$$= [0.130 \quad 0.155 \quad 0.715]$$

21. a. $T^2 = TT = \begin{bmatrix} \frac{1}{7} & \frac{6}{7} \\ \frac{3}{7} & \frac{4}{7} \end{bmatrix}\begin{bmatrix} \frac{1}{7} & \frac{6}{7} \\ \frac{3}{7} & \frac{4}{7} \end{bmatrix} = \begin{bmatrix} \frac{19}{49} & \frac{30}{49} \\ \frac{15}{49} & \frac{34}{49} \end{bmatrix}$

$T^3 = T^2T = \begin{bmatrix} \frac{19}{49} & \frac{30}{49} \\ \frac{15}{49} & \frac{34}{49} \end{bmatrix}\begin{bmatrix} \frac{1}{7} & \frac{6}{7} \\ \frac{3}{7} & \frac{4}{7} \end{bmatrix}$

$= \begin{bmatrix} \frac{109}{343} & \frac{234}{343} \\ \frac{117}{343} & \frac{226}{343} \end{bmatrix}$

b. From T^2, entry in row 1, column 2, is $\dfrac{30}{49}$.

c. From T^3, entry in row 2, column 1, is $\dfrac{117}{343}$.

23. $T^T - I = \begin{bmatrix} \frac{1}{3} & \frac{2}{3} \\ \frac{2}{3} & \frac{1}{3} \end{bmatrix} - \begin{bmatrix} 1 & 0 \\ 0 & 1 \end{bmatrix} = \begin{bmatrix} -\frac{2}{3} & \frac{2}{3} \\ \frac{2}{3} & -\frac{2}{3} \end{bmatrix}$

$\begin{bmatrix} -\frac{2}{3} & \frac{2}{3} & \vdots & 0 \\ \frac{2}{3} & -\frac{2}{3} & \vdots & 0 \\ 1 & 1 & \vdots & 1 \end{bmatrix} \to \cdots \to \begin{bmatrix} 1 & 0 & \vdots & \frac{1}{2} \\ 0 & 1 & \vdots & \frac{1}{2} \\ 0 & 0 & \vdots & 0 \end{bmatrix}$

$Q = \begin{bmatrix} \frac{1}{2} & \frac{1}{2} \end{bmatrix}$

25. $\quad \mathbf{T} = \begin{array}{c} \\ \text{Japanese} \\ \text{Non - Japanese} \end{array} \overset{\begin{array}{cc} \text{Japanese} & \text{Non - Japanese} \end{array}}{\begin{bmatrix} 0.8 & 0.2 \\ 0.6 & 0.4 \end{bmatrix}}$

a. $\quad \mathbf{T}^2 = \begin{bmatrix} 0.8 & 0.2 \\ 0.6 & 0.4 \end{bmatrix}\begin{bmatrix} 0.8 & 0.2 \\ 0.6 & 0.4 \end{bmatrix}$

$\quad = \begin{bmatrix} 0.76 & 0.24 \\ 0.72 & 0.28 \end{bmatrix}$

From row 1, column 1, the probability that a person who presently owns a Japanese car will buy a Japanese car two cars later is 0.76.

b. $\quad \mathbf{X}_2 = \mathbf{X}_0\mathbf{T}^2 = [0.6 \quad 0.4]\begin{bmatrix} 0.76 & 0.24 \\ 0.72 & 0.28 \end{bmatrix}$

$\quad = [0.744 \quad 0.256]$

In two years, we expect 74.4% Japanese, 25.6% non-Japanese.

c. $\quad \mathbf{T}^T - \mathbf{I} = \begin{bmatrix} 0.8 & 0.6 \\ 0.2 & 0.4 \end{bmatrix} - \begin{bmatrix} 1 & 0 \\ 0 & 1 \end{bmatrix}$

$\quad = \begin{bmatrix} -0.2 & 0.6 \\ 0.2 & -0.6 \end{bmatrix}$

$\quad \begin{bmatrix} -0.2 & 0.6 & \vdots & 0 \\ 0.2 & -0.6 & \vdots & 0 \\ 1 & 1 & \vdots & 1 \end{bmatrix} \rightarrow \ldots$

$\quad \rightarrow \begin{bmatrix} 1 & 0 & \vdots & 0.75 \\ 0 & 1 & \vdots & 0.25 \\ 0 & 0 & \vdots & 0 \end{bmatrix}$

$\mathbf{Q} = [0.75 \quad 0.25]$

In the long run, 75% Japanese, 25% non-Japanese

Mathematical Snapshot Chapter 10

1. For $\mathbf{X}_0 = [0 \quad 1 \quad 0 \quad 0]$ or $[0 \quad 0 \quad 1 \quad 0]$, the first entry of the state vector is greater than 0.5 for $n = 7$ or greater. If $\mathbf{X}_0 = [0 \quad 1 \quad 0 \quad 0]$, then
$\mathbf{X}_0\mathbf{T}^7 \approx [0.5217 \quad 0.0000 \quad 0.4783 \quad 0.0000]$.

3. Against Always Defect,
$$\mathbf{T} = \begin{array}{c} 1 \\ 2 \\ 3 \\ 4 \end{array}\overset{\begin{array}{cccc} 1 & 2 & 3 & 4 \end{array}}{\begin{bmatrix} 0 & 1 & 0 & 0 \\ 0 & 0.1 & 0 & 0.9 \\ 0 & 1 & 0 & 0 \\ 0 & 0.1 & 0 & 0.9 \end{bmatrix}}.$$

Against Always Cooperate,
$$\mathbf{T} = \begin{array}{c} 1 \\ 2 \\ 3 \\ 4 \end{array}\overset{\begin{array}{cccc} 1 & 2 & 3 & 4 \end{array}}{\begin{bmatrix} 1 & 0 & 0 & 0 \\ 0.1 & 0 & 0.9 & 0 \\ 1 & 0 & 0 & 0 \\ 0.1 & 0 & 0.9 & 0 \end{bmatrix}}.$$

Against regular Tit-for-tat,
$$\mathbf{T} = \begin{array}{c} 1 \\ 2 \\ 3 \\ 4 \end{array}\overset{\begin{array}{cccc} 1 & 2 & 3 & 4 \end{array}}{\begin{bmatrix} 1 & 0 & 0 & 0 \\ 0.1 & 0 & 0.9 & 0 \\ 0 & 1 & 0 & 0 \\ 0 & 0.1 & 0 & 0.9 \end{bmatrix}}.$$

Chapter 11

Principles in Practice 11.1

1. The graph of the greatest integer function is shown.

$$10$$

$$-10 \qquad 10$$

$$-10$$

$\lim_{x \to a} f(x)$ does not exist when a is an integer since the limits are different depending on the side from which you approach the integer. $\lim_{x \to a} f(x)$ exists for all numbers which are not integers.

2. $\lim_{r \to 1} V(r) = \lim_{r \to 1} \frac{4}{3}\pi r^3 = \frac{4}{3}\pi \lim_{r \to 1} r^3$

$= \frac{4}{3}\pi(1)^3 = \frac{4}{3}\pi$

3. $\lim_{x \to 8} R(x) = \lim_{x \to 8}\left(500x - 6x^2\right)$

$= \lim_{x \to 8} 500x - \lim_{x \to 8} 6x^2$

$= 500 \lim_{x \to 8} x - 6 \lim_{x \to 8} x^2 = 500(8) - 6(8)^2$

$= 4000 - 384 = 3616$

4. $\lim_{t \to 2} p = \lim_{t \to 2} \dfrac{50\left(t^2 + 4t\right)}{t^2 + 3t + 20} = \dfrac{\lim_{t \to 2}\left[50\left(t^2 + 4t\right)\right]}{\lim_{t \to 2}\left(t^2 + 3t + 20\right)}$

$= \dfrac{50\left[2^2 + 4(2)\right]}{2^2 + 3(2) + 20} = \dfrac{600}{30} = 20$

5. As $h \to 0$, both the numerator and denominator approach 0. For $h \neq 0$,

$\lim_{h \to 0} \dfrac{125 + 2(x + h) - (125 + 2x)}{h}$

$= \lim_{h \to 0} \dfrac{125 + 2x + 2h - 125 - 2x}{h} = \lim_{h \to 0} \dfrac{2h}{h}$

$= \lim_{h \to 0} 2 = 2.$

Exercise 11.1

1. **a.** 1

   b. 0

   c. 1

3. **a.** 1

   b. does not exist

   c. 3

5. $f(0.9) = 2.8$ $f(1.1) = 3.2$
   $f(0.99) = 2.98$ $f(1.01) = 3.02$
   $f(0.999) = 2.998$ $f(1.001) = 3.002$
   estimate of limit: 3

7. $f(-0.1) \approx 0.9516$ $f(0.1) \approx 1.0517$
   $f(-0.01) \approx 0.9950$ $f(0.01) \approx 1.0050$
   $f(-0.001) \approx 0.9995$ $f(0.001) \approx 1.0005$
   estimate of limit: 1

9. $\lim\limits_{x \to 2} 16 = 16$

11. $\lim\limits_{t \to -5} \left(t^2 - 5\right) = (-5)^2 - 5 = 25 - 5 = 20$

13. $\lim\limits_{x \to -1} \left(x^3 - 3x^2 - 2x + 1\right)$
    $= (-1)^3 - 3(-1)^2 - 2(-1) + 1 = -1 - 3 + 2 + 1 = -1$

15. $\lim\limits_{t \to -3} \dfrac{t-2}{t+5} = \dfrac{\lim\limits_{t \to -3}(t-2)}{\lim\limits_{t \to -3}(t+5)} = \dfrac{-3-2}{-3+5} = \dfrac{-5}{2} = -\dfrac{5}{2}$

17. $\lim\limits_{h \to 0} \dfrac{h}{h^2 - 7h + 1} = \dfrac{\lim\limits_{h \to 0} h}{\lim\limits_{h \to 0}\left(h^2 - 7h + 1\right)}$

    $= \dfrac{0}{0^2 - 7(0) + 1} = 0$

19. $\lim\limits_{p \to 4} \sqrt{p^2 + p + 5} = \sqrt{\lim\limits_{p \to 4}\left(p^2 + p + 5\right)}$
    $= \sqrt{4^2 + 4 + 5} = \sqrt{25} = 5$

21. $\lim\limits_{x \to -2} \dfrac{x^2 + 2x}{x+2} = \lim\limits_{x \to -2} \dfrac{x(x+2)}{x+2} = \lim\limits_{x \to -2} x = -2$

23. $\lim\limits_{x \to 2} \dfrac{x^2 - x - 2}{x - 2} = \lim\limits_{x \to 2} \dfrac{(x-2)(x+1)}{x-2}$
    $= \lim\limits_{x \to 2}(x+1) = 3$

25. $\displaystyle\lim_{x\to-1}\frac{x^2+2x+1}{x+1}=\lim_{x\to-1}\frac{(x+1)^2}{x+1}$
$\displaystyle=\lim_{x\to-1}(x+1)=0$

27. $\displaystyle\lim_{x\to3}\frac{x-3}{x^2-9}=\lim_{x\to3}\frac{x-3}{(x+3)(x-3)}$
$\displaystyle=\lim_{x\to3}\frac{1}{x+3}=\frac{1}{6}$

29. $\displaystyle\lim_{x\to4}\frac{x^2-9x+20}{x^2-3x-4}=\lim_{x\to4}\frac{(x-4)(x-5)}{(x-4)(x+1)}$
$\displaystyle=\lim_{x\to4}\frac{x-5}{x+1}=-\frac{1}{5}$

31. $\displaystyle\lim_{x\to2}\frac{3x^2-x-10}{x^2+5x-14}=\lim_{x\to2}\frac{(3x+5)(x-2)}{(x+7)(x-2)}$
$\displaystyle=\lim_{x\to2}\frac{3x+5}{x+7}=\frac{11}{9}$

33. $\displaystyle\lim_{h\to0}\frac{(2+h)^2-2^2}{h}=\lim_{h\to0}\frac{\left[4+4h+h^2\right]-4}{h}$
$\displaystyle=\lim_{h\to0}\frac{4h+h^2}{h}=\lim_{h\to0}\frac{h(4+h)}{h}=\lim_{h\to0}4+h=4$

35. $\displaystyle\lim_{h\to0}\frac{(x+h)^2-x^2}{h}=\lim_{h\to0}\frac{2xh+h^2}{h}$
$\displaystyle=\lim_{h\to0}(2x+h)=2x$

37. $\displaystyle\lim_{h\to0}\frac{f(x+h)-f(x)}{h}$
$\displaystyle=\lim_{h\to0}\frac{[4-(x+h)]-(4-x)}{h}$
$\displaystyle=\lim_{h\to0}\frac{-h}{h}=\lim_{h\to0}-1=-1$

39. $\displaystyle\lim_{h\to0}\frac{f(x+h)-f(x)}{h}$
$\displaystyle=\lim_{h\to0}\frac{\left[(x+h)^2-3\right]-\left(x^2-3\right)}{h}$
$\displaystyle=\lim_{h\to0}\frac{x^2+2xh+h^2-3-\left(x^2-3\right)}{h}$
$\displaystyle=\lim_{h\to0}\frac{2xh+h^2}{h}=\lim_{h\to0}(2x+h)=2x$

41. $\displaystyle\lim_{h\to0}\frac{f(x+h)-f(x)}{h}=\lim_{h\to0}\frac{\left[(x+h)^2-3(x+h)\right]-\left(x^2-3x\right)}{h}$
$\displaystyle=\lim_{h\to0}\frac{x^2+2xh+h^2-3x-3h-\left(x^2-3x\right)}{h}=\lim_{h\to0}\frac{2xh+h^2-3h}{h}$
$\displaystyle=\lim_{h\to0}\frac{h(2x+h-3)}{h}=\lim_{h\to0}(2x+h-3)=2x-3$

43. $\displaystyle\lim_{x\to6}\frac{\sqrt{x-2}-2}{x-6}=\lim_{x\to6}\frac{\left(\sqrt{x-2}-2\right)\left(\sqrt{x-2}+2\right)}{(x-6)\left(\sqrt{x-2}+2\right)}$
$\displaystyle=\lim_{x\to6}\frac{(x-2)-4}{(x-6)\left(\sqrt{x-2}+2\right)}=\lim_{x\to6}\frac{x-6}{(x-6)\left(\sqrt{x-2}+2\right)}$
$\displaystyle=\lim_{x\to6}\frac{1}{\sqrt{x-2}+2}=\frac{1}{4}$

45. a. $\lim\limits_{T_c \to 0} \dfrac{T_h - T_c}{T_h} = \dfrac{T_h - 0}{T_h} = \dfrac{T_h}{T_h} = 1$

   b. $\lim\limits_{T_c \to T_h} \dfrac{T_h - T_c}{T_h} = \dfrac{T_h - T_h}{T_h} = \dfrac{0}{T_h} = 0$

47.

11.00

49.

−7.00

51. The graph of $C(p)$ is shown. (Negative amounts of impurities and money are not reasonable, so only the first quadrant is shown.)

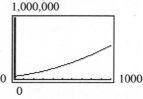

As p gets closer and closer to 0, the values of $C(p)$ increase without bound, so $\lim\limits_{p \to 0} C(p)$ does not exist.

Principles in Practice 11.2

1. The graph of $p(x)$ is shown.

From the graph, it is apparent that $\lim\limits_{x \to \infty} p(x) = 0$. The graph starts out high and quickly drops down toward zero. According to this function, a low price corresponds to a high demand and a high price corresponds to a low standard.

2. The graph of $y(x)$ is shown.

From the graph, it is apparent that $\lim\limits_{x \to \infty} y(x) = 500$. The greatest yearly sales that the company can expect is $500,000, even with unlimited spending on advertising.

3. The graph of $C(x)$ is shown.

From the graph it is apparent that $\lim\limits_{x \to \infty} C(x) = \infty$. This indicates that the cost increases without bound the more units that you make.

4. $\lim\limits_{x\to 1} f(x)$ does not exist since

$\lim\limits_{x\to 1^-} f(x) = \lim\limits_{x\to 1^-} 100 = 100$ while

$\lim\limits_{x\to 1^+} f(x) = \lim\limits_{x\to 1^+} 175 = 175$.

$\lim\limits_{x\to 2.5} f(x) = 250$ since

$\lim\limits_{x\to 2.5^-} f(x) = \lim\limits_{x\to 2.5^+} = 250$

Exercise 11.2

1. a.   2

   b.   3

   c.   does not exist

   d. $-\infty$

   e. ∞

   f. ∞

   g. ∞

   h.   0

   i.   1

   j.   1

   k.   1

3. $\lim\limits_{x\to 3^+} (x-2)$

As $x\to 3^+$, then $x-2\to 1$.

5. $\lim\limits_{x\to -\infty} 5x$

As x becomes very negative, so does $5x$.
Thus $\lim\limits_{x\to -\infty} 5x = -\infty$.

7. $\lim\limits_{x\to 0^-} \dfrac{6x}{x^4} = \lim\limits_{x\to 0^-} \dfrac{6}{x^3} = -\infty$ since x^3 is

negative and close to 0 for $x\to 0^-$.

9. $\lim\limits_{x\to -\infty} x^2 = \infty$ since x^2 is positive for

$x\to -\infty$.

11. $\lim\limits_{h\to 0^+} \sqrt{h}$

If h is positive and close to 0, then $\sqrt{h}$ is close to 0.

13. $\lim\limits_{x\to 5^-} \dfrac{3}{x-5} = -\infty$

$\lim\limits_{x\to 5^+} \dfrac{3}{x-5} = \infty$

So $\lim\limits_{x\to 5} \dfrac{3}{x-5} = -\infty$ does not exist.

15. $\lim\limits_{x\to 1^+} \left(4\sqrt{x-1}\right)$. As $x\to 1^+$, then $x-1$

approaches 0 through positive values. So
$\sqrt{x-1}\to 0$. Thus

$\lim\limits_{x\to 1^+} \left(4\sqrt{x-1}\right) = 4\cdot \lim\limits_{x\to 1^+} \sqrt{x-1} = 4\cdot 0 = 0$.

17. $\lim\limits_{x\to\infty} \sqrt{x+10}$

As x becomes very large, so does $x+10$.
Because square roots of very large numbers
are very large, $\lim\limits_{x\to\infty} \sqrt{x+10} = \infty$.

19. $\lim\limits_{x\to\infty} \dfrac{3}{\sqrt{x}} = 3 \lim\limits_{x\to\infty} \dfrac{1}{x^{\frac{1}{2}}} = 3\cdot 0 = 0$

21. $\lim\limits_{x\to\infty} \dfrac{x+8}{x-3} = \lim\limits_{x\to\infty} \dfrac{x}{x} = \lim\limits_{x\to\infty} 1 = 1$

23. $\lim\limits_{x\to-\infty} \dfrac{x^2-1}{x^3+4x-3} = \lim\limits_{x\to-\infty} \dfrac{x^2}{x^3} = \lim\limits_{x\to-\infty} \dfrac{1}{x} = 0$

25. $\lim\limits_{t\to\infty} \dfrac{5t^2+2t+1}{4t+7} = \lim\limits_{t\to\infty} \dfrac{5t^2}{4t} = \lim\limits_{t\to\infty} \dfrac{5t}{4}$

$= \lim\limits_{t\to\infty}\left(\dfrac{5}{4}t\right) = \infty$

27. $\lim\limits_{x\to\infty} \dfrac{7}{2x+1} = \lim\limits_{x\to\infty} \dfrac{7}{2x} = \dfrac{7}{2}\cdot\lim\limits_{x\to\infty} \dfrac{1}{x} = \dfrac{7}{2}\cdot 0 = 0$

29. $\lim\limits_{x\to\infty} \dfrac{3-4x-2x^3}{5x^3-8x+1} = \lim\limits_{x\to\infty} \dfrac{-2x^3}{5x^3}$

$= \lim\limits_{x\to\infty} \dfrac{-2}{5} = -\dfrac{2}{5}$

31. $\lim\limits_{x\to 3^-} \dfrac{x+2}{x^2-9} = \lim\limits_{x\to 3^-} \dfrac{x+3}{(x+3)(x-3)}$

$= \lim\limits_{x\to 3^-} \dfrac{1}{x-3} = -\infty$

33. $\lim\limits_{w\to\infty} \dfrac{2w^2-3w+4}{5w^2+7w-1} = \lim\limits_{w\to\infty} \dfrac{2w^2}{5w^2} = \lim\limits_{w\to\infty} \dfrac{2}{5} = \dfrac{2}{5}$

35. $\lim\limits_{x\to\infty} \dfrac{6-4x^2+x^3}{4+5x-7x^2} = \lim\limits_{x\to\infty} \dfrac{x^3}{-7x^2} = \lim\limits_{x\to\infty} \dfrac{x}{-7} = -\infty$

37. $\lim\limits_{x\to -5} \dfrac{2x^2+9x-5}{x^2+5x} = \lim\limits_{x\to -5} \dfrac{(2x-1)(x+5)}{x(x+5)}$

$= \lim\limits_{x\to -5} \dfrac{2x-1}{x} = \dfrac{11}{5}$

39. $\lim\limits_{x\to 1} \dfrac{x^2-3x+1}{x^2+1} = \dfrac{\lim\limits_{x\to 1}\left(x^2-3x+1\right)}{\lim\limits_{x\to 1}\left(x^2+1\right)} = \dfrac{-1}{2} = -\dfrac{1}{2}$

41. As $x\to 1^+$, then $\dfrac{1}{x-1}\to\infty$. Thus $\lim\limits_{x\to 1^+}\left[1+\dfrac{1}{x-1}\right] = \infty$

43. $\lim\limits_{x\to -7^-} \dfrac{x^2+1}{\sqrt{x^2-49}}$. As $x\to -7^-$, then $x^2+1\to 50$ and $\sqrt{x^2-49}$

approaches 0 through positive values. Thus $\dfrac{x^2+1}{\sqrt{x^2-49}}\to\infty$.

45. As $x \to 0^+$, $x + x^2$ approaches 0 through positive values. Thus $\dfrac{5}{x + x^2} \to \infty$.

47. $\displaystyle\lim_{x \to 1^-} \frac{x}{x-1} = -\infty$

$\displaystyle\lim_{x \to 1^+} \frac{x}{x-1} = \infty$

Answer: does not exist

49. As $x \to 0^+$, $\dfrac{3}{x} \to \infty$. Thus $-\dfrac{3}{x} \to -\infty$.

Answer: $-\infty$

51. $\displaystyle\lim_{x \to 0^+} |x| = \lim_{x \to 0^+} x = 0$; $\displaystyle\lim_{x \to 0^-} |x| = \lim_{x \to 0^-} (-x) = 0$. Thus $\displaystyle\lim_{x \to 0} |x| = 0$.

53. $\displaystyle\lim_{x \to -\infty} \frac{x+1}{x} = \lim_{x \to -\infty} \frac{x}{x} = \lim_{x \to -\infty} 1 = 1$

55. $f(x) = \begin{cases} 2 & \text{if } x \le 2 \\ 1 & \text{if } x > 2 \end{cases}$

   a. $\displaystyle\lim_{x \to 2^+} f(x) = \lim_{x \to 2^+} 1 = 1$

   b. $\displaystyle\lim_{x \to 2^-} f(x) = \lim_{x \to 2^+} 2 = 2$

   c. $\displaystyle\lim_{x \to 2^+} f(x) \ne \lim_{x \to 2^-} f(x)$, so $\displaystyle\lim_{x \to 2} f(x)$ does not exist.

   d. $\displaystyle\lim_{x \to \infty} f(x) = \lim_{x \to \infty} 1 = 1$

   e. $\displaystyle\lim_{x \to -\infty} f(x) = \lim_{x \to -\infty} 2 = 2$

57. $g(x) = \begin{cases} x & \text{if } x < 0 \\ -x & \text{if } x > 0 \end{cases}$

   a. $\displaystyle\lim_{x \to 0^+} g(x) = \lim_{x \to 0^+} -x = 0$

   b. $\displaystyle\lim_{x \to 0^-} g(x) = \lim_{x \to 0^-} x = 0$

   c. $\displaystyle\lim_{x \to 0^+} g(x) = \lim_{x \to 0^-} g(x) = 0$, so $\displaystyle\lim_{x \to 0} g(x) = 0$

   d. $\displaystyle\lim_{x \to \infty} g(x) = \lim_{x \to \infty} -x = -\infty$

   e. $\displaystyle\lim_{x \to -\infty} g(x) = \lim_{x \to -\infty} x = -\infty$

59. $\displaystyle\lim_{q \to -\infty} \bar{c} = \lim_{q \to \infty} \left(\frac{5000}{q} + 6 \right)$

$= 0 + 6 = 6$

61. $\displaystyle\lim_{t \to \infty} \left[20{,}000 + \frac{10{,}000}{(t+2)^2} \right] = 20{,}000 + 0$

$= 20{,}000$

63. $\lim\limits_{x\to\infty} y = \lim\limits_{x\to\infty} \dfrac{900x}{10+45x} = \lim\limits_{x\to\infty} \dfrac{900x}{45x}$
$= \lim\limits_{x\to\infty} 20 = 20$

65. $1, 0.5, 0.525, 0.631, 0.912, 0.986, 0.998$;
conclude limit is 1.

67.

69.

a. 11

b. 9

c. does not exist

Exercise 11.3

1. $S = 4000e^{0.055(6)} \approx \$5563.87$
$5563.87 - 4000 = \$1563.87$

3. $P = 2500e^{-0.0675(8)} \approx \$1456.87$

5. $e^{0.04} - 1 \approx 0.0408$
Answer: 4.08%

7. $e^{0.03} - 1 \approx 0.0305$
Answer: 3.05%

9. $S = 100e^{0.045(2)} \approx \$109.42$

11. $P = 1,000,000e^{-0.05(5)} \approx \$778,800.78$

13. a. $10,000(1+0.04)^{20} \approx \$21,911$

   b. $P = 21,911e^{-(0.06)(20)} \approx \$6599$

15. Effective rate $= e^r - 1$. Thus $0.05 = e^r - 1$,
$e^r = 1.05$, $r = \ln 1.05 \approx 0.0488$.
Answer: 4.88%

17. $100\dfrac{1-e^{-0.05(20)}}{0.05} \approx \$1264$

19. $3P = Pe^{0.07t}$
$3 = e^{0.07t}$
$0.07t = \ln 3$
$t = \dfrac{\ln 3}{0.07} \approx 16$
Answer: 16 years

21. The accumulated amounts under each option
are:

   a. $1000e^{(0.035)(2)} \approx \$1072.51$

   b. $1020(1.0175)^4 \approx \$1093.30$

   c. $500e^{(0.035)(2)} + 500(1.0175)^4$
   $\approx 536.25 + 535.93 = \$1072.18$

23. a. $9000(1.0125)^4 \approx \$9458.51$

   b. After one year the accumulated amount
   of the investment is
   $10,000e^{0.055} \approx \$10,565.41$. The payoff
   for the loan (including interest) is
   $1000 + 1000(0.08) = \$1080$. The net
   return is $10,565.41 - 1080 = \$9485.41$.
   Thus, this strategy is better by
   $9485.41 - 9458.51 = \$26.90$.

Exercise 11.4

1. $f(x) = x^3 - 5x; x = 2$

　(i)　f is defined at $x = 2$: $f(2) = -2$

　(ii)　$\lim\limits_{x \to 2} f(x) = \lim\limits_{x \to 2}\left(x^3 - 5x\right) = 2^3 - 5(2) = -2$, which exists

　(iii)　$\lim\limits_{x \to 2} f(x) = -2 = f(2)$
　　　Thus f is continuous at $x = 2$.

3. $g(x) = \sqrt{2 - 3x}$; $x = 0$

　(i)　g is defined at $x = 0$; $g(0) = \sqrt{2}$.

　(ii)　$\lim\limits_{x \to 0} g(x) = \lim\limits_{x \to 0} \sqrt{2 - 3x} = \sqrt{2}$, which
　　　exists

　(iii)　$\lim\limits_{x \to 0} g(x) = \sqrt{2} = g(0)$
　　　Thus g is continuous at $x = 0$.

5. $h(x) = \dfrac{x - 4}{x + 4}$; $x = 4$

　(i)　h is defined at $x = 4$, $h(4) = 0$.

　(ii)　$\lim\limits_{x \to 4} h(x) = \lim\limits_{x \to 4} \dfrac{x - 4}{x + 4} = \dfrac{0}{8} = 0$, which
　　　exists.

　(iii)　$\lim\limits_{x \to 4} h(x) = 0 = h(4)$
　　　Thus h is continuous at $x = 4$.

7. Continuous at -2 and 0 because f is a rational function and at neither point is the denominator zero.

9. Discontinuous at 3 and -3 because at both points the denominator of this rational function is zero.

11. $F(x) = \begin{cases} x + 2 & \text{if } x \geq 2 \\ x^2 & \text{if } x < 2 \end{cases}$

　　F is defined at $x = 2$ and $x = 0$; $F(2) = 4$,
　　$F(0) = 0$.
　　Because $\lim\limits_{x \to 2^+} F(x) = \lim\limits_{x \to 2^+} (x + 2) = 4$ and
　　$\lim\limits_{x \to 2^-} F(x) = \lim\limits_{x \to 2^-} x^2 = 4$, we have
　　$\lim\limits_{x \to 2} F(x) = 4$. In addition,
　　$\lim\limits_{x \to 0} F(x) = \lim\limits_{x \to 0} x^2 = 0$. Since
　　$\lim\limits_{x \to 2} F(x) = 4 = F(2)$ and
　　$\lim\limits_{x \to 0} F(x) = 0 = F(0)$, F is continuous at
　　both 2 and 0.
　　Answer: Continuous at 2 and 0.

13. f is a polynomial function.

15. f is a rational function and the denominator is never zero.

17. None, because f is a polynomial function.

19. The denominator of this rational function is zero only when $x = -4$. Thus f is discontinuous only at $x = -4$.

21. None, because g is a polynomial function.

23. $x^2 + 2x - 15 = 0$, $(x + 5)(x - 3) = 0$, $x = -5$ or 3. Discontinuous at -5 and 3.

25. $x^3 - x = 0$, $x(x^2 - 1) = 0$,

$x(x + 1)(x - 1) = 0$, $x = 0, \pm 1$.
Discontinuous at $0, \pm 1$.

27. $x^2 + 1 = 0$ has no real roots, so no
discontinuity exists.

29. $f(x) = \begin{cases} 1 & \text{if } x \ge 0 \\ -1 & \text{if } x < 0 \end{cases}$

For $x < 0, f(x) = -1$, which is a polynomial
and hence continuous. For $x > 0, f(x) = 1$,
which is a polynomial and hence
continuous. Because
$\lim\limits_{x \to 0^-} f(x) = \lim\limits_{x \to 0^-} (-1) = -1$ and
$\lim\limits_{x \to 0^+} f(x) = \lim\limits_{x \to 0^+} 1 = 1$, $\lim\limits_{x \to 0} f(x)$ does not
exist. Thus f is discontinuous at $x = 0$.
Answer: 0

31. $f(x) = \begin{cases} 0 & \text{if } x \le 1 \\ x - 1 & \text{if } x > 1 \end{cases}$

For $x < 1, f(x) = 0$, which is a polynomial
and hence continuous. For $x > 1$,
$f(x) = x - 1$, which is a polynomial and
hence continuous. For $x = 1, f$ is defined
$[f(1) = 0]$. Because $\lim\limits_{x \to 1^-} f(x) = \lim\limits_{x \to 1^-} 0 = 0$
and $\lim\limits_{x \to 1^+} f(x) = \lim\limits_{x \to 1^+} (x - 1) = 0$, then
$\lim\limits_{x \to 1} f(x) = 0$. Since $\lim\limits_{x \to 1} f(x) = 0 = f(0)$, f
is continuous at $x = 1$.
Answer: none

33. $f(x) = \begin{cases} x^2 & \text{if } x > 2 \\ x - 1 & \text{if } x < 2 \end{cases}$

For $x < 2, f(x) = x - 1$, which is a polynomial
and hence continuous. For $x > 2$, $f(x) = x^2$,
which is a polynomial and hence
continuous. Because f is not defined at $x = 2$,
it is discontinuous there.
Answer: 2

35.

Discontinuous at 1, 2, 3, 4.

37.

f is continuous at 2.
f is discontinuous at 5.
f is discontinuous at 10.
Ans. yes, no, no

Principles in Practice 11.5

1. We need to solve $V(x) > 0$. The zeros of $V(x)$
occur when $x = 0$, $8 - 2x = 0$, and
$10 - 2x = 0$, or $x = 0, 4$, and 5. These zeros
determine the intervals $(-\infty, 0)$ $(0, 4)$, $(4, 5)$,
and $(5, \infty)$. Using $x = -1, 1, 4.5$, and 6 for
test points, we find the sign of $V(x)$:
$V(-1) = (-)(+)(+) = -$, so $V(x) < 0$ on
$(-\infty, 0)$; $V(1) = (+)(+)(+) = +$, so $V(x) > 0$
on $(0, 4)$; $V(4.5) = (+)(-)(+) = -$, so
$V(x) < 0$ on $(4, 5)$; $V(6) = (+)(-)(-) = +$,
so $V(x) > 0$ on $(5, \infty)$. The volume is positive
when $0 < x < 4$ or $5 < x$. However, $x > 5$ is
unrealistic (as is $x < 0$) since the longest side
of the piece of metal has length
$2(5) = 10$ inches. Thus, the volume is
positive when $0 < x < 4$.

Exercise 11.5

1. $x^2 - 3x - 4 > 0$

$f(x) = x^2 - 3x - 4 = (x+1)(x-4)$ has zeros -1 and 4. By considering the intervals $(-\infty, -1)$, $(-1, 4)$, and $(4, \infty)$, we find $f(x) > 0$ on $(-\infty, -1)$ and $(4, \infty)$.

Answer: $(-\infty, -1)$, $(4, \infty)$

3. $x^2 - 5x + 6 \le 0$

$f(x) = x^2 - 5x + 6 = (x-2)(x-3)$ has zeros 2 and 3. By considering the intervals $(-\infty, 2)$, $(2, 3)$, and $(3, \infty)$, we find $f(x) < 0$ on $(2, 3)$.

Answer: $[2, 3]$

5. $2x^2 + 11x + 14 < 0$

$f(x) = 2x^2 + 11x + 14 = (2x+7)(x+2)$ has zeros $-\dfrac{7}{2}$ and -2. By considering the intervals $\left(-\infty, -\dfrac{7}{2}\right)$, $\left(-\dfrac{7}{2}, -2\right)$, and $(-2, \infty)$, we find $f(x) < 0$ on $\left(-\dfrac{7}{2}, -2\right)$.

Answer: $\left(-\dfrac{7}{2}, -2\right)$

7. $x^2 + 4 < 0$. Since $x^2 + 4$ is always positive, the inequality $x^2 + 4 < 0$ has no solution.

Answer: no solution

9. $(x+2)(x-3)(x+6) \le 0$

$f(x) = (x+2)(x-3)(x+6)$ has zeros -2, 3, and -6. By considering the intervals $(-\infty, -6)$, $(-6, -2)$, $(-2, 3)$, and $(3, \infty)$, we find $f(x) < 0$ on $(-\infty, -6)$ and $(-2, 3)$.

Answer: $(-\infty, -6]$, $[-2, 3]$

11. $-x(x-5)(x+4) > 0$, or equivalently, $x(x-5)(x+4) < 0$. $f(x) = x(x-5)(x+4)$ has zeros, 0, 5, and -4. By considering the intervals $(-\infty, -4)$, $(-4, 0)$, $(0, 5)$, and $(5, \infty)$, we find $f(x) < 0$ on $(-\infty, -4)$ and $(0, 5)$.

Answer: $(-\infty, -4)$, $(0, 5)$

13. $x^3 + 4x \ge 0$

$f(x) = x\left(x^2 + 4\right)$ has 0 as the only (real) zero. By considering the intervals $(-\infty, 0)$ and $(0, \infty)$, we find $f(x) > 0$ on $(0, \infty)$.

Answer: $[0, \infty)$

15. $x^3 + 2x^2 - 3x > 0$

$f(x) = x(x+3)(x-1)$ has zeros 0, -3, and 1. By considering the intervals $(-\infty, -3)$, $(-3, 0)$ $(0, 1)$, and $(1, \infty)$, we find $f(x) > 0$ on $(-3, 0)$ and $(1, \infty)$.

Answer: $(-3, 0)$, $(1, \infty)$

17. $\dfrac{x}{x^2 - 9} < 0$

$f(x) = \dfrac{x}{x^2 - 9}$ is discontinuous when $x = \pm 3$; f has 0 as a zero. By considering the intervals $(-\infty, -3)$, $(-3, 0)$, $(0, 3)$, and $(3, \infty)$, we find $f(x) < 0$ on $(-\infty, -3)$ and $(0, 3)$.

Answer: $(-\infty, -3)$, $(0, 3)$

19. $\dfrac{4}{x-1} \ge 0$

$f(x) = \dfrac{4}{x-1}$ is discontinuous when $x = 1$, and $f(x) = 0$ has no root. By considering the intervals $(-\infty, 1)$ and $(1, \infty)$, we find $f(x) > 0$ on $(1, \infty)$. Note also that $f(x) \ne 0$ for any x.

Answer: $(1, \infty)$

21. $\dfrac{x^2 - x - 6}{x^2 + 4x - 5} \ge 0$

$f(x) = \dfrac{x^2 - x - 6}{x^2 + 4x - 5} = \dfrac{(x-3)(x+2)}{(x+5)(x-1)}$ is discontinuous at $x = -5$ and $x = 1$; f has zeros 3 and -2. By considering the intervals $(-\infty, -5)$, $(-5, -2)$, $(-2, 1)$, $(1, 3)$, and $(3, \infty)$, we find $f(x) > 0$ on $(-\infty, -5)$, $(-2, 1)$, and $(3, \infty)$.

Answer: $(-\infty, -5)$, $[-2, 1)$, $[3, \infty)$

23. $\dfrac{3}{x^2 + 6x + 5} \le 0$

$f(x) = \dfrac{3}{x^2 + 6x + 5} = \dfrac{3}{(x+5)(x+1)}$ is never

zero, but is discontinuous at $x = -5$ and
$x = -1$. By considering the intervals
$(-\infty, -5)$, $(-5, -1)$, and $(-1, \infty)$, we find that
$f(x) < 0$ on $(-5, -1)$.
Answer: $(-5, -1)$

25. $x^2 + 2x \ge 2$, or equivalently,

$x^2 + 2x - 2 \ge 0$. $f(x) = x^2 + 2x - 2$ has

zeros $-1 \pm \sqrt{3}$. By considering the intervals

$\left(-\infty, -1-\sqrt{3}\right)$ $\left(-1-\sqrt{3}, -1+\sqrt{3}\right)$, and

$\left(-1+\sqrt{3}, \infty\right)$, we find $f(x) > 0$ on

$\left(-\infty, -1-\sqrt{3}\right)$ and $\left(-1+\sqrt{3}, \infty\right)$.

Answer: $\left(-\infty, -1-\sqrt{3}\right], \left[-1+\sqrt{3}, \infty\right)$

27. Revenue = (no. of units)(price per unit).
We want $q(20 - 0.1q) \ge 750$

$0.1q^2 - 20q + 750 \le 0$

$q^2 - 200q + 7500 \le 0$

$(q - 50)(q - 150) \le 0$.
Solving gives $50 \le q \le 150$.
Answer: between 50 and 150 units, inclusive

29.

If x is the length of a side of the piece of
aluminum, then the box will be 4 by $x - 8$ by
$x - 8$.

$4(x - 8)^2 \ge 324$

$(x - 8)^2 \ge 81$

$x^2 - 16x - 17 \ge 0$

$(x - 17)(x + 1) \ge 0$

Solving $x \le -1$ or $x \ge 17$. Since x must be
positive, we have $x \ge 17$.
Answer: 17 in. by 17 in.

31.

$(-\infty, -7.72]$

33.

$(-\infty, -0.5), (0.667, \infty)$

Chapter 11 Review Problems

1. $\displaystyle\lim_{x \to -1} \left(2x^2 + 6x - 1\right) = 2(-1)^2 + 6(-1) - 1 = -5$

3. $\displaystyle\lim_{x \to 3} \dfrac{x^2 - 9}{x^2 - 3x} = \lim_{x \to 3} \dfrac{(x+3)(x-3)}{x(x-3)}$

$= \displaystyle\lim_{x \to 3} \dfrac{x+3}{x} = \dfrac{6}{3} = 2$

5. $\lim\limits_{h \to 0} (x + h) = x + 0 = x$

7. $\lim\limits_{x \to -4} \dfrac{x^3 + 4x^2}{x^2 + 2x - 8} = \lim\limits_{x \to -4} \dfrac{x^2(x + 4)}{(x + 4)(x - 2)}$

$\lim\limits_{x \to -4} \dfrac{x^2}{x - 2} = \dfrac{16}{-6} = -\dfrac{8}{3}$

9. As $x \to \infty$, $x + 1 \to \infty$. Thus $\lim\limits_{x \to \infty} \dfrac{2}{x + 1} = 0$.

Answer: 0

11. $\lim\limits_{x \to \infty} \dfrac{3x - 2}{7x + 3} = \lim\limits_{x \to \infty} \dfrac{3x}{7x} = \lim\limits_{x \to \infty} \dfrac{3}{7} = \dfrac{3}{7}$

13. $\lim\limits_{t \to 3^-} \dfrac{2t - 3}{t - 3} = -\infty$ and $\lim\limits_{t \to 3^+} \dfrac{2t - 3}{t - 3} = \infty$.

Thus $\lim\limits_{t \to 3} \dfrac{2t - 3}{t - 3}$ does not exist.

Answer: Limit does not exist

15. $\lim\limits_{x \to -\infty} \dfrac{x + 3}{1 - x} = \lim\limits_{x \to -\infty} \dfrac{x}{-x} = \lim\limits_{x \to -\infty} (-1) = -1$

17. $\lim\limits_{x \to \infty} \dfrac{x^2 - 1}{(3x + 2)^2} = \lim\limits_{x \to \infty} \dfrac{x^2 - 1}{9x^2 + 12x + 4}$

$= \lim\limits_{x \to \infty} \dfrac{x^2}{9x^2} = \lim\limits_{x \to \infty} \dfrac{1}{9} = \dfrac{1}{9}$

19. $\lim\limits_{x \to 3^-} \dfrac{x + 3}{x^2 - 9} = \lim\limits_{x \to 3^-} \dfrac{x + 3}{(x + 3)(x - 3)}$

$= \lim\limits_{x \to 3^-} \dfrac{1}{x - 3} = -\infty$

21. $\lim\limits_{x \to \infty} \sqrt{3x}$. As x becomes large, so does $3x$.

Because the square roots of large numbers are also large, $\lim\limits_{x \to \infty} \sqrt{3x} = \infty$.

Answer: ∞

23. $\lim\limits_{x \to \infty} \dfrac{x^{100} + \frac{1}{x^2}}{e - x^{98}} = \lim\limits_{x \to \infty} \dfrac{x^2\left(x^{100} + \frac{1}{x^2}\right)}{x^2\left(e - x^{98}\right)}$

$= \lim\limits_{x \to \infty} \dfrac{x^{102}}{ex^2 - x^{100}} = \lim\limits_{x \to \infty} \dfrac{x^{102}}{-x^{100}}$

$= \lim\limits_{x \to \infty} \left(-x^2\right) = -\infty$

25. $\lim\limits_{x \to 1^-} f(x) = \lim\limits_{x \to 1^-} x^2 = 1$

$\lim\limits_{x \to 1^+} f(x) = \lim\limits_{x \to 1^+} x = 1$

Thus $\lim\limits_{x \to 1} f(x) = 1$.

Answer: 1

27. $\lim\limits_{x \to 4^+} \dfrac{\sqrt{x^2 - 16}}{4 - x} = \lim\limits_{x \to 4^+} \dfrac{\sqrt{x - 4}\sqrt{x + 4}}{-(x - 4)}$

$= \lim\limits_{x \to 4^+} -\dfrac{\sqrt{x + 4}}{\sqrt{x - 4}}$

As $x \to 4^+$, $\sqrt{x - 4}$ approaches 0 through positive values and $\sqrt{x + 4} \to \sqrt{8}$. Thus

$-\dfrac{\sqrt{x + 4}}{\sqrt{x - 4}} \to -\infty$.

Answer: $-\infty$

29. $\lim\limits_{h \to 0} \dfrac{f(x + h) - f(x)}{h}$

$= \lim\limits_{h \to 0} \dfrac{[8(x + h) - 2] - [8x - 2]}{h}$

$= \lim\limits_{h \to 0} \dfrac{8h}{h} = \lim\limits_{h \to 0} 8 = 8$

31. $y = 23\left(1 - \dfrac{1}{1+2x}\right)$

Considering $\dfrac{1}{1+2x}$, we have $\lim\limits_{x\to\infty} \dfrac{1}{1+2x} = \dfrac{1}{2} \cdot \lim\limits_{x\to\infty} \dfrac{1}{x} = \dfrac{1}{2} \cdot 0 = 0$.

Thus $\lim\limits_{x\to\infty} y = \lim\limits_{x\to\infty}\left[23\left(1 - \dfrac{1}{1+2x}\right)\right] = 23(1-0) = 23$

Answer: 23

33. a. $S = 2500e^{0.05(14)} \approx \$5034.38$

b. $P = 2500e^{-0.05(14)} \approx \$1241.46$

35. Effective rate $= e^{0.06} - 1 \approx 0.0618$

Answer: 6.18%

37. $S = Pe^{rt}$, $2P = Pe^{0.05t}$, $2 = e^{0.05t}$, $0.05t = \ln 2$

$t = \dfrac{\ln 2}{0.05} = 20 \ln 2$

Answer: 20 ln 2

39. $f(x) = x + 5; x = 7$

(i) f is defined at $x = 7; f(7) = 12$

(ii) $\lim\limits_{x\to 7} f(x) = \lim\limits_{x\to 7}(x+5) = 7 + 5 = 12$,
which exists

(iii) $\lim\limits_{x\to 7} f(x) = 12 = f(7)$
Thus f is continuous at $x = 7$.

41. Since $f(x) = \dfrac{1}{4}x$ is polynomial function, it is continuous everywhere.

43. $f(x) = \dfrac{x^2}{x+3}$ is a rational function and the denominator is zero at $x = -3$. Thus f is discontinuous at $x = -3$.
Answer: $x = -3$

45. Since $f(x) = \dfrac{x-1}{2x^2+3}$ is a rational function whose denominator is never zero, f is continuous everywhere.
Answer: none

47. $f(x) = \dfrac{4-x^2}{x^2+3x-4} = \dfrac{4-x^2}{(x+4)(x-1)}$ is a rational function and the denominator is zero only when $x = -4$ or $x = 1$, so f is discontinuous there.
Answer: $x = -4, 1$

49. $f(x) = \begin{cases} x+4 & \text{if } x > -2 \\ 3x+6 & \text{if } x \le -2 \end{cases}$

For $x < -2, f(x) = 3x + 6$, which is a polynomial and hence continuous. For $x > -2, f(x) = x + 4$, which is a polynomial and hence continuous. Because
$\lim\limits_{x\to -2^-} f(x) = \lim\limits_{x\to -2^-}(3x+6) = 0$ and
$\lim\limits_{x\to -2^+} f(x) = \lim\limits_{x\to -2^+}(x+4) = 2$, $\lim\limits_{x\to -2} f(x)$
does not exist. Thus f is discontinuous at $x = -2$.
Answer: $x = -2$

51. $x^2 + 4x - 12 > 0$

$f(x) = x^2 + 4x - 12 = (x + 6)(x - 2)$ has zeros –6 and 2. By considering the intervals $(-\infty, -6)$, $(-6, 2)$, and $(2, \infty)$, we find $f(x) > 0$ on $(-\infty, -6)$ and $(2, \infty)$.
Answer: $(-\infty, -6)$, $(2, \infty)$

53. $x^3 \geq 2x^2$, $x^3 - 2x^2 \geq 0$

$f(x) = x^3 - 2x^2 = x^2(x - 2)$ has zeros 0 and 2. By considering the intervals $(-\infty, 0)$, $(0, 2)$, and $(2, \infty)$, we find $f(x) > 0$ on $(2, \infty)$.
Answer: $[2, \infty)$, $x = 0$

55. $\dfrac{x + 5}{x^2 - 1} < 0$. $f(x) = \dfrac{x + 5}{(x + 1)(x - 1)}$ is

discontinuous when $x = \pm 1$, and f has –5 as a zero. By considering the intervals $(-\infty, -5)$, $(-5, -1)$, $(-1, 1)$, and $(1, \infty)$, we find $f(x) < 0$ on $(-\infty, -5)$ and $(-1, 1)$.
Answer: $(-\infty, -5)$, $(-1, 1)$

57. $\dfrac{x^2 + 3x}{x^2 + 2x - 8} \geq 0$, or $\dfrac{x(x + 3)}{(x + 4)(x - 2)} \geq 0$.

We consider the intervals determined by $x = 0, -3, -4$, and 2, namely $(-\infty, -4)$, $(-4, -3)$, $(-3, 0)$, $(0, 2)$, and $(2, \infty)$. We find $f(x) > 0$ on $(-\infty, -4)$, $(-3, 0)$, and $(2, \infty)$.
Answer: $(-\infty, -4)$, $[-3, 0]$, $(2, \infty)$

59.

1.00

61.

0

63.

$[2.00, \infty)$

Mathematical Snapshot Chapter 11

1. $D = 5345e^{-rt}$

A year from now, $t = 1$ and $D = 4500$. Thus

$4500 = 5345e^{-r}$

$e^{-r} = \dfrac{4500}{5345}$

$-r = \ln \dfrac{4500}{5345}$

$r = -\ln \dfrac{4500}{5345} \approx 0.17$

The rate is 17%.

3. An exponential model assumes a fixed repayment rate. In reality, the repayment rate is constantly changing as a result of changing fiscal policy and other factors.

Chapter 12

Principles in Practice 12.1

1. $\dfrac{dH}{dt} = \dfrac{d}{dt}\left(6 + 40t - 16t^2\right)$

$= \lim_{h \to 0} \dfrac{H(t+h) - H(t)}{h}$

$= \lim_{h \to 0} \dfrac{\left[6 + 40(t+h) - 16(t+h)^2\right] - \left(6 + 40t - 16t^2\right)}{h}$

$= \lim_{h \to 0} \dfrac{6 + 40t + 40h - 16t^2 - 32th - 16h^2 - 6 - 40t + 16t^2}{h}$

$= \lim_{h \to 0} \dfrac{40h - 32th - 16h^2}{h} = \lim_{h \to 0} (40 - 32t - 16h)$

$= 40 - 32t$

$\dfrac{dH}{dt} = 40 - 32t$

Exercise 12.1

1. a. $f(x) = x^3 + 3$, $P = (2, 11)$

To begin, if $x = 3$, then $m_{PQ} = \dfrac{\left(3^3 + 3\right) - 11}{3 - 2} = 19$. If $x = 2.5$, then $m_{PQ} = \dfrac{\left[(2.5)^3 + 3\right] - 11}{2.5 - 2} = 15.25$.

Continuing in this manner, we complete the table:

x-value of Q	3	2.5	2.2	2.1	2.01	2.001
m_{PQ}	19	15.25	13.24	12.61	12.0601	12.0060

b. We estimate that $m_{\tan}$ at P is 12.

3. $f(x) = x$

$f'(x) = \lim_{h \to 0} \dfrac{f(x+h) - f(x)}{h}$

$= \lim_{h \to 0} \dfrac{(x+h) - x}{h}$

$= \lim_{h \to 0} \dfrac{h}{h} = \lim_{h \to 0} 1 = 1$

5. $y = 4x + 7$. Let $y = f(x)$.

$$\frac{dy}{dx} = \lim_{h \to 0} \frac{f(x+h) - f(x)}{h}$$

$$= \lim_{h \to 0} \frac{[4(x+h)+7] - [4x+7]}{h}$$

$$= \lim_{h \to 0} \frac{4x + 4h + 7 - 4x - 7}{h}$$

$$= \lim_{h \to 0} \frac{4h}{h} = \lim_{h \to 0} 4 = 4$$

7. Let $f(x) = 5 - 4x$.

$$\frac{d}{dx}(5 - 4x) = \lim_{h \to 0} \frac{f(x+h) - f(x)}{h}$$

$$= \lim_{h \to 0} \frac{[5 - 4(x+h)] - [5 - 4x]}{h}$$

$$= \lim_{h \to 0} \frac{-4h}{h} = \lim_{h \to 0} (-4) = -4$$

9. $f(x) = 3$

$$f'(x) = \lim_{h \to 0} \frac{f(x+h) - f(x)}{h}$$

$$= \lim_{h \to 0} \frac{3 - 3}{h} = \lim_{h \to 0} \frac{0}{h} = \lim_{h \to 0} 0 = 0$$

11. $f(x) = x^2 + 4x - 8$

$$\frac{d}{dx}\left(x^2 + 4 - 8\right)$$

$$= \lim_{h \to 0} \frac{f(x+h) - f(x)}{h}$$

$$= \lim_{h \to 0} \frac{\left[(x+h)^2 + 4(x+h) - 8\right] - \left[x^2 + 4x - 8\right]}{h}$$

$$= \lim_{h \to 0} \frac{x^2 + 2xh + h^2 + 4x + 4h - 8 - x^2 - 4x + 8}{h}$$

$$= \lim_{h \to 0} \frac{2xh + h^2 + 4h}{h}$$

$$= \lim_{h \to 0} (2x + h + 4) = 2x + 0 + 4 = 2x + 4$$

13. $p = f(q) = 2q^2 + 5q - 1$

$\dfrac{dp}{dq} = \lim\limits_{h \to 0} \dfrac{f(q+h) - f(q)}{h}$

$= \lim\limits_{h \to 0} \dfrac{\left[2(q+h)^2 + 5(q+h) - 1\right] - \left[2q^2 + 5q - 1\right]}{h}$

$= \lim\limits_{h \to 0} \dfrac{4qh + 2h^2 + 5h}{h}$

$= \lim\limits_{h \to 0} (4q + 2h + 5) = 4q + 0 + 5 = 4q + 5$

15. $y = f(x) = \dfrac{6}{x}$

$y' = \lim\limits_{h \to 0} \dfrac{f(x+h) - f(x)}{h} = \lim\limits_{h \to 0} \dfrac{\frac{6}{x+h} - \frac{6}{x}}{h}$

Multiplying the numerator and denominator by $x(x + h)$ gives

$y' = \lim\limits_{h \to 0} \dfrac{6x - 6(x+h)}{hx(x+h)} = \lim\limits_{h \to 0} \dfrac{-6h}{hx(x+h)}$

$= \lim\limits_{h \to 0} \left[-\dfrac{6}{x(x+h)} \right] = -\dfrac{6}{x(x+0)} = -\dfrac{6}{x^2}$

17. $f(x) = \sqrt{x+2}$

$f'(x) = \lim\limits_{h \to 0} \dfrac{f(x+h) - f(x)}{h}$

$= \lim\limits_{h \to 0} \dfrac{\sqrt{x+h+2} - \sqrt{x+2}}{h}$

Rationalizing the numerator gives

$\dfrac{\sqrt{x+h+2} - \sqrt{x+2}}{h}$

$= \dfrac{\sqrt{x+h+2} - \sqrt{x+2}}{h} \cdot \dfrac{\sqrt{x+h+2} + \sqrt{x+2}}{\sqrt{x+h+2} + \sqrt{x+2}}$

$= \dfrac{(x+h+2) - (x+2)}{h\left(\sqrt{x+h+2} + \sqrt{x+2}\right)} = \dfrac{1}{\sqrt{x+h+2} + \sqrt{x+2}}$

Thus $f'(x) = \lim\limits_{h \to 0} \dfrac{1}{\sqrt{x+h+2} + \sqrt{x+2}} = \dfrac{1}{2\sqrt{x+2}}$

19. $y = f(x) = x^2 + 4$

$$y' = \lim_{h \to 0} \frac{f(x+h) - f(x)}{h}$$

$$= \lim_{h \to 0} \frac{\left[(x+h)^2 + 4\right] - \left[x^2 + 4\right]}{h}$$

$$= \lim_{h \to 0} \frac{2xh + h^2}{h} = \lim_{h \to 0} (2x + h) = 2x + 0 = 2x$$

The slope at $(-2, 8)$ is $y'(-2) = 2(-2) = -4$.

21. $y = 4x^2 - 5$

$$y' = \lim_{h \to 0} \frac{\left[4(x+h)^2 - 5\right] - \left[4x^2 - 5\right]}{h}$$

$$= \lim_{h \to 0} \frac{8xh + 4h^2}{h} = \lim_{h \to 0} (8x + 4h) = 8x$$

The slope when $x = 0$ is $y'(0) = 8(0) = 0$.

23. $y = x + 4$

$$y' = \lim_{h \to 0} \frac{[(x+h) + 4] - [x + 4]}{h} = \lim_{h \to 0} \frac{h}{h} = 1$$

If $x = 3$, then $y' = 1$. The tangent line at the point $(3, 7)$ is $y - 7 = 1(x - 3)$, or $y = x + 4$.

25. $y = 3x^2 + 3x - 4$

$$y' = \lim_{h \to 0} \frac{\left[3(x+h)^2 + 3(x+h) - 4\right] - \left[3x^2 + 3x - 4\right]}{h}$$

$$= \lim_{h \to 0} \frac{6xh + 3h^2 + 3h}{h} = \lim_{h \to 0} (6x + 3h + 3) = 6x + 3$$

If $x = -1$, then $y' = 6(-1) + 3 = -3$. The tangent line at the point $(-1, -4)$ is $y + 4 = -3(x + 1)$, or $y = -3x - 7$.

27. $y = \dfrac{3}{x - 1}$

$$y' = \lim_{h \to 0} \frac{\frac{3}{(x+h)-1} - \frac{3}{x-1}}{h}$$

$$= \lim_{h \to 0} \frac{\frac{3(x-1) - 3(x+h-1)}{(x+h-1)(x-1)}}{h}$$

$$= \lim_{h \to 0} \frac{-3h}{h(x+h-1)(x-1)} = \lim_{h \to 0} \frac{-3}{(x+h-1)(x-1)}$$

$$= -\frac{3}{(x-1)^2}$$

If $x = 2$, then $y' = -\dfrac{3}{1} = -3$. The tangent line at $(2, 3)$ is $y - 3 = -3(x - 2)$, or $y = -3x + 9$.

29. $r = \left(\dfrac{\eta}{1+\eta}\right)\left(r_L - \dfrac{dC}{dD}\right)$

$(1+\eta)r = \eta\left(r_L - \dfrac{dC}{dD}\right)$

$r + \eta r = \eta\left(r_L - \dfrac{dC}{dD}\right)$

$r = \eta\left(r_L - \dfrac{dC}{dD}\right) - \eta r$

$r = \eta\left(r_L - \dfrac{dC}{dD} - r\right)$

$\eta = \dfrac{r}{r_L - r - \frac{dC}{dD}}$

31. $-3.000, 13.445$

33. $-5.120, 0.038$

35.

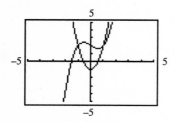

For the x-values of the points where the tangent to the graph of f is horizontal, the corresponding values of $f'(x)$ are 0. This is expected because the slope of a horizontal line is zero and the derivative gives the slope of the tangent line.

Principles in Practice 12.2

1. $r'(q) = \dfrac{d}{dq}(50q) - \dfrac{d}{dq}\left(0.3q^2\right)$

$= 50\dfrac{d}{dq}(q) - 0.3\dfrac{d}{dq}\left(q^2\right)$

$= 50(1) - 0.3(2q) = 50 - 0.6q$

The marginal revenue is $r'(q) = 50 - 0.6q$.

Exercise 12.2

1. $f(x) = 5$ is a constant function, so $f'(x) = 0$

3. $y = x^6$, $y' = 6x^{6-1} = 6x^5$

5. $y = x^{80}$, $\dfrac{dy}{dx} = 80x^{80-1} = 80x^{79}$

7. $f(x) = 9x^2$, $f'(x) = 9\left(2x^{2-1}\right) = 18x$

9. $g(w) = 4w^5$, $g'(w) = 4\left(5w^{5-1}\right) = 20w^4$

11. $y = \frac{2}{3}x^4$, $y' = \frac{2}{3}\left(4x^{3-1}\right) = \frac{8}{3}x^3$

13. $f(t) = \frac{1}{18}t^9$, $f'(t) = \frac{1}{18}\left(9t^{9-1}\right) = \frac{1}{2}t^8$

15. $f(x) = x + 3$, $f'(x) = 1 + 0 = 1$

17. $f'(x) = 4(2x) - 2(1) + 0 = 8x - 2$

19. $g'(p) = 4p^{4-1} - 3\left(3p^{3-1}\right) - 0 = 4p^3 - 9p^2$

21. $y' = -\left(8x^{8-1}\right) + 5x^{5-1} = -8x^7 + 5x^4$

23. $y' = -13\left(3x^2\right) + 14(2x) - 2(1) + 0$

$= -39x^2 + 28x - 2$

25. $f'(x) = 2\left(0 - 4x^3\right) = -8x^3$

27. $g(x) = \frac{1}{3}\left(13 - x^4\right)$,

$g'(x) = \frac{1}{3}\left(0 - 4x^3\right) = -\frac{4}{3}x^3$

29. $h(x) = 4x^4 + x^3 - \dfrac{9}{2}x^2 + 8x$

$h'(x) = 4(4x^3) + 3x^2 - \dfrac{9}{2}(2x) + 8(1)$

$= 16x^3 + 3x^2 - 9x + 8$

31. $f(x) = \dfrac{3}{10}x^4 + \dfrac{7}{3}x^3$

$f'(x) = \dfrac{3}{10}(4x^3) + \dfrac{7}{3}(3x^2) = \dfrac{6}{5}x^3 + 7x^2$

33. $f'(x) = \dfrac{7}{2}x^{\left(\frac{7}{2}\right)-1} = \dfrac{7}{2}x^{\frac{5}{2}}$

35. $y' = \dfrac{3}{4}x^{\left(\frac{3}{4}\right)-1} + 2\left(\dfrac{5}{3}\right)x^{\left(\frac{5}{3}\right)-1} = \dfrac{3}{4}x^{-\frac{1}{4}} + \dfrac{10}{3}x^{\frac{2}{3}}$

37. $f(x) = 11\sqrt{x} = 11x^{\frac{1}{2}}$,

$f'(x) = 11\left(\dfrac{1}{2}\right)x^{\left(\frac{1}{2}\right)-1} = \dfrac{11}{2}x^{-\frac{1}{2}} = \dfrac{11}{2\sqrt{x}}$

39. $f(r) = 6r^{\frac{1}{3}}$, $f'(r) = 6\left(\dfrac{1}{3}r^{-\frac{2}{3}}\right) = 2r^{-\frac{2}{3}}$

41. $f'(x) = -4x^{-4-1} = -4x^{-5}$

43. $f'(x) = -3x^{-3-1} + \left(-5x^{-5-1}\right) - 2\left(-6x^{-6-1}\right)$

$= -3x^{-4} - 5x^{-6} + 12x^{-7}$

45. $y = \dfrac{1}{x} = x^{-1}$

$\dfrac{dy}{dx} = -1 \cdot x^{-1-1} = -x^{-2} = -\dfrac{1}{x^2}$

47. $y = \dfrac{8}{x^5} = 8x^{-5}$

$y' = 8\left(-5x^{-6}\right) = -40x^{-6}$

49. $g(x) = \dfrac{4}{3x^3} = \dfrac{4}{3}x^{-3}$

$g'(x) = \dfrac{4}{3}\left(-3x^{-4}\right) = -4x^{-4}$

51. $f(t) = \dfrac{1}{2}\left(\dfrac{1}{t}\right) = \dfrac{1}{2}t^{-1}$

$f'(t) = \dfrac{1}{2}\left(-1 \cdot t^{-2}\right) = -\dfrac{1}{2}t^{-2}$

53. $f(x) = \dfrac{1}{7}x + 7x^{-1}$

$f'(x) = \dfrac{1}{7}(1) + 7\left(-1x^{-2}\right) = \dfrac{1}{7} - 7x^{-2}$

55. $f'(x) = -9\left(\dfrac{1}{3}x^{-\frac{2}{3}}\right) + 5\left(-\dfrac{2}{5}x^{-\frac{7}{5}}\right)$

$= -3x^{-\frac{2}{3}} - 2x^{-\frac{7}{5}}$

57. $q(x) = \dfrac{1}{\sqrt[5]{x}} = \dfrac{1}{x^{\frac{1}{5}}} = x^{-\frac{1}{5}}$

$q'(x) = -\dfrac{1}{5}x^{-\frac{6}{5}}$

59. $y = \dfrac{2}{x^{\frac{1}{2}}} = 2x^{-\frac{1}{2}}$

$y' = 2\left(-\dfrac{1}{2}x^{-\frac{1}{2}}\right) = -x^{-\frac{3}{2}}$

61. $y = x^2\sqrt{x} = x^2\left(x^{\frac{1}{2}}\right) = x^{2+\left(\frac{1}{2}\right)} = x^{\frac{5}{2}}$

$y' = \dfrac{5}{2}x^{\frac{3}{2}}$

63. $f(x) = x\left(3x^2 - 10x + 7\right) = 3x^3 - 10x^2 + 7x$

$f'(x) = 9x^2 - 20x + 7$

65. $f(x) = x^3(3x)^2 = x^3\left(9x^2\right) = 9x^5$

$f'(x) = 45x^4$

67. $v(x) = x^{-\frac{2}{3}}(x + 5) = x^{\frac{1}{3}} + 5x^{-\frac{2}{3}}$

$v'(x) = \dfrac{1}{3}x^{-\frac{2}{3}} - \dfrac{10}{3}x^{-\frac{5}{3}} = \dfrac{1}{3}x^{-\frac{5}{3}}(x - 10)$

69. $f(q) = \dfrac{4q^3 + 7q - 4}{q} = \dfrac{4q^3}{q} + \dfrac{7q}{q} - \dfrac{4}{q}$

$= 4q^2 + 7 - 4q^{-1}$

$f'(q) = 8q + 4q^{-2} = 8q + \dfrac{4}{q^2}$

71. $f(x) = (x+1)(x+3) = x^2 + 4x + 3$

$f'(x) = 2x + 4 = 2(x+2)$

73. $w(x) = \dfrac{x^2 + x^3}{x^2} = \dfrac{x^2}{x^2} + \dfrac{x^3}{x^2} = 1 + x$

$w'(x) = 0 + 1 = 1$

75. $y' = 6x + 4$

$y'\big|_{x=0} = 4$

$y'\big|_{x=2} = 16, \; y'\big|_{x=-3} = -14$

77. y is a constant, so $y' = 0$ for all x.

79. $y = 4x^2 + 5x + 6$

$y' = 8x + 5$

$y'\big|_{x=1} = 13$

An equation of the tangent line is
$y - 15 = 13(x - 1)$, or $y = 13x + 2$.

81. $y = \dfrac{2}{x^2} = 2x^{-2}$

$y' = 2(-2x^{-3}) = \dfrac{-4}{x^3}$

$y'\big|_{x=1} = -4$

An equation of the tangent line is
$y - 2 = -4(x - 1)$, or $y = -4x + 6$.

83. $y = 3 + x - 5x^2 + x^4$

$y' = 1 - 10x + 4x^3$.

When $x = 0$, then $y = 3$ and $y' = 1$. Thus an
equation of the tangent line is
$y - 3 = 1(x - 0)$, or $y = x + 3$.

85. $y = \dfrac{1}{3}x^3 - x^2$

$y' = x^2 - 2x$

A horizontal tangent line has slope 0, so we
set $x^2 - 2x = 0$. Then $x(x - 2) = 0$, $x = 0$ or
$x = 2$. If $x = 0$, then $y = 0$. If $x = 2$, then

$y = -\dfrac{4}{3}$. This gives the points $(0, 0)$ and

$\left(2, -\dfrac{4}{3}\right)$.

87. $y = x^2 - 5x + 3$

$y' = 2x - 5$

Setting $2x - 5 = 1$ gives $2x = 6$, $x = 3$. When
$x = 3$, then $y = -3$. This gives the point
$(3, -3)$.

89. $f(x) = \sqrt{x} + \dfrac{1}{\sqrt{x}} = x^{\frac{1}{2}} + x^{-\frac{1}{2}}$

$f'(x) = \dfrac{1}{2}x^{-\frac{1}{2}} - \dfrac{1}{2}x^{-\frac{3}{2}}$

$= \dfrac{1}{2\sqrt{x}} - \dfrac{1}{2x\sqrt{x}} = \dfrac{x-1}{2x\sqrt{x}}$

Thus $\dfrac{x-1}{2x\sqrt{x}} - f'(x)$

$= \dfrac{x-1}{2x\sqrt{x}} - \dfrac{x-1}{2x\sqrt{x}} = 0$

91. $y = x^3 - 3x$

$y'(x) = 3x^2 - 3$

$y'\big|_{x=2} = 3\left(2^2\right) - 3 = 9$

The tangent line at $(2, 2)$ is given by
$y - 2 = 9(x - 2)$, or $y = 9x - 16$.

Principles in Practice 12.3

1. Here $\dfrac{dP}{dp} = 5$ and $\Delta p = 25.5 - 25 = 0.5$. $\Delta P \approx \dfrac{dP}{dp}\Delta p = 5(0.5) = 2.5$

   The profit increases by 2.5 units when the price is changed from 25 to 25.5 per unit.

2. $\dfrac{dy}{dt} = \dfrac{d}{dt}\left(16t - 16t^2\right) = 16 - 16(2t) = 16 - 32t$

   $\left.\dfrac{dy}{dt}\right|_{t=0.5} = 16 - 32(0.5) = 16 - 16 = 0$

   The graph of $y(t)$ is shown.

   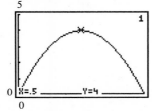

   When $t = 0.5$, the object is at the peak of its flight.

3. $V'(r) = \dfrac{4}{3}\pi\left(3r^2\right) + 4\pi(2r) = 4\pi r^2 + 8\pi r$

   When $r = 2$, $V'(r) = 4\pi(2)^2 + 8\pi(2) = 32\pi$ and $V(r) = \dfrac{4}{3}\pi(2)^3 + 4\pi(2)^2 = \dfrac{32\pi}{3} + 16\pi = \dfrac{80}{3}\pi$.

   The relative rate of change of the volume when $r = 2$ is $\dfrac{V'(2)}{V(2)} = \dfrac{32\pi}{\frac{80}{3}\pi} = \dfrac{6}{5} = 1.2$. Multiplying 1.2 by

   100 gives the percentage rate of change: $(1.2)(100) = 120\%$.

Exercise 12.3

1. $s = f(t) = t^3 + 2t$.

If $\Delta t = 1$, then over [1, 2] we have $\dfrac{\Delta s}{\Delta t} = \dfrac{f(2) - f(1)}{\Delta t} = \dfrac{\left(2^3 + 2 \cdot 2\right) - (1 + 2 \cdot 1)}{1} = 9$.

If $\Delta t = 0.5$, then over [1, 1.5] we have $\dfrac{\Delta s}{\Delta t} = \dfrac{f(1.5) - f(1)}{\Delta t} = \dfrac{\left[(1.5)^3 + 2 \cdot 1.5\right] - 3}{0.5} = 6.75$.

If $\Delta t = 0.2$, then over [1, 1.2] we have $\dfrac{\Delta s}{\Delta t} = \dfrac{f(1.2) - f(1)}{\Delta t} = \dfrac{\left[(1.2)^3 + 2 \cdot 1.2\right] - 3}{0.2} = 5.64$.

Continuing in this way we obtain the following table:

Δt	1	0.5	0.2	0.1	0.01	0.001
$\dfrac{\Delta s}{\Delta t}$	9	6.75	5.64	5.31	5.0301	5.003001

We estimate the velocity when $t = 1$ to be 5.0000 m/s. With differentiation we get $v = \dfrac{ds}{dt} = 3t^2 + 2$.

$\left.\dfrac{ds}{dt}\right|_{t=1} = 3\left(1^2\right) + 2 = 5$ m/s

3. $s = f(t) = t^2 - 3t$

   a.   When $t = 4$, then $s = 4^2 - 3(4) = 4$ m.

   b. $\dfrac{\Delta s}{\Delta t} = \dfrac{f(4.5) - f(4)}{0.5} = \dfrac{\left[(4.5)^2 - 3(4.5)\right] - 4}{0.5} = 5.5$ m/s

   c. $v = \dfrac{ds}{dt} = 2t - 3$. If $t = 4$, then $v = 2(4) - 3 = 5$ m/s

5. $s = 2t^3 + 6$

   a.   When $t = 1$, $s = 2(1)^3 + 6 = 8$ m.

   b. $\dfrac{\Delta s}{\Delta t} = \dfrac{f(1.02) - f(1)}{0.02} = \dfrac{\left[2(1.02)^3 + 6\right] - 8}{0.02} = 6.1208$ m/s

   c. $v = \dfrac{ds}{dt} = 6t^2$. If $t = 1$, then $v = 6(1)^2 = 6$ m/s

7. $s = t^4 - 2t^3 + t$

    a.   When $t = 2$, $s = 2^4 - 2\left(2^3\right) + 2 = 2$ m.

    b. $\dfrac{\Delta s}{\Delta t} = \dfrac{f(2.1) - f(2)}{0.1} = \dfrac{\left[(2.1)^4 - 2(2.1)^3 + 2.1\right] - 2}{0.1} = 10.261$ m/s

    c. $v = 4t^3 - 6t^2 + 1$

        $v\big|_{t=2} = 4\left(2^3\right) - 6\left(2^2\right) + 1 = 9$ m/s

9. $i = 2.6\sqrt{P} = 2.6P^{\frac{1}{2}}$

    $\dfrac{di}{dP} = 1.3P^{-\frac{1}{2}} = \dfrac{1.3}{\sqrt{P}}$

    When $P = 4$, then $\dfrac{di}{dP} = \dfrac{1.3}{\sqrt{4}} = 0.65$.

11. $\dfrac{dy}{dx} = \dfrac{25}{2}x^{\frac{3}{2}}$. If $x = 9$,

    $\dfrac{dy}{dx} = \dfrac{25}{2}(27) = 337.50$.

13. $\dfrac{dT}{dT_e} = 0 + 0.27(1 - 0) = 0.27$

15. $c = 500 + 10q$, $\dfrac{dc}{dq} = 10$. When $q = 100$,

    $\dfrac{dc}{dq} = 10$.

17. $\dfrac{dc}{dq} = 0.3(2q) + 2 = 0.6q + 2$. When $q = 3$,

    $\dfrac{dc}{dq} = 0.6(3) + 2 = 3.8$.

19. $\dfrac{dc}{dq} = 2q + 50$. Evaluating when $q = 15$, 16 and 17 gives 80, 82 and 84, respectively.

21. $\bar{c} = 0.01q + 5 + \dfrac{500}{q}$

    $c = \bar{c}q = 0.01q^2 + 5q + 500$

    $\dfrac{dc}{dq} = 0.02q + 5$

    $\dfrac{dc}{dq}\bigg|_{q=50} = 6$

    $\dfrac{dc}{dq}\bigg|_{q=100} = 7$

23. $c = \bar{c}q = 0.00002q^3 - 0.01q^2 + 6q + 20{,}000$

    $\dfrac{dc}{dq} = 0.00006q^2 - 0.02q + 6$

    If $q = 100$, then $\dfrac{dc}{dq} = 4.6$. If $q = 500$, then $\dfrac{dc}{dq} = 11$.

25. $\dfrac{dr}{dq} = 0.7$ for all q

27. $\dfrac{dr}{dq} = 250 + 90q - 3q^2$. Evaluating when $q = 5$, 10 and 25 gives 625, 850 and 625, respectively.

29. $\dfrac{dc}{dq} = 6.750 - 0.000328(2q) = 6.750 - 0.000656q$

$\dfrac{dc}{dq}\bigg|_{q=5000} = 6.750 - 0.000656(5000) = 3.47$

31. $PR^{0.93} = 5,000,000$

$P = 5,000,000R^{-0.93}$

$\dfrac{dP}{dR} = -4,650,000R^{-1.93}$

33. a. $\dfrac{dy}{dx} = -1.5 - x$

$\dfrac{dy}{dx}\bigg|_{x=6} = -1.5 - 6 = -7.5$

b. Setting $-1.5 - x = -6$ gives $x = 4.5$.

35. a. $y' = 1$

b. $\dfrac{y'}{y} = \dfrac{1}{x+4}$

c. $y'(5) = 1$

d. $\dfrac{1}{5+4} = \dfrac{1}{9} \approx 0.111$

e. 11.1%

37. a. $y' = 6x$

b. $\dfrac{y'}{y} = \dfrac{6x}{3x^2 + 7}$

c. $y'(2) = 6(2) = 12$

d. $\dfrac{12}{12+7} = \dfrac{12}{19} \approx 0.632$

e. 63.2%

39. a. $y' = -3x^2$

b. $\dfrac{y'}{y} = \dfrac{-3x^2}{8 - x^3}$

c. $y'(1) = -3$

d. $-\dfrac{3}{7} \approx -0.429$

e. -42.9%

41. $c = 0.2q^2 + 1.2q + 4$

$\dfrac{dc}{dq} = 0.4q + 1.2$

If $q = 5$, then $\dfrac{dc}{dq} = 0.4(5) + 1.2 = 3.2$.

If $q = 5$, then $c = 15$ and

$\dfrac{\frac{dc}{dq}}{c}(100) = \dfrac{3.2}{15}(100) \approx 21.3\%$.

43. a. $\dfrac{dr}{dq} = 30 - 0.6q$

b. If $q = 10$,

$\dfrac{r'}{r} = \dfrac{30 - 6}{300 - 30} = \dfrac{24}{270} = \dfrac{4}{45} \approx 0.09$.

c. 9%

45. $\dfrac{W'}{W} = \dfrac{0.864t^{-0.568}}{2t^{0.432}} = \dfrac{0.432}{t}$

47. The cost of $q = 20$ bikes is
$q\bar{c} = 20(150) = \$3000$. The marginal cost,
$\$125$, is the approximate cost of one
additional bike. Thus the approximate cost
of producing 21 bikes is
$\$3000 + \$125 = \$3125$.

49. $\$5.07$ per unit

Principles in Practice 12.5

1. $\dfrac{dR}{dx} = (2 - 0.15x)\dfrac{d}{dx}(225 + 20x) + (225 + 20x)\dfrac{d}{dx}(2 - 0.15x)$

    $= (2 - 0.15x)(20) + (225 + 20x)(-0.15)$

    $= 40 - 3x - 33.75 - 3x = 6.25 - 6x$

    $\dfrac{dR}{dx} = 6.25 - 6x$

2. $T(x) = x^2 - \dfrac{1}{3}x^3$

    $T'(x) = 2x - x^2$

    When the dosage is 1 milligram the
sensitivity is $T'(1) = 2(1) - 1^2 = 1$.

Exercise 12.5

1. $f'(x) = (4x + 1)(6) + (6x + 3)(4)$

    $= 24x + 6 + 24x + 12$

    $= 48x + 18 = 6(8x + 3)$

3. $s'(t) = (8 - 7t)(2t) + \left(t^2 - 2\right)(-7)$

    $= 16t - 14t^2 - 7t^2 + 14$

    $= 14 + 16t - 21t^2$

9. $y' = \left(x^2 + 3x - 2\right)(4x - 1) + \left(2x^2 - x - 3\right)(2x + 3)$

    $= \left(4x^3 + 12x^2 - 8x - x^2 - 3x + 2\right) + \left(4x^3 - 2x^2 - 6x + 6x^2 - 3x - 9\right)$

    $= 8x^3 + 15x^2 - 20x - 7$

11. $f'(w) = \left(8w^2 + 2w - 3\right)\left(15w^2\right) + \left(5w^3 + 2\right)(16w + 2)$

    $= 120w^4 + 30w^3 - 45w^2 + 80w^4 + 10w^3 + 32w + 4$

    $= 200w^4 + 40w^3 - 45w^2 + 32w + 4$

13. $y' = \left(x^2 - 1\right)\left(9x^2 - 6\right) + \left(3x^3 - 6x + 5\right)(2x) - 4(8x + 2)$

    $= 15x^4 - 27x^2 - 22x - 2$

5. $f'(r) = \left(3r^2 - 4\right)(2r - 5) + \left(r^2 - 5r + 1\right)(6r)$

    $= 6r^3 - 15r^2 - 8r + 20 + 6r^3 - 30r^2 + 6r$

    $= 12r^3 - 45r^2 - 2r + 20$

7. Without the product rule we have

    $f(x) = x^2\left(2x^2 - 5\right) = 2x^4 - 5x^2$

    $f'(x) = 8x^3 - 10x$

15. $f'(p) = \dfrac{3}{2}\left[\left(p^{\frac{1}{2}} - 4\right)(4) + (4p - 5)\left(\dfrac{1}{2}p^{-\frac{1}{2}}\right)\right]$

$\quad = \dfrac{3}{2}\left[4p^{\frac{1}{2}} - 16 + 2p^{\frac{1}{2}} - \dfrac{5}{2}p^{-\frac{1}{2}}\right]$

$\quad = \dfrac{3}{2}\left[6p^{\frac{1}{2}} - 16 - \dfrac{5}{2}p^{-\frac{1}{2}}\right]$

$\quad = \dfrac{3}{4}\left(12p^{\frac{1}{2}} - 5p^{-\frac{1}{2}} - 32\right)$

17. $y = 7 \cdot \dfrac{2}{3}$ is a constant function, so $y' = 0$.

19. $y = (2x - 1)(3x + 4)(x + 7)$

$\quad = [(2x - 1)(3x + 4)](x + 7)$

$\quad y' = [(2x - 1)(3x + 4)](1) + (x + 7)[(2x - 1)(3) + (3x + 4)(2)]$

$\quad = 6x^2 + 5x - 4 + (x + 7)[12x + 5]$

$\quad = 6x^2 + 5x - 4 + 12x^2 + 89x + 35$

$\quad = 18x^2 + 94x + 31$

21. $f'(x) = \dfrac{(x - 1)(5) - (5x)(1)}{(x - 1)^2} = -\dfrac{5}{(x - 1)^2}$

23. $f(x) = \dfrac{3}{2x^6} = \dfrac{3}{2}x^{-6}$

$\quad f'(x) = \dfrac{3}{2}\left(-6x^{-7}\right) = -\dfrac{9}{x^7}$

25. $y' = \dfrac{(x - 1)(1) - (x + 2)(1)}{(x - 1)^2}$

$\quad = \dfrac{x - 1 - x - 2}{(x - 1)^2}$

$\quad = -\dfrac{3}{(x - 1)^2}$

27. $h'(z) = \dfrac{\left(z^2 - 4\right)(-2) - (6 - 2z)(2z)}{\left(z^2 - 4\right)^2}$

$\quad = \dfrac{-2z^2 + 8 - 12z + 4z^2}{\left(z^2 - 4\right)^2} = \dfrac{2z^2 - 12z + 8}{\left(z^2 - 4\right)^2}$

$\quad = \dfrac{2\left(z^2 - 6z + 4\right)}{\left(z^2 - 4\right)^2}$

29. $y' = \dfrac{\left(x^2 - 5x\right)(16x - 2) - \left(8x^2 - 2x + 1\right)(2x - 5)}{\left(x^2 - 5x\right)^2}$

$\quad = \dfrac{16x^3 - 82x^2 + 10x - \left(16x^3 - 44x^2 + 12x - 5\right)}{\left(x^2 - 5x\right)^2} = \dfrac{-38x^2 - 2x + 5}{\left(x^2 - 5x\right)^2}$

31. $y' = \dfrac{\left(2x^2 - 3x + 2\right)(2x - 4) - \left(x^2 - 4x + 3\right)(4x - 3)}{\left(2x^2 - 3x + 2\right)^2}$

$= \dfrac{4x^3 - 6x^2 + 4x - 8x^2 + 12x - 8 - \left(4x^3 - 16x^2 + 12x - 3x^2 + 12x - 9\right)}{\left(2x^2 - 3x + 2\right)^2}$

$= \dfrac{5x^2 - 8x + 1}{\left(2x^2 - 3x + 2\right)^2}$

33. $g'(x) = \dfrac{\left(x^{100} + 7\right)(0) - (1)\left(100x^{99}\right)}{\left(x^{100} + 7\right)^2} = -\dfrac{100x^{99}}{\left(x^{100} + 7\right)^2}$

35. $u(v) = \dfrac{v^5 - 8}{v} = \dfrac{v^5}{v} - \dfrac{8}{v} = v^4 - 8v^{-1}$

$u'(v) = 4v^3 + 8v^{-2} = 4\left(v^3 + \dfrac{2}{v^2}\right) + \dfrac{4\left(v^5 + 2\right)}{v^2}$

37. $y = \dfrac{3x^2 - x - 1}{\sqrt[3]{x}} = \dfrac{3x^2 - x - 1}{x^{\frac{1}{3}}} = 3x^{\frac{5}{3}} - x^{\frac{2}{3}} - x^{-\frac{1}{3}}$

$y' = 5x^{\frac{2}{3}} - \dfrac{2}{3}x^{-\frac{1}{3}} + \dfrac{1}{3}x^{-\frac{4}{3}} = 5x^{\frac{2}{3}} - \dfrac{2}{3x^{\frac{1}{3}}} + \dfrac{1}{3x^{\frac{4}{3}}}$

$= \dfrac{15x^2 - 2x + 1}{3x^{\frac{4}{3}}}$

39. $y' = -\dfrac{(x - 8)(0) - (4)(1)}{(x - 8)^2} + \dfrac{(3x + 1)(2) - (2x)(3)}{(3x + 1)^2}$

$= \dfrac{4}{(x - 8)^2} + \dfrac{2}{(3x + 1)^2}$

41. $y' = \dfrac{[(x + 2)(x - 4)](1) - (x - 5)(2x - 2)}{[(x + 2)(x - 4)]^2}$

$= \dfrac{x^2 - 2x - 8 - \left(2x^2 - 12x + 10\right)}{[(x + 2)(x - 4)]^2}$

$= \dfrac{-\left(x^2 - 10x + 18\right)}{[(x + 2)(x - 4)]^2}$

43. $s'(t) = \dfrac{\left[\left(t^2 - 1\right)\left(t^3 + 7\right)\right](2t + 3) - \left(t^2 + 3t\right)\left(5t^4 - 3t^2 + 14t\right)}{\left[\left(t^2 - 1\right)\left(t^3 + 7\right)\right]^2}$

$= \dfrac{-3t^6 - 12t^5 + t^4 + 6t^3 - 21t^2 - 14t - 21}{\left[\left(t^2 - 1\right)\left(t^3 + 7\right)\right]^2}$

45. $y = 3x - \dfrac{\frac{2}{x} - \frac{3}{x-1}}{x - 2} = 3x - \dfrac{\frac{2(x-1)-3x}{x(x-1)}}{x - 2}$

$= 3x + \dfrac{x + 2}{x(x - 1)(x - 2)} = 3x + \dfrac{x + 2}{x^3 - 3x^2 + 2x}$

$y' = 3 + \dfrac{(x^3 - 3x^2 + 2x)(1) - (x + 2)(3x^2 - 6x + 2)}{[x(x - 1)(x - 2)]^2}$

$= 3 - \dfrac{2x^3 + 3x^2 - 12x + 4}{[x(x - 1)(x - 2)]^2}$

47. $f'(x) = \dfrac{(a + x)(-1) - (a - x)(1)}{(a + x)^2} = -\dfrac{2a}{(a + x)^2}$

49. $y = \left(4x^2 + 2x - 5\right)\left(x^3 + 7x + 4\right)$

$y' = \left(4x^2 + 2x - 5\right)\left(3x^2 + 7\right) + \left(x^3 + 7x + 4\right)(8x + 2)$

$y'(-1) = (-3)(10) + (-4)(-6) = -6$

51. $y = \dfrac{6}{x - 1}$

$y' = \dfrac{(x - 1)(0) - (6)(1)}{(x - 1)^2} = -\dfrac{6}{(x - 1)^2}$

$y'(3) = -\dfrac{6}{2^2} = -\dfrac{3}{2}$

The tangent is $y - 3 = -\dfrac{3}{2}(x - 3)$, or $y = -\dfrac{3}{2}x + \dfrac{15}{2}$.

53. $y = (2x + 3)\left[2\left(x^4 - 5x^2 + 4\right)\right]$

$y' = (2x + 3)\left[2\left(4x^3 - 10x\right)\right] + \left[2\left(x^4 - 5x^2 + 4\right)\right](2)$

$y'(0) = (3)(0) + [2(4)](2) = 16$

The tangent line is $y - 24 = 16(x - 0)$, or $y = 16x + 24$.

55. $y = \dfrac{x}{2x-6}$

$y' = \dfrac{(2x-6)(1) - x(2)}{(2x-6)^2} = \dfrac{-6}{(2x-6)^2}$

If $x = 1$, then $y = \dfrac{1}{2-6} = -\dfrac{1}{4}$ and

$y' = \dfrac{-6}{(-4)^2} = \dfrac{-6}{16} = -\dfrac{3}{8}$.

Thus $\dfrac{y'}{y} = \dfrac{-\frac{3}{8}}{-\frac{1}{4}} = \dfrac{3}{2} = 1.5$.

57. $s = \dfrac{2}{t^3 + 1}$. When $t = 1$, then $s = 1$ m.

$v = \dfrac{(t^3 + 1)(0) - 2(3t^2)}{(t^3 + 1)^2} = -\dfrac{6t^2}{(t^3 + 1)^2}$

If $t = 1$, then $v = -\dfrac{6}{4} = -1.5$ m/s.

59. $p = 25 - 0.02q$

$r = pq = 25q - 0.02q^2$

$\dfrac{dr}{dq} = 25 - 0.04q$

61. $p = \dfrac{108}{q+2} - 3$

$r = pq = \dfrac{108q}{q+2} - 3q$

$\dfrac{dr}{dq} = \dfrac{(q+2)(108) - (108q)(1)}{(q+2)^2} - 3$

$= \dfrac{216}{(q+2)^2} - 3$

63. $\dfrac{dC}{dI} = 0.672$

65. $C = 2 + 2I^{\frac{1}{2}}$

$\dfrac{dC}{dI} = 0 + 2\left(\dfrac{1}{2} I^{-\frac{1}{2}}\right) = \dfrac{1}{\sqrt{I}}$

When $I = 16$, then $\dfrac{dC}{dI} = \dfrac{1}{\sqrt{16}} = \dfrac{1}{4}$ and

$\dfrac{dS}{dI} = 1 - \dfrac{1}{4} = \dfrac{3}{4}$

67. $\dfrac{dC}{dI} = \dfrac{\left(\sqrt{I} + 4\right)\left(\frac{8}{\sqrt{I}} + 1.2\sqrt{I} - 0.2\right) - \left(16\sqrt{I} + 0.8\sqrt{I^3} - 0.2I\right)\left(\frac{1}{2\sqrt{I}}\right)}{\left(\sqrt{I} + 4\right)^2}$

$\left.\dfrac{dC}{dI}\right|_{I=36} \approx 0.615$, so $\dfrac{dS}{dI} = 1 - 0.615 = 0.385$ when $I = 36$.

69. Simplifying gives $C = 10 + 0.7I - 0.2I^{\frac{1}{2}}$

a. $\dfrac{dC}{dI} = 0.7 - 0.1I^{-\frac{1}{2}} = 0.7 - \dfrac{0.1}{\sqrt{I}}$

$\dfrac{dS}{dI} = 1 - \dfrac{dC}{dI} = 0.3 + \dfrac{0.1}{\sqrt{I}}$

$\left.\dfrac{dS}{dI}\right|_{I=25} = 0.3 + \dfrac{0.1}{5} = 0.32$

b. $\dfrac{\frac{dC}{dI}}{C}$ when $I = 25$ is $\dfrac{0.7 - \frac{0.1}{5}}{10 + 0.7(25) - 0.2(5)} \approx 0.026$

71. $\dfrac{dc}{dq} = 5 \cdot \dfrac{(q+3)(2q) - q^2(1)}{(q+3)^2} = 5 \cdot \dfrac{q^2 + 6q}{(q+3)^2}$

$\qquad = \dfrac{5q(q+6)}{(q+3)^2}$

73. $y = \dfrac{900x}{10 + 45x}$

$\qquad \dfrac{dy}{dx} = \dfrac{(10 + 45x)(900) - (900x)(45)}{(10 + 45x)^2}$

$\qquad \dfrac{dy}{dx}\bigg|_{x=2} = \dfrac{(100)(900) - (1800)(45)}{(100)^2} = \dfrac{9}{10}$

75. $y = \dfrac{0.7355x}{1 + 0.02744x}$

$\qquad \dfrac{dy}{dx} = \dfrac{(1 + 0.02744x)(0.7355) - (0.7355x)(0.02744)}{(1 + 0.02744x)^2}$

$\qquad = \dfrac{0.7355}{(1 + 0.02744x)^2}$

77. $\dfrac{d\bar{c}}{dq} = \dfrac{d}{dq}\left(\dfrac{c}{q}\right) = \dfrac{q \cdot \frac{dc}{dq} - c(1)}{q^2}$. When $q = 20$ we have $\dfrac{\frac{d\bar{c}}{dq}}{\bar{c}} = \dfrac{\frac{q \cdot \frac{dc}{dq} - c}{q^2}}{\bar{c}} = \dfrac{\frac{20(125) - 20(150)}{(20)^2}}{150} = -\dfrac{1}{120}$

79. $\dfrac{dy}{dx} = (2x - 1)(x - 2)(1) + (2x - 1)(1)(x + 3) + 2(x - 2)(x + 3)$

$\qquad = \left(2x^2 - 5x + 2\right) + \left(2x^2 + 5x - 3\right) + \left(2x^2 + 2x - 12\right)$

$\qquad = 6x^2 + 2x - 13$

Principles in Practice 12.6

1. By the chain rule,

$\dfrac{dy}{dt} = \dfrac{dy}{dx} \cdot \dfrac{dx}{dt} = \dfrac{d}{dx}\left(4x^2\right) \cdot \dfrac{d}{dt}(6t) = (8x)(6) = 48x$.

Since $x = 6t$, $\dfrac{dy}{dt} = 48(6t) = 288t$.

Exercise 12.6

1. $\dfrac{dy}{dx} = \dfrac{dy}{du} \cdot \dfrac{du}{dx} = (2u - 2)(2x - 1)$. Expressing the answer in terms of x, we have

$(2u - 2)(2x - 1) = \left[2\left(x^2 - x\right) - 2\right](2x - 1)$

$\qquad = \left(2x^2 - 2x - 2\right)(2x - 1)$

$\qquad = 4x^3 - 2x^2 - 4x^2 + 2x - 4x + 2$

$\qquad = 4x^3 - 6x^2 - 2x + 2$

3. $y = w^{-2}$, so $\dfrac{dy}{dw} = -2w^{-3} = -\dfrac{2}{w^3}$.

$\dfrac{dw}{dx} = -1$. Thus $\dfrac{dy}{dx} = \dfrac{dy}{dw} \cdot \dfrac{dw}{dx} = \left(-\dfrac{2}{w^3}\right)(-1) = \dfrac{2}{w^3} = \dfrac{2}{(2 - x)^3}$

5. $\dfrac{dw}{dt} = \dfrac{dw}{du} \cdot \dfrac{du}{dt} = (2u)\left[\dfrac{(t-1)-(t+1)}{(t-1)^2}\right]$

$\quad = 2u\left[\dfrac{-2}{(t-1)^2}\right]$. If $t = 3$, then $u = \dfrac{3+1}{3-1} = 2$,

$\quad$ so $\dfrac{dw}{dt}\Big|_{t=3} = 2(2)\left[\dfrac{-2}{4}\right] = -2$.

7. $\dfrac{dy}{dx} = \dfrac{dy}{dw} \cdot \dfrac{dw}{dx} = (6w - 8)(4x)$. If $x = 0$, then

$\quad \dfrac{dy}{dx} = 0$.

9. $y' = 6(3x+2)^5 \cdot \dfrac{d}{dx}(3x+2)$

$\quad = 6(3x+2)^5(3) = 18(3x+2)^5$

11. $y' = 3\left(5 - x^2\right)^2 \cdot \dfrac{d}{dx}\left(5 - x^2\right)$

$\quad = 3\left(5 - x^2\right)^2(-2x) = -6x\left(5 - x^2\right)^2$

13. $y' = 2 \cdot 100\left(x^3 - 8x^2 + x\right)^{99} \cdot \dfrac{d}{dx}\left(x^3 - 8x^2 + x\right)$

$\quad = 200\left(x^3 - 8x^2 + x\right)^{99}\left(3x^2 - 16x + 1\right)$

$\quad = 200\left(3x^2 - 16x + 1\right)\left(x^3 - 8x^2 + x\right)^{99}$

15. $y' = -3\left(x^2 - 2\right)^{-4} \cdot \dfrac{d}{dx}\left(x^2 - 2\right)$

$\quad = -3\left(x^2 - 2\right)^{-4}(2x) = -6x\left(x^2 - 2\right)^{-4}$

17. $y' = 3\left(-\dfrac{10}{3}\right)\left(2x^2 - 3x - 1\right)^{-\frac{13}{3}}(4x - 3)$

$\quad = -10(4x - 3)\left(2x^2 - 3x - 1\right)^{-\frac{13}{3}}$

19. $y = \sqrt{5x^2 - x} = \left(5x^2 - x\right)^{\frac{1}{2}}$

$\quad y' = \dfrac{1}{2}\left(5x^2 - x\right)^{-\frac{1}{2}}(10x - 1)$

$\quad = \dfrac{1}{2}(10x - 1)\left(5x^2 - x\right)^{-\frac{1}{2}}$

21. $y = \sqrt[4]{2x - 1} = (2x - 1)^{\frac{1}{4}}$

$\quad y' = \dfrac{1}{4}(2x - 1)^{-\frac{3}{4}}(2) = \dfrac{1}{2}(2x - 1)^{-\frac{3}{4}}$

23. $y = 2\sqrt[5]{\left(x^3 + 1\right)^2} = 2\left(x^3 + 1\right)^{\frac{2}{5}}$

$\quad y' = 2\left(\dfrac{2}{5}\right)\left(x^3 + 1\right)^{-\frac{3}{5}}\left(3x^2\right)$

$\quad = \dfrac{12}{5}x^2\left(x^3 + 1\right)^{-\frac{3}{5}}$

25. $y = \dfrac{6}{2x^2 - x + 1} = 6\left(2x^2 - x + 1\right)^{-1}$

$\quad y' = 6(-1)\left(2x^2 - x + 1\right)^{-2}(4x - 1)$

$\quad = -6(4x - 1)\left(2x^2 - x + 1\right)^{-2}$

27. $y = \dfrac{1}{\left(x^2 - 3x\right)^2} = \left(x^2 - 3x\right)^{-2}$

$\quad y' = -2\left(x^2 - 3x\right)^{-3}(2x - 3)$

$\quad = -2(2x - 3)\left(x^2 - 3x\right)^{-3}$

29. $y = \dfrac{2}{\sqrt{8x-1}} = 2(8x-1)^{-\frac{1}{2}}$

$y' = 2\left(-\dfrac{1}{2}\right)(8x-1)^{-\frac{3}{2}}(8) = -8(8x-1)^{-\frac{3}{2}}$

31. $y = \sqrt[3]{7x} + \sqrt[3]{7}\,x = (7x)^{\frac{1}{3}} + \sqrt[3]{7}\,x$

$y' = \dfrac{1}{3}(7x)^{-\frac{2}{3}}(7) + \sqrt[3]{7}(1) = \dfrac{7}{3}(7x)^{-\frac{2}{3}} + \sqrt[3]{7}$

33. By the product rule,

$y' = x^2\left[5(x-4)^4(1)\right] + (x-4)^5(2x).$

Factoring out $x(x-4)^4$ from both terms gives

$y' = x(x-4)^4[5x + 2(x-4)]$

$\quad = x(x-4)^4(7x-8)$

35. $y = 2x\sqrt{6x-1} = 2x(6x-1)^{\frac{1}{2}}$ By the product rule,

$y' = 2x\left(\dfrac{1}{2}(6x-1)^{-\frac{1}{2}}(6)\right) + \sqrt{6x-1}(2)$

$\quad = 6x(6x-1)^{-\frac{1}{2}} + 2\sqrt{6x-1}$

37. By the product rule,

$y' = \left(x^2 + 2x - 1\right)^3(5) + (5x)\left[3\left(x^2 + 2x - 1\right)^2(2x+2)\right]$

$\quad = 5\left(x^2 + 2x - 1\right)^2\left[\left(x^2 + 2x - 1\right) + 3x(2x+2)\right]$

$\quad = 5\left(x^2 + 2x - 1\right)^2\left(7x^2 + 8x - 1\right)$

39. $y' = (8x-1)^3\left[4(2x+1)^3(2)\right] + (2x+1)^4\left[3(8x-1)^2(8)\right]$

$\quad = 8(8x-1)^2(2x+1)^3[(8x-1) + 3(2x+1)]$

$\quad = 8(8x-1)^2(2x+1)^3(14x+2)$

$\quad = 16(8x-1)^2(2x+1)^3(7x+1)$

41. $y' = 10\left(\dfrac{x-7}{x+4}\right)^9\left[\dfrac{(x+4)(1) - (x-7)(1)}{(x+4)^2}\right]$

$\quad = 10\left(\dfrac{x-7}{x+4}\right)^9\left[\dfrac{11}{(x+4)^2}\right] = \dfrac{110(x-7)^9}{(x+4)^9(x+4)^2} = \dfrac{110(x-7)^9}{(x+4)^{11}}$

43. $y' = \dfrac{1}{2}\left(\dfrac{x-2}{x+3}\right)^{-\frac{1}{2}}\left[\dfrac{(x+3)(1) - (x-2)(1)}{(x+3)^2}\right]$

$\quad = \dfrac{5}{2(x+3)^2}\left(\dfrac{x-2}{x+3}\right)^{-\frac{1}{2}} = \dfrac{5}{2(x+3)^2}\sqrt{\dfrac{x+3}{x-2}}$

45. $y' = \dfrac{\left(x^2+4\right)^3(2)-(2x-5)\left[3\left(x^2+4\right)^2(2x)\right]}{\left(x^2+4\right)^6}$

Factoring out $\left(x^2+4\right)^2$ from the numerator and canceling,

$y' = \dfrac{\left(x^2+4\right)^2\left\{\left(x^2+4\right)(2)-(2x-5)[3(2x)]\right\}}{\left(x^2+4\right)^6}$

$= \dfrac{\left(x^2+4\right)(2)-(2x-5)(6x)}{\left(x^2+4\right)^4}$

$= \dfrac{2x^2+8-12x^2+30x}{\left(x^2+4\right)^4} = \dfrac{-10x^2+30x+8}{\left(x^2+4\right)^4}$

$= \dfrac{-2\left(5x^2-15x-4\right)}{\left(x^2+4\right)^4}$

47. $y' = \dfrac{(3x-1)^3\left[5(8x-1)^4(8)\right]-(8x-1)^5\left[3(3x-1)^2(3)\right]}{(3x-1)^6}$

$= \dfrac{(3x-1)^2\left[(3x-1)(40)(8x-1)^4-(8x-1)^5(9)\right]}{(3x-1)^6}$

$= \dfrac{(3x-1)(40)(8x-1)^4-(8x-1)^5(9)}{(3x-1)^4}$

$= \dfrac{(8x-1)^4[40(3x-1)-(8x-1)(9)]}{(3x-1)^4}$

$= \dfrac{(8x-1)^4(48x-31)}{(3x-1)^4}$

49. $y = 6\left(5x^2 + 2\right)\sqrt{x^4 + 5} = 6\left[\left(5x^2 + 2\right)\left(x^4 + 5\right)^{\frac{1}{2}}\right]$

$y' = 6\left[\left(5x^2 + 2\right) \cdot \frac{1}{2}\left(x^4 + 5\right)^{-\frac{1}{2}}\left(4x^3\right) + \left(x^4 + 5\right)^{\frac{1}{2}}(10x)\right]$

$= 6\left[\left(5x^2 + 2\right)\left(x^4 + 5\right)^{-\frac{1}{2}}\left(2x^3\right) + \left(x^4 + 5\right)^{\frac{1}{2}}(10x)\right]$

$= 12x\left[\left(5x^2 + 2\right)\left(x^4 + 5\right)^{-\frac{1}{2}}\left(x^2\right) + \left(x^4 + 5\right)^{\frac{1}{2}}(5)\right]$

Factoring out $\left(x^4 + 5\right)^{-\frac{1}{2}}$ gives

$y' = 12x\left(x^4 + 5\right)^{-\frac{1}{2}}\left[\left(5x^2 + 2\right)\left(x^2\right) + \left(x^4 + 5\right)(5)\right]$

$= 12x\left(x^4 + 5\right)^{-\frac{1}{2}}\left(10x^4 + 2x^2 + 25\right)$

51. $y' = 8 + \dfrac{(t+4)(1) - (t-1)(1)}{(t+4)^2} - 2\left(\dfrac{8t-7}{4}\right)\left(\dfrac{1}{4} \cdot 8\right)$

$= 8 + \dfrac{5}{(t+4)^2} - (8t - 7) = 15 - 8t + \dfrac{5}{(t+4)^2}$

53. $y' = \dfrac{\left(x^2 - 7\right)^4\left[(2x+1)(2)(3x-5)(3) + (3x-5)^2(2)\right] - (2x+1)(3x-5)^2\left[4\left(x^2-7\right)^3(2x)\right]}{\left(x^2-7\right)^8}$

55. $\dfrac{dy}{dx} = \dfrac{dy}{du} \cdot \dfrac{du}{dx} = \left[3(5u+6)^2(5)\right]\left[4\left(x^2+1\right)^3(2x)\right]$

When $x = 0$, then $\dfrac{dy}{dx} = 0$.

57. $y' = 3\left(x^2 - 7x - 8\right)^2(2x - 7)$

If $x = 8$, then

slope $= y' = 3(64 - 56 - 8)^2(16 - 7) = 0$.

59. $y = \left(x^2 - 8\right)^{\frac{2}{3}}$

$y' = \frac{2}{3}\left(x^2 - 8\right)^{-\frac{1}{3}}(2x) = \dfrac{4x}{3\left(x^2 - 8\right)^{\frac{1}{3}}}$

If $x = 3$, then $y' = \dfrac{12}{3(1)} = 4$. Thus the tangent

is $y - 1 = 4(x - 3)$, or $y = 4x - 11$.

61. $y' = \dfrac{(x+1)\left(\frac{1}{2}\right)(7x+2)^{-\frac{1}{2}}(7) - \sqrt{7x+2}\,(1)}{(x+1)^2}$

$= \dfrac{(x+1)\left(\frac{7}{2}\right)\frac{1}{\sqrt{7x+2}} - \sqrt{7x+2}}{(x+1)^2}$

If $x = 1$, then $y' = \dfrac{2\left(\frac{7}{2}\right)\left(\frac{1}{3}\right) - 3}{4} = -\dfrac{1}{6}$. The

tangent line is $y - \dfrac{3}{2} = -\dfrac{1}{6}(x - 1)$, or

$y = -\dfrac{1}{6}x + \dfrac{5}{3}$.

63. $y = \left(x^2 + 9\right)^3$ and $y' = 6x\left(x^2 + 9\right)^2$. When $x = 4$, then $y = (25)^3$ and $y' = 6(4)(25)^2$, so

$$\frac{y'}{y}(100) = \frac{6(4)(25)^2}{(25)^3}(100) = \frac{24}{25}(100) = 96\%$$

65. Given $q = 2m$, $p = -0.5q + 20$; $m = 5$.

$$\frac{dr}{dm} = \frac{dr}{dq} \cdot \frac{dq}{dm}$$

Since $r = pq = -0.5q^2 + 20q$, we have $\frac{dr}{dq} = -q + 20$. For $m = 5$, then $q = 2(5) = 10$, so

$\left.\frac{dr}{dq}\right|_{m=5} = -10 + 20 = 10$. Also, $\frac{dq}{dm} = 2$. Thus $\left.\frac{dr}{dm}\right|_{m=5} = (10)(2) = 20$.

67. $q = \dfrac{10m^2}{\sqrt{m^2 + 9}}$

$p = \dfrac{525}{q + 3}$; $m = 4$

$\dfrac{dr}{dm} = \dfrac{dr}{dq} \cdot \dfrac{dq}{dm}$

$r = pq = \dfrac{525q}{q + 3}$, so $\dfrac{dr}{dq} = 525 \cdot \dfrac{(q+3)(1) - q(1)}{(q+3)^2} = \dfrac{1575}{(q+3)^2}$.

If $m = 4$, then $q = 32$, so $\left.\dfrac{dr}{dq}\right|_{m=4} = \dfrac{1575}{1225} = \dfrac{9}{7}$.

$$\frac{dq}{dm} = \frac{\left(m^2+9\right)^{\frac{1}{2}}(20m) - 10m^2 \cdot \frac{1}{2}\left(m^2+9\right)^{-\frac{1}{2}}(2m)}{m^2 + 9}$$

$$= \frac{\left(m^2+9\right)^{-\frac{1}{2}}\left[20m\left(m^2+9\right) - 10m^3\right]}{m^2 + 9}$$

$$= \frac{10m^3 + 180m}{\left(m^2+9\right)^{\frac{3}{2}}}$$

When $m = 4$, then $\dfrac{dq}{dm} = \dfrac{10(64) + 180(4)}{(25)^{\frac{3}{2}}} = \dfrac{1360}{125} = \dfrac{272}{25}$. Thus $\left.\dfrac{dr}{dm}\right|_{m=4} = \dfrac{9}{7} \cdot \dfrac{272}{25} \approx 13.99$.

69. a. $\dfrac{dp}{dq} = 0 - \dfrac{1}{2}\left(q^2 + 20\right)^{-\frac{1}{2}}(2q) = \dfrac{-q}{\sqrt{q^2 + 20}}$

b. $\dfrac{\frac{dp}{dq}}{p} = \dfrac{\dfrac{-q}{\sqrt{q^2+20}}}{100 - \sqrt{q^2 + 20}}$

$= -\dfrac{q}{\sqrt{q^2+20}\left(100 - \sqrt{q^2 + 20}\right)}$

$= -\dfrac{q}{100\sqrt{q^2 + 20} - q^2 - 20}$

c. $r = pq = 100q - q\sqrt{q^2 + 20}$

$\dfrac{dr}{dq}$

$= 100 - \left[q \cdot \dfrac{1}{2}\left(q^2 + 20\right)^{-\frac{1}{2}}(2q) + \sqrt{q^2 + 20}\,(1)\right]$

$= 100 - \dfrac{q^2}{\sqrt{q^2 + 20}} - \sqrt{q^2 + 20}$

71. $\dfrac{dc}{dp} = \dfrac{dc}{dq} \cdot \dfrac{dq}{dp} = (10 + 0.2q)(-2.5)$

When $p = 80$, then $q = 600$, so $\left.\dfrac{dc}{dp}\right|_{p=80} = -325$.

73. $\dfrac{dc}{dq} = \dfrac{\left(q^2 + 3\right)^{\frac{1}{2}}(10q) - \left(5q^2\right)\left[\frac{1}{2}\left(q^2 + 3\right)^{-\frac{1}{2}}(2q)\right]}{q^2 + 3}$

Multiplying numerator and denominator by $\left(q^2 + 3\right)^{\frac{1}{2}}$ gives $\dfrac{dc}{dq} = \dfrac{\left(q^2 + 3\right)(10q) - 5q^2(q)}{\left(q^2 + 3\right)^{\frac{3}{2}}}$

$= \dfrac{5q^3 + 30q}{\left(q^2 + 3\right)^{\frac{3}{2}}} = \dfrac{5q\left(q^2 + 6\right)}{\left(q^2 + 3\right)^{\frac{3}{2}}}.$

75. $\dfrac{dV}{dt} = \dfrac{dV}{dr} \cdot \dfrac{dr}{dt} = \left(4\pi r^2\right)\left[10^{-8}(2t) + 10^{-7}\right]$. When $t = 10$, then

$r = 10^{-8}\left(10^2\right) + 10^{-7}(10) = 10^{-6} + 10^{-6} = 2(10)^{-6}$. Thus

$\dfrac{dV}{dt}\bigg|_{t=10} = 4\pi\left[2(10)^{-6}\right]^2\left[10^{-8}(2)(10) + 10^{-7}\right] = 4\pi\left[4(10)^{-12}\right]\left[3\left(10^{-7}\right)\right] = 48\pi(10)^{-19}$

77. a. $\dfrac{d}{dx}\left(l_x\right) = -0.001424x^3 + 0.01338x^2 + 1.692x - 34.8$

If $x = 36$, $\dfrac{d}{dx}\left(l_x\right) \approx -22.986$.

b. If $x = 36$, $\dfrac{\frac{d}{dx}\left(l_x\right)}{l} \approx \dfrac{-22.986}{19,453.758} \approx -0.001$.

79. By the chain rule, $\dfrac{dc}{dp} = \dfrac{dc}{dq} \cdot \dfrac{dq}{dp}$. We are given that $q = \dfrac{100}{p} = 100p^{-1}$, so $\dfrac{dq}{dp} = -100p^{-2} = \dfrac{-100}{p^2}$.

Thus $\dfrac{dc}{dp} = \dfrac{dc}{dq}\left[\dfrac{-100}{p^2}\right]$. When $q = 200$, then $p = \dfrac{100}{200} = \dfrac{1}{2}$ and we are given that $\dfrac{dc}{dq} = 0.01$.

Therefore $\dfrac{dc}{dp} = 0.01\left[\dfrac{-100}{\left(\frac{1}{2}\right)^2}\right] = -4$.

81. $\dfrac{dy}{dt} = \dfrac{dy}{dx} \cdot \dfrac{dx}{dt} = f'(x)g'(t)$. We are given that $g(2) = 3$, so $x = 3$ when $t = 2$.

Thus $\dfrac{dy}{dt}\bigg|_{t=2} = \dfrac{dy}{dx}\bigg|_{x=g(2)} \cdot \dfrac{dx}{dt}\bigg|_{t=2} = f'(3)g'(2) = 10(4) = 40$.

83. $86,111.22$

Chapter 12 Review Problems

1. $f(x) = 2 - x^2$

$f'(x) = \displaystyle\lim_{h \to 0} \dfrac{f(x+h) - f(x)}{h} = \lim_{h \to 0} \dfrac{\left[2 - (x+h)^2\right] - \left(2 - x^2\right)}{h}$

$= \displaystyle\lim_{h \to 0} \dfrac{\left[2 - x^2 - 2hx - h^2\right] - \left(2 - x^2\right)}{h} = \lim_{h \to 0} \dfrac{-2hx - h^2}{h}$

$= \displaystyle\lim_{h \to 0} \dfrac{-h(2x + h)}{h} = \lim_{h \to 0} -(2x + h) = -2x$

3. $f(x) = \sqrt{3x}$

$$f'(x) = \lim_{h \to 0} \frac{f(x+h) - f(x)}{h} = \lim_{h \to 0} \frac{\sqrt{3(x+h)} - \sqrt{3x}}{h}$$

$$= \lim_{h \to 0} \frac{\sqrt{3(x+h)} - \sqrt{3x}}{h} \cdot \frac{\sqrt{3(x+h)} + \sqrt{3x}}{\sqrt{3(x+h)} + \sqrt{3x}}$$

$$= \lim_{h \to 0} \frac{3(x+h) - 3x}{h\left(\sqrt{3(x+h)} + \sqrt{3x}\right)} = \lim_{h \to 0} \frac{3h}{h\left(\sqrt{3(x+h)} + \sqrt{3x}\right)}$$

$$= \lim_{h \to 0} \frac{3}{\sqrt{3(x+h)} + \sqrt{3x}}$$

$$= \frac{3}{\sqrt{3x} + \sqrt{3x}} = \frac{3}{2\sqrt{3x}} = \frac{\sqrt{3}}{2\sqrt{x}}$$

5. y is a constant function, so $y' = 0$.

7. $y' = 7\left(4x^3\right) - 6\left(3x^2\right) + 5(2x) + 0$

$\quad = 28x^3 - 18x^2 + 10x = 2x\left(14x^2 - 9x + 5\right)$

9. $f(s) = s^2\left(s^2 + 2\right) = s^4 + 2s^2$

$\quad f'(s) = 4s^3 + 2(2s) = 4s^3 + 4s = 4s\left(s^2 + 1\right)$

11. $y = \dfrac{1}{5}\left(x^2 + 1\right)$

$\quad y' = \dfrac{1}{5}(2x) = \dfrac{2x}{5}$

13. $y' = \left(x^2 + 6x\right)\left(3x^2 - 12x\right) + \left(x^3 - 6x^2 + 4\right)(2x + 6)$

$\quad = 3x^4 + 6x^3 - 72x^2 + \left(2x^4 + 6x^3 - 12x^3 - 36x^2 + 8x + 24\right)$

$\quad = 5x^4 - 108x^2 + 8x + 24$

15. $f'(x) = 100\left(2x^2 + 4x\right)^{99}(4x + 4)$

$\quad = 400(x + 1)[(2x)(x + 2)]^{99}$

17. $y = 3(2x + 1)^{-1}$

$\quad y' = 3(-1)(2x + 1)^{-2}(2) = -\dfrac{6}{(2x + 1)^2}$

19. $y' = (8 + 2x)\left[(4)\left(x^2 + 1\right)^3(2x)\right] + \left(x^2 + 1\right)^4(2)$

$= 2\left(x^2 + 1\right)^3\left[4x(8 + 2x) + \left(x^2 + 1\right)\right]$

$= 2\left(x^2 + 1\right)^3\left(32x + 8x^2 + x^2 + 1\right)$

$= 2\left(x^2 + 1\right)^3\left(9x^2 + 32x + 1\right)$

21. $f'(z) = \dfrac{\left(z^2 + 4\right)(2z) - \left(z^2 - 1\right)(2z)}{\left(z^2 + 4\right)^2} = \dfrac{10z}{\left(z^2 + 4\right)^2}$

23. $y = (4x - 1)^{\frac{1}{3}}$

$y' = \frac{1}{3}(4x - 1)^{-\frac{2}{3}}(4) = \frac{4}{3}(4x - 1)^{-\frac{2}{3}}$

25. $y = (1 - x)^{-\frac{1}{2}}$

$y' = \left(-\frac{1}{2}\right)(1 - x)^{-\frac{3}{2}}(-1) = \frac{1}{2}(1 - x)^{-\frac{3}{2}}$

27. $h'(x) = (x - 6)^4\left[3(x + 5)^2\right] + (x + 5)^3\left[4(x - 6)^3\right]$

$= (x - 6)^3(x + 5)^2[3(x - 6) + 4(x + 5)]$

$= (x - 6)^3(x + 5)^2(7x + 2)$

29. $y' = \dfrac{(x + 6)(5) - (5x - 4)(1)}{(x + 6)^2} = \dfrac{34}{(x + 6)^2}$

31. $y' = 2\left(-\frac{3}{8}\right)x^{-\frac{11}{8}} + \left(-\frac{3}{8}\right)(2x)^{-\frac{11}{8}}(2)$

$= -\frac{3}{4}x^{-\frac{11}{8}} - \frac{3}{4}\left(2^{-\frac{11}{8}}\right)x^{-\frac{11}{8}}$

$= -\frac{3}{4}x^{-\frac{11}{8}}\left(1 + 2^{-\frac{11}{8}}\right) = -\frac{3}{4}\left(1 + 2^{-\frac{11}{8}}\right)x^{-\frac{11}{8}}$

33. $y' = \dfrac{\left(x^2+5\right)^{\frac{1}{2}}(2x) - \left(x^2+6\right)\left(\frac{1}{2}\right)\left(x^2+5\right)^{-\frac{1}{2}}(2x)}{x^2+5}$

Multiplying the numerator and denominator by $\left(x^2+5\right)^{\frac{1}{2}}$ gives

$y' = \dfrac{\left(x^2+5\right)(2x) - x\left(x^2+6\right)}{\left(x^2+5\right)^{\frac{3}{2}}}$

$= \dfrac{x^3+4x}{\left(x^2+5\right)^{\frac{3}{2}}} = \dfrac{x\left(x^2+4\right)}{\left(x^2+5\right)^{\frac{3}{2}}}$

35. $y' = \dfrac{3}{5}\left(x^3+6x^2+9\right)^{-\frac{2}{5}}\left(3x^2+12x\right)$

$= \dfrac{3}{5}\left(x^3+6x^2+9\right)^{-\frac{2}{5}}(3x)(x+4)$

$= \dfrac{9}{5}x(x+4)\left(x^3+6x^2+9\right)^{-\frac{2}{5}}$

37. $g(z) = -7z(z-1) = -7\left(z^2-z\right)$

$g'(z) = -7(2z-1) = 7(1-2z)$

39. $y = x^2 - 6x + 4$

$y' = 2x - 6$

When $x = 1$, then $y = -1$ and $y' = -4$. An equation of the tangent line is
$y - (-1) = -4(x-1)$, or $y = -4x+3$.

41. $y = x^{\frac{1}{3}}$

$y' = \dfrac{1}{3}x^{-\frac{2}{3}}$

When $x = 8$, then $y = 2$ and $y' = \dfrac{1}{12}$. An equation of the tangent line is
$y - 2 = \dfrac{1}{12}(x-8)$, or $y = \dfrac{1}{12}x + \dfrac{4}{3}$.

43. $f(x) = 4x^2 + 2x + 8$

$f'(x) = 8x + 2$

$f(1) = 14$ and $f'(1) = 10$. The relative rate of change is $\dfrac{f'(1)}{f(1)} = \dfrac{10}{14} = \dfrac{5}{7} \approx 0.714$, so the percentage rate of change is 71.4%.

45. $r = q(20-0.1q) = 20q - 0.1q^2$

$\dfrac{dr}{dq} = 20 - 0.2q$

47. $\dfrac{dC}{dI} = 0.6 - 0.25\left(\dfrac{1}{2}\right)I^{-\frac{1}{2}} = 0.6 - \dfrac{1}{8\sqrt{I}}$

$\left.\dfrac{dC}{dI}\right|_{I=16} \approx 0.569$

Thus the marginal propensity to consume is 0.569, so the marginal propensity to save is $1 - 0.569 = 0.431$.

49. Since $p = -0.5q + 450$, then
$r = pq = -0.5q^2 + 450q$. Thus
$\dfrac{dr}{dq} = 450 - q$.

51. $\dfrac{dc}{dq} = 0.125 + 0.00878q$

$\left.\dfrac{dc}{dq}\right|_{q=70} = 0.7396$

53. $\dfrac{dy}{dx} = 42x^2 - 34x - 16$

$\left.\dfrac{dy}{dx}\right|_{x=2} = 84$ eggs/mm

55. a. $\dfrac{dt}{dT}$ when $T = 38$ is

$\dfrac{d}{dT}\left[\dfrac{4}{3}T - \dfrac{175}{4}\right]_{T=38} = \left.\dfrac{4}{3}\right|_{T=38} = \dfrac{4}{3}$.

b. $\dfrac{dt}{dT}$ when $T = 35$ is

$\dfrac{d}{dT}\left[\dfrac{1}{24}T + \dfrac{11}{4}\right]_{T=35} = \left.\dfrac{1}{24}\right|_{T=35} = \dfrac{1}{24}$.

57. $V' = \dfrac{1}{2}\pi d^2$. If $d = 4$ ft, then $V' = 8\pi\,\dfrac{\text{ft}^3}{\text{ft}}$.

59. $c = \bar{c}q = 2q^2 + \dfrac{10,000}{q} = 2q^2 + 10,000q^{-1}$

$\dfrac{dc}{dq} = 4q - 10,000q^{-2} = 4q - \dfrac{10,000}{q^2}$

61. a. $q = 10\sqrt{m^2 + 3600} - 600$

$p = \sqrt{7200 - 9q}$; $m = 80$

$\dfrac{dr}{dm} = \dfrac{dr}{dq} \cdot \dfrac{dq}{dm}$.

$r = pq = q\sqrt{7200 - 9q}$, so $\dfrac{dr}{dq} = q\left(\dfrac{1}{2}\right)(7200 - 9q)^{-\frac{1}{2}}(-9) + \sqrt{7200 - 9q}\,(1)$. If $m = 80$, then $q = 400$,

so $\left.\dfrac{dr}{dq}\right|_{m=80} = 30$. $\dfrac{dq}{dm} = 10 \cdot \dfrac{1}{2}\left(m^2 + 3600\right)^{-\frac{1}{2}}(2m)$. $\left.\dfrac{dq}{dm}\right|_{m=80} = 8$. Thus $\left.\dfrac{dr}{dm}\right|_{m=80} = (30)(8) = 240$

b. $\left.\dfrac{\frac{dr}{dm}}{r}\right|_{m=80} = \left.\dfrac{240}{r}\right|_{q=400} = \dfrac{240}{400\sqrt{3600}} = \dfrac{1}{100}$

c. No. The extra cost of $300 would exceed the extra revenue [approximately $240, from part (a)].

63. 0.305

65. −0.32

Mathematical Snapshot Chapter 12

1. In Problems 63 and 64 of Sec. 12.5, the slope is ≈ 0.7. In Fig. 12.15 the slope is above 0.9. More is spent; less is saved.

3. The slope of the family consumption curve is $\dfrac{112,040}{\sqrt{1.9667 \times 10^{10} + 224,080x}}$, which for $x = 25,000$ equals about 0.705. You would expect the family to spend $705 and save $295.

5. Answers may vary.

Chapter 13

Principles in Practice 13.1

1. $\dfrac{dq}{dp} = \dfrac{d}{dp}\left[25 + 2\ln\left(3p^2 + 4\right)\right]$

$= 0 + 2\dfrac{d}{dp}\left[\ln\left(3p^2 + 4\right)\right]$

$= 2\left(\dfrac{1}{3p^2 + 4}\right)\dfrac{d}{dp}\left(3p^2 + 4\right) = \dfrac{2}{3p^2 + 4}(6p)$

$= \dfrac{12p}{3p^2 + 4}$

2. With $I_0 = 1$, $R(I) = \log I$.

$\dfrac{dR}{dI} = \dfrac{d}{dI}[\log I] = \dfrac{d}{dI}\left[\dfrac{\ln I}{\ln 10}\right]$

$= \dfrac{1}{\ln 10} \cdot \dfrac{1}{I} = \dfrac{1}{I \ln 10}$

Exercise 13.1

1. $\dfrac{dy}{dx} = 4 \cdot \dfrac{d}{dx}(\ln x) = 4 \cdot \dfrac{1}{x} = \dfrac{4}{x}$

3. $\dfrac{dy}{dx} = \dfrac{1}{3x - 7}(3) = \dfrac{3}{3x - 7}$

5. $y = \ln x^2 = 2\ln x$

$\dfrac{dy}{dx} = 2 \cdot \dfrac{1}{x} = \dfrac{2}{x}$

7. $\dfrac{dy}{dx} = \dfrac{1}{1 - x^2}(-2x) = -\dfrac{2x}{1 - x^2}$

9. $f'(p) = \dfrac{1}{2p^3 + 3p}\left(6p^2 + 3\right)$

$= \dfrac{6p^2 + 3}{2p^3 + 3p} = \dfrac{3\left(2p^2 + 1\right)}{p\left(2p^2 + 3\right)}$

11. $f'(t) = t\left(\dfrac{1}{t}\right) + (\ln t)(1) = 1 + \ln t$

13. $\dfrac{dy}{dx} = x^2\left[\dfrac{1}{4x + 3}(4)\right] + [\ln(4x + 3)](2x)$

$= \dfrac{4x^2}{4x + 3} + 2x\ln(4x + 3)$

15. $y = \log_3(8x - 1) = \dfrac{\ln(8x - 1)}{\ln 3}$

$\dfrac{dy}{dx} = \dfrac{1}{\ln 3} \cdot \dfrac{d}{dx}[\ln(8x - 1)]$

$= \dfrac{1}{\ln 3} \cdot \dfrac{1}{8x - 1}(8) = \dfrac{8}{(8x - 1)(\ln 3)}$

17. $y = x^2 + \log_2\left(x^2 + 4\right) = x^2 + \dfrac{\ln\left(x^2 + 4\right)}{\ln 2}$

$\dfrac{dy}{dx} = 2x + \dfrac{1}{\ln 2}\left[\dfrac{1}{x^2 + 4}(2x)\right]$

$= 2x\left[1 + \dfrac{1}{(\ln 2)\left(x^2 + 4\right)}\right]$

19. $f'(z) = \dfrac{z\left(\frac{1}{z}\right) - (\ln z)(1)}{z^2} = \dfrac{1 - \ln z}{z^2}$

21. $\dfrac{dy}{dx} = \dfrac{(\ln x)(2x) - \left(x^2 - 1\right)\left(\frac{1}{x}\right)}{\ln^2 x}$

$= \dfrac{2x^2 \ln(x) - x^2 + 1}{x\ln^2 x}$

23. $y = \ln\left(x^2 + 4x + 5\right)^3 = 3\ln\left(x^2 + 4x + 5\right)$

$\dfrac{dy}{dx} = 3 \cdot \dfrac{1}{x^2 + 4x + 5}(2x + 4)$

$= \dfrac{3(2x + 4)}{x^2 + 4x + 5} = \dfrac{6(x + 2)}{x^2 + 4x + 5}$

25. $y = 9\ln\sqrt{1 + x^2} = \dfrac{9}{2}\ln\left(1 + x^2\right)$

$\dfrac{dy}{dx} = \dfrac{9}{2} \cdot \dfrac{1}{1 + x^2}(2x) = \dfrac{9x}{1 + x^2}$

27. $f(l) = \ln\left(\dfrac{1+l}{1-l}\right) = \ln(1+l) - \ln(1-l)$

$f'(l) = \dfrac{1}{1+l} - \dfrac{1}{1-l}(-1)$

$= \dfrac{(1-l)+(1+l)}{(1+l)(1-l)} = \dfrac{2}{1-l^2}$

29. $y = \ln\sqrt[4]{\dfrac{1+x^2}{1-x^2}} = \dfrac{1}{4}\left[\ln\left(1+x^2\right) - \ln\left(1-x^2\right)\right]$

$\dfrac{dy}{dx} = \dfrac{1}{4}\left[\dfrac{2x}{1+x^2} - \dfrac{-2x}{1-x^2}\right]$

$= \dfrac{1}{4}\left[\dfrac{2x\left(1-x^2\right)+2x\left(1+x^2\right)}{\left(1+x^2\right)\left(1-x^2\right)}\right] = \dfrac{x}{1-x^4}$

31. $y = \ln\left[\left(x^2+2\right)^2\left(x^3+x-1\right)\right]$

$= 2\ln\left(x^2+2\right) + \ln\left(x^3+x-1\right)$

$\dfrac{dy}{dx} = 2 \cdot \dfrac{1}{x^2+2}(2x) + \dfrac{1}{x^3+x-1}\left(3x^2+1\right)$

$= \dfrac{4x}{x^2+2} + \dfrac{3x^2+1}{x^3+x-1}$

33. $y = 5\ln\left(x\sqrt{2x+1}\right) = 5\ln x + 5\ln(2x+1)^{\frac{1}{2}}$

$= 5\ln x + \dfrac{5}{2}\ln(2x+1)$

$\dfrac{dy}{dx} = \dfrac{5}{x} + \dfrac{5}{2} \cdot \dfrac{1}{2x+1}(2) = \dfrac{5}{x} + \dfrac{5}{2x+1}$

35. $\dfrac{dy}{dx} = \left(x^2+1\right)\left[\dfrac{1}{2x+1}(2)\right] + \ln(2x+1) \cdot [2x]$

$= \dfrac{2\left(x^2+1\right)}{2x+1} + 2x\ln(2x+1)$

37. $y = \ln x^3 + \ln^3 x = 3\ln x + (\ln x)^3$

$\dfrac{dy}{dx} = 3 \cdot \dfrac{1}{x} + 3(\ln x)^2 \cdot \dfrac{1}{x} = \dfrac{3}{x} + \dfrac{3(\ln x)^2}{x}$

$= \dfrac{3\left(1+\ln^2 x\right)}{x}$

39. $y = \ln^4(ax) = [\ln(ax)]^4$

$\dfrac{dy}{dx} = 4[\ln(ax)]^3\left(\dfrac{1}{ax} \cdot a\right) = \dfrac{4\ln^3(ax)}{x}$

41. $y = x\ln\sqrt{x-1} = \dfrac{1}{2}x\ln(x-1)$

By the product rule,

$\dfrac{dy}{dx} = \dfrac{1}{2}\left[x\left(\dfrac{1}{x-1}\right) + \ln(x-1) \cdot [1]\right]$

$= \dfrac{x}{2(x-1)} + \ln\sqrt{x-1}$

43. $y = \sqrt{4+3\ln x} = (4+3\ln x)^{\frac{1}{2}}$

$\dfrac{dy}{dx} = \dfrac{1}{2}(4+3\ln x)^{-\frac{1}{2}} \cdot \dfrac{3}{x} = \dfrac{3}{2x\sqrt{4+3\ln x}}$

45. $y = \ln\left(x^2-2x-2\right)$

$y' = \dfrac{2x-2}{x^2-2x-2}$

The slope of the tangent line at $x=3$ is

$y'(3) = \dfrac{6-2}{9-6-2} = 4$. Also, if $x=3$, then

$y = \ln(9-6-2) = \ln 1 = 0$. Thus an equation of the tangent line is $y-0 = 4(x-3)$, or $y = 4x-12$.

47. $y = \dfrac{x}{\ln x}$

$y' = \dfrac{(\ln x)(1) - x\left(\frac{1}{x}\right)}{\ln^2 x} = \dfrac{\ln x - 1}{\ln^2 x}$

When $x=3$ the slope is $y'(3) = \dfrac{(\ln 3)-1}{\ln^2 3}$.

49. $c = 25\ln(q+1) + 12$

$\dfrac{dc}{dq} = \dfrac{25}{q+1}$, so $\dfrac{dc}{dq}\bigg|_{q=6} = \dfrac{25}{7}$.

51. $\dfrac{dq}{dp} = \dfrac{d}{dp}[25 + 10\ln(2p+1)]$

$= 0 + 10\dfrac{d}{dp}[\ln(2p+1)] = 10\left(\dfrac{1}{2p+1}\right)\dfrac{d}{dp}[2p+1]$

$= \dfrac{10}{2p+1}(2) = \dfrac{20}{2p+1}$

53. $A = 6\ln\left(\dfrac{T}{a-T} - a\right)$. Rate of change of A with respect to T:

$\dfrac{dA}{dT} = 6 \cdot \dfrac{1}{\frac{T}{a-T} - a}\left[\dfrac{(a-T)(1) - T(-1)}{(a-T)^2}\right]$

$= 6 \cdot \dfrac{1}{\frac{T-a(a-T)}{a-T}}\left[\dfrac{a}{(a-T)^2}\right]$

$= 6 \cdot \dfrac{a-T}{T-a^2+aT} \cdot \dfrac{a}{(a-T)^2}$

$= \dfrac{6a}{\left(T-a^2+aT\right)(a-T)}$

55. $\dfrac{d}{dx}\left(\log_b u\right) = \dfrac{d}{dx}\left(\dfrac{\ln u}{\ln b}\right)$

$= \dfrac{1}{\ln b} \cdot \dfrac{d}{dx}(\ln u) = \dfrac{1}{\ln b}\left(\dfrac{1}{u} \cdot \dfrac{du}{dx}\right)$

$= \left(\log_b e\right)\left(\dfrac{1}{u} \cdot \dfrac{du}{dx}\right) = \dfrac{1}{u}\left(\log_b e\right)\dfrac{du}{dx}$

57. $f'(x) = \dfrac{1-\ln 2x}{x^2}$

$f'(x) = 0$ for $x \approx 1.36$

Principles in Practice 13.2

1. The rate of change of temperature with respect to time is $\dfrac{dT}{dt}$. $T(t)$ has the form Ce^u where C is a constant and $u = kt$.

$\dfrac{dT}{dt} = \dfrac{d}{dt}\left[Ce^{kt}\right] = C\dfrac{d}{dt}\left[e^{kt}\right]$

$= C\left(e^{kt}\right)\dfrac{d}{dt}[kt] = Ce^{kt}(k) = Cke^{kt}$

Exercise 13.2

1. $y' = 7 \cdot \dfrac{d}{dx}\left(e^x\right) = 7e^x$

3. $y' = e^{x^2+4}(2x) = 2xe^{x^2+4}$

5. $y' = e^{9-5x} \cdot \dfrac{d}{dx}(9-5x)$

$= e^{9-5x}(-5) = -5e^{9-5x}$

7. $f'(r) = e^{3r^2+4r+4}(6r+4)$

$= 2(3r+2)e^{3r^2+4r+4}$

9. By the product rule,

$y' = x\left(e^x\right) + e^x(1) = e^x(x+1)$

11. $y' = x^2\left[e^{-x^2}(-2x)\right] + e^{-x^2}[2x]$

$= 2xe^{-x^2}\left(1 - x^2\right)$

13. $y = \dfrac{1}{3}\left(e^x + e^{-x}\right)$

$y' = \dfrac{1}{3}\left[e^x + e^{-x}(-1)\right] = \dfrac{e^x - e^{-x}}{3}$

15. $\dfrac{d}{dx}\left(4^{3x^2}\right) = \dfrac{d}{dx}\left[e^{(\ln 4)3x^2}\right]$

$\quad = e^{(\ln 4)3x^2}[(\ln 4)(6x)]$

$\quad = (6x)4^{3x^2}\ln 4$

17. $f'(w) = \dfrac{w^2\left[e^{2w}(2)\right] - e^{2w}[2w]}{w^4}$

$\quad = \dfrac{2e^{2w}(w-1)}{w^3}$

19. $y' = e^{1+\sqrt{x}}\left(\dfrac{1}{2}x^{-\frac{1}{2}}\right) = \dfrac{e^{1+\sqrt{x}}}{2\sqrt{x}}$

21. $y = x^5 - 5^x = x^5 - e^{(\ln 5)x}$

$\quad y' = 5x^4 - e^{(\ln 5)x}(\ln 5) = 5x^4 - 5^x\ln 5$

23. $\dfrac{dy}{dx} = \dfrac{\left(e^x+1\right)\left[e^x\right]-\left(e^x-1\right)\left[e^x\right]}{\left(e^x+1\right)^2}$

$\quad = \dfrac{2e^x}{\left(e^x+1\right)^2}$

25. $y = e^{\ln x} = x$ (by the property $e^{\ln a} = a$).

Thus $y' = 1$.

27. $y' = e^{x\ln x}\left[x\cdot\dfrac{1}{x} + (\ln x)(1)\right] = (1+\ln x)e^{x\ln x}$

29. $f(x) = ee^x e^{x^2} = e^{1+x+x^2}$

$\quad f'(x) = e^{1+x+x^2}(1+2x) = (1+2x)e^{1+x+x^2}$

$\quad f'(-1) = [1+2(-1)]e^{1+(-1)+(-1)^2} = -e$

31. $y = e^x$, $y' = e^x$. When $x = -2$, then $y = e^{-2}$ and $y' = e^{-2}$. Thus an equation of the tangent line is $y - e^{-2} = e^{-2}(x+2)$, or $y = e^{-2}x + 3e^{-2}$

33. $\dfrac{dp}{dq} = 15e^{-0.001q}(-0.001) = -0.015e^{-0.001q}$

$\quad \dfrac{dp}{dq}\bigg|_{q=500} = -0.015e^{-0.5}$

35. $\bar{c} = \dfrac{7000e^{\frac{q}{700}}}{q}$, so $c = \bar{c}q = 7000e^{\frac{q}{700}}$.

The marginal cost function is

$\quad \dfrac{dc}{dq} = 7000e^{\frac{q}{700}}\left(\dfrac{1}{700}\right) = 10e^{\frac{q}{700}}$. Thus

$\quad \dfrac{dc}{dq}\bigg|_{q=350} = 10e^{0.5}$ and $\dfrac{dc}{dq}\bigg|_{q=700} = 10e$.

37. $w = e^{x^3-4x} + x\ln(x-1)$ and $x = \dfrac{t+1}{t-1}$

By the chain rule, $\dfrac{dw}{dt} = \dfrac{dw}{dx}\cdot\dfrac{dx}{dt}$

$= \left[e^{x^3-4x}\left(3x^2-4\right) + x\left(\dfrac{1}{x-1}\right) + [\ln(x-1)(1)]\right]\cdot\left[\dfrac{(t-1)(1)-(t+1)(1)}{(t-1)^2}\right]$

$= \left[\left(3x^2-4\right)e^{x^3-4x} + \dfrac{x}{x-1} + \ln(x-1)\right]\left[\dfrac{-2}{(t-1)^2}\right]$.

When $t = 3$, then $x = \dfrac{3+1}{3-1} = \dfrac{4}{2} = 2$ and $\dfrac{dw}{dt} = [8+2+0]\left[-\dfrac{1}{2}\right] = -5$.

39. $\dfrac{d}{dx}\left(c^x - x^c\right) = \dfrac{d}{dx}\left[\left(e^{\ln c}\right)^x - x^c\right]$

$= \dfrac{d}{dx}\left[e^{(\ln c)x} - x^c\right]$

$= (\ln c)e^{(\ln c)x} - cx^{c-1} = (\ln c)c^x - cx^{c-1}$

When $x = 1$, this derivative is 0. Thus
$(\ln c)c - c = 0$, or $c[\ln(c) - 1] = 0$. Since
$c > 0$, we must have $\ln(c) - 1 = 0$, $\ln c = 1$,
or $c = e$.

41. $q = 500\left(1 - e^{-0.2t}\right)$

$\dfrac{dq}{dt} = 500\left(-e^{-0.2t}\right)(-0.2) = 100e^{-0.2t}$

Thus $\dfrac{dq}{dt}\bigg|_{t=10} = 100e^{-2}$

43. $P = 1.92e^{0.0176t}$

$\dfrac{dP}{dt} = 1.92e^{0.0176t}(0.0176) = P(0.0176)$

$= 0.0176P = kP$ for $k = 0.0176$.

45. Since $S = Pe^{rt}$, then $\dfrac{dS}{dt} = Pe^{rt}r = rPe^{rt}$.

Thus $\dfrac{\frac{dS}{dt}}{S} = \dfrac{rPe^{rt}}{Pe^{rt}} = r$.

47. $N = 10^A 10^{-bM} = 10^{A-bM} = e^{(\ln 10)(A-bM)}$

$\dfrac{dN}{dM} = e^{(\ln 10)(A-bM)}(\ln 10)(-b)$, so

$\dfrac{dN}{dM} = 10^{A-bM}(\ln 10)(-b) = -b\left(10^{A-bM}\right)\ln 10$

49. $C(t) = C_0 e^{-\left(\frac{r}{V}\right)t}$

$\dfrac{dC}{dt} = C_0 e^{-\left(\frac{r}{V}\right)t}\left(-\dfrac{r}{V}\right)$

$= [C(t)]\left(-\dfrac{r}{V}\right) = -\left(\dfrac{r}{V}\right)C(t)$

51. $f(t) = 1 - e^{-0.008t}$

$f'(t) = 0.008e^{-0.008t}$

$f'(100) = 0.008e^{-0.8} \approx 0.0036$

53. $f'(x) = \left(4x^3 + 4x - 4\right)e^{x^4 + 2x^2 - 4x}$

$f'(x) = 0$ for $x \approx 0.68$

Principles in Practice 13.3

1. Assume that P is a function of t and
differentiate both sides of $\ln\left(\dfrac{P}{1-P}\right) = 0.5t$
with respect to t.

$\dfrac{d}{dt}\left[\ln\left(\dfrac{P}{1-P}\right)\right] = \dfrac{d}{dt}[0.5t]$

$\left(\dfrac{1}{\frac{P}{1-P}}\right)\dfrac{d}{dt}\left[\dfrac{P}{1-P}\right] = 0.5$

$\dfrac{1-P}{P} \cdot \dfrac{(1)(1-P) - P(-1)}{(1-P)^2} \cdot \dfrac{dP}{dt} = 0.5$

$\dfrac{1-P+P}{P(1-P)} \cdot \dfrac{dP}{dt} = 0.5$

$\dfrac{dP}{dt} = 0.5P(1-P)$

2. $\dfrac{dV}{dt} = \dfrac{d}{dt}\left[\dfrac{4}{3}\pi r^3\right] = \dfrac{4}{3}\pi\left(3r^2\right)\dfrac{dr}{dt} = 4\pi r^2 \dfrac{dr}{dt}$

When $\dfrac{dr}{dt} = 5$ and $r = 12$,

$\dfrac{dV}{dt} = 4\pi(12)^2(5) = 2880\pi$. The balloon is
increasing at the rate of 2880π cubic
inches/minute.

3. The hypotenuse is the length of the ladder,
so $x^2 + y^2 = 100$. Differentiate both sides of
the equation with respect to t.

$\dfrac{d}{dt}\left[x^2 + y^2\right] = \dfrac{d}{dt}[100]$

$2x\dfrac{dx}{dt} + 2y\dfrac{dy}{dt} = 0$

When $y = 8$, we can find x by using the
Pythagorean theorem.

$x^2 + 8^2 = 100$

$x^2 = 100 - 64 = 36$

$x = 6$

When $x = 6$, $y = 8$, and $\frac{dx}{dt} = 3$, we have

$$2(6)(3) + 2(8)\frac{dy}{dt} = 0$$

$$36 + 16\frac{dy}{dt} = 0$$

$$\frac{dy}{dt} = -\frac{36}{16} = -\frac{9}{4}$$

$\frac{dy}{dt} = -\frac{9}{4}$, thus the top of the ladder is

sliding down the wall at the rate of $\frac{9}{4}$

feet/sec.

Exercise 13.3

1. $2x + 8yy' = 0$

   $x + 4yy' = 0$

   $4yy' = -x$

   $y' = -\frac{x}{4y}$

3. $12y^3 y' - 7 = 0$

   $y' = \frac{7}{12y^3}$

5. $\frac{1}{2}x^{-\frac{1}{2}} + \frac{1}{2}y^{-\frac{1}{2}}y' = 0$

   $x^{-\frac{1}{2}} + y^{-\frac{1}{2}}y' = 0$

   $y^{-\frac{1}{2}}y' = -x^{-\frac{1}{2}}$

   $y' = -\frac{x^{-\frac{1}{2}}}{y^{-\frac{1}{2}}} = -\frac{y^{\frac{1}{2}}}{x^{\frac{1}{2}}} = -\frac{\sqrt{y}}{\sqrt{x}} = -\sqrt{\frac{y}{x}}$

7. $\left(\frac{3}{4}\right)x^{-\frac{1}{4}} + \left(\frac{3}{4}\right)y^{-\frac{1}{4}}y' = 0$

   $y' = -\frac{y^{\frac{1}{4}}}{x^{\frac{1}{4}}}$

9. By the product rule $xy' + y(1) = 0$, $xy' = -y$,

   $y' = -\frac{y}{x}$

11. $xy' + y(1) - y' - 11 = 0$

    $y'(x - 1) = 11 - y$

    $y' = \frac{11 - y}{x - 1}$

13. $6x^2 + 3y^2 y' - 12(xy' + y) = 0$

    $3y^2 y' - 12xy' = 12y - 6x^2$

    $y'(3y^2 - 12x) = 12y - 6x^2$

    $y'(y^2 - 4x) = 4y - 2x^2$

    $y' = \frac{4y - 2x^2}{y^2 - 4x}$

15. $1 = \frac{1}{2}y^{-\frac{1}{2}}y' + \frac{1}{3}y^{-\frac{2}{3}}y'$

    $6 = y'\left(\frac{3}{y^{\frac{1}{2}}} + \frac{2}{y^{\frac{2}{3}}}\right)$

    $6 = y'\left(\frac{3y^{\frac{1}{6}} + 2}{y^{\frac{2}{3}}}\right)$

    $y' = \frac{6y^{\frac{2}{3}}}{3y^{\frac{1}{6}} + 2}$

17. $3x^2\left(3y^2 y'\right) + y^3(6x) - 1 + y' = 0$

    $9x^2 y^2 y' + y' = 1 - 6xy^3$

    $y'\left(9x^2 y^2 + 1\right) = 1 - 6xy^3$

    $y' = \frac{1 - 6xy^3}{1 + 9x^2 y^2}$

19. $y\left(\frac{1}{x}\right) + (\ln x)y' = x\left(e^y y'\right) + e^y(1)$

    $\left[\ln(x) - xe^y\right]y' = e^y - \frac{y}{x}$

    $\left[\ln(x) - xe^y\right]y' = \frac{xe^y - y}{x}$

    $y' = \frac{xe^y - y}{x\left[\ln(x) - xe^y\right]}$

21. $\left[x\left(e^y y'\right)+e^y(1)\right]+y'=0$

$xe^y y'+e^y+y'=0$

$\left(xe^y+1\right)y'=-e^y$

$y'=-\dfrac{e^y}{xe^y+1}$

23. $2\left(1+e^{3x}\right)\left(3e^{3x}\right)=\dfrac{1}{x+y}(1+y')$

$6e^{3x}\left(1+e^{3x}\right)(x+y)=1+y'$

$y'=6e^{3x}\left(1+e^{3x}\right)(x+y)-1$

25. $1+[xy'+y(1)]+2yy'=0$

$xy'+2yy'=-1-y$

$(x+2y)y'=-(1+y)$

$y'=-\dfrac{1+y}{x+2y}$

At the point (1, 2), $y'=-\dfrac{1+2}{1+4}=-\dfrac{3}{5}$

27. $8x+18yy'=0$

$y'=-\dfrac{8x}{18y}=-\dfrac{4x}{9y}$

Thus at $\left(0,\dfrac{1}{3}\right)$, $y'=0$; at $\left(x_0, y_0\right)$,

$y'=-\dfrac{4x_0}{9y_0}$.

29. $3x^2+2yy'=0$

$y'=-\dfrac{3x^2}{2y}$

At (−1, 2), $y'=-\dfrac{3}{4}$. The tangent is given by

$y-2=-\dfrac{3}{4}(x+1)$, or $y=-\dfrac{3}{4}x+\dfrac{5}{4}$.

31. $p=100-q^2$

$\dfrac{d}{dp}(p)=\dfrac{d}{dp}\left(100-q^2\right)$

$1=-2q\cdot\dfrac{dq}{dp}$

$\dfrac{dq}{dp}=-\dfrac{1}{2q}$

33. $p=\dfrac{20}{(q+5)^2}$

$\dfrac{d}{dp}(p)=\dfrac{d}{dp}\left[\dfrac{20}{(q+5)^2}\right]$

$\dfrac{d}{dp}(p)=\dfrac{d}{dp}\left[20(q+5)^{-2}\right]$

$1=-\dfrac{40}{(q+5)^3}\cdot\dfrac{dq}{dp}$

$\dfrac{dq}{dp}=-\dfrac{(q+5)^3}{40}$

35. $\ln\dfrac{I}{I_0}=-\lambda t$

$\ln I-\ln I_0=-\lambda t$

$\dfrac{1}{I}\dfrac{dI}{dt}=-\lambda$

$\dfrac{dI}{dt}=-\lambda I$

37. $1.5M=\log\left(\dfrac{E}{2.5\times10^{11}}\right)$

$1.5M=\log E-\log\left(2.5\times10^{11}\right)$

$\dfrac{d}{dM}(1.5M)=\dfrac{d}{dM}\left[\log E-\log\left(2.5\times10^{11}\right)\right]$

$\dfrac{d}{dM}(1.5M)=\dfrac{d}{dM}\left[\dfrac{\ln E}{\ln 10}-\log\left(2.5\times10^{11}\right)\right]$

$1.5=\dfrac{1}{\ln 10}\left(\dfrac{1}{E}\cdot\dfrac{dE}{dM}\right)$

$\dfrac{dE}{dM}=1.5E\ln 10$

39. $TV^{0.4}=1500$. Differentiating implicitly with respect to T:

$T\left(0.4V^{-0.6}\dfrac{dV}{dT}\right)+V^{0.4}(1)=0$,

$0.4TV^{-0.6}\dfrac{dV}{dT}=-V^{0.4}$,

$\dfrac{dV}{dT}=-\dfrac{V^{0.4}}{0.4TV^{-0.6}}=-\dfrac{V}{0.4T}=-2.5\dfrac{V}{T}$.

41. $S^2 + \frac{1}{4}I^2 = SI + I$. Differentiating implicitly with respect to I: $2S\frac{dS}{dI} + \frac{1}{2}I = \left[S(1) + I\frac{dS}{dI}\right] + 1$,

$2S\frac{dS}{dI} - I\frac{dS}{dI} = S + 1 - \frac{I}{2}$, $(2S - I)\frac{dS}{dI} = \frac{2S + 2 - I}{2}$, $\frac{dS}{dI} = \frac{2S + 2 - I}{2(2S - I)}$.

Marginal propensity to consume $= \frac{dC}{dI} = 1 - \frac{dS}{dI}$. Thus $\frac{dC}{dI} = 1 - \frac{2S + 2 - I}{2(2S - I)}$.

When $I = 16$ and $S = 12$, $\frac{dC}{dI} = 1 - \frac{24 + 2 - 16}{2(24 - 16)} = 1 - \frac{10}{16} = \frac{6}{16} = \frac{3}{8}$.

Exercise 13.4

1. $y = (x + 1)^2(x - 2)\left(x^2 + 3\right)$. Taking natural logarithms of both sides gives

$\ln y = \ln\left[(x + 1)^2(x - 2)\left(x^2 + 3\right)\right]$.

Using properties of logarithms on the right side gives

$\ln y = 2\ln(x + 1) + \ln(x - 2) + \ln\left(x^2 + 3\right)$.

Differentiating both sides with respect to x,

$\dfrac{y'}{y} = \dfrac{2}{x + 1} + \dfrac{1}{x - 2} + \dfrac{2x}{x^2 + 3}$.

Solving for y',

$y' = y\left[\dfrac{2}{x + 1} + \dfrac{1}{x - 2} + \dfrac{2x}{x^2 + 3}\right]$.

Expressing y' in terms of x,

$y' = (x + 1)^2(x - 2)\left(x^2 + 3\right)\left[\dfrac{2}{x + 1} + \dfrac{1}{x - 2} + \dfrac{2x}{x^2 + 3}\right]$

3. $\ln y = \ln\left[\left(3x^3 - 1\right)^2(2x + 5)^3\right]$

$= 2\ln\left(3x^3 - 1\right) + 3\ln(2x + 5)$

$\dfrac{y'}{y} = 2 \cdot \dfrac{9x^2}{3x^3 - 1} + 3 \cdot \dfrac{2}{2x + 5}$

$y' = y\left[\dfrac{18x^2}{3x^3 - 1} + \dfrac{6}{2x + 5}\right]$

$y' = \left(3x^3 - 1\right)^2(2x + 5)^3\left[\dfrac{18x^2}{3x^3 - 1} + \dfrac{6}{2x + 5}\right]$

5. $y = \sqrt{x + 1}\sqrt{x^2 - 2}\sqrt{x + 4}$

$\ln y = \ln\left(\sqrt{x + 1}\sqrt{x^2 - 2}\sqrt{x + 4}\right)$

$\ln y = \dfrac{1}{2}\ln(x + 1) + \dfrac{1}{2}\ln\left(x^2 - 2\right)$

$\qquad + \dfrac{1}{2}\ln(x + 4)$

$\dfrac{y'}{y} = \dfrac{1}{2}\left[\dfrac{1}{x + 1} + \dfrac{2x}{x^2 - 2} + \dfrac{1}{x + 4}\right]$

$y' = \dfrac{y}{2}\left[\dfrac{1}{x + 1} + \dfrac{2x}{x^2 - 2} + \dfrac{1}{x + 4}\right]$

$= \dfrac{\sqrt{x + 1}\sqrt{x^2 - 2}\sqrt{x + 4}}{2}$

$\qquad \cdot \left[\dfrac{1}{x + 1} + \dfrac{2x}{x^2 - 2} + \dfrac{1}{x + 4}\right]$

7. $\ln y = \ln \dfrac{\sqrt{1-x^2}}{1-2x} = \dfrac{1}{2} \ln\left(1-x^2\right) - \ln(1-2x)$

$\dfrac{y'}{y} = \dfrac{1}{2} \cdot \dfrac{-2x}{1-x^2} - \dfrac{-2}{1-2x}$

$y' = y\left[-\dfrac{x}{1-x^2} + \dfrac{2}{1-2x}\right]$

$y' = \dfrac{\sqrt{1-x^2}}{1-2x}\left[\dfrac{x}{x^2-1} + \dfrac{2}{1-2x}\right]$

9. $y = \dfrac{\left(2x^2+2\right)^2}{(x+1)^2(3x+2)}$

$\ln y = \ln\left[\dfrac{\left(2x^2+2\right)^2}{(x+1)^2(3x+2)}\right]$

$= 2\ln\left(2x^2+2\right) - 2\ln(x+1) - \ln(3x+2)$

$\dfrac{y'}{y} = 2 \cdot \dfrac{4x}{2x^2+2} - 2 \cdot \dfrac{1}{x+1} - \dfrac{3}{3x+2}$

$y' = y\left[\dfrac{8x}{2x^2+2} - \dfrac{2}{x+1} - \dfrac{3}{3x+2}\right]$

$= \dfrac{\left(2x^2+2\right)^2}{(x+1)^2(3x+2)}\left[\dfrac{4x}{x^2+1} - \dfrac{2}{x+1} - \dfrac{3}{3x+2}\right]$

11. $\ln y = \ln\sqrt{\dfrac{(x-1)(x+1)}{3x-4}}$

$= \dfrac{1}{2}[\ln(x-1) + \ln(x+1) - \ln(3x-4)]$

$\dfrac{y'}{y} = \dfrac{1}{2}\left[\dfrac{1}{x-1} + \dfrac{1}{x+1} - \dfrac{3}{3x-4}\right]$

$y' = \dfrac{y}{2}\left[\dfrac{1}{x-1} + \dfrac{1}{x+1} - \dfrac{3}{3x-4}\right]$

$y' = \dfrac{1}{2}\sqrt{\dfrac{(x-1)(x+1)}{3x-4}}\left[\dfrac{1}{x-1} + \dfrac{1}{x+1} - \dfrac{3}{3x-4}\right]$

13. $y = x^{2x+1}$. Thus

$\ln y = \ln x^{2x+1} = (2x+1)\ln x$.

$\dfrac{y'}{y} = (2x+1)\dfrac{1}{x} + (\ln x)(2)$

$y' = y\left[\dfrac{2x+1}{x} + 2\ln x\right]$

$y' = x^{2x+1}\left[\dfrac{2x+1}{x} + 2\ln x\right]$

15. $y = x^{\frac{1}{x}}$. Thus $\ln y = \dfrac{1}{x}\ln x = \dfrac{\ln x}{x}$.

$\dfrac{y'}{y} = \dfrac{x\left(\frac{1}{x}\right) - (\ln x)(1)}{x^2}$

$y' = y\left[\dfrac{1-\ln x}{x^2}\right]$

$y' = \dfrac{x^{\frac{1}{x}}(1-\ln x)}{x^2}$

17. $y = (3x+1)^{2x}$. Thus

$\ln y = \ln\left[(3x+1)^{2x}\right] = 2x\ln(3x+1)$

$\dfrac{y'}{y} = 2\left\{x\left(\dfrac{3}{3x+1}\right) + [\ln(3x+1)](1)\right\}$

$y' = 2y\left[\dfrac{3x}{3x+1} + \ln(3x+1)\right]$

$= 2(3x+1)^{2x}\left[\dfrac{3x}{3x+1} + \ln(3x+1)\right]$

19. $y = 4e^x x^{3x}$. Thus

$\ln y = \ln 4 + \ln\left(e^x x^{3x}\right) = \ln 4 + \ln e^x + \ln x^{3x}$

$= \ln 4 + x + 3x\ln x$

$\dfrac{y'}{y} = 1 + 3\left[x\left(\dfrac{1}{x}\right) + (\ln x)(1)\right]$

$y' = y(4 + 3\ln x)$

$y' = 4e^x x^{3x}(4 + 3\ln x)$

21. $y = (4x - 3)^{2x+1}$

$\ln y = \ln(4x - 3)^{2x+1} = (2x + 1)\ln(4x - 3)$

$\dfrac{y'}{y} = (2x + 1)\left[\dfrac{4}{4x - 3}\right] + [\ln(4x - 3)](2)$

$y' = y\left[\dfrac{4(2x + 1)}{4x - 3} + 2\ln(4x - 3)\right]$

When $x = 1$, then $\dfrac{dy}{dx} = 1\left[\dfrac{12}{1} + 2\ln(1)\right] = 12$.

23. $y = (x + 1)(x + 2)^2 (x + 3)^2$

$\ln y = \ln(x + 1) + 2\ln(x + 2) + 2\ln(x + 3)$

$\dfrac{y'}{y} = \dfrac{1}{x + 1} + \dfrac{2}{x + 2} + \dfrac{2}{x + 3}$

$y' = y\left[\dfrac{1}{x + 1} + \dfrac{2}{x + 2} + \dfrac{2}{x + 3}\right]$

When $x = 0$, then $y = 36$ and $y' = 96$. Thus an equation of the tangent line is
$y - 36 = 96(x - 0)$, or $y = 96x + 36$.

25. $y = 3e^x\left(x^2 - x + 1\right)^x$

$\ln y = \ln 3 + \ln e^x + \ln\left(x^2 - x + 1\right)^x$

$= \ln(3) + x + x\ln\left(x^2 - x + 1\right)$

$\dfrac{y'}{y} = 1 + \left[x\left(\dfrac{2x - 1}{x^2 - x + 1}\right)\right] + \left[\ln\left(x^2 - x + 1\right)(1)\right]$

$y' = y\left[1 + \dfrac{x(2x - 1)}{x^2 - x + 1} + \ln\left(x^2 - x + 1\right)\right]$

When $x = 1$, then $y = 3e$ and
$y' = 3e[1 + 1 + \ln(1)] = 6e$. Thus an equation
of the tangent line is $y - 3e = 6e(x - 1)$, or
$y = 6ex - 3e$.

27. $y = (3x)^{-2x}$

$\ln y = -2x\ln(3x)$

$\dfrac{y'}{y} = -2\left\{x\left[\dfrac{1}{3x}(3)\right] + [\ln(3x)](1)\right\}$

$= -2[1 + \ln(3x)]$

$\dfrac{y'}{y} \cdot 100$ gives the percentage rate of change.

Thus $-2[1 + \ln(3x)](100) = 60$

$1 + \ln(3x) = -0.3$

$\ln(3x) = -1.3$

$3x = e^{-1.3}$

$x = \dfrac{1}{3e^{1.3}}$

Principles in Practice 13.5

1. $\dfrac{dh}{dt} = 0 - 16(2t) = -32t$ ft/sec

$\dfrac{d^2h}{dt^2} = \dfrac{d}{dt}[-32t] = -32$ feet/sec^2

The acceleration of the rock at time t is
-32 feet/sec^2 or 32 feet/sec^2 downward.

2. The rate of change of the marginal cost
function with respect to x is $c''(q)$.

$c'(q) = 14q + 11$

$c'' = 14$

When $x = 3$, the rate of change of the
marginal cost function is 14 dollars/unit^2.

Exercise 13.5

1. $y' = 12x^2 - 24x + 6$

$y'' = 24x - 24$

$y''' = 24$

3. $\dfrac{dy}{dx} = -1$

$\dfrac{d^2y}{dx^2} = 0$

5. $y' = 3x^2 + e^x$

$y'' = 6x + e^x$

$y''' = 6 + e^x$

$y^{(4)} = e^x$

7. $f(x) = x^2\ln x$

$f'(x) = x^2\left(\dfrac{1}{x}\right) + (\ln x)(2x) = x(1 + 2\ln x)$

$f''(x) = x\left(\dfrac{2}{x}\right) + (1 + 2\ln x)(1) = 3 + 2\ln x$

9. $f(p) = \dfrac{1}{6p^3} = \dfrac{1}{6} p^{-3}$

$f'(p) = -\dfrac{1}{2} p^{-4}$

$f''(p) = 2p^{-5}$

$f'''(p) = -10p^{-6} = -\dfrac{10}{p^6}$

11. $f(r) = \sqrt{9-r} = (9-r)^{\frac{1}{2}}$

$f'(r) = -\dfrac{1}{2}(9-r)^{-\frac{1}{2}}$

$f''(r) = -\dfrac{1}{4}(9-r)^{-\frac{3}{2}} = -\dfrac{1}{4(9-r)^{\frac{3}{2}}}$

13. $y = \dfrac{1}{5x-6} = (5x-6)^{-1}$

$\dfrac{dy}{dx} = (-1)(5x-6)^{-2}(5) = -5(5x-6)^{-2}$

$\dfrac{d^2y}{dx^2} = -5(-2)(5x-6)^{-3}(5)$

$= 50(5x-6)^{-3} = \dfrac{50}{(5x-6)^3}$

15. $y = \dfrac{x+1}{x-1}$

$y' = \dfrac{(x-1)(1)-(x+1)(1)}{(x-1)^2}$

$= -\dfrac{2}{(x-1)^2} = -2(x-1)^{-2}$

$y'' = 4(x-1)^{-3} = \dfrac{4}{(x-1)^3}$

17. $y = \ln[x(x+6)] = \ln(x) + \ln(x+6)$

$y' = \dfrac{1}{x} + \dfrac{1}{x+6} = x^{-1} + (x+6)^{-1}$

$y'' = -x^{-2} + (-1)(x+6)^{-2} = -\left[\dfrac{1}{x^2} + \dfrac{1}{(x+6)^2}\right]$

19. $f(z) = z^2 e^z$

$f'(z) = z^2\left(e^z\right) + e^z(2z) = \left(ze^z\right)(z+2)$

$f''(z) = \left(ze^z\right)(1) + (z+2)\left[ze^z + e^z(1)\right]$

$= e^z\left(z^2 + 4z + 2\right)$

21. $y = e^{2x}$

$\dfrac{dy}{dx} = 2e^{2x}$

$\dfrac{d^2y}{dx^2} = 4e^{2x}$

$\dfrac{d^3y}{dx^3} = 8e^{2x}$

$\dfrac{d^4y}{dx^4} = 16e^{2x}$

$\dfrac{d^5y}{dx^5} = 32e^{2x}$

$\left.\dfrac{d^5y}{dx^5}\right|_{x=0} = 32e^0 = 32$

23. $x^2 + 4y^2 - 16 = 0$

$2x + 8yy' = 0$

$8yy' = -2x$

$y' = -\dfrac{x}{4y}$

$y'' = -\dfrac{4y(1) - x(4y')}{16y^2}$

$= -\dfrac{4y - 4x\left(-\frac{x}{4y}\right)}{16y^2} = -\dfrac{4y^2 + x^2}{16y^3}$

$= -\dfrac{16}{16y^3} = -\dfrac{1}{y^3}$

25. $y^2 = 4x$

$2yy' = 4$

$y' = \dfrac{2}{y} = 2y^{-1}$

$y'' = -2y^{-2}y' = -2y^{-2}\left(2y^{-1}\right) = -\dfrac{4}{y^3}$

27. $\sqrt{x} + 4\sqrt{y} = 4$

$x^{\frac{1}{2}} + 4y^{\frac{1}{2}} = 4$

$\frac{1}{2}x^{-\frac{1}{2}} + 2y^{-\frac{1}{2}}y' = 0$

$2y^{-\frac{1}{2}}y' = -\frac{1}{2}x^{-\frac{1}{2}}$

$y' = -\frac{1}{2} \cdot \frac{x^{-\frac{1}{2}}}{2y^{-\frac{1}{2}}} = -\frac{1}{4} \cdot \frac{y^{\frac{1}{2}}}{x^{\frac{1}{2}}}$

$y'' = -\frac{1}{4}\left[\dfrac{x^{\frac{1}{2}}\left(\frac{1}{2}y^{-\frac{1}{2}}y'\right) - y^{\frac{1}{2}}\left(\frac{1}{2}x^{-\frac{1}{2}}\right)}{x}\right]$

$= -\frac{1}{8}\left[\dfrac{\dfrac{x^{\frac{1}{2}}}{y^{\frac{1}{2}}}\left(-\dfrac{y^{\frac{1}{2}}}{4x^{\frac{1}{2}}}\right) - \dfrac{y^{\frac{1}{2}}}{x^{\frac{1}{2}}}}{x}\right] = -\frac{1}{8}\left[\dfrac{-\dfrac{1}{4} - \dfrac{y^{\frac{1}{2}}}{x^{\frac{1}{2}}}}{x}\right]$

$= \frac{1}{8}\left[\dfrac{\dfrac{1}{4} + \dfrac{y^{\frac{1}{2}}}{x^{\frac{1}{2}}}}{x}\right] = \frac{1}{8}\left[\dfrac{x^{\frac{1}{2}} + 4y^{\frac{1}{2}}}{4x^{\frac{3}{2}}}\right]$

$= \frac{1}{8}\left[\dfrac{4}{4x^{\frac{3}{2}}}\right] = \dfrac{1}{8x^{\frac{3}{2}}}$

29. $xy + y - x = 4$

$xy' + y(1) + y' - 1 = 0$

$xy' + y' = 1 - y$

$(x+1)y' = 1 - y$

$y' = \dfrac{1-y}{1+x}$

$y'' = \dfrac{(1+x)(-y') - (1-y)(1)}{(1+x)^2}$

$= \dfrac{(1+x)\left[-\frac{(1-y)}{(1+x)}\right] - (1-y)}{(1+x)^2}$

$= \dfrac{-(1-y) - (1-y)}{(1+x)^2} = \dfrac{-2(1-y)}{(1+x)^2} = \dfrac{2(y-1)}{(1+x)^2}$

31. $y = e^{x+y}$

$y' = e^{x+y}(1 + y')$

$y' - e^{x+y}y' = e^{x+y}$

$y'\left(1 - e^{x+y}\right) = e^{x+y}$

$y' = \dfrac{e^{x+y}}{1 - e^{x+y}}$

$y' = \dfrac{y}{1-y}$

$y'' = \dfrac{(1-y)y' - y(-y')}{(1-y)^2} = \dfrac{y'}{(1-y)^2}$

$= \dfrac{\frac{y}{1-y}}{(1-y)^2} = \dfrac{y}{(1-y)^3}$

33. $x^2 + 8y = y^2$

$2x + 8y' = 2yy'$

$x + 4y' = yy'$

$x = yy' - 4y'$

$x = y'(y - 4)$

$y' = \dfrac{x}{y-4}$

$y'' = \dfrac{(y-4)(1) - x(y')}{(y-4)^2} = \dfrac{y - 4 - x\left(\frac{x}{y-4}\right)}{(y-4)^2}$

$= \dfrac{(y-4)^2 - x^2}{(y-4)^3}$

When $x = 3$ and $y = -1$, then

$y'' = \dfrac{(-5)^2 - 3^2}{(-5)^3} = -\dfrac{16}{125}.$

35. $f(x) = (5x - 3)^4$

$f'(x) = 20(5x - 3)^3$

$f''(x) = 300(5x - 3)^2$

37. $\dfrac{dc}{dq} = 0.6q + 2$

$\dfrac{d^2c}{dq^2} = 0.6$

$\left.\dfrac{d^2c}{dq^2}\right|_{q=100} = 0.6$

39. $f(x) = x^4 - 6x^2 + 5x - 6$

$f'(x) = 4x^3 - 12x + 5$

$f''(x) = 12x^2 - 12 = 12(x+1)(x-1)$

Clearly $f'(x) = 0$ when $x = \pm 1$.

41. $f'(x) = 6e^x - 3x^2 - 30x$

$f''(x) = 6\left(e^x - x - 5\right)$

$f''(x) = 0$ when $x \approx -4.99$ or 1.94.

Chapter 13 Review Problems

1. $y = 2e^x + e^2 + e^{x^2}$

$y' = 2e^x + 0 + e^{x^2}(2x) = 2\left(e^x + xe^{x^2}\right)$

3. $f'(r) = \dfrac{1}{r^2 + 5r}(2r + 5) = \dfrac{2r+5}{r(r+5)}$

5. $y = e^{x^2 + 4x + 5}$

$y' = e^{x^2+4x+5}(2x+4) = 2(x+2)e^{x^2+4x+5}$

7. $y' = e^x(2x) + \left(x^2 + 2\right)e^x = e^x\left(x^2 + 2x + 2\right)$

9. $y = \sqrt{(x-6)(x+5)(9-x)}$

$\ln y = \ln \sqrt{(x-6)(x+5)(9-x)}$

$= \frac{1}{2}[\ln(x-6) + \ln(x+5) + \ln(9-x)]$

$\dfrac{y'}{y} = \frac{1}{2}\left[\dfrac{1}{x-6} + \dfrac{1}{x+5} + \dfrac{-1}{9-x}\right]$

$y' = \dfrac{y}{2}\left[\dfrac{1}{x-6} + \dfrac{1}{x+5} - \dfrac{1}{9-x}\right]$

$= \dfrac{\sqrt{(x-6)(x+5)(9-x)}}{2}\left[\dfrac{1}{x-6} + \dfrac{1}{x+5} + \dfrac{1}{x-9}\right]$

11. $y' = \dfrac{e^x\left(\frac{1}{x}\right) - (\ln x)\left(e^x\right)}{e^{2x}}$

$= \dfrac{e^x - xe^x \ln x}{xe^{2x}} = \dfrac{1 - x\ln x}{xe^x}$

13. $f(q) = \ln\left[(q+1)^2(q+2)^3\right]$

$= 2\ln(q+1) + 3\ln(q+2)$

$f'(q) = \dfrac{2}{q+1} + \dfrac{3}{q+2}$

15. $y = e^{(2-7x)(\ln 10)}$

$y' = e^{(2-7x)(\ln 10)}(-7\ln 10) = -7(\ln 10)10^{2-7x}$

17. $y = \dfrac{4e^{3x}}{xe^{x-1}} = \dfrac{4e^{2x+1}}{x}$

$y' = 4 \cdot \dfrac{x\left[e^{2x+1}(2)\right] - e^{2x+1}[1]}{x^2} = \dfrac{4e^{2x+1}(2x-1)}{x^2}$

19. $y = \log_2(8x+5)^2 = 2\log_2(8x+5)$

$= 2 \cdot \dfrac{\ln(8x+5)}{\ln 2}$

$y' = 2 \cdot \dfrac{1}{\ln 2} \cdot \dfrac{8}{8x+5} = \dfrac{16}{(8x+5)\ln 2}$

21. $f(l) = \ln\left(1 + l + l^2 + l^3\right)$

$f'(l) = \dfrac{1}{1+l+l^2+l^3}\left[1 + 2l + 3l^2\right]$

$= \dfrac{1 + 2l + 3l^2}{1+l+l^2+l^3}$

23. $y = (x+1)^{x+1}$

$\ln y = (x+1)\ln(x+1)$

$\dfrac{y'}{y} = (x+1)\dfrac{1}{x+1} + \ln(x+1)[1]$

$= 1 + \ln(x+1)$

$y' = y[1 + \ln(x+1)]$

$= (x+1)^{x+1}[1 + \ln(x+1)]$

25. $f(t) = \ln\left(t^2\sqrt{2-t}\right) = 2\ln t + \dfrac{1}{2}\ln(2-t)$

$f'(t) = 2\left(\dfrac{1}{t}\right) + \dfrac{1}{2}\left(\dfrac{1}{2-t}\right)(-1)$

$= \dfrac{2}{t} + \dfrac{1}{2(t-2)} = \dfrac{5t-8}{2t(t-2)}$

27. $y = \dfrac{\left(x^2+2\right)^{\frac{3}{2}}\left(x^2+9\right)^{\frac{4}{9}}}{\left(x^3+6x\right)^{\frac{4}{11}}}$

$\ln y = \dfrac{3}{2}\ln\left(x^2+2\right) + \dfrac{4}{9}\ln\left(x^2+9\right) - \dfrac{4}{11}\ln\left(x^3+6x\right)$

$\dfrac{y'}{y} = \dfrac{3}{2}\left(\dfrac{1}{x^2+2}\right)(2x) + \dfrac{4}{9}\left(\dfrac{1}{x^2+9}\right)(2x) - \dfrac{4}{11}\left(\dfrac{1}{x^3+6x}\right)(3x^2+6)$

$y' = y\left[\dfrac{3x}{x^2+2} + \dfrac{8x}{9\left(x^2+9\right)} - \dfrac{12\left(x^2+2\right)}{11x\left(x^2+6\right)}\right]$

$= \dfrac{\left(x^2+2\right)^{\frac{3}{2}}\left(x^2+9\right)^{\frac{4}{9}}}{\left(x^3+6x\right)^{\frac{4}{11}}} \cdot \left[\dfrac{3x}{x^2+2} + \dfrac{8x}{9\left(x^2+9\right)} - \dfrac{12\left(x^2+2\right)}{11x\left(x^2+6\right)}\right]$

29. $y = \left(x^x\right)^x = x^{x^2}$

$\ln y = \ln x^{x^2} = x^2 \ln x$

$\dfrac{y'}{y} = x^2 \left(\dfrac{1}{x}\right) + (\ln x)(2x) = x + 2x \ln x$

$y' = y(x + 2x \ln x) = \left(x^x\right)^x (x + 2x \ln x)$

31. $y = (x+1)\ln x^2 = 2(x+1)\ln x$

$y' = 2\left[(x+1)\left(\dfrac{1}{x}\right) + (\ln x)(1)\right] = 2\left[\dfrac{x+1}{x} + \ln x\right]$

When $x = 1$, then $y' = 2\left[\dfrac{2}{1} + \ln 1\right] = 4$.

33. $y = e^{e + x \ln\left(\frac{1}{x}\right)} = e^{e - x \ln x}$

$y' = e^{e - x \ln x}\left(-\left[x\left(\dfrac{1}{x}\right) + (\ln x)(1)\right]\right)$

$= -(1 + \ln x)e^{e - x \ln x}$

When $x = e$, then $y' = -(1 + \ln e)e^{e - e \ln e} = -(2)e^0 = -2$.

35. $y = 3e^x$

$y' = 3e^x$

If $x = \ln 2$, then $y = 3e^{\ln 2} = 6$ and

$y' = 3e^{\ln 2} = 6$.

An equation of the tangent line is
$y - 6 = 6(x - \ln 2)$, $y = 6x + 6 - 6 \ln 2$,
$y = 6x + 6(1 - \ln 2)$. Alternatively, since
$6 \ln 2 = \ln 2^6 = \ln 64$, the tangent line can be
written as $y = 6x + 6 - \ln 64$.

37. $y = x\left(2^{2-x^2}\right)$. To find y' we shall use
logarithmic differentiation.

$\ln y = \ln\left[x\left(2^{2-x^2}\right)\right] = \ln x + \left(2 - x^2\right)\ln 2$

$\dfrac{y'}{y} = \dfrac{1}{x} + (-2x)\ln 2$

$y' = y\left[\dfrac{1}{x} - 2(\ln 2)x\right]$

When $x = 1$, then $y = 2$ and $y' = 2(1 - 2\ln 2)$.
Equation of tangent line is
$y - 2 = 2(1 - 2\ln 2)(x - 1)$. The y-intercept
of the tangent line corresponds to the point
where $x = 0$:
$y - 2 = 2(1 - 2\ln 2)(-1) = -2 + 4\ln 2$
Thus $y = 4\ln 2$ and then y-intercept is
$(0, 4\ln 2)$.

39. $y = e^{x^2-4}$

$y' = e^{x^2-4}[2x] = 2xe^{x^2-4}$

$y'' = 2\left(xe^{x^2-4}[2x] + e^{x^2-4} \cdot 1\right)$

$\quad = 2e^{x^2-4}\left(2x^2 + 1\right)$

At $(2, 1)$, $y'' = 2e^0(9) = 18$

41. $y = \ln(2x)$

$y' = \dfrac{1}{2x}(2) = x^{-1}$

$y'' = -1 \cdot x^{-2} = -x^{-2}$

$y''' = -(-2)x^{-3} = \dfrac{2}{x^3}$

At $(1, \ln 2)$, $y''' = \dfrac{2}{1^3} = 2$

43. $2xy + y^2 = 10$

$2(xy' + y) + 2yy' = 0$

$2xy' + 2yy' = -2y$

$(x + y)y' = -y$

$y' = -\dfrac{y}{x + y}$

45. $\ln\left(xy^2\right) = xy$

$\ln x + 2\ln y = xy$

$\dfrac{1}{x} + \dfrac{2}{y}y' = xy' + y$

$y + 2xy' = x^2yy' + xy^2$

$2xy' - x^2yy' = xy^2 - y$

$\left(2x - x^2y\right)y' = xy^2 - y$

$y' = \dfrac{xy^2 - y}{2x - x^2y}$

47. $x + xy + y = 5$

$1 + xy' + y(1) + y' = 0$

$(x + 1)y' = -1 - y$

$y' = -\dfrac{1 + y}{x + 1}$

$y'' = -\dfrac{(x + 1)y' - (1 + y)}{(x + 1)^2}$

At $(2, 1)$, $y' = -\dfrac{1 + 1}{2 + 1} = -\dfrac{2}{3}$ and

$y'' = -\dfrac{3\left(-\frac{2}{3}\right) - 2}{9} = \dfrac{4}{9}$

49. $e^y = (y + 1)e^x$

$e^y y' = (y + 1)e^x + e^x(y')$

$e^y y' - e^x y' = (y + 1)e^x$

$\left(e^y - e^x\right)y' = (y + 1)e^x$

$y' = \dfrac{(y + 1)e^x}{e^y - e^x} = \dfrac{(y + 1)\left(\frac{e^y}{y+1}\right)}{e^y - \left(\frac{e^y}{y+1}\right)} = \dfrac{e^y}{e^y - \frac{e^y}{y+1}}$

$\quad = \dfrac{1}{1 - \frac{1}{y+1}} = \dfrac{y + 1}{y}$

$y'' = \dfrac{y(y') - (y + 1)(y')}{y^2} = \dfrac{-y'}{y^2} = -\dfrac{\frac{y+1}{y}}{y^2}$

$\quad = -\dfrac{y + 1}{y^3}$

51. $f'(t) = 0.8e^{-0.01t}(-0.01) - 0.2e^{-0.0002t}(-0.0002)$

$\quad = 0.008e^{-0.0.1t} + 0.00004e^{-0.0002t}$

53. $f'(x) = 12\left(3x^3 + x^2 - 3\right)e^{9x^4 + 4x^3 - 36x}$

$f'(x) = 0$ when $x \approx 0.90$

Mathematical Snapshot Chapter 13

1. Figure 13.4 does not readily show how long
    it takes for the population to reach its final
    size. Fig. 13.5 shows that this takes about
    45 days.

3. Even if the graph starts out exactly
    coinciding with the ideal curve, a line
    segment tangent to the curve at one end must
    (in general) lie slightly off the curve at the
    other end. This introduces errors that
    accumulate over successive iterations. The
    amount of cumulative error could be reduced
    by taking smaller time steps, such as
    1 month instead of 1 year, and
    correspondingly drawing shorter line
    segments.

Chapter 14

Principles in Practice 14.1

1. The graph of $c(q) = 2q^3 - 21q^2 + 60q + 500$ is shown.

There looks to be a relative maximum at $q = 2$ and a relative minimum at $q = 5$.
$$c'(q) = 6q^2 - 42q + 60 = 6(q^2 - 7q + 10)$$
$$= 6(q - 5)(q - 2)$$
$c'(q) = 0$ when $q = 2$ or $q = 5$. If $q < 2$, then $c'(q) = 6(-)(-) = +$, so $c(q)$ is increasing. If $2 < q < 5$, then $c'(q) = 6(+)(-) = -$, so $c(q)$ is decreasing. If $5 < q$, then $c'(q) = 6(+)(+) = +$, so $c(q)$ is increasing. When $q = 2$, there is a relative maximum, since $c'(q)$ changes from + to −. The relative maximum value is
$$2(2)^3 - 21(2)^2 + 60(2) + 500 = 552.$$ When $q = 5$, there is a relative minimum, since $c'(q)$ changes from − to +. The relative minimum value is
$$2(5)^3 - 21(5)^2 + 60(5) + 500 = 525.$$

2. First, find $C'(t)$, with $C(t) = \dfrac{0.14t}{(t+2)^2}$.

$$C'(t) = \frac{0.14(t+2)^2 - 0.14t(2)(t+2)}{(t+2)^4}$$
$$= \frac{0.14(t+2) - 0.28t}{(t+2)^3} = \frac{0.28 - 0.14t}{(t+2)^3}$$
$$= \frac{0.14(2-t)}{(t+2)^3}$$

$C'(t) = 0$ when $t = 2$ and is undefined when $t = -2$. However, since t denotes the number of hours after an injection, negative values of t are not reasonable. If $0 \le t < 2$,
$C'(t) = \dfrac{+}{+} = +$, so $C(t)$ is increasing. If $2 < t$,
$C'(t) = \dfrac{-}{+} = -$, so $C(t)$ is decreasing. When $t = 2$, there is a relative maximum, since $C'(t)$ changes from + to −. The drug is at its greatest concentration 2 hours after the injection.

Exercise 14.1

1. Decreasing on $(-\infty, -1)$ and $(3, \infty)$; increasing on $(-1, 3)$; relative minimum $(-1, -1)$; relative maximum $(3, 4)$.

3. Decreasing on $(-\infty, -2)$ and $(0, 2)$; increasing on $(-2, 0)$ and $(2, \infty)$; relative minimum $(-2, 1)$ and $(2, 1)$; no relative maximum.

5. $f'(x) = (x+1)(x-3)$
$f'(x) = 0$ when $x = -1, 3$.
CV: $x = -1, 3$

$$\begin{array}{ccc} + & - & + \\ \hline & & \\ -1 & & 3 \end{array}$$

Increasing on $(-\infty, -1)$ and $(3, \infty)$; decreasing on $(-1, 3)$; relative maximum when $x = -1$; relative minimum when $x = 3$.

7. $f'(x) = (x+1)(x-3)^2$
CV: $x = -1, 3$

$$\begin{array}{ccc} - & + & + \\ \hline & & \\ -1 & & 3 \end{array}$$

Decreasing on $(-\infty, -1)$; increasing on $(-1, 3)$ and $(3, \infty)$; relative minimum when $x = -1$.

9. $y = x^3 + 3$

$y' = 3x^2$

CV: $x = 0$

$$\frac{\quad + \quad\quad + \quad}{0}$$

Increasing on $(-\infty, 0)$; increasing on $(0, \infty)$; no relative maximum or minimum.

11. $y = x - x^2 + 2$

$y' = 1 - 2x$

CV: $x = \dfrac{1}{2}$

$$\frac{\quad + \quad\quad - \quad}{\frac{1}{2}}$$

Increasing on $\left(-\infty, \dfrac{1}{2}\right)$; decreasing on

$\left(\dfrac{1}{2}, \infty\right)$; relative maximum when $x = \dfrac{1}{2}$.

13. $y = -\dfrac{x^3}{3} - 2x^2 + 5x - 2$

$y' = -x^2 - 4x + 5 = -\left(x^2 + 4x - 5\right)$

$\quad = -(x + 5)(x - 1)$

CV: $x = -5, 1$

$$\frac{\quad - \quad + \quad - \quad}{-5 \quad\quad 1}$$

Decreasing on $(-\infty, -5)$ and $(1, \infty)$; increasing on $(-5, 1)$; relative minimum when $x = -5$; relative maximum when $x = 1$.

15. $y = x^4 - 2x^2$

$y' = 4x^3 - 4x = 4x\left(x^2 - 1\right) = 4x(x + 1)(x - 1)$

CV: $x = 0, \pm 1$

$$\frac{\quad - \quad + \quad - \quad + \quad}{-1 \quad 0 \quad 1}$$

Decreasing on $(-\infty, -1)$ and $(0, 1)$; increasing on $(-1, 0)$ and $(1, \infty)$; relative maximum when $x = 0$; relative minima when $x = \pm 1$.

17. $y = x^3 - 6x^2 + 9x$

$y' = 3x^2 - 12x + 9 = 3\left(x^2 - 4x + 3\right)$

$\quad = 3(x - 1)(x - 3)$

CV: $x = 1, 3$

$$\frac{\quad + \quad - \quad + \quad}{1 \quad\quad 3}$$

Increasing on $(-\infty, 1)$ and $(3, \infty)$; decreasing on $(1, 3)$; relative maximum when $x = 1$; relative minimum when $x = 3$.

19. $y = 2x^3 - \dfrac{11}{2}x^2 - 10x + 2$

$y' = 6x^2 - 11x - 10 = (2x - 5)(3x + 2)$

CV: $x = -\dfrac{2}{3}, \dfrac{5}{2}$

$$\frac{\quad + \quad - \quad + \quad}{-\frac{2}{3} \quad \frac{5}{2}}$$

Increasing on $\left(-\infty, -\dfrac{2}{3}\right)$ and $\left(\dfrac{5}{2}, \infty\right)$;

decreasing on $\left(-\dfrac{2}{3}, \dfrac{5}{2}\right)$; relative maximum

when $x = -\dfrac{2}{3}$; relative minimum when

$x = \dfrac{5}{2}$.

21. $y = x^3 + 2x^2 - x - 1$

$y' = 3x^2 + 4x - 1$

Setting $y' = 0$ gives $3x^2 + 4x - 1 = 0$. By the quadratic formula,

$x = \dfrac{-4 \pm 2\sqrt{7}}{6} = \dfrac{-2 \pm \sqrt{7}}{3}$.

CV: $x = \dfrac{-2 \pm \sqrt{7}}{3}$

$$\frac{\quad + \quad - \quad + \quad}{\frac{-2 - \sqrt{7}}{3} \quad \frac{-2 + \sqrt{7}}{3}}$$

Increasing on $\left(-\infty, \dfrac{-2-\sqrt{7}}{3}\right)$ and

$\left(\dfrac{-2+\sqrt{7}}{3}, \infty\right)$; decreasing on

$\left(\dfrac{-2-\sqrt{7}}{3}, \dfrac{-2+\sqrt{7}}{3}\right)$; relative maximum

when $x = \dfrac{-2-\sqrt{7}}{3}$; relative minimum when

$x = \dfrac{-2+\sqrt{7}}{3}$.

23. $y = 3x^5 - 5x^3$

$y' = 15x^4 - 15x^2 = 15x^2(x+1)(x-1)$

CV: $x = 0, \pm1$

$$\begin{array}{ccccc} + & - & - & + \\ \hline & -1 & 0 & 1 \end{array}$$

Increasing on $(-\infty, -1)$ and $(1, \infty)$; decreasing on $(-1, 0)$ and $(0, 1)$; relative maximum when $x = -1$; relative minimum when $x = 1$.

25. $y = -x^5 - 5x^4 + 200$

$y' = -5x^4 - 20x^3 = -5x^3(x+4)$

CV: $x = 0, -4$

$$\begin{array}{ccc} - & + & - \\ \hline & -4 & 0 \end{array}$$

Decreasing on $(-\infty, -4)$ and $(0, \infty)$; increasing on $(-4, 0)$; relative minimum when $x = -4$; relative maximum when $x = 0$.

27. $y = 8x^4 - x^8$

$y' = 32x^3 - 8x^7 = 8x^3\left(4 - x^4\right)$

$= 8x^3\left(2 + x^2\right)\left(2 - x^2\right)$

$= 8x^3\left(2 + x^2\right)\left(\sqrt{2} - x\right)\left(\sqrt{2} + x\right)$

CV: $x = 0, \pm\sqrt{2}$

$$\begin{array}{cccc} + & - & + & - \\ \hline & -\sqrt{2} & 0 & \sqrt{2} \end{array}$$

Increasing on $\left(-\infty, -\sqrt{2}\right)$ and $\left(0, \sqrt{2}\right)$;

decreasing on $\left(-\sqrt{2}, 0\right)$ and $\left(\sqrt{2}, \infty\right)$;

relative maximum when $x = \pm\sqrt{2}$, relative minimum when $x = 0$.

29. $y = \left(x^3 + 1\right)^3$

$y' = 9x^2\left(x^3 + 1\right)^2$

$= 9x^2(x+1)^2\left(x^2 - x + 1\right)^2$

CV: $0, -1$

$$\begin{array}{ccc} + & + & + \\ \hline & -1 & 0 \end{array}$$

Increasing on $(-\infty, -1)$, $(-1, 0)$, and $(0, \infty)$; never decreasing; no relative extremum.

31. $y = \dfrac{5}{x-1} = 5(x-1)^{-1}$

$y' = -5(x-1)^{-2} = -\dfrac{5}{(x-1)^2}$

CV: None, but $x = 1$ must be included in the sign chart because it is a point of discontinuity of y.

$$\begin{array}{cc} - & - \\ \hline & \boxed{1} \end{array}$$

Decreasing on $(-\infty, 1)$ and $(1, \infty)$; no relative extremum.

33. $y = \dfrac{10}{\sqrt{x}} = 10x^{-\frac{1}{2}}$. [Note: $x > 0$]

$y' = -5x^{-\frac{3}{2}} = -\dfrac{5}{\sqrt{x^3}} < 0$ for $x > 0$.

Decreasing on $(0, \infty)$; no relative extremum.

35. $y = \dfrac{x^2}{2-x}$

$y' = \dfrac{(2-x)(2x) - x^2(-1)}{(2-x)^2} = \dfrac{x(4-x)}{(2-x)^2}$

CV: $x = 0, 4$, but $x = 2$ must be included in the sign chart because it is a point of discontinuity of y.

$$\begin{array}{cccc} - & + & + & - \\ \hline & 0 & \boxed{2} & 4 \end{array}$$

Decreasing on $(-\infty, 0)$ and $(4, \infty)$; increasing on $(0, 2)$ and $(2, 4)$; relative minimum when $x = 0$; relative maximum when $x = 4$.

37. $y = \dfrac{x^2 - 3}{x + 2}$

$$y' = \dfrac{(x+2)(2x) - \left(x^2 - 3\right)(1)}{(x+2)^2}$$

$$= \dfrac{x^2 + 4x + 3}{(x+2)^2} = \dfrac{(x+1)(x+3)}{(x+2)^2}$$

CV: $x = -3, -1$, but $x = -2$ must be included in the sign chart because it is a point of discontinuity of y.

$$\begin{array}{ccccc} + & - & - & + \\ \hline & -3 & \boxed{-2} & -1 & \end{array}$$

Increasing on $(-\infty, -3)$ and $(-1, \infty)$; decreasing on $(-3, -2)$ and $(-2, -1)$; relative maximum when $x = -3$; relative minimum when $x = -1$.

39. $y = \dfrac{5x + 2}{x^2 + 1}$

$$y' = \dfrac{\left(x^2 + 1\right)(5) - (5x + 2)(2x)}{\left(x^2 + 1\right)^2}$$

$$= \dfrac{-5x^2 - 4x + 5}{\left(x^2 + 1\right)^2}$$

$y' = 0$ when $-5x^2 - 4x + 5 = 0$; by the

quadratic formula, $x = \dfrac{-2 \pm \sqrt{29}}{5}$

CV: $x = \dfrac{-2 \pm \sqrt{29}}{5}$

$$\begin{array}{ccc} - & + & - \\ \hline \frac{-2-\sqrt{29}}{5} & & \frac{-2+\sqrt{29}}{5} \end{array}$$

Decreasing on $\left(-\infty, \dfrac{-2 - \sqrt{29}}{5}\right)$ and

$\left(\dfrac{-2 + \sqrt{29}}{5}, \infty\right)$; increasing on

$\left(\dfrac{-2 - \sqrt{29}}{5}, \dfrac{-2 + \sqrt{29}}{5}\right)$; relative minimum

when $x = \dfrac{-2 - \sqrt{29}}{5}$; relative maximum

when $x = \dfrac{-2 + \sqrt{29}}{5}$.

41. $y = (x + 2)^3 (x - 5)^2$

y'

$$= (x+2)^3 [(2)(x-5)] + (x-5)^2 \left[(3)\left(x+2\right)^2\right]$$

$$= (x+2)^2 (x-5)[2(x+2) + 3(x-5)]$$

$$= (x+2)^2 (x-5)(5x - 11)$$

CV: $x = -2, 5, \dfrac{11}{5}$

$$\begin{array}{cccc} + & + & - & + \\ \hline -2 & \frac{11}{5} & 5 & \end{array}$$

Increasing on $(-\infty, -2)$, $\left(-2, \dfrac{11}{5}\right)$ and $(5, \infty)$;

decreasing on $\left(\dfrac{11}{5}, 5\right)$; relative maximum

when $x = \dfrac{11}{5}$; relative minimum when $x = 5$.

43. $y = x^3 (x - 6)^4$

$$y' = x^3 \left[4(x - 6)^3\right] + (x - 6)^4 \left(3x^2\right)$$

$$= x^2 (x - 6)^3 [4x + 3(x - 6)]$$

$$= x^2 (x - 6)^3 (7x - 18)$$

CV: $x = 0, 6, \dfrac{18}{7}$

$$\begin{array}{cccc} + & + & - & + \\ \hline 0 & \frac{18}{7} & 6 & \end{array}$$

Increasing on $(-\infty, 0)$, $\left(0, \dfrac{18}{7}\right)$, and $(6, \infty)$;

decreasing on $\left(\dfrac{18}{7}, 6\right)$; relative maximum

when $x = \dfrac{18}{7}$; relative minimum when $x = 6$.

45. $y = e^{-2x}$

$y' = -2e^{-2x} < 0$ for all x. Thus decreasing on $(-\infty, \infty)$; no relative extremum.

47. $y = x^2 - 9\ln x$. [Note: $x > 0$.]

$y' = 2x - \dfrac{9}{x} = \dfrac{2x^2 - 9}{x}$

CV: $x = \dfrac{3\sqrt{2}}{2}$

$$\begin{array}{c} \quad - \quad + \\ \hline \quad | \quad \\ 0 \;\; \frac{3\sqrt{2}}{2} \end{array}$$

Decreasing on $\left(0, \dfrac{3\sqrt{2}}{2}\right)$; increasing on

$\left(\dfrac{3\sqrt{2}}{2}, \infty\right)$; relative minimum when

$x = \dfrac{3\sqrt{2}}{2}$.

49. $y = e^x + e^{-x}$

$y' = e^x - e^{-x}$

Setting $y' = 0$ gives $e^x - e^{-x} = 0$,

$e^x = e^{-x}$,

$x = -x$, $x = 0$

CV: $x = 0$

$$\begin{array}{c} \quad - \quad + \\ \hline \quad | \quad \\ 0 \end{array}$$

Decreasing on $(-\infty, 0)$; increasing on $(0, \infty)$; relative minimum when $x = 0$.

51. $y = x\ln x - x$. [Note: $x > 0$.]

$y' = \left[x \cdot \dfrac{1}{x} + (\ln x)(1)\right] - 1 = \ln x$

CV: $x = 1$

$$\begin{array}{c} \quad - \quad + \\ \hline \quad | \quad | \\ 0 \;\; 1 \end{array}$$

Decreasing on $(0, 1)$; increasing on $(1, \infty)$; relative minimum when $x = 1$; no relative maximum.

53. $y = x^2 - 6x - 7 = (x - 7)(x + 1)$

Intercepts $(7, 0)$, $(-1, 0)$, $(0, -7)$

$y' = 2x - 6 = 2(x - 3)$

CV: $x = 3$

Decreasing on $(-\infty, 3)$; increasing on $(3, \infty)$; relative minimum when $x = 3$.

55. $y = 3x - x^3 = x\left(\sqrt{3} + x\right)\left(\sqrt{3} - x\right)$

Intercepts: $(0, 0)$, $\left(\pm\sqrt{3}, 0\right)$

Symmetric about origin.

$y' = 3 - 3x^2 = 3(1 + x)(1 - x)$

CV: $x = \pm 1$

Decreasing on $(-\infty, -1)$ and $(1, \infty)$; increasing on $(-1, 1)$; relative minimum when $x = -1$; relative maximum when $x = 1$.

57. $y = 2x^3 - 9x^2 + 12x = x\left(2x^2 - 9x + 12\right)$

Note that $2x^2 - 9x + 12 = 0$ has no real roots. The only intercept is $(0, 0)$.

$y' = 6x^2 - 18x + 12 = 6\left(x^2 - 3x + 2\right)$

$= 6(x - 2)(x - 1)$

CV: $x = 1, 2$

Increasing on $(-\infty, 1)$ and $(2, \infty)$; decreasing on $(1, 2)$; relative maximum when $x = 1$; relative minimum when $x = 2$.

59. $y = x^4 + 4x^3 + 4x^2 = x^2(x + 2)^2$

Intercepts $(0, 0)$, $(-2, 0)$

$y' = 4x^3 + 12x^2 + 8x = 4x(x + 1)(x + 2)$

CV: $x = 0, -1, -2$

Increasing on $(-2, -1)$ and $(0, \infty)$; decreasing on $(-\infty, -2)$ and $(-1, 0)$; relative maximum when $x = -1$; relative minimum when $x = -2$ or $x = 0$.

61. $y = (x - 1)^2(x + 2)^2$

Intercepts: $(1, 0)$, $(-2, 0)$, $(0, 4)$

$y' = (x - 1)^2 \cdot 2(x + 2) + (x + 2)^2 \cdot 2(x - 1)$

$= 2(x - 1)(x + 2)[(x - 1) + (x + 2)]$

$= 2(x - 1)(x + 2)(2x + 1)$

CV: $x = 1, -2, -\dfrac{1}{2}$

Decreasing on $(-\infty, -2)$ and $\left(-\dfrac{1}{2}, 1\right)$;

increasing on $\left(-2, -\dfrac{1}{2}\right)$ and $(1, \infty)$;

relative minimum when $x = -2$ or $x = 1$;

relative maximum when $x = -\dfrac{1}{2}$.

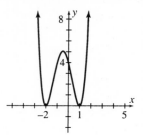

63. $y = 2\sqrt{x} - x = \sqrt{x}\left(2 - \sqrt{x}\right)$. [Note: $x \geq 0$.]

Intercepts $(0, 0)$, $(4, 0)$

$y' = \dfrac{1}{\sqrt{x}} - 1 = \dfrac{1 - \sqrt{x}}{\sqrt{x}}$

CV: $x = 0, 1$

Increasing on $(0, 1)$; decreasing on $(1, \infty)$; relative maximum when $x = 1$.

65.

67. $c_f = 25,000$

$\bar{c}_f = \dfrac{c_f}{q} = \dfrac{25,000}{q}$

$\dfrac{d}{dq}\left(\bar{c}_f\right) = -\dfrac{25,000}{q^2} < 0$ for $q > 0$, so $\bar{c}_f$ is a

decreasing function for $q > 0$.

69. $p = 400 - 2q$

Revenue is given by $r = pq = (400 - 2q)q$.

$$= 400q - 2q^2$$

Marginal revenue is $r' = 400 - 4q$. Marginal revenue is increasing when its derivative is positive. But $(r')' = -4 < 0$. Thus marginal revenue is never increasing.

71. $r = 240q + 57q^2 - q^3$

$r' = 240 + 114q - 3q^2 = 0$

$3(40 - q)(2 + q) = 0$

Since $q \geq 0$, we have $q = 40$ as the only CV. Since r is increasing on $(0, 40)$ and decreasing on $(40, \infty)$, r is a maximum when output is 40.

73. $E = 0.71\left(1 - \dfrac{T_c}{T_h}\right)$

$\dfrac{dE}{dT_h} = 0.71\left(\dfrac{T_c}{T_h^2}\right) > 0$, so as T_h increases,

E increases.

75. $C(k) = 100\left[100 + 9k + \dfrac{144}{k}\right]$, $1 \leq k \leq 100$

a. $C(1) = 25,300$

b. $C'(k) = 100\left[9 - \dfrac{144}{k^2}\right]$

$= 100\left[\dfrac{9k^2 - 144}{k^2}\right]$

$= 100\left[\dfrac{9(k + 4)(k - 4)}{k^2}\right]$

Since $k \geq 1$, the only critical value is $k = 4$. If $1 \leq k < 4$, then $C'(k) < 0$ and C is decreasing. If $4 < k \leq 100$, then $C'(k) > 0$ and C is increasing. Thus C has an absolute minimum for $k = 4$.

c. $C(4) = 17,200$

77. Relative minimum: $(-4.10, -2.21)$

79. Relative maximum: $(2.74, 3.74)$; relative minimum: $(-2.74, -3.74)$

81. Relative minimum: 0, 1.50, 2.00; relative maximum: 0.57, 1.77

83. a. $f'(x) = 4 - 6x - 3x^2$

b.

c. $f'(x) > 0$ on $(-2.53, 0.53)$; $f'(x) < 0$ on $(-\infty, -2.53)$, $(0.53, \infty)$, f is inc. on $(-2.53, 0.53)$; f is dec. on $(-\infty, -2.53)$, $(0.53, \infty)$.

d.

Exercise 14.2

1. $f(x) = x^2 - 2x + 3$ and f is continuous over $[0, 3]$.

$f'(x) = 2x - 2 = 2(x - 1)$

The only critical value on the interval $[0, 3]$ is $x = 1$. We evaluate f at this point and at the endpoints: $f(0) = 3$, $f(1) = 2$, and $f(3) = 6$.

Absolute maximum: $f(3) = 6$; absolute minimum: $f(1) = 2$

3. $f(x) = \dfrac{1}{3}x^3 - x^2 - 3x + 1$ and f is

continuous over [0, 2].

$f'(x) = x^2 - 2x - 3 = (x+1)(x-3)$

There are no critical values on (0, 2), so we only have to evaluate f at the endpoints:

$f(0) = 1$ and $f(2) = -\dfrac{19}{3}$.

Absolute maximum: $f(0) = 1$;

absolute minimum: $f(2) = -\dfrac{19}{3}$

5. $f(x) = 4x^3 + 3x^2 - 18x + 3$ and f is

continuous over $\left[\dfrac{1}{2}, 3\right]$.

$f'(x) = 12x^2 + 6x - 18 = 6\left(2x^2 + x - 3\right)$

$= 6(2x+3)(x-1)$

The only critical value on $\left(\dfrac{1}{2}, 3\right)$ is $x = 1$.

We evaluate f at this point and the

endpoints: $f\left(\dfrac{1}{2}\right) = -\dfrac{19}{4}$;

$f(1) = -8$, $f(3) = 84$.

Absolute maximum: $f(3) = 84$;

absolute minimum: $f(1) = -8$

7. $f(x) = -3x^5 + 5x^3$ and f is continuous over

[–2, 0].

$f'(x) = -15x^4 + 15x^2 = 15x^2\left(1 - x^2\right)$

$= 15x^2(1+x)(1-x)$

The only critical value on (–2, 0) is

$x = -1$. We have $f(-2) = 56$, $f(-1) = -2$,

and $f(0) = 0$.

Absolute maximum: $f(-2) = 56$;

absolute minimum: $f(-1) = -2$.

9. $f(x) = 3x^4 - x^6$ and f is continuous over

[–1, 2].

$f'(x) = 12x^3 - 6x^5 = 6x^3\left(2 - x^2\right)$

$= 6x^3\left(\sqrt{2} - x\right)\left(\sqrt{2} + x\right)$

The only critical values on (–1, 2) are $x = 0$,

$\sqrt{2}$. We have $f(-1) = 2$, $f(0) = 0$,

$f\left(\sqrt{2}\right) = 4$, and $f(2) = -16$.

Absolute maximum: $f\left(\sqrt{2}\right) = 4$;

absolute minimum: $f(2) = -16$

11. $f(x) = x^4 - 9x^2 + 2$ and f is continuous

over [–1, 3].

$f'(x) = 4x^3 - 18x = 2x\left(2x^2 - 9\right)$

$= 2x\left(\sqrt{2}x - 3\right)\left(\sqrt{2}x + 3\right)$

The only critical values on (–1, 3) are $x = 0$

and $x = \dfrac{3}{\sqrt{2}} = \dfrac{3\sqrt{2}}{2}$. We have $f(-1) = -6$,

$f(0) = 2$, $f\left(\dfrac{3\sqrt{2}}{2}\right) = -\dfrac{73}{4}$, and $f(3) = 2$.

Thus there is an absolute maximum when

$x = 0$ or $x = 3$, and an absolute minimum

when $x = \dfrac{3\sqrt{2}}{2}$.

Absolute maximum: $f(0) = f(3) = 2$;

absolute minimum: $f\left(\dfrac{3\sqrt{2}}{2}\right) = -\dfrac{73}{4}$

13. $f(x) = x^{\frac{2}{3}}$ and f is continuous over [–2, 3].

Absolute maximum: $f(3) \approx 2.08$;

absolute minimum: $f(0) = 0$

15.

a. −3.22, −0.78

b. 2.75

c. 9

d. 14,283

Exercise 14.3

1. $f(x) = x^4 - 3x^3 + 7x - 5$

$f''(x) = 6x(2x - 3)$

$f''(x)$ is 0 when $x = 0, \frac{3}{2}$. Sign chart for

f'':

$$\begin{array}{ccc} + & - & + \\ \hline & 0 & \frac{3}{2} \end{array}$$

Concave up on $(-\infty, 0)$ and $\left(\frac{3}{2}, \infty\right)$; concave

down on $\left(0, \frac{3}{2}\right)$. Inflection points when

$x = 0, \frac{3}{2}$.

3. $f(x) = \dfrac{2 + x - x^2}{x^2 - 2x + 1}$

$f''(x) = \dfrac{2(7 - x)}{(x - 1)^4}$

$f''(x)$ is 0 when $x = 7$. Although f'' is not
defined when $x = 1$, f is not continuous at
$x = 1$. So there is no inflection point when
$x = 1$, but $x = 1$ must be considered in
concavity analysis. Sign chart for f'':

$$\begin{array}{ccc} + & + & - \\ \hline & \boxed{1} & 7 \end{array}$$

Concave up on $(-\infty, 1)$ and $(1, 7)$; concave
down on $(7, \infty)$. Inflection point when $x = 7$.

5. $f(x) = \dfrac{x^2 + 1}{x^2 - 2}$

$f''(x) = \dfrac{6(3x^2 + 2)}{(x^2 - 2)^3} = \dfrac{6(3x^2 + 2)}{\left[(x - \sqrt{2})(x + \sqrt{2})\right]^3}$

$f''(x)$ is never 0. Although f'' is not
defined when $x = \pm\sqrt{2}$, f is not continuous
at $x = \pm\sqrt{2}$. So there is no inflection point
when $x = \pm\sqrt{2}$, but $x = \pm\sqrt{2}$ must be
considered in concavity analysis. Sign chart
of f'':

$$\begin{array}{ccc} + & - & + \\ \hline & \boxed{-\sqrt{2}} & \boxed{\sqrt{2}} \end{array}$$

Concave up on $\left(-\infty, -\sqrt{2}\right)$ and $\left(\sqrt{2}, \infty\right)$;
concave down on $\left(-\sqrt{2}, \sqrt{2}\right)$. No inflection
point.

7. $y = -2x^2 + 4x$

$y' = -4x + 4$

$y'' = -4 < 0$ for all x, so the graph is
concave down for all x, that is, on $(-\infty, \infty)$.

9. $y = 4x^3 + 12x^2 - 12x$

$y' = 12x^2 + 24x - 12$

$y'' = 24x + 24 = 24(x + 1)$

Possible inflection point when $x = -1$.
Concave down on $(-\infty, -1)$: concave up on
$(-1, \infty)$; inflection point when $x = -1$.

11. $y = 4x^3 - 21x^2 + 5x$

$y' = 12x^2 - 42x + 5$

$y'' = 24x - 42 = 24\left(x - \frac{7}{4}\right)$

Possible inflection point when $x = \frac{7}{4}$.

Concave down on $\left(-\infty, \frac{7}{4}\right)$; concave up on

$\left(\frac{7}{4}, \infty\right)$; inflection point when $x = \frac{7}{4}$.

13. $y = x^4 - 6x^2 + 5x - 6$

$y' = 4x^3 - 12x + 5$

$y'' = 12x^2 - 12 = 12(x^2 - 1) = 12(x + 1)(x - 1)$

Possible inflection points when $x = \pm 1$.
Concave up on $(-\infty, -1)$ and $(1, \infty)$; concave down on $(-1, 1)$; inflection points when $x = \pm 1$.

15. $y = 2x^{\frac{1}{5}}$

$y' = \frac{2}{5} x^{-\frac{4}{5}}$

$y'' = -\frac{8}{25} x^{-\frac{9}{5}} = -\frac{8}{25x^{\frac{9}{5}}}$

y'' is not defined when $x = 0$ and y is continuous there. Thus there is a possible inflection point when $x = 0$. Concave up on $(-\infty, 0)$; concave down on $(0, \infty)$; inflection point when $x = 0$.

17. $y = \frac{x^4}{2} + \frac{19x^3}{6} - \frac{7x^2}{2} + x + 5$

$y' = 2x^3 + \frac{19}{2} x^2 - 7x + 1$

$y'' = 6x^2 + 19x - 7 = (3x - 1)(2x + 7)$

Possible inflection points when $x = -\frac{7}{2}, \frac{1}{3}$.

Concave up on $\left(-\infty, -\frac{7}{2}\right)$ and $\left(\frac{1}{3}, \infty\right)$;

concave down on $\left(-\frac{7}{2}, \frac{1}{3}\right)$; inflection points

when $x = -\frac{7}{2}, \frac{1}{3}$.

19. $y = \frac{1}{20} x^5 - \frac{1}{4} x^4 + \frac{1}{6} x^3 - \frac{1}{2} x - \frac{2}{3}$

$y' = \frac{1}{4} x^4 - x^3 + \frac{1}{2} x^2 - \frac{1}{2}$

$y'' = x^3 - 3x^2 + x = x(x^2 - 3x + 1)$

y'' is 0 when $x = 0$ or $x^2 - 3x + 1 = 0$.
Using the quadratic formula to solve

$x^2 - 3x + 1 = 0$ gives $x = \frac{3 \pm \sqrt{5}}{2}$.

Thus possible inflection points occur when

$x = 0, \frac{3 \pm \sqrt{5}}{2}$. Concave down on $(-\infty, 0)$

and $\left(\frac{3 - \sqrt{5}}{2}, \frac{3 + \sqrt{5}}{2}\right)$; concave up on

$\left(0, \frac{3 - \sqrt{5}}{2}\right)$ and $\left(\frac{3 + \sqrt{5}}{2}, \infty\right)$; inflection

points when $x = 0, \frac{3 \pm \sqrt{5}}{2}$.

21. $y = \frac{1}{30} x^6 - \frac{7}{12} x^4 + 5x^2 + 2x - 1$

$y' = \frac{1}{5} x^5 - \frac{7}{3} x^3 + 10x + 2$

$y'' = x^4 - 7x^2 + 10 = (x^2 - 2)(x^2 - 5)$

$= (x + \sqrt{2})(x - \sqrt{2})(x + \sqrt{5})(x - \sqrt{5})$

Possible inflection points when
$x = \pm\sqrt{2}, \pm\sqrt{5}$. Concave up on

$(-\infty, -\sqrt{5}), (-\sqrt{2}, \sqrt{2})$, and $(\sqrt{5}, \infty)$;

concave down on $(-\sqrt{5}, -\sqrt{2})$ and

$(\sqrt{2}, \sqrt{5})$; inflection points when

$x = \pm\sqrt{5}, \pm\sqrt{2}$.

23. $y = \frac{x + 1}{x - 1}$

$y' = \frac{-2}{(x - 1)^2}$

$y'' = \frac{4}{(x - 1)^3}$

No possible inflection point, but we consider $x = 1$ in the concavity analysis. Concave down on $(-\infty, 1)$; concave up on $(1, \infty)$.

25. $y = \dfrac{4x^2}{x^2 + 1}$

$y' = \dfrac{\left(x^2 + 1\right)(8x) - 4x^2(2x)}{\left(x^2 + 1\right)^2} = \dfrac{8x}{\left(x^2 + 1\right)^2}$

$y'' = \dfrac{\left(x^2 + 1\right)^2(8) - 2x(2)\left(x^2 + 1\right)(8x)}{\left(x^2 + 1\right)^4}$

$= \dfrac{\left(x^2 + 1\right)(8) - 32x^2}{\left(x^2 + 1\right)^3}$

$= \dfrac{8\left(1 - 3x^2\right)}{\left(x^2 + 1\right)^3} = \dfrac{8\left(1 + \sqrt{3}x\right)\left(1 - \sqrt{3}x\right)}{\left(x^2 + 1\right)^3}$

Possible inflection points when $x = \pm\dfrac{1}{\sqrt{3}}$.

Concave down on $\left(-\infty, -\dfrac{1}{\sqrt{3}}\right)$ and

$\left(\dfrac{1}{\sqrt{3}}, \infty\right)$; concave up on $\left(-\dfrac{1}{\sqrt{3}}, \dfrac{1}{\sqrt{3}}\right)$;

inflection points when $x = \pm\dfrac{1}{\sqrt{3}}$.

27. $y = \dfrac{21x + 40}{6(x + 3)^2}$

$y' = \dfrac{1}{6} \cdot \dfrac{(x + 3)^2(21) - (21x + 40)[2(x + 3)]}{(x + 3)^4}$

$= \dfrac{1}{6} \cdot \dfrac{(x + 3)(21) - (21x + 40)(2)}{(x + 3)^3}$

$= \dfrac{1}{6} \cdot \dfrac{-21x - 17}{(x + 3)^3} = -\dfrac{1}{6} \cdot \dfrac{21x + 17}{(x + 3)^3}$

$y'' = -\dfrac{1}{6} \cdot \dfrac{(x + 3)^3(21) - (21x + 17)\left[3(x + 3)^2\right]}{(x + 3)^6}$

$= -\dfrac{1}{6} \cdot \dfrac{(x + 3)(21) - (21x + 17)(3)}{(x + 3)^4}$

$= -\dfrac{1}{6} \cdot \dfrac{-42x + 12}{(x + 3)^4} = \dfrac{7x - 2}{(x + 3)^4}$

Possible inflection point when $x = \dfrac{2}{7}$

($x = -3$ must be considered in concavity analysis). Concave down on $(-\infty, -3)$ and

$\left(-3, \dfrac{2}{7}\right)$; concave up on $\left(\dfrac{2}{7}, \infty\right)$; inflection

point when $x = \dfrac{2}{7}$.

29. $y = 5e^x$

$y' = 5e^x$

$y'' = 5e^x$

Thus $y'' > 0$ for all x. Concave up on $(-\infty, \infty)$.

31. $y = 3xe^x$

$y' = 3xe^x + 3e^x = 3e^x(x + 1)$

$y'' = 3e^x(1) + 3(x + 1)e^x = 3e^x(x + 2)$

$y'' = 0$ if $x = -2$. Concave down on $(-\infty, -2)$; concave up on $(-2, \infty)$; inflection point when $x = -2$.

33. $y = \dfrac{\ln x}{2x}$.   (Note: $x > 0$.)

$y' = \dfrac{2x \cdot \frac{1}{x} - (\ln x)(2)}{4x^2} = \dfrac{1 - \ln x}{2x^2}$

$y'' = \dfrac{2x^2\left(-\frac{1}{x}\right) - (1 - \ln x)(4x)}{4x^4}$

$= \dfrac{-2x - (1 - \ln x)(4x)}{4x^4}$

$= \dfrac{-1 - (1 - \ln x)(2)}{2x^3} = \dfrac{2\ln(x) - 3}{2x^3}$

y'' is 0 if $2\ln(x) - 3 = 0$, $\ln x = \dfrac{3}{2}$, $x = e^{\frac{3}{2}}$.

Concave down on $\left(0, e^{\frac{3}{2}}\right)$; concave up on

$\left(e^{\frac{3}{2}}, \infty\right)$; inflection point when $x = e^{\frac{3}{2}}$.

35. $y = x^2 + 4x + 3 = (x+3)(x+1)$

Intercepts $(-3, 0)$, $(-1, 0)$, and $(0, 3)$.

$y' = 2x + 4 = 2(x+2)$

CV: $x = -2$

Decreasing on $(-\infty, -2)$; increasing on $(-2, \infty)$; relative minimum at $(-2, -1)$.

$y'' = 2$

No possible inflection point. Concave up on $(-\infty, \infty)$.

37. $y = 4x - x^2 = x(4-x)$

Intercepts $(0, 0)$ and $(4, 0)$

$y' = 4 - 2x = 2(2-x)$

CV: $x = 2$

Increasing on $(-\infty, 2)$; decreasing on $(2, \infty)$; relative maximum at $(2, 4)$.

$y'' = -2$

No possible inflection point. Concave down on $(-\infty, \infty)$.

39. $y = x^3 - 9x^2 + 24x - 19$

The x-intercepts are not convenient to find; the y-intercept is $(0, -19)$.

$y' = 3x^2 - 18x + 24 = 3(x-2)(x-4)$

CV: $x = 2$ and $x = 4$

Increasing on $(-\infty, 2)$ and $(4, \infty)$; decreasing on $(2, 4)$; relative maximum at $(2, 1)$; relative minimum at $(4, -3)$.

$y'' = 6x - 18 = 6(x-3)$

Possible inflection point when $x = 3$. Concave down on $(-\infty, 3)$; concave up on $(3, \infty)$; inflection point at $(3, -1)$.

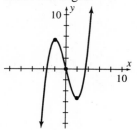

41. $y = \dfrac{x^3}{3} - 4x = \dfrac{x^3 - 12x}{3}$

$= \dfrac{1}{3}x\left(x + 2\sqrt{3}\right)\left(x - 2\sqrt{3}\right)$

Intercepts $(0, 0)$ and $\left(\pm 2\sqrt{3}, 0\right)$

$y' = x^2 - 4 = (x+2)(x-2)$

CV: $x = \pm 2$

Increasing on $(-\infty, -2)$ and $(2, \infty)$; decreasing on $(-2, 2)$; relative maximum at $\left(-2, \dfrac{16}{3}\right)$; relative minimum at $\left(2, -\dfrac{16}{3}\right)$.

$y'' = 2x$

Possible inflection point when $x = 0$. Concave down on $(-\infty, 0)$; concave up on $(0, \infty)$; inflection point at $(0, 0)$. Symmetric about the origin.

43. $y = x^3 - 3x^2 + 3x - 3$

Intercept $(0, -3)$

$y' = 3x^2 - 6x + 3 = 3(x-1)^2$

CV: $x = 1$

Increasing on $(-\infty, 1)$ and $(1, \infty)$; no relative maximum or minimum

$y'' = 6(x-1)$

Possible inflection point when $x = 1$.

Concave down on $(-\infty, 1)$; concave up on $(1, \infty)$; inflection point at $(1, -2)$.

45. $y = 4x^3 - 3x^4 = x^3(4 - 3x)$

Intercepts $(0, 0)$, $\left(\frac{4}{3}, 0\right)$

$y' = 12x^2 - 12x^3 = 12x^2(1 - x)$

CV: $x = 0$ and $x = 1$

Increasing on $(-\infty, 0)$ and $(0, 1)$; decreasing on $(1, \infty)$; relative maximum at $(1, 1)$.

$y'' = 24x - 36x^2 = 12x(2 - 3x)$

Possible inflection points at $x = 0$ and $x = \frac{2}{3}$. Concave down on $(-\infty, 0)$ and $\left(\frac{2}{3}, \infty\right)$; concave up on $\left(0, \frac{2}{3}\right)$; inflection point at $(0, 0)$ and $\left(\frac{2}{3}, \frac{16}{27}\right)$

47. $y = -2 + 12x - x^3$

Intercept $(0, -2)$

$y' = 12 - 3x^2 = 3(2 + x)(2 - x)$

CV: $x = \pm 2$

Decreasing on $(-\infty, -2)$ and $(2, \infty)$; increasing on $(-2, 2)$; relative minimum at $(-2, -18)$; relative maximum at $(2, 14)$.

$y'' = -6x$

Possible inflection point when $x = 0$.

Concave up on $(-\infty, 0)$; concave down on $(0, \infty)$; inflection point at $(0, -2)$.

49. $y = x^3 - 6x^2 + 12x - 6$

Intercept $(0, -6)$

$y' = 3x^2 - 12x + 12 = 3(x-2)^2$

CV: $x = 2$

Increasing on $(-\infty, 2)$ and $(2, \infty)$.

$y'' = 6(x - 2)$

Possible inflection point when $x = 2$.

Concave down on $(-\infty, 2)$; concave up on $(2, \infty)$; inflection point at $(2, 2)$.

51. $y = 5x - x^5 = x\left(5 - x^4\right)$

$= x\left(\sqrt{5} + x^2\right)\left(\sqrt{5} - x^2\right)$

$= x\left(\sqrt{5} + x^2\right)\left(\sqrt[4]{5} + x\right)\left(\sqrt[4]{5} - x\right)$

Intercepts $(0, 0)$ and $\left(\pm\sqrt[4]{5}, 0\right)$

Symmetric about the origin.

$y' = 5 - 5x^4 = 5\left(1 - x^4\right) = 5\left(1 - x^2\right)\left(1 + x^2\right)$

$= 5(1 - x)(1 + x)\left(1 + x^2\right)$

CV: $x = \pm 1$

Decreasing on $(-\infty, -1)$ and $(1, \infty)$;
increasing on $(-1, 1)$; relative minimum at
$(-1, -4)$; relative maximum at $(1, 4)$.

$y'' = -20x^3$

Possible inflection point when $x = 0$.
Concave up on $(-\infty, 0)$; concave down on
$(0, \infty)$; inflection point at $(0, 0)$.

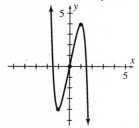

53. $y = 3x^4 - 4x^3 + 1$

Intercepts $(0, 1)$ and $(1, 0)$ [the latter is
found by inspection of the equation].
No symmetry.

$y' = 12x^3 - 12x^2 = 12x^2(x - 1)$

CV: $x = 0$ and $x = 1$

Decreasing on $(-\infty, 0)$ and $(0, 1)$; increasing
on $(1, \infty)$; relative minimum at $(1, 0)$.

$y'' = 36x^2 - 24x = 12x(3x - 2)$

Possible inflection points at $x = 0$ and

$x = \frac{2}{3}$. Concave up on $(-\infty, 0)$ and $\left(\frac{2}{3}, \infty\right)$;

concave down on $\left(0, \frac{2}{3}\right)$; inflection points

at $(0, 1)$ and $\left(\frac{2}{3}, \frac{11}{27}\right)$.

55. $y = 4x^2 - x^4 = x^2(2 + x)(2 - x)$

Intercepts $(0, 0)$ and $(\pm 2, 0)$
Symmetric about the y-axis.

$y' = 8x - 4x^3 = 4x\left(2 - x^2\right)$

$= 4x\left(\sqrt{2} + x\right)\left(\sqrt{2} - x\right)$

CV: $x = 0, \pm\sqrt{2}$

Increasing on $\left(-\infty, -\sqrt{2}\right)$ and $\left(0, \sqrt{2}\right)$;

decreasing on $\left(-\sqrt{2}, 0\right)$ and $\left(\sqrt{2}, \infty\right)$;

relative maxima at $\left(\pm\sqrt{2}, 4\right)$; relative

minimum at $(0, 0)$.

$y'' = 8 - 12x^2 = 12\left[\frac{2}{3} - x^2\right]$

$= 12\left(\sqrt{\frac{2}{3}} - x\right)\left(\sqrt{\frac{2}{3}} + x\right)$

Possible inflection points when $x = \pm\sqrt{\frac{2}{3}}$.

Concave down on $\left(-\infty, -\sqrt{\frac{2}{3}}\right)$ and

$\left(\sqrt{\frac{2}{3}}, \infty\right)$; concave up on $\left(-\sqrt{\frac{2}{3}}, \sqrt{\frac{2}{3}}\right)$;

inflection points at $\left(\pm\sqrt{\frac{2}{3}}, \frac{20}{9}\right)$.

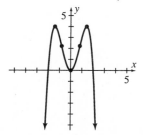

57. $y = x^{1/3}(x - 8)$

Intercepts $(0, 0)$ and $(8, 0)$

Since $y = x^{4/3} - 8x^{1/3}$

$y' = \dfrac{4}{3}x^{1/3} - \dfrac{8}{3}x^{-2/3}$

$= \dfrac{4}{3}\left[x^{1/3} - \dfrac{2}{x^{2/3}}\right] = \dfrac{4(x - 2)}{3x^{2/3}}$

CV: $x = 0, 2$

Decreasing on $(-\infty, 0)$ and $(0, 2)$; increasing on $(2, \infty)$; relative minimum at

$\left(2, -6\sqrt[3]{2}\right) \approx (2, -7.56)$.

$y'' = \dfrac{4}{9}x^{-2/3} + \dfrac{16}{9}x^{-5/3}$

$= \dfrac{4}{9}\left[\dfrac{1}{x^{2/3}} + \dfrac{4}{x^{5/3}}\right] = \dfrac{4(x + 4)}{9x^{5/3}}$

Possible inflection points when $x = -4, 0$.
Concave up on $(-\infty, -4)$ and $(0, \infty)$; concave down on $(-4, 0)$; inflection points at $\left(-4, 12\sqrt[3]{4}\right)$ and $(0, 0)$. Observe that at the origin the tangent line exists but it is vertical.

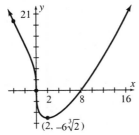

59. $y = 4x^{1/3} + x^{4/3} = x^{1/3}(4 + x)$

Intercepts $(0, 0)$ and $(-4, 0)$

$y' = \dfrac{4}{3}x^{-2/3} + \dfrac{4}{3}x^{1/3} = \dfrac{4}{3}\left[\dfrac{1}{x^{2/3}} + x^{1/3}\right]$

$= \dfrac{4(1 + x)}{3x^{2/3}}$

CV: $x = 0, -1$

Decreasing on $(-\infty, -1)$; increasing on $(-1, 0)$ and $(0, \infty)$; rel. min at $(-1, -3)$

$y'' = -\dfrac{8}{9}x^{-5/3} + \dfrac{4}{9}x^{-2/3} = \dfrac{4}{9}\left[\dfrac{1}{x^{2/3}} - \dfrac{2}{x^{5/3}}\right]$

$= \dfrac{4(x - 2)}{9x^{5/3}}$

Possible inflection points when $x = 0, 2$.
Concave up on $(-\infty, 0)$ and $(2, \infty)$; concave down on $(0, 2)$; inflection point at $(0, 0)$ and $\left(2, 6\sqrt[3]{2}\right)$. Observe that at the origin the tangent line exists but it is vertical.

61. $y = 2x + 3x^{2/3} = 2x^{2/3}\left(x^{1/3} + \dfrac{3}{2}\right)$

Intercepts $(0, 0)$ and $\left(-\dfrac{27}{8}, 0\right)$

$y' = 2 + 2x^{-1/3} = 2\left(1 + \dfrac{1}{\sqrt[3]{x}}\right)$

$= 2\left(\dfrac{\sqrt[3]{x} + 1}{\sqrt[3]{x}}\right)$

CV: $x = 0, -1$

Increasing on $(-\infty, -1)$ and $(0, \infty)$; decreasing on $(-1, 0)$; relative maximum at $(-1, 1)$; relative minimum at $(0, 0)$.

$y'' = -\dfrac{2}{3}x^{-4/3} = -\dfrac{2}{3x^{4/3}}$

Possible inflection point at $x = 0$. Concave down on $(-\infty, 0)$ and $(0, \infty)$. Observe that at the origin the tangent line exists but it is vertical.

63.

65.

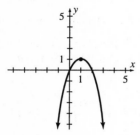

67. $p = \dfrac{100}{q+2}$

$\dfrac{dp}{dq} = -\dfrac{100}{(q+2)^2} < 0$ for $q > 0$, so p is

decreasing. Since $\dfrac{d^2p}{dq^2} = \dfrac{200}{(q+2)^3} > 0$ for

$q > 0$, the demand curve is concave up.

69. $S = f(A) = 12\sqrt[4]{A}$, $0 \le A \le 625$. For the

given values of A we have $S' = 3A^{-\frac{3}{4}} > 0$

and $S'' = -\left(\dfrac{9}{4}\right)A^{-\frac{7}{4}} < 0$. Thus y is increasing

and concave down.

71. $y = 12.5 + 5.8(0.42)^x$

$y' = 5.8(0.42)^x \ln(0.42)$

Since $\ln(0.42) < 0$, we have $y' < 0$, so the
function is decreasing.

$y'' = 5.8(0.42)^x \ln^2(0.42) > 0$, so the
function is concave up.

73. $n = f(r) = 0.1\ln(r) + \dfrac{7}{r} - 0.8$, $1 \le r \le 10$

a. $\dfrac{dn}{dr} = \dfrac{0.1}{r} - \dfrac{7}{r^2} = \dfrac{0.1r - 7}{r^2}$

$= \dfrac{0.1(r - 70)}{r^2} < 0$

for $1 \le r \le 10$. Thus the graph of f is
always falling. Also,

$\dfrac{d^2n}{dr^2} = -\dfrac{0.1}{r^2} + \dfrac{14}{r^3} = \dfrac{14 - 0.1r}{r^3}$

$= \dfrac{0.1(140 - r)}{r^3} > 0$

for $1 \le r \le 10$. Thus the graph is
concave up.

b.

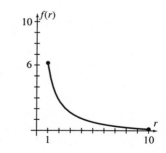

c. $\dfrac{dn}{dr}\bigg|_{r=5} = -0.26$, so the rate of decrease

is 0.26.

75.

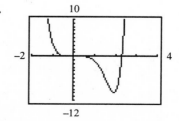

Two inflection points

77. $y = x^3 - 2x^2 + x + 3$

$y' = 3x^2 - 4x + 1$

When $x = 2$, then $y = 5$ and $y' = 5$. Thus an equation of the tangent line at $x = 2$ is $y - 5 = 5(x - 2)$, or $y = 5x - 5$. Graphing the curve and the tangent line indicates that the curve lies above the tangent line around $x = 2$. Thus the curve is concave up at $x = 2$.

79. $f(x) = x^6 + 3x^5 - 4x^4 + 2x^2 + 1$

$f'(x) = 6x^5 + 15x^4 - 16x^3 + 4x$

$f''(x) = 30x^4 + 60x^3 - 48x^2 + 4$

Inflection points of f when $x \approx -2.61, -0.26$.

Exercise 14.4

1. $y = x^2 - 5x + 6$

$y' = 2x - 5$

CV: $x = \dfrac{5}{2}$

$y'' = 2$

$y''\left(\dfrac{5}{2}\right) = 2 > 0$

Thus there is a relative minimum when $x = \dfrac{5}{2}$. Because there is only one relative extremum and f is continuous, the relative minimum is an absolute minimum.

3. $y = -4x^2 + 2x - 8$

$y' = -8x + 2$

CV: $x = \dfrac{1}{4}$

$y'' = -8$

$y''\left(\dfrac{1}{4}\right) = -8 < 0$

Thus there is a relative maximum when $x = \dfrac{1}{4}$. Because there is only one relative extremum and f is continuous, the relative maximum is an absolute maximum.

5. $y = x^3 - 27x + 1$

$y' = 3x^2 - 27 = 3\left(x^2 - 9\right) = 3(x + 3)(x - 3)$

CV: $x = \pm 3$

$y'' = 6x$

$y''(-3) = -18 < 0 \Rightarrow$ relative maximum when $x = -3$

$y''(3) = 18 > 0 \Rightarrow$ relative minimum when $x = 3$

7. $y = -x^3 + 3x^2 + 1$

$y' = -3x^2 + 6x = -3x(x - 2)$

CV: $x = 0, 2$

$y'' = -6x + 6$

$y''(0) = 6 > 0 \Rightarrow$ relative minimum when $x = 0$

$y''(2) = -6 < 0 \Rightarrow$ relative maximum when $x = 2$

9. $y = 3x^4 + 3$

$y' = 12x^3$

CV: $x = 0$

$y'' = 36x^2$

Since $y''(0) = 0$, the second-derivative test fails. Using the first-derivative test, we see that f decreases for $x < 0$ and f increases for $x > 0$, so there is a relative minimum when $x = 0$.

11. $y = 81x^5 - 5x$

$y' = 81 \cdot 5x^4 - 5 = 5\left(81x^4 - 1\right)$

$\quad = 5\left(9x^2 - 1\right)\left(9x^2 + 1\right)$

$\quad = 5(3x + 1)(3x - 1)\left(9x^2 + 1\right)$

CV: $x = \pm\frac{1}{3}$

$y'' = 81 \cdot 5 \cdot 4x^3$

$y''\left(-\frac{1}{3}\right) = -60 < 0 \Rightarrow$ relative maximum

when $x = -\frac{1}{3}$

$y''\left(\frac{1}{3}\right) = 60 > 0 \Rightarrow$ relative minimum when

$x = \frac{1}{3}$

13. $y = \left(x^2 + 7x + 10\right)^2$

$y' = 2\left(x^2 + 7x + 10\right)(2x + 7)$

$\quad = 2(x + 2)(x + 5)(2x + 7)$

CV: $x = -2, -5, -\frac{7}{2}$

$y'' = 2\left[\left(x^2 + 7x + 10\right)(2) + (2x + 7)(2x + 7)\right]$

$y''(-5) = 18 > 0 \Rightarrow$ relative minimum when

$x = -5$

$y''\left(-\frac{7}{2}\right) = -9 < 0 \Rightarrow$ relative maximum

when $x = -\frac{7}{2}$

$y''(-2) = 18 > 0 \Rightarrow$ relative minimum when

$x = -2$

Exercise 14.5

1. $y = f(x) = \dfrac{x}{x - 1}$

When $x = 1$ the denominator is zero but the numerator is not zero. Thus the line $x = 1$ is a vertical asymptote. Testing for horizontal asymptotes,

$\lim\limits_{x \to \infty} \dfrac{x}{x - 1} = \lim\limits_{x \to \infty} \dfrac{x}{x} = \lim\limits_{x \to \infty} 1 = 1.$

Similarly $\lim\limits_{x \to -\infty} f(x) = 1.$ Thus the line

$y = 1$ is a horizontal asymptote.

3. $f(x) = \dfrac{x - 1}{2x + 3}$

When $x = -\frac{3}{2}$ the denominator is zero but

the numerator is not. Thus $x = -\frac{3}{2}$ is a

vertical asymptote.

$\lim\limits_{x \to \infty} f(x) = \lim\limits_{x \to \infty} \dfrac{x}{2x} = \lim\limits_{x \to \infty} \dfrac{1}{2} = \dfrac{1}{2}.$

Similarly $\lim\limits_{x \to -\infty} f(x) = \dfrac{1}{2}.$ Thus $y = \dfrac{1}{2}$ is a

horizontal asymptote.

5. $y = f(x) = \dfrac{4}{x}$

When $x = 0$ the denominator is zero but the numerator is not zero, so $x = 0$ is a vertical asymptote. Taking limits at infinity,

$\lim\limits_{x \to \infty}\left(\dfrac{4}{x}\right) = 0 = \lim\limits_{x \to -\infty}\left(\dfrac{4}{x}\right),$ so the line $y = 0$ is

a horizontal asymptote.

7. $y = f(x) = \dfrac{1}{x^2 - 1} = \dfrac{1}{(x - 1)(x + 1)}$

Vertical asymptotes are $x = 1$ and $x = -1$.

$\lim\limits_{x \to \infty} \dfrac{1}{x^2 - 1} = 0.$ Similarly, $\lim\limits_{x \to -\infty} f(x) = 0.$

Thus $y = 0$ is a horizontal asymptote.

9. $y = f(x) = x^2 - 5x + 5$ is a polynomial function, so there are no horizontal or vertical asymptotes.

11. $f(x) = \dfrac{2x^2}{x^2 + x - 6} = \dfrac{2x^2}{(x + 3)(x - 2)}$

Vertical asymptotes are $x = -3$ and $x = 2$.

$\lim\limits_{x \to \infty} f(x) = \lim\limits_{x \to \infty} \dfrac{2x^2}{x^2} = \lim\limits_{x \to \infty} 2 = 2,$ and

$\lim\limits_{x \to -\infty} f(x) = 2.$ Thus $y = 2$ is a horizontal

asymptote.

13. $y = f(x) = \dfrac{4 + 2x - 7x^2}{x^2 - 8}$

$= \dfrac{4 + 2x - 7x^2}{\left(x - 2\sqrt{2}\right)\left(x + 2\sqrt{2}\right)}$

When $x = -2\sqrt{2}$ or $x = 2\sqrt{2}$, the denominator is zero but the numerator is not. Thus $x = -2\sqrt{2}$ and $x = 2\sqrt{2}$ are vertical asymptotes.

$\displaystyle\lim_{x\to\infty} f(x) = \dfrac{-7x^2}{x^2} = \lim_{x\to\infty} -7 = -7$.

Similarly, $\displaystyle\lim_{x\to-\infty} f(x) = -7$. Thus $y = -7$ is a horizontal asymptote.

15. $y = f(x) = \dfrac{4}{x - 6} + 7 = \dfrac{7x - 38}{x - 6}$

From the denominator we find that the line $x = 6$ is a vertical asymptote. Taking limits at infinity,

$\displaystyle\lim_{x\to\infty} f(x) = \lim_{x\to\infty} \dfrac{7x}{x} = \lim_{x\to\infty} 7 = 7$, and

$\displaystyle\lim_{x\to-\infty} f(x) = 7$. Thus $y = 7$ is a horizontal asymptote.

17. $f(x) = \dfrac{3 - x^4}{x^3 + x^2} = \dfrac{3 - x^4}{x^2(x + 1)}$

Vertical asymptotes are $x = 0$ and $x = -1$. Because the degree of the numerator (4) is greater than the degree of the denominator (3), there is no horizontal asymptote.

19. $y = f(x) = \dfrac{x^2 - 3x - 4}{1 + 4x + 4x^2} = \dfrac{x^2 - 3x - 4}{(1 + 2x)^2}$

From the denominator, $x = -\dfrac{1}{2}$ is a vertical asymptote. Also,

$\displaystyle\lim_{x\to\infty} f(x) = \lim_{x\to\infty} \dfrac{x^2}{4x^2} = \lim_{x\to\infty} \dfrac{1}{4} = \dfrac{1}{4}$, and

$\displaystyle\lim_{x\to-\infty} f(x) = \dfrac{1}{4}$, so $y = \dfrac{1}{4}$ is a horizontal asymptote.

21. $y = f(x) = \dfrac{9x^2 - 16}{2(3x + 4)^2} = \dfrac{(3x + 4)(3x - 4)}{2(3x + 4)^2}$

When $x = -\dfrac{4}{3}$, both the numerator and denominator are zero. Since

$\displaystyle\lim_{x\to-4/3^+} f(x) = \lim_{x\to-4/3^+} \dfrac{3x - 4}{2(3x + 4)} = -\infty$, the

line $x = -\dfrac{4}{3}$ is a vertical asymptote.

$\displaystyle\lim_{x\to\infty} \dfrac{9x^2 - 16}{2(3x + 4)^2} = \lim_{x\to\infty} \dfrac{9x^2}{18x^2} = \lim_{x\to\infty} \dfrac{1}{2} = \dfrac{1}{2}$.

Similarly, $\displaystyle\lim_{x\to-\infty} f(x) = \dfrac{1}{2}$. Thus $y = \dfrac{1}{2}$ is a horizontal asymptote.

23. $y = f(x) = 2e^{x+2} + 4$

We have $\displaystyle\lim_{x\to\infty} f(x) = +\infty$ and

$\displaystyle\lim_{x\to-\infty} f(x) = 2 \cdot \lim_{x\to-\infty} e^x + \lim_{x\to-\infty} 4$
$= 2(0) + 4 = 4$

Thus $y = 4$ is a horizontal asymptote. There is no vertical asymptote because $f(x)$ neither increases nor decreases without bound around any fixed value of x.

25. $y = \dfrac{3}{x}$

Symmetric about the origin. Vertical

asymptote is $x = 0$. $\displaystyle\lim_{x\to\infty} \dfrac{3}{x} = 0 = \lim_{x\to-\infty}\dfrac{3}{x}$,

so $y = 0$ is a horizontal asymptote.

$y' = -\dfrac{3}{x^2}$

CV: None, however $x = 0$ must be included in the inc.-dec. analysis. Decreasing on $(-\infty, 0)$ and $(0, \infty)$.

$y'' = \dfrac{6}{x^3}$

No possible inflection point, but we include $x = 0$ in the concavity analysis. Concave down on $(-\infty, 0)$; concave up on $(0, \infty)$.

27. $y = \dfrac{x}{x+1}$

Intercept $(0, 0)$

Vertical asymptote is $x = -1$

$\displaystyle\lim_{x\to\infty} y = 1 = \lim_{x\to-\infty} y$, so $y = 1$ is a horizontal

asymptote.

$y' = \dfrac{(x+1)(1) - x(1)}{(x+1)^2} = \dfrac{1}{(x+1)^2}$

CV: None, but $x = -1$ must be included in the inc.-dec. analysis. Increasing on $(-\infty, -1)$ and $(-1, \infty)$.

$y'' = -\dfrac{2}{(x+1)^3}$

No possible inflection point, but $x = -1$ must be included in concavity analysis. Concave up on $(-\infty, -1)$, concave down on $(-1, \infty)$.

29. $y = x^2 + \dfrac{1}{x^2} = \dfrac{x^4 + 1}{x^2}$

$x \ne 0$, so there is no y-intercept. Setting $y = 0 \Rightarrow$ no x-intercept. Replacing x by $-x$ yields symmetry about the y-axis. Setting $x^2 = 0$ gives $x = 0$ as the only vertical asymptote. Because the degree of the numerator is greater than the degree of the denominator, no horizontal asymptote exists.

$y = x^2 + x^{-2}$

$y' = 2x - 2x^{-3} = 2x - \dfrac{2}{x^3} = \dfrac{2x^4 - 2}{x^3}$

$\quad = \dfrac{2\left(x^4 - 1\right)}{x^3}$

$\quad = \dfrac{2\left(x^2 + 1\right)(x+1)(x-1)}{x^3}.$

CV: $x = \pm 1$, but $x = 0$ must be included in the inc.-dec. analysis. Decreasing on $(-\infty, -1)$ and $(0, 1)$; increasing on $(-1, 0)$ and $(1, \infty)$; relative minima at $(-1, 2)$ and $(1, 2)$,

$y'' = 2 + \dfrac{6}{x^4} > 0$

for all $x \ne 0$. Concave up on $(-\infty, 0)$ and $(0, \infty)$.

31. $y = \dfrac{1}{x^2 - 1} = \dfrac{1}{(x+1)(x-1)}$

Intercept $(0, -1)$

Symmetric about the y-axis.

Vertical asymptotes are $x = -1$ and $x = 1$.

$\displaystyle\lim_{x \to \infty} \frac{1}{x^2 - 1} = 0 = \lim_{x \to -\infty} \frac{1}{x^2 - 1}$, so $y = 0$ is a horizontal asymptote.

$y' = -\dfrac{2x}{\left(x^2 - 1\right)^2}$

CV: $x = 0$, but $x = \pm 1$ must be included in the inc.-dec. analysis. Increasing on $(-\infty, -1)$ and $(-1, 0)$; decreasing on $(0, 1)$ and $(1, \infty)$; relative maximum at $(0, -1)$.

$y'' = -2 \cdot \dfrac{\left(x^2 - 1\right)^2 (1) - x\left[4x\left(x^2 - 1\right)\right]}{\left(x^2 - 1\right)^4}$

$ = -2 \cdot \dfrac{\left(x^2 - 1\right)\left[\left(x^2 - 1\right) - 4x^2\right]}{\left(x^2 - 1\right)^4}$

$ = \dfrac{2\left(3x^2 + 1\right)}{\left(x^2 - 1\right)^3} = \dfrac{2\left(3x^2 + 1\right)}{[(x+1)(x-1)]^3}$

No possible inflection point, but $x = \pm 1$ must be considered in the concavity analysis. Concave up: $(-\infty, -1)$, $(1, \infty)$; concave down: $(-1, 1)$.

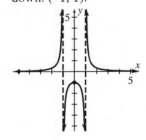

33. $y = \dfrac{1+x}{1-x}$

Intercepts: Setting $x = 0 \Rightarrow y = 1$; setting $y = 0 \Rightarrow x = -1$. Thus the intercepts are $(0, 1)$ and $(-1, 0)$. Setting $1 - x = 0 \Rightarrow x = 1$ is the only vertical asymptote. Since

$\displaystyle\lim_{x \to \infty} \frac{1+x}{1-x} = \lim_{x \to \infty} \frac{x}{-x} = \lim_{x \to \infty} -1 = -1$
$\displaystyle = \lim_{x \to -\infty} \frac{1+x}{1-x}$

the only horizontal asymptote is $y = -1$.

$y' = \dfrac{(1-x)(1) - (1+x)(1)}{(1-x)^2} = \dfrac{2}{(1-x)^2}$

No critical values, but $x = 1$ must be considered in the ind.-dec. analysis. Increasing on $(-\infty, 1)$ and $(1, \infty)$.

$y'' = \dfrac{4}{(1-x)^3}$

No possible inflection point, but $x = 1$ must be included in the concavity analysis. Concave up on $(-\infty, 1)$; concave down on $(1, \infty)$.

35. $y = \dfrac{x^2}{7x+4}$

Intercept: $(0, 0)$

Vertical asymptote is $x = -\dfrac{4}{7}$. Because the degree of the numerator is greater than the degree of the denominator, no horizontal asymptote exists.

$$y' = \frac{(7x+4)(2x) - x^2(7)}{(7x+4)^2}$$

$$= \frac{7x^2 + 8x}{(7x+4)^2} = \frac{x(7x+8)}{(7x+4)^2}$$

CV: $x = 0, -\dfrac{8}{7}$, but $x = -\dfrac{4}{7}$ must be included in the inc.-dec. analysis. Increasing on $\left(-\infty, -\dfrac{8}{7}\right)$ and $(0, \infty)$; decreasing on $\left(-\dfrac{8}{7}, -\dfrac{4}{7}\right)$ and $\left(-\dfrac{4}{7}, 0\right)$; relative maximum at $\left(-\dfrac{8}{7}, -\dfrac{16}{49}\right)$; relative minimum at $(0, 0)$.

$$y'' = \frac{\left(7x^2+4\right)^2(14x+8) - \left(7x^2+8x\right)[14(7x+4)]}{(7x+4)^4}$$

$$= \frac{(7x+4)\left[(7x+4)(14x+8) - 14\left(7x^2+8x\right)\right]}{(7x+4)^4}$$

$$= \frac{32}{(7x+4)^3}$$

No possible inflection point but $x = -\dfrac{4}{7}$ must be included in concavity analysis. Concave down on $\left(-\infty, -\dfrac{4}{7}\right)$; concave up on $\left(-\dfrac{4}{7}, \infty\right)$.

37. $y = \dfrac{9}{9x^2 - 6x - 8} = \dfrac{9}{(3x+2)(3x-4)}$

Intercept: $\left(0, -\dfrac{9}{8}\right)$

Vertical asymptote: $x = -\dfrac{2}{3}$, $x = \dfrac{4}{3}$

$$\lim_{x \to \infty} y = \lim_{x \to \infty} \frac{9}{9x^2} = \lim_{x \to \infty} \frac{1}{x^2} = 0 = \lim_{x \to -\infty} y$$

Thus $y = 0$ is a horizontal asymptote. Since $y = 9\left(9x^2 - 6x - 8\right)^{-1}$,

$$y' = 9(-1)\left(9x^2 - 6x - 8\right)^{-2}(18x - 6)$$

$$= -\frac{54(3x - 1)}{[(3x+2)(3x-4)]^2}$$

CV: $x = \dfrac{1}{3}$, but $x = -\dfrac{2}{3}$ and $x = \dfrac{4}{3}$ must be included in inc.-dec. analysis.

Increasing on $\left(-\infty, -\dfrac{2}{3}\right)$ and $\left(-\dfrac{2}{3}, \dfrac{1}{3}\right)$; decreasing on $\left(\dfrac{1}{3}, \dfrac{4}{3}\right)$ and $\left(\dfrac{4}{3}, \infty\right)$; relative maximum

at $\left(\dfrac{1}{3}, -1\right)$. Finding y'' gives:

$$y'' = -54 \cdot \frac{\left(9x^2 - 6x - 8\right)^2(3) - (3x - 1)\left[2\left(9x^2 - 6x - 8\right)(18x - 6)\right]}{\left(9x^2 - 6x - 8\right)^4}$$

$$= -54 \cdot \frac{3\left(9x^2 - 6x - 8\right)\left[\left(9x^2 - 6x - 8\right) - 4(3x - 1)(3x - 1)\right]}{\left(9x^2 - 6x - 8\right)^4}$$

$$= \frac{-162\left(-27x^2 + 18x - 12\right)}{\left(9x^2 - 6x - 8\right)^3} = \frac{486\left(9x^2 - 6x + 4\right)}{[(3x+2)(3x-4)]^3}$$

Since $9x^2 - 6x + 4 = 0$ has no real roots, y'' is never zero. No possible inflection points,

but $x = -\dfrac{2}{3}$ and $x = \dfrac{4}{3}$ must be included in concavity analysis. Concave up on $\left(-\infty, -\dfrac{2}{3}\right)$

and $\left(\dfrac{4}{3}, \infty\right)$; concave down on $\left(-\dfrac{2}{3}, \dfrac{4}{3}\right)$.

39. $y = \dfrac{2x-3}{(2x-9)^2}$

Intercepts: $\left(\dfrac{3}{2}, 0\right), \left(0, -\dfrac{1}{27}\right)$

Vertical asymptote is $x = \dfrac{9}{2}$.

$$\lim_{x \to \infty} y = \lim_{x \to \infty} \frac{2x}{4x^2} = \lim_{x \to \infty} \frac{1}{2x} = 0 = \lim_{x \to -\infty} y$$

Thus $y = 0$ is horiz. asymptote.

$$y' = \frac{(2x-9)^2(2) - (2x-3)[4(2x-9)]}{(2x-9)^4}$$

$$= \frac{2(2x-9)[(2x-9) - 2(2x-3)]}{(2x-9)^4}$$

$$= \frac{2(-2x-3)}{(2x-9)^3} = -2 \cdot \frac{2x+3}{(2x-9)^3}$$

CV: $x = -\dfrac{3}{2}$, but $x = \dfrac{9}{2}$ must be included in inc.-dec. analysis. Decreasing on $\left(-\infty, -\dfrac{3}{2}\right)$ and $\left(\dfrac{9}{2}, \infty\right)$; increasing on $\left(-\dfrac{3}{2}, \dfrac{9}{2}\right)$; relative minimum at $\left(-\dfrac{3}{2}, -\dfrac{1}{24}\right)$.

$$y'' = -2 \cdot \frac{(2x-9)^3(2) - (2x+3)\left[6(2x-9)^2\right]}{(2x-9)^6}$$

$$= -2 \cdot \frac{2(2x-9)^2[(2x-9) - 3(2x+3)]}{(2x-9)^6}$$

$$= -4 \cdot \frac{-4x-18}{(2x-9)^4} = 8 \cdot \frac{2x+9}{(2x-9)^4}$$

Possible inflection point when $x = -\dfrac{9}{2}$, but $x = \dfrac{9}{2}$ must be included in concavity analysis. Concave down on $\left(-\infty, -\dfrac{9}{2}\right)$; concave up on $\left(-\dfrac{9}{2}, \dfrac{9}{2}\right)$ and $\left(\dfrac{9}{2}, \infty\right)$; inflection point at $\left(-\dfrac{9}{2}, -\dfrac{1}{27}\right)$.

41. $y = \dfrac{x^2 - 1}{x^3} = \dfrac{(x+1)(x-1)}{x^3}$

Intercepts are $(-1, 0)$ and $(1, 0)$.
Symmetric about the origin.
Vertical asymptote $x = 0$.

$$\lim_{x \to \infty} \frac{x^2-1}{x^3} = \lim_{x \to \infty} \frac{x^2}{x^3} = \lim_{x \to \infty} \frac{1}{x}$$

$$= 0 = \lim_{x \to -\infty} \frac{1-x}{x^2}, \text{ so } y = 0 \text{ is the only}$$

horizontal asymptote. Since $y = x^{-1} - x^{-3}$, then

$$y' = -x^{-2} + 3x^{-4} = x^{-4}\left(-x^2 + 3\right) = \frac{3 - x^2}{x^4}$$

CV: $x = \pm\sqrt{3}$, but $x = 0$ must be included in the inc.-dec. analysis. Increasing on $\left(-\sqrt{3}, 0\right)$ and $\left(0, \sqrt{3}\right)$; decreasing on $\left(-\infty, -\sqrt{3}\right)$ and $\left(\sqrt{3}, \infty\right)$; relative maximum at $\left(\sqrt{3}, \dfrac{2\sqrt{3}}{9}\right)$; relative minimum at $\left(-\sqrt{3}, -\dfrac{2\sqrt{3}}{9}\right)$.

$$y'' = 2x^{-3} - 12x^{-5} = 2x^{-5}\left(x^2 - 6\right)$$

$$= \frac{2\left(x^2 - 6\right)}{x^5}$$

Possible inflection points when $x = \pm\sqrt{6}$, but $x = 0$ must be included in the concavity analysis. Concave down on $\left(-\infty, -\sqrt{6}\right)$ and $\left(0, \sqrt{6}\right)$; concave up on $\left(-\sqrt{6}, 0\right)$ and $\left(\sqrt{6}, \infty\right)$; inflection points at $\left(\sqrt{6}, \frac{5\sqrt{6}}{36}\right)$ and $\left(-\sqrt{6}, \frac{-5\sqrt{6}}{36}\right)$.

43. $y = x + \dfrac{1}{x+1} = \dfrac{x^2 + x + 1}{x+1}$

Intercepts: Setting $x = 0 \Rightarrow y = 1$; setting $y = 0$ yields no real roots. Thus the only intercept is $(0, 1)$.

$x = -1$ is the only vertical asymptote. Because the degree of the numerator is greater than the degree of the denominator, there is no horizontal asymptote.

$$y' = \frac{(x+1)(2x+1) - \left(x^2 + x + 1\right)}{(x+1)^2} = \frac{x^2 + 2x}{(x+1)^2} = \frac{x(x+2)}{(x+1)^2}$$

CV: 0 and –2, but $x = -1$ must be included in the inc.-dec. analysis. Increasing on $(-\infty, -2)$ and $(0, \infty)$; decreasing on $(-2, -1)$ and $(-1, 0)$; relative maximum at $(-2, -3)$; relative minimum at $(0, 1)$.

$$y'' = \frac{(x+1)^2(2x+2) - \left(x^2 + 2x\right)[2(x+1)]}{(x+1)^4} = \frac{(x+1)(2x+2) - \left(x^2 + 2x\right)[2]}{(x+1)^3} = \frac{2}{(x+1)^3}$$

No possible inflection point, but $x = -1$ must be included in the concavity analysis. Concave down on $(-\infty, -1)$; concave up on $(-1, \infty)$.

45. $y = \dfrac{-3x^2 + 2x - 5}{3x^2 - 2x - 1} = \dfrac{-3x^2 + 2x - 5}{(3x+1)(x-1)}$

Note that $-3x^2 + 2x - 5$ is never zero.

Intercept: $(0, 5)$

Vertical asymptotes are $x = -\frac{1}{3}$ and $x = 1$.

$$\lim_{x \to \infty} y = \lim_{x \to \infty} \frac{-3x^2}{3x^2} = \lim_{x \to \infty} -1 = -1 = \lim_{x \to -\infty} y$$

Thus $y = -1$ is horizontal asymptote.

$$y' = \frac{\left(3x^2 - 2x - 1\right)(-6x + 2) - \left(-3x^2 + 2x - 5\right)(6x - 2)}{\left(3x^2 - 2x - 1\right)^2}$$

$$= \frac{2(3x - 1)\left[\left(3x^2 - 2x - 1\right)(-1) - \left(-3x^2 + 2x - 5\right)\right]}{\left(3x^2 - 2x - 1\right)^2}$$

$$= \frac{12(3x - 1)}{\left(3x^2 - 2x - 1\right)^2} = \frac{12(3x - 1)}{[(3x + 1)(x - 1)]^2}$$

CV: $x = \frac{1}{3}$, but $x = -\frac{1}{3}$ and $x = 1$ must be included in inc.-dec. analysis.

Decreasing on $\left(-\infty, -\frac{1}{3}\right)$ and $\left(-\frac{1}{3}, \frac{1}{3}\right)$; increasing on $\left(\frac{1}{3}, 1\right)$ and $(1, \infty)$; relative minimum at $\left(\frac{1}{3}, \frac{7}{2}\right)$.

$$y'' = 12 \cdot \frac{\left(3x^2 - 2x - 1\right)^2 (3) - (3x - 1)\left[2\left(3x^2 - 2x - 1\right)(6x - 2)\right]}{\left(3x^2 - 2x - 1\right)^4}$$

$$= 12 \cdot \frac{\left(3x^2 - 2x - 1\right)\left[3\left(3x^2 - 2x - 1\right) - 2(3x - 1)(6x - 2)\right]}{\left(3x^2 - 2x - 1\right)^4}$$

$$= 12 \cdot \frac{-27x^2 + 18x - 7}{\left(3x^2 - 2x - 1\right)^3} = \frac{-12\left(27x^2 - 18x + 7\right)}{[(3x + 1)(x - 1)]^3}$$

Since $27x^2 - 18x + 7$ is never zero, there is no possible inflection point, but $x = -\frac{1}{3}$ and $x = 1$ must be included in concavity analysis. Concave down on $\left(-\infty, -\frac{1}{3}\right)$ and $(1, \infty)$; concave up on $\left(-\frac{1}{3}, 1\right)$.

47.

49.

51. $\lim\limits_{x\to\infty}\dfrac{x}{a+bx}=\lim\limits_{x\to\infty}\dfrac{x}{bx}=\lim\limits_{x\to\infty}\dfrac{1}{b}=\dfrac{1}{b}$

Thus $y=\dfrac{1}{b}$ is a horizontal asymptote.

53. $\lim\limits_{t\to\infty}\left(150-76e^{-t}\right)=\lim\limits_{t\to\infty}\left(150-\dfrac{76}{e^{t}}\right)$

$=150-0=150$

Thus $y=150$ is a horizontal asymptote.

55.

$x\approx\pm2.45,\ x\approx0.67,\ y=2$

57.

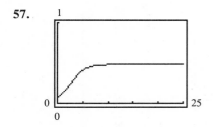

From the graph, it appears that
$\lim\limits_{x\to\infty}y\approx0.48$. Thus a horizontal asymptote
is $y\approx0.48$. Algebraically, we have

$\lim\limits_{x\to\infty}\dfrac{0.34e^{0.7x}}{4.2+0.71e^{0.7x}}=\lim\limits_{x\to\infty}\dfrac{\frac{0.34e^{0.7x}}{e^{0.7x}}}{\frac{4.2+0.71e^{0.7x}}{e^{0.7x}}}$

$=\lim\limits_{x\to\infty}\dfrac{0.34}{\frac{4.2}{e^{0.7x}}+0.71}=\dfrac{0.34}{0+0.71}\approx0.48$

Chapter 14 Review Problems

1. $y=\dfrac{3x^2}{x^2-16}=\dfrac{3x^2}{(x+4)(x-4)}$

When $x=\pm4$ the denominator is zero and the
numerator is not zero. Thus $x=4$ and $x=-4$
are vertical asymptotes.

$\lim\limits_{x\to\infty}\dfrac{3x^2}{x^2-16}=\lim\limits_{x\to\infty}\dfrac{3x^2}{x^2}=\lim\limits_{x\to\infty}3=3$

Similarly, $\lim\limits_{x\to-\infty}y=3$. Thus $y=3$ is the
only horizontal asymptote.

3. $y=\dfrac{5x^2-3}{(3x+2)^2}=\dfrac{5x^2-3}{9x^2+12x+4}$

When $x=-\dfrac{2}{3}$, the denominator is zero and
the numerator is not zero. Thus $x=-\dfrac{2}{3}$ is a
vertical asymptote.

$\lim\limits_{x\to\infty}y=\lim\limits_{x\to\infty}\dfrac{5x^2}{9x^2}=\lim\limits_{x\to\infty}\dfrac{5}{9}=\dfrac{5}{9}$

Similarly, $\lim\limits_{x\to-\infty}y=\dfrac{5}{9}$. Thus $y=\dfrac{5}{9}$ is the
only horizontal asymptote.

5. $f(x)=\dfrac{7x^2}{2-x}$

$f'(x)=\dfrac{(2-x)(14x)-7x^2(-1)}{(2-x)^2}$

$=\dfrac{7x[2(2-x)+x]}{(2-x)^2}=\dfrac{7x(4-x)}{(2-x)^2}$

Thus $x=0$ and $x=4$ are the critical values.
Note: Although $f'(2)$ is not defined, 2 is
not a critical value because 2 is not in the
domain of f.

7. $f(x)=\dfrac{\sqrt[3]{x+1}}{3-4x}$

$f'(x)=\dfrac{(3-4x)\left[\frac{1}{3}(x+1)^{-\frac{2}{3}}\right]-(x+1)^{\frac{1}{3}}(-4)}{(3-4x)^2}$

$=\dfrac{\frac{1}{3}(x+1)^{-\frac{2}{3}}[(3-4x)+12(x+1)]}{(3-4x)^2}$

$=\dfrac{8x+15}{3(x+1)^{\frac{2}{3}}(3-4x)^2}$

$f'(x)$ is zero when $x=-\dfrac{15}{8}$; $f'(x)$ is not
defined when $x=-1$ or $x=\dfrac{3}{4}$. However $\dfrac{3}{4}$
is not in the domain of f. Thus $x=-\dfrac{15}{8}$ and
$x=-1$ are critical values.

9. $f(x) = -x^3 + 6x^2 - 9x$

$f'(x) = -3x^2 + 12x - 9$

$= -3(x^2 - 4x + 3) = -3(x-1)(x-3)$

CV: $x = 1$ and $x = 3$. Increasing on $(1, 3)$;
decreasing on $(-\infty, 1)$ and $(3, \infty)$.

11. $f(x) = \dfrac{6x^4}{x^2 - 3}$

$f'(x) = 6 \cdot \dfrac{(x^2 - 3)(4x^3) - x^4(2x)}{(x^2 - 3)^2}$

$= \dfrac{12x^3[2(x^2 - 3) - x^2]}{(x^2 - 3)^2} = \dfrac{12x^3(x^2 - 6)}{(x^2 - 3)^2}$

$= \dfrac{12x^3(x + \sqrt{6})(x - \sqrt{6})}{[(x + \sqrt{3})(x - \sqrt{3})]^2}$

CV: $x = 0, \pm\sqrt{6}$, but $x = \pm\sqrt{3}$ are also
considered in the inc.-dec. analysis.
Decreasing on $(-\infty, -\sqrt{6})$, $(0, \sqrt{3})$, and
$(\sqrt{3}, \sqrt{6})$; increasing on $(-\sqrt{6}, -\sqrt{3})$,
$(-\sqrt{3}, 0)$ and $(\sqrt{6}, \infty)$.

13. $f(x) = x^4 - x^3 - 14$

$f'(x) = 4x^3 - 3x^2$

$f''(x) = 12x^2 - 6x = 6x(2x - 1)$

$f''(x) = 0$ when $x = 0$ or $x = \dfrac{1}{2}$. Concave

up on $(-\infty, 0)$ and $\left(\dfrac{1}{2}, \infty\right)$; concave down on

$\left(0, \dfrac{1}{2}\right)$.

15. $f(x) = \dfrac{1}{2x - 1} = (2x - 1)^{-1}$

$f'(x) = -2(2x - 1)^{-2}$

$f'' = 8(2x - 1)^3 = \dfrac{8}{(2x - 1)^3}$

$f''(x)$ is not defined when $x = \dfrac{1}{2}$. Concave

down on $\left(-\infty, \dfrac{1}{2}\right)$; concave up on $\left(\dfrac{1}{2}, \infty\right)$.

17. $f(x) = (4x + 1)^3(4x + 9)$

$f'(x) = (4x + 1)^3(4) + (4x + 9)\left[12(4x + 1)^2\right]$

$= 4(4x + 1)^2[(4x + 1) + 3(4x + 9)]$

$= 4(4x + 1)^2(16x + 28) = 16(4x + 1)^2(4x + 7)$

$f''(x) = 16\left\{(4x + 1)^2(4) + (4x + 7)[8(4x + 1)]\right\}$

$= 64(4x + 1)[(4x + 1) + 2(4x + 7)]$

$= 64(4x + 1)(12x + 15) = 192(4x + 1)(4x + 5)$

$f''(x) = 0$ when $x = -\dfrac{1}{4}$ or $x = -\dfrac{5}{4}$. Concave up on $\left(-\infty, -\dfrac{5}{4}\right)$ and $\left(-\dfrac{1}{4}, \infty\right)$; concave down on

$\left(-\dfrac{5}{4}, -\dfrac{1}{4}\right)$.

19. $f(x) = 2x^3 - 9x^2 + 12x + 7$

$f'(x) = 6x^2 - 18x + 12 = 6(x^2 - 3x + 2)$

$= 6(x - 1)(x - 2)$

CV: $x = 1$ and $x = 2$

Increasing on $(-\infty, 1)$ and $(2, \infty)$; decreasing on $(1, 2)$. Relative maximum when $x = 1$; relative minimum when $x = 2$.

21. $f(x) = \dfrac{x^6}{6} + \dfrac{x^3}{3}$

$f'(x) = x^5 + x^2 = x^2(x^3 + 1)$

CV: $x = 0$ and $x = -1$

Decreasing on $(-\infty, -1)$; increasing on $(-1, 0)$ and $(0, \infty)$; relative minimum when $x = -1$.

23. $f(x) = x^{\frac{2}{3}}(x + 1) = x^{\frac{5}{3}} + x^{\frac{2}{3}}$

$f'(x) = \dfrac{5}{3}x^{\frac{2}{3}} + \dfrac{2}{3}x^{-\frac{1}{3}} = \dfrac{1}{3}x^{-\frac{1}{3}}(5x + 2)$

$= \dfrac{5x + 2}{3x^{\frac{1}{3}}}$

CV: $x = 0$ and $x = -\dfrac{2}{5}$

Increasing on $\left(-\infty, -\dfrac{2}{5}\right)$ and $(0, \infty)$;

decreasing on $\left(-\dfrac{2}{5}, 0\right)$. Relative maximum

when $x = -\dfrac{2}{5}$; relative minimum when

$x = 0$.

25. $y = x^5 - 5x^4 + 3x$

$y' = 5x^4 - 20x^3 + 3$

$y'' = 20x^3 - 60x^2 = 20x^2(x - 3)$

Possible inflection points occur when $x = 0$ or $x = 3$. Concave down on $(-\infty, 0)$ and $(0, 3)$; concave up on $(3, \infty)$. Concavity changes around $x = 3$, so there is an inflection point at $x = 3$.

27. $y = 4(3x - 5)(x^4 + 2)$

$= 12x^5 - 20x^4 + 24x - 40$

$y' = 60x^4 - 80x^3 + 24$

$y'' = 240x^3 - 240x^2 = 240x^2(x - 1)$

Possible inflection points occur when $x = 0$ or $x = 1$. Concave down on $(-\infty, 0)$ and $(0, 1)$; concave up on $(1, \infty)$. Inflection point when $x = 1$.

29. $y = \dfrac{x^2}{5e^x} = \dfrac{1}{5} \cdot x^2 e^{-x}$

$y' = \dfrac{1}{5} \cdot x^2(-e^{-x}) + \dfrac{1}{5} \cdot e^{-x}(2x)$

$= -\dfrac{1}{5}e^{-x}(x^2 - 2x)$

$y'' = -\dfrac{1}{5}\left[e^{-x}(2x - 2) + (x^2 - 2x)(-e^{-x})\right]$

$= \dfrac{1}{5}e^{-x}\left[-(2x - 2) + (x^2 - 2x)\right]$

$= \dfrac{1}{5}e^{-x}(x^2 - 4x + 2)$

y'' is defined for all x and y'' is zero only when $x^2 - 4x + 2 = 0$. By the quadratic formula the only possible points of inflection occur when $x = 2 \pm \sqrt{2}$. Concave up on $\left(-\infty, 2 - \sqrt{2}\right)$ and $\left(2 + \sqrt{2}, \infty\right)$; concave down on $\left(2 - \sqrt{2}, 2 + \sqrt{2}\right)$. Inflection points when $x = 2 \pm \sqrt{2}$.

31. $f(x) = 3x^4 - 4x^3$ and f is continuous on $[0, 2]$.

$f'(x) = 12x^3 - 12x^2 = 12x^2(x - 1)$

The only critical value on $(0, 2)$ is $x = 1$. Evaluating f at this value and at the endpoints gives $f(0) = 0, f(1) = -1$, and $f(2) = 16$. Absolute maximum: $f(2) = 16$; absolute minimum $f(1) = -1$.

33. $f(x) = \dfrac{x}{(5x-6)^2}$ and f is continuous on $[-2, 0]$.

$$f'(x) = \frac{(5x-6)^2(1) - x[10(5x-6)]}{(5x-6)^4}$$

$$= \frac{(5x-6)[(5x-6) - 10x]}{(5x-6)^4} = \frac{-5x-6}{(5x-6)^3}$$

$$= -\frac{5x+6}{(5x-6)^3}$$

The only critical value on $(-2, 0)$ is $x = -\dfrac{6}{5}$. Evaluating f at this value and at the endpoints gives

$f(-2) = -\dfrac{1}{128}$, $f\left(-\dfrac{6}{5}\right) = -\dfrac{1}{120}$ and $f(0) = 0$. Absolute maximum: $f(0) = 0$;

absolute minimum: $f\left(-\dfrac{6}{5}\right) = -\dfrac{1}{120}$.

35. $f(x) = \left(x^2 + 1\right)e^{-x}$

a. $f'(x) = \left(x^2 + 1\right)\left(-e^{-x}\right) + e^{-x}(2x)$

$$= -e^{-x}\left[\left(x^2 + 1\right) - 2x\right] = -e^{-x}\left(x^2 - 2x + 1\right)$$

$$= -e^{-x}(x-1)^2$$

CV: $x = 1$

Decreasing on $(-\infty, 1)$ and $(1, \infty)$. No relative extrema.

b. $f''(x) = -\left\{e^{-x}[2(x-1)] + (x-1)^2\left(-e^{-x}\right)\right\}$

$$= e^{-x}(x-1)[-2 + (x-1)]$$

$$= e^{-x}(x-1)(x-3)$$

Possible inflection points when $x = 1, 3$. Concave up on $(-\infty, 1)$ and $(3, \infty)$; concave down on $(1, 3)$.

Inflection points at $(1, f(1)) = \left(1, 2e^{-1}\right)$ and $(3, f(3)) = \left(3, 10e^{-3}\right)$.

37. $y = x^2 - 2x - 24 = (x+4)(x-6)$
Intercepts: $(-4, 0)$, $(6, 0)$, $(0, -24)$
No symmetry. No asymptotes.
$y' = 2(x-1)$
CV: $x = 1$
Increasing on $(1, \infty)$; decreasing on $(-\infty, 1)$;
relative minimum at $(1, -25)$.
$y'' = 2$
No possible inflection point. Concave up on
$(-\infty, \infty)$.

39. $y = x^3 - 12x + 20$

Intercept: $(0, 20)$

No symmetry; no asymptotes

$y' = 3x^2 - 12$

$= 3(x^2 - 4) = 3(x + 2)(x - 2)$

CV: $x = \pm 2$

Increasing on $(-\infty, -2)$ and $(2, \infty)$; decreasing on $(-2, 2)$; relative maximum at $(-2, 36)$; relative minimum at $(2, 4)$.

$y'' = 6x$

Possible inflection point when $x = 0$. Concave up on $(0, \infty)$; concave down on $(-\infty, 0)$; inflection point at $(0, 20)$.

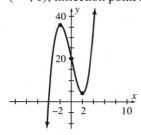

41. $y = x^3 + x = x(x^2 + 1)$

Intercept $(0, 0)$

Symmetric about the origin. No asymptotes.

$y' = 3x^2 + 1$

CV: None

Increasing on $(-\infty, \infty)$.

$y'' = 6x$

Possible inflection point when $x = 0$. Concave down on $(-\infty, 0)$; concave up on $(0, \infty)$; inflection point at $(0, 0)$.

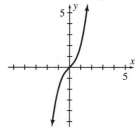

43. $y = f(x) = \dfrac{100(x + 5)}{x^2}$

Intercept: $(-5, 0)$

No symmetry.

$x = 0$ is the only vertical asymptote.

$\lim\limits_{x \to \infty} y = 100 \lim\limits_{x \to \infty} \dfrac{x}{x^2} = 100 \lim\limits_{x \to \infty} \dfrac{1}{x} = 0$, and $\lim\limits_{x \to -\infty} y = 0$, so $y = 0$ is the only horizontal asymptote.

$y = 100\left[x^{-1} + 5x^{-2}\right]$

$y' = 100\left[-x^{-2} - 10x^{-3}\right] = -100\left[\dfrac{1}{x^2} + \dfrac{10}{x^3}\right]$

$= \dfrac{-100(x + 10)}{x^3}$

CV: $x = -10$ but $x = 0$ must be included in analysis for inc-dec. Increasing on $(-10, 0)$; decreasing on $(-\infty, -10)$ and $(0, \infty)$; relative minimum at $(-10, -5)$.

$y'' = 100\left[2x^{-3} + 30x^{-4}\right] = 200\left[\dfrac{1}{x^3} + \dfrac{15}{x^4}\right]$

$= \dfrac{200(x + 15)}{x^4}$

Possible inflection point when $x = -15$, but $x = 0$ must also be considered in concavity analysis. Concave up on $(-15, 0)$ and $(0, \infty)$; concave down on $(-\infty, -15)$; inflection point at $\left(-15, -\dfrac{40}{9}\right)$

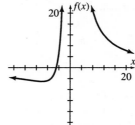

45. $y = \dfrac{x}{(2x-1)^3}$

Intercept: $(0, 0)$

No symmetry. Vertical asymptote is $x = \dfrac{1}{2}$.

$$\lim_{x\to\infty} y = \lim_{x\to\infty} \frac{x}{8x^3} = \lim_{x\to\infty} \frac{1}{8x^2}$$
$$= 0 = \lim_{x\to-\infty} y, \text{ so } y = 0 \text{ is a horizontal}$$

asymptote.

$$y' = \frac{(2x-1)^3(1) - x\left[6(2x-1)^2\right]}{(2x-1)^6}$$

$$= \frac{(2x-1)^2[(2x-1) - 6x]}{(2x-1)^6}$$

$$= -\frac{4x+1}{(2x-1)^4}$$

CV: $x = -\dfrac{1}{4}$, but $x = \dfrac{1}{2}$ must be considered

in inc.-dec. analysis. Increasing on

$\left(-\infty, -\dfrac{1}{4}\right)$; decreasing on $\left(-\dfrac{1}{4}, \dfrac{1}{2}\right)$ and

$\left(\dfrac{1}{2}, \infty\right)$; relative maximum at $\left(-\dfrac{1}{4}, \dfrac{2}{27}\right)$.

$$y'' = -\frac{(2x-1)^4(4) - (4x+1)\left[8(2x-1)^3\right]}{(2x-1)^8}$$

$$= -\frac{4(2x-1)^3[(2x-1) - 2(4x+1)]}{(2x-1)^8}$$

$$= -\frac{4(-6x-3)}{(2x-1)^5} = \frac{12(2x+1)}{(2x-1)^5}$$

Possible inflection point when $x = -\dfrac{1}{2}$, but

$x = \dfrac{1}{2}$ must be considered in concavity

analysis. Concave up on $\left(-\infty, -\dfrac{1}{2}\right)$ and

$\left(\dfrac{1}{2}, \infty\right)$; concave down on $\left(-\dfrac{1}{2}, \dfrac{1}{2}\right)$;

inflection point at $\left(-\dfrac{1}{2}, \dfrac{1}{16}\right)$.

$\left(-\dfrac{1}{2}, \dfrac{1}{16}\right)\left(-\dfrac{1}{4}, \dfrac{2}{27}\right)$

47. $f(x) = \dfrac{e^x + e^{-x}}{2}$

Intercept $(0, 1)$

Symmetric about the y-axis. No asymptotes.

$$f'(x) = \frac{e^x - e^{-x}}{2}$$

Setting

$$f'(x) = 0 \Rightarrow e^x = e^{-x} \Rightarrow x = -x \Rightarrow x = 0$$

CV: $x = 0$

Increasing on $(0, \infty)$; decreasing on $(-\infty, 0)$;

relative minimum at $(0, 1)$. Finding $f''(x)$

gives: $f''(x) = \dfrac{e^x + e^{-x}}{2}$. $f''(x) > 0$ for all

x. No possible inflection point. Concave up

on $(-\infty, \infty)$.

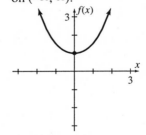

49. a. False. $f'(x_0) = 0$ only indicates the
possibility of a relative extremum at x_0,
For example, if $f(x) = x^3$, then
$f'(x) = 3x^2$ and $f'(0) = 0$. However
there is no relative extremum at $x = 0$.

b. False. For example, let $x_1 = -1$ and
$x_2 = 1$. Then $x_1 < x_2$ and
$f(x_1) = -1 < f(x_2) = 1$.

c. True. The absolute minimum is $f(0) = 0$ and the absolute maximum is $f(1) = 1$.

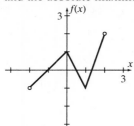

d. False. If concavity does not change around x_0, then $\left(x_0, f(x_0)\right)$ is not an inflection point. For example, consider $f(x) = x^4$. If $x_0 = 0$, then $f''(x_0) = 0$, but $\left(x_0, f(x_0)\right)$ is not an inflection point. See graph in part (c).

e. False. Consider the function f whose graph is shown. On $(-2, 2)$ it has exactly one relative maximum [at the point $(0, 1)$] but no absolute maximum.

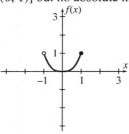

51. $c = q^3 - 6q^2 + 12q + 18$

Marginal cost $= \dfrac{dc}{dq} = 3q^2 - 12q + 12$.

Marginal cost is increasing when its derivative, which is $\dfrac{d^2c}{dq^2}$, is positive.

$\dfrac{d^2c}{dq^2} = 6q - 12 = 6(q - 2)$

$\dfrac{d^2c}{dq^2} > 0$ for $q > 2$. Thus marginal cost is increasing for $q > 2$.

53. $p = 150 - \dfrac{\sqrt{q}}{10}$, $q > 0$. The revenue function r is given by

$$r = pq = \left(150 - \frac{\sqrt{q}}{10}\right)q = 150q - \frac{q^{\frac{3}{2}}}{10}.$$

$$r' = 150 - \frac{3}{20}q^{\frac{1}{2}}$$

$$r'' = -\frac{3}{40}q^{-\frac{1}{2}} = -\frac{3}{40\sqrt{q}}$$

Since $r'' < 0$ for $q > 0$, the graph of the revenue function is concave down for $q > 0$.

55. $f(t) = At^3 + Bt^2 + Ct + D$

$f'(t) = 3At^2 + 2Bt + C$

$f''(t) = 6At + 2B$, which gives an inflection point when $6At + 2B = 0$, that is for $t_0 = -\dfrac{B}{3A}$. This value of t_0 must be such that $f'(t_0) = 0$.

$$3A\left(-\frac{B}{3A}\right)^2 + 2B\left(-\frac{B}{3A}\right) + C = 0$$

$$\frac{1}{3}\left(\frac{B^2}{A}\right) - \frac{2}{3}\left(\frac{B^2}{A}\right) + C = 0$$

$$C = \frac{1}{3}\left(\frac{B^2}{A}\right)$$

$$3AC = B^2,$$

which was to be shown.

57.

Relative maximum $(-1.32, 12.28)$; relative minimum $(0.44, 1.29)$

59.

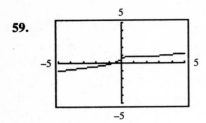

The x-value of the inflection point of f
corresponds to the x-intercept of f''.
Thus the x-value of the inflection point is
$x = -0.60$.

Mathematical Snapshot Chapter 14

1. The data for 1998–2000 fall into the same
   pattern as the 1959–1969 data.

Chapter 15

1. Let the numbers be x and $26 - x$. Then if
$P = x(26 - x) = 26x - x^2$, we have
$P' = 26 - 2x$. Setting $P' = 0 \Rightarrow x = 13$.
Since $P''(13) = -2 < 0$, there is a maximum
when $x = 13$. Because $26 - x = 13$, the
required numbers are 13 and 13.

3. We are given that $15x + 9(2y) = 9000$, or
$y = \dfrac{9000 - 15x}{18}$. We want to maximize area
A, where $A = xy$.
$$A = xy = x\left(\frac{9000 - 15x}{18}\right) = \frac{1}{18}\left(9000x - 15x^2\right)$$
$$A' = \frac{1}{18}(9000 - 30x)$$
Setting $A' = 0 \Rightarrow x = 300$. Since
$A''(300) = \dfrac{1}{18}(-30) < 0$, we have a
maximum at $x = 300$. Thus
$y = \dfrac{9000 - 15(300)}{18} = 250$. The dimensions
are 300 ft by 250 ft.

5. $c = 0.05q^2 + 5q + 500$
Avg. Cost per unit
$$= \bar{c} = \frac{c}{q} = 0.05q + 5 + \frac{500}{q}$$
$\bar{c}' = 0.05 - \dfrac{500}{q^2}$. Setting $\bar{c}' = 0$ yields
$0.05 = \dfrac{500}{q^2}$, $q^2 = 10{,}000$, $q = \pm 100$. We
exclude $q = -100$ because q represents the
number of units. Since $\bar{c}'' = \dfrac{1000}{q^3} > 0$ for
$q > 0$, $\bar{c}$ is an absolute minimum when
$q = 100$ units.

7. $p = -5q + 30$
Since total revenue = (price)(quantity),
$$r = pq = (-5q + 30)q = -5q^2 + 30q$$
Setting $r' = -10q + 30 = 0 \Rightarrow q = 3$. Since
$r'' = -10 < 0$, r is maximum at $q = 3$ units,
for which the corresponding price is
$p = -5(3) + 30 = \$15$.

9. $f(p) = 160 - p - \dfrac{900}{p + 10}$, where $0 \le p \le 100$.
Setting $f'(p) = 0$ gives $-1 + \dfrac{900}{(p + 10)^2} = 0$,
$\dfrac{900}{(p + 10)^2} = 1$, $(p + 10)^2 = 900$,
$p + 10 = \pm 30$, from which $p = 20$.

a. Since $f''(p) = \dfrac{-1800}{(p + 10)^3} < 0$ for
$p = 20$, we have an absolute maximum
of $f(20) = 110$ grams.

b. $f(0) = 70$ and $f(100) = 51\dfrac{9}{11}$, so we
have an absolute minimum of
$f(100) = 51\dfrac{9}{11}$ grams.

11. $p = 72 - 0.04q$
$c = 500 + 30q$
Profit = Total Revenue − Total Cost
$P = pq - c = (72 - 0.04q)q - (500 + 30q)$
$\quad = -\left(0.04q^2 - 42q + 500\right)$
Setting $P' = -(0.08q - 42) = 0$ yields
$q = 525$. Since P is increasing on $[0, 525)$
and decreasing on $(525, \infty)$, P is maximum
when $q = 525$ units. This corresponds to a
price of $p = 72 - 0.04(525) = \$51$ and a
profit of $P = \$10{,}525$.

13. $p = 42 - 4q$

$\bar{c} = 2 + \dfrac{80}{q}$

Total Cost $= c = \bar{c}q = 2q + 80$

Profit = Total Revenue − Total Cost

$P = pq - c = (42 - 4q)q - (2q + 80)$

$\quad = -\left(4q^2 - 40q + 80\right)$

$P' = -(8q - 40)$

Setting $P' = -(8q - 40) = 0$ gives $q = 5$. We find that $P'' = -8 < 0$, so P has a maximum value when $q = 5$. The corresponding price p is $42 - 4(5) = \$22$.

15. $p = q^2 - 100q + 3200$ on $[0, 120]$

$\bar{c} = \dfrac{2}{3}q^2 - 40q + \dfrac{10,000}{q}$

Profit = Total Revenue − Total Cost

Since total revenue $r = pq$ and total cost $= c = \bar{c}q$,

$P = pq - \bar{c}q$

$\quad = q^3 - 100q^2 + 3200q - \left(\dfrac{2}{3}q^3 - 40q^2 + 10,000\right)$

$\quad = \dfrac{1}{3}q^3 - 60q^2 + 3200q - 10,000$

$P' = q^2 - 120q + 3200 = (q - 40)(q - 80)$

Setting $P' = 0$ gives $q = 40$ or 80.

Evaluating profit at $q = 0, 40, 80,$ and 120 gives

$P(0) = -10,000$

$P(40) = \dfrac{130,000}{3} = 43,333\dfrac{1}{3}$

$P(80) = \dfrac{98,000}{3} = 32,666\dfrac{2}{3}$

$P(120) = 86,000$

Thus the profit maximizing output is $q = 120$ units, and the corresponding maximum profit is \$86,000.

17. Total fixed costs = \$1200, material-labor costs/unit = \$2, and the demand equation is $p = \dfrac{100}{\sqrt{q}}$.

Profit = Total Revenue − Total Cost

$P = pq - c$

$P = \dfrac{100}{\sqrt{q}} \cdot q - (2q + 1200)$

$\quad = 100\sqrt{q} - 2q - 1200$

$\quad = 2\left(50\sqrt{q} - q - 600\right)$

Setting $P' = 2\left(\dfrac{25}{\sqrt{q}} - 1\right) = 0$ yields $q = 625$.

We see that $P'' = -25q^{-\frac{3}{2}} < 0$ for $q > 0$, so P is maximum when $q = 625$. When MR equals MC, then $\dfrac{50}{\sqrt{q}} = 2$ or, equivalently, $q = 625$. When $q = 625$, then $p = \$4$.

19. If $x =$ number of \$0.50 decreases, where $0 \le x \le 36$, then the monthly fee for each subscriber is $18 - 0.50x$, and the total number of subscribers is $4800 + 150x$. Let r be the total (monthly) revenue. revenue = (monthly rate)(number of subscribers)

$r = (18 - 0.50x)(4800 + 150x)$

$r' = (18 - 0.50x)(150)$

$\quad +(4800 + 150x)(-0.50)$

$\quad = 300 - 150x = 150(2 - x)$

Setting $r' = 0$ yields $x = 2$.

Evaluating r when $x = 0, 2,$ and 36, we find that r is a maximum when $x = 2$. This corresponds to a monthly fee of $18 - 0.50(2) = \$17$ and a monthly revenue r of \$86,700.

21. See Fig. 15.6 in the text. Given that $x^2 y = 32$, we want to minimize

$S = 4(xy) + x^2$. Since $y = \dfrac{32}{x^2}$, where $x > 0$,

we have $S = 4x\left(\dfrac{32}{x^2}\right) + x^2 = \left(\dfrac{128}{x}\right) + x^2$,

from which $S' = \left(-\dfrac{128}{x^2}\right) + 2x$. Setting

$S' = 0$ gives $2x^3 = 128$, $x^3 = 64$, $x = 4$.

Since $S'' = \left(\dfrac{256}{x^3}\right) + 2$, we get $S''(4) > 0$,

so $x = 4$ gives a minimum. If $x = 4$, then

$y = \dfrac{32}{16} = 2$. The dimensions are

$4 \text{ ft} \times 4 \text{ ft} \times 2 \text{ ft}$.

23. $V = x(12 - 2x)^2$

$= 144x - 48x^2 + 4x^3$

$= 4\left(36x - 12x^2 + x^3\right)$

where $0 < x < 6$.

$V' = 4\left(36 - 24x + 3x^2\right)$

$= 12\left(x^2 - 8x + 12\right)$

$= 12(x - 6)(x - 2)$

For $0 < x < 6$, setting $V' = 0$ gives $x = 2$.
Since $V' > 0$ on $(0, 2)$ and $V' < 0$ on $(2, 6)$,
V is maximum when $x = 2$. Thus the length
of the side of the square must be 2 in., which
results in a volume of

$(12 - 4)^2 (2) = 128 \text{ in}^3$.

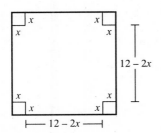

25. See Fig. 15.9 in text.

$V = K = \pi r^2 h$ (1)

$S = 2\pi rh + \pi r^2$ (2)

From Equation (1) $h = \dfrac{K}{\pi r^2}$.

Thus Equation (2) becomes

$S = \dfrac{2K}{r} + \pi r^2$

$\dfrac{dS}{dr} = -\dfrac{2K}{r^2} + 2\pi r = \dfrac{2\left(\pi r^3 - K\right)}{r^2}$.

If $S' = 0$, then $\pi r^3 - K = 0$, $\pi r^3 = K$,

$r = \sqrt[3]{\dfrac{K}{\pi}}$. Thus

$h = \dfrac{K}{\pi\left(\frac{K}{\pi}\right)^{\frac{2}{3}}} = \left(\dfrac{K}{\pi}\right)^{\frac{1}{3}} = \sqrt[3]{\dfrac{K}{\pi}}$.

Note that since $S'' = 2\pi + \dfrac{4K}{r^3} > 0$ for $r > 0$,

we have a minimum.

27. $p = 600 - 2q$

$c = 0.2q^2 + 28q + 200$

Profit = Total Revenue − Total Cost

$P = pq - c$

$P = (600 - 2q)q - \left(0.2q^2 + 28q + 200\right)$

$= -\left(2.2q^2 - 572q + 200\right)$

$P' = -(4.4q - 572)$

Setting $P' = 0$ yields $q = 130$. Since
$P'' = -4.4 < 0$, P is maximum when
$q = 130$ units. The corresponding price is
$p = 600 - 2(130) = \$340$, and the profit is
$P = \$36,980$. If a tax of \$22/unit is imposed
on the manufacturer, then the cost equation
is

$c_1 = 0.2q^2 + 28q + 200 + 22q$

$= 0.2q^2 + 50q + 200$.

The demand equation remains the same.
Thus

$P_1 = pq - c_1$

$= (600 - 2q)q - \left(0.2q^2 + 50q + 200\right)$

$= -\left(2.2q^2 - 550q + 200\right)$

$P'_1 = -(4.4q - 550)$

Setting $P'_1 = 0$ yields $q = 125$. Since $P''_1 = -4.4 < 0$, P_1 is maximum when $q = 125$ units. The corresponding price is $p = \$350$ and the profit is $P_1 = \$34,175$.

29. Let q = number of units in a production run. Since inventory is depleted at a uniform rate, assume that the average inventory is $\frac{q}{2}$. The value of average inventory is $10\left(\frac{q}{2}\right)$, and carrying costs are $0.128\left[10\left(\frac{q}{2}\right)\right]$. The number of production runs per year is $\frac{1000}{q}$, and total set-up costs are $40\left(\frac{1000}{q}\right)$. We want to minimize the sum C of carry costs and set-up costs.

$$C = 0.128\left[10\left(\frac{q}{2}\right)\right] + 40\left(\frac{1000}{q}\right)$$

$$= 0.64q + \frac{40,000}{q}$$

$$C' = 0.64 - \frac{40,000}{q^2}$$

Setting $C' = 0$ yields

$$q^2 = \frac{40,000}{0.64} = 62,500,$$

$q = 250$ (since $q > 0$). Since

$$C'' = \frac{80,000}{q^3} > 0,$$

C is minimum when $q = 250$. Thus the economic lot size is 250/lot (4 lots).

31. Let x = number of people over the 30.
Note: $0 \le x \le 10$.
Revenue = r
= (number attending)(charge/person)
= $(30 + x)(50 - 1.25x)$
= $1500 + 12.5x - 1.25x^2$
$r' = 12.5 - 2.5x$
Setting $r' = 0$ yields $x = 5$. Since $r'' = -2.5 < 0$, r is maximum when $x = 5$, that is, when 35 attend.

33. The cost per mile of operating the truck is $0.165 + \frac{s}{200}$. Driver's salary is $\$18$/hr. The number of hours for 700 mi trip is $\frac{700}{s}$.

Driver's salary for trip is $18\left(\frac{700}{s}\right)$, or $\frac{12,600}{s}$. The cost of operating the truck for the trip is $700\left[0.165 + \frac{s}{200}\right]$.

Total cost of trip is

$$C = \frac{12,600}{s} + 700\left(0.165 + \frac{s}{200}\right)$$

Setting $C' = -\frac{12,600}{s^2} + \frac{7}{2} = 0$ yields

$s^2 = 3600$,
or $s = 60$ (since $s > 0$). Since

$$C'' = \frac{25,200}{s^3} > 0$$

for $s > 0$, C is a minimum when $s = 60$ mi/h.

35. Profit P is given by
P = Total revenue – Total cost
= Total revenue – (salaries + fixed cost)
= $50q - (750m + 2500)$
= $50\left(m^3 - 12m^2 + 60m\right) - 750m - 2500$
= $50\left(m^3 - 12m^2 + 45m - 50\right)$, where
$0 \le m \le 7$
$P' = 50\left(3m^2 - 24m + 45\right)$
= $150\left(m^2 - 8m + 15\right) = 150(m - 3)(m - 5)$

Setting $P' = 0$ gives the critical values 3 and 5. We now evaluate P at these critical values and also at the endpoints 0 and 7.
$P(0) = -2500$
$P(3) = 200$
$P(5) = 0$
$P(7) = 1000$
Thus Ms. Jones should hire 7 salespeople to obtain a maximum weekly profit of $\$1000$.

37. x = tons of chemical A ($x \le 4$),

$y = \dfrac{24 - 6x}{5 - x}$ = tons of chemical B, profit on

A = \$2000/ton, and profit on B = \$1000/ton.

Total Profit = $P_T = 2000x + 1000\left(\dfrac{24 - 6x}{5 - x}\right)$

$= 2000\left[x + \dfrac{12 - 3x}{5 - x}\right]$

$P'_T = 2000\left[1 + \dfrac{(5 - x)(-3) - (12 - 3x)(-1)}{(5 - x)^2}\right]$

$= 2000\left[1 - \dfrac{3}{(5 - x)^2}\right]$

$= 2000\left[\dfrac{x^2 - 10x + 22}{(5 - x)^2}\right]$

Setting $P'_T = 0$ yields (by the quadratic formula)

$x = \dfrac{10 \pm 2\sqrt{3}}{2} = 5 \pm \sqrt{3}$

Because $x \le 4$, choose $x = 5 - \sqrt{3}$. Since P_T is increasing on $\left[0,\, 5 - \sqrt{3}\right)$ and decreasing on $\left(5 - \sqrt{3},\, 4\right]$, P_T is a maximum for $x = 5 - \sqrt{3}$ tons. If profit on A is P/ton and profit on B is $\dfrac{P}{2}$/ton, then

$P_T = Px + \dfrac{P}{2}\left(\dfrac{24 - 6x}{5 - x}\right) = P\left[x + \dfrac{12 - 3x}{5 - x}\right]$

$P'_T = P\left[\dfrac{x^2 - 10x + 22}{(5 - x)^2}\right]$

Setting $P'_T = 0$ and using an argument similar to that above, we find that P_T is a maximum when $x = 5 - \sqrt{3}$ tons.

39. $P(j) = Aj\dfrac{L^4}{V} + B\dfrac{V^3 L^2}{1 + j}$

$\dfrac{dP}{dj} = \dfrac{AL^4}{V} - \dfrac{BV^3 L^2}{(1 + j)^2} = 0$

Solving for $(1 + j)^2$ gives $(1 + j)^2 = \dfrac{BV^4}{AL^2}$

41. $\bar{c} = \dfrac{c}{q} = 3q + 50 - 18\ln(q) + \dfrac{120}{q}$, $q > 0$

$\dfrac{d\bar{c}}{dq} = 3 - \dfrac{18}{q} - \dfrac{120}{q^2} = \dfrac{3q^2 - 18q - 120}{q^2}$

$= \dfrac{3\left(q^2 - 6q - 40\right)}{q^2}$

$= \dfrac{3(q - 10)(q + 4)}{q^2}$

Critical value is $q = 10$ since $q \ge 0$.

Since $\dfrac{d\bar{c}}{dq} < 0$ for $0 < q < 10$, and $\dfrac{d\bar{c}}{dq} > 0$ for $q > 10$, we have a minimum when $q = 10$ cases. This minimum average cost is $3(10) + 50 - 18\ln 10 + 12 \approx \$50.55$.

Exercise 15.2

1. $y = 3x - 4$

$dy = \dfrac{d}{dx}(3x - 4)dx = 3\ dx$

3. $d[f(x)] = f'(x)dx = \dfrac{1}{2}\left(x^4 + 6\right)^{-1/2}\left(4x^3\right)dx$

$= \dfrac{2x^3}{\sqrt{x^4 + 6}}dx$

5. $u = x^{-2}$

$du = \dfrac{d}{dx}\left(x^{-2}\right)dx = -2x^{-3}dx = -\dfrac{2}{x^3}dx$

7. $dp = \dfrac{d}{dx}\left[\ln\left(x^2 + 7\right)\right]dx = \dfrac{1}{x^2 + 7}(2x)dx$

$= \dfrac{2x}{x^2 + 7}dx$

9. $dy = y'dx$

$= \left[(9x + 3)e^{2x^2 + 3}(4x) + e^{2x^2 + 3}(9)\right]dx$

$= 3e^{2x^2 + 3}[(3x + 1)(4x) + 3]dx$

$= 3e^{2x^2 + 3}\left(12x^2 + 4x + 3\right)dx$

11. $\Delta y = [4 - 7(3.02)] - [4 - 7(3)] = -0.14$

$dy = -7\ dx = -7(0.02) = -0.14$

13. $\Delta y = \left[4(-0.75)^2 - 3(-0.75) + 10\right]$
$$-\left[4(-1)^2 - 3(-1) + 10\right] = -2.5$$
$dy = (8x - 3)\, dx = [8(-1) - 3]\,(0.25) = -2.75$

15. $\Delta y = \sqrt{25 - (2.9)^2} - \sqrt{25 - 3^2} \approx 0.073$
$$dy = \frac{-x}{\sqrt{25 - x^2}}\, dx = \frac{-3}{\sqrt{16}}(-0.1) = \frac{3}{40}$$
$$= 0.075$$

17. **a.** $f(x) = \dfrac{x + 5}{x + 1}$
$$f'(x) = \frac{(x + 1)(1) - (x + 5)(1)}{(x + 1)^2} = \frac{-4}{(x + 1)^2}$$
$$f'(1) = \frac{-4}{4} = -1$$

   b. We use $f(x + dx) \approx f(x) + dy$ with $x = 1$, $dx = 0.1$.
$$f(1.1) = f(1 + 0.1) \approx f(1) + f'(1)dx$$
$$= \frac{6}{2} + (-1)(0.1) = 2.9$$

19. Let $y = f(x) = \sqrt{x}$
$$f(x + dx) \approx f(x) + dy = \sqrt{x} + \frac{1}{2\sqrt{x}}\, dx$$
If $x = 100$ and $dx = -1$, then
$$\sqrt{99} = f(100 - 1) \approx \sqrt{100} + \frac{1}{2\sqrt{100}}(-1)$$
$$= 9.95$$

21. Let $y = f(x) = \sqrt[3]{x}$
$$f(x + dx) \approx f(x) + dy = \sqrt[3]{x} + \frac{1}{3x^{\frac{2}{3}}}\, dx$$
If $x = 64$ and $dx = 1.5$, then
$$\sqrt[3]{65.5} = f(64 + 1.5) \approx \sqrt[3]{64} + \frac{1}{3\left(\sqrt[3]{64}\right)^2}(1.5)$$
$$= 4 + \frac{1.5}{3 \cdot 4^2} = 4\frac{1}{32}$$

23. Let $y = f(x) = \ln x$
$$f(x + dx) \approx f(x) + dy = \ln(x) + \frac{1}{x}\, dx$$
If $x = 1$ and $dx = -0.03$, then
$$\ln(0.97) = f(1 + (-0.03))$$
$$\approx \ln(1) + \frac{1}{1}(-0.03) = -0.03$$

25. Let $y = f(x) = e^x$
$$f(x + dx) \approx f(x) + dy = e^x + e^x dx$$
If $x = 0$ and $dx = 0.01$, then
$$e^{0.01} = f(0 + 0.01) \approx e^0 + e^0(0.01) = 1.01$$

27. $\dfrac{dy}{dx} = 2$, so $\dfrac{dx}{dy} = \dfrac{1}{\frac{dy}{dx}} = \dfrac{1}{2}$

29. $\dfrac{dq}{dp} = 6p\left(p^2 + 5\right)^2$, so $\dfrac{dp}{dq} = \dfrac{1}{6p\left(p^2 + 5\right)^2}$

31. $q = p^{-1}$, $\dfrac{dq}{dp} = -1p^{-2} = \dfrac{-1}{p^2}$, so $\dfrac{dp}{dq} = -p^2$

33. $\dfrac{dx}{dy} = \dfrac{1}{\frac{dy}{dx}} = \dfrac{1}{10x + 3}$
   If $x = 3$, then $\dfrac{dx}{dy} = \dfrac{1}{33}$

35. $p = \dfrac{500}{q + 2}$
$$\frac{dp}{dq} = \frac{-500}{(q + 2)^2}$$
$$\frac{dq}{dp} = -\frac{(q + 2)^2}{500}$$
$$\left.\frac{dq}{dp}\right|_{q=18} = -\left.\frac{(q + 2)^2}{500}\right|_{q=18} = -\frac{4}{5}$$

37. $P = 396q - 2.2q^2 - 400$, q changes from 80 to 81.
$$\Delta P \approx dP = P'\, dq = (396 - 4.4q)dq$$
Choosing $q = 80$ and $dq = 1$,
$$\Delta P \approx [396 - 4.4(80)](1) = 44.$$
True change is
$$P(81) - P(80) = 17{,}241.80 - 17{,}200 = 41.80$$

39. $p = \dfrac{10}{\sqrt{q}}$. We approximate p when $q = 24$.

$$p(q + dq) \approx p + dp = \frac{10}{\sqrt{q}} - \frac{5}{\sqrt{q^3}}\, dq$$

If $q = 25$ and $dq = -1$, then

$$\frac{10}{\sqrt{24}} = p(25 + (-1)) \approx \frac{10}{\sqrt{25}} - \frac{5}{\sqrt{(25)^3}}(-1)$$

$$= 2 + \frac{1}{25} = \frac{51}{25} = 2.04$$

41. $c = \dfrac{q^4}{2} + 3q + 400$

If $q = 10$ and $dq = 2$,

$$\frac{dc}{c} = \frac{\left(2q^3 + 3\right)dq}{\frac{q^4}{2} + 3q + 400} = \frac{(2003)(2)}{5430} \approx 0.7$$

43. $V = \dfrac{4}{3}\pi r^3$

$dV = 4\pi r^2 dr$

Now, the change in r is

$$dr = \left(6.6 \times 10^{-4}\right) - \left(6.5 \times 10^{-4}\right)$$

$$= 0.1 \times 10^{-4} = 10^{-5}$$

Thus $dV = 4\pi\left(6.5 \times 10^{-4}\right)^2\left(10^{-5}\right)$

$$\approx \left(1.69 \times 10^{-11}\right)\pi \text{ cm}^3.$$

45. a. We substitute $q = 40$ and $p = 20$

$$2 + \frac{40^2}{200} = \frac{4000}{20^2}$$

$$2 + 8 = 10$$

$$10 = 10$$

b. We differentiate implicitly with respect to p.

$$0 + \frac{1}{200}\left(2q \frac{dq}{dp}\right) = -\frac{8000}{p^3}$$

From part (a) $q = 40$ when $p = 20$.
Substituting gives

$$\frac{1}{200}\left(2 \cdot 40 \frac{dq}{dp}\right) = -\frac{8000}{20^3}$$

$$\frac{dq}{dp} = -2.5$$

c. $q(p + dp) \approx q(p) + dq$

$$= q(p) + q'(p)dp$$

$$q(19.20) = q(20 + (-0.8))$$

$$\approx q(20) + q'(20)dp$$

$$= 40 + (-2.5)(-0.8) = 42 \text{ units}$$

Exercise 15.3

1. $\eta = \dfrac{\frac{p}{q}}{\frac{dp}{dq}} = \dfrac{\frac{p}{q}}{-2}$.

When $q = 5$ then $p = 40 - 2(5) = 30$, so

$$\eta = \frac{\frac{30}{5}}{-2} = -3$$

Because $|\eta| > 1$, demand is elastic.

3. $p = \dfrac{3500}{q} = 3500q^{-1}$

$$\frac{dp}{dq} = -3500q^{-2} = -\frac{3500}{q^2}$$

$$\eta = \frac{\frac{p}{q}}{\frac{dp}{dq}} = \frac{\frac{p}{q}}{-\frac{3500}{q^2}} = \frac{\frac{(3500/q)}{q}}{-\frac{3500}{q^2}} = -1$$

Because $|\eta| = 1$, demand has unit elasticity.

5. $\eta = \dfrac{\frac{p}{q}}{\frac{dp}{dq}} = \dfrac{\frac{p}{q}}{-\frac{500}{(q+2)^2}} = \dfrac{\frac{[500/(q+2)]}{q}}{-\frac{500}{(q+2)^2}} = -\frac{q+2}{q}$

When $q = 104$, then $\eta = -\dfrac{106}{104} = -\dfrac{53}{52}$.

Because $|\eta| > 1$, demand is elastic.

7. $\eta = \dfrac{\frac{p}{q}}{\frac{dp}{dq}} = \dfrac{\frac{p}{q}}{-\frac{e^{\frac{q}{100}}}{100}}$

When $q = 100$, then $p = 150 - e$ and

$$\eta = \frac{\frac{150-e}{100}}{-\frac{e}{100}} = -\left(\frac{150}{e} - 1\right). \text{ Because } |\eta| > 1,$$

demand is elastic.

9. $q = 600 - 100p$

$$\eta = \frac{\frac{p}{q}}{\frac{dp}{dq}} = \frac{p}{q} \cdot \frac{dq}{dp} = \frac{p}{q}(-100)$$

If $p = 3$, then $q = 600 - 100(3) = 300$, so $\eta = \frac{3}{300}(-100) = -1$. Since $|\eta| = 1$, demand has unit elasticity.

11. $q = \sqrt{2500 - p}$

$$\eta = \frac{\frac{p}{q}}{\frac{dp}{dq}} = \frac{p}{q} \cdot \frac{dq}{dp}$$

$$\frac{dq}{dp} = \frac{1}{2}(2500 - p)^{-\frac{1}{2}}(-1) = \frac{-1}{2\sqrt{2500 - p}}$$

$$= -\frac{1}{2q}$$

$$\eta = \frac{p}{q}\left(-\frac{1}{2q}\right) = -\frac{p}{2q^2}$$

If $p = 900$, then $q = \sqrt{2500 - 900} = 40$, so

$$\eta = -\frac{900}{3200} = -\frac{9}{32}. \ |\eta| < 1, \text{ so demand is}$$

inelastic.

13. $q = \frac{(p - 100)^2}{2}$

$$\eta = \frac{\frac{p}{q}}{\frac{dp}{dq}} = \frac{p}{q} \cdot \frac{dq}{dp}$$

$$\frac{dq}{dp} = \frac{1}{2}(2)(p - 100)(1) = p - 100, \text{ so}$$

$\eta = \frac{p}{q}(p - 100)$. If $p = 20$, then

$$q = \frac{(20 - 100)^2}{2} = 3200. \text{ Thus}$$

$$\eta = \frac{20}{3200}(20 - 100) = -\frac{1}{2}. \text{ Demand is}$$

inelastic.

15. $p = 13 - 0.05q$

$$\eta = \frac{\frac{p}{q}}{\frac{dp}{dq}} = -\frac{p}{0.05q}$$

p	q	η	demand
10	60	$-\dfrac{10}{3}$	elastic
3	200	$-\dfrac{3}{10}$	inelastic
6.50	130	-1	unit elasticity

17. $q = 500 - 40p + p^2$

$$\eta = \frac{\frac{p}{q}}{\frac{dp}{dq}} = \frac{p}{q} \cdot \frac{dq}{dp}$$

$$\frac{dq}{dp} = -40 + 2p, \text{ so } \eta = \frac{p}{q}(2p - 40).$$

When $p = 15$, then
$q = 500 - 40(15) + 15^2 = 125$, so

$$\eta|_{p=15} = \frac{15}{125}(30 - 40) = -\frac{6}{5} = -1.2. \text{ Now,}$$

(% change in price) $\cdot$ (η) = % change in demand. Thus if the price of 15 increases

$\frac{1}{2}$%, then the change in demand is

approximately $\left(\frac{1}{2}\%\right)(-1.2) = -0.6\%$. Thus demand decreases approximately 0.6%.

19. $p = 500 - 2q$

$$\eta = \frac{\frac{p}{q}}{\frac{dp}{dq}} = \frac{\frac{500 - 2q}{q}}{-2} = \frac{q - 250}{q}$$

If demand is elastic, then $\eta = \frac{q - 250}{q} < -1$.

For $q > 0$, we have $q - 250 < -q$, $2q < 250$, so $q < 125$. Thus, if $0 < q < 125$, demand is elastic. If demand is inelastic, then

$$\eta = \frac{q - 250}{q} > -1. \text{ For } q > 0, \text{ the inequality}$$

implies $q > 125$. Thus if $125 < q < 250$, then demand is inelastic.

Since Total Revenue

$= r = pq = 500q - 2q^2$, then

$r' = 500 - 4q = 4(125 - q)$. If $0 < q < 125$,

then $r' > 0$, so r is increasing. If

$125 < q < 250$, then $r' < 0$, so r is

decreasing.

21. $p = \dfrac{1000}{q^2}$

$r = pq = \dfrac{1000}{q}$

$\dfrac{dr}{dq} = -1000q^{-2} = -\dfrac{1000}{q^2}$

$\eta = \dfrac{\frac{p}{q}}{\frac{dp}{dq}} = \dfrac{\frac{1000}{q^3}}{-\frac{2000}{q^3}} = -\dfrac{1}{2}$

$p\left(1 + \dfrac{1}{\eta}\right) = \dfrac{1000}{q^2}(1 - 2) = -\dfrac{1000}{q^2} = \dfrac{dr}{dq}$

23. **a.** $p = \dfrac{200}{\sqrt{6000 + 10q^2}}$

Substituting $p = 2$ and $q = 20$:

$2 = \dfrac{200}{\sqrt{6000 + 10(20)^2}}$

$2 = \dfrac{200}{100}$

$2 = 2$

b. $\dfrac{dp}{dq} = 200\left(-\dfrac{1}{2}\right)\left(6000 + 10q^2\right)^{-\frac{3}{2}}(20q)$

$= \dfrac{-2000q}{\left(6000 + 10q^2\right)^{\frac{3}{2}}}$

$= \dfrac{200}{\sqrt{6000 + 10q^2}} \cdot \dfrac{-10q}{6000 + 10q^2}$

$= \dfrac{-10pq}{6000 + 10q^2}$

Thus

$\eta = \dfrac{\frac{p}{q}}{\frac{dp}{dq}} = \dfrac{\frac{p}{q}}{\frac{-10pq}{6000+10q^2}} = \dfrac{-\left(6000 + 10q^2\right)}{10q^2}$

When $p = 2$ we have $q = 20$, so

$\eta\big|_{p=2} = \dfrac{-\left[6000 + 10(20)^2\right]}{10(20)^2} = -2.5$

Thus demand is elastic.

c. If the price (when $p = 2$) is decreased by 2%, then the percentage change in demand is $(-2)(-2.5) = 5\%$. Since $q = 20$ when $p = 2$, this means that q will increase approximately by 5% of 20, which is 1. That is, demand increases by 1 unit (approx).

d. Total revenue will increase when the price is lowered because demand is elastic (see the discussion of elasticity and revenue in the text).

25. **a.** $q = \dfrac{60}{p} + \ln\left(65 - p^3\right)$

$\eta = \dfrac{\frac{p}{q}}{\frac{dp}{dq}} = \dfrac{p}{q}\dfrac{dq}{dp} = \dfrac{p}{q}\left[-\dfrac{60}{p^2} - \dfrac{3p^2}{65 - p^3}\right]$

If $p = 4$, then $q = \dfrac{60}{4} + \ln 1 = 15$, so

$\eta = \dfrac{4}{15}\left[-\dfrac{60}{16} - \dfrac{3(16)}{65 - 64}\right] = -\dfrac{207}{15}$

≈ -13.8, elastic

b. The percentage change in q is $(-2)(-13.8) = 27.6\%$, so q increases by approximately 27.6%.

c. Lowering the price increases revenue because demand is elastic.

27. The percentage change in price is
$\frac{-5}{80} \cdot 100 = -\frac{25}{4}\%$ and the percentage

change in quantity is $\frac{50}{500} \cdot 100 = 10\%$ thus,

since (elasticity)(% change in price) $\approx$ (% change in demand),

(elasticity) $\left(-\frac{25}{4}\right) \approx 10$

elasticity $\approx -\frac{40}{25} = -\frac{8}{5} = -1.6$

To estimate $\frac{dr}{dq}$ when $p = 80$, we have

$$\frac{dr}{dq} = p\left(1 + \frac{1}{\eta}\right) = 80\left(1 + \frac{1}{-\frac{8}{5}}\right) = 30$$

29. $\frac{dp}{dq} = 200(-1)(q+5)^{-2} = \frac{-200}{(q+5)^2}$

Thus $\eta = \frac{\frac{p}{q}}{\frac{dp}{dq}} = \frac{\frac{200}{q(q+5)}}{-\frac{200}{(q+5)^2}} = -\frac{q+5}{q}$.

For $5 \le q \le 95$, $|\eta| = \frac{q+5}{q} = 1 + \frac{5}{q}$ and

$|\eta|' = -\frac{5}{q^2}$.

Since $|\eta|' < 0$, $|\eta|$ is decreasing on $[5, 95]$, and thus $|\eta|$ is maximum at $q = 5$ and minimum at $q = 95$.

Principles in Practice 15.4

1. Let $f(x) = 20x - 0.01x^2 - 850 + 3\ln x$, then $f'(x) = 20 - 0.02x + \frac{3}{x}$. $f(10) \approx -644$ and $f(50) \approx 137$, so we use 50 to be the first approximation, x_1, to find the break-even quantity between 10 and 50.

$$x_{n+1} = x_n - \frac{f(x_n)}{f'(x_n)} = x_n - \frac{20x_n - 0.01x_n^2 - 850 + 3\ln x_n}{20 - 0.02x_n + 3x_n^{-1}}$$

$$= x_n - \frac{20x_n^2 - 0.01x_n^3 - 850x_n + 3x_n \ln x_n}{20x_n - 0.02x_n^2 + 3}$$

$$= \frac{20x_n^2 - 0.02x_n^3 + 3x_n - \left(20x_n^2 - 0.01x_n^3 - 850x_n + 3x_n \ln x_n\right)}{20x_n - 0.02x_n^2 + 3}$$

$$= \frac{-0.01x_n^3 + 853x_n - 3x_n \ln x_n}{20x_n - 0.02x_n^2 + 3}$$

$x_2 = 50 - \frac{f(50)}{f'(50)} \approx 42.82602$

$x_3 = 42.82602 - \frac{f(42.82602)}{f'(42.82602)} \approx 42.85459$

$x_4 = 42.85459 - \frac{f(42.85459)}{f'(42.85459)} \approx 42.85459$

Since the values of x_3 and x_4 differ by less than 0.0001, we take the first break-even quantity to be $x \approx 42.85459$ or 43 televisions.

$f(1900) \approx 1073$ and $f(2000) \approx -827$, so we use 2000 to be the first approximation, x_1, for the break-even quantity between 1900 and 2000.

$$x_2 = 2000 - \frac{f(2000)}{f'(2000)} \approx 1958.63703$$

$$x_3 = 1958.63703 - \frac{f(1958.63703)}{f'(1958.63703)} \approx 1957.74457$$

$$x_4 = 1957.74457 - \frac{f(1957.74457)}{f'(1957.74457)} \approx 1957.74415$$

$$x_5 = 1957.74415 - \frac{f(1957.74415)}{f'(1957.74415)} \approx 1957.74415$$

Since the values of x_4 and x_5 differ by less than 0.0001, we take the second break-even quantity to be $x \approx 1957.74415$ or 1958 televisions.

Exercise 15.4

1. We want a root of $f(x) = x^3 - 4x + 1 = 0$. We see that $f(0) = 1$ and $f(1) = -2$ have opposite signs, so there must be a root between 0 and 1. Moreover, $f(0)$ is closer to 0 than is $f(1)$, so we select $x_1 = 0$ as our initial estimate. Since $f'(x) = 3x^2 - 4$, the recursion formula is

$$x_{n+1} = x_n - \frac{f(x_n)}{f'(x_n)} = x_n - \frac{x_n^3 - 4x_n + 1}{3x_n^2 - 4}.$$

Simplifying gives $x_{n+1} = \frac{2x_n^3 - 1}{3x_n^2 - 4}$. Thus we obtain:

n	x_n	x_{n+1}
1	0.00000	0.25000
2	0.25000	0.25410
3	0.25410	0.25410

Because $|x_4 - x_3| < 0.0001$, the root is approximately $x_4 = 0.25410$.

3. Let $f(x) = x^3 - x - 1$. We have $f(1) = -1$ and $f(2) = 5$ (note the sign change). Since $f(1)$ is closer to 0 than is $f(2)$, we choose $x_1 = 1$. We have $f'(x) = 3x^2 - 1$, so the recursion formula is

$$x_{n+1} = x_n - \frac{f(x_n)}{f'(x_n)} = x_n - \frac{x_n^3 - x_n - 1}{3x_n^2 - 1}$$
$$= \frac{2x_n^3 + 1}{3x_n^2 - 1}$$

n	x_n	x_{n+1}
1	1.00000	1.50000
2	1.50000	1.34783
3	1.34783	1.32520
4	1.32520	1.32472
5	1.32472	1.32472

Since $|x_6 - x_5| < 0.0001$, the root is approximately $x_6 = 1.32472$.

5. Let $f(x) = x^3 + x + 16$. We have
$f(-3) = -14$ and $f(-2) = 6$ (note the sign change). Since $f(-2)$ is closer to 0 than is $f(-3)$, we choose $x_1 = -2$. Since
$f'(x) = 3x^2 + 1$, the recursion formula is

$$x_{n+1} = x_n - \frac{f(x)}{f'(x_n)} = x_n - \frac{x_n^3 + x_n + 16}{3x_n^2 + 1}$$
$$= \frac{2x_n^3 - 16}{3x_n^2 + 1}$$

n	x_n	x_{n+1}
1	−2.00000	−2.46154
2	−2.46154	−2.38977
3	−2.38977	−2.38769
4	−2.38769	−2.38769

Because $|x_5 - x_4| < 0.0001$, the root is approximately $x_5 = -2.38769$.

7. $x^4 = 3x - 1$, so use $f(x) = x^4 - 3x + 1 = 0$.
Since $f(0) = 1$ and $f(1) = -1$ (note the sign change), $f(0)$ and $f(1)$ are equally close to 0. We shall choose $x_1 = 0$. Since
$f'(x) = 4x^3 - 3$, the recursion formula is

$$x_{n+1} = x_n - \frac{f(x_n)}{f'(x_n)} = x_n - \frac{x_n^4 - 3x_n + 1}{4x_n^3 - 3}$$
$$= \frac{3x_n^4 - 1}{4x_n^3 - 3}$$

n	x_n	x_{n+1}
1	0.00000	0.33333
2	0.33333	0.33766
3	0.33766	0.33767

Because $|x_4 - x_3| < 0.0001$, the root is approximately $x_4 = 0.33767$.

9. Let $f(x) = x^4 - 2x^3 + x^2 - 3$. $f(1) = -3$ and $f(2) = 1$ (note the sign change), so $f(2)$ is closer to 0 than is $f(1)$. We choose $x_1 = 2$. Since $f'(x) = 4x^3 - 6x^2 + 2x$, the recursion formula is

$$x_{n+1} = x_n - \frac{f(x)}{f'(x_n)}$$
$$= x_n - \frac{x_n^4 - 2x_n^3 + x_n^2 - 3}{4x_n^3 - 6x_n^2 + 2x_n}$$

n	x_n	x_{n+1}
1	2.00000	1.91667
2	1.91667	1.90794
3	1.90794	1.90785

Because $|x_4 - x_3| < 0.0001$, the root is approximately $x_4 = 1.90785$.

11. The desired number is x, where $x^3 = 71$, or $x^3 - 71 = 0$. Thus we want to find a root of $f(x) = x^3 - 71 = 0$. Since $4^3 = 64$, the solution should be close to 4, so we choose $x_1 = 4$ as our initial estimate. We have $f'(x) = 3x^2$, so the recursion formula is

$$x_{n+1} = x_n - \frac{f(x_n)}{f'(x_n)} = x_n - \frac{x_n^3 - 71}{3x_n^2}$$
$$= \frac{2x_n^3 + 71}{3x_n^2}$$

n	x_n	x_{n+1}
1	4	4.146
2	4.146	4.141
3	4.141	4.141

Thus to three decimal places, $\sqrt[3]{71} = 4.141$.

13. We want real solutions to $e^x = x + 5$. Thus we want to find roots of

$f(x) = e^x - x - 5 = 0$. A rough sketch of the

exponential function $y = e^x$ and the line

$y = x + 5$ shows that there are two intersection points: one when x is near -5, and the other when x is near 3. Thus we must find two roots. Since $f'(x) = e^x - 1$, the recursion formula is

$$x_{n+1} = x_n - \frac{f(x_n)}{f'(x_n)} = x_n - \frac{e^{x_n} - x_n - 5}{e^{x_n} - 1}$$

If $x_1 = -5$, we obtain

n	x_n	x_{n+1}
1	-5	-4.99
2	-4.99	-4.99

If $x_1 = 3$, we obtain:

n	x_n	x_{n+1}
1	3	2.37
2	2.37	2.03
3	2.03	1.94
4	1.94	1.94

Thus the solutions are -4.99 and 1.94.

15. The break-even quantity is the value of q when total revenue and total cost are equal: $r = c$, or $r - c = 0$. Thus we must find a root of $3q - \left(250 + 2q - 0.1q^3\right) = 0$, or

$f(q) = q - 250 + 0.1q^3 = 0$, so

$f'(q) = 1 + 0.3q^2$. The recursion formula is

$$q_{n+1} = q_n - \frac{f(q_n)}{f'(q_n)}$$

$$= q_n - \frac{q_n - 250 + 0.1q_n^3}{1 + 0.3q_n^2}$$

We choose $q_1 = 13$, as suggested.

n	x_n	x_{n+1}
1	13	13.33
2	13.33	13.33

Thus $q \approx 13.33$.

17. The equilibrium quantity is the value of q for which supply and demand are equal, that is, it is a root of $2q + 5 = \dfrac{100}{q^2 + 1}$, or of

$f(q) = 2q + 5 - \dfrac{100}{q^2 + 1} = 0$. Since

$f'(q) = 2 + \dfrac{200q}{\left(q^2 + 1\right)^2}$, the recursion

formula is

$$q_{n+1} = q_n - \frac{f(q_n)}{f'(q_n)} = q_n - \frac{2q_n + 5 - \frac{100}{q_n^2 + 1}}{2 + \frac{200q_n}{\left(q_n^2 + 1\right)^2}}$$

A rough sketch shows that the graph of the supply equation intersects the graph of the demand equation when q is near 3. Thus we select $q_1 = 3$.

n	x_n	x_{n+1}
1	3	2.875
2	2.875	2.880
3	2.880	2.880

Thus $q \approx 2.880$.

19. For a critical value of

$f(x) = \dfrac{x^3}{3} - x^2 - 5x + 1$, we want a root of

$f'(x) = x^2 - 2x - 5 = 0$. Since

$\dfrac{d}{dx}[f'(x)] = 2x - 2$, the recursion formula

is $x_{n+1} = x_n - \dfrac{x_n^2 - 2x_n - 5}{2x_n - 2}$.

For the given interval [3, 4], note that
$f'(3) = -2$ and $f'(4) = 3$ have opposite
signs. Thus there is a root x between 3 and 4.
Since 3 is closer to 0, we shall select $x_1 = 3$.

n	x_n	x_{n+1}
1	3.0	3.5
2	3.5	3.45
3	3.45	3.45

Thus $x \approx 3.45$.

Chapter 15 Review Problems

1. $q = 80m^2 - 0.1m^4$

$\dfrac{dq}{dm} = 160m - 0.4m^3 = 0.4m\left(400 - m^2\right)$

$= 0.4m(20 + m)(20 - m)$. Setting $\dfrac{dq}{dm} = 0$

yields $m = 0$ or $m = 20$ (for $m \geq 0$). We find
that q is increasing on (0, 20) and decreasing
on (20, ∞), so q is maximum at $m = 20$.

3. $p = \sqrt{600 - q}$, where $100 \leq q \leq 300$.

Total Revenue $= r = pq = q\sqrt{600 - q}$

$r' = q\left(\dfrac{1}{2}\right)(600 - q)^{-\frac{1}{2}}(-1) + \sqrt{600 - q}(1)$

$= \dfrac{1}{2}(600 - q)^{-\frac{1}{2}}[-q + 2(600 - q)]$

$= \dfrac{1200 - 3q}{2\sqrt{600 - q}} = \dfrac{3(400 - q)}{2\sqrt{600 - q}}$

No critical values over [100, 300]. Since
$r' > 0$ on [100, 300], r is increasing on
[100, 300], so r must have a maximum at
$q = 300$.

5. $p = 400 - 2q$

$\bar{c} = q + 160 + \dfrac{2000}{q}$

Total Cost $= c = \bar{c}q = q^2 + 160q + 2000$
Profit = Total Revenue – Total Cost
$P = pq - c$

$= (400 - 2q)q - \left(q^2 + 160q + 2000\right)$

$= -\left(3q^2 - 240q + 2000\right)$

$P' = -(6q - 240) = -6(q - 40)$

Setting $P' = 0$ yields $q = 40$. Since
$P'' = -6 < 0$, P is maximum when $q = 40$,
and the corresponding profit is

$P = -\left[3 \cdot 40^2 - 240(40) + 2000\right] = \$2800$.

7. $2x + 4y = 800$; thus $x = 400 - 2y$
Area $= A = xy = (400 - 2y)y$

$= 400y - 2y^2$

$\dfrac{dA}{dy} = 400 - 4y = 4(100 - y)$

Setting $\dfrac{dA}{dy} = 0$ gives $y = 100$. Since

$\dfrac{d^2A}{dy^2} = -4 < 0$, A is maximum when

$y = 100$. When $y = 100$, then $x = 200$.
The dimensions are 200 ft by 100 ft.

9. a. $c = 2q^3 - 9q^2 + 12q + 20$, where
$\dfrac{3}{4} \leq q \leq 6$.

$\dfrac{dc}{dq} = 6q^2 - 18q + 12 = 6\left(q^2 - 3q + 2\right)$

$= 6(q - 1)(q - 2)$

Setting $\dfrac{dc}{dq} = 0$ gives $q = 1$ or 2.

Evaluating c at these critical values and the endpoints: $c\left(\dfrac{3}{4}\right) = \dfrac{793}{32} \approx 24.78$, $c(1) = 25$, $c(2) = 24$, $c(6) = 200$. Thus a minimum occurs at $q = 2$, which corresponds to 200 stands and a total cost of \$24,000. This gives an average cost per stand of $\dfrac{24{,}000}{200} = \$120$.

b. There are no critical values of $3 \le q \le 6$, so we only evaluate c at the endpoints: $c(3) = 29$, $c(6) = 200$. Thus a minimum occurs at $q = 3$, which gives 300 stands.

11. $d\left[x^2 \ln(x+5)\right] = \dfrac{d}{dx}\left[x^2 \ln(x+5)\right]dx$

$= \left[\dfrac{x^2}{x+5} + 2x \ln(x+5)\right]dx$

13. $F = \dfrac{9}{5}C + 32$

$dF = F'\,dC = \dfrac{9}{5}\,dC$, so when

$dC = \dfrac{1}{2}^\circ$, $dF = \dfrac{9}{5}\left(\dfrac{1}{2}\right)^\circ = \left(\dfrac{9}{10}\right)^\circ$.

15. Let $y = f(x) = e^x$

$f(x+dx) \approx f(x) + dy = e^x + e^x\,dx$

If $x = 0$ and $dx = -0.01$, then

$e^{-0.01} = f(0 + (-0.01)) \approx e^0 + e^0(-0.01)$

$= 1 - 0.01 = 0.99$

17. $x = 4y^2 + 7y - 3$

$\dfrac{dy}{dx} = \dfrac{1}{\frac{dx}{dy}} = \dfrac{1}{8y+7}$

19. $p = 900 - q^2$

$\eta = \dfrac{\frac{p}{q}}{\frac{dp}{dq}} = \dfrac{\frac{900-q^2}{q}}{-2q} = -\dfrac{900-q^2}{2q^2}$

When $q = 10$, then $\eta = -4$. Since $|\eta| > 1$, demand is elastic.

21. $p = 30 - \sqrt{q}$

$\eta = \dfrac{\frac{p}{q}}{\frac{dp}{dq}} = \dfrac{\frac{p}{q}}{-\frac{1}{2\sqrt{q}}} = \dfrac{-2p}{\sqrt{q}} = \dfrac{-2p}{30-p} = \dfrac{2p}{p-30}$

a. When $p = 10$, then $\eta = \dfrac{2(10)}{10-30} = -1$.

b. $\eta = \dfrac{2p}{p-30}$

If $0 < p < 10$, then $-1 < \eta < 0$, so $|\eta| < 1$ and demand is inelastic.

23. a. $\eta = \dfrac{\frac{p}{q}}{\frac{dp}{dq}} = \dfrac{p}{q} \cdot \dfrac{dq}{dp}$

$q = \sqrt{100 - p}$, where $0 < p < 100$.

$\dfrac{dq}{dp} = \dfrac{-1}{2\sqrt{100-p}}$. Thus

$\eta = \dfrac{p}{\sqrt{100-p}} \cdot \dfrac{-1}{2\sqrt{100-p}}$

$= \dfrac{-p}{2(100-p)} = \dfrac{p}{2p-200}$

For elastic demand we want

$\dfrac{p}{2p-200} < -1$. Noting that the denominator is negative for $0 < p < 100$, we multiply both sides of the inequality by $2p - 200$ and reverse the direction of the inequality

$p > -2p + 200$, $3p > 200$, $p > \dfrac{200}{3}$

Thus $\dfrac{200}{3} < p < 100$ for elastic demand.

b. $\eta\big|_{p=40} = \dfrac{40}{80-200} = -\dfrac{1}{3}$

% change in $q \approx$ (% change in price)(η)

$= 5\left(-\dfrac{1}{3}\right)\% = -\dfrac{5}{3}\% = -1.67\%$. Thus demand decreases by approximately 1.67%.

25. We want real solutions of $e^x = 3x$. Thus we want to find roots of $f(x) = e^x - 3x = 0$. A rough sketch of the exponential function $y = e^x$ and the line $y = 3x$ shows that there are two intersection points: one when x is near 0.5, and the other when x is near 1.5. Thus we must find two roots. Since $f'(x) = e^x - 3$, the recursion formula is

$$x_{n+1} = x_n - \frac{f(x_n)}{f'(x_n)} = x_n - \frac{e^{x_n} - 3x_n}{e^{x_n} - 3}$$

If $x_1 = 0.5$, we obtain

n	x_n	x_{n+1}
1	0.5	0.610
2	0.610	0.619
3	0.619	0.619

If $x_1 = 1.5$, we obtain

n	x_n	x_{n+1}
1	1.5	1.512
2	1.512	1.512

Thus the solutions are 0.619 and 1.512.

Mathematical Snapshot Chapter 15

1. In Example 5 of Sec. 15.1, the production run setup cost plays the role of the fixed order cost, F. The production cost per unit plays the role of the unit value, V. Yes, the Wilson formula can be used:

$$q = \sqrt{\frac{2FD}{RV}} = \sqrt{\frac{2(40)(10,000)}{(0.10)(20)}} \approx 632.5$$

3. It makes no difference, because the safety margin represents a fixed number of units stored at a constant cost per year. The remaining units are then ordered just as if there were no safety margin.

Chapter 16

Principles in Practice 16.1

1. $\int 28.3 \, dq = 28.3q + C$

The form of the cost function is $28.3q + C$.

2. $\int 0.12t^2 dt = 0.12 \frac{t^3}{3} + C = 0.04t^3 + C$

The revenue function is $R(t) = 0.04t^3 + C$.

3. Let $S(t)$ = the number of subscribers t months after the competition entered the market, then $S'(t) = -\frac{480}{t^3}$.

$S(t) = \int -\frac{480}{t^3} \, dt = -480 \int t^{-3} dt$

$= -480 \left(\frac{t^{-2}}{-2} \right) + C = 240t^{-2} + C = \frac{240}{t^2} + C$

The number of subscribers is

$S(t) = \frac{240}{t^2} + C$.

4. $\int \left(500 + 300\sqrt{t} \right) dt = \int \left(500 + 300t^{\frac{1}{2}} \right) dt$

$= 500t + \frac{t^{\frac{3}{2}}}{\frac{3}{2}} + C = 500t + \frac{2}{3}t^{\frac{3}{2}} + C$

The population is $N(t) = 500t + \frac{2}{3}t^{\frac{3}{2}} + C$

5. The amount of money saved is $\int \frac{dS}{dt} \, dt$.

$\int \left(2.1t^2 - 65.4t + 491.6 \right) dt$

$= 2.1 \left(\frac{t^3}{3} \right) - 65.4 \left(\frac{t^2}{2} \right) + 491.6t + C$

$= 0.7t^3 - 32.7t^2 + 491.6t + C$

The amount of money saved is

$S(t) = 0.7t^3 - 32.7t^2 + 491.6t + C$

Exercise 16.1

1. $\int 5 \, dx = 5x + C$

3. $\int x^8 dx = \frac{x^{8+1}}{8+1} + C = \frac{x^9}{9} + C$

5. $\int 5x^{-7} dx = 5 \int x^{-7} dx = 5 \cdot \frac{x^{-7+1}}{-7+1} + C$

$= 5 \cdot \frac{x^{-6}}{-6} + C = -\frac{5}{6x^6} + C$

7. $\int \frac{2}{x^{10}} \, dx = 2 \int x^{-10} dx = 2 \cdot \frac{x^{-10+1}}{-10+1} + C$

$= \frac{2x^{-9}}{-9} + C = -\frac{2}{9x^9} + C$

9. $\int \frac{1}{y^{\frac{11}{5}}} \, dy = \int y^{-\frac{11}{5}} dy = \frac{y^{\frac{-11}{5}+1}}{\frac{-11}{5}+1} + C$

$= \frac{y^{-\frac{6}{5}}}{-\frac{6}{5}} + C = -\frac{5}{6y^{\frac{6}{5}}} + C$

11. $\int (8 + u) du = \int 8 \, du + \int u \, du$

$= 8u + \frac{u^{1+1}}{1+1} + C = 8u + \frac{u^2}{2} + C$

13. $\int \left(y^5 - 5y \right) dy = \int y^5 dy - \int 5y \, dy$

$= \frac{y^{5+1}}{5+1} - 5 \cdot \frac{y^{1+1}}{1+1} + C$

$= \frac{y^6}{6} - 5 \cdot \frac{y^2}{2} + C = \frac{y^6}{6} - \frac{5y^2}{2} + C$

15. $\int \left(3t^2 - 4t + 5 \right) dt$

$= 3 \int t^2 dt - 4 \int t \, dt + \int 5 \, dt$

$= 3 \cdot \frac{t^3}{3} - 4 \cdot \frac{t^2}{2} + 5t + C = t^3 - 2t^2 + 5t + C$

17. Since $7 + e$ is a constant,

$\int (7 + e) dx = (7 + e)x + C$.

19. $\int\left(\frac{x}{7}-\frac{3}{4}x^4\right)dx = \frac{1}{7}\int x\,dx - \frac{3}{4}\int x^4 dx$

$\qquad = \frac{1}{7}\cdot\frac{x^2}{2} - \frac{3}{4}\cdot\frac{x^5}{5} + C$

$\qquad = \frac{x^2}{14} - \frac{3x^5}{20} + C$

21. $\int 6e^x dx = 6\int e^x dx = 6e^x + C$

23. $\int\left(x^{8.3}-9x^6+3x^{-4}+x^{-3}\right)dx$

$\qquad = \frac{x^{9.3}}{9.3} - 9\cdot\frac{x^7}{7} + 3\cdot\frac{x^{-3}}{-3} + \frac{x^{-2}}{-2} + C$

$\qquad = \frac{x^{9.3}}{9.3} - \frac{9x^7}{7} - \frac{1}{x^3} - \frac{1}{2x^2} + C$

25. $\int\frac{-2\sqrt{x}}{3}dx = -\frac{2}{3}\int x^{\frac{1}{2}}dx = -\frac{2}{3}\cdot\frac{x^{\frac{1}{2}+1}}{\frac{1}{2}+1} + C$

$\qquad = -\frac{2}{3}\cdot\frac{x^{\frac{3}{2}}}{\frac{3}{2}} + C = -\frac{4x^{\frac{3}{2}}}{9} + C$

27. $\int\frac{1}{4\sqrt[8]{x^7}}dx = \frac{1}{4}\int x^{-\frac{7}{8}}dx = \frac{1}{4}\cdot\frac{x^{\frac{-7}{8}+1}}{\frac{-7}{8}+1} + C$

$\qquad = \frac{1}{4}\cdot\frac{x^{\frac{1}{8}}}{\frac{1}{8}} + C = 2\sqrt[8]{x} + C$

29. $\int\left(\frac{x^3}{3}-\frac{3}{x^3}\right)dx = \frac{1}{3}\int x^3 dx - 3\int x^{-3}dx$

$\qquad = \frac{1}{3}\cdot\frac{x^{3+1}}{3+1} - 3\cdot\frac{x^{-3+1}}{-3+1} + C$

$\qquad = \frac{1}{3}\cdot\frac{x^4}{4} - 3\cdot\frac{x^{-2}}{-2} + C = \frac{x^4}{12} + \frac{3}{2x^2} + C$

31. $\int\left(\frac{3w^2}{2}-\frac{2}{3w^2}\right)dw$

$\qquad = \frac{3}{2}\int w^2 dw - \frac{2}{3}\int w^{-2}dw$

$\qquad = \frac{3}{2}\cdot\frac{w^3}{3} - \frac{2}{3}\cdot\frac{w^{-1}}{-1} + C = \frac{w^3}{2} + \frac{2}{3w} + C$

33. $\int\frac{2z-5}{7}dz = \frac{1}{7}\int(2z-5)dz$

$\qquad = \frac{1}{7}\left(2\int z\,dz - \int 5\,dz\right)$

$\qquad = \frac{1}{7}\left(2\cdot\frac{z^{1+1}}{1+1} - 5z\right) + C$

$\qquad = \frac{1}{7}\left(2\cdot\frac{z^2}{2} - 5z\right) + C = \frac{1}{7}\left(z^2 - 5z\right) + C$

35. $\int\left(x^e + 10e^x\right)dx = \int x^e dx + 10\int e^x dx$

$\qquad = \frac{x^{e+1}}{e+1} + 10e^x + C$

37. $\int\left(2\sqrt{x}-3\sqrt[4]{x}\right)dx = \int\left(2x^{\frac{1}{2}}-3x^{\frac{1}{4}}\right)dx$

$\qquad = 2\int x^{\frac{1}{2}}dx - 3\int x^{\frac{1}{4}}dx$

$\qquad = 2\cdot\frac{x^{\frac{1}{2}+1}}{\frac{1}{2}+1} - 3\cdot\frac{x^{\frac{1}{4}+1}}{\frac{1}{4}+1} + C$

$\qquad = 2\cdot\frac{x^{\frac{3}{2}}}{\frac{3}{2}} - 3\cdot\frac{x^{\frac{5}{4}}}{\frac{5}{4}} + C = \frac{4x^{\frac{3}{2}}}{3} - \frac{12x^{\frac{5}{4}}}{5} + C$

39. $\int\left(-\frac{\sqrt[3]{x^2}}{5} - \frac{7}{2\sqrt{x}} + 6x\right)dx$

$\qquad = \int\left(-\frac{x^{\frac{2}{3}}}{5} - \frac{7x^{-\frac{1}{2}}}{2} + 6x\right)dx$

$\qquad = -\frac{1}{5}\int x^{\frac{2}{3}}dx - \frac{7}{2}\int x^{-\frac{1}{2}}dx + 6\int x\,dx$

$\qquad = -\frac{1}{5}\cdot\frac{x^{\frac{5}{3}}}{\frac{5}{3}} - \frac{7}{2}\cdot\frac{x^{\frac{1}{2}}}{\frac{1}{2}} + 6\cdot\frac{x^2}{2} + C$

$\qquad = -\frac{3x^{\frac{5}{3}}}{25} - 7x^{\frac{1}{2}} + 3x^2 + C$

41. $\int\left(x^2 + 5\right)(x-3)dx$

$\qquad = \int\left(x^3 - 3x^2 + 5x - 15\right)dx$

$\qquad = \frac{x^4}{4} - 3\cdot\frac{x^3}{3} + 5\cdot\frac{x^2}{2} - 15x + C$

$\qquad = \frac{x^4}{4} - x^3 + \frac{5x^2}{2} - 15x + C$

43. $\int \sqrt{x}(x+3)dx = \int \left(x^{\frac{3}{2}} + 3x^{\frac{1}{2}} \right) dx$

$= \dfrac{x^{\frac{5}{2}}}{\frac{5}{2}} + 3 \cdot \dfrac{x^{\frac{3}{2}}}{\frac{3}{2}} + C$

$= \dfrac{2x^{\frac{5}{2}}}{5} + 2x^{\frac{3}{2}} + C$

45. $\int (2u+1)^2 \, du = \int \left(4u^2 + 4u + 1 \right) du$

$= 4 \cdot \dfrac{u^3}{3} + 4 \cdot \dfrac{u^2}{2} + u + C$

$= \dfrac{4u^3}{3} + 2u^2 + u + C$

47. $\int v^{-2} \left(2v^4 + 3v^2 - 2v^{-3} \right) dv$

$= \int \left(2v^2 + 3 - 2v^{-5} \right) dv$

$= 2 \cdot \dfrac{v^3}{3} + 3v - 2 \cdot \dfrac{v^{-4}}{-4} + C$

$= \dfrac{2v^3}{3} + 3v + \dfrac{1}{2v^4} + C$

49. $\int \dfrac{z^4 + 10z^3}{2z^2} \, dz = \dfrac{1}{2} \int \left(\dfrac{z^4}{z^2} + \dfrac{10z^3}{z^2} \right) dz$

$= \dfrac{1}{2} \int \left(z^2 + 10z \right) dz$

$= \dfrac{1}{2} \left(\dfrac{z^3}{3} + 10 \cdot \dfrac{z^2}{2} \right) + C = \dfrac{z^3}{6} + \dfrac{5z^2}{2} + C$

51. $\int \dfrac{e^x + e^{2x}}{e^x} \, dx = \int \left(\dfrac{e^x}{e^x} + \dfrac{e^{2x}}{e^x} \right) dx$

$= \int \left(1 + e^x \right) dx = x + e^x + C$

53. No, $F(x) - G(x)$ must be a constant.

55. Because an antiderivative of the derivative of a function is the function itself, we have

$\int \dfrac{d}{dx} \left[\dfrac{1}{\sqrt{x^2+1}} \right] dx = \dfrac{1}{\sqrt{x^2+1}} + C.$

Principles in Practice 16.2

1. $N(t) = \int \dfrac{dN}{dt} \, dt = \int \left(800 + 200e^t \right) dt$

$= 800t + 200e^t + C$

Since $N(5) = 40{,}000$, we have

$40{,}000 = 800(5) + 200e^5 + C$, so

$C = 40{,}000 - \left(4000 + 200e^5 \right)$

$= 36{,}000 - 200e^5 \approx 6317.37$

$N(t) = 800t + 200e^t + 6317.37$

2. Since $y'' = \dfrac{d}{dt}(y') = 84t + 24$

$y' = \int (84t + 24) dt = 84 \left(\dfrac{t^2}{2} \right) + 24t + C_1$

$= 42t^2 + 24t + C_1$

Since $y'(8) = 2891$, we have

$2891 = 42(8)^2 + 24(8) + C_1 = 2880 + C_1$, so

$C_1 = 2891 - 2880 = 11$, and

$y' = 42t^2 + 24t + 11.$

$y(t) = \int y' \, dt = \int \left(42t^2 + 24t + 11 \right) dt$

$= 42 \left(\dfrac{t^3}{3} \right) + 24 \left(\dfrac{t^2}{2} \right) + 11t + C_2$

$= 14t^3 + 12t^2 + 11t + C_2$

Since $y(2) = 185$, we have

$185 = 14(2)^3 + 12(2)^2 + 11(2) + C_2$

$= 182 + C_2$, so $C_2 = 185 - 182 = 3.$

$y(t) = 14t^3 + 12t^2 + 11t + 3$

Exercise 16.2

1. $\dfrac{dy}{dx} = 3x - 4$

$y = \int (3x - 4) dx = \dfrac{3x^2}{2} - 4x + C$

Using $y(-1) = \dfrac{13}{2}$ gives

$\dfrac{13}{2} = \dfrac{3(-1)^2}{2} - 4(-1) + C$

$\dfrac{13}{2} = \dfrac{11}{2} + C$

Thus $C = 1$, so $y = \dfrac{3x^2}{2} - 4x + 1.$

3. $y' = \dfrac{4}{\sqrt{x}}$

$y = \displaystyle\int \dfrac{4}{\sqrt{x}} \, dx = \int 4x^{-\frac{1}{2}} dx = 4 \cdot \dfrac{x^{\frac{1}{2}}}{\frac{1}{2}} + C$

Thus $y = 8x^{\frac{1}{2}} + C$. Now, $y(4) = 10$ implies

$10 = 8 \cdot (4)^{\frac{1}{2}} + C$, $10 = 16 + C$, $C = -6$. Thus
$y = 8\sqrt{x} - 6$. Evaluating at $x = 9$ gives
$y(9) = 8 \cdot 3 - 6 = 18$.

5. $y'' = -x^2 - 2x$

$y' = \displaystyle\int \left(-x^2 - 2x\right) dx = -\dfrac{x^3}{3} - x^2 + C_1$

$y'(1) = 0$ implies $0 = -\dfrac{1}{3} - 1 + C_1$, so

$C_1 = \dfrac{4}{3}$. Thus $y' = -\dfrac{x^3}{3} - x^2 + \dfrac{4}{3}$.

Now we integrate again to find y.

$y = \displaystyle\int \left(-\dfrac{x^3}{3} - x^2 + \dfrac{4}{3}\right) dx$

$= -\dfrac{x^4}{12} - \dfrac{x^3}{3} + \dfrac{4x}{3} + C_2$

$y(1) = 1$, so $1 = -\dfrac{1}{12} - \dfrac{1}{3} + \dfrac{4}{3} + C_2$, from

which $C_2 = \dfrac{1}{12}$. Thus we have

$y = -\dfrac{x^4}{12} - \dfrac{x^3}{3} + \dfrac{4x}{3} + \dfrac{1}{12}$.

7. $y''' = 2x$

$y'' = \displaystyle\int 2x \, dx = x^2 + C_1$

$y''(-1) = 3$ implies that $3 = 1 + C_1$,
so $C_1 = 2$.

$y' = \displaystyle\int \left(x^2 + 2\right) dx = \dfrac{x^3}{3} + 2x + C_2$

$y'(3) = 10$ implies $10 = 9 + 6 + C_2$,
so $C_2 = -5$.

Thus

$y = \displaystyle\int \left(\dfrac{x^3}{3} + 2x - 5\right) dx$

$= \dfrac{x^4}{12} + x^2 - 5x + C_3$.

$y(0) = 13$ implies that $13 = 0 + 0 - 0 + C_3$, so

$C_3 = 13$. Therefore $y = \dfrac{x^4}{12} + x^2 - 5x + 13$.

9. $\dfrac{dr}{dq} = 0.7$

$r = \displaystyle\int 0.7 \, dq = 0.7q + C$

If $q = 0$, r must be 0, so $0 = 0 + C$, $C = 0$.
Thus $r = 0.7q$. Since $r = pq$, we have

$p = \dfrac{r}{q} = \dfrac{0.7q}{q} = 0.7$. The demand function

is $p = 0.7$.

11. $\dfrac{dr}{dq} = 275 - q - 0.3q^2$

Thus $r = \displaystyle\int \left(275 - q - 0.3q^2\right) dq$

$= 275q - 0.5q^2 - 0.1q^3 + C$. When $q = 0$,
r must be 0. Thus $0 = 0 - 0 - 0 + C$, so $C = 0$
and $r = 275q - 0.5q^2 - 0.1q^3$. Since $r = pq$,

then $p = \dfrac{r}{q} = 275 - 0.5q - 0.1q^2$. Thus the

demand function is $p = 275 - 0.5q - 0.1q^2$.

13. $\dfrac{dc}{dq} = 1.35$

$c = \displaystyle\int 1.35 \, dq = 1.35q + C$

When $q = 0$, then $c = 200$, so $200 = 0 + C$, or
$C = 200$. Thus $c = 1.35q + 200$.

15. $\dfrac{dc}{dq} = 0.09q^2 - 1.2q + 4.5$

$c = \displaystyle\int \left(0.09q^2 - 1.2q + 4.5\right) dq$

$= 0.03q^3 - 0.6q^2 + 4.5q + C$. If $q = 0$, then
$c = 7700$, from which $C = 7700$. Hence
$c = 0.03q^3 - 0.6q^2 + 4.5q + 7700$. If
$q = 10$, substituting gives $c = 7715$.

17. $G = \int \left[-\frac{P}{25} + 2 \right] dP = -\frac{P^2}{50} + 2P + C$

When $P = 10$, then $G = 38$, so
$38 = -2 + 20 + C$, from which $C = 20$. Thus
$G = -\frac{1}{50}P^2 + 2P + 20$.

19. $v = \int -\frac{(P_1 - P_2)r}{2l\eta} dr = -\frac{(P_1 - P_2)r^2}{4l\eta} + C$

Since $v = 0$ when $r = R$, then

$0 = -\frac{(P_1 - P_2)R^2}{4l\eta} + C$, so $C = \frac{(P_1 - P_2)R^2}{4l\eta}$.

Thus $v = -\frac{(P_1 - P_2)r^2}{4l\eta} + \frac{(P_1 - P_2)R^2}{4l\eta}$

$= \frac{(P_1 - P_2)(R^2 - r^2)}{4l\eta}$.

21. $\frac{dc}{dq} = 0.003q^2 - 0.4q + 40$

$c = \int \left(0.003q^2 - 0.4q + 40 \right) dq$

$= 0.003 \cdot \frac{q^3}{3} - 0.4 \cdot \frac{q^2}{2} + 40q + C$

$= 0.001q^3 - 0.2q^2 + 40q + C$

When $q = 0$, then $c = 5000$, so
$5000 = 0 - 0 + 0 + C$, or $C = 5000$. Thus
$c = 0.001q^3 - 0.2q^2 + 40q + 5000$. When
$q = 100$, then $c = 8000$. Since

Avg. Cost $= \bar{c} = \frac{\text{Total Cost}}{\text{Quantity}} = \frac{c}{q}$, when

$q = 100$, we have $\bar{c} = \frac{8000}{100} = \$80$.

(Observe that knowing $\frac{dc}{dq} = 27.50$ when

$q = 50$ is not relevant to the problem.)

Principles in Practice 16.3

1. Using the values given,
$\frac{dT}{dt} = -0.5(70 - 60)e^{-0.5t} = -5e^{-0.5t}$

$T(t) = \int \frac{dT}{dt} dt = \int -5e^{-0.5t} dt$

$= 10e^{-0.5t} + C$

2. The number of words memorized is $v(t)$.

$v(t) = \int \frac{35}{t+1} dt = 35 \ln|t + 1| + C$.

Exercise 16.3

1. Let $u = x + 5 \Rightarrow du = 1dx = dx$

$\int (x + 5)^7 [dx] = \int u^7 du = \frac{u^8}{8} + C$

$= \frac{(x+5)^8}{8} + C$

3. Let $u = x^2 + 3 \Rightarrow du = 2x\ dx$

$\int 2x \left(x^2 + 3 \right)^5 dx$

$= \int \left(x^2 + 3 \right)^5 [2x\ dx] = \int u^5 du = \frac{u^6}{6} + C$

$= \frac{\left(x^2 + 3 \right)^6}{6} + C$

5. Let $u = y^3 + 3y^2 + 1 \Rightarrow du = \left(3y^2 + 6y \right) dy$

$\int \left(3y^2 + 6y \right) \left(y^3 + 3y^2 + 1 \right)^{\frac{2}{3}} dy$

$= \int \left(y^3 + 3y^2 + 1 \right)^{\frac{2}{3}} \left[\left(3y^2 + 6y \right) dy \right]$

$= \int u^{\frac{2}{3}} du = \frac{u^{\frac{5}{3}}}{\frac{5}{3}} + C$

$= \frac{3}{5} \left(y^3 + 3y^2 + 1 \right)^{\frac{5}{3}} + C$

7. Let $u = 3x - 1 \Rightarrow du = 3\ dx$

$$\int \frac{5}{(3x-1)^3}\ dx = \frac{5}{3}\int \frac{1}{(3x-1)^3}[3\ dx]$$

$$= \frac{5}{3}\int \frac{1}{u^3}\ du = \frac{5}{3}\int u^{-3}\ du$$

$$= \frac{5}{3}\cdot\frac{u^{-2}}{-2} + C = -\frac{5(3x-1)^{-2}}{6} + C$$

9. Let $u = 2x - 1 \Rightarrow du = 2\ dx$.

$$\int \sqrt{2x-1}\ dx = \int (2x-1)^{\frac{1}{2}}\ dx$$

$$= \frac{1}{2}\int (2x-1)^{\frac{1}{2}}[2\ dx]$$

$$= \frac{1}{2}\int u^{\frac{1}{2}}\ du = \frac{1}{2}\cdot\frac{u^{\frac{3}{2}}}{\frac{3}{2}} + C = \frac{1}{3}(2x-1)^{\frac{3}{2}} + C$$

11. Let $u = 7x - 6 \Rightarrow du = 7\ dx$

$$\int (7x-6)^4\ dx = \frac{1}{7}\int (7x-6)^4[7\ dx]$$

$$= \frac{1}{7}\int u^4\ du = \frac{1}{7}\cdot\frac{u^5}{5} + C$$

$$= \frac{(7x-6)^5}{35} + C$$

13. Let $u = x^2 + 3 \Rightarrow du = 2x\ dx$

$$\int x\left(x^2+3\right)^{12}\ dx = \frac{1}{2}\int \left(x^2+3\right)^{12}[2x\ dx]$$

$$= \frac{1}{2}\int u^{12}\ du$$

$$= \frac{1}{2}\cdot\frac{u^{13}}{13} + C = \frac{\left(x^2+3\right)^{13}}{26} + C$$

15. Let $u = 27 + x^5 \Rightarrow du = 5x^4\ dx$

$$\int 4x^4\left(27+x^5\right)^{\frac{1}{3}}\ dx = \frac{4}{5}\int \left(27+x^5\right)^{\frac{1}{3}}\left[5x^4\ dx\right]$$

$$= \frac{4}{5}\int u^{\frac{1}{3}}\ du = \frac{4}{5}\cdot\frac{u^{\frac{4}{3}}}{\frac{4}{3}} + C$$

$$= \frac{3}{5}\left(27+x^5\right)^{\frac{4}{3}} + C$$

17. Let $u = 3x \Rightarrow du = 3\ dx$

$$\int 3e^{3x}\ dx = \int e^{3x}[3\ dx]$$

$$= \int e^u\ du = e^u + C = e^{3x} + C$$

19. Let $u = t^2 + t \Rightarrow du = (2t+1)dt$

$$\int (2t+1)e^{t^2+t}\ dt = \int e^{t^2+t}[(2t+1)\ dt]$$

$$= \int e^u\ du = e^u + C = e^{t^2+t} + C$$

21. $\displaystyle\int xe^{7x^2}\ dx = \frac{1}{14}\int e^{7x^2}[14x\ dx]$

$$= \frac{1}{14}e^{7x^2} + C$$

23. $\displaystyle\int 6e^{-2x}\ dx = 6\left(-\frac{1}{2}\right)\int e^{-2x}[-2\ dx]$

$$= -3e^{-2x} + C$$

25. Let $u = x + 5 \Rightarrow du = dx$

$$\int \frac{1}{x+5}[dx] = \int \frac{1}{u}\ du = \ln|u| + C$$

$$= \ln|x+5| + C$$

27. $\displaystyle\int \frac{3x^2+4x^3}{x^3+x^4}\ dx$

$$= \int \frac{1}{x^3+x^4}\left[\left(3x^2+4x^3\right)dx\right]$$

$$= \ln\left|x^3+x^4\right| + C$$

29. $\displaystyle\int \frac{6z}{\left(z^2-6\right)^5}\ dz = 6\cdot\frac{1}{2}\int \left(z^2-6\right)^{-5}[2z\ dz]$

$$= 3\cdot\frac{\left(z^2-6\right)^{-4}}{-4} + C$$

$$= -\frac{3}{4}\left(z^2-6\right)^{-4} + C$$

31. $\displaystyle\int \frac{4}{x}\ dx = 4\int \frac{1}{x}\ dx = 4\ln|x| + C$

33. $\int \frac{s^2}{s^3+5}\,ds = \frac{1}{3}\int \frac{1}{s^3+5}\left[3s^2\,ds\right]$

$= \frac{1}{3}\ln\left|s^3+5\right| + C$

35. $\int \frac{8}{5-3x}\,dx = 8\left(-\frac{1}{3}\right)\int \frac{1}{5-3x}[-3\,dx]$

$= -\frac{8}{3}\ln\left|5-3x\right| + C$

37. $\int \sqrt{5x}\,dx = \frac{1}{5}\int (5x)^{\frac{1}{2}}[5\,dx] = \frac{1}{5}\cdot\frac{(5x)^{\frac{3}{2}}}{\frac{3}{2}} + C$

$= \frac{2}{15}(5x)^{\frac{3}{2}} + C = \frac{2}{15}(5x)(5x)^{\frac{1}{2}} + C$

$= \frac{2}{3}x\sqrt{5x} + C = \frac{2\sqrt{5}}{3}x^{\frac{3}{2}} + C$

39. $\int \frac{x}{\sqrt{x^2-4}}\,dx = \frac{1}{2}\int \left(x^2-4\right)^{-\frac{1}{2}}[2x\,dx]$

$= \frac{1}{2}\cdot\frac{\left(x^2-4\right)^{\frac{1}{2}}}{\frac{1}{2}} + C$

$= \sqrt{x^2-4} + C$

41. $\int 2y^3 e^{y^4+1}\,dy = 2\int y^3 e^{y^4+1}\,dy$

$= 2\cdot\frac{1}{4}\int e^{y^4+1}\left[4y^3\,dy\right]$

$= 2\cdot\frac{1}{4}\cdot e^{y^4+1} + C = \frac{1}{2}e^{y^4+1} + C$

43. $\int v^2 e^{-2v^3+1}\,dv = -\frac{1}{6}\int e^{-2v^3+1}\left[-6v^2\,dv\right]$

$= -\frac{1}{6}e^{-2v^3+1} + C$

45. $\int \left(e^{-5x} + 2e^x\right)dx = \int e^{-5x}\,dx + 2\int e^x\,dx$

$= -\frac{1}{5}\int e^{-5x}[-5\,dx] + 2\int e^x\,dx$

$= -\frac{1}{5}e^{-5x} + 2e^x + C$

47. $\int (x+1)\left(3-3x^2-6x\right)^3 dx$

$= -\frac{1}{6}\int \left(3-3x^2-6x\right)^3[(-6x-6)dx]$

$= -\frac{1}{6}\cdot\frac{\left(3-3x^2-6x\right)^4}{4} + C$

$= -\frac{1}{24}\left(3-3x^2-6x\right)^4 + C$

49. $\int \frac{x^2+2}{x^3+6x}\,dx = \frac{1}{3}\int \frac{1}{x^3+6x}\left[\left(3x^2+6\right)dx\right]$

$= \frac{1}{3}\ln\left|x^3+6x\right| + C$

51. $\int \frac{16s-4}{3-2s+4s^2}\,dx$

$= 2\int \frac{1}{3-2s+4s^2}[(8s-2)ds]$

$= 2\ln\left|3-2s+4s^2\right| + C$

53. $\int x\left(2x^2+1\right)^{-1}dx = \int \frac{x}{2x^2+1}\,dx$

$= \frac{1}{4}\int \frac{1}{2x^2+1}[4x\,dx]$

$= \frac{1}{4}\ln\left(2x^2+1\right) + C$

55. $\int -\left(x^2-2x^5\right)\left(x^3-x^6\right)^{-10}dx$

$= -\frac{1}{3}\int \left(x^3-x^6\right)^{-10}\left[3\left(x^2-2x^5\right)dx\right]$

$= -\frac{1}{3}\cdot\frac{\left(x^3-x^6\right)^{-9}}{-9} + C$

$= \frac{1}{27}\left(x^3-x^6\right)^{-9} + C$

57. $\int \left(2x^3+x\right)\left(x^4+x^2\right)dx$

$= \frac{1}{2}\int \left(x^4+x^2\right)^1\left[2\left(2x^3+x\right)dx\right]$

$= \frac{1}{2}\cdot\frac{\left(x^4+x^2\right)^2}{2} + C = \frac{1}{4}\left(x^4+x^2\right)^2 + C$

59. $\int \dfrac{18+12x}{\left(4-9x-3x^2\right)^5}\,dx$

$= -2\int \left(4-9x-3x^2\right)^{-5}[(-9-6x)\,dx]$

$= -2 \cdot \dfrac{\left(4-9x-3x^2\right)^{-4}}{-4} + C$

$= \dfrac{1}{2}\left(4-9x-3x^2\right)^{-4} + C$

61. $u = 4x^3 + 3x^2 - 4$

$du = \left(12x^2 + 6x\right)dx = 6x(2x+1)dx$

$\int x(2x+1)e^{4x^3+3x^2-4}\,dx$

$= \dfrac{1}{6}\int e^{4x^3+3x^2-4}[6x(2x+1)dx]$

$= \dfrac{1}{6}\int e^u\,du = \dfrac{1}{6}e^u + C = \dfrac{1}{6}e^{4x^3+3x^2-4} + C$

63. $\int x\sqrt{\left(8-5x^2\right)^3}\,dx$

$= -\dfrac{1}{10}\int \left(8-5x^2\right)^{\frac{3}{2}}[-10x\,dx]$

$= -\dfrac{1}{10} \cdot \dfrac{\left(8-5x^2\right)^{\frac{5}{2}}}{\frac{5}{2}} + C$

$= -\dfrac{1}{25}\left(8-5x^2\right)^{\frac{5}{2}} + C$

65. $\int\left(\sqrt{2x} - \dfrac{1}{\sqrt{2x}}\right)dx = \int \sqrt{2x}\,dx - \int \dfrac{1}{\sqrt{2x}}\,dx$

$= \dfrac{1}{2}\int (2x)^{\frac{1}{2}}[2\,dx] - \dfrac{1}{2}\int (2x)^{-\frac{1}{2}}[2\,dx]$

$= \dfrac{1}{2} \cdot \dfrac{(2x)^{\frac{3}{2}}}{\frac{3}{2}} - \dfrac{1}{2} \cdot \dfrac{(2x)^{\frac{1}{2}}}{\frac{1}{2}} + C$

$= \dfrac{(2x)^{\frac{3}{2}}}{3} - \sqrt{2x} + C$

$= \dfrac{2\sqrt{2}}{3}x^{\frac{3}{2}} - \sqrt{2}x^{\frac{1}{2}} + C$

67. $\int \left(x^2+1\right)^2 dx = \int\left(x^4+2x^2+1\right)dx$

$= \dfrac{x^5}{5} + \dfrac{2x^3}{3} + x + C$

69. $\int\left[\dfrac{x}{x^2+1} + \dfrac{x^5}{\left(x^6+1\right)^2}\right]dx$

$= \int \dfrac{x}{x^2+1}\,dx + \int \dfrac{x^5}{\left(x^6+1\right)^2}\,dx$

$= \dfrac{1}{2}\int \dfrac{1}{x^2+1}[2x\,dx] + \dfrac{1}{6}\int\left(x^6+1\right)^{-2}[6x^5dx] = \dfrac{1}{2}\ln\left(x^2+1\right) + \dfrac{1}{6} \cdot \dfrac{\left(x^6+1\right)^{-1}}{-1} + C$

$= \dfrac{1}{2}\ln\left(x^2+1\right) - \dfrac{1}{6\left(x^6+1\right)} + C$

71. $\displaystyle \int\left[\frac{1}{3x-5}-\left(x^2-2x^5\right)\left(x^3-x^6\right)^{-10}\right]dx$

$\displaystyle =\frac{1}{3}\int\frac{1}{3x-5}[3\ dx]-\frac{1}{3}\int\left(x^3-x^6\right)^{-10}\left[\left(3x^2-6x^5\right)dx\right]$

$\displaystyle =\frac{1}{3}\ln|3x-5|-\frac{1}{3}\cdot\frac{\left(x^3-x^6\right)^{-9}}{-9}+C$

$\displaystyle =\frac{1}{3}\ln|3x-5|+\frac{1}{27}\left(x^3-x^6\right)^{-9}+C$

73. $\displaystyle \int\left[\sqrt{3x+1}-\frac{x}{x^2+3}\right]dx$

$\displaystyle =\int(3x+1)^{\frac{1}{2}}dx-\int\frac{x}{x^2+3}dx$

$\displaystyle =\frac{1}{3}\int(3x+1)^{\frac{1}{2}}[3\ dx]-\frac{1}{2}\int\frac{1}{x^2+3}[2x\ dx]$

$\displaystyle =\frac{1}{3}\cdot\frac{(3x+1)^{\frac{3}{2}}}{\frac{3}{2}}-\frac{1}{2}\ln\left(x^2+3\right)+C$

$\displaystyle =\frac{2}{9}(3x+1)^{\frac{3}{2}}-\ln\sqrt{x^2+3}+C$

75. Let $u=\sqrt{x}\Rightarrow du=\frac{1}{2}x^{-\frac{1}{2}}dx=\frac{1}{2\sqrt{x}}dx$.

$\displaystyle \int\frac{e^{\sqrt{x}}}{\sqrt{x}}dx=2\int e^{\sqrt{x}}\left[\frac{1}{2\sqrt{x}}dx\right]$

$\displaystyle =2\int e^u du=2e^u+C=2e^{\sqrt{x}}+C$

77. $\displaystyle \int\frac{1+e^{2x}}{4e^x}dx=\frac{1}{4}\int\left(\frac{1}{e^x}+\frac{e^{2x}}{e^x}\right)dx$

$\displaystyle =\frac{1}{4}\int\left(e^{-x}+e^x\right)dx$

$\displaystyle =-\frac{1}{4}\int e^{-x}[-1\ dx]+\frac{1}{4}\int e^x dx$

$\displaystyle =-\frac{1}{4}e^{-x}+\frac{1}{4}e^x+C$

79. Let

$\displaystyle u=\ln\left(x^2+2x\right)\Rightarrow du=\frac{1}{x^2+2x}(2x+2)dx$

$\displaystyle \int\frac{x+1}{x^2+2x}\ln\left(x^2+2x\right)dx$

$\displaystyle =\frac{1}{2}\int\ln\left(x^2+2x\right)\left[\frac{2x+2}{x^2+2x}dx\right]$

$\displaystyle =\frac{1}{2}\int u\ du=\frac{1}{2}\cdot\frac{u^2}{2}+C$

$\displaystyle =\frac{1}{4}\ln^2\left(x^2+2x\right)+C$

81. $\displaystyle y=\int(3-2x)^2 dx=-\frac{1}{2}\int(3-2x)^2[-2\ dx]$

$\displaystyle =-\frac{1}{2}\cdot\frac{(3-2x)^3}{3}+C=-\frac{1}{6}(3-2x)^3+C$

$y(0)=1$ implies $1=-\frac{1}{6}(27)+C$, so

$C=\frac{11}{2}$. Thus $y=-\frac{1}{6}(3-2x)^3+\frac{11}{2}$.

83. $\displaystyle y''=\frac{1}{x^2}$

$\displaystyle y'=\int x^{-2}dx=-x^{-1}+C_1$

$y'(-1)=1$ implies $1=1+C_1$, so $C_1=0$.

Thus $y'=-x^{-1}$.

$\displaystyle y=\int\left(-x^{-1}\right)dx=-\int\frac{1}{x}dx=-\ln|x|+C_2$

$y(1)=0$ implies that $0=0+C_2$, so $C_2=0$.

Thus $y=-\ln|x|=\ln\left|\frac{1}{x}\right|$.

85. $V(t) = \int \dfrac{dV}{dt} dt = \int 8e^{0.05t} dt$

$= 8\left(\dfrac{e^{0.05t}}{0.05}\right) + C = 160e^{0.05t} + C$

The house cost \$350,000 to build, so
$V(0) = 350$.
$350 = 160e^0 + C = 160 + C$
$190 = C$
$V(t) = 160e^{0.05t} + 190$

87. Note that $r > 0$.

$C = \int \left[\dfrac{Rr}{2K} + \dfrac{B_1}{r}\right] dr = \int \dfrac{Rr}{2K} dr + \int \dfrac{B_1}{r} dr$

$= \dfrac{R}{2K} \int r \, dr + B_1 \int \dfrac{1}{r} dr$

$= \dfrac{R}{2K} \cdot \dfrac{r^2}{2} + B_1 \ln|r| + B_2$

Thus we obtain $C = \dfrac{Rr^2}{4K} + B_1 \ln|r| + B_2$.

Exercise 16.4

1. $\int \dfrac{2x^4 + 3x^3 - x^2}{x^3} dx$

$= \int \left(\dfrac{2x^4}{x^3} + \dfrac{3x^3}{x^3} - \dfrac{x^2}{x^3}\right) dx$

$= \int \left(2x + 3 - \dfrac{1}{x}\right) dx = 2 \cdot \dfrac{x^2}{2} + 3x - \ln|x| + C$

$= x^2 + 3x - \ln|x| + C$

3. $\int (3x^2 + 2)\sqrt{2x^3 + 4x + 1}\, dx$

$= \dfrac{1}{2} \int \left(2x^3 + 4x + 1\right)^{\frac{1}{2}} \left[2\left(3x^2 + 2\right) dx\right]$

$= \dfrac{1}{2} \cdot \dfrac{\left(2x^3 + 4x + 1\right)^{\frac{3}{2}}}{\frac{3}{2}} + C$

$= \dfrac{1}{3}\left(2x^3 + 4x + 1\right)^{\frac{3}{2}} + C$

5. $\int \dfrac{15}{\sqrt{4 - 5x}} dx = 15 \int (4 - 5x)^{-\frac{1}{2}} dx$

$= 15 \cdot \left(-\dfrac{1}{5}\right) \int (4 - 5x)^{-\frac{1}{2}} [-5 \, dx]$

$= -3 \cdot \dfrac{(4 - 5x)^{\frac{1}{2}}}{\frac{1}{2}} + C = -6\sqrt{4 - 5x} + C$

7. $\int 4^{7x} dx = \int \left(e^{\ln 4}\right)^{7x} dx = \int e^{(\ln 4)(7x)} dx$

$= \dfrac{1}{7 \ln 4} \int e^{(\ln 4)(7x)} [7 \ln 4 \, dx]$

$= \dfrac{1}{7 \ln 4} \cdot e^{(\ln 4)(7x)} + C$

$= \dfrac{1}{7 \ln 4}\left(e^{\ln 4}\right)^{(7x)} + C = \dfrac{4^{7x}}{7 \ln 4} + C$

9. $\int 2x\left(7 - e^{\frac{x^2}{4}}\right) dx = \int \left(14x - 2xe^{\frac{x^2}{4}}\right) dx$

$= 14 \int x \, dx - 2 \int xe^{\frac{x^2}{4}} dx$

$= 14 \int x \, dx - 2 \cdot 2 \int e^{\frac{x^2}{4}}\left[\dfrac{1}{2} x \, dx\right]$

$= 14 \cdot \dfrac{x^2}{2} - 4 \cdot e^{\frac{x^2}{4}} + C = 7x^2 - 4e^{\frac{x^2}{4}} + C$

11. By long division,

$\dfrac{6x^2 - 11x + 5}{3x - 1} = 2x - 3 + \dfrac{2}{3x - 1}$. Thus

$\int \dfrac{6x^2 - 11x + 5}{3x - 1} dx = \int \left(2x - 3 + \dfrac{2}{3x - 1}\right) dx$

$= 2 \int x \, dx - \int 3 \, dx + 2 \cdot \dfrac{1}{3} \int \dfrac{1}{3x - 1}[3 \, dx]$

$= x^2 - 3x + \dfrac{2}{3} \ln|3x - 1| + C$

13. $\int \dfrac{3e^{2x}}{e^{2x} + 1} dx = \dfrac{3}{2} \int \dfrac{1}{e^{2x} + 1}\left[2e^{2x} dx\right]$

$= \dfrac{3}{2} \ln\left(e^{2x} + 1\right) + C$

15. $\int \dfrac{e^{\frac{7}{x}}}{x^2} dx = \int e^{\frac{7}{x}} \cdot \dfrac{1}{x^2} dx = -\dfrac{1}{7} \int e^{\frac{7}{x}}\left[-\dfrac{7}{x^2} dx\right]$

$= -\dfrac{1}{7} e^{\frac{7}{x}} + C$

17. By using long division on the integrand,

$$\int \frac{2x^3}{x^2-4}dx = \int \left(2x + \frac{8x}{x^2-4}\right)dx$$

$$= \int 2x\,dx + 4\int \frac{1}{x^2-4}[2x\,dx]$$

$$= x^2 + 4\ln\left|x^2-4\right| + C.$$

19. $\int \frac{\left(\sqrt{x}+2\right)^2}{3\sqrt{x}}dx = \frac{2}{3}\int \left(\sqrt{x}+2\right)^2 \left[\frac{1}{2\sqrt{x}}dx\right]$

$$= \frac{2}{3} \cdot \frac{\left(\sqrt{x}+2\right)^3}{3} + C = \frac{2}{9}\left(\sqrt{x}+2\right)^3 + C$$

21. $\int \frac{5\left(x^{\frac{1}{3}}+2\right)^4}{\sqrt[3]{x^2}}dx = 3\int 5\left(x^{\frac{1}{3}}+2\right)^4\left[\frac{1}{3}x^{-\frac{2}{3}}dx\right]$

$$= 3\left(x^{\frac{1}{3}}+2\right)^5 + C$$

23. $\int \frac{\ln x}{x}dx = \int (\ln x)\left[\frac{1}{x}dx\right] = \frac{(\ln x)^2}{2} + C$

$$= \frac{1}{2}\left(\ln^2 x\right) + C$$

25. $\int \frac{\ln^2(r+1)}{r+1}dr = \int [\ln(r+1)]^2\left(\frac{1}{r+1}dr\right)$

$$= \frac{1}{3}\ln^3(r+1) + C$$

27. $\int \frac{3^{\ln x}}{x}dx = \int \frac{\left(e^{\ln 3}\right)^{\ln x}}{x}dx$

$$= \frac{1}{\ln 3}\int e^{(\ln 3)\ln x}\left[\frac{\ln 3}{x}dx\right]$$

$$= \frac{1}{\ln 3} \cdot e^{(\ln 3)\ln x} + C$$

$$= \frac{1}{\ln 3}\left(e^{\ln 3}\right)^{\ln x} + C = \frac{3^{\ln x}}{\ln 3} + C$$

29. $\int x\sqrt{e^{x^2+3}}\,dx = \int x\left(e^{x^2+3}\right)^{\frac{1}{2}}dx$

$$= \int e^{\frac{\left(x^2+3\right)}{2}}[x\,dx] = e^{\frac{\left(x^2+3\right)}{2}} + C$$

31. $\int \frac{8}{(x+3)\ln(x+3)}dx$

$$= 8\int \frac{1}{\ln(x+3)}\left[\frac{1}{x+3}dx\right]$$

$$= 8\ln|\ln(x+3)| + C$$

33. By using long division on the integrand,

$$\int \frac{x^3+x^2-x-3}{x^2-3}dx = \int \left(x+1+\frac{2x}{x^2-3}\right)dx$$

$$= \int (x+1)dx + \int \frac{1}{x^2-3}[2x\,dx]$$

$$= \frac{x^2}{2} + x + \ln\left|x^2-3\right| + C$$

35. $\int \frac{6x\sqrt{\ln\left(x^2+1\right)^2}}{x^2+1}dx$

$$= \frac{3}{2}\int \left[2\ln\left(x^2+1\right)\right]^{\frac{1}{2}}\left[\frac{4x}{x^2+1}dx\right]$$

$$= \frac{3}{2} \cdot \frac{\left[2\ln\left(x^2+1\right)\right]^{\frac{3}{2}}}{\frac{3}{2}} + C$$

$$= \ln^{\frac{3}{2}}\left[\left(x^2+1\right)^2\right] + C$$

37. $\int \left[\frac{x^3}{\sqrt{x^4-1}} - \ln 4\right]dx$

$$= \frac{1}{4}\int \left(x^4-1\right)^{-\frac{1}{2}}\left[4x^3dx\right] - \int (\ln 4)dx$$

$$= \frac{1}{4} \cdot \frac{\left(x^4-1\right)^{\frac{1}{2}}}{\frac{1}{2}} - (\ln 4)x + C$$

$$= \frac{1}{2}\sqrt{x^4-1} - (\ln 4)x + C$$

39. $\displaystyle\int \frac{2x^4 - 8x^3 - 6x^2 + 4}{x^3}\, dx$

$\displaystyle = \int \left(2x - 8 - \frac{6}{x} + \frac{4}{x^3}\right) dx$

$\displaystyle = 2\int x\, dx - \int 8\, dx - 6\int \frac{1}{x}\, dx + 4\int x^{-3}\, dx$

$\displaystyle = 2 \cdot \frac{x^2}{2} - 8x - 6\ln|x| + 4 \cdot \frac{x^{-2}}{-2} + C$

$\displaystyle = x^2 - 8x - 6\ln|x| - \frac{2}{x^2} + C$

41. By using long division on the integrand,

$\displaystyle\int \frac{x}{x-1}\, dx = \int \left(1 + \frac{1}{x-1}\right) dx$

$\displaystyle = x + \ln|x-1| + C$

43. $\displaystyle\int \frac{xe^{x^2}}{\sqrt{e^{x^2}+2}}\, dx = \frac{1}{2}\int \left(e^{x^2}+2\right)^{-\frac{1}{2}}\left[2xe^{x^2}\, dx\right]$

$\displaystyle = \frac{1}{2} \cdot \frac{\left(e^{x^2}+2\right)^{\frac{1}{2}}}{\frac{1}{2}} + C = \sqrt{e^{x^2}+2} + C$

45. $\displaystyle\int \frac{\left(e^{-x}+6\right)^2}{e^x}\, dx = -\int \left(e^{-x}+6\right)^2 \left[-e^{-x}dx\right]$

$\displaystyle = -\frac{\left(e^{-x}+6\right)^3}{3} + C$

47. $\displaystyle\int \left(x^3 + ex\right)\sqrt{x^2+e}\, dx$

$\displaystyle = \int x\left(x^2+e\right)\left(x^2+e\right)^{\frac{1}{2}} dx$

$\displaystyle = \frac{1}{2}\int \left(x^2+e\right)^{\frac{3}{2}}[2x\, dx] = \frac{1}{2} \cdot \frac{\left(x^2+e\right)^{\frac{5}{2}}}{\frac{5}{2}} + C$

$\displaystyle = \frac{1}{5}\left(x^2+e\right)^{\frac{5}{2}} + C$

49. $\displaystyle\int \sqrt{x}\sqrt{(8x)^{\frac{3}{2}}+3}\, dx = \int \left(8^{\frac{3}{2}}x^{\frac{3}{2}}+3\right)^{\frac{1}{2}} \cdot x^{\frac{1}{2}}\, dx$

$\displaystyle = \frac{2}{3 \cdot 8^{\frac{3}{2}}}\int \left(8^{\frac{3}{2}}x^{\frac{3}{2}}+3\right)^{\frac{1}{2}}\left[8^{\frac{3}{2}} \cdot \frac{3}{2} \cdot x^{\frac{1}{2}}dx\right]$

$\displaystyle = \frac{2}{3 \cdot 16\sqrt{2}} \cdot \frac{\left(8^{\frac{3}{2}}x^{\frac{3}{2}}+3\right)^{\frac{3}{2}}}{\frac{3}{2}} + C$

$\displaystyle = \frac{1}{36\sqrt{2}}\left[(8x)^{\frac{3}{2}}+3\right]^{\frac{3}{2}} + C$

51. $\displaystyle\int \frac{\sqrt{s}}{e^{\sqrt{s^3}}}\, ds = -\frac{2}{3}\int e^{-s^{\frac{3}{2}}}\left[-\frac{3}{2}s^{\frac{1}{2}}ds\right]$

$\displaystyle = -\frac{2}{3}e^{-\sqrt{s^3}} + C$

53. $e^{\ln(x+2)}$ is simply $x + 2$. Thus

$\displaystyle\int e^{\ln(x+2)}dx = \int (x+2)dx = \frac{x^2}{2} + 2x + C$

55. $\displaystyle\int \frac{\ln\left(xe^x\right)}{x}\, dx = \int \frac{\ln x + \ln e^x}{x}\, dx$

$\displaystyle = \int \frac{\ln x + x}{x}\, dx = \int \left(\frac{\ln x}{x} + 1\right)dx$

$\displaystyle = \int (\ln x)\left[\frac{1}{x}\, dx\right] + \int 1\, dx = \frac{\ln^2 x}{2} + x + C$

57. $\displaystyle\frac{dr}{dq} = \frac{200}{(q+2)^2}$

$\displaystyle r = \int 200(q+2)^{-2}\, dq = 200 \cdot \frac{(q+2)^{-1}}{-1} + C$

$\displaystyle = -\frac{200}{q+2} + C$

When $q = 0$, then $r = 0$, so $0 = -100 + C$, or
$C = 100$. Hence $\displaystyle r = -\frac{200}{q+2} + 100 = \frac{100q}{q+2}$.

Since $r = pq$, then $\displaystyle p = \frac{r}{q} = \frac{100}{q+2}$.

Answer: $\displaystyle p = \frac{100}{q+2}$

59. $\dfrac{dc}{dq} = \dfrac{20}{q+5}$

$c = \displaystyle\int \dfrac{20}{q+5}\, dq = 20 \int \dfrac{1}{q+5}\, dq$

$= 20\ln|q+5| + C$

When $q = 0$, then $c = 2000$, so

$2000 = 20\ln(5) + C$, or $C = 2000 - 20\ln 5$.

Hence $c = 20\ln|q+5| + 2000 - 20\ln 5$

$= 20\left(\ln|q+5| - \ln 5\right) + 2000$

$= 20\ln\left|\dfrac{q+5}{5}\right| + 2000$

Answer: $c = 20\ln\left|\dfrac{q+5}{5}\right| + 2000$

61. $\dfrac{dC}{dI} = \dfrac{1}{\sqrt{I}}$

$C = \displaystyle\int I^{-\frac{1}{2}}\, dI = \dfrac{I^{\frac{1}{2}}}{\frac{1}{2}} + C_1 = 2\sqrt{I} + C_1$

$C(9) = 8$ implies that $8 = 2 \cdot 3 + C_1$, or

$C_1 = 2$. Thus $C = 2\sqrt{I} + 2 = 2\left(\sqrt{I} + 1\right)$.

Answer: $C = 2\left(\sqrt{I} + 1\right)$

63. $\dfrac{dC}{dI} = \dfrac{3}{4} - \dfrac{1}{6\sqrt{I}}$

$C = \displaystyle\int \left[\dfrac{3}{4} - \dfrac{I^{-\frac{1}{2}}}{6}\right] dI = \int \dfrac{3}{4}\, dI - \dfrac{1}{6}\int I^{-\frac{1}{2}}\, dI$

$= \dfrac{3}{4}I - \dfrac{1}{6} \cdot \dfrac{I^{\frac{1}{2}}}{\frac{1}{2}} + C_1 = \dfrac{3}{4}I - \dfrac{\sqrt{I}}{3} + C_1$

Thus $C = \dfrac{3}{4}I - \dfrac{\sqrt{I}}{3} + C_1$. $C(25) = 23$ implies

that $23 = \dfrac{3}{4} \cdot 25 - \dfrac{5}{3} + C_1$, so $C_1 = \dfrac{71}{12}$.

Answer: $C = \dfrac{3}{4}I - \dfrac{1}{3}\sqrt{I} + \dfrac{71}{12}$

65. $\dfrac{dc}{dq} = \dfrac{100q^2 - 4998q + 50}{q^2 - 50q + 1}$

a. $\dfrac{dc}{dq}\bigg|_{q=50} = \dfrac{100(50)^2 - 4998(50) + 50}{(50)^2 - 50(50) + 1} = \$150 \text{ per unit}$

b. To find c, we integrate $\dfrac{dc}{dq}$ by using long division:

$c = \displaystyle\int \dfrac{100q^2 - 4998q + 50}{q^2 - 50q + 1}\, dq = \int \left(100 + \dfrac{2q - 50}{q^2 - 50q + 1}\right) dq$

$= \displaystyle\int 100\, dq + \int \dfrac{1}{q^2 - 50q + 1} [(2q - 50)dq]$

Thus $c = 100q + \ln|q^2 - 50q + 1| + C$. When $q = 0$, then $c = 10{,}000$,

so $10{,}000 = 0 + \ln(1) + C$, so $C = 10{,}000$. Hence $c = 100q + \ln|q^2 - 50q + 1| + 10{,}000$.

When $q = 50$, then $c = 5000 + \ln(1) + 10{,}000 = \$15{,}000$.

c.   If $c = f(q)$, then $f(q + dq) \approx g(q) + dc = f(q) + \dfrac{dc}{dq} dq$

Letting $q = 50$ and $dq = 2$, we have

$$f(52) = f(50 + 2) \approx f(50) + \left.\dfrac{dc}{dq}\right|_{q=50} \cdot (2)$$

$$= 15{,}000 + 150(2) = \$15{,}300$$

67. $\dfrac{dV}{dt} = \dfrac{8t^3}{\sqrt{0.2t^4 + 8000}}$

$V = \displaystyle\int \dfrac{8t^3}{\sqrt{0.2t^4 + 8000}}\, dt$

$= \displaystyle\int \left(0.02t^4 + 8000\right)^{-\frac{1}{2}} \cdot 8t^3 dt$

$= 10\displaystyle\int \left(0.2t^4 + 8000\right)^{-\frac{1}{2}} \left[0.8t^3\right] dt$

$= 10\dfrac{\left(0.2t^4 + 8000\right)^{\frac{1}{2}}}{\frac{1}{2}} + C$

Thus $V = 20\sqrt{0.2t^4 + 8000} + C$. If $t = 0$,

then $V = 500$, so $500 = 20\sqrt{8000} + C$,

$500 = 20\sqrt{1600 \cdot 5} + C$, $500 = 800\sqrt{5} + C$,

or $C = 500 - 800\sqrt{5}$. Hence

$V = 20\sqrt{0.02t^4 + 8000} + 500 - 800\sqrt{5}$.

When $t = 10$, then

$V = 20\sqrt{10{,}000} + 500 - 800\sqrt{5}$

$= 20(100) + 500 - 800\sqrt{5} \approx \$711$ per acre.

69. $S = \displaystyle\int \dfrac{dS}{dI}\, dI = \displaystyle\int \dfrac{5}{(I + 2)^2}\, dI$

$= 5\displaystyle\int (I + 2)^{-2}\, dI = 5 \cdot \dfrac{(I + 2)^{-1}}{-1} + C_1$

Thus $S = -\dfrac{5}{I + 2} + C_1$. If C is the total

national consumption (in billions of dollars),

then $C + S = I$, or $C = I - S$. Hence

$C = I + \dfrac{5}{I + 2} - C_1$. When $I = 8$, then

$C = 7.5$, so $7.5 = 8 + \dfrac{1}{2} - C_1$, or $C_1 = 1$.

Thus $S = 1 - \dfrac{5}{I + 2}$. If $S = 0$, then

$$0 = 1 - \dfrac{5}{I + 2} \Rightarrow \dfrac{5}{I + 2}$$

$$= 1 \Rightarrow 5 = I + 2 \Rightarrow I = 3$$

Exercise 16.5

1. $5 + 6 + 7 + 8 + 9 = 35$

3. $(-1) + 1 + (-1) + 1 + (-1) + 1 + (-1) + 1$
    $+ (-1) + 1 = 0$

5. $5 + 20 = 25$

7. $\left(-\dfrac{1}{2}\right) + \dfrac{5}{16} = -\dfrac{3}{16}$

9. $0 + \dfrac{3}{2} + \left(-\dfrac{8}{3}\right) = -\dfrac{7}{6}$

11. $\displaystyle\sum_{k=1}^{19} k$

13. $\displaystyle\sum_{k=1}^{4} (2k - 1)$

15. $\displaystyle\sum_{k=1}^{10} k^2$

17. $\displaystyle\sum_{k=1}^{450} k = \dfrac{450(451)}{2} = 101{,}475$

19. $\displaystyle\sum_{j=1}^{6} 4j = 4\displaystyle\sum_{j=i}^{6} j = 4 \cdot \dfrac{6(7)}{2} = 84$

21. $\displaystyle\sum_{i=1}^{6} 3i^2 = 3\sum_{i=1}^{6} i^2 = 3 \cdot \frac{6(7)(13)}{6} = 273$

23. After n years,
Total maint. cost = $100 + 200 + \ldots + 100n$
$= 100(1 + 2 + \ldots + n)$
$= 100 \cdot \dfrac{n(n+1)}{2} = 50n(n+1)$
Thus total cost after n years = $3200 + 50n(n+1)$
Avg. annual total cost is $C = \dfrac{3200 + 50n(n+1)}{n} = \dfrac{3200}{n} + 50(n+1)$
$\dfrac{dC}{dn} = -\dfrac{3200}{n^2} + 50 = \dfrac{50n^2 - 3200}{n^2} = \dfrac{50(n-8)(n+8)}{n^2}$
We want $n > 0$, so the critical point to consider is $n = 8$. Since $\dfrac{dC}{dn} < 0$ for $0 < n < 8$ and $\dfrac{dC}{dn} > 0$
for $n > 8$, then C is minimum when $n = 8$. At this value, $C = 850$.
Answer: 8, $850

Principles in Practice 16.6

1. Divide the interval $[0, 10]$ into n subintervals of equal length Δx, so $\Delta x = \dfrac{10}{n}$. The endpoints of the

subintervals are 0, $\dfrac{10}{n}$, $2\left(\dfrac{10}{n}\right)$, $3\left(\dfrac{10}{n}\right)$, $\ldots$, $(n-1)\left(\dfrac{10}{n}\right)$, and $n\left(\dfrac{10}{n}\right) = 10$. Letting S_n denote the sum
of the areas of the rectangles corresponding to right-hand endpoints, we have
$S_n = \dfrac{10}{n} R\left(\dfrac{10}{n}\right) + \dfrac{10}{n} R\left[2\left(\dfrac{10}{n}\right)\right] + \ldots + \dfrac{10}{n} R\left[n\left(\dfrac{10}{n}\right)\right]$
$= \dfrac{10}{n}\left[\left\{600 - 0.5\left(\dfrac{10}{n}\right)\right\} + \left\{600 - 0.5(2)\left(\dfrac{10}{n}\right)\right\} + \ldots + \left\{600 - 0.5(n)\left(\dfrac{10}{n}\right)\right\}\right]$
$= \dfrac{10}{n}\left[600n - 0.5\left(\dfrac{10}{n}\right)\{1 + 2 + \ldots + n\}\right]$
$= \dfrac{10}{n}\left[600n - 0.5\left(\dfrac{10}{n}\right)\dfrac{n(n+1)}{2}\right]$
$= \dfrac{10}{n}[600n - 2.5(n+1)]$
$= 6000 - 25\left(\dfrac{n+1}{n}\right)$
Now take the limit of S_n as $n \to \infty$
$\displaystyle\lim_{n\to\infty} S_n = \lim_{n\to\infty}\left[6000 - 25\left(\dfrac{n+1}{n}\right)\right]$
$= \displaystyle\lim_{n\to\infty}\left[6000 - 25\left(1 + \dfrac{1}{n}\right)\right] = 6000 - 25$
$= 5975$
The total revenue for selling 10 units is $5975.

Exercise 16.6

1. $f(x) = x, y = 0, x = 1$

$S_3, \Delta x = \frac{1}{3}$

$S_3 = \frac{1}{3} f\left(\frac{1}{3}\right) + \frac{1}{3} f\left(\frac{2}{3}\right) + \frac{1}{3} f\left(\frac{3}{3}\right) = \frac{1}{3}\left[f\left(\frac{1}{3}\right) + f\left(\frac{2}{3}\right) + f\left(\frac{3}{3}\right)\right]$

$= \frac{1}{3}\left[\frac{1}{3} + \frac{2}{3} + \frac{3}{3}\right] = \frac{1}{3} \cdot \frac{6}{3} = \frac{2}{3}$ Answer: $\frac{2}{3}$ sq unit

3. $f(x) = x^2, y = 0, x = 1$

$S_3, \Delta x = \frac{1}{3}$

$S_3 = \frac{1}{3} f\left(\frac{1}{3}\right) + \frac{1}{3} f\left(\frac{2}{3}\right) + \frac{1}{3} f\left(\frac{3}{3}\right) = \frac{1}{3}\left[\frac{1}{9} + \frac{4}{9} + \frac{9}{9}\right]$

$= \frac{1}{3} \cdot \frac{14}{9} = \frac{14}{27}$

Answer: $\frac{14}{27}$ sq unit

5. $f(x) = 4x; [0, 1]$

$\Delta x = \frac{1}{n}$

$S_n = \frac{1}{n} f\left(\frac{1}{n}\right) + \ldots + \frac{1}{n} f\left(n \cdot \frac{1}{n}\right)$

$= \frac{1}{n}\left[f\left(\frac{1}{n}\right) + \ldots + f\left(n \cdot \frac{1}{n}\right)\right]$

$= \frac{1}{n}\left[4 \cdot \frac{1}{n} + \ldots + 4 \cdot \frac{n}{n}\right]$

$= \frac{4}{n^2}[1 + \ldots + n] = \frac{4}{n^2} \cdot \frac{n(n+1)}{2}$

$= \frac{2(n+1)}{n}$

7. a. $S_n = \frac{1}{n}\left[\left(\frac{1}{n} + 1\right) + \left(\frac{2}{n} + 1\right) + \ldots + \left(\frac{n}{n} + 1\right)\right]$

$= \frac{1}{n}\left[\frac{1}{n}(1 + 2 + \ldots + n) + n\right]$

$= \frac{1}{n}\left[\frac{1}{n} \cdot \frac{n(n+1)}{2} + n\right]$

$= \frac{n+1}{2n} + 1$

b. $\lim_{n \to \infty} S_n = \lim_{n \to \infty}\left[\frac{n+1}{2n} + 1\right]$

$= \lim_{n \to \infty}\left[\frac{1}{2} + \frac{1}{2n} + 1\right]$

$= \frac{1}{2} + 0 + 1 = \frac{3}{2}$

9. $f(x) = x, y = 0, x = 1$

$\Delta x = \frac{1}{n}$

$S_n = \frac{1}{n} f\left(\frac{1}{n}\right) + \ldots + \frac{1}{n} f\left(n \cdot \frac{1}{n}\right)$

$= \frac{1}{n}\left[f\left(\frac{1}{n}\right) + \ldots + f\left(n \cdot \frac{1}{n}\right)\right]$

$= \frac{1}{n}\left[\frac{1}{n} + \ldots + \frac{n}{n}\right] = \frac{1}{n^2}[1 + \ldots + n]$

$= \frac{1}{n^2} \cdot \frac{n(n+1)}{2}$

$= \frac{1}{2} \cdot \frac{n+1}{n} = \frac{1}{2}\left[1 + \frac{1}{n}\right]$

$\lim_{n \to \infty} S_n = \frac{1}{2}$

Answer: $\frac{1}{2}$ sq unit

11. $f(x) = x^2, y = 0, x = 1$

$\Delta x = \frac{1}{n}$

$S_n = \frac{1}{n} f\left(\frac{1}{n}\right) + \ldots + \frac{1}{n} f\left(n \cdot \frac{1}{n}\right)$

$= \frac{1}{n}\left[\left(\frac{1}{n}\right)^2 + \ldots + \left(n \cdot \frac{1}{n}\right)^2\right]$

$= \frac{1}{n^3}[1^2 + \ldots + n^2] = \frac{1}{n^3} \cdot \frac{n(n+1)(2n+1)}{6}$

$= \frac{1}{6} \cdot \frac{2n^2 + 3n + 1}{n^2}$

$= \frac{1}{6}\left[2 + \frac{3}{n} + \frac{1}{n^2}\right]$

$\lim_{n \to \infty} S_n = \frac{1}{3}$

Answer: $\frac{1}{3}$ sq unit

13. $f(x) = 2x^2$, $y = 0$, $x = 2$

$\Delta x = \dfrac{2}{n}$

$S_n = \dfrac{2}{n} f\left(\dfrac{2}{n}\right) + \ldots + \dfrac{2}{n} f\left(n \cdot \dfrac{2}{n}\right)$

$\quad = \dfrac{2}{n}\left[f\left(\dfrac{2}{n}\right) + \ldots + f\left(n \cdot \dfrac{2}{n}\right)\right]$

$\quad = \dfrac{2}{n}\left[2\left(\dfrac{2}{n}\right)^2 + \ldots + 2\left(n \cdot \dfrac{2}{n}\right)^2\right]$

$\quad = \dfrac{16}{n^3}\left[1^2 + \ldots + n^2\right]$

$\quad = \dfrac{16}{n^3} \cdot \dfrac{n(n+1)(2n+1)}{6} = \dfrac{8}{3} \cdot \dfrac{2n^2 + 3n + 1}{n^2}$

$\quad = \dfrac{8}{3}\left[2 + \dfrac{3}{n} + \dfrac{1}{n^2}\right]$

$\lim_{n \to \infty} S_n = \dfrac{16}{3}$

Answer: $\dfrac{16}{3}$ sq units

15. $\displaystyle\int_0^2 3x \, dx$

Let $f(x) = 3x$.

$\Delta x = \dfrac{2}{n}$

$S_n = \dfrac{2}{n} f\left(\dfrac{2}{n}\right) + \ldots + \dfrac{2}{n} f\left(n \cdot \dfrac{2}{n}\right)$

$\quad = \dfrac{2}{n}\left[3\left(\dfrac{2}{n}\right) + \ldots + 3\left(n \cdot \dfrac{2}{n}\right)\right]$

$\quad = \dfrac{12}{n^2}[1 + \ldots + n] = \dfrac{12}{n^2} \cdot \dfrac{n(n+1)}{2}$

$\quad = 6 \cdot \dfrac{n+1}{n} = 6\left[1 + \dfrac{1}{n}\right]$

$\displaystyle\int_0^2 3x \, dx = \lim_{n \to \infty} S_n = 6$

Answer: 6

17. $\displaystyle\int_0^3 -4x \, dx$

Let $f(x) = -4x$.

$\Delta x = \dfrac{3}{n}$

$S_n = \dfrac{3}{n} f\left(\dfrac{3}{n}\right) + \ldots + \dfrac{3}{n} f\left(n \cdot \dfrac{3}{n}\right)$

$\quad = \dfrac{3}{n}\left[f\left(\dfrac{3}{n}\right) + \ldots + f\left(n \cdot \dfrac{3}{n}\right)\right]$

$\quad = \dfrac{3}{n}\left[-4\left(\dfrac{3}{n}\right) - \ldots - 4\left(n \cdot \dfrac{3}{n}\right)\right] = -\dfrac{36}{n^2}[1 + \ldots + n]$

$\quad = -\dfrac{36}{n^2} \cdot \dfrac{n(n+1)}{2} = -18 \cdot \dfrac{n+1}{n} = -18\left[1 + \dfrac{1}{n}\right]$

$\displaystyle\int_0^3 -4x \, dx = \lim_{n \to \infty} S_n = -18$

Answer: -18

19. $\displaystyle\int_0^1 \left(x^2 + x\right) dx$

Let $f(x) = x^2 + x$.

$\Delta x = \dfrac{1}{n}$

$S_n = \dfrac{1}{n} f\left(\dfrac{1}{n}\right) + \ldots + \dfrac{1}{n} f\left(n \cdot \dfrac{1}{n}\right)$

$\quad = \dfrac{1}{n}\left\{\left[\left(\dfrac{1}{n}\right)^2 + \dfrac{1}{n}\right] + \ldots + \left[\left(n \cdot \dfrac{1}{n}\right)^2 + n \cdot \dfrac{1}{n}\right]\right\}$

$\quad = \dfrac{1}{n}\left\{\left(\dfrac{1}{n}\right)^2 \left[1^2 + \ldots + n^2\right] + \dfrac{1}{n}[1 + \ldots + n]\right\}$

$\quad = \dfrac{1}{n^3} \cdot \dfrac{n(n+1)(2n+1)}{6} + \dfrac{1}{n^2} \cdot \dfrac{n(n+1)}{2}$

$\quad = \dfrac{1}{6} \cdot \dfrac{2n^2 + 3n + 1}{n^2} + \dfrac{1}{2} \cdot \dfrac{n+1}{n}$

$\quad = \dfrac{1}{6}\left[2 + \dfrac{3}{n} + \dfrac{1}{n^2}\right] + \dfrac{1}{2}\left[1 + \dfrac{1}{n}\right]$

$$\int_0^1 \left(x^2 + x\right)dx = \lim_{n\to\infty} S_n = \frac{1}{3} + \frac{1}{2} = \frac{5}{6}$$

Answer: $\frac{5}{6}$

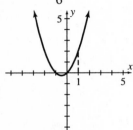

21. $\int_2^3 \sqrt{x^2 + 1}\, dx$ is simply a real number. Thus

$$D_x\left[\int_2^3 \sqrt{x^2 + 1}dx\right] = D_x \text{ (real number)} = 0.$$

Answer: 0

23. $f(x) = \begin{cases} 1 & \text{if} & x \le 1 \\ 2 - x & \text{if} & 1 \le x \le 2 \\ -1 + \frac{x}{2} & \text{if} & x > 2 \end{cases}$

f is continuous and $f(x) \ge 0$ on $[-1, 3]$.

Thus $\int_{-1}^3 f(x)dx$ gives the area A bounded by $y = f(x)$, $y = 0$, $x = -1$, and $x = 3$. From the diagram, this area is composed of three subareas, A_1, A_2, and A_3 and $A = A_1 + A_2 + A_3$.

A_1 = area of rectangle = $(2)(1) = 2$ sq units

A_2 = area of triangle = $\frac{1}{2}(1)(1) = \frac{1}{2}$ sq unit

A_3 = area of triangle = $\frac{1}{2}(1)\left(\frac{1}{2}\right) = \frac{1}{4}$ sq unit

Since $A = A_1 + A_2 + A_3 = 2 + \frac{1}{2} + \frac{1}{4}$

$= \frac{11}{4}$ sq units, we have $\int_{-1}^3 f(x)dx = \frac{11}{4}$.

Answer: $\frac{11}{4}$

3 ↑y

$y = f(x)$ A_3

A_1 $\frac{1}{2}$ A_2 x

3

25. 4.3 sq units

27. 2.4

29. -25.5

Principles in Practice 16.7

1. $\int_3^6 10,000e^{0.02t}\, dt = \left(10,000\, \frac{e^{0.02t}}{0.02}\right)\Big|_3^6$

$= \left(500,000e^{0.02t}\right)\Big|_3^6$

$= 500,000\left(e^{0.02(6)} - e^{0.02(3)}\right)$

$= 500,000\left(e^{0.12} - e^{0.06}\right) \approx 32,830$

The total income for the chain between the third and sixth years was about \$32,830.

2. The total cost for the first 5 years is $M(5)$ or

$$M(5) - M(0) = \int_0^5 M'(x)dx$$

$$\int_0^5 \left(90x^2 + 5000\right)dx = \left(90\frac{x^3}{3} + 5000x\right)\Big|_0^5$$

$$= \left(30x^3 + 5000x\right)\Big|_0^5 = 30(5)^3 + 5000(5) - 0$$

$= 3750 + 25,000 = 28,750$

The total cost for the first 5 years is \$28,750.

Exercise 16.7

1. $\int_0^2 7\,dx = 7x\Big|_0^2 = 7(2) - 7(0) = 14 - 0 = 14$

3. $\int_1^2 5x\,dx = 5 \cdot \frac{x^2}{2}\Big|_1^2 = 10 - \frac{5}{2} = \frac{15}{2}$

5. $\int_{-3}^1 (2x-3)dx = \left(x^2 - 3x\right)\Big|_{-3}^1 = -2 - (18)$
$= -20$

7. $\int_2^3 \left(y^2 - 2y + 1\right)dy = \int_2^3 (y-1)^2\,dy$
$= \frac{1}{3}(y-1)^3\Big|_2^3$
$= \frac{8}{3} - \frac{1}{3} = \frac{7}{3}$

9. $\int_{-2}^{-1}\left(3w^2 - w - 1\right)dw = \left(w^3 - \frac{w^2}{2} - w\right)\Big|_{-2}^{-1}$
$= -\frac{1}{2} - (-8) = \frac{15}{2}$

11. $\int_1^2 \left(-4t^{-4}\right) = dt = \frac{4}{3}t^{-3}\Big|_1^2 = \frac{4}{3t^3}\Big|_1^2 = \frac{1}{6} - \frac{8}{6}$
$= -\frac{7}{6}$

13. $\int_{-1}^1 \sqrt[3]{x^5}\,dx = \int_{-1}^1 x^{\frac{5}{3}}dx = \frac{3x^{\frac{8}{3}}}{8}\Big|_{-1}^1 = \frac{3}{8} - \frac{3}{8} = 0$

15. $\int_{1/2}^3 \frac{1}{x^2}\,dx = -\frac{1}{x}\Big|_{1/2}^3 = -\frac{1}{3} - (-2) = \frac{5}{3}$

17. $\int_{-1}^1 (z+1)^5\,dz = \frac{(z+1)^6}{6}\Big|_{-1}^1 = \frac{32}{3} - 0 = \frac{32}{3}$

19. $\int_0^1 2x^2\left(x^3 - 1\right)^3 dx = \frac{2}{3}\int_0^1 \left(x^3 - 1\right)^3\left[3x^2 dx\right]$
$= \frac{1}{6}\left(x^3 - 1\right)^4\Big|_0^1 = 0 - \frac{1}{6} = -\frac{1}{6}$

21. $\int_1^8 \frac{4}{y}\,dy = 4\ln|y|\Big|_1^8 = 4(\ln 8 - \ln 1)$
$= 4(\ln 8 - 0) = 4\ln 8$

23. $\int_0^1 e^5\,dx = e^5 x\Big|_0^1 = e^5 - 0 = e^5$

25. $\int_0^2 x^2 e^{x^3}\,dx = \frac{1}{3}\int_0^2 e^{x^3}\left[3x^2 dx\right]$
$= \frac{1}{3}e^{x^3}\Big|_0^2 = \frac{1}{3}\left(e^8 - e^0\right) = \frac{1}{3}\left(e^8 - 1\right)$

27. $\int_4^5 \frac{2}{(x-3)^3}\,dx = 2\int_4^5 (x-3)^{-3}\,dx$
$= 2 \cdot \frac{(x-3)^{-2}}{-2}\Big|_4^5$
$= -\frac{1}{(x-3)^2}\Big|_4^5 = -\frac{1}{4} - (-1) = \frac{3}{4}$

29. $\int_{1/3}^2 \sqrt{10 - 3p}\,dp = -\frac{1}{3}\int_{1/3}^2 (10 - 3p)^{\frac{1}{2}}[-3\,dp]$
$= -\frac{2}{9}(10 - 3p)^{\frac{3}{2}}\Big|_{1/3}^2 = -\frac{2}{9}(8 - 27) = \frac{38}{9}$

31. $\int_0^1 x^2\sqrt[3]{7x^3 + 1}\,dx$
$= \frac{1}{21}\int_0^1 \left(7x^3 + 1\right)^{\frac{1}{3}}\left[21x^2 dx\right]$
$= \frac{1}{21} \cdot \frac{\left(7x^3 + 1\right)^{\frac{4}{3}}}{\frac{4}{3}}\Big|_0^1 = \frac{\left(7x^3 + 1\right)^{\frac{4}{3}}}{28}\Big|_0^1$
$= \frac{16}{28} - \frac{1}{28} = \frac{15}{28}$

33. $\displaystyle\int_0^1 \frac{2x^3+x}{x^2+x^4+1}\,dx$

$= \dfrac{1}{2}\displaystyle\int_0^1 \frac{1}{x^4+x^2+1}\left[2\left(2x^3+x\right)dx\right]$

$= \dfrac{1}{2}\ln\left(x^4+x^2+1\right)\Big|_0^1 = \dfrac{1}{2}[\ln 3 - \ln 1]$

$= \dfrac{1}{2}\ln 3$

35. $\displaystyle\int_0^1\left(e^x - e^{-2x}\right)dx$

$= \displaystyle\int_0^1 e^x\,dx - \left(-\dfrac{1}{2}\right)\int_0^1 e^{-2x}[-2\ dx]$

$= \left(e^x + \dfrac{e^{-2x}}{2}\right)\Big|_0^1 = \left(e + \dfrac{e^{-2}}{2}\right) - \left(1 + \dfrac{1}{2}\right)$

$= e + \dfrac{1}{2e^2} - \dfrac{3}{2}$

37. $\displaystyle\int_1^e 2\left(x^{-1} + x^{-2} - x^{-3}\right)dx$

$= 2\left(\ln|x| + \dfrac{x^{-1}}{-1} - \dfrac{x^{-2}}{-2}\right)\Big|_1^e$

$= 2\left(1 - \dfrac{1}{e} + \dfrac{1}{2e^2}\right) - 2\left(0 - 1 + \dfrac{1}{2}\right)$

$= 3 - \dfrac{2}{e} + \dfrac{1}{e^2}$

39. $\displaystyle\int_1^3 (x+1)e^{x^2+2x}\,dx$

$= \dfrac{1}{2}\displaystyle\int_1^3 e^{x^2+2x}[2(x+1)dx]$

$= \dfrac{1}{2}e^{x^2+2x}\Big|_1^3 = \dfrac{1}{2}\left(e^{15} - e^3\right) = \dfrac{e^3}{2}\left(e^{12}-1\right)$

41. Using long division on the integrand, we obtain

$\displaystyle\int_0^2\left[x^3 + x + \frac{3x^2+5}{x^3+5x+1}\right]dx$

$= \left[\dfrac{x^4}{4} + \dfrac{x^2}{2} + \ln\left|x^3+5x+1\right|\right]\Big|_0^2$

$= (6 + \ln 19) - 0 = 6 + \ln 19$

43. $\displaystyle\int_0^2 f(x)dx = \int_0^{1/2} 4x^2\,dx + \int_{1/2}^2 2x\ dx$

$= \dfrac{4x^3}{3}\Big|_0^{1/2} + x^2\Big|_{1/2}^2 = \left(\dfrac{1}{6} - 0\right) + \left(4 - \dfrac{1}{4}\right) = \dfrac{47}{12}$

45. $f(x) = \displaystyle\int_1^x 3\dfrac{1}{t^2}\,dt = -\dfrac{3}{t}\Big|_1^x = -\dfrac{3}{x} + 3 = 3 - \dfrac{3}{x}$

$\displaystyle\int_e^1 f(x)dx = \int_e^1\left(3 - \dfrac{3}{x}\right)dx = (3x - 3\ln|x|)\Big|_e^1$

$= (3 - 0) - (3e - 3) = 6 - 3e$

47. $\displaystyle\int_1^3 f(x)dx = \int_1^2 f(x)dx + \int_2^3 f(x)dx$, so

$\displaystyle\int_1^2 f(x)dx = \int_1^3 f(x)dx - \int_2^3 f(x)dx$

$= \displaystyle\int_1^3 f(x)dx + \int_3^2 f(x)dx = 4 + 3 = 7$

49. $\displaystyle\int_1^2 e^{x^2}\,dx$ is a constant, so $\dfrac{d}{dx}\displaystyle\int_1^2 e^{x^2}\,dx$ is 0. Thus

$\displaystyle\int_1^2\left[\dfrac{d}{dx}\int_1^2 e^{x^2}\,dx\right]dx = \int_1^2 0\ dx = C\Big|_1^2 = C - C$

$= 0$

51. $\displaystyle\int_0^T \alpha^{\frac{5}{2}}\,dt = \alpha^{\frac{5}{2}}t\Big|_0^T = \alpha^{\frac{5}{2}}T - 0 = \alpha^{\frac{5}{2}}T$

53. The total number receiving between a and b dollars equals the number $N(a)$ receiving a or more dollars minus the number $N(b)$ receiving b or more dollars. Thus

$N(a) - N(b) = \displaystyle\int_b^a -Ax^{-B}\,dx$.

55. $\displaystyle\int_0^5 2000e^{-0.06t}\,dt$

$= 2000\cdot\dfrac{1}{-0.06}\displaystyle\int_0^5 e^{-0.06t}[-0.06\ dt]$

$= -\dfrac{2000}{0.06}e^{-0.06t}\Big|_0^5 = -\dfrac{2000}{0.06}\left(e^{-0.03} - 1\right)$

$\approx \$8639$

57. $\displaystyle\int_{36}^{64} 10,000\sqrt{100-t}\,dt = (-1)(10,000)\int_{36}^{64}(100-t)^{\frac{1}{2}}[(-1)\ dt]$

$\quad = -\frac{2}{3}(10,000)(100-t)^{\frac{3}{2}}\Big|_{36}^{64} = -\frac{2}{3}(10,000)[216-512]$

$\quad \approx 1,973,333$

59. $\displaystyle\int_{65}^{75}(0.2q+8)dq = \left(0.1q^2+8q\right)\Big|_{65}^{75}$

$\quad = 1162.5 - 942.5 = \$220$

61. $\displaystyle\int_{400}^{900}\frac{1000}{\sqrt{100q}}\,dq = \int_{400}^{900}\frac{1000}{10\sqrt{q}}\,dq = 100\int_{400}^{900}q^{-\frac{1}{2}}\,dq$

$\quad = 100\cdot\frac{q^{\frac{1}{2}}}{\frac{1}{2}}\Big|_{400}^{900} = 200\sqrt{q}\,\Big|_{400}^{900} = 200(30-20) = \$2000$

63. $\displaystyle\int_{0}^{12}(8t+10)dt = \left(4t^2+10t\right)\Big|_{0}^{12} = 696-0 = 696$

$\quad \displaystyle\int_{6}^{12}(8t+10)dt = \left(4t^2+10t\right)\Big|_{6}^{12} = 696-204 = 492$

65. $\displaystyle G = \int_{-R}^{R} i\ dx = ix\Big|_{-R}^{R} = iR-(-iR) = 2Ri$

67. $\displaystyle A = \frac{\int_{0}^{R}(m+x)[1-(m+x)]dx}{\int_{0}^{R}[1-(m+x)]dx} = \frac{\int_{0}^{R}\left(m+x-m^2-2mx-x^2\right)dx}{\int_{0}^{R}(1-m-x)dx}$

$\quad = \dfrac{\left[mx+\frac{x^2}{2}-m^2x-mx^2-\frac{x^3}{3}\right]\Big|_{0}^{R}}{\left[x-mx-\frac{x^2}{2}\right]\Big|_{0}^{R}}$

$\quad = \dfrac{\left[mR+\frac{R^2}{2}-m^2R-mR^2-\frac{R^3}{3}\right]-0}{\left[R-mR-\frac{R^2}{2}\right]-0}$

$\quad = \dfrac{R\left[m+\frac{R}{2}-m^2-mR-\frac{R^2}{3}\right]}{R\left[1-m-\frac{R}{2}\right]} = \dfrac{m+\frac{R}{2}-m^2-mR-\frac{R^2}{3}}{1-m-\frac{R}{2}}$

69. $\displaystyle\int_0^4 \frac{1}{(4x+4)^2}\,dx = \frac{1}{4}\int_0^4 (4x+4)^{-2}[4\ dx] = \frac{1}{4}\cdot\frac{(4x+4)^{-1}}{-1}\bigg|_0^4$

$\displaystyle = -\frac{1}{4}\cdot\frac{1}{4x+4}\bigg|_0^4 = -\frac{1}{16}\cdot\frac{1}{x+1}\bigg|_0^4 = -\frac{1}{16}\left(\frac{1}{5}-1\right) = \frac{1}{20} = 0.05$

71. 3.52

73. 55.39

Exercise 16.8

In Problems 1–34, answers are assumed to be
expressed in square units.

1. $y = 4x,\ x = 2$

$\displaystyle\text{Area} = \int_0^2 4x\ dx = 2x^2\bigg|_0^2 = 8 - 0 = 8$

3. $y = 3x + 2,\ x = 2,\ x = 3$

$\displaystyle\text{Area} = \int_2^3 (3x+2)\,dx = \left(\frac{3x^2}{2}+2x\right)\bigg|_2^3$

$\displaystyle = \frac{39}{2} - 10 = \frac{19}{2}$

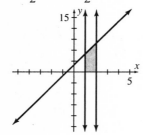

5. $y = x - 1,\ x = 5$

$\displaystyle\text{Area} = \int_1^5 (x-1)\,dx = \left(\frac{x^2}{2}-x\right)\bigg|_1^5$

$\displaystyle = \frac{15}{2} - \left(-\frac{1}{2}\right) = \frac{16}{2} = 8$

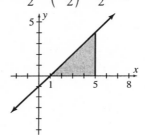

7. $y = x^2,\ x = 2,\ x = 3$

$\displaystyle\text{Area} = \int_2^3 x^2\,dx = \frac{x^3}{3}\bigg|_2^3 = 9 - \frac{8}{3} = \frac{19}{3}$

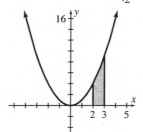

9. $y = x^2 + 2$, $x = -1$, $x = 2$

$$\text{Area} = \int_{-1}^{2}\left(x^2 + 2\right)dx = \left(\frac{x^3}{3} + 2x\right)\Bigg|_{-1}^{2}$$

$$= \frac{20}{3} - \left(-\frac{7}{3}\right) = \frac{27}{3} = 9$$

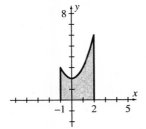

11. $y = x^2 - 2x$, $x = -3$, $x = -1$

$$\text{Area} = \int_{-3}^{-1}\left(x^2 - 2x\right)dx = \left(\frac{x^3}{3} - x^2\right)\Bigg|_{-3}^{-1}$$

$$= -\frac{4}{3} - (-18) = \frac{50}{3}$$

13. $y = 9 - x^2$

$$\text{Area} = \int_{-3}^{3}\left(9 - x^2\right)dx = \left(9x - \frac{x^3}{3}\right)\Bigg|_{-3}^{3}$$

$$= 18 - (-18) = 36$$

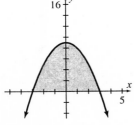

15. $y = 1 - x - x^3$, $x = -2$, $x = 0$

$$\text{Area} = \int_{-2}^{0}\left(1 - x - x^3\right)dx$$

$$= \left(x - \frac{x^2}{2} - \frac{x^4}{4}\right)\Bigg|_{-2}^{0} = 0 - (-8) = 8$$

17. $A = 3 + 2x - x^2$

$$\text{Area} = \int_{-1}^{3}\left(3 + 2x - x^2\right)dx$$

$$= \left(3x + x^2 - \frac{x^3}{3}\right)\Bigg|_{-1}^{3} = 9 - \left(-\frac{5}{3}\right) = \frac{32}{3}$$

19. $y = \frac{1}{x}$, $x = 1$, $x = e$

$$\text{Area} = \int_{1}^{e}\frac{1}{x}dx = \ln|x|\Big\|_{1}^{e} = \ln e - \ln 1$$

$$= 1 - 0 = 1$$

21. $y = \sqrt{x+9}$, $x = -9$, $x = 0$

Area $= \int_{-9}^{0} \sqrt{x+9}\,dx = \int_{-9}^{0}(x+9)^{\frac{1}{2}}\,dx$

$= \dfrac{(x+9)^{\frac{3}{2}}}{\frac{3}{2}}\Bigg|_{-9}^{0} = \dfrac{2(x+9)^{\frac{3}{2}}}{3}\Bigg|_{-9}^{0}$

$= 18 - 0 = 18$

23. $y = \sqrt{2x-1}$, $x = 1$, $x = 5$

Area $= \int_{1}^{5} \sqrt{2x-1}\,dx$

$= \dfrac{1}{2}\int_{1}^{5}(2x-1)^{\frac{1}{2}}[2\ dx]$

$= \dfrac{(2x-1)^{\frac{3}{2}}}{3}\Bigg|_{1}^{5} = 9 - \dfrac{1}{3} = \dfrac{26}{3}$

25. $y = \sqrt[3]{x}$, $x = 2$

Area

$= \int_{0}^{2}\sqrt[3]{x}\,dx = \int_{0}^{2}x^{\frac{1}{3}}\,dx = \dfrac{3x^{\frac{4}{3}}}{4}\Bigg|_{0}^{2} = \dfrac{3(2)^{\frac{4}{3}}}{4} - 0$

$= \dfrac{3\left(2\sqrt[3]{2}\right)}{4} = \dfrac{3}{2}\sqrt[3]{2}$

27. $y = e^{x}$, $x = 0$, $x = 2$

Area $= \int_{0}^{2} e^{x}\,dx = e^{x}\Big|_{0}^{2} = e^{2} - 1$

29. $y = x + \dfrac{2}{x}$, $x = 1$, $x = 2$

Area $= \int_{1}^{2}\left(x + \dfrac{2}{x}\right)dx = \left(\dfrac{x^{2}}{2} + 2\ln|x|\right)\Bigg|_{1}^{2}$

$= (2 + 2\ln 2) - \dfrac{1}{2} = \dfrac{3}{2} + 2\ln 2 = \dfrac{3}{2} + \ln 4$

31. $y = x^3$, $x = -2$, $x = 4$

$$\text{Area} = \int_{-2}^{0} -x^3\, dx + \int_{0}^{4} x^3\, dx$$

$$= -\frac{x^4}{4}\Big|_{-2}^{0} + \frac{x^4}{4}\Big|_{0}^{4}$$

$$= [0 - (-4)] + [64 - 0] = 68$$

33. $y = 2x - x^2$, $x = 1$, $x = 3$

$$\text{Area} = \int_{1}^{2} \left(2x - x^2\right) dx + \int_{2}^{3} -\left(2x - x^2\right) dx$$

$$= \left(x^2 - \frac{x^3}{3}\right)\Big|_{1}^{2} - \left(x^2 - \frac{x^3}{3}\right)\Big|_{2}^{3}$$

$$= \left[\frac{4}{3} - \frac{2}{3}\right] - \left[0 - \frac{4}{3}\right] = \frac{6}{3} = 2$$

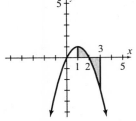

35. $f(x) = \begin{cases} 3x^2 & \text{if} \quad 0 \le x \le 2 \\ 16 - 2x & \text{if} \quad x \ge 2 \end{cases}$

$$\text{Area} = \int_{0}^{3} f(x)\, dx = \int_{0}^{2} 3x^2\, dx + \int_{2}^{3}(16 - 2x)\, dx$$

$$= x^3\Big|_{0}^{2} + \left(16x - x^2\right)\Big|_{2}^{3}$$

$$= [8 - 0] + [39 - 28] = 19 \text{ sq units}$$

37. a. $P(0 \le x \le 1) = \int_{0}^{1} \frac{1}{8} x\, dx = \frac{x^2}{16}\Big|_{0}^{1}$

$$= \frac{1}{16} - 0 = \frac{1}{16}$$

b. $P(2 \le x \le 4) = \int_{2}^{4} \frac{1}{8} x\, dx = \frac{x^2}{16}\Big|_{2}^{4}$

$$= 1 - \frac{1}{4} = \frac{3}{4}$$

c. $P(x \ge 3) = \int_{3}^{4} \frac{1}{8} x\, dx = \frac{x^2}{16}\Big|_{3}^{4}$

$$= 1 - \frac{9}{16} = \frac{7}{16}$$

39. a. $P(3 \le x \le 5) = \int_{3}^{5} \frac{1}{x}\, dx = \ln|x|\Big|_{3}^{5}$

$$= \ln 5 - \ln 3 = \ln \frac{5}{3}$$

b. $P(x \le 4) = \int_{e}^{4} \frac{1}{x}\, dx = \ln|x|\Big|_{e}^{4}$

$$= \ln(4) - \ln e = \ln(4) - 1$$

c. $P(x \ge 3) = \int_{3}^{e^2} \frac{1}{x}\, dx = \ln|x|\Big|_{3}^{e^2}$

$$= \ln e^2 - \ln 3 = 2 - \ln 3$$

d. $P\left(e \le x \le e^2\right) = \int_{e}^{e^2} \frac{1}{x}\, dx$

$$= \ln|x|\Big|_{e}^{e^2} - \ln e^2 - \ln e$$

$$= 2 - 1 = 1$$

41. 1.89 sq units

43. The x-intercept on $[1, 3]$ is $A \approx 2.190327947$

$$\text{Area} = \int_1^A -\left(x^4 - 2x^3 - 2\right)dx + \int_A^3 \left(x^4 - 2x^3 - 2\right)dx$$

≈ 11.41 sq units.

Exercise 16.9

1. Area

$$= \int_a^b \left(y_{\text{UPPER}} - y_{\text{LOWER}}\right)dx$$

$$= \int_{-2}^3 \left[(x+6) - x^2\right]dx$$

3. Intersection points:

$x^2 - x = 2x$, $x^2 - 3x = 0$,

$x(x-3) = 0 \Rightarrow x = 0$ or $x = 3$

Area

$$= \int_0^3 \left(y_{\text{UPPER}} - y_{\text{LOWER}}\right)dx$$

$$+ \int_3^4 \left(y_{\text{UPPER}} - y_{\text{LOWER}}\right)dx$$

$$= \int_0^3 \left[2x - \left(x^2 - x\right)\right]dx$$

$$+ \int_3^4 \left[\left(x^2 - x\right) - 2x\right]dx$$

5. The graphs of $y = 1 - x^2$ and $y = x - 1$
intersect when $1 - x^2 = x - 1$,
$0 = x^2 + x - 2$, $0 = (x-1)(x+2) \Rightarrow x = 1$
or $x = -2$. When $x = 1$, then $y = 0$. We use
horizontal elements, where y ranges from 0
to 1. Solving $y = x - 1$ for x gives
$x = y + 1$, and solving $y = 1 - x^2$ for x gives

$x^2 = 1 - y$, $x = \pm\sqrt{1 - y}$. We must choose
$x = \sqrt{1 - y}$ because x is not negative over
the given region.

$$\text{Area} = \int_0^1 \left(x_{\text{RIGHT}} - x_{\text{LEFT}}\right)dy$$

$$= \int_0^1 \left[(y+1) - \sqrt{1 - y}\right]dy$$

7. The graphs of $y = x^2 - 4$ and $y = 11 - 2x^2$
intersect when $x^2 - 4 = 11 - 2x^2$, $3x^2 = 15$,
$x^2 = 5$, so $x = \pm\sqrt{5}$. We use vertical
elements.

$$\text{Area} = \int_{-\sqrt{5}}^2 \left(y_{\text{UPPER}} - y_{\text{LOWER}}\right)dx$$

$$= \int_{-\sqrt{5}}^2 \left[\left(11 - 2x^2\right) - \left(x^2 - 4\right)\right]dx$$

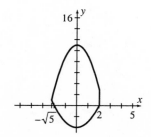

In Problems 9–33, the answers are assumed to be expressed in square units.

9. $y = x^2$, $y = 2x$
Region appears below.
Intersection: $x^2 = 2x$, $x^2 - 2x = 0$,
$x(x - 2) = 0$, so $x = 0$ or 2.
$$\text{Area} = \int_0^2 \left(2x - x^2\right) dx = \left(x^2 - \frac{x^3}{3}\right)\Big|_0^2$$
$$= \left(4 - \frac{8}{3}\right) - 0 = \frac{4}{3}$$

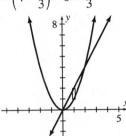

11. $y = x^2$, $x = 0$, $y = 4$ ($x \geq 0$). Region appears below.
Intersection: $x^2 = 4$, so $x = \pm 2$
$$\text{Area} = \int_0^2 \left(4 - x^2\right) dx = \left(4x - \frac{x^3}{3}\right)\Big|_0^2$$
$$= \left(8 - \frac{8}{3}\right) - 0 = \frac{16}{3}$$

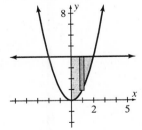

13. $y = x^2 + 2$, $y = 8$. Region appears below.
Intersection: $x^2 + 2 = 8$, $x^2 = 6$, so
$x = \pm\sqrt{6}$
Area
$$= \int_{-\sqrt{6}}^{\sqrt{6}} \left[8 - \left(x^2 + 2\right)\right] dx = \int_{-\sqrt{6}}^{\sqrt{6}} \left(6 - x^2\right) dx$$
$$= \left(6x - \frac{x^3}{3}\right)\Big|_{-\sqrt{6}}^{\sqrt{6}}$$
$$= \left(6\sqrt{6} - \frac{6\sqrt{6}}{3}\right) - \left(-6\sqrt{6} + \frac{6\sqrt{6}}{3}\right) = 8\sqrt{6}$$

15. $x = 8 + 2y$, $x = 0$, $y = -1$, $y = 3$. Region appears below.
$$\text{Area} = \int_{-1}^3 (8 + 2y) dy = \left(8y + y^2\right)\Big|_{-1}^3$$
$$= (24 + 9) - (-8 + 1) = 40$$

17. $y = 4 - x^2$, $y = -3x$. Region appears below.

Intersection: $-3x = 4 - x^2$, $x^2 - 3x - 4 = 0$,

$(x + 1)(x - 4) = 0$, so $x = -1$ or 4.

Area $\int_{-1}^{4}\left[\left(4 - x^2\right) - (-3x)\right]dx$

$= \left(4x - \dfrac{x^3}{3} + \dfrac{3x^2}{2}\right)\Bigg|_{-1}^{4}$

$= \left(16 - \dfrac{64}{3} + 24\right) - \left(-4 + \dfrac{1}{3} + \dfrac{3}{2}\right) = \dfrac{125}{6}$

19. $y^2 = x$, $y = x - 2$. Region appears below.

Intersection: $y^2 = y + 2$, $y^2 - y - 2 = 0$,

$(y + 1)(y - 2) = 0$, so $y = -1$ or 2.

Area

$= \int_{-1}^{2}\left[(y + 2) - y^2\right]dy = \left(\dfrac{y^2}{2} + 2y - \dfrac{y^3}{3}\right)\Bigg|_{-1}^{2}$

$= \left(2 + 4 - \dfrac{8}{3}\right) - \left(\dfrac{1}{2} - 2 + \dfrac{1}{3}\right) = \dfrac{9}{2}$

21. $2y = 4x - x^2$, $2y = x - 4$. Region appears below.

Intersection: $x - 4 = 4x - x^2$,

$x^2 - 3x - 4 = 0$,

$(x + 1)(x - 4) = 0$, so $x = -1$ or 4. Note that the y-values of the curves are given by

$y = \dfrac{4x - x^2}{2}$ and $y = \dfrac{x - 4}{2}$.

Area $= \int_{-1}^{4}\left[\left(\dfrac{4x - x^2}{2}\right) - \left(\dfrac{x - 4}{2}\right)\right]dx$

$= \int_{-1}^{4}\left(\dfrac{3}{2}x - \dfrac{x^2}{2} + 2\right)dx$

$= \left(\dfrac{3x^2}{4} - \dfrac{x^3}{6} + 2x\right)\Bigg|_{-1}^{4}$

$= \left(12 - \dfrac{64}{6} + 8\right) - \left(\dfrac{3}{4} + \dfrac{1}{6} - 2\right)$

$= \dfrac{125}{12}$

23. $y^2 = x$, $3x - 2y = 1$ (or $x = \dfrac{1 + 2y}{3}$). Region appears below.

Intersection: $y^2 = \dfrac{1 + 2y}{3}$, $3y^2 = 1 + 2y$,

$3y^2 - 2y - 1 = 0$, $(3y + 1)(y - 1) = 0$, so

$y = -\dfrac{1}{3}$ or 1.

Area $= \int_{-1/3}^{1}\left[\left(\dfrac{1 + 2y}{3}\right) - y^2\right]dx$

$= \int_{-1/3}^{1}\left(\dfrac{1}{3} + \dfrac{2y}{3} - y^2\right)dy$

$= \left(\dfrac{y}{3} + \dfrac{y^2}{3} - \dfrac{y^3}{3}\right)\Bigg|_{-1/3}^{1}$

$= \left(\dfrac{1}{3} + \dfrac{1}{3} - \dfrac{1}{3}\right) - \left(-\dfrac{1}{9} + \dfrac{1}{27} + \dfrac{1}{81}\right) = \dfrac{32}{81}$

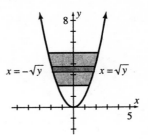

25. $y = 8 - x^2$, $y = x^2$, $x = -1$, $x = 1$. Region appears below.

Intersection: $x^2 = 8 - x^2$, $2x^2 = 8$, $x^2 = 4$, so

$x = \pm 2$.

Area

$$= \int_{-1}^{1} \left[\left(8 - x^2 \right) - x^2 \right] dx = \int_{-1}^{1} \left(8 - 2x^2 \right) dx$$

$$= \left(8x - \frac{2x^3}{3} \right) \Big|_{-1}^{1} = \left(8 - \frac{2}{3} \right) - \left(-8 + \frac{2}{3} \right) = \frac{44}{3}$$

27. $y = x^2$, $y = 2$, $y = 5$. Region appears below.

Area

$$= \int_{2}^{5} \left[\sqrt{y} - \left(-\sqrt{y} \right) \right] dy = \int_{2}^{5} 2\sqrt{y} \, dy = 2 \cdot \frac{y^{\frac{3}{2}}}{\frac{3}{2}} \Big|_{2}^{5}$$

$$= \frac{4 y^{\frac{3}{2}}}{3} \Big|_{2}^{5} = \frac{4 \cdot 5\sqrt{5}}{3} - \frac{4 \cdot 2\sqrt{2}}{3}$$

$$= \frac{4}{3} \left(5\sqrt{5} - 2\sqrt{2} \right)$$

29. $y = x^3 - 1$, $y = x - 1$. Region appears below. Intersection: $x^3 = x$, $x^3 - x = 0$,

$x \left(x^2 - 1 \right) = 0$,

$x(x + 1)(x - 1) = 0$, so $x = 0$ or $x = \pm 1$.

Area $= \int_{-1}^{0} \left(x^3 - x \right) dx + \int_{0}^{1} \left(x - x^3 \right) dx$

$$= \left(\frac{x^4}{4} - \frac{x^2}{2} \right) \Big|_{-1}^{0} + \left(\frac{x^2}{2} - \frac{x^4}{4} \right) \Big|_{0}^{1}$$

$$= \left[0 - \left(\frac{1}{4} - \frac{1}{2} \right) \right] + \left[\left(\frac{1}{2} - \frac{1}{4} \right) - 0 \right] = \frac{1}{2}$$

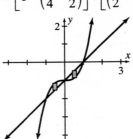

31. $y = \dfrac{-17 - 4x}{4}$, $y = \dfrac{1}{x}$. Region appears

below. Intersection: $\dfrac{-17 - 4x}{4} = \dfrac{1}{x}$,

$-17x - 4x^2 = 4$, $4x^2 + 17x + 4 = 0$, $(4x + 1)(x + 4) = 0$, so $x = -\dfrac{1}{4}$ or -4.

Area $= \displaystyle\int_{-4}^{-1/4}\left[\dfrac{1}{x} - \left(\dfrac{17 - 4x}{4}\right)\right]dx$

$= \left(\ln|x| - \dfrac{17}{4}x + \dfrac{x^2}{2}\right)\Bigg|_{-4}^{-1/4}$

$= \left(\ln\dfrac{1}{4} - \dfrac{17}{16} + \dfrac{1}{32}\right) - (\ln 4 - 17 + 8)$

$= \dfrac{255}{32} - 4\ln 2$

33. $y = x - 1$, $y = 5 - 2x$. Region appears below. Intersection: $x - 1 = 5 - 2x$, $3x = 6$, so $x = 2$.

Area $= \displaystyle\int_0^2[(5 - 2x) - (x - 1)]dx$

$+ \displaystyle\int_2^4[(x - 1) - (5 - 2x)]dx$

$= \displaystyle\int_0^2(6 - 3x)dx + \int_2^4(3x - 6)dx$

$= -\dfrac{1}{3}\displaystyle\int_0^2(6 - 3x)[-3\,dx] + \dfrac{1}{3}\int_2^4(3x - 6)[3\,dx]$

$= -\dfrac{(6 - 3x)^2}{6}\Bigg|_0^2 + \dfrac{(3x - 6)^2}{6}\Bigg|_2^4$

$= -[0 - 6] + [6 - 0] = 6 + 6 = 12$

35. $\dfrac{\text{Area between curve and diag.}}{\text{Area under diagonal}} = \dfrac{\displaystyle\int_0^1\left[x - \left(\frac{20}{21}x^2 + \frac{1}{21}x\right)\right]dx}{\displaystyle\int_0^1 x\,dx}$

Numerator $= \displaystyle\int_0^1\left[\dfrac{20}{21}x - \dfrac{20}{21}x^2\right]dx = \dfrac{20}{21}\int_0^1\left(x - x^2\right)dx$

$= \dfrac{20}{21}\left(\dfrac{x^2}{2} - \dfrac{x^3}{3}\right)\Bigg|_0^1 = \dfrac{20}{21}\left[\left(\dfrac{1}{2} - \dfrac{1}{3}\right) - 0\right] = \dfrac{20}{21}\cdot\dfrac{1}{6} = \dfrac{10}{63}$

Denominator $= \displaystyle\int_0^1 x\,dx = \dfrac{x^2}{2}\Bigg|_0^1 = \dfrac{1}{2}$

Coefficient of inequality $= \dfrac{\frac{10}{63}}{\frac{1}{2}} = \dfrac{20}{63}$

37. $y^2 = 4x$, $y = mx$

Intersection: $(mx)^2 = 4x$ $m^2x^2 = 4x$,

$m^2x^2 - 4x = 0$, $x(m^2x - 4) = 0$, $x = 0$ or

$x = \dfrac{4}{m^2}$.

If $x = 0$, then $y = 0$; if $x = \dfrac{4}{m^2}$, then $y = \dfrac{4}{m}$.

With horizontal elements,

$$\text{Area} = \int_0^{4/m}\left(\frac{y}{m} - \frac{y^2}{4}\right)dy = \left(\frac{y^2}{2m} - \frac{y^3}{12}\right)\Bigg|_0^{4/m}$$

$$= \frac{8}{3m^3} - \frac{16}{3m^3} = \frac{8}{3m^3} \text{ square units}$$

Note: with vertical elements,

$$\text{Area} = \int_0^{4/m^2}\left(2\sqrt{x} - mx\right)dx$$

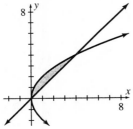

39. $y = x^2$ and $y = k$ intersect when

$x^2 = k$, $x = \pm\sqrt{k}$. Equating areas gives

$$\int_{-\sqrt{k}}^{\sqrt{k}}\left(k - x^2\right)dx = \frac{1}{2}\int_{-2}^{2}\left(4 - x^2\right)dx$$

$$\left(kx - \frac{x^3}{3}\right)\Bigg|_{-\sqrt{k}}^{\sqrt{k}} = \frac{1}{2}\left(4x - \frac{x^3}{3}\right)\Bigg|_{-2}^{2}$$

$$\frac{4}{3}k^{\frac{3}{2}} = \frac{16}{3}$$

$$k^{\frac{3}{2}} = 4 \Rightarrow k = 4^{\frac{3}{2}} = \left(2^2\right)^{\frac{3}{2}} = 2^{\frac{4}{3}}$$

41. 4.76 sq units

43. With vertical elements, two integrals are involved.
Answer: 7.26 sq units

Exercise 16.10

1. D: $p = 22 - 0.8q$
S: $p = 6 + 1.2q$

Equilibrium pt. $= (q_0,\ p_0) = (8,\ 15.6)$

$$CS = \int_0^{q_0}\left[f(q) - p_0\right]dq$$

$$= \int_0^8 [(22 - 0.8q) - 15.6] = \int_0^8 (6.4 - 0.8q)dq$$

$$= \left(6.4q - 0.4q^2\right)\Big|_0^8 = (51.2 - 25.6) - 0$$

$$= 25.6$$

$$PS = \int_0^{q_0}\left[p_0 - g(q)\right]dq$$

$$= \int_0^8 [15.6 - (6 + 1.2q)]dq$$

$$= \int_0^8 (9.6 - 1.2q)dq$$

$$= \left(9.6q - 0.6q^2\right)\Big|_0^8 = (76.8 - 38.4) - 0$$

$$= 38.4$$

3. D: $p = \frac{50}{q+5}$
   S: $p = \frac{q}{10} + 4.5$

Equilibrium pt. $= (q_0, p_0) = (5, 5)$

$CS = \int_0^{q_0} [f(q) - p_0]dq$

$= \int_0^5 \left[\frac{50}{q+5} - 5 \right]dq = \left(50\ln|q+5| - 5q\right)\Big|_0^5$

$= [50\ln(10) - 25] - [50\ln(5)]$
$= 50[\ln(10) - \ln(5)] - 25 = 50\ln(2) - 25$

$PS = \int_0^{q_0} [p_0 - g(q)]dq$

$= \int_0^5 \left[5 - \left(\frac{q}{10} + 4.5\right)\right]dq = \int_0^5 \left(0.5 - \frac{q}{10}\right)dq$

$= \left(0.5q - \frac{q^2}{20}\right)\Big|_0^5 = (2.5 - 1.25) - 0 = 1.25$

5. D: $p = 100(10 - p)$
   S: $p = 80(p - 10)$

Equilibrium pt. $= (q_0, p_0) = (400, 6)$

We use horizontal strips and integrate with respect to p.

$CS = \int_6^{10} 100(10 - p)dp$

$= 100\left(10p - \frac{p^2}{2}\right)\Big|_6^{10}$

$= 100[(100 - 50) - (60 - 18)]$
$= 800$

$PS = \int_1^6 80(p - 1)dp$

$= 80\left(\frac{p^2}{2} - p\right)\Big|_1^6$

$= 80\left[(18 - 6) - \left(\frac{1}{2} - 1\right)\right] = 1000$

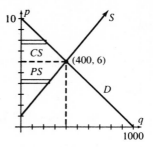

7. We integrate with respect to p. From the demand equation, when $q = 0$, then $p = 100$.

$CS = \int_{84}^{100} 10\sqrt{100 - p}\,dp$

$= \int_{84}^{100} -10(100 - p)^{\frac{1}{2}}[-dp]$

$= -\frac{20}{3}(100 - p)^{\frac{3}{2}}\Big|_{84}^{100}$

$= -\frac{20}{3}\left[0 - (16)^{\frac{3}{2}}\right] = -\frac{20}{3}(-64)$

$= 426\frac{2}{3} \approx \$426.67$

9. At equilibrium,
$2^{11-q} = 2^{q+1} \Rightarrow 11 - q = q + 1 \Rightarrow q = 5$, so
$p = 2^{11-5} = 64$

$CS = \int_0^5 \left(2^{11-q} - 64\right)dq = \left(-\frac{2^{11-q}}{\ln 2} - 64q\right)\Big|_0^5$

$= -\frac{64}{\ln 2} - 320 - \left(-\frac{2^{11}}{\ln 2} - 0\right)$

≈ 2542.307 hundred $\approx \$254,000$

11. $CS \approx 1197$; $PS \approx 477$

Chapter 16 Review Problems

1. $\int \left(x^3 + 2x - 7\right)dx = \frac{x^4}{4} + 2 \cdot \frac{x^2}{2} - 7x + C$

$= \frac{x^4}{4} + x^2 - 7x + C$

3. $\displaystyle\int_0^9 \left(\sqrt{x}+x\right)dx = \int_0^9 \left(x^{\frac{1}{2}}+x\right)dx$

$\displaystyle = \left(\frac{2x^{\frac{3}{2}}}{3}+\frac{x^2}{2}\right)\Bigg|_0^9$

$\displaystyle = \left(18+\frac{81}{2}\right) = \frac{117}{2}$

5. $\displaystyle\int \frac{6}{(x+5)^3}dx = 6\int (x+5)^{-3}dx$

$\displaystyle = \frac{6(x+5)^{-2}}{-2}+C$

$\displaystyle = -3(x+5)^{-2}+C$

7. $\displaystyle\int \frac{6x^2-12}{x^3-6x+1}dx$

$\displaystyle = 2\int \frac{1}{x^3-6x+1}\left[\left(3x^2-6\right)dx\right]$

$\displaystyle = 2\ln\left|x^3-6x+1\right|+C$

9. $\displaystyle\int_0^1 \sqrt[3]{3t+8}\,dt = \frac{1}{3}\int_0^1 (3t+8)^{\frac{1}{3}}[3\ dt]$

$\displaystyle = \frac{1}{3}\cdot\frac{(3t+8)^{\frac{4}{3}}}{\frac{4}{3}}\Bigg|_0^1$

$\displaystyle = \frac{(3t+8)^{\frac{4}{3}}}{4}\Bigg|_0^1 = \frac{11\sqrt[3]{11}}{4}-4$

11. $\displaystyle\int y(y+1)^2\,dy = \int\left(y^3+2y^2+y\right)dy$

$\displaystyle = \frac{y^4}{4}+\frac{2y^3}{3}+\frac{y^2}{2}+C$

13. $\displaystyle\int \frac{\sqrt[4]{z}-\sqrt[3]{z}}{\sqrt{z}}\,dz = \int\left(\frac{z^{\frac{1}{4}}}{z^{\frac{1}{2}}}-\frac{z^{\frac{1}{3}}}{z^{\frac{1}{2}}}\right)dz$

$\displaystyle = \int\left(z^{-\frac{1}{4}}-z^{-\frac{1}{6}}\right)dz$

$\displaystyle = \frac{z^{\frac{3}{4}}}{\frac{3}{4}}-\frac{z^{\frac{5}{6}}}{\frac{5}{6}}+C = \frac{4z^{\frac{3}{4}}}{3}-\frac{6z^{\frac{5}{6}}}{5}+C$

15. $\displaystyle\int_1^2 \frac{t^3}{2+t^3}\,dt = \frac{1}{3}\int_1^2 \frac{1}{2+t^3}\left[3t^2\,dt\right]$

$\displaystyle = \frac{1}{3}\ln\left|2+t^3\right|\Big|_1^2$

$\displaystyle = \frac{1}{3}(\ln 10-\ln 3) = \frac{1}{3}\ln\frac{10}{3}$

17. $\displaystyle\int x^2\sqrt{3x^3+2}\,dx = \frac{1}{9}\int\left(3x^3+2\right)^{\frac{1}{2}}\left[9x^2\,dx\right]$

$\displaystyle = \frac{1}{9}\cdot\frac{\left(3x^3+2\right)^{\frac{3}{2}}}{\frac{3}{2}}+C = \frac{2}{27}\left(3x^3+2\right)^{\frac{3}{2}}+C$

19. $\displaystyle\int\left(e^{2y}-e^{-2y}\right)dy$

$\displaystyle = \frac{1}{2}\int e^{2y}[2\ dy]-\left(-\frac{1}{2}\right)\int e^{-2y}[-2\ dy]$

$\displaystyle = \frac{1}{2}e^{2y}+\frac{1}{2}e^{-2y}+C = \frac{1}{2}\left(e^{2y}+e^{-2y}\right)+C$

21. $\displaystyle\int\left(\frac{1}{x}+\frac{2}{x^2}\right)dx = \int\frac{1}{x}\,dx+2\int x^{-2}\,dx$

$\displaystyle = \ln|x|+2\cdot\frac{x^{-1}}{-1}+C$

$\displaystyle = \ln|x|-\frac{2}{x}+C$

23. $\displaystyle\int_{-2}^1 10\left(y^4-y+1\right)dy = 10\left(\frac{y^5}{5}-\frac{y^2}{2}+y\right)\Bigg|_{-2}^1$

$\displaystyle = 10\left(\frac{1}{5}-\frac{1}{2}+1\right)-10\left(-\frac{32}{5}-2-2\right) = 111$

25. $\displaystyle\int_{\sqrt{3}}^2 7x\sqrt{4-x^2}\,dx = 7\int_{\sqrt{3}}^2 x\left(4-x^2\right)^{\frac{1}{2}}dx$

$\displaystyle = 7\cdot\left(-\frac{1}{2}\right)\Bigg|_{\sqrt{3}}^2 \left(4-x^2\right)^{\frac{1}{2}}[-2x\ dx]$

$\displaystyle = -\frac{7}{2}\cdot\frac{\left(4-x^2\right)^{\frac{3}{2}}}{\frac{3}{2}}\Bigg|_{\sqrt{3}}^2$

$\displaystyle = -\frac{7}{3}\cdot\left(4-x^2\right)^{\frac{3}{2}}\Bigg|_{\sqrt{3}}^2 = -\frac{7}{3}(0-1) = \frac{7}{3}$

27. $\displaystyle\int_0^1\left[2x-\frac{1}{(x+1)^{\frac{2}{3}}}\right]dx$

$\displaystyle=2\int_0^1 x\,dx-\int_0^1(x+1)^{-\frac{2}{3}}[dx]$

$\displaystyle=\left[2\cdot\frac{x^2}{2}-\frac{(x+1)^{\frac{1}{3}}}{\frac{1}{3}}\right]\Bigg|_0^1=\left[x^2-3(x+1)^{\frac{1}{3}}\right]\Bigg|_0^1$

$\displaystyle=\left[1-3\sqrt[3]{2}\right]-[0-3]=4-3\sqrt[3]{2}$

29. $\displaystyle\int\frac{\sqrt{t}-3}{t^2}dt=\int\left[\frac{t^{\frac{1}{2}}}{t^2}-\frac{3}{t^2}\right]dt$

$\displaystyle=\int\left(t^{-\frac{3}{2}}-3t^{-2}\right)dt$

$\displaystyle=\frac{t^{-\frac{1}{2}}}{-\frac{1}{2}}-3\cdot\frac{t^{-1}}{-1}+C=-2t^{-\frac{1}{2}}+3t^{-1}+C$

$\displaystyle=\frac{3}{t}-\frac{2}{\sqrt{t}}+C$

31. $\displaystyle\int_{-1}^0\frac{x^2+4x-1}{x+2}dx=\int_{-1}^0\left(x+2-\frac{5}{x+2}\right)dx$

$\displaystyle=\left(\frac{x^2}{2}+2x-5\ln|x+2|\right)\Bigg|_{-1}^0$

$\displaystyle=(-5\ln 2)-\left(\frac{1}{2}-2-0\right)$

$\displaystyle=\frac{3}{2}-5\ln 2$

33. $\displaystyle\int 9\sqrt{x}\sqrt{x^{\frac{3}{2}}+1}\,dx$

$\displaystyle=9\cdot\frac{2}{3}\int\left(x^{\frac{3}{2}}+1\right)^{\frac{1}{2}}\left[\frac{3}{2}x^{\frac{1}{2}}dx\right]$

$\displaystyle=6\cdot\frac{\left(x^{\frac{3}{2}}+1\right)^{\frac{3}{2}}}{\frac{3}{2}}+C=4\left(x^{\frac{3}{2}}+1\right)^{\frac{3}{2}}+C$

35. $\displaystyle\int_1^e\frac{e^{\ln x}}{x^2}dx=\int_1^e\frac{x}{x^2}dx=\int_1^e\frac{1}{x}dx=\ln|x|\Big|_1^e$

$\displaystyle=\ln e-\ln 1$

$\displaystyle=1-0=1$

37. $\displaystyle\int\frac{\left(1+e^{3x}\right)^2}{e^{-3x}}dx=\frac{1}{3}\int\left(1+e^{3x}\right)^2\left[3e^{3x}dx\right]$

$\displaystyle=\frac{\left(1+e^{3x}\right)^3}{9}+C$

39. $\displaystyle\int 3\sqrt{10^{3x}}\,dx=3\int 10^{\frac{3x}{2}}dx$

$\displaystyle=3\cdot\frac{2}{3}\int 10^{\frac{3x}{2}}\left[\frac{3}{2}dx\right]$

$\displaystyle=2\cdot\frac{10^{\frac{3x}{2}}}{\ln 10}+C=\frac{2\sqrt{10^{3x}}}{\ln 10}+C$

41. $\displaystyle y=\int\left(e^{2x}+3\right)dx=\int e^{2x}dx+\int 3\,dx$

$\displaystyle=\frac{1}{2}\int e^{2x}[2\,dx]+\int 3\,dx$

$\displaystyle=\frac{1}{2}e^{2x}+3x+C$

$y(0)=-\frac{1}{2}$ implies that $-\frac{1}{2}=\frac{1}{2}+0+C$, so

$C=-1$. Thus $y=\frac{1}{2}e^{2x}+3x-1$

43. $y=x^2-1$, $x=2$, $y\ge 0$. Region appears below.

$\displaystyle\text{Area}=\int_1^2\left(x^2-1\right)dx=\left(\frac{x^3}{3}-x\right)\Bigg|_1^2$

$\displaystyle=\left(\frac{8}{3}-2\right)-\left(\frac{1}{3}-1\right)=\frac{4}{3}$

45. $y = \sqrt{x+4}$, $x = 0$. Region appears below.

$$\text{Area} = \int_{-4}^{0} \sqrt{x+4}\,dx = \int_{-4}^{0} (x+4)^{\frac{1}{2}}\,[dx]$$

$$= \frac{(x+4)^{\frac{3}{2}}}{\frac{3}{2}}\Bigg|_{-4}^{0} = \frac{2(x+4)^{\frac{3}{2}}}{3}\Bigg|_{-4}^{0}$$

$$= \frac{16}{3} - 0 = \frac{16}{3}$$

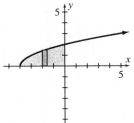

47. $y = 5x - x^2$. Region appears below.

$$\text{Area} = \int_{0}^{5} \left(5x - x^2\right) dx = \left(\frac{5x^2}{2} - \frac{x^3}{3}\right)\Bigg|_{0}^{5}$$

$$= \left(\frac{125}{2} - \frac{125}{3}\right) - 0 = \frac{125}{6}$$

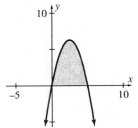

49. $y = \frac{1}{x} + 3$, $x = 1$, $x = 3$. Region appears below.

$$\text{Area} = \int_{1}^{3} \left(\frac{1}{x} + 3\right) dx = \left(\ln|x| + 3x\right)\Bigg|_{1}^{3}$$

$$= [\ln(3) + 9] - 3 = 6 + \ln 3$$

51. $y^2 = 4x$, $x = 0$, $y = 2$. Region appears below.

$$\text{Area} = \int_{0}^{2} \frac{y^2}{4}\,dy = \frac{y^3}{12}\Bigg|_{0}^{2} = \frac{8}{12} - 0 = \frac{2}{3}$$

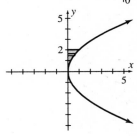

53. $y = x^2 + 4x - 5$, $y = 0$. Region appears below.
$x^2 + 4x - 5 = 0$, $(x+5)(x-1) = 0$, so $x = -5, 1$.

$$\text{Area} = \int_{-5}^{1} -\left(x^2 + 4x - 5\right) dx$$

$$= -\left(\frac{x^3}{3} + 2x^2 - 5x\right)\Bigg|_{-5}^{1}$$

$$= -\left(\frac{1}{3} + 2 - 5\right) + \left(-\frac{125}{3} + 50 + 25\right) = 36$$

55. $y = x^2 - 2x$, $y = 12 - x^2$. Region appears below.

$x^2 - 2x = 12 - x^2$, $2x^2 - 2x - 12 = 0$,

$2(x + 2)(x - 3) = 0$, so $x = -2, 3$

Area $\int_{-2}^{3} \left[\left(12 - x^2 \right) - \left(x^2 - 2x \right) \right] dx$

$= 2\int_{-2}^{3} \left(6 + x - x^2 \right) dx$

$= 2\left(6x + \frac{x^2}{2} - \frac{x^3}{3} \right)\Big|_{-2}^{3}$

$= 2\left[\left(18 + \frac{9}{2} - 9 \right) - \left(-12 + 2 + \frac{8}{3} \right) \right] = \frac{125}{3}$

57. $y = \ln x$, $x = 0$, $y = 0$, $y = 1$. Region appears below.

$y = \ln x \Rightarrow x = e^y$

Area $= \int_{0}^{1} e^y dy = e^y \Big|_{0}^{1} = e - 1$

59. $r = \int \left(100 - \frac{3}{2}\sqrt{2q} \right) dq$

$= \int 100 dq - \frac{3}{2}\sqrt{2} \int q^{\frac{1}{2}} dq$

$= 100q - \frac{3}{2}\sqrt{2} \cdot \frac{q^{\frac{3}{2}}}{\frac{3}{2}} + C = 100q - \sqrt{2}q^{\frac{3}{2}} + C$

When $q = 0$, then $r = 0$. Thus $0 = 0 - 0 + C$,

so $C = 0$. Hence $r = 100q - \sqrt{2}q^{\frac{3}{2}}$. Since $r = pq$, then

$p = \frac{r}{q} = 100 - \sqrt{2}q^{\frac{1}{2}} = 100 - \sqrt{2q}$. Thus

$p = 100 - \sqrt{2q}$.

61. $\int_{10}^{20} \left(275 - q - 0.3q^2 \right) dq$

$= \left(275q - \frac{q^2}{2} - \frac{0.3q^3}{3} \right)\Big|_{10}^{20}$

$= (5500 - 200 - 800) - (2750 - 50 - 100)$

$= \$1900$

63. $\int_{0}^{100} 0.008e^{-0.008t} dt$

$= -\int_{0}^{100} e^{0.008t} [-0.008 \ dt]$

$= -e^{-0.008t}\Big|_{0}^{100} = -e^{-0.8} + 1 \approx 0.5507$

65. $y = 9 - 2x$, $y = x$; from $x = 0$ to $x = 4$. Region appears below. Intersection: $x = 9 - 2x$, $3x = 9$, so $x = 3$.

Area $= \int_{0}^{3} [(9 - 2x) - x] dx$

$\quad + \int_{3}^{4} [x - (9 - 2x)] dx$

$= \int_{0}^{3} (9 - 3x) dx + \int_{3}^{4} (3x - 9) dx$

$= \left(9x - \frac{3x^2}{2} \right)\Big|_{0}^{3} + \left(\frac{3x^2}{2} - 9x \right)\Big|_{3}^{4}$

$= \left[\left(27 - \frac{27}{2} \right) - 0 \right] + \left[(24 - 36) - \left(\frac{27}{2} - 27 \right) \right]$

$= 15$ square units

67. $D\!: p = 0.01q^2 - 1.1q + 30$
$\phantom{\textbf{67.}}\ \ S\!: p = 0.01q^2 + 8$

Equil. pt. $= (q_0,\ p_0) = (20,\ 12)$

$CS = \displaystyle\int_0^{q_0} [f(q) - p_0]dq$

$= \displaystyle\int_0^{20} \left[\left(0.01q^2 - 1.1q + 30\right) - 12\right]dq$

$= \displaystyle\int_0^{20} \left(0.01q^2 - 1.1q + 18\right)dq$

$= \left(\dfrac{0.01q^3}{3} - \dfrac{1.1q^2}{2} + 18q\right)\Bigg|_0^{20}$

$= \left(\dfrac{80}{3} - 220 + 360\right) - 0 = 166\dfrac{2}{3}$

$PS = \displaystyle\int_0^{q_0} [p_0 - g(q)]dq$

$= \displaystyle\int_0^{20} \left[12 - \left(0.01q^2 + 8\right)\right]dq$

$= \displaystyle\int_0^{20} \left(4 - 0.01q^2\right)dq = \left(4q - \dfrac{0.01q^3}{3}\right)\Bigg|_0^{20}$

$= \left(80 - \dfrac{80}{3}\right) - 0 = 53\dfrac{1}{3}$

69. $\displaystyle\int_{q_0}^{q_n} \dfrac{dq}{q - \hat{q}} = -(u+v)\int_0^n dt$

$\ln|q - \hat{q}|\Big\|_{q_0}^{q_n} = -(u+v)t\big|_0^n$

$\ln|q_n - \hat{q}| - \ln|q_0 - \hat{q}| = -(u+v)n$

$\ln|q_0 - \hat{q}| - \ln|q_n - \hat{q}| = (u+v)n$

$\ln\left|\dfrac{q_0 - \hat{q}}{q_n - \hat{q}}\right| = (u+v)n$

$n = \dfrac{1}{u+v}\ln\left|\dfrac{q_0 - \hat{q}}{q_n - \hat{q}}\right|$

as was to be shown.

71. Case 1. $r \neq -1$

$g(x) = \dfrac{1}{k}\displaystyle\int_1^{1/x} ku^r\, du = \int_1^{1/x} u^r\, du = \dfrac{u^{r+1}}{r+1}\Bigg|_1^{1/x}$

$= \dfrac{1}{r+1}\left(x^{-r-1} - 1\right)$

$g'(x) = \dfrac{1}{r+1}\left[-(r+1)x^{-r-2}\right] = -\dfrac{1}{x^{r+2}}$

Case 2. $r = -1$

$g(x) = \dfrac{1}{k}\displaystyle\int_1^{1/x} ku^{-1}\, du = \int_1^{1/x} \dfrac{1}{u}\, du$

$= \ln|u|\Big|_1^{1/x} = \ln\left(\dfrac{1}{x}\right) - 0 = -\ln x$

$g'(x) = -\dfrac{1}{x} = -\dfrac{1}{x^{r+2}}$

73. With vertical elements, two integrals are involved.
Answer: 24.71 sq units

75. $CS \approx 1148;\ PS \approx 251$

Mathematical Snapshot Chapter 16

1. a. $\displaystyle\int_0^5 f(t)dt = \int_0^5 (50 - 2t)dt = \left(50t - t^2\right)\Big|_0^5$

$= (250 - 25) - 0 = 225$

b. $\displaystyle\int_{10}^{15} f(t)dt = \int_{10}^{15} (50 - 2t)dt$

$= \left(50t - t^2\right)\Big|_{10}^{15}$

$= (750 - 225) - (500 - 100) = 125$

3. a. Total revenue

$$= \int_0^R (m+st)f(t)dt = \int_0^{30} (100+t)(900-t^2)dt$$

$$= \int_0^{30} \left(90,000 + 900t - 100t^2 - t^3\right)dt$$

$$= 90,000t + 450t^2 - \frac{100}{3}t^3 - \frac{1}{4}t^4 \Big|_0^{30}$$

$$= 2,700,000 + 405,000 - 900,000 - 202,500$$

$$= \$2,002,500$$

b. Total number of units sold

$$= \int_0^R f(t)dt = \int_0^{30} \left(900-t^2\right)dt$$

$$= \left(900t - \frac{1}{3}t^3\right)\Big|_0^{30} = 27,000 - 9000$$

$$= 18,000$$

c. Average delivered price $= \dfrac{\text{total revenue}}{\text{total number of units sold}}$

$$= \frac{2,002,500}{18,000} = \$111.25$$

Chapter 17

1. $S(t) = \int -4te^{0.1t} dt$

   Let $u = -4t$ and $dv = e^{0.1t} dt$, so $du = -4dt$,

   and $v = \int e^{0.1t} dt = \frac{1}{0.1} e^{0.1t} = 10e^{0.1t}$.

   $\int -4te^{0.1t} dt = (-4t)(10e^{0.1t})$

   $-\int (10e^{0.1t})(-4)dt$

   $= -40te^{0.1t} + \int 40e^{0.1t} dt$

   $= -40te^{0.1t} + 40\frac{e^{0.1t}}{0.1} + C$

   $= -40te^{0.1t} + 400e^{0.1t} + C$

   $S(t) = -40te^{0.1t} + 400e^{0.1t} + C$ and

   $S(0) = 5000$

   $5000 = 0 + 400e^0 + C$

   $C = 4600$

   $S(t) = -40te^{0.1t} + 400e^{0.1t} + 4600$

2. $P(t) = \int 0.1t(\ln t)^2 dt$

   Let $u = (\ln t)^2$ and $dv = 0.1t \, dt$, so

   $du = 2(\ln t)\left(\frac{1}{t}\right)dt = \frac{2\ln t}{t} dt$ and

   $v = \int 0.1t \, dt = 0.1\frac{t^2}{2} = 0.05t^2$

   $\int 0.1t(\ln t)^2 dt$

   $= 0.05t^2(\ln t)^2 - \int (0.05t^2)\left(\frac{2\ln t}{t}\right)dt$

   $= 0.05(t \ln t)^2 - \int 0.1t \ln t \, dt$

   For $\int 0.1t \ln t \, dt$, let $u = \ln t$ and

   $dv = 0.1t \, dt$, so $du = \frac{1}{t} dt$ and $v = 0.05t^2$.

$\int 0.1t \ln t \, dt = 0.05t^2 \ln t - \int (0.05t^2)\left(\frac{1}{t}\right)dt$

$= 0.05t^2 \ln t - \int 0.05t \, dt$

$= 0.05t^2 \ln t - 0.05\frac{t^2}{2} + C$

$= 0.05t^2 \ln t - 0.025t^2 + C$

Thus,

$P(t) = 0.05(t \ln t)^2$

$- \left(0.05t^2 \ln t - 0.025t^2\right) + C$

$= 0.05(t \ln t)^2 - 0.05t^2 \ln t + 0.025t^2 + C$

Exercise 17.1

1. $\int f(x)dx = uv - \int v \, du$

   $= x \cdot \frac{2}{3}(x+5)^{\frac{3}{2}} - \int \frac{2}{3}(x+5)^{\frac{3}{2}} dx$

   $= \frac{2}{3}x(x+5)^{\frac{3}{2}} - \frac{2}{3} \cdot \frac{2}{5}(x+5)^{\frac{5}{2}} + C$

   $= \frac{2}{3}x(x+5)^{\frac{3}{2}} - \frac{4}{15}(x+5)^{\frac{5}{2}} + C$

3. $\int xe^{-x} dx$

   Letting $u = x$, $dv = e^{-x} dx$, then $du = dx$,

   $v = -e^{-x}$.

   $\int xe^{-x} dx = -xe^{-x} - \int -e^{-x} dx$

   $= -xe^{-x} - \int e^{-x}[-dx] = -xe^{-x} - e^{-x} + C$

   $= -e^{-x}(x+1) + C$

5. $\int y^3 \ln y \, dy$

Letting $u = \ln y$, $dv = y^3 dy$, then

$du = \left(\dfrac{1}{y}\right) dy$, $v = \dfrac{y^4}{4}$

$\int y^3 \ln y \, dy = \dfrac{y^4 \ln y}{4} - \int \dfrac{y^4}{4}\left(\dfrac{1}{y} dy\right)$

$= \dfrac{y^4 \ln y}{4} - \int \dfrac{y^3}{4} dy = \dfrac{y^4 \ln y}{4} - \dfrac{y^4}{16} + C$

$= \dfrac{y^4}{4}\left[\ln(y) - \dfrac{1}{4}\right] + C$

7. $\int \ln(4x) \, dx$

Letting $u = \ln(4x)$, $dv = dx$, then

$du = \left(\dfrac{1}{x}\right) dx$,

$v = x$.

$\int \ln(4x) dx = x \ln(4x) - \int x\left(\dfrac{1}{x} dx\right)$

$= x \ln(4x) - \int dx = x \ln(4x) - x + C$

$= x[\ln(4x) - 1] + C$

9. $\int 15x\sqrt{x+1} \, dx$

Let $u = 15x$, $dv = \sqrt{x+1} \, dx$, then du

$= 15dx$, $v = \dfrac{2}{3}(x+1)^{\frac{3}{2}}$

$\int 15x\sqrt{x+1} \, dx$

$= 15x \cdot \dfrac{2(x+1)^{\frac{3}{2}}}{3} - \int \dfrac{2(x+1)^{\frac{3}{2}}}{3} \cdot 15dx$

$= 10x(x+1)^{\frac{3}{2}} - 4(x+1)^{\frac{5}{2}} + C$

$= 2(x+1)^{\frac{3}{2}}[5x - 2(x+1)] + C$

$= 2(x+1)^{\frac{3}{2}}(3x - 2) + C$

11. $\int \dfrac{x}{(2x+1)^2} \, dx$

Letting $u = x$, $dv = (2x+1)^{-2} dx$, then

$du = dx$, $v = \dfrac{(2x+1)^{-1}}{-2} = -\dfrac{1}{2(2x+1)}$

$\int \dfrac{x}{(2x+1)^2} \, dx = -\dfrac{x}{2(2x+1)}$

$-\int -\dfrac{1}{2(2x+1)} \, dx$

$= -\dfrac{x}{2(2x+1)} + \dfrac{1}{2} \cdot \dfrac{1}{2}\int \dfrac{1}{2x+1}[2 \, dx]$

$= -\dfrac{x}{2(2x+1)} + \dfrac{1}{4} \ln|2x+1| + C$

13. $\int \dfrac{\ln x}{x^2} \, dx$

Letting $u = \ln x$, $dv = x^{-2} dx$, then

$du = \dfrac{1}{x} dx$, $v = -x^{-1}$.

$\int \dfrac{\ln x}{x^2} \, dx = -\dfrac{\ln x}{x} - \int -x^{-1}\left(\dfrac{1}{x} dx\right)$

$= -\dfrac{\ln x}{x} + \int x^{-2} dx = -\dfrac{\ln x}{x} - \dfrac{1}{x} + C$

$= -\dfrac{1}{x}(1 + \ln x) + C$

15. $\int_1^2 4xe^{2x} dx$

Letting $u = 4x$, $dv = e^{2x} dx$, then $du = 4dx$,

$v = \dfrac{1}{2} e^{2x}$

$\int_1^2 4xe^{2x} dx = \left[2xe^{2x} - \int 2e^{2x} dx\right]_1^2$

$= \left[2xe^{2x} - e^{2x}\right]_1^2 = e^{2x}(2x-1)\Big|_1^2$

$= e^4(3) - e^2(1) = e^2\left(3e^2 - 1\right)$

17. $\int_0^1 xe^{-x^2} dx = -\dfrac{1}{2}\int_0^1 e^{-x^2}(-2x \, dx)$

(Form: $\int e^u du$)

$= -\dfrac{1}{2} e^{-x^2}\Big|_0^1 = -\dfrac{1}{2}\left(e^{-1} - 1\right) = \dfrac{1}{2}\left(1 - e^{-1}\right)$

19. $\displaystyle\int_1^2 \frac{3x}{\sqrt{4-x}}\,dx$

Letting $u = 3x$, $dv = (4-x)^{-\frac{1}{2}}\,dx$, then

$du = 3dx$, $v = -2(4-x)^{\frac{1}{2}}$.

$\displaystyle\int_1^2 \frac{3x}{\sqrt{4-x}}\,dx$

$\displaystyle = \left[-6x(4-x)^{\frac{1}{2}} - \int -2(4-x)^{\frac{1}{2}}(3\,dx)\right]_1^2$

$\displaystyle = \left[-6x(4-x)^{\frac{1}{2}} - 4(4-x)^{\frac{3}{2}}\right]_1^2$

$\displaystyle = \left\{-2\sqrt{4-x}\,[3x + 2(4-x)]\right\}\Big|_1^2$

$\displaystyle = \left\{-2\sqrt{4-x}\,(x+8)\right\}\Big|_1^2 = -2\left(10\sqrt{2} - 9\sqrt{3}\right)$

$\displaystyle = 2\left(9\sqrt{3} - 10\sqrt{2}\right)$

21. $\displaystyle\int 2(2x-1)\ln(x-1)\,dx$

Letting $u = 2\ln(x-1)$, $dv = (2x-1)dx$, then

$\displaystyle du = \frac{2}{x-1}\,dx$, $v = x^2 - x = x(x-1)$.

$\displaystyle\int 2(2x-1)\ln(x-1)\,dx$

$\displaystyle = 2x(x-1)\ln(x-1) - \int x(x-1)\frac{2}{x-1}\,dx$

$\displaystyle = 2x(x-1)\ln(x-1) - \int 2x\,dx$

$\displaystyle = 2x(x-1)\ln(x-1) - x^2 + C$

23. $\displaystyle\int x^2 e^x\,dx$

Letting $u = x^2$, $dv = e^x dx$, then $du = 2x\,dx$
and $v = e^x$.

$\displaystyle\int x^2 e^x\,dx = x^2 e^x - \int e^x(2x\,dx)$

$\displaystyle = x^2 e^x - 2\int xe^x dx$

For $\displaystyle\int xe^x dx$, let $u = x$, $dv = e^x dx$. Then

$du = dx$, $v = e^x$ and

$\displaystyle\int xe^x dx = xe^x - \int e^x dx = xe^x - e^x + C_1$

$= e^x(x-1) + C_1$. Thus

$\displaystyle\int x^2 e^x dx = x^2 e^x - 2\left[e^x(x-1)\right] + C$

$\displaystyle = e^x\left(x^2 - 2x + 2\right) + C.$

25. $\displaystyle\int\left(x - e^{-x}\right)^2 dx = \int\left(x^2 - 2xe^{-x} + e^{-2x}\right)dx$

$\displaystyle = \frac{x^3}{3} - \frac{e^{-2x}}{2} - 2\int xe^{-x} dx$

Using Problem 3 for $\displaystyle\int xe^{-x} dx$,

$\displaystyle\int\left(x - e^{-x}\right)^2 dx$

$\displaystyle = \frac{x^3}{3} - \frac{e^{-2x}}{2} + 2e^{-x}(x+1) + C$

27. $\displaystyle\int x^3 e^{x^2} dx$

Letting $u = x^2$, $dv = xe^{x^2} dx$, then

$\displaystyle du = 2x\,dx$, $v = \left(\frac{1}{2}\right)e^{x^2}$.

$\displaystyle\int x^3 e^{x^2} dx = \frac{x^2 e^{x^2}}{2} - \int \frac{e^{x^2}}{2}(2x\,dx)$

$\displaystyle = \frac{x^2 e^{x^2}}{2} - \frac{e^{x^2}}{2} + C = \frac{e^{x^2}}{2}\left(x^2 - 1\right) + C$

29. $\displaystyle\int\left(2^x + x\right)^2 dx = \int\left(2^{2x} + 2x2^x + x^2\right)dx$

$\displaystyle = \int 2^{2x} dx + \int x2^{x+1} dx + \int x^2 dx$

For $\displaystyle\int x2^{x+1} dx$, let $u = x$, $dv = 2^{x+1} dx$.

Then $du = dx$, $\displaystyle v = \frac{1}{\ln 2}\cdot 2^{x+1}$ and

$\displaystyle\int x2^{x+1} dx = \frac{x}{\ln 2}\cdot 2^{x+1} - \frac{1}{\ln 2}\int 2^{x+1} dx$

$\displaystyle = \frac{x}{\ln 2}\cdot 2^{x+1} - \frac{1}{\ln^2 2}\cdot 2^{x+1} + C_1$. Thus

$\displaystyle\int\left(2^x + x\right)^2 dx$

$\displaystyle = \int 2^{2x} dx + \int x2^{x+1} dx + \int x^2 dx$

$\displaystyle = \frac{1}{2}\int 2^{2x}[2\,dx] + \int x2^{x+1} dx + \int x^2 dx$

379

$$= \frac{1}{2\ln 2} \cdot 2^{2x} + \frac{x}{\ln 2} \cdot 2^{x+1} - \frac{1}{\ln^2 2} \cdot 2^{x+1}$$

$$+ \frac{x^3}{3} + C$$

31. area $= \int_1^{e^3} (\ln x)dx$. Letting $u = \ln x$, $dv = dx$,

then $du = \left(\frac{1}{x}\right)dx$, $v = x$.

area $= \int_1^{e^3} (\ln x)dx = \left[(x\ln x) - \int x \cdot \frac{1}{x} dx\right]_1^{e^3}$

$= \left[(x\ln x) - \int dx\right]_1^{e^3} = [x\ln(x) - x]_1^{e^3}$

$= \left[e^3 \cdot 3 - e^3\right] - [1 \cdot 0 - 1] = 2e^3 + 1$

Answer: $2e^3 + 1$ sq units

33. area $= \int_0^4 x\sqrt{2x+1}\, dx$. Letting $u = x$,

$dv = (2x+1)^{\frac{1}{2}} dx$, then $du = dx$,

$v = \frac{1}{3}(2x+1)^{\frac{3}{2}}$.

area $= \int_0^4 x\sqrt{2x+1}\, dx$

$= \left[\frac{x}{3}(2x+1)^{\frac{3}{2}} - \frac{1}{3}\int (2x+1)^{\frac{3}{2}} dx\right]_0^4$

$= \left[\frac{x}{3}(2x+1)^{\frac{3}{2}} - \frac{1}{3} \cdot \frac{1}{2}\int (2x+1)^{\frac{3}{2}}(2\, dx)\right]_0^4$

$= \left[\frac{x}{3}(2x+1)^{\frac{3}{2}} - \frac{1}{15}(2x+1)^{\frac{5}{2}}\right]_0^4$

$= \left[\frac{4}{3}(27) - \frac{1}{15}(243)\right] - \left[0 - \frac{1}{15}\right] = \frac{298}{15}$

Answer: $\frac{298}{15}$ sq units

35. a. Consider $\int p\, dq$. Letting $u = p$,

$dv = dq$, then $du = \frac{dp}{dq} dq$, $v = q$. Thus

$\int p\, dq = pq - \int q\frac{dp}{dq} dq = r - \int q\frac{dp}{dq} dq$

(since $r = pq$).

b. From (a), $r = \int p\, dq + \int q\frac{dp}{dq} dq$.

Combining the integrals gives

$r = \int \left(p + q\frac{dp}{dq}\right)dq$.

c. From (b), $\frac{dr}{dq} = p + q\frac{dp}{dq}$. Thus

$\int_0^{q_0} \left(p + q\frac{dp}{dq}\right)dq$

$= \int_0^{q_0} \frac{dr}{dq} dq = r(q_0) - r(0) = r(q_0)$

[since $r(0) = 0$].

Principles in Practice 17.2

1. $r(q) = \int r'(q)dq = \int \frac{5(q+4)}{q^2 + 4q + 3} dq$

Express $\frac{5(q+4)}{q^2 + 4q + 3}$ as a sum of partial

fractions.

$\frac{5(q+4)}{q^2 + 4q + 3} = \frac{5(q+4)}{(q+1)(q+3)} = \frac{A}{q+1} + \frac{B}{q+3}$

$5(q+4) = A(q+3) + B(q+1)$

When $q = -3$, we get $5(1) = -2B$, so

$B = -\frac{5}{2}$. When $q = -1$, we get $5(3) = A(2)$,

so $A = \frac{15}{2}$.

$$r(q) = \int \frac{5(q+4)}{q^2 + 4q + 3} dx = \int \frac{\frac{15}{2}}{q+1} dq$$

$$- \int \frac{\frac{5}{2}}{q+3} dq$$

$$= \frac{15}{2} \ln|q+1| - \frac{5}{2} \ln|q+3| + C$$

$$= \frac{5}{2} \ln\left|\frac{(q+1)^3}{q+3}\right| + C$$

Since $r(0) = 0$, $0 = \frac{5}{2} \ln\left|\frac{1}{3}\right| + C$ so $C = \frac{5}{2} \ln 3$

and $r(q) = \frac{5}{2} \ln\left|\frac{3(q+1)^3}{q+3}\right|$.

2. $V(t) = \int V'(t) dt = \int \frac{300t^3}{t^2 + 6} dt$

Since the degree of the numerator is greater than the degree of the denominator, we first divide $300t^3$ by $t^2 + 6$ to reduce the fraction.

$$\frac{300t^3}{t^2 + 6} = \frac{300t^3 + 1800t - 1800t}{t^2 + 6}$$

$$= \frac{300t(t^2 + 6) - 1800t}{t^2 + 6} = 300t - \frac{1800t}{t^2 + 6}$$

$t^2 + 6$ is irreducible. To integrate $\frac{1800t}{t^2 + 6}$, let

$u = t^2 + 6$, so $du = 2t\, dt$

$$\int \frac{300t^3}{t^2 + 6} dt = \int 300t\, dt - \int \frac{1800t}{t^2 + 6} dt$$

$$= 150t^2 - 900 \ln|t^2 + 6| + C$$

$$V(t) = 150t^2 - 900 \ln(t^2 + 6) + C$$

Exercise 17.2

1. $\frac{10x}{x^2 + 7x + 6} = \frac{10x}{(x+6)(x+1)} = \frac{A}{x+6} + \frac{B}{x+1}$

$10x = A(x+1) + B(x+6)$

If $x = -1$, then $-10 = 5B$, or $B = -2$. If $x = -6$, then $-60 = -5A$, or $A = 12$.

Answer $\frac{12}{x+6} - \frac{2}{x+1}$

3. $\frac{x^2}{x^2 + 6x + 8} = 1 + \frac{-6x - 8}{x^2 + 6x + 8}$ (by long division).

$$\frac{-6x - 8}{x^2 + 6x + 8} = \frac{-6x - 8}{(x+2)(x+4)}$$

$$= \frac{A}{x+2} + \frac{B}{x+4}$$

$-6x - 8 = A(x+4) + B(x+2)$

If $x = -4$, then $16 = -2B$, or $B = -8$. If $x = -2$, then $4 = 2A$, or $A = 2$.

Answer: $1 + \frac{2}{x+2} - \frac{8}{x+4}$

5. $\frac{4x-5}{x^2 + 2x + 1} = \frac{4x-5}{(x+1)^2} = \frac{A}{x+1} + \frac{B}{(x+1)^2}$

$4x - 5 = A(x+1) + B$

If $x = -1$, then $-9 = B$. If $x = 0$, then $-5 = A + B$, $-5 = A - 9$, or $A = 4$.

Answer: $\frac{4}{x+1} - \frac{9}{(x+1)^2}$

7. $\frac{x^2 + 3}{x^3 + x} = \frac{x^2 + 3}{x(x^2 + 1)} = \frac{A}{x} + \frac{Bx + C}{x^2 + 1}$

$x^2 + 3 = A(x^2 + 1) + (Bx + C)x$

$x^2 + 3 = (A + B)x^2 + Cx + A$

Thus $A + B = 1$, $C = 0$, $A = 3$. This gives $A = 3$, $B = -2$, $C = 0$.

Answer: $\frac{3}{x} - \frac{2x}{x^2 + 1}$

9. $\frac{5x-2}{x^2 - x} = \frac{5x-2}{x(x-1)} = \frac{A}{x} + \frac{B}{x-1}$

$5x - 2 = A(x-1) + Bx$

If $x = 1$, then $3 = B$. If $x = 0$, then $-2 = -A$, or $A = 2$.

$$\int \frac{5x-2}{x^2 - x} dx = \int \left(\frac{2}{x} + \frac{3}{x-1}\right) dx$$

Answer:

$2 \ln|x| + 3 \ln|x-1| + C = \ln|x^2(x-1)^3| + C$

11. $\dfrac{x+10}{x^2-x-2}=\dfrac{x+10}{(x+1)(x-2)}=\dfrac{A}{x+1}+\dfrac{B}{x-2}$

$x+10=A(x-2)+B(x+1)$

If $x=2$, then $12=3B$, or $B=4$. If $x=-1$,
then $9=-3A$, or $A=-3$.

$\displaystyle\int\dfrac{x+10}{x^2-x-2}\,dx=\int\left(\dfrac{-3}{x+1}+\dfrac{4}{x-2}\right)dx$

Answer: $-3\ln|x+1|+4\ln|x-2|+C$

$=\ln\left|\dfrac{(x-2)^4}{(x+1)^3}\right|+C$

13. $\dfrac{3x^3-3x+4}{4x^2-4}=\dfrac{1}{4}\cdot\dfrac{3x^3-3x+4}{x^2-1}$

$=\dfrac{1}{4}\left(3x+\dfrac{4}{x^2-1}\right)$

$\dfrac{4}{x^2-1}=\dfrac{4}{(x-1)(x+1)}=\dfrac{A}{x-1}+\dfrac{B}{x+1}$

$4=A(x+1)+B(x-1)$

If $x=-1$, then $4=-2B$, or $B=-2$. If $x=1$,
then $4=2A$, or $A=2$.

$\displaystyle\int\dfrac{3x^3-3x+4}{4x^2-4}\,dx=\dfrac{1}{4}\int\left(3x+\dfrac{2}{x-1}+\dfrac{-2}{x+1}\right)dx$

Answer:

$\left(\dfrac{1}{4}\right)\left[\left(\dfrac{3x^2}{2}\right)+2\ln|x-1|-2\ln|x+1|\right]+C$

$\left(\dfrac{1}{4}\right)\left[\left(\dfrac{3x^2}{2}\right)+\ln\left|\dfrac{x-1}{x+1}\right|^2\right]+C$

15. $\dfrac{17x-12}{x^3-x^2-12x}=\dfrac{17x-12}{x(x-4)(x+3)}$

$=\dfrac{A}{x}+\dfrac{B}{x-4}+\dfrac{C}{x+3}$

$17x-12$

$=A(x-4)(x+3)+Bx(x+3)+Cx(x-4)$

If $x=0$, then $-12=-12A$, or $A=1$. If $x=4$,
then $56=28B$, or $B=2$. If $x=-3$, then
$-63=21C$, or $C=-3$.

$\displaystyle\int\dfrac{17x-12}{x^3-x^2-12x}\,dx=\int\left(\dfrac{1}{x}+\dfrac{2}{x-4}+\dfrac{-3}{x+3}\right)dx$

Answer:

$\ln|x|+2\ln|x-4|-3\ln|x+3|+C$

$=\ln\left|\dfrac{x(x-4)^2}{(x+3)^3}\right|+C$

17. $\displaystyle\int\dfrac{2(3x^5+4x^3-x)}{x^6+2x^4-x^2-2}\,dx$

$=\displaystyle\int\dfrac{1}{x^6+2x^4-x^2-2}\left[2\!\left(3x^5+4x^3-x\right)dx\right]$

$\left(\text{Form: }\displaystyle\int\left(\dfrac{1}{u}\right)du\right)$ (Partial fractions not

required.)

Answer: $\ln\left|x^6+2x^4-x^2-2\right|+C$

19. $\dfrac{2x^2-5x-2}{(x-2)^2(x-1)}=\dfrac{A}{x-1}+\dfrac{B}{x-2}+\dfrac{C}{(x-2)^2}$

$2x^2-5x-2$

$=A(x-2)^2+B(x-1)(x-2)+C(x-1)$

If $x=1$, then $-5=A$. If $x=2$, then $-4=C$.

If $x=0$, then $-2=4A+2B-C$,

$-2=-20+2B+4$, or $B=7$.

$\displaystyle\int\dfrac{2x^2-5x-2}{(x-2)^2(x-1)}\,dx$

$=\displaystyle\int\left[\dfrac{-5}{x-1}+\dfrac{7}{x-2}+\dfrac{-4}{(x-2)^2}\right]dx$

Answer:

$\left[\dfrac{4}{(x-2)}\right]-5\ln|x-1|+7\ln|x-2|+C$

$=\left[\dfrac{4}{(x-2)}\right]+\ln\left|\dfrac{(x-2)^7}{(x-1)^5}\right|+C$

21. $\dfrac{2(x^2+8)}{x^3+4x}=\dfrac{2x^2+16}{x(x^2+4)}=\dfrac{A}{x}+\dfrac{Bx+C}{x^2+4}$

$2x^2+16=A(x^2+4)+(Bx+C)x$

$2x^2+16=(A+B)x^2+Cx+4A$

Thus $A+B=2$, $C=0$, $4A=16$. This gives $A=4$, $B=-2$, $C=0$.

$\displaystyle\int\dfrac{2(x^2+8)}{x^3+4x}\,dx=\int\left(\dfrac{4}{x}+\dfrac{-2x}{x^2+4}\right)dx\;=4\int\dfrac{1}{x}\,dx-\int\dfrac{1}{x^2+4}[2x\,dx]$

Answer: $4\ln|x|-\ln(x^2+4)+C=\ln\left[\dfrac{x^4}{x^2+4}\right]+C$

23. $\dfrac{-x^3+8x^2-9x+2}{(x^2+1)(x-3)^2}=\dfrac{Ax+B}{x^2+1}+\dfrac{C}{x-3}+\dfrac{D}{(x-3)^2}$

$-x^3+8x^2-9x+2=(Ax+B)(x-3)^2+C(x-3)(x^2+1)+D(x^2+1)$

$=(Ax+B)(x^2-6x+9)+C(x^3-3x^2+x-3)+D(x^2+1)$

$=(A+C)x^3+(B-6A-3C+D)x^2+(9A-6B+C)x+(9B-3C+D)$

Thus $A+C=-1$, $B-6A-3C+D=8$, $9A-6B+C=-9$, $9B-3C+D=2$.

This gives $A=-1$, $B=0$, $C=0$, $D=2$.

$\displaystyle\int\dfrac{-x^3+8x^2-9x+2}{(x^2+1)(x-3)^2}\,dx=\int\left(\dfrac{-x}{x^2+1}+\dfrac{0}{x-3}+\dfrac{2}{(x-3)^2}\right)dx$

Answer: $\left(-\frac{1}{2}\right)\ln(x^2+1)-\left[\dfrac{2}{(x-3)}\right]+C$

25. $\dfrac{14x^3+24x}{(x^2+1)(x^2+2)}=\dfrac{Ax+B}{x^2+1}+\dfrac{Cx+D}{x^2+2}$

$14x^3+24x=(x^2+2)(Ax+B)+(x^2+1)(Cx+D)=(A+C)x^3+(B+D)x^2+(2A+C)x+(2B+D)$

Thus $A+C=14$, $B+D=0$, $2A+C=24$, $2B+D=0$.

This gives $A=10$, $B=0$, $C=4$, $D=0$.

$\displaystyle\int\dfrac{14x^3+24x}{(x^2+1)(x^2+2)}\,dx=\int\left(\dfrac{10x}{x^2+1}+\dfrac{4x}{x^2+2}\right)dx=5\int\dfrac{1}{x^2+1}[2\,dx]+2\int\dfrac{1}{x^2+2}[2\,dx]$

Answer:

$5\ln(x^2+1)+2\ln(x^2+2)+C\;=\ln\left[(x^2+1)^5(x^2+2)^2\right]+C$

27. $\dfrac{3x^3 + x}{\left(x^2 + 1\right)^2} = \dfrac{Ax + B}{x^2 + 1} + \dfrac{Cx + D}{\left(x^2 + 1\right)^2}$

$3x^3 + x = (Ax + B)\left(x^2 + 1\right) + (Cx + D)$

$= Ax^3 + Bx^2 + (A + C)x + (B + D)$

Thus $A = 3$, $B = 0$, $A + C = 1$, $B + D = 0$.

This gives $A = 3$, $B = 0$, $C = -2$, $D = 0$.

$\displaystyle\int \dfrac{3x^3 + x}{\left(x^2 + 1\right)^2}\, dx = \int \left[\dfrac{3x}{x^2 + 1} + \dfrac{-2x}{\left(x^2 + 1\right)^2}\right] dx$

Answer: $\dfrac{3}{2}\ln\!\left(x^2 + 1\right) + \dfrac{1}{x^2 + 1} + C$

29. $\dfrac{2 - 2x}{x^2 + 7x + 12} = \dfrac{2 - 2x}{(x + 3)(x + 4)}$

$= \dfrac{A}{x + 3} + \dfrac{B}{x + 4}$

$2 - 2x = A(x + 4) + B(x + 3)$

If $x = -4$, then $10 = -B$, or $B = -10$.

If $x = -3$, then $8 = A$.

$\displaystyle\int_0^1 \dfrac{2 - 2x}{x^2 + 7x + 12}\, dx = \int_0^1 \left(\dfrac{8}{x + 3} + \dfrac{-10}{x + 4}\right) dx$

$= \Big[8\ln|x + 3| - 10\ln|x + 4|\Big]_0^1$

Answer: $18\ln(4) - 10\ln(5) - 8\ln(3)$

31. Note that $\dfrac{6\!\left(x^2 + 1\right)}{(x + 2)^2} \geq 0$ on $[0, 1]$.

Area $= \displaystyle\int_0^1 \dfrac{6(x^2 + 1)}{(x + 2)^2}\, dx$

$\dfrac{6(x^2 + 1)}{(x + 2)^2} = 6 + \dfrac{-24x - 18}{(x + 2)^2}$ (by long division)

$\dfrac{-24x - 18}{(x + 2)^2} = \dfrac{A}{x + 2} + \dfrac{B}{(x + 2)^2}$

$-24x - 18 = A(x + 2) + B$

If $x = -2$, then $30 = B$. If $x = 0$, then

$-18 = 2A + B$, $-18 = 2A + 30$, or $A = -24$.

Area $= \displaystyle\int_0^1 \dfrac{6\!\left(x^2 + 1\right)}{(x + 2)^2}\, dx$

$= \displaystyle\int_0^1 \left[6 + \dfrac{-24}{x + 2} + \dfrac{30}{(x + 2)^2}\right] dx$

$= \left[6x - 24\ln|x + 2| - \dfrac{30}{x + 2}\right]_0^1$

Answer: $11 + 24\ln\dfrac{2}{3}$ sq units

Exercise 17.3

1. Let $u = x$, $a^2 = 9$. Then $du = dx$.

$\displaystyle\int \dfrac{dx}{(9 - x^2)^{3/2}} = \dfrac{x}{9\sqrt{9 - x^2}} + C$

3. Let $u = 4x$, $a^2 = 3$. Then $du = 4\,dx$.

$\displaystyle\int \dfrac{dx}{x^2\sqrt{16x^2 + 3}} = 4\int \dfrac{(4\,dx)}{(4x)^2\sqrt{(4x)^2 + 3}}$

$= 4\left[-\dfrac{\sqrt{(4x)^2 + 3}}{3(4x)}\right] + C$

$= -\dfrac{\sqrt{16x^2 + 3}}{3x} + C$

5. Formula 5 with $u = x$, $a = 6$, $b = 7$. Then $du = dx$.

$\displaystyle\int \dfrac{dx}{x(6 + 7x)} = \dfrac{1}{6}\ln\left|\dfrac{x}{6 + 7x}\right| + C$

7. Formula 28 with $u = x$, $a = 3$. Then $du = dx$.

$\displaystyle\int \dfrac{dx}{x\sqrt{x^2 + 9}} = \dfrac{1}{3}\ln\left|\dfrac{\sqrt{x^2 + 9} - 3}{x}\right| + C$

9. Formula 12 with $u = x$, $a = 2$, $b = 3$, $c = 4$, $k = 5$. Then $du = dx$.

$\displaystyle\int \dfrac{x\,dx}{(2 + 3x)(4 + 5x)}$

$= \dfrac{1}{2}\left[\dfrac{4}{5}\ln|4 + 5x| - \dfrac{2}{3}\ln|2 + 3x|\right] + C$

11. Formula 45 with $u = x$, $a = 4$, $b = 3$, $c = 2$.
Then $du = dx$.
$$\int \frac{dx}{4 + 3e^{2x}} = \frac{1}{8}\left(2x - \ln\left[4 + 3e^{2x}\right]\right) + C$$

13. Formula 9 with $u = x$, $a = 1$, $b = 1$.
Then $du = dx$.
$$\int \frac{2\,dx}{x(1+x)^2} = 2\int \frac{dx}{x(1+x)^2}$$
$$= 2\left[\frac{1}{1+x} + \ln\left|\frac{x}{1+x}\right|\right] + C$$

15. Formula 3 with $u = x$, $a = 2$, $b = 1$.
Then $du = dx$.
$$\int_0^1 \frac{x\,dx}{2+x} = \left(x - 2\ln|2 + x|\right)\Big|_0^1$$
$$= 1 - 2\ln 3 + 2\ln 2$$
$$= 1 - \ln 9 + \ln 4.$$
$$= 1 + \ln\left(\frac{4}{9}\right)$$

17. Formula 23 with $u = x$, $a^2 = 3$.
Then $du = dx$.
$$\int \sqrt{x^2 - 3}\,dx$$
$$= \frac{1}{2}\left(x\sqrt{x^2 - 3} - 3\ln\left|x + \sqrt{x^2 - 3}\right|\right) + C$$

19. Formula 38 with $u = x$, $a = 12$.
Then $du = dx$.
$$\int_0^{1/12} xe^{12x}\,dx = \frac{e^{12x}}{144}(12x - 1)\Big|_0^{1/12}$$
$$= \frac{1}{144}[e(0) - 1(-1)]$$
$$= \frac{1}{144}$$

21. Formula 39 with $u = x$, $n = 2$, $a = 1$.
Then $du = dx$.
$$\int x^2 e^x\,dx = x^2 e^x - 2\int xe^x\,dx$$

Applying Formula 38 on $\int xe^x\,dx$ with
$u = x$, $a = 1$ (so $du = dx$) gives
$\int xe^x\,dx = e^x(x - 1) + C_1$. Thus
$$\int x^2 e^x\,dx = x^2 e^x - 2\left[e^x(x - 1)\right] + C$$
$$= e^x\left[x^2 - 2(x - 1)\right] + C$$
$$= e^x\left(x^2 - 2x + 2\right) + C$$

23. Formula 26 with $u = 2x$, $a^2 = 1$.
Then $du = 2\,dx$.
$$\int \frac{\sqrt{4x^2 + 1}}{x^2}\,dx = 2\int \frac{\sqrt{(2x)^2 + 1}}{(2x)^2}(2\,dx)$$
$$= 2\left(-\frac{\sqrt{4x^2 + 1}}{2x} + \ln\left|2x + \sqrt{4x^2 + 1}\right|\right) + C$$

25. Formula 7 with $u = x$, $a = 1$, $b = 3$.
Then $du = dx$.
$$\int \frac{x\,dx}{(1 + 3x)^2} = \frac{1}{9}\left(\ln|1 + 3x| + \frac{1}{1 + 3x}\right) + C$$

27. Formula 34 with $u = \sqrt{5}x$, $a = \sqrt{7}$.
Then $du = \sqrt{5}dx$.
$$\int \frac{dx}{7 - 5x^2} = \frac{1}{\sqrt{5}}\int \frac{1}{\left(\sqrt{7}\right)^2 - \left(\sqrt{5}x\right)^2}\left(\sqrt{5}dx\right)$$
$$= \frac{1}{\sqrt{5}}\left(\frac{1}{2\sqrt{7}}\ln\left|\frac{\sqrt{7} + \sqrt{5}x}{\sqrt{7} - \sqrt{5}x}\right|\right) + C$$

29. Formula 42 with $u = 3x$, $n = 5$.
Then $du = 3\,dx$.
$$\int 36x^5 \ln(3x)\,dx = 36\int x^5 \ln(3x)\,dx$$
$$= \frac{36}{3^6}\int (3x)^5 \ln(3x)(3\,dx)$$
$$= \frac{4}{81}\left[\frac{(3x)^6 \ln(3x)}{6} - \frac{(3x)^6}{36}\right] + C$$
$$= x^6[6\ln(3x) - 1] + C$$

31. Formula 13 with $u = x$, $a = 1$, $b = 3$.
Then $du = dx$.

$$\int 270x\sqrt{1+3x}\,dx = 270\int x\sqrt{1+3x}\;dx$$

$$= 270\left[\frac{2(9x-2)(1+3x)^{\frac{3}{2}}}{15\cdot 9}\right] + C$$

$$= 4(9x-2)(1+3x)^{\frac{3}{2}} + C$$

33. Formula 27 with $u = 2x$, $a^2 = 13$.
Then $du = 2\,dx$.

$$\int \frac{dx}{\sqrt{4x^2-13}} = \frac{1}{2}\int \frac{1}{\sqrt{(2x)^2-13}}(2\,dx)$$

$$= \frac{1}{2}\ln\left|2x + \sqrt{4x^2-13}\right| + C$$

35. Formula 21 with $u = 2x$, $a^2 = 9$.
Then $du = 2\,dx$.

$$\int \frac{dx}{x^2\sqrt{9-4x^2}} = 2\int \frac{(2\,dx)}{(2x)^2\sqrt{9-(2x)^2}}$$

$$= 2\left[-\frac{\sqrt{9-4x^2}}{9(2x)}\right] + C$$

$$= -\frac{\sqrt{9-4x^2}}{9x} + C$$

37. Formula 45 with
$u = \sqrt{x}$, $a = \pi$, $b = 7$, $c = 4$.
Then $du = \frac{1}{2\sqrt{x}}\,dx$

$$\int \frac{dx}{\sqrt{x}\left(\pi + 7e^{4\sqrt{x}}\right)} = 2\int \frac{1}{\pi + 7e^{4\sqrt{x}}}\left(\frac{1}{2\sqrt{x}}\,dx\right)$$

$$= 2\left[\frac{1}{4\pi}\left(4\sqrt{x} - \ln\left|\pi + 7e^{4\sqrt{x}}\right|\right)\right] + C$$

$$= \frac{1}{2\pi}\left(4\sqrt{x} - \ln\left|\pi + 7e^{4\sqrt{x}}\right|\right) + C$$

39. Can be put in the form $\int \frac{1}{u}\,du$.

$$\int \frac{x\,dx}{x^2+1} = \frac{1}{2}\int \frac{1}{x^2+1}(2x\,dx)$$

$$= \frac{1}{2}\ln\left(x^2+1\right) + C$$

41. Can be put in the form $\int u^n du$.

$$\int 6x\sqrt{2x^2+1}\,dx = \frac{3}{2}\int \left(2x^2+1\right)^{\frac{1}{2}}(4x\,dx)$$

$$= \frac{3}{2}\cdot \frac{\left(2x^2+1\right)^{\frac{3}{2}}}{\frac{3}{2}} + C$$

$$= \left(2x^2+1\right)^{\frac{3}{2}} + C$$

43. Formula 11 or partial fractions. For partial fractions,

$$\int \frac{1}{x^2-5x+6}\,dx = \int\left[\frac{1}{x-3} + \frac{-1}{x-2}\right]dx.$$

$$= \ln\left|\frac{x-3}{x-2}\right| + C$$

45. Integration by parts or formula 42. For formula 42, let $u = x$, $n = 3$. Then $du = dx$.

$$\int x^3 \ln x\,dx = \frac{x^4}{4}\left[\ln(x) - \frac{1}{4}\right] + C$$

47. Integration by parts or formula 38. For formula 38, let $u = 2x$, $a = 1$. Then $du = 2\,dx$.

$$\int 4xe^{2x}\,dx = e^{2x}(2x-1) + C$$

49. Integration by parts (applied twice) or formula 43 and then formula 41. For formula 43, let $u = x$, $n = 0$, $m = 2$. Then $du = dx$.

$$\int \ln^2 x\;dx = x\ln^2 x - 2\int \ln x\;dx$$

Now we apply formula 41 to the last integral with $u = x$ (so $du = dx$).

$$\int \ln^2 x\,dx = x(\ln x)^2 - 2x(\ln x) + 2x + C$$

51. Integration by parts or formula 15. For formula 15, let $u = x$, $a = 4$, $b = -1$. Then $du = dx$.

$$\int_1^2 \frac{x\,dx}{\sqrt{4-x}} = \frac{2(-x-8)\sqrt{4-x}}{3}\bigg|_1^2$$

$$= \frac{2}{3}\left(9\sqrt{3} - 10\sqrt{2}\right)$$

53. Can be put in the form $\int u^n\,du$.

$$\int_0^1 \frac{2x\,dx}{\sqrt{8-x^2}} = -\int_0^1 \left(8-x^2\right)^{-\frac{1}{2}}(-2x\,dx)$$

$$= -\frac{\left(8-x^2\right)^{\frac{1}{2}}}{\frac{1}{2}}\bigg|_0^1$$

$$= -2\left(8-x^2\right)^{\frac{1}{2}}\bigg|_0^1 = -2\left(\sqrt{7}-\sqrt{8}\right)$$

$$= -2\left(\sqrt{7}-2\sqrt{2}\right)$$

$$= 2\left(2\sqrt{2}-\sqrt{7}\right)$$

55. Integration by parts or formula 42. For formula 42, let $u = 2x$, $n = 1$. Then $du = 2\,dx$.

$$\int_1^2 x\ln(2x)\,dx = \frac{1}{4}\int_1^2 (2x)\ln(2x)[2\,dx]$$

$$= \frac{1}{4}\left[\frac{(2x)^2\ln(2x)}{2} - \frac{(2x)^2}{4}\right]\bigg|_1^2$$

$$= 2\ln(4) - \frac{1}{2}\ln(2) - \frac{3}{4}$$

$$= 2\ln\left(2^2\right) - \frac{1}{2}\ln(2) - \frac{3}{4}$$

$$= 4\ln(2) - \frac{1}{2}\ln(2) - \frac{3}{4}$$

$$= \frac{7}{2}(\ln 2) - \frac{3}{4}$$

57. Partial fractions or formula 5. For formula 5, let $u = q$, $a = 1$, $b = -1$. Then $du = dq$.

$$\int_{q_0}^{q_n} \frac{dq}{q(1-q)} = \ln\left|\frac{q}{1-q}\right|\bigg|_{q_0}^{q_n}$$

$$= \ln\left|\frac{q_n}{1-q_n}\right| - \ln\left|\frac{q_0}{1-q_0}\right|$$

$$= \ln\left|\frac{q_n(1-q_0)}{q_0(1-q_n)}\right|$$

59. a. For $\int_0^{10} 5000e^{-0.06t}\,dt$, the form $\int e^u\,du$ can be applied.

$$\int_0^{10} 5000e^{-0.06t}\,dt$$

$$= -\frac{5000}{0.06}\int_0^{10} e^{-0.06t}(-0.06\,dt)$$

$$= -\frac{5000}{0.06}e^{-0.06t}\bigg|_0^{10} = -\frac{5000}{0.06}\left(e^{-0.6}-1\right)$$

$$\approx \$37{,}599$$

b. Use formula 38 with $u = t$ and $a = -0.05$, so $du = dt$.

$$\int_0^8 200te^{-0.05t}\,dt = 200\int_0^8 te^{-0.05t}\,dt$$

$$= 200\left[\frac{e^{-0.05t}}{0.0025}(-0.05t-1)\right]\bigg|_0^8$$

$$= \frac{200}{0.0025}\left[e^{-0.4}(-1.4)+1\right] \approx \$4924$$

61. a. $\displaystyle\int_0^{10} 400e^{0.06(10-t)}dt$

$\displaystyle= 400\int_0^{10} e^{0.6-0.06t}dt$

$\displaystyle= 400\int_0^{10} e^{0.6}e^{-0.06t}dt$

$\displaystyle= 400e^{0.6}\int_0^{10} e^{-0.06t}dt$

$\displaystyle= 400e^{0.6}\left(\frac{1}{-0.06}\right)\int_0^{10} e^{-0.06t}(-0.06\ dt)$

$\displaystyle= \frac{400e^{0.6}}{-0.06}e^{-0.06t}\Big|_0^{10}$

$\displaystyle= \frac{400e^{0.6}}{-0.06}\left[e^{-0.6}-1\right]$

$\approx \$5481$

b. Use formula 38 with $u = t$ and
$a = -0.04$, so $du = dt$.

$\displaystyle\int_0^5 40te^{0.04(5-t)}dt = 40\int_0^5 te^{0.2}e^{-0.04t}dt$

$\displaystyle= 40e^{0.2}\int_0^5 te^{-0.04t}dt$

$\displaystyle= 40e^{0.2}\left[\frac{e^{-0.04t}}{0.0016}(-0.04t-1)\right]\Big|_0^5$

$\displaystyle= \frac{40e^{0.2}}{0.0016}\left[e^{-0.2}(-0.2-1)-1(-1)\right]$

$\approx \$535$

Exercise 17.4

1. $\displaystyle\bar{f} = \frac{1}{4-0}\int_0^4 x^2dx = \frac{1}{4}\cdot\frac{x^3}{3}\Big|_0^4 = \frac{16}{3}-0 = \frac{16}{3}$

3. $\displaystyle\bar{f} = \frac{1}{2-(-1)}\int_{-1}^2 \left(2-3x^2\right)dx$

$\displaystyle= \frac{1}{3}\left(2x-x^3\right)\Big|_{-1}^2 = -1$

5. $\displaystyle\bar{f} = \frac{1}{2-(-2)}\int_{-2}^2 4t^3dt = \frac{1}{4}t^4\Big|_{-2}^2 = 4-4 = 0$

7. $\displaystyle\bar{f} = \frac{1}{9-1}\int_1^9 6\sqrt{x}\,dx = \frac{1}{8}\left(4x^{\frac{3}{2}}\right)\Big|_1^9 = 13$

9. $\displaystyle\bar{P} = \frac{1}{100-0}\int_0^{100}\left(396q-2.1q^2-400\right)dq$

$\displaystyle= \frac{1}{100}\left(198q^2-0.7q^3-400q\right)\Big|_0^{100}$

$\displaystyle= \frac{1}{100}(1,980,000-700,000-40,000)-0$

$= 12,400$

Answer: $12,400

11. $\displaystyle\frac{1}{2-0}\int_0^2 3000e^{0.05t}dt$

$\displaystyle= \frac{3000}{2}\cdot\frac{1}{0.05}\int_0^2 e^{0.05t}[0.05\ dt]$

$\displaystyle= 30,000e^{0.05t}\Big|_0^2 = 30,000\left(e^{0.1}-1\right)\approx \$3155$

Answer: $3155

13. Average value $\displaystyle= \frac{1}{q_0-0}\int\frac{dr}{dq}dq.$

$\displaystyle= \frac{1}{q_0}\left[r(q_0)-r(0)\right]$

But $r(0) = 0$, so avg. value $\displaystyle= \frac{r(q_0)}{q_0}.$

Since $r(q_0)$
= [price per unit when q_0 units are sold] $\cdot q_0$,
we have

avg. value $= \dfrac{\left[\begin{array}{c}\text{price per unit}\\\text{when }q_0\text{ units}\\\text{are sold}\end{array}\right]\cdot q_0}{q_0}$

= price per unit when $\cdot q_0$ units are sold.

Principles in Practice 17.5

1. In this case, $f(t) = \dfrac{60}{\sqrt{t^2+9}}$, $n = 5$, $a = 0$,
and $b = 5$. Thus $h = \dfrac{b-a}{n} = \dfrac{5-0}{5} = 1$.
The terms to be added are

$$f(0) = \frac{60}{\sqrt{0^2 + 9}} = \frac{60}{3} = 20$$

$$2f(1) = \frac{2(60)}{\sqrt{1^2 + 9}} = \frac{120}{\sqrt{10}} \approx 37.9473$$

$$2f(2) = \frac{2(60)}{\sqrt{2^2 + 9}} = \frac{120}{\sqrt{13}} \approx 33.2820$$

$$2f(3) = \frac{2(60)}{\sqrt{3^2 + 9}} = \frac{120}{\sqrt{18}} \approx 28.2843$$

$$2f(4) = \frac{2(60)}{\sqrt{4^2 + 9}} = \frac{120}{5} = 24$$

$$f(5) = \frac{60}{\sqrt{5^2 + 9}} = \frac{60}{\sqrt{34}} \approx 10.2899$$

The sum of the above terms is 153.8035.
The estimate of the radius after 5 seconds is

$$\int_0^5 \frac{60}{\sqrt{t^2 + 9}}\, dt \approx \frac{1}{2}(153.8035) \approx 76.90 \text{ feet.}$$

2. In this case, $f(t) = 0.3e^{0.2t^2}$, $n = 8$, $a = 0$, and $b = 4$. Thus, $h = \frac{b-a}{n} = \frac{4}{8} = 0.5$.
The terms to be added are

$$f(0) = 0.3e^0 = 0.3$$

$$4f(0.5) = 4(0.3)e^{0.05} \approx 1.2615$$

$$2f(1) = 2(0.3)e^{0.2} \approx 0.7328$$

$$4f(1.5) = 4(0.3)e^{0.45} \approx 1.8820$$

$$2f(2) = 2(0.3)e^{0.8} \approx 1.3353$$

$$4f(2.5) = 4(0.3)e^{1.25} \approx 4.1884$$

$$2f(3) = 2(0.3)e^{1.8} \approx 3.6298$$

$$4f(3.5) = 4(0.3)e^{2.45} \approx 13.9060$$

$$f(4) = 0.3e^{3.2} \approx 7.3598$$

The sum of the above terms is 34.5956. The estimate of the amount the culture grew over the first four hours is

$$\int_0^4 0.3e^{0.2t^2}\, dt \approx \frac{0.5}{3}(34.5956) \approx 5.77 \text{ grams.}$$

Exercise 17.5

1. $f(x) = \frac{170}{1 + x^2}$, $n = 6$, $a = -2$, $b = 4$.
Trapezoidal

$$h = \frac{b-a}{n} = \frac{4 - (-2)}{6} = \frac{6}{6} = 1$$

$$
\begin{aligned}
f(-2) &= 34 = 34 \\
2f(-1) &= 2(85) = 170 \\
2f(0) &= 2(170) = 340 \\
2f(1) &= 2(85) = 170 \\
2f(2) &= 2(34) = 68 \\
2f(3) &= 2(17) = 34 \\
f(4) &= 10 = \underline{10} \\
& 826
\end{aligned}
$$

$$\int_{-2}^4 \frac{170}{1 + x^2}\, dx \approx \frac{1}{2}(826) = 413$$

3. $f(x) = x^2$, $n = 5$, $a = 0$, $b = 1$
Trapezoidal

$$h = \frac{b-a}{n} = \frac{1-0}{5} = \frac{1}{5} = 0.2$$

$$
\begin{aligned}
f(0) &= 0.0000 \\
2f(0.2) &= 0.0800 \\
2f(0.4) &= 0.3200 \\
2f(0.6) &= 0.7200 \\
2f(0.8) &= 1.2800 \\
f(1) &= \underline{1.0000} \\
& 3.4000
\end{aligned}
$$

$$\int_0^1 x^2\, dx \approx \frac{0.2}{2}(3.4000) = 0.340$$

Actual value: $\int_0^1 x^2\, dx = \left.\frac{x^3}{3}\right|_0^1 = \frac{1}{3} \approx 0.333$

5. $f(x) = \frac{1}{x}$, $n = 6$, $a = 1$, $b = 4$

Simpson's

$h = \frac{b-a}{n} = \frac{4-1}{6} = 0.5$

Finding the appropriate sum, we have

$\quad\quad f(1) = 1.0000$

$\quad 4f(1.5) = 2.6667$

$\quad\quad 2f(2) = 1.0000$

$\quad 4f(2.5) = 1.6000$

$\quad\quad 2f(3) = 0.6667$

$\quad 2f(3.5) = 1.1429$

$\quad\quad\quad f(4) = 0.2500$

$\quad\quad\quad\quad\quad \overline{8.3263}$

$\int_1^4 \frac{1}{x}\,dx \approx \frac{0.5}{3}(8.3263) \approx 1.388$

Actual value:

$\int_1^4 \frac{1}{x}\,dx = \ln|x|\Big|_1^4 = \ln 4 - \ln 1$

$= \ln 4 - 0 = \ln 4$

≈ 1.386

7. $f(x) = \frac{x}{x+1}$, $n = 4$, $a = 0$, $b = 2$

Trapezoidal

$h = \frac{b-a}{n} = \frac{2}{4} = 0.5$

$\quad\quad f(0) = 0.0000$

$\quad 2f(0.5) = 0.6667$

$\quad\quad 2f(1) = 1.0000$

$\quad 2f(1.5) = 1.2000$

$\quad\quad\quad f(2) = \underline{0.6667}$

$\quad\quad\quad\quad\quad 3.5334$

Thus

$\int_0^2 \frac{x}{x+1}\,dx \approx \frac{0.5}{2}(3.5334) \approx 0.883$

9. $\int_{15}^{40} l(t)\,dt$, males, $n = 5$, $a = 15$, $b = 40$

$h = \frac{40-15}{5} = 5$

$\quad\quad l(15) = \quad 96,672$

$\quad 2l(20) = 191,922$

$\quad 2l(25) = 190,000$

$\quad 2l(30) = 188,194$

$\quad 2l(35) = 186,134$

$\quad\quad l(40) = \underline{\quad 91,628}$

$\quad\quad\quad\quad\quad\quad 944,550$

$\int_{15}^{40} l(t)\,dt \approx \frac{5}{2}(944,550) = 2,361,375$

11. $a = 1$, $b = 5$, $h = 1$

$\quad\quad f(1) = 0.4 \quad\quad = 0.4$

$\quad 4f(2) = 4(0.6) = 2.4$

$\quad 2f(3) = 2(1.2) = 2.4$

$\quad 4f(4) = 4(0.8) = 3.2$

$\quad\quad f(5) = 0.5 \quad\quad = \underline{0.5}$

$\quad\quad\quad\quad\quad\quad\quad\quad 8.9$

$\int_1^5 f(x)\,dx \approx \frac{1}{3}(8.9) \approx 3.0$

The area is about 3.0 square units.

13. $\int_1^3 f(x)\,dx$, $n = 4$, $a = 1$, $b = 3$

$h = \frac{3-1}{4} = 0.5$

$\quad\quad f(1) = 1 \quad\quad\quad = \quad 1$

$\quad 4f(1.5) = 4(2) \quad = \quad 8$

$\quad 2f(2) = 2(2) \quad\quad = \quad 4$

$\quad 4f(2.5) = 4(0.5) = \quad 2$

$\quad\quad f(3) = 1 \quad\quad\quad = \underline{\quad 1}$

$\quad\quad\quad\quad\quad\quad\quad\quad\quad 16$

$\int_1^3 f(x)\,dx \approx \frac{0.5}{3}(16) = \frac{8}{3}$

15. $f(x) = \sqrt{1-x^2}$, $a = 0$, $b = 1$, $n = 4$

$h = \dfrac{1-0}{4} = 0.25$

Simpson

$f(0) = 1.0000$

$4f(0.25) = 3.8730$

$2f(0.50) = 1.7321$

$4f(0.75) = 2.6458$

$\underline{\quad f(1) = 0.0000 \quad}$

9.2509

$\displaystyle\int_0^1 \sqrt{1-x^2}\,dx \approx \dfrac{0.25}{3}(9.2509) \approx 0.771$

17. Let $f(x)$ = distance from near to far shore at point x on highway. Then area $\approx \displaystyle\int_0^4 f(x)\,dx$.

Using Simpson's rule with $h = 0.5$:

$\begin{aligned}
f(0) &= 0.5 - 0.5 &&= 0 &&= 0 \\
4f(0.5) &= 4(2.3 - 0.3) &&= 4(2) &&= 8 \\
2f(1) &= 2(2.2 - 0.7) &&= 2(1.5) &&= 3 \\
4f(1.5) &= 4(3 - 1) &&= 4(2) &&= 8 \\
2f(2) &= 2(2.5 - 0.5) &&= 2(2) &&= 4 \\
4f(2.5) &= 4(2.2 - 0.2) &&= 4(2) &&= 8 \\
2f(3) &= 2(1.5 - 0.5) &&= 2(1) &&= 2 \\
4f(3.5) &= 4(1.3) - 0.8) &&= 4(0.5) &&= 2 \\
f(4) &= 1 - 1 &&= 0 &&= \underline{\;0\;} \\
& && && \;\;35
\end{aligned}$

Area $\approx \displaystyle\int_0^4 f(x)\,dx \approx \dfrac{0.5}{3}(35) = \dfrac{35}{6}\,\text{km}^2$

19. a. $\text{MC} = \dfrac{dc}{dq}$

$\displaystyle\int_0^{120} \dfrac{dc}{dq}\,dq = c(120) - c(0)$

= (total cost of 120 units) – (fixed costs)

= total variable costs of 120 units

Using the trapezoidal rule with $h = 20$

and $f(q) = \dfrac{dc}{dq}$ to estimate the integral:

$\begin{aligned}
f(0) &= 260 &&= 260 \\
2f(20) &= 2(255) &&= 510 \\
2f(40) &= 2(240) &&= 480 \\
2f(60) &= 2(240) &&= 480 \\
2f(80) &= 2(245) &&= 490 \\
2f(100) &= 2(250) &&= 500 \\
f(120) &= 255 &&= \underline{255} \\
& && \;\;2975
\end{aligned}$

$\displaystyle\int_0^{120} \dfrac{dc}{dq}\,dq \approx \dfrac{20}{2}(2975) = \$29{,}750$

b. $\text{MR} = \dfrac{dr}{dq}$

$\displaystyle\int_0^{120} \dfrac{dr}{dq}\,dq = r(120) - r(0) = r(120)$

[since $r(0) = 0$]

= total revenue from sale of 120 units

Using Simpson's rule with $h = 20$ and

$g(q) = \dfrac{dr}{dq}$ to estimate the integral:

$\begin{aligned}
g(0) &= 415 &&= 415 \\
4g(20) &= 4(360) &&= 1440 \\
2g(40) &= 2(320) &&= 640 \\
4g(60) &= 4(290) &&= 1160 \\
2g(80) &= 2(270) &&= 540 \\
4g(100) &= 4(260) &&= 1040 \\
g(120) &= 255 = &&= \underline{255} \\
& && \;\;5490
\end{aligned}$

$\displaystyle\int_0^{120} \dfrac{dr}{dq}\,dq \approx \dfrac{20}{3}(5490) = \$36{,}600$

c. At $q = 120$:

total revenue $\approx 36{,}600$

total cost = (tot. var. costs)

+ (fixed costs)

$\approx 29{,}750 + 1500 = 31{,}250$

Thus maximum profit

= (total rev.) – (total costs)

$\approx 36{,}600 - 31{,}250 = \$5350$

Principles in Practice 17.6

1. Separating variables, we have

$$\frac{dI}{dx} = -0.0085I$$

$$\frac{dI}{I} = -0.0085dx$$

$$\int \frac{1}{I} dI = -\int 0.0085 \ dx$$

$$\ln|I| + C_1 - 0.0085x$$

To solve for I, we convert to exponential Formula

$$I = e^{C_1 - 0.0085x} = Ce^{-0.0085x} \text{ since } I = I_0$$

when $x = 0$, $I_0 = Ce^0 = C$, so

$$I(x) = I_0 e^{0.0085x}$$

Exercise 17.6

1. $y' = 2xy^2$

$$\frac{dy}{dx} = 2xy^2$$

$$\frac{dy}{y^2} = 2x \ dx$$

$$\int y^{-2} dy = \int 2x \ dx$$

$$-\frac{1}{y} = x^2 + C$$

$$y = -\frac{1}{x^2 + C}$$

3. $\dfrac{dy}{dx} - 3x\sqrt{x^2 + 1} = 0$

$$dy = 3x\left(x^2 + 1\right)^{\frac{1}{2}} dx$$

$$\int dy = 3\int x\left(x^2 + 1\right)^{\frac{1}{2}} dx$$

$$\int dy = \frac{3}{2}\int \left(x^2 + 1\right)^{\frac{1}{2}}[2x \ dx]$$

$$y = \frac{3}{2} \cdot \frac{\left(x^2 + 1\right)^{\frac{3}{2}}}{\frac{3}{2}} + C$$

$$y = \left(x^2 + 1\right)^{\frac{3}{2}} + C$$

5. $\dfrac{dy}{dx} = y$, where $y > 0$.

$$\frac{dy}{y} = dx$$

$$\int \frac{dy}{y} = \int dx$$

$$\ln y = x + C_1$$

$$y = e^{x + C_1} = e^{C_1}e^x = Ce^x, \text{ where } C = e^{C_1}.$$

Thus $y = Ce^x$, where $C > 0$.

7. $y' = \dfrac{y}{x}$, where $x, y > 0$.

$$\frac{dy}{dx} = \frac{y}{x}$$

$$\frac{dy}{y} = \frac{dx}{x}$$

$$\int \frac{dy}{y} = \int \frac{dx}{x}$$

$$\ln y = \ln x + C_1$$

$$\ln y = \ln x + \ln C, \text{ where } C > 0.$$

$$\ln y = \ln(Cx) \Rightarrow y = Cx, \text{ where } C > 0.$$

9. $y' = \dfrac{1}{y}$, where $y > 0$ and $y(2) = 2$

$$\frac{dy}{dx} = \frac{1}{y}$$

$$y \ dy = dx$$

$$\int y \ dy = \int dx$$

$$\frac{y^2}{2} = x + C$$

Given $y(2) = 2$, we obtain $\dfrac{2^2}{2} = 2 + C$, so

$C = 0$. Thus $y^2 = 2x$, $y = \pm\sqrt{2x}$. But given

that $y > 0$, we must choose $y = \sqrt{2x}$.

11. $e^y y' - x^2 = 0$, where $y = 0$ when $x = 0$.

$$e^y \frac{dy}{dx} = x^2$$

$$e^y dy = x^2 dx$$

$$\int e^y dy = \int x^2 dx$$

$$e^y = \frac{x^3}{3} + C$$

Given that $y(0) = 0$, we have $e^0 = 0 + C$, so

$$1 = C \Rightarrow e^y = \frac{x^3}{3} + 1, \ e^y = \frac{x^3 + 3}{3}, \text{ so}$$

$$y = \ln \frac{x^3 + 3}{3}.$$

13. $\left(4x^2 + 3\right)^2 \frac{dy}{dx} - 4xy^2 = 0$

$$\left(4x^2 + 3\right)^2 \frac{dy}{dx} = 4xy^2$$

$$\frac{dy}{y^2} = \frac{4x}{\left(4x^2 + 3\right)^2} dx$$

$$\int \frac{dy}{y^2} = \int \frac{4x}{\left(4x^2 + 3\right)^2} dx$$

$$\int y^{-2} dy = 4 \cdot \frac{1}{8} \int \left(4x^2 + 3\right)^{-2} [8x \ dx]$$

$$-\frac{1}{y} = -\frac{1}{2\left(4x^2 + 3\right)} + C$$

Now, $y(0) = \frac{3}{2}$ implies $-\frac{1}{\frac{3}{2}} = -\frac{1}{2(3)} + C$,

so $C = -\frac{1}{2}$. Thus

$$-\frac{1}{y} = -\frac{1}{2\left(4x^2 + 3\right)} - \frac{1}{2}$$

$$= -\frac{1 + \left(4x^2 + 3\right)}{2\left(4x^2 + 3\right)} = -\frac{4x^2 + 4}{2\left(4x^2 + 3\right)}$$

$$= -\frac{2\left(x^2 + 1\right)}{4x^2 + 3}.$$

Hence $y = \frac{4x^2 + 3}{2\left(x^2 + 1\right)}.$

15. $\frac{dy}{dx} = \frac{3x\sqrt{1 + y^2}}{y}$, where $y > 0$ and

$y(1) = \sqrt{8}$.

$$\frac{y \ dy}{\sqrt{1 + y^2}} = 3x \ dx$$

$$\frac{1}{2} \int \left(1 + y^2\right)^{-\frac{1}{2}} [2y \ dy] = 3 \int x \ dx$$

$$\left(1 + y^2\right)^{\frac{1}{2}} = \frac{3x^2}{2} + C$$

$$y(1) = \sqrt{8} \Rightarrow (1 + 8)^{\frac{1}{2}} = \frac{3}{2} + C$$

$$C = \frac{3}{2}$$

Thus

$$\left(1 + y^2\right)^{\frac{1}{2}} = \frac{3x^2}{2} + \frac{3}{2}$$

$$1 + y^2 = \left[\frac{3x^2}{2} + \frac{3}{2}\right]^2$$

$$y^2 = \left[\frac{3x^2}{2} + \frac{3}{2}\right]^2 - 1$$

Since $y > 0$, $y = \sqrt{\left[\frac{3x^2}{2} + \frac{3}{2}\right]^2 - 1}$.

17. $2\frac{dy}{dx} = \frac{xe^{-y}}{\sqrt{x^2 + 3}}$, where $y(1) = 0$.

$$dye^y = \frac{1}{2} x\left(x^2 + 3\right)^{-\frac{1}{2}} dy$$

$$\int e^y dy = \frac{1}{2} \cdot \frac{1}{2} \int \left(x^2 + 3\right)^{-\frac{1}{2}} [2x \ dx]$$

$$e^y = \frac{1}{2}\left(x^2 + 3\right)^{\frac{1}{2}} + C$$

Now, $y(1) = 0 \Rightarrow e^0 = \frac{1}{2}(2) + C$, so $C = 0$.

Thus

$$e^y = \frac{1}{2}\left(x^2 + 3\right)^{\frac{1}{2}} \Rightarrow y = \ln\left(\frac{1}{2}\sqrt{x^2 + 3}\right).$$

19. $(q+1)^2 \dfrac{dc}{dq} = cq$

$$\int \frac{1}{c}\,dc = \int \frac{q}{(q+1)^2}\,dq$$

Using partial fractions or formula 7 for

$\displaystyle\int \frac{q}{(q+1)^2}\,dq$, we obtain

$c = \ln(q+1) + \dfrac{1}{q+1} + C$. Now, fixed cost is

given to be e, which means that $c = e$ when $q = 0$. This implies $1 + 0 = 1 + C$, so $C = 0$.
Thus

$$\ln c = \ln(q+1) + \frac{1}{q+1} \Rightarrow c = \frac{e^{\ln(q+1)+1}}{(q+1)},$$

$c = \dfrac{e^{\ln(q+1)}e^1}{(q+1)}$, or $c = (q+1)e^{\frac{1}{(q+1)}}$.

21. $\dfrac{dy}{dt} = -0.05y$

$$\int \frac{1}{y}\,dy = -0.05\int dt$$

$\ln|y| = -0.05t + C$

Given that $y = 900$ when $t = 0$, we have
$\ln 900 = -0 + C = C$. Thus
$\ln|y| = -0.05t + \ln 900$. To find t when
money is 90% new, we note that y would be
$10\%(900) = 90$. Solving
$\ln 90 = -0.05t + \ln 900$ gives
$t = \dfrac{\ln 900 - \ln 90}{0.05} \approx 46\,\text{weeks}.$

23. Let N be the population at time t, where $t = 0$
corresponds to 1985. Since N follows
exponential growth, $N = N_0 e^{kt}$. Now,
$N = 40{,}000$ when $t = 0$, so $N_0 = 40{,}000$.
Therefore $N = 40{,}000e^{kt}$. Since $N = 48{,}000$
when $t = 10$, we have $48{,}000 = 40{,}000e^{10k}$,
$1.2 = e^{10k}$, $\ln 1.2 = 10k$, $k = \dfrac{\ln 1.2}{10}$

Thus

$N = 40{,}000e^{\ln(1.2)\left(\frac{t}{10}\right)}$ (*)

$N = 40{,}000e^{0.18\left(\frac{t}{10}\right)}$

$N = 40{,}000e^{0.018t}$ (First form)

From (*), we have $N = 40{,}000\left[e^{\ln 1.2}\right]^{\frac{t}{10}}$, so

$N = 40{,}000(1.2)^{\frac{t}{10}}$ (Second form)

At year 2005, $t = 20$ and so

$N = 40{,}000(1.2)^{\frac{20}{10}} = 40{,}000(1.2)^2$

$= 57{,}600.$

25. Let N be the population (in billions) at time
t, where t is the number of years past 1930.
N follows exponential growth, so
$N = N_0 e^{kt}$. When $t = 0$, then $N = 2$, so
$N_0 = 2$. Thus $N = 2e^{kt}$. Since $N = 3$ when
$t = 30$, then

$3 = 2e^{30k}$

$\dfrac{3}{2} = e^{30k}$

$30k = \ln\dfrac{3}{2}$

$k = \dfrac{\ln\frac{3}{2}}{30}$

Thus $N = 2e^{\frac{t}{30}\ln\frac{3}{2}}$.
In 2010, $t = 80$ and so

$N = 2e^{\frac{80}{30}\ln\frac{3}{2}} \approx 2e^{1.08124}$ billion.

27. Let N be amount of sample that remains
after t seconds. Then $N = N_0 e^{-\lambda t}$, where
N_0 is the initial amount present. When
$t = 100$, then $N = 0.3N_0$. Thus

$0.3N_0 = N_0 e^{-100\lambda}$

$0.3 = e^{-100\lambda}$

$-100\lambda = \ln 0.3$

$\lambda = -\dfrac{\ln 0.3}{100}$

Thus $\lambda \approx 0.01204$. The half-life is

$\dfrac{\ln 2}{\lambda} = \dfrac{\ln 2}{-\frac{\ln 0.3}{100}} = -100\dfrac{\ln 2}{\ln 0.3} \approx 57.57\,\text{s}.$

29. Let N be the amount of ^{14}C present in the scroll t years after it was made. Then $N = N_0 e^{-\lambda t}$, where N_0 is amount of ^{14}C present when $t = 0$. We must find t when $N = 0.7 N_0$.

$$0.7 N_0 = N_0 e^{-\lambda t}$$
$$0.7 = e^{-\lambda t}$$
$$-\lambda t = \ln 0.7$$

so $t = -\dfrac{\ln 0.7}{\lambda}$. By Eq. 15 in text,

$\lambda = \dfrac{\ln 2}{5600}$, so

$$t = -\frac{\ln 0.7}{\frac{\ln 2}{5600}} = -\frac{5600 \ln 0.7}{\ln 2} \approx 2900 \text{ years.}$$

31. $\dfrac{dN}{dt} = kN$

$$N = Ae^{kt}$$
$$N_0 = Ae^{kt_0}$$
$$A = \frac{N_0}{e^{kt_0}}$$

Thus $N = \dfrac{N_0}{e^{kt_0}}\left(e^{kt}\right) = N_0 e^{kt - kt_0}$, or

$$N = N_0 e^{k(t - t_0)}, \text{ where } t \geq t_0.$$

33. $N = N_0 e^{-\lambda t}$

When $t = 2$, then $N = 10$. Thus

$10 = N_0 e^{-2\lambda}$, $N_0 = 10 e^{2\lambda}$. By Equation 15,

$$6 = \frac{\ln 2}{\lambda}$$
$$\lambda = \frac{\ln 2}{6}$$

Thus $N_0 = 10 e^{2\frac{\ln 2}{6}} = 10 e^{\frac{\ln 2}{3}} \approx 12.6$ units.

35. $\dfrac{dA}{dt} = 200 - 0.50A$

$$\int \frac{dA}{200 - 0.50A}$$
$$= \int dt - \frac{1}{0.50} \ln(200 - 0.50A) = t + C_1$$
$$\ln(200 - 0.50A) = -0.50t - 0.50C_1$$
$$= -0.50t + C_2$$

Thus

$$200 - 0.50A = e^{-0.50t + C_2} = e^{-0.50t} e^{C_2}$$
$$200 - \frac{A}{2} = Ce^{-0.50t}$$

Given that $A = 0$ when $t = 0$, we have

$C = 200$, so $200 - \dfrac{A}{2} = 200 e^{-\frac{t}{2}}$

$$200 - 200 e^{-\frac{t}{2}} = \frac{A}{2}$$
$$200\left(1 - e^{-\frac{t}{2}}\right) = \frac{A}{2}$$

Thus $A = 400\left(1 - e^{-\frac{t}{2}}\right)$. If $t = 1$,

$$A = 400\left(1 - e^{-\frac{1}{2}}\right) \approx 157 \text{ gm.}$$

37. a. $\dfrac{dV}{dt} = kV$

$$\int \frac{1}{V} dV = \int k \, dt$$
$$\ln V = kt + C_1$$
$$V = e^{kt} e^{C_1}$$

or $V = Ce^{kt}$. Now $t = 0$ corresponds to July 1, 2000 where
$V = 0.70 \cdot 30,000 = 21,000$, so
$21,000 = C(1)$. Thus $V = 21,000 e^{kt}$.
Also $V = 18,900$ for $t = \dfrac{1}{2}$, so

$$18,900 = 21,000 e^{\frac{k}{2}}$$
$$0.9 = e^{\frac{k}{2}}$$
$$\frac{k}{2} = \ln 0.9$$
$$k = 2 \ln 0.9$$

Thus $V = 21,000 e^{(2 \ln 0.9)t}$.

b. $14,000 = 21,000 e^{(2 \ln 0.9)t}$

$$\frac{2}{3} = e^{(2 \ln 0.9)t}$$
$$\ln \frac{2}{3} = (2 \ln 0.9)t$$
$$t = \frac{\ln \frac{2}{3}}{2 \ln 0.9} \approx 1.924$$

This corresponds to about 23 months after July 1, 2000 $\Rightarrow$ June 2002.

Exercise 17.7

1. $N = \dfrac{M}{1 + be^{-ct}}$

$M = 80,000$

Since $N = 40,000$ at $t = 0$ (1995), we have

$40,000 = \dfrac{80,000}{1+b}$, so $1 + b = \dfrac{80,000}{40,000} = 2$,

or $b = 1$. Hence $N = \dfrac{80,000}{1 + e^{-ct}}$. If $t = 5$, then

$N = 50,000$, so

$50,000 = \dfrac{80,000}{1 + e^{-5c}}$

$1 + e^{-5c} = \dfrac{80,000}{50,000} = \dfrac{8}{5}$

$e^{-5c} = \dfrac{8}{5} - 1 = \dfrac{3}{5}$

$e^{-c} = \left(\dfrac{3}{5}\right)^{\frac{1}{5}}$

Hence $N = \dfrac{80,000}{1 + \left(\frac{3}{5}\right)^{\frac{t}{5}}}$. In 2005, $t = 10$ so

$N = \dfrac{80,000}{1 + \left(\frac{3}{5}\right)^2} \approx 58,800$.

3. $N = \dfrac{M}{1 + be^{-ct}}$

$M = 6,000,000$, and $N = 100$ when $t = 0$, so

$100 = \dfrac{6,000,000}{1+b}$

$1 + b = \dfrac{6,000,000}{100} = 60,000$

$b = 59,999$

Hence $N = \dfrac{6,000,000}{1 + 59,999e^{-ct}}$. Since

$N = 10,000$ when $t = 1$,

$10,000 = \dfrac{6,000,000}{1 + 59,999e^{-c}}$,

$1 + 59,999e^{-c} = \dfrac{6,000,000}{10,000} = 600$

$e^{-c} = \dfrac{599}{59,999}$

Hence $N = \dfrac{6,000,000}{1 + 59,999\left(\frac{599}{59,999}\right)^t}$. If $t = 2$,

then $N = \dfrac{6,000,000}{1 + 59,999\left(\frac{599}{59,999}\right)^2} \approx 860,000$.

5. $N = \dfrac{M}{1 + be^{-ct}}$

$M = 100,000$, and since $N = 500$ when $t = 0$, we have

$500 = \dfrac{100,000}{1+b}$

$1 + b = \dfrac{100,000}{500} = 200$

$b = 199$

Hence $N = \dfrac{100,000}{1 + 199e^{-ct}}$. If $t = 1$, then

$N = 1000$. Thus

$1000 = \dfrac{100,000}{1 + 199e^{-c}}$

$1 + 199e^{-c} = \dfrac{100,000}{1000} = 100$

$199e^{-c} = 99$

$e^{-c} = \dfrac{99}{199}$

Hence $N = \dfrac{100,000}{1 + 199\left(\frac{99}{199}\right)^t}$. If $t = 2$, then

$N = \dfrac{100,000}{1 + 199\left(\frac{99}{199}\right)^2} \approx 1990$.

7. a. $N = \dfrac{375}{1 + e^{5.2-2.3t}} = \dfrac{375}{1 + e^{5.2}e^{-2.3t}}$

$\approx \dfrac{375}{1 + 181.27e^{-2.3t}}$

b. $\displaystyle\lim_{t \to \infty} N = \dfrac{375}{1 + 181.27(0)} = 375$

9. $\dfrac{dT}{dt} = k(T - a)$ where $a = 10$.

$\dfrac{dT}{T - a} = k\,dt$

$\displaystyle\int \dfrac{dT}{T - a} = \int k\,dt$

Thus $\ln(T - 10) = kt + C$. At $t = 0$, we have
$T = 32$, so $\ln(32 - 10) = 0 + C$, $C = \ln 22$, so
$\ln(T - 10) = kt + \ln 22$
$\ln(T - 10) - \ln 22 = kt$. Hence
$\ln\left(\dfrac{T - 10}{22}\right) = kt$. If $t = 1$, then $T = 30$. Thus
$\ln\left(\dfrac{30 - 10}{22}\right) = k \cdot 1$, so $k = \ln\dfrac{20}{22} = \ln\dfrac{10}{11}$.

Hence $\ln\left(\dfrac{T - 10}{22}\right) = \left(\ln\dfrac{10}{11}\right)t$. If $T = 37$, then
$\ln\left(\dfrac{27}{22}\right) = \left(\ln\dfrac{10}{11}\right)t$

$t = \dfrac{\ln\frac{27}{22}}{\ln\frac{10}{11}} \approx -2.15$ hr

which corresponds to 2 hr 9 min. Time of
murder: 3:15 A.M. − 2 hr 9 min = 1:06 A.M.

11. $\dfrac{dx}{dt} = k(70{,}000 - x)$

$\displaystyle\int \dfrac{dx}{70{,}000 - x} = \int k \, dt$

$-\ln(70{,}000 - x) = kt + C$

$\ln(70{,}000 - x) = -kt - C$

$70{,}000 - x = e^{-kt - C} = e^{-C}e^{-kt} = Ae^{-kt}$,

where $A = e^{-C}$. Thus $x = 70{,}000 - Ae^{-kt}$.
If $t = 0$, then $x = 10{,}000$, so
$10{,}000 = 70{,}000 - A \Rightarrow A = 60{,}000$. Thus

$x = 70{,}000 - 60{,}000e^{-kt}$. If $t = 1$, then

$x = 40{,}000$, so

$40{,}000 = 70{,}000 - 60{,}000e^{-k}$

$60{,}000e^{-k} = 30{,}000$

$e^{-k} = \dfrac{30{,}000}{60{,}000} = \dfrac{1}{2}$

Thus $x = 70{,}000 - 60{,}000\left(\dfrac{1}{2}\right)^{t}$. If $t = 3$,

then $x = 70{,}000 - 60{,}000\left(\dfrac{1}{8}\right) = \$62{,}500$.

13. $\dfrac{dN}{dt} = k(M - N)$

$\displaystyle\int \dfrac{dN}{M - N} = \int k \, dt$

$-\ln(M - N) = kt + C$

If $t = 0$, then $N = N_0$, so $-\ln(M - N_0) = C$.

Thus we have
$-\ln(M - N) = kt - \ln(M - N_0)$
$\ln(M - N_0) - \ln(M - N) = kt$
$\ln\dfrac{M - N_0}{M - N} = kt$
$\ln\dfrac{M - N}{M - N_0} = -kt$
$\dfrac{M - N}{M - N_0} = e^{-kt}$
$M - N = (M - N_0)e^{-kt}$
$N = M - (M - N_0)e^{-kt}$

Principles in Practice 17.8

1. $\displaystyle\int_0^\infty \left(3e^{-0.1t} - 3e^{-0.3t}\right)dt$

$= \displaystyle\lim_{r \to \infty}\int_0^r \left(3e^{-0.1t} - 3e^{-0.3t}\right)dt$

$= \displaystyle\lim_{r \to \infty}\left(-30e^{-0.1t} + 10e^{-0.3t}\right)\Big|_0^r$

$= \displaystyle\lim_{r \to \infty}\left[-\dfrac{30}{e^{0.1r}} + \dfrac{10}{e^{0.3r}} - \left(-30e^0 + 10e^0\right)\right]$

$= \displaystyle\lim_{r \to \infty}\left[-\dfrac{30}{e^{0.1r}} + \dfrac{10}{e^{0.3r}} - (-20)\right]$

$= 0 + 0 + 20 = 20$

The total amount of the drug that is
eliminated is approximately 20 milliliters.

Exercise 17.8

1. $\displaystyle\int_3^\infty \dfrac{1}{x^2}\,dx = \lim_{r \to \infty}\int_3^r x^{-2}\,dx$

$= \displaystyle\lim_{r \to \infty}\dfrac{x^{-1}}{-1}\Big|_3^r = \lim_{r \to \infty}\left(-\dfrac{1}{x}\right)\Big|_3^r$

$= \displaystyle\lim_{r \to \infty}\left(-\dfrac{1}{r} + \dfrac{1}{3}\right) = 0 + \dfrac{1}{3} = \dfrac{1}{3}$

3. $\displaystyle\int_1^\infty \dfrac{1}{x}\,dx = \lim_{r \to \infty}\int_1^r \dfrac{1}{x}\,dx = \lim_{r \to \infty}\ln|x|\Big|_1^r$

$= \displaystyle\lim_{r \to \infty}\left(\ln|r| - 0\right)$

$= \displaystyle\lim_{r \to \infty}\ln|r| = \infty \Rightarrow$ diverges

5. $\displaystyle\int_1^\infty e^{-x}\,dx = \lim_{r\to\infty} -\int_1^r e^{-x}[-dx]$

$\displaystyle= \lim_{r\to\infty} (-e^{-x})\Big|_1^r$

$\displaystyle= \lim_{r\to\infty}\left(-e^{-r}+e^{-1}\right) = \lim_{r\to\infty}\left(-\frac{1}{e^r}+\frac{1}{e}\right)$

$\displaystyle= 0 + \frac{1}{e} = \frac{1}{e}$

7. $\displaystyle\int_1^\infty \frac{1}{\sqrt{x}}\,dx = \lim_{r\to\infty}\int_1^r x^{-\frac{1}{2}}\,dx = \lim_{r\to\infty} 2x^{\frac{1}{2}}\Big|_1^r$

$\displaystyle= \lim_{r\to\infty}\left(2\sqrt{r}-2\right) = \infty \Rightarrow \text{diverges}$

9. $\displaystyle\int_{-\infty}^{-2}\frac{1}{(x+1)^3}\,dx = \lim_{r\to\infty}\int_r^{-2}(x+1)^{-3}\,dx$

$\displaystyle= \lim_{r\to\infty}\frac{(x+1)^{-2}}{-2}\Big|_r^{-2}$

$\displaystyle= \lim_{r\to-\infty} -\frac{1}{2(x+1)^2}\Big|_r^{-2}$

$\displaystyle= \lim_{r\to-\infty}\left[-\frac{1}{2}+\frac{1}{2(r+1)^2}\right]$

$\displaystyle= -\frac{1}{2}+0 = -\frac{1}{2}$

11. $\displaystyle\int_{-\infty}^\infty xe^{-x^2}\,dx = \int_{-\infty}^0 xe^{-x^2}\,dx + \int_0^\infty xe^{-x^2}\,dx$

$\displaystyle\int_{-\infty}^0 xe^{-x^2}\,dx = \lim_{r\to-\infty} -\frac{1}{2}\int_r^0 e^{-x^2}[-2x\,dx]$

$\displaystyle= \lim_{r\to-\infty} -\frac{1}{2}e^{-x^2}\Big|_r^0$

$\displaystyle= \lim_{r\to-\infty}\left[-\frac{1}{2}+\frac{1}{2e^{r^2}}\right] = -\frac{1}{2}+0 = -\frac{1}{2}$

$\displaystyle\int_0^\infty xe^{-x^2}\,dx = \lim_{r\to\infty} -\frac{1}{2}\int_0^r e^{-x^2}[-2x\,dx]$

$\displaystyle= \lim_{r\to\infty} -\frac{1}{2}e^{-x^2}\Big|_o^r$

$\displaystyle= \lim_{r\to\infty}\left[-\frac{1}{2e^{r^2}}+\frac{1}{2}\right] = 0 + \frac{1}{2} = \frac{1}{2}$

Thus $\displaystyle\int_{-\infty}^\infty xe^{-x^2}\,dx = -\frac{1}{2}+\frac{1}{2} = 0$.

13. a. $\displaystyle\int_{800}^\infty \frac{k}{x^2}\,dx = 1$

$\displaystyle\lim_{r\to\infty} k\int_{800}^r x^{-2}\,dx = 1$

$\displaystyle\lim_{r\to\infty} -\frac{k}{x}\Big|_{800}^r = 1$

$\displaystyle\lim_{r\to\infty}\left(-\frac{k}{r}+\frac{k}{800}\right) = 1$

$\displaystyle0 + \frac{k}{800} = 1$

$k = 800$

b. $\displaystyle\int_{1200}^\infty \frac{800}{x^2}\,dx = \lim_{r\to\infty} 800\int_{1200}^r x^{-2}\,dx$

$\displaystyle= \lim_{r\to\infty} -\frac{800}{x}\Big|_{1200}^r$

$\displaystyle= \lim_{r\to\infty}\left(-\frac{800}{r}+\frac{800}{1200}\right) = 0 + \frac{2}{3} = \frac{2}{3}$

15. $\displaystyle\int_0^\infty 240{,}000e^{-0.06t}\,dt$

$\displaystyle= \lim_{r\to\infty}\frac{240{,}000}{-0.06}\int_0^r e^{-0.06t}[-0.06\,dt]$

$\displaystyle= \lim_{r\to\infty} -\frac{240{,}000}{0.06}e^{-0.06t}\Big|_0^r$

$\displaystyle= \lim_{r\to\infty} -\frac{240{,}000}{0.06}\left(\frac{1}{e^{-0.06r}}-1\right)$

$\displaystyle= -\frac{240{,}000}{0.06}(-1) = 4{,}000{,}000$

17. area $= \int_0^\infty e^{-2x} dx = \lim_{r \to \infty} -\frac{1}{2} \int_0^r e^{-2x}[-2 \ dx] = \lim_{r \to \infty} - \frac{e^{-2x}}{2}\bigg|_0^r$

$$= \lim_{r \to \infty} \left[-\frac{1}{2e^{2r}} + \frac{1}{2} \right] = 0 + \frac{1}{2} = \frac{1}{2} \text{ square unit}$$

19. $\int_0^\infty \frac{40,000}{(t+2)^2} dt = \lim_{r \to \infty} \int_0^r \frac{40,000}{(t+2)^2} dt = \lim_{r \to \infty} -\frac{40,000}{t+2}\bigg|_0^r = \lim_{r \to \infty} \left[-\frac{40,000}{r+2} + \frac{40,000}{2} \right]$

$$= 0 + \frac{40,000}{2} = 20,000 \text{ increase}$$

Chapter 17 Review Problems

1. Integration by parts or formula 42. For integration by parts, let $u = \ln x$, $dv = x \ dx$.

Then $du = \frac{1}{x} dx$ and $v = \frac{x^2}{2}$. Thus $\int x \ln x \ dx = \ln x \left(\frac{x^2}{2} \right) - \int \frac{x^2}{2} \cdot \frac{1}{x} dx = \frac{x^2}{2} \ln(x) - \int \frac{x}{2} dx$

$= \frac{x^2}{2} \ln(x) - \frac{x^2}{4} + C = \frac{x^2}{4}[2\ln(x) - 1] + C$

[Or, with formula 42, let $u = x$ (so $du = dx$) and $n = 1$.]

3. Formula 23 with $u = 2x$, $a^2 = 9$.

Then $du = 2 \ dx$.

$\int_0^2 \sqrt{4x^2 + 9} dx = \frac{1}{2} \int_0^2 \sqrt{(2x)^2 + 9}(2 \ dx)$

$= \frac{1}{2} \left[\frac{1}{2} \left((2x)\sqrt{4x^2 + 9} + 9 \ln\left| 2x + \sqrt{4x^2 + 9} \right| \right) \right]_0^2 = \left(5 + \frac{9}{4} \ln 9 \right) - \left(0 + \frac{9}{4} \ln 3 \right)$

$= 5 + \frac{9}{4} \ln 3^2 - \frac{9}{4} \ln 3$

$= 5 + \frac{18}{4} \ln 3 - \frac{9}{4} \ln 3 = 5 + \frac{9}{4} \ln 3$

5. By partial fractions,

$\int \frac{21x \ dx}{(2+3x)(3+x)} = \int \left[\frac{-6}{2+3x} + \frac{9}{3+x} \right] dx$

$= -2 \ln|2 + 3x| + 9 \ln|3 + x| + C$

Alternatively, by formula 12 with $u = x$
(so $du = dx$), $a = 2$, $b = 3$, $c = 3$, and $k = 1$,

$\int \frac{21x \ dx}{(2+3x)(3+x)} = 21 \int \frac{x \ dx}{(2+3x)(3+x)}$

$= 21 \cdot \frac{1}{7} \left[3 \ln|3 + x| - \frac{2}{3} \ln|2 + 3x| \right] + C$

$= 9 \ln|3 + x| - 2 \ln|2 + 3x| + C$

7. Partial fractions or formula 9. For formula 9, let $u = x$ (so $du = dx$), $a = 2$, and $b = 1$. For partial fractions,

$\int \frac{dx}{x(x+2)^2} = \int \left[\frac{\frac{1}{4}}{x} + \frac{-\frac{1}{4}}{x+2} + \frac{-\frac{1}{2}}{(x+2)^2} \right] dx$

$= \frac{1}{4} \ln|x| - \frac{1}{4} \ln|x + 2| + \frac{1}{2(x+2)} + C$

$= \frac{1}{2(x+2)} + \frac{1}{4} \ln\left| \frac{x}{x+2} \right| + C$

9. Formula 21 with $u = 4x$ (so $du = 4\,dx$) and $a^2 = 9$.

$$\int \frac{dx}{x^2\sqrt{9-16x^2}} = 4\int \frac{(4\,dx)}{(4x)^2\sqrt{9-(4x)^2}}$$

$$= 4\left[-\frac{\sqrt{9-16x^2}}{9(4x)}\right] + C$$

$$= -\frac{\sqrt{9-16x^2}}{9x} + C$$

11. Partial fractions or formula 35. For partial fractions

$$\int \frac{9\,dx}{x^2-9} = \int\left[\frac{\frac{3}{2}}{x-3} + \frac{-\frac{3}{2}}{x+3}\right]dx$$

$$= \frac{3}{2}\ln|x-3| - \frac{3}{2}\ln|x+3| + C$$

$$= \frac{3}{2}\ln\left|\frac{x-3}{x+3}\right| + C.$$

To apply formula 35, first write the integral as $9\int \frac{dx}{x^2-9}$ and then set $u = x$ (so $du = dx$) and $a = 3$.

13. Integration by parts or formula 38. With parts, let $u = 7x$ and $dv = 7e^{7x}dx$. Then $du = 7dx$ and $v = e^{7x}$. Thus

$$\int 49xe^{7x}dx = 7xe^{7x} - \int 7e^{7x}dx$$

$$= 7xe^{7x} - e^{7x} + C = e^{7x}(7x-1) + C.$$

With formula 38, let $u = 7x$ (so $du = 7dx$) and $a = 1$.

15. The integral has the form $\int \frac{1}{u}\,du$.

$$\int \frac{dx}{2x\ln 2x} = \frac{1}{2}\int \frac{1}{\ln 2x}\left[\frac{2}{2x}\,dx\right]$$

$$= \frac{1}{2}\ln|\ln 2x| + C$$

17. Long division or formula 3. For long division,

$$\int \frac{2x}{3+2x}\,dx = \int\left[1 - \frac{3}{3+2x}\right]dx$$

$$= x - 3\cdot\frac{1}{2}\int \frac{1}{3+2x}[2\,dx]$$

$$= x - \frac{3}{2}\ln|3+2x| + C.$$

To apply formula 3, write the integral as $2\int \frac{x}{3+2x}\,dx$ and $u = x$ (so $du = dx$), $a = 3$ and $b = 2$.

19. Partial fractions

$$\int \frac{5x^2+2}{x^3+x}\,dx = \int\left[\frac{2}{x} + \frac{3x}{x^2+1}\right]dx$$

$$= 2\ln|x| + \frac{3}{2}\ln\left(x^2+1\right) + C$$

21. Integration by parts
$u = \ln(x+1)$
$dv = (x+1)^{-\frac{1}{2}}dx$
Then $du = \frac{1}{x+1}dx$ and $v = 2(x+1)^{\frac{1}{2}}$.

$$\int \frac{\ln(x+1)}{\sqrt{x+1}}\,dx$$

$$= 2(x+1)^{\frac{1}{2}}\ln(x+1) - 2\int (x+1)^{-\frac{1}{2}}dx$$

$$= 2(x+1)^{\frac{1}{2}}\ln(x+1) - 4(x+1)^{\frac{1}{2}} + C$$

$$= 2\sqrt{x+1}[\ln(x+1) - 2] + C$$

23. $\bar{f} = \frac{1}{4-2}\int_2^4 \left(3x^2+2x\right)dx = \frac{1}{2}\left(x^3+x^2\right)\Big|_2^4$

$$= \frac{1}{2}[(64+16)-(8+4)] = 34$$

25. $f(x) = \frac{1}{x+1}$
$n = 6$, $a = 0$, $b = 3$
$h = \frac{b-a}{n} = \frac{3-0}{6} = 0.5$

a. Trapezoidal
$f(0) = 1.0000$
$2f(0.5) = 1.3333$
$2f(1) = 1.0000$
$2f(1.5) = 0.8000$
$2f(2) = 0.6667$
$2f(2.5) = 0.5714$
$f(3) = 0.2500$

$\overline{\quad 5.6214\quad}$

$\frac{0.5}{2}(5.6214) \approx 1.405$

b. Simpson's

$$f(0) = 1.0000$$
$$4f(0.5) = 2.6667$$
$$2f(1) = 1.0000$$
$$4f(1.5) = 1.6000$$
$$2f(2) = 0.6667$$
$$4f(2.5) = 1.1429$$
$$f(3) = 0.2500$$
$$\overline{8.3263}$$

$$\frac{0.5}{3}(8.3263) \approx 1.388$$

27. $y' = 3x^2y + 2xy$, $y > 0$

$$\frac{dy}{y} = \left(3x^2 + 2x\right)dx$$

$$\int \frac{dy}{y} = \int \left(3x^2 + 2x\right)dx$$

$\ln y = x^3 + x^2 + C_1$, from which

$y = e^{x^3 + x^2 + C_1}$, $y = Ce^{x^3 + x^2}$, where $C > 0$.

29. $\displaystyle\int_3^\infty \frac{1}{x^3}\,dx = \lim_{r \to \infty} \int_3^r x^{-3}\,dx$

$$= \lim_{r \to \infty} \frac{x^{-2}}{-2}\bigg|_3^t = \lim_{r \to \infty} -\frac{1}{2x^2}\bigg|_3^r$$

$$= \lim_{r \to \infty}\left[-\frac{1}{2r^2} + \frac{1}{18}\right] = 0 + \frac{1}{18} = \frac{1}{18}$$

31. $\displaystyle\int_1^\infty \frac{1}{2x}\,dx = \lim_{r \to \infty}\int_1^r \frac{1}{2x}\,dx = \lim_{r \to \infty}\frac{1}{2}\ln|x|\bigg|_1^r$

$$= \lim_{r \to \infty}\left[\frac{1}{2}\ln|r| - 0\right] = \infty \Rightarrow \text{diverges}$$

33. $N = N_0 e^{kt}$

Since $N = 100,000$ when $t = 0$ (1985),

$N_0 = 100,000$. Thus $N = 100,000e^{kt}$.

Since $N = 120,000$ when $t = 15$, then

$$120,000 = 100,000e^{15k}$$

$$1.2 = e^{15k}$$

$\ln 1.2 = 15k$, or $k = \dfrac{\ln 1.2}{15}$. Thus

$$N = 100,000e^{t\frac{\ln 1.2}{15}} = 100,000\left(e^{\ln 1.2}\right)^{\frac{t}{15}}$$

$$= 100,000(1.2)^{\frac{t}{15}}$$

For the year 2015 we have $t = 30$ and

$$N = 100,000(1.2)^{\frac{30}{15}} = 100,000(1.2)^2$$
$$= 144,000$$

35. $N = N_0 e^{-\lambda t}$, where N_0 is the original amount present. When $t = 100$, then $N = 0.95N_0$, so we have

$$0.95N_0 = N_0 e^{-100\lambda}$$

$$0.95 = e^{-100\lambda}$$

$$100\lambda = \ln 0.95$$

$$\lambda = -\frac{\ln 0.95}{100} \approx 0.0005 \text{ (decay constant)}.$$

After 200 years, $N = N_0 e^{-200\lambda}$. Thus

$$\frac{N}{N_0} = e^{-200\lambda} = e^{-200\left[-\frac{\ln 0.95}{100}\right]} = e^{2\ln 0.95}$$

$$\approx 0.90 = 90\%$$

37. $N = \dfrac{450}{1 + be^{-ct}}$

If $t = 0$, then $N = 2$. Thus $2 = \dfrac{450}{1 + b}$,

$1 + b = \dfrac{450}{2} = 225$, $b = 224$, so

$N = \dfrac{450}{1 + 224e^{-ct}}$. If $t = 6$, then

$N = 300 \Rightarrow 300 = \dfrac{450}{1 + 224e^{-6c}}$

$$1 + 224e^{-6c} = \frac{450}{300} = \frac{3}{2}$$

$$224e^{-6c} = \frac{3}{2} - 1 = \frac{1}{2}$$

$$e^{-6c} = \frac{1}{448}$$

$$e^{6c} = 448$$

$$6c = \ln 448$$

$$c = \frac{\ln 448}{6} \approx 1.02$$

Thus $N \approx \dfrac{450}{1 + 224e^{-1.02t}}$.

39. $\dfrac{dT}{dt} = k(T - 25)$

$\dfrac{dT}{T - 25} = k\ dt$

$\displaystyle\int \dfrac{dT}{T - 25} = \int k\ dt$

$\ln(T - 25) = kt + C$

If $t = 0$, then $T = 35$. Thus $\ln 10 = C$, so $\ln\left(\dfrac{T - 25}{10}\right) = kt$. If $t = 1$, then $T = 34$ and $\ln\left(\dfrac{9}{10}\right) = k$.

Thus $\ln\left(\dfrac{T - 25}{10}\right) = (\ln 0.9)t$.

If $T = 37$,

$\ln \dfrac{12}{10} = (\ln 0.9)t$

$\ln 1.2 = (\ln 0.9)t,$

$t = \dfrac{\ln 1.2}{\ln 0.9} \approx -1.73$

Note that 1.73 hr corresponds approximately to 1 hr 44 min. Thus 6:00 P.M. − 1 hr 44 min = 4:16 P.M.

41. $\displaystyle\int_{o}^{\infty} f(x)\,dx$

$= \displaystyle\lim_{r \to \infty} \int_{0}^{r}\left(0.008e^{-0.01x} + 0.00004e^{-0.0002x}\right)dx$

$= \displaystyle\lim_{r \to \infty}\left(-0.8e^{-0.01x} - 0.2e^{-0.0002x}\right)\Big|_{0}^{r}$

$= \displaystyle\lim_{r \to \infty}\left(-\dfrac{0.8}{e^{0.01r}} - \dfrac{0.2}{e^{0.0002r}} + 0.8 + 0.2\right)$

$= 0 - 0 + 0.8 + 0.2 = 1$

43. a. Total revenue

$= r(12) - r(0) = \displaystyle\int_{0}^{12} \dfrac{dr}{dq}\,dq.\ \ f(q) = \dfrac{dr}{dq}$

$n = 4,\ a = 0,\ b = 12$

$h = \dfrac{b - a}{n} = \dfrac{12 - 0}{4} = 3$

Trapezoidal

$\begin{aligned}
f(0) &= \ 25 \\
2f(3) &= \ 44 \\
2f(6) &= \ 36 \\
2f(9) &= \ 26 \\
f(12) &= \ \underline{\ 7\ } \\
&\ \ \ \ \ 138
\end{aligned}$

$TR \approx \dfrac{3}{2}(138) = 207$

Simpson's

$\begin{aligned}
f(0) &= \ 25 \\
4f(3) &= \ 88 \\
2f(6) &= \ 36 \\
4f(9) &= \ 52 \\
f(12) &= \ \underline{\ 7\ } \\
&\ \ \ \ \ 208
\end{aligned}$

$TR \approx \dfrac{3}{3}(208) = 208$

b. Total variable cost

$$c(12) - c(0) = \int_0^{12} \frac{dc}{dq}\, dq$$

$$f(q) = \frac{dc}{dq}$$

$a = 0, b = 12$

Using as little data as possible, we choose $n = 1$ for Trapezoidal and $n = 2$ for Simpson (n must be even).

Trapezoidal ($n = 1$)

$$h = \frac{b-a}{n} = \frac{12-0}{1} = 12$$

$$f(0) = 15$$
$$f(12) = \underline{7}$$
$$ 22$$

$$VC \approx \frac{12}{2}(22) = 132$$

Simpson's ($n = 2$)

$$h = \frac{b-a}{n} = \frac{12-0}{2} = 6$$

$$f(0) = 15$$
$$4f(6) = 48$$
$$f(12) = \underline{7}$$
$$ 70$$

$$VC \approx \frac{6}{3}(70) = 140$$

To each of our results we must add on the fixed cost of 25 to obtain total cost. Thus for trapezoidal we get $TC \approx 132 + 25 = 157$, and for Simpson we have $TC \approx 140 + 25 = 165$.

c. We use the relation

$$P(12) = \int_0^{12}\left[\frac{dr}{dq} - \frac{dc}{dq}\right]dq - 25.$$ First we

determine variable cost for each rule

with $n = 4$ and $h = \dfrac{b-a}{n} = \dfrac{12-0}{4} = 3$.

Trapezoidal
$$f(0) = 15$$
$$2f(3) = 28$$
$$2f(6) = 24$$
$$2f(9) = 20$$
$$f(12) = \underline{7}$$
$$ 94$$

$$VC \approx \frac{3}{2}(94) = 141$$

Simpson's
$$f(0) = 15$$
$$4f(3) = 56$$
$$2f(6) = 24$$
$$4f(12) = 40$$
$$f(12) = \underline{7}$$
$$ 142$$

$$VC \approx \frac{3}{3}(142) = 142$$

Using these results and those of part (a), we have:

Trapezoidal
$$P(12) \approx 207 - 141 - 25 = 41$$
Simpson's
$$P(12) \approx 208 - 142 - 25 = 41$$

Mathematical Snapshot Chapter 17

1. $C = 2000$, $w_0 = 200$

$$w_{eq} = \frac{C}{17.5} = \frac{2000}{17.5} \approx 114$$

$$w(t) = \frac{C}{17.5} + \left(w_0 - \frac{C}{17.5}\right)e^{-0.005t}$$

$$= \frac{2000}{17.5} + \left(200 - \frac{2000}{17.5}\right)e^{-0.005t}$$

Letting $w(t) = 175$ and solving for t gives

$$175 = \frac{2000}{17.5} + \left(200 - \frac{2000}{17.5}\right)e^{-0.005t}$$

$$175 - \frac{2000}{17.5} = \left(200 - \frac{2000}{17.5}\right)e^{-0.005t}$$

$$\frac{175 - \frac{2000}{17.5}}{200 - \frac{2000}{17.5}} = e^{-0.005t}$$

$$-0.005t = \ln\left[\frac{175 - \frac{2000}{17.5}}{200 - \frac{2000}{17.5}}\right]$$

$$t = \frac{\ln\left[\frac{175 - \frac{2000}{17.5}}{200 - \frac{2000}{17.5}}\right]}{-0.005} \approx 69$$

Thus $w_{eq} = 114$ and $t = 69$ days.

3. $w(t) = \frac{C}{17.5} + \left(w_0 - \frac{C}{17.5}\right)e^{-0.005t}$

Since $\frac{C}{17.5} = w_{eq}$, we have

$$w(t) = w_{eq} + \left(w_0 - w_{eq}\right)e^{-0.005t}.$$

Simplifying the equation

$$w(t+d) = w(t) - \frac{1}{2}\left[w(t) - w_{eq}\right] \text{ gives}$$

$$w(t+d) = \frac{1}{2}\left[w(t) + w_{eq}\right]. \text{ Thus}$$

$$w_{eq} + \left(w_0 - w_{eq}\right)e^{-0.005(t+d)}$$

$$= \frac{1}{2}\left[w_{eq} + \left(w_0 - w_{eq}\right)e^{-0.005t} + w_{eq}\right], \text{ or}$$

$$w_{eq} + \left(w_0 - w_{eq}\right)e^{-0.005(t+d)}$$

$$= w_{eq} + \frac{1}{2}\left(w_0 - w_{eq}\right)e^{-0.005t}$$

Solving for d gives

$$e^{-0.005(t+d)} = \frac{1}{2}e^{-0.005t}$$

$$e^{-0.005t}e^{-0.005d} = \frac{1}{2}e^{-0.005t}$$

$$e^{-0.005d} = \frac{1}{2}$$

$$-0.005d = \ln\frac{1}{2} = -\ln 2$$

$$d = \frac{\ln 2}{0.005}$$

as was to be shown.

5. Answers may vary.

Chapter 18

Principles in Practice 18.1

1. The uniform density function is given by $f(x) = \begin{cases} \frac{1}{60}, & \text{if } 0 \le x < 60 \\ 0, & \text{otherwise.} \end{cases}$

    The probability of waiting between 25 and 45 minutes is

    $$P(25 \le X \le 45) = \int_{25}^{45} \frac{1}{60}\,dx = \frac{x}{60}\Big|_{25}^{45}$$

    $$= \frac{45-25}{60} = \frac{20}{60} = \frac{1}{3}.$$

2. The exponential density function is given by $f(x) = \begin{cases} \frac{1}{10}e^{-\frac{x}{10}}, & \text{if } x \ge 0 \\ 0, & \text{if } x < 0. \end{cases}$

    The probability that the break pads will break down after the warranty period is

    $$P(5 < X) = 1 - P(0 \le X \le 5) = 1 - \int_0^5 \frac{1}{10}e^{-\frac{x}{10}}\,dx = 1 - \left(-e^{-\frac{x}{10}}\Big|_0^5 \right)$$

    $$= 1 - \left(-e^{-\frac{5}{10}} + e^0 \right) = 1 + e^{-\frac{1}{2}} - 1 = e^{-\frac{1}{2}} \approx 0.607$$

3. The exponential density function is given by $f(x) = \begin{cases} 0.2e^{-0.2x}, & \text{for } x \ge 0 \\ 0, & \text{otherwise.} \end{cases}$

    The mean is given by $\mu = \frac{1}{k} = \frac{1}{0.2} = 5.$

    The standard deviation is given by $\sigma = \frac{1}{k} = \frac{1}{0.2} = 5.$

Exercise 18.1

1. **a.** $P(1 < X < 2) = \int_1^2 \frac{1}{6}(x+1)\,dx$

    $$= \frac{(x+1)^2}{12}\Big|_1^2$$

    $$= \frac{9}{12} - \frac{4}{12} = \frac{5}{12}$$

    b. $P(X < 2.5) = \int_1^{2.5} \frac{1}{6}(x+1)\,dx$

    $$= \frac{(x+1)^2}{12}\Big|_1^{2.5}$$

    $$= \frac{49}{48} - \frac{4}{12} = \frac{11}{16} = 0.6875.$$

    c. $P\left(X \ge \frac{3}{2}\right) = \int_{3/2}^3 \frac{1}{6}(x+1)\,dx$

    $$= \frac{(x+1)^2}{12}\Big|_{3/2}^3$$

    $$= \frac{16}{12} - \frac{25}{48} = \frac{13}{16} = 0.8125$$

d. $\int_1^c \frac{1}{6}(x+1)dx = \frac{1}{2}$

$\dfrac{(x+1)^2}{12}\Big|_1^c = \frac{1}{2}$

$\dfrac{(c+1)^2}{12} - \frac{1}{3} = \frac{1}{2}$

$(c+1)^2 - 4 = 6$

$(c+1)^2 = 10$

$c+1 = \pm\sqrt{10}$

$c = -1 \pm \sqrt{10}$

We choose $c = -1 + \sqrt{10}$ since $1 < c < 3$.

3. a. $f(x) = \begin{cases} \frac{1}{3}, & \text{if } 1 \le x \le 4 \\ 0, & \text{otherwise} \end{cases}$

b. $\dfrac{3-2}{4-1} = \frac{1}{3}$

c. $P(0 < X < 1) = \int_0^1 0\,dx = 0$

d. $P(X \le 3.5) = P(1 \le X \le 3.5)$

$= \dfrac{3.5-1}{4-1} = \dfrac{2.5}{3} = \dfrac{5}{6}$

e. $P(X > 3) = P(3 < X \le 4) = \dfrac{4-3}{4-1} = \dfrac{1}{3}$

f.   0

g. $P(X < 5) = P(1 \le X \le 4) = \dfrac{4-1}{4-1} = 1$

h. $\mu = \int_1^4 x\left(\frac{1}{3}\right)dx = \dfrac{x^2}{6}\Big|_1^4 = \dfrac{5}{2}$

i. $\sigma^2 = \int_1^4 x^2\left(\frac{1}{3}\right)dx - \mu^2 = \dfrac{x^3}{9}\Big|_1^4 - \left(\frac{5}{2}\right)^2$

$= \left[\frac{64}{9} - \frac{1}{9}\right] - \frac{25}{4} = 7 - \frac{25}{4} = \frac{3}{4}$

Thus $\sigma = \dfrac{\sqrt{3}}{2}$.

j.   If $1 \le x \le 4$,

$F(x) = \int_1^x \frac{1}{3}\,dt = \dfrac{t}{3}\Big|_1^x = \dfrac{x-1}{3}$

Thus $F(x) = \begin{cases} 0, & \text{if } x < 1 \\ \frac{x-1}{3}, & \text{if } 1 \le x \le 4 \\ 1, & \text{if } x > 4 \end{cases}$

$P(X < 2) = F(2) = \dfrac{2-1}{3} = \dfrac{1}{3}$

$P(1 < X < 3) = F(3) - F(1) = \dfrac{2}{3} - 0 = \dfrac{2}{3}$

5. a. $f(x) = \begin{cases} \frac{1}{b-a}, & \text{if } a \le x \le b \\ 0, & \text{otherwise} \end{cases}$

b. $\mu = \int_a^b x\left(\frac{1}{b-a}\right)dx = \dfrac{x^2}{2(b-a)}\Big|_a^b$

$= \dfrac{b^2 - a^2}{2(b-a)} = \dfrac{a+b}{2}$

c. $\sigma^2 = \int_a^b x^2\left(\frac{1}{b-a}\right)dx - \mu^2$

$= \dfrac{x^3}{3(b-a)}\Big|_a^b - \left(\frac{a+b}{2}\right)^2$

$= \dfrac{b^3 - a^3}{3(b-a)} - \dfrac{(a+b)^2}{4}$

$= \dfrac{b^2 + ab + a^2}{3} - \dfrac{a^2 + 2ab + b^2}{4}$

$= \dfrac{b^2 - 2ab + a^2}{12} = \dfrac{(b-a)^2}{12}$

Thus $\sigma = \dfrac{b-a}{\sqrt{12}}$.

7. $f(x) = \begin{cases} 2e^{-2x}, & \text{if } x \geq 0 \\ 0, & \text{if } x < 0 \end{cases}$

a. $P(1 < X < 3) = \int_1^3 2e^{-2x}\,dx = -e^{-2x}\Big|_1^3$

$= -e^{-6} + e^{-2} \approx 0.133$

b. $P(X < 2) = \int_0^2 2e^{-2x}\,dx = -e^{-2x}\Big|_0^2$

$= -e^{-4} + 1 \approx 0.982$

c. $P(X > 4.5) = 1 - P(X \leq 4.5)$

$= 1 - \int_0^{4.5} 2e^{-2x}\,dx$

$= 1 - \left(-e^{-2x}\right)\Big|_0^{4.5} = 1 - \left(-e^{-9} + 1\right)$

≈ 0.0001

d. From the text, $\mu = \sigma = \frac{1}{k} = \frac{1}{2}$

$P(\mu - \sigma < X < \mu + \sigma) = P(0 < X < 1)$

$= \int_0^1 2e^{-2x}\,dx = -e^{-2x}\Big|_0^1$

$= -e^{-2} + 1 \approx 0.865$

e. $\int_0^{\infty} 2e^{-2x}\,dx = \lim_{r \to \infty} \int_0^r 2e^{-2x}\,dx$

$= \lim_{r \to \infty} -e^{-2x}\Big|_0^r$

$= \lim_{r \to \infty} \left(-e^{-2r} + 1\right) = 0 + 1 = 1$

9. a. $\int_0^4 kx\,dx = 1$

$\frac{kx^2}{2}\Big|_0^4 = 1$

$8k = 1$

$k = \frac{1}{8}$

b. $P(2 < X < 3) = \int_2^3 \frac{x}{8}\,dx = \frac{x^2}{16}\Big|_2^3$

$= \frac{9}{16} - \frac{4}{16} = \frac{5}{16}$

c. $P(X > 2.5) = \int_{2.5}^4 \frac{x}{8}\,dx = \frac{x^2}{16}\Big|_{2.5}^4$

$= 1 - \frac{25}{64} = \frac{39}{64} \approx 0.609$

d. $P(X > 0) = P(0 \leq X \leq 4) = 1$

e. $\mu = \int_0^4 x\left(\frac{x}{8}\right)dx = \frac{x^3}{24}\Big|_0^4 = \frac{64}{24} - 0 = \frac{8}{3}$

f. $\sigma^2 = \int_0^4 x^2\left(\frac{x}{8}\right)dx - \mu^2 = \frac{x^4}{32}\Big|_0^4 - \left(\frac{8}{3}\right)^2$

$= 8 - \frac{64}{9} = \frac{8}{9}$

Thus $\sigma = \frac{\sqrt{8}}{3} = \frac{2\sqrt{2}}{3}$

g. $P(X < c) = \frac{1}{2}$

$\int_0^c \frac{x}{8}\,dx = \frac{1}{2}$

$\frac{x^2}{16}\Big|_0^c = \frac{1}{2}$

$\frac{c^2}{16} = \frac{1}{2}$

$c^2 = 8$

$c = \pm 2\sqrt{2}$

We choose $c = 2\sqrt{2}$ since $0 < c < 4$.

h. $P(3 < X < 5) = P(3 < X < 4) = \int_3^4 \frac{x}{8}\,dx$

$= \frac{x^2}{16}\Big|_3^4 = \frac{16}{16} - \frac{9}{16} = \frac{7}{16}$

11. $P(X \le 7) = \int_0^7 \frac{1}{10}\,dx = \frac{x}{10}\Big|_0^7 = \frac{7}{10}$

$E(X) = \int_0^{10} x\left(\frac{1}{10}\right)dx = \frac{x^2}{20}\Big|_0^{10} = 5$ min.

13. $P(X > 1) = 1 - P(X \le 1)$

$= 1 - \int_0^1 3e^{-3x}\,dx = 1 - \left(-e^{-3x}\right)\Big|_0^1$

$= 1 - \left(-e^{-3} + 1\right) \approx 0.050$

Exercise 18.2

1. a. $P(0 < Z < 1.8) = A(1.8) = 0.4641$

b. $P(0.45 < Z < 2.81) = A(2.81) - A(0.45)$
$= 0.4975 - 0.1736 = 0.3239$

c. $P(Z > -1.27) = 0.5 + A(1.27)$
$= 0.5 + 0.3980 = 0.8980$

d. $P(Z \le 2.93) = 0.5 + A(2.93)$
$= 0.5 + 0.4983 = 0.9983$

e. $P(-2.61 < Z \le 1.4) = A(2.61) + A(1.4)$
$= 0.4955 + 0.4192 = 0.9147$

f. $P(Z > 0.07) = 0.5 - A(0.07)$
$= 0.5 - 0.0279 = 0.4721$

3. $P(Z < z_0) = 0.5517$
$0.5 + A(z_0) = 0.5517$
$A(z_0) = 0.0517$
$z_0 = 0.13$

5. $P(Z > z_0) = 0.8599$
$0.5 + A(-z_0) = 0.8599$
$A(-z_0) = 0.3599$
$-z_0 = 1.08$
$z_0 = -1.08$

7. $P(-z_0 < Z < z_0) = 0.2662$
$2A(z_0) = 0.2662$
$A(z_0) = 0.1331$
$z_0 = 0.34$

9. a. $P(X < 27) = P\left(Z < \frac{27-16}{4}\right)$
$= P(Z < 2.75) = 0.5 + A(2.75)$
$= 0.5 + 0.4970 = 0.9970$

b. $P(X < 10) = P\left(Z < \frac{10-16}{4}\right)$
$= P(Z < -1.5) = 0.5 - A(1.5)$
$= 0.5 - 0.4332 = 0.0668$

c. $P(10.8 < X < 12.4)$
$= P\left(\frac{10.8-16}{4} < Z < \frac{12.4-16}{4}\right)$
$= P(-1.3 < Z < -0.9) = A(1.3) - A(0.9)$
$= 0.4032 - 0.3159 = 0.0873$

11. $P(X > -2) = P\left(Z > \frac{-2-(-3)}{2}\right)$
$= P\left(Z > \frac{1}{2}\right) = 0.5 - A\left(\frac{1}{2}\right)$
$= 0.5 - 0.1915 = 0.3085$

13. Since $\sigma^2 = 9$, $\sigma = 3$. Thus
$P(19 < X \le 28) = P\left(\frac{19-25}{3} < Z \le \frac{28-25}{3}\right)$
$= P(-2 < Z \le 1) = A(2) + A(1)$
$= 0.4772 + 0.3413 = 0.8185$

15. $P(X > 54) = P(Z > z_0) = 0.0401$
$0.5 - A(z_0) = 0.0401$
$A(z_0) = 0.4599$
$z_0 = 1.75$
Since $\frac{54-40}{\sigma} = 1.75$
$\frac{14}{\sigma} = 1.75$
so $\sigma = \frac{14}{1.75} = 8$.

17. Let X be score on test. Then
$P(X > 630) = P\left(Z > \frac{630-500}{100}\right)$
$= P(Z > 1.3) = 0.5 - A(1.3) = 0.5 - 0.4032$
$= 0.0968 \Rightarrow 9.68\%$

19. Let X be height of an adult. Then

$$P(X < 72) = P\left(Z < \frac{72 - 68}{3}\right) = P(Z < 1.33)$$

$$= 0.5 + A(1.33) = 0.5 + 0.4082 = 0.9082$$

$$\Rightarrow 90.82\%$$

21. Let X be I.Q. of a child in population.

a. $P(X > 125) = P\left(Z > \frac{125 - 100.4}{11.6}\right)$

$$= P(Z > 2.12) = 0.5 - A(2.12)$$

$$= 0.5 - 0.4830 = 0.0170. \text{ Thus } 1.7\%$$
of the children have I.Q.'s greater than 125.

b. If x_0 is the value, then

$$P(X > x_0) = 0.90. \text{ Thus}$$

$$P\left(Z > \frac{x_0 - 100.4}{11.6}\right) = 0.90 \text{ or}$$

$$0.5 + A\left(-\frac{x_0 - 100.4}{11.6}\right) = 0.90. \text{ Hence}$$

$$A\left(-\frac{x_0 - 100.4}{11.6}\right) = 0.4, \text{ so}$$

$$-\frac{x_0 - 100.4}{11.6} = 1.28 \text{ or}$$

$$x_0 = 85.552 \approx 85.6.$$

Principles in Practice 18.3

1. X is the number of winners and X is binomial with $n = 60$ and $p = \frac{1}{4}$. To find $P(X = 20)$, use the normal approximation to the binomial distribution with

$$\mu = np = 60\left(\frac{1}{4}\right) = 15 \text{ and}$$

$$\sigma\sqrt{npq} = \sqrt{60\left(\frac{1}{4}\right)\left(\frac{3}{4}\right)} = \sqrt{\frac{45}{4}} \approx 3.35.$$

Converting the correct X-values 19.5 and 20.5 to Z-values gives

$$z_1 = \frac{19.5 - 15}{\sqrt{\frac{45}{4}}} \approx 1.34$$

$$z_2 = \frac{20.5 - 15}{\sqrt{\frac{45}{4}}} \approx 1.64$$

Thus $P(X = 20) \approx P(1.34 \le Z \le 1.64)$
$= A(1.64) - A(1.34) = 0.4495 - 0.4099$
$= 0.0396$
The probability of 20 winners out of 60 contestants is 0.0396.

Exercise 18.3

1. $n = 150$, $p = 0.4$, $q = 0.6$, $\mu = np$
$= 150(0.04) = 60$,
$$\sigma = \sqrt{npq} - \sqrt{150(0.4)(0.6)} = \sqrt{36} = 6$$
$$P(X \le 52) = P(X < 52.5)$$
$$z = \frac{52.5 - 60}{6} = -1.25$$
$$P(X \le 52) = P(X \le 52.5)$$
$$\approx P(Z \le -1.25) = 0.5 - A(1.25)$$
$$= 0.5 - 0.3944 = 0.1056$$
$$P(X \ge 74) = P(X \ge 73.5) \approx P\left(Z \ge \frac{73.5 - 60}{6}\right)$$
$$= P(Z \ge 2.25)$$
$$= 0.5 - A(2.25)$$
$$= 0.5 - 0.4878 = 0.0122$$

3. $n = 200$, $p = 0.6$, $q = 0.4$, $\mu = np = 120$
$$\sigma = \sqrt{npq} = \sqrt{48} \approx 6.93$$
$$P(X = 125) = P(124.5 \le X \le 125.5)$$
$$\approx P\left(\frac{124.5 - 120}{6.93} \le Z \le \frac{125.5 - 120}{6.93}\right)$$
$$= P(0.65 \le Z \le 0.79)$$
$$= A(0.79) - A(0.65)$$
$$= 0.2852 - 0.2422 = 0.0430$$
$$P(110 \le X \le 135) = P(109.5 \le X \le 135.5)$$
$$\approx P\left(\frac{109.5 - 120}{6.93} \le Z \le \frac{135.5 - 120}{6.93}\right)$$
$$= P(-1.52 \le Z \le 2.24) = A(1.52) + A(2.24)$$
$$= 0.4357 + 0.4875 = 0.9232$$

5. Let $X =$ no. of times 5 occurs. Then X is binomial with $n = 300$, $p = \frac{1}{6}$, $q = \frac{5}{6}$,
$$\mu = np = 50, \ \sigma = \sqrt{npq} = \sqrt{41.666} \approx 6.45.$$
$$P(45 \le X \le 60) = P(44.5 \le X \le 60.5)$$
$$\approx P\left(\frac{44.5 - 50}{6.45} \le Z \le \frac{60.5 - 50}{6.45}\right)$$
$$= P(-0.85 \le Z \le 1.63) = A(0.85) + A(1.63)$$
$$= 0.3023 + 0.4484 = 0.7507$$

7. Let X = no. of trucks out of service. Then X can be considered binomial with $n = 60$, $p = 0.1$, $q = 0.9$, $\mu = np = 6$,

$$\sigma = \sqrt{npq} = \sqrt{5.4} \approx 2.32$$

$$P(X \geq 7) = P(X \geq 6.5) \approx P\left(Z \geq \frac{6.5 - 6}{2.32}\right)$$

$$= P(Z \geq 0.22) = 0.5 - A(0.22)$$

$$= 0.5 - 0.0871 = 0.4129$$

9. Let X = no. of correct answers. Then X is binomial and $p = 0.5$, $q = 0.5$. If $n = 20$, then $\mu = np = 20(0.05) = 10$,

$$\sigma = \sqrt{npq} = \sqrt{20(0.5)(0.5)} = \sqrt{5} \approx 2.24 \text{ and}$$

$$P(X \geq 12) = P(X \geq 11.5)$$

$$\approx P\left(Z \geq \frac{11.5 - 10}{2.24}\right) = P(Z \geq 0.67)$$

$$= 0.5 - A(0.67) = 0.5 - 0.2486 = 0.2514. \text{ If}$$

$n = 100$, then $\mu = np = 100(0.5) = 50$,

$$\sigma = \sqrt{npq} = \sqrt{100(0.5)(0.5)} = \sqrt{25} = 5,$$

and

$$P(X \geq 60) = P(X \geq 59.5)$$

$$\approx P\left(Z \geq \frac{59.5 - 50}{5}\right) = P(Z \geq 1.9)$$

$$= 0.5 - A(1.9)$$

$$= 0.5 - 0.4713 = 0.0287$$

11. Let X = no. of deals consisting of three cards of one suit and two cards of another suit. Then X is binomial with $n = 100$, $p = 0.1$, $q = 0.9$,

$$\mu = np = 10, \ \sigma = \sqrt{npq} = \sqrt{9} = 3.$$

$$P(X \geq 16) = P(X \geq 15.5)$$

$$\approx P\left(Z \geq \frac{15.5 - 10}{3}\right)$$

$$= P(Z \geq 1.83)$$

$$= 0.5 - A(1.83)$$

$$= 0.5 - 0.4664 = 0.0336$$

Chapter 18 Review Problems

1. a. $P(0 \leq X \leq 1) = 1$

$$\int_0^1 \left(\frac{1}{3} + kx^2\right)dx = 1$$

$$\left(\frac{x}{3} + \frac{kx^3}{3}\right)\Bigg|_0^1 = 1$$

$$\frac{1}{3} + \frac{k}{3} = 1$$

$$\frac{k}{3} = \frac{2}{3}$$

$$k = 2$$

b. $P\left(\frac{1}{2} < X < \frac{3}{4}\right) = \int_{1/2}^{3/4}\left(\frac{1}{3} + 2x^2\right)dx$

$$= \left(\frac{x}{3} + \frac{2x^3}{3}\right)\Bigg|_{1/2}^{3/4} = \frac{1}{3}\left(x + 2x^3\right)\Bigg|_{1/2}^{3/4}$$

$$\frac{1}{3}\left[\left(\frac{3}{4} + \frac{27}{32}\right) - \left(\frac{1}{2} + \frac{1}{4}\right)\right] = \frac{9}{32}$$

c. $P\left(X \geq \frac{1}{2}\right) = \int_{1/2}^1 \left(\frac{1}{3} + 2x^2\right)dx$

$$= \left(\frac{x}{3} + \frac{2x^3}{3}\right)\Bigg|_{1/2}^1 = \frac{1}{3}\left(x + 2x^3\right)\Bigg|_{1/2}^1$$

$$= \frac{1}{3}\left[(1 + 2) - \left(\frac{1}{2} + \frac{1}{4}\right)\right] = \frac{3}{4}$$

d. If $0 \leq x \leq 1$, $F(x) = \int_0^x\left(\frac{1}{3} + 2t^2\right)dt$

$$= \left(\frac{t}{3} + \frac{2t^3}{3}\right)\Bigg|_0^x = \frac{x}{3} + \frac{2x^3}{3}$$

Therefore,

$$F(x) = \begin{cases} 0, & \text{if } x < 0 \\ \frac{x}{3} + \frac{2x^3}{3}, & \text{if } 0 \leq x \leq 1 \\ 1, & \text{if } x > 1 \end{cases}$$

3. a. $\mu = \int_0^4 x\left(\frac{1}{8}x\right)dx = \left.\frac{x^3}{24}\right|_0^4 = \frac{8}{3}$

b. $\sigma^2 = \int_0^4 x^2\left(\frac{1}{8}x\right)dx - \mu^2$

$= \left.\frac{x^4}{32}\right|_0^4 - \left(\frac{8}{3}\right)^2$

$= 8 - \frac{64}{9} = \frac{8}{9}$

Thus $\sigma = \frac{2\sqrt{2}}{3} \approx 0.94$.

5. $P(X > 22) = P\left(Z > \frac{22-20}{4}\right)$

$= P(Z > 0.5) = 0.5 - A(0.5)$

$= 0.5 - 0.1915 = 0.3085$

7. $P(14 < X < 18) = P\left(\frac{14-20}{4} < Z < \frac{18-20}{4}\right)$

$= P(-1.5 < Z < -0.5)$

$= A(1.5) - A(0.5) = 0.4332 - 0.1915$

$= 0.2417$

9. $P(X < 16) = P\left(Z < \frac{16-20}{4}\right)$

$= P(Z < -1) = 0.5 - A(1)$

$= 0.5 - 0.3413 = 0.1587$

11. $n = 100, p = 0.35, q = 0.65, \mu = np = 35,$

$\sigma = \sqrt{npq} = \sqrt{22.75} \approx 4.77$

$P(25 \le X \le 47) = P(24.5 \le X \le 47.5)$

$\approx P\left(\frac{24.5-35}{4.77} \le Z \le \frac{47.5-35}{4.77}\right)$

$= P(-2.20 \le Z \le 2.62) = A(2.20) + A(2.62)$

$= 0.4956 + 0.4861 = 0.9817$

13.   Let X = height of an individual. X is normally distributed with $\mu = 68$ and $\sigma = 2$.

$P(X > 72) = P\left(Z > \frac{72-68}{2}\right)$

$= P(Z > 2) = 0.5 - A(2)$

$= 0.5 - 0.4772 = 0.0228$

Mathematical Snapshot Chapter 18

1. The result should correspond to the known distribution function.

3. The list of earthquake magnitudes will appear to have a normal density function. This is surprising, since one would expect something more like an exponential density function, with most earthquakes being very low-magnitude. Presumably, the explanation for the normal density function is that as magnitude declines, the likelihood of a quake's being reported and thus appearing on the list also goes down.

Chapter 19

Principles in Practice 19.1

1. a. $c(500, 700) = 160 + 2(500) + 3(700)$
$= 160 + 1000 + 2100 = 3260$
The cost of manufacturing 500
12-ounce and 700 20-ounce mugs is
$3260.

b. $c(1000, 750) = 160 + 2(1000) + 3(750)$
$= 160 + 2000 + 2250 = 4410$
The cost of manufacturing 1000
12-ounce mugs and 750 20-ounce mugs
is $4410.

Exercise 19.1

1. $f(1, 2) = 4(1) - (2)^2 + 3 = 4 - 4 + 3 = 3$

3. $g(0, -4, 2) = e^0 (2[-4] + 3[2]) = 1(-8 + 6)$
$= -2$

5. $h(-3, 3, 5, 4) = \dfrac{-3(3)}{5^2 - 4^2} = \dfrac{-9}{25 - 16} = \dfrac{-9}{9}$
$= -1$

7. $g(4, 8) = 2(4)\left(4^2 - 5\right) = 2(4)(11) = 88$

9. $F(2, 0, -1) = 3$

11. $f(x, y) = 2x - 5y + 4$
$f\left(x_0 + h, y_0\right) = 2\left(x_0 + h\right) - 5y_0 + 4$
$= 2x_0 + 2h - 5y_0 + 4$

13. $f(400, 400, 80) = \dfrac{400(400)}{80} = 2000$

15. A plane parallel to the x, z-plane has the
form $y = $ constant. Because $(0, -4, 0)$ lies on
the plane, the equation is $y = -4$.

17. A plane parallel to the x, y-plane has the
form $z = $ constant. Because $(2, 7, 6)$ lies on
the plane, the equation is $z = 6$.

19. $x + y + z = 1$ can be put in the form
$Ax + By + Cz + D = 0$, so the graph is a
plane. The intercepts are $(1, 0, 0)$, $(0, 1, 0)$,
and $(0, 0, 1)$.

21. $3x + 6y + 2z = 12$ can be put in the form
$Ax + By + Cz + D = 0$, so the graph is a
plane. The intercepts are $(4, 0, 0)$, $(0, 2, 0)$,
and $(0, 0, 6)$.

23. $x + 2y = 2$ can be put in the form
$Ax + By + Cz + D = 0$, so the graph is a
plane. There are only two intercepts:
$(2, 0, 0)$ and $(0, 1, 0)$. The x, y-trace is
$x + 2y = 2$, which is a line. For any fixed
value of z, we obtain the line $x + 2y = 2$.

25. $z = 4 - x^2$. The x, z-trace is $z = 4 - x^2$, which is a parabola. For any fixed value of y, we obtain the parabola $z = 4 - x^2$.

27. $x^2 + y^2 + z^2 = 1$. The x, y-trace is $x^2 + y^2 = 1$, which is a circle. The x, z-trace is $x^2 + z^2 = 1$, which is a circle. The y, z-trace is $y^2 + z^2 = 1$, which is a circle. The surface is a sphere with only the top hemisphere shown in the diagram.

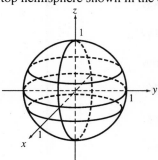

Exercise 19.2

1. $f(x, y) = 4x^2 + 3y^2 - 7$
$f_x(x, y) = 4(2x) + 0 + 0 = 8x$
$f_y(x, y) = 0 + 3(2y) + 0 = 6y$

3. $f(x, y) = 2y + 1$
$f_x(x, y) = 0 + 0 = 0$
$f_y(x, y) = 2(1) + 0 = 2$

5. $g(x, y) = x^3 y^2 + 2x^2 y - 4xy + 3y$
$g_x(x, y) = \left(3x^2\right)y^2 + 2(2x)y - 4(1)y + 0$
$= 3x^2 y^2 + 4xy - 4y$
$g_y(x, y) = x^3(2y) + 2x^2(1) - 4x(1) + 3(1)$
$= 2x^3 y + 2x^2 - 4x + 3$

7. $g(p, q) = \sqrt{pq} = (pq)^{\frac{1}{2}}$
$g_p(p, q) = \frac{1}{2}(pq)^{-\frac{1}{2}} \cdot q = \frac{q}{2\sqrt{pq}}$
$g_q(p, q) = \frac{1}{2}(pq)^{-\frac{1}{2}} \cdot p = \frac{p}{2\sqrt{pq}}$

9. $h(s, t) = \frac{s^2 + 4}{t - 3}$
$h_s(s, t) = \frac{1}{t-3}(2s) = \frac{2s}{t-3}$
Rewriting $h(s, t)$ as $\left(s^2 + 4\right)(t - 3)^{-1}$, we have
$h_t(s, t) = \left(s^2 + 4\right)\left[(-1)(t-3)^{-2}(1)\right]$
$= -\frac{s^2 + 4}{(t-3)^2}$

11. $u(q_1, q_2) = \frac{3}{4}\ln q_1 + \frac{1}{4}\ln q_2$
$u_{q_1}(q_1, q_2) = \frac{3}{4} \cdot \frac{1}{q_1} + 0 = \frac{3}{4q_1}$
$u_{q_2}(q_1, q_2) = 0 + \frac{1}{4} \cdot \frac{1}{q_2} = \frac{1}{4q_2}$

13. $h(x, y) = \dfrac{x^2 + 3xy + y^2}{\sqrt{x^2 + y^2}}$

$$h_x(x, y) = \frac{\left(x^2 + y^2\right)^{\frac{1}{2}}[2x + 3y] - \left(x^2 + 3xy + y^2\right)\left[\frac{1}{2}\left(x^2 + y^2\right)^{-\frac{1}{2}}(2x)\right]}{\left[\left(x^2 + y^2\right)^{\frac{1}{2}}\right]^2}$$

$$= \frac{\left(x^2 + y^2\right)^{-\frac{1}{2}}\left[\left(x^2 + y^2\right)(2x + 3y) - \left(x^2 + 3xy + y^2\right)x\right]}{x^2 + y^2}$$

$$= \frac{2x^3 + 3x^2y + 2xy^2 + 3y^3 - x^3 - 3x^2y - xy^2}{\left(x^2 + y^2\right)^{\frac{3}{2}}} = \frac{x^3 + xy^2 + 3y^3}{\left(x^2 + y^2\right)^{\frac{3}{2}}}$$

$$h_y(x, y) = \frac{\left(x^2 + y^2\right)^{\frac{1}{2}}[3x + 2y] - \left(x^2 + 3xy + y^2\right)\left[\frac{1}{2}\left(x^2 + y^2\right)^{-\frac{1}{2}}(2y)\right]}{\left[\left(x^2 + y^2\right)^{\frac{1}{2}}\right]^2}$$

$$= \frac{\left(x^2 + y^2\right)^{-\frac{1}{2}}\left[\left(x^2 + y^2\right)(3x + 2y) - \left(x^2 + 3xy + y^2\right)y\right]}{x^2 + y^2}$$

$$= \frac{3x^3 + 2x^2y + 3xy^2 + 2y^3 - x^2y - 3xy^2 - y^3}{\left(x^2 + y^2\right)^{\frac{3}{2}}} = \frac{3x^3 + x^2y + y^3}{\left(x^2 + y^2\right)^{\frac{3}{2}}}$$

15. $z = 5x \ln(x^2 + y)$

$\dfrac{\partial z}{\partial x} = e^{5xy}(5y) = 5ye^{5xy}$; $\dfrac{\partial z}{\partial y} = e^{5xy}(5x) = 5xe^{5xy}$

17. $z = 5x \ln\left(x^2 + y\right)$

$$\frac{\partial z}{\partial x} = 5\left\{x\left[\frac{1}{x^2 + y}(2x)\right] + \ln\left(x^2 + y\right)[1]\right\} = 5\left[\frac{2x^2}{x^2 + y} + \ln\left(x^2 + y\right)\right]$$

$$\frac{\partial z}{\partial y} = 5x\left(\frac{1}{x^2 + y}[1]\right) = \frac{5x}{x^2 + y}$$

19. $f(r, s) = (r + 2s)^{\frac{1}{2}}\left(r^3 - 2rs + s^2\right)$

$f_r(r, s) = (r + 2s)^{\frac{1}{2}}\left[3r^2 - 2s\right] + \left(r^3 - 2rs + s^2\right)\left[\frac{1}{2}(r + 2s)^{-\frac{1}{2}}(1)\right]$

$= \sqrt{r + 2s}\left(3r^2 - 2s\right) + \dfrac{r^3 - 2rs + s^2}{2\sqrt{r + 2s}}$

$f_s(r, s) = (r + 2s)^{\frac{1}{2}}\left[-2r + 2s\right] + \left(r^3 - 2rs + s^2\right)\left[\frac{1}{2}(r + 2s)^{-\frac{1}{2}}(2)\right]$

$= 2(s - r)\sqrt{r + 2s} + \dfrac{r^3 - 2rs + s^2}{\sqrt{r + 2s}}$

21. $f(r, s) = e^{3-r}\ln(7 - s)$

$f_r(r, s) = \ln(7 - s)\left[e^{3-r}(-1)\right]$

$= -e^{3-r}\ln(7 - s)$

$f_s(r, s) = e^{3-r}\left[\dfrac{1}{7 - s}(-1)\right] = \dfrac{e^{3-r}}{s - 7}$

23. $g(x, y, z) = 3x^2 y + 2xy^2 z + 3z^3$

$g_x(x, y, z) = 3y(2x) + 2y^2 z(1) + 0$

$= 6xy + 2y^2 z$

$g_y(x, y, z) = 3x^2(1) + 2xz(2y) + 0$

$= 3x^2 + 4xyz$

$g_z(x, y, z) = 0 + 2xy^2(1) + 3\left(3z^2\right)$

$= 2xy^2 + 9z^2$

25. $g_r(r, s, t) = e^{s+t}[2r + 0] = 2re^{s+t}$

$g_s(r, s, t) = e^{s+t}\left[0 + 21s^2\right]$

$+ \left(r^2 + 7s^3\right)\left[e^{s+t}(1)\right]$

$= \left(7s^3 + 21s^2 + r^2\right)e^{s+t}$

$g_t(r, s, t) = \left(r^2 + 7s^3\right)\left[e^{s+t}(1)\right]$

$= e^{s+t}\left(r^2 + 7s^3\right)$

27. $f(x, y) = x^3 y + 7x^2 y^2$

$f_x(x, y) = 3x^2 y + 14xy^2$

$f_x(1, -2) = 50$

29. $g(x, y, z) = e^x\sqrt{y + 2z}$

$g_z(x, y, z) = e^x\left[\dfrac{1}{2}(y + 2z)^{-\frac{1}{2}}(2)\right]$

$= \dfrac{e^x}{\sqrt{y + 2z}}$

$g_z(0, 6, 4) = \dfrac{1}{\sqrt{6 + 8}} = \dfrac{1}{\sqrt{14}}$

31. $h(r, s, t, u) = \left(s^2 + tu\right)\ln(2r + 7st)$

$h_s(r, s, t, u) = \dfrac{7t\left(s^2 + tu\right)}{2r + 7st} + 2s\ln(2r + 7st)$

$h_s(1, 0, 0, 1) = 0$

33. $f(r, s, t) = rst\left(r^2 + s^3 + t^4\right)$

$= r^3 st + rs^4 t + rst^5$

$f_s(r, s, t) = r^3(1)t + r\left(4s^3\right)t + r(1)t^5$

$= r^3 t + 4rs^3 t + rt^5$

$f_s(1, -1, 2) = 2 + (-8) + 32 = 26$

35. $z = xe^{x-y} - ye^{y-x}$

$\dfrac{\partial z}{\partial x} = \left[xe^{x-y} + e^{x-y}\right] - \left[ye^{y-x}(-1)\right]$

$\dfrac{\partial z}{\partial y} = \left[xe^{x-y}(-1)\right] - \left[ye^{y-x} + e^{y-x}\right]$

Thus $\dfrac{\partial z}{\partial x} + \dfrac{\partial z}{\partial y} = e^{x-y} - e^{y-x}$, as was to be shown.

37. $F(b, C, T, i) = \dfrac{bT}{C} + \dfrac{iC}{2}$

$\dfrac{\partial F}{\partial C} = \dfrac{\partial}{\partial C}\left[\dfrac{bT}{C}\right] + \dfrac{\partial}{\partial C}\left[\dfrac{iC}{2}\right] = -\dfrac{bT}{C^2} + \dfrac{i}{2}$

39. $R = f(r, a, n) = \dfrac{r}{1 + a\left(\frac{n-1}{2}\right)}$

$= r\left[1 + a\left(\dfrac{n-1}{2}\right)\right]^{-1}$

$\dfrac{\partial R}{\partial n} = r(-1)\left[1 + a\left(\dfrac{n-1}{2}\right)\right]^{-2} \cdot \dfrac{a}{2}$

$= -\dfrac{ra}{2\left[1 + a\left(\frac{n-1}{2}\right)\right]^2}$

Exercise 19.3

1. $c = 7x + 0.3y^2 + 2y + 900$

$\dfrac{\partial c}{\partial y} = 0.6y + 2$

When $x = 20$ and $y = 30$, then

$\dfrac{\partial c}{\partial y} = 0.6(30) + 2 = 20$.

3. $c = 0.03(x + y)^3 - 0.6(x + y)^2 + 9.5(x + y)$
   $+ 7700$

$\dfrac{\partial c}{\partial x} = 0.09(x + y)^2 - 1.2(x + y) + 9.5$

When $x = 50$ and $y = 80$, then

$\dfrac{\partial c}{\partial x} = 0.09(130)^2 - 1.2(130) + 9.5 = 1374.5$.

5. $\dfrac{\partial P}{\partial k} = 1.582(0.764)l^{0.192}k^{-0.236}$

$= 1.208648l^{0.192}k^{-0.236}$

$\dfrac{\partial P}{\partial l} = 1.582(0.192)l^{-0.808}k^{0.764}$

$= 0.303744l^{-0.808}k^{0.764}$

7. $\dfrac{\partial q_A}{\partial p_A} = -50,\ \dfrac{\partial q_A}{\partial p_B} = 2,\ \dfrac{\partial q_B}{\partial q_A} = 4,$

$\dfrac{\partial q_B}{\partial p_B} = -20$

Since $\dfrac{\partial q_A}{\partial q_B} > 0$ and $\dfrac{\partial q_B}{\partial q_A} > 0$ the products
are competitive.

9. $q_A = 100p_A^{-1}p_B^{-\frac{1}{2}}$

$q_B = 500p_B^{-1}p_A^{-\frac{1}{3}}$

$\dfrac{\partial q_A}{\partial p_A} = 100(-1)p_A^{-2}p_B^{-\frac{1}{2}} = \dfrac{-100}{p_A^2 p_B^{\frac{1}{2}}}$

$\dfrac{\partial q_A}{\partial p_B} = 100\left(-\dfrac{1}{2}\right)p_A^{-1}p_B^{-\frac{3}{2}} = \dfrac{-50}{p_A p_B^{\frac{3}{2}}}$

$\dfrac{\partial q_B}{\partial p_A} = 500\left(-\dfrac{1}{3}\right)p_B^{-1}p_A^{-\frac{4}{3}} = \dfrac{-500}{3p_B p_A^{\frac{4}{3}}}$

$\dfrac{\partial q_B}{\partial p_B} = 500(-1)p_B^{-2}p_A^{-\frac{1}{3}} = -\dfrac{500}{p_B^2 p_A^{\frac{1}{3}}}$

Since $\dfrac{\partial q_A}{\partial p_B} < 0$ and $\dfrac{\partial q_B}{\partial p_A} < 0$, the products
are complementary.

11. $\dfrac{\partial P}{\partial B} = 0.01A^{0.27}B^{-0.99}C^{0.01}D^{0.23}E^{0.09}F^{0.27}$

$\dfrac{\partial P}{\partial C} = 0.01A^{0.27}B^{0.01}C^{-0.99}D^{0.23}E^{0.09}F^{0.27}$

13. $\dfrac{\partial z}{\partial x} = 4480$. If a staff manager with an M.B.A. degree had an extra year of work experience before the degree, the manager would receive \$4480 per year in extra compensation.

15. a. $\dfrac{\partial R}{\partial w} = -1.015$; $\dfrac{\partial R}{\partial s} = -0.846$

b. One for which $w = w_0$ and $s = s_0$ since increasing w by 1 while holding s fixed decreases the reading ease score.

17. $\dfrac{\partial g}{\partial x} = \dfrac{1}{V_F} > 0$ for $V_F > 0$. Thus if x increases and V_F and V_S are fixed, then g increases.

19. a. $\dfrac{\partial q_A}{\partial p_A} = 30\sqrt{p_B}\left(-\dfrac{2}{3}p_A^{-\frac{5}{3}}\right)$

$\dfrac{\partial q_A}{\partial p_B} = \dfrac{30}{p_A^{\frac{2}{3}}}\left(\dfrac{1}{2}p_B^{-\frac{1}{2}}\right)$

When $p_A = 8$ and $p_B = 64$, then

$\dfrac{\partial q_A}{\partial p_A} = 30(8)\left(-\dfrac{2}{3}\cdot\dfrac{1}{32}\right) = -5$

$\dfrac{\partial q_A}{\partial p_B} = \dfrac{30}{4}\left(\dfrac{1}{2}\cdot\dfrac{1}{8}\right) = \dfrac{15}{32}.$

b. From (a), when $p_A = 8$ and $p_B = 64$,

then $\dfrac{\partial q_A}{\partial p_B} = \dfrac{15}{32}$. Hence each

$1 reduction in p_B decreases q_A by

approximately $\dfrac{15}{32}$ unit. Thus a

$4 reduction in p_B (from \$64 to \$60)

decreases the demand for A by

approximately $\dfrac{15}{32}(4) = \dfrac{15}{8}$ units.

21. a. $\dfrac{\partial R}{\partial E_r} = 2.5945 - 0.1608E_r - 0.02771I_r$

If $E_r = 18.8$ and $I_r = 10$, then

$\dfrac{\partial R}{\partial E_r} = -0.70564$. Since $\dfrac{\partial R}{\partial E_r} < 0$,

such a candidate should not be so advised.

b. $\dfrac{\partial R}{\partial N} = 0.8579 - 0.0122N$

If $\dfrac{\partial R}{\partial N} < 0$, then $N > 70.3 \approx 70\%$

23. $q_A = 1000 - 50p_A + 2p_B(-50)$

$\eta_{p_A} = \left(\dfrac{p_A}{q_A}\right)\dfrac{\partial q_A}{\partial p_A} = \left(\dfrac{p_A}{q_A}\right)(-50)$

$\eta_{p_B} = \left(\dfrac{p_B}{q_A}\right)\dfrac{\partial q_A}{\partial p_B} = \left(\dfrac{p_B}{q_A}\right)(2)$

When $p_A = 2$ and $p_B = 10$, then

$q_A = 920$, from which $\eta_{p_A} = -\dfrac{5}{46}$ and

$\eta_{p_B} = \dfrac{1}{46}$

25. $q_A = \dfrac{100}{p_A\sqrt{p_B}}$

$\eta_{p_A} = \left(\dfrac{p_A}{q_A}\right)\dfrac{\partial q_A}{\partial p_A} = \left(\dfrac{p_A}{q_A}\right)\left(\dfrac{-100}{p_A^2\sqrt{p_B}}\right)$

$\eta_{p_B} = \left(\dfrac{p_B}{q_A}\right)\dfrac{\partial q_A}{\partial p_B} = \left(\dfrac{p_B}{q_A}\right)\left(\dfrac{-50}{p_A\sqrt{p_B^3}}\right)$

When $p_A = 1$ and $p_B = 4$, then $q_A = 50$.

This gives $\eta_{p_A} = -1$ and $\eta_{p_B} = -\dfrac{1}{2}$.

Exercise 19.4

1. $2x + 0 + 2z\dfrac{\partial z}{\partial x} = 0$.

$2z\dfrac{\partial z}{\partial x} = -2x$, $\dfrac{\partial z}{\partial x} = -\dfrac{2x}{2z} = -\dfrac{x}{z}$

3. $6z^2\dfrac{\partial z}{\partial y} - 0 - 8y = 0$

$\dfrac{\partial z}{\partial y} = \dfrac{8y}{6z^2} = \dfrac{4y}{3z^2}$

5. $x^2 - 2y - z^2 + y\left(x^2z^2\right) = 20$

$2x - 0 - 2z\dfrac{\partial z}{\partial x} + y\left[x^2\cdot 2z\dfrac{\partial z}{\partial x} + z^2\cdot 2x\right] = 0$

$\left(2x^2yz - 2z\right)\dfrac{\partial z}{\partial x} = -2x - 2xyz^2$

$\dfrac{\partial z}{\partial x} = \dfrac{-2x\left(1 + yz^2\right)}{2z\left(x^2y - 1\right)} = \dfrac{x\left(yz^2 + 1\right)}{z\left(1 - x^2y\right)}$

7. $0 + e^y + e^z \dfrac{\partial z}{\partial y} = 0$

$\dfrac{\partial z}{\partial y} = -\dfrac{e^y}{e^z} = -e^{y-z}$

9. $\dfrac{1}{z}\dfrac{\partial z}{\partial x} + 9\dfrac{\partial z}{\partial x} - y = 0$

$\left(\dfrac{1}{z} + 9\right)\dfrac{\partial z}{\partial x} = y$

$\left(\dfrac{1+9z}{z}\right)\dfrac{\partial z}{\partial x} = y$

$\dfrac{\partial z}{\partial x} = \dfrac{yz}{9+z}$

11. $\left(2z\dfrac{\partial z}{\partial y} + 6x\right)\sqrt{x^3 + 5} = 0$

$2z\dfrac{\partial z}{\partial y} + 6x = 0$

$\dfrac{\partial z}{\partial y} = \dfrac{-6x}{2z} = -\dfrac{3x}{z}$

13. $\left[x \cdot 2z\dfrac{\partial z}{\partial x} + z^2 \cdot 1\right] + y\dfrac{\partial z}{\partial x} - 0 = 0$.

$(2xz + y)\dfrac{\partial z}{\partial x} = -z^2$

$\dfrac{\partial z}{\partial x} = -\dfrac{z^2}{2xz + y}$

If $x = 2$, $y = -2$, $z = 3$, then

$\dfrac{\partial z}{\partial x} = -\dfrac{9}{12-2} = -\dfrac{9}{10}$.

15. $e^{yz} \cdot y\dfrac{\partial z}{\partial x} = -y\left[x\dfrac{\partial z}{\partial x} + z \cdot 1\right]$.

$\left(ye^{yz} + xy\right)\dfrac{\partial z}{\partial x} = -yz$

$\dfrac{\partial z}{\partial x} = -\dfrac{yz}{y\left(e^{yz} + x\right)}$

$\dfrac{\partial z}{\partial x} = -\dfrac{z}{e^{yz} + x}$

If $x = -\dfrac{e^2}{2}$, $y = 1$, $z = 2$, then

$\dfrac{\partial z}{\partial x} = -\dfrac{2}{e^2 + \frac{-e^2}{2}} = -\dfrac{2}{\frac{e^2}{2}} = -\dfrac{4}{e^2}$.

17. $\dfrac{1}{z}\dfrac{\partial z}{\partial x} = 4 + 0$

$\dfrac{\partial z}{\partial x} = 4z$

If $x = 5$, $y = -20$, $z = 1$, then $\dfrac{\partial z}{\partial x} = 4$.

19. $\dfrac{(rs)\left[2t\frac{\partial t}{\partial r}\right] - \left(s^2 + t^2\right)[s]}{(rs)^2} = 0$.

$2rst\dfrac{\partial t}{\partial r} - s\left(s^2 + t^2\right) = 0$

$2rst\dfrac{\partial t}{\partial r} = s\left(s^2 + t^2\right)$

$\dfrac{\partial t}{\partial r} = \dfrac{s\left(s^2 + t^2\right)}{2rst} = \dfrac{s^2 + t^2}{2rt}$

If $r = 1$, $s = 2$, $t = 4$, then

$\dfrac{\partial t}{\partial r} = \dfrac{4+16}{2 \cdot 1 \cdot 4} = \dfrac{20}{8} = \dfrac{5}{2}$.

21. $c + \sqrt{c} = 12 + q_A\sqrt{9 + q_B^2}$

a. If $q_A = 6$ and $q_B = 4$, then

$c + \sqrt{c} = 12 + 6(5) = 42$, $\sqrt{c} = 42 - c$,

$c = (42 - c)^2 = 42^2 - 84c + c^2$,

$c^2 - 85c + 1764 = 0$,

$c = \dfrac{85 \pm \sqrt{(-85)^2 - 4(1)(1764)}}{2}$

$= \dfrac{85 \pm \sqrt{169}}{2} = \dfrac{85 \pm 13}{2}$. Thus $c = 49$ or

$c = 36$. However $c = 49$ is extraneous but $c = 36$ is not. Thus $c = 36$.

b. Differentiating with respect to q_A:

$\dfrac{\partial c}{\partial q_A} + \dfrac{1}{2\sqrt{c}} \cdot \dfrac{\partial c}{\partial q_A} = \sqrt{9 + q_B^2}$.

$\left(1 + \dfrac{1}{2\sqrt{c}}\right)\dfrac{\partial c}{\partial q_A} = \sqrt{9 + q_B^2}$.

When $q_A = 6$ and $q_B = 4$, then $c = 36$

and $\left(1 + \dfrac{1}{12}\right)\dfrac{\partial c}{\partial q_A} = 5$, $\dfrac{13}{12} \cdot \dfrac{\partial c}{\partial q_A} = 5$, or

$\dfrac{\partial c}{\partial q_A} = \dfrac{60}{13}$.

Differentiating with respect to q_B:

$$\frac{\partial c}{\partial q_B} + \frac{1}{2\sqrt{c}} \cdot \frac{\partial c}{\partial q_B} = q_A \cdot \frac{q_B}{\sqrt{9 + q_B^2}}$$

$$\left(1 + \frac{1}{2\sqrt{c}}\right) \frac{\partial c}{\partial q_B} = \frac{q_A q_B}{\sqrt{9 + q_B^2}}$$

When $q_A = 6$ and $q_B = 4$, then $c = 36$ and

$$\left(1 + \frac{1}{12}\right) \frac{\partial c}{\partial q_B} = \frac{24}{5}, \frac{13}{12} \cdot \frac{\partial c}{\partial q_B} = \frac{24}{5}, \text{ or } \frac{\partial c}{\partial q_B} = \frac{288}{65}.$$

Exercise 19.5

1. $f_x(x,\ y) = 4(2x)y = 8xy$
$f_{xy}(x,\ y) = 8x$

3. $f_y(x,\ y) = 3$
$f_{yy}(x,\ y) = 0$
$f_{yyx}(x,\ y) = 0$

5. $f_y(x,\ y) = 9\left[e^{2xy}(2x)\right] = 18xe^{2xy}$
$f_{yx}(x,\ y) = 18\left[x\left(e^{2xy} \cdot 2y\right) + e^{2xy}(1)\right] = 18e^{2xy}(2xy + 1)$
$f_{yxy}(x,\ y) = 18\left[e^{2xy}(2x) + (2xy + 1)\left(e^{2xy} \cdot 2x\right)\right]$
$= 18e^{2xy}(2x)[1 + (2xy + 1)] = 18e^{2xy}(2x)[2 + 2xy]$
$= 72x(1 + xy)e^{2xy}$

7. $f(x,\ y) = (x + y)^2(xy) = \left(x^2 + 2xy + y^2\right)(xy)$
$= x^3y + 2x^2y^2 + xy^3$
$f_x(x,\ y) = 3x^2y + 4xy^2 + y^3$
$f_y(x,\ y) = x^3 + 4x^2y + 3xy^2$
$f_{xx}(x,\ y) = 6xy + 4y^2$
$f_{yy}(x,\ y) = 4x^2 + 6xy$

9. $\frac{\partial z}{\partial x} = \frac{1}{2}\left(x^2 + y^2\right)^{-\frac{1}{2}}[2x] = x\left(x^2 + y^2\right)^{-\frac{1}{2}}$
$\frac{\partial^2 z}{\partial x^2} = x\left[-\frac{1}{2}\left(x^2 + y^2\right)^{-\frac{3}{2}}[2x]\right] + \left(x^2 + y^2\right)^{-\frac{1}{2}}[1]$
$= \left(x^2 + y^2\right)^{-\frac{3}{2}}\left[-x^2 + \left(x^2 + y^2\right)\right] = y^2\left(x^2 + y^2\right)^{-\frac{3}{2}}$

11. $f_y(x, y, z) = 0$

$f_{yx}(x, y, z) = 0$

$f_{yxx}(x, y, z) = 0$

Thus $f_{yxx}(4, 3, -2) = 0$.

13. $f_k(l, k) = 30l^3 k^5 - 7lk^6$

$f_{kk}(l, k) = 150l^3 k^4 - 42lk^5$

$f_{kkl}(l, k) = 450l^2 k^4 - 42k^5$

Thus

$f_{kkl}(8, 1) = 450(64)(1) - (42)(1) = 28,758$.

15. $f_x(x, y) = y^2 e^x + \dfrac{1}{x}$

$f_{xy}(x, y) = 2ye^x$

$f_{xyy}(x, y) = 2e^x$

Thus $f_{xyy}(1, 1) = 2e$.

17. $\dfrac{\partial c}{\partial q_B} = \dfrac{1}{3}\left(3q_A^2 + q_B^3 + 4\right)^{-\frac{2}{3}}\left(3q_B^2\right)$

$= q_B^2\left(3q_A^2 + q_B^3 + 4\right)^{-\frac{2}{3}}$

$\dfrac{\partial^2 c}{\partial q_A \partial q_B} = -\dfrac{2}{3} q_B^2\left(3q_A^2 + q_B^3 + 4\right)^{-\frac{5}{3}}\left(6q_A\right)$

$= -4q_A q_B^2\left(3q_A^2 + q_B^3 + 4\right)^{-\frac{5}{3}}$

When $p_A = 25$ and $p_B = 4$, then

$q_A = 10 - 25 + 16 = 1$ and

$q_B = 20 + 25 - 44 = 1$, and

$\dfrac{\partial^2 c}{\partial q_A \partial q_B} = -4(8)^{-\frac{5}{3}} = -\dfrac{4}{32} = -\dfrac{1}{8}$.

19. $f_x(x, y) = 24x^2 + 4xy^2$

$f_y(x, y) = 4x^2 y + 20y^3$

$f_{xy}(x, y) = 8xy$

$f_{yx}(x, y) = 8xy$

Thus $f_{xy}(x, y) = f_{yx}(x, y)$.

21. $\dfrac{\partial z}{\partial x} = \dfrac{2x}{x^2 + y^2}$

$\dfrac{\partial^2 z}{\partial x^2} = \dfrac{\left(x^2 + y^2\right)(2) - (2x)(2x)}{\left(x^2 + y^2\right)^2}$

$= \dfrac{2\left(y^2 - x^2\right)}{\left(x^2 + y^2\right)^2}$

$\dfrac{\partial z}{\partial y} = \dfrac{2y}{x^2 + y^2}$

$\dfrac{\partial^2 z}{\partial y^2} = \dfrac{\left(x^2 + y^2\right)(2) - (2y)(2y)}{\left(x^2 + y^2\right)^2}$

$= \dfrac{2\left(x^2 - y^2\right)}{\left(x^2 + y^2\right)^2}$

$\dfrac{\partial^2 z}{\partial x^2} + \dfrac{\partial^2 z}{\partial y^2} = \dfrac{2\left(y^2 - x^2\right)}{\left(x^2 + y^2\right)^2} + \dfrac{2\left(x^2 - y^2\right)}{\left(x^2 + y^2\right)^2} = 0$

23. $2z\dfrac{\partial z}{\partial y} + 2y = 0$

$\dfrac{\partial z}{\partial y} = -\dfrac{2y}{2z} = -\dfrac{y}{z}$

$\dfrac{\partial^2 z}{\partial y^2} = -\dfrac{z(1) - y \cdot \frac{\partial z}{\partial y}}{z^2} = -\dfrac{z - y\left(-\frac{y}{z}\right)}{z^2}$

$= -\dfrac{z^2 + y^2}{z^3}$

From original equation, $z^2 + y^2 = 3x^2$.

Thus $\dfrac{\partial^2 z}{\partial y^2} = -\dfrac{3x^2}{z^3}$.

Exercise 19.6

1. $z = 5x + 3y$, $x = 2r + 3s$, $y = r - 2s$

$\dfrac{\partial z}{\partial r} = \dfrac{\partial z}{\partial x}\dfrac{\partial x}{\partial r} + \dfrac{\partial z}{\partial y}\dfrac{\partial y}{\partial r} = (5)(2) + (3)(1) = 13$

$\dfrac{\partial z}{\partial s} = \dfrac{\partial z}{\partial x}\dfrac{\partial x}{\partial s} + \dfrac{\partial z}{\partial y}\dfrac{\partial y}{\partial s} = (5)(3) + (3)(-2) = 9$

3. $z = e^{x+y}$, $x = t^2 + 3$, $y = \sqrt{t^3}$

$\dfrac{dz}{dt} = \dfrac{\partial z}{\partial x}\dfrac{dx}{dt} + \dfrac{\partial z}{\partial y}\dfrac{dy}{dt} = e^{x+y}(2t) + e^{x+y}\left(\dfrac{3}{2}t^{\frac{1}{2}}\right)$

$= \left(2t + \dfrac{3}{2}\sqrt{t}\right)e^{x+y}$

5. $w = x^2 z^2 + xyz + yz^2$, $x = 5t$, $y = 2t + 3$, $z = 6 - t$

$\dfrac{dw}{dt} = \dfrac{\partial w}{\partial x}\dfrac{dx}{dt} + \dfrac{\partial w}{\partial y}\dfrac{dy}{dt} + \dfrac{\partial w}{\partial t}\dfrac{dz}{dt}$

$= \left(2xz^2 + yz\right)(5) + \left(xz + z^2\right)(2) + \left(2x^2 z + xy + 2yz\right)(-1)$

$= 5\left(2xz^2 + yz\right) + 2\left(xz + z^2\right) - \left(2x^2 z + xy + 2yz\right)$

7. $z = \left(x^2 + xy^2\right)^3$, $x = r + s + t$, $y = 2r - 3s + 8t$

$\dfrac{\partial z}{\partial t} = \dfrac{\partial z}{\partial x}\dfrac{\partial x}{\partial t} + \dfrac{\partial z}{\partial y}\dfrac{\partial y}{\partial t}$

$= 3\left(x^2 + xy^2\right)^2\left(2x + y^2\right)[1] + 3\left(x^2 + xy^2\right)^2(2xy)[8]$

$= 3\left(x^2 + xy^2\right)^2\left(2x + y^2 + 16xy\right)$

9. $w = x^2 + xyz + y^3 z^2$, $x = r - s^2$, $y = rs$, $z = 2r - 5s$

$\dfrac{\partial w}{\partial s} = \dfrac{\partial w}{\partial x}\dfrac{\partial x}{\partial s} + \dfrac{\partial w}{\partial y}\dfrac{\partial y}{\partial s} + \dfrac{\partial w}{\partial z}\dfrac{\partial z}{\partial s}$

$= (2x + yz)(-2s) + \left(xz + 3y^2 z^2\right)(r) + \left(xy + 2y^3 z\right)(-5)$

$= -2s(2x + yz) + r\left(xz + 3y^2 z^2\right) - 5\left(xy + 2y^3 z\right)$

11. $y = x^2 - 7x + 5$, $x = 19rs + 2s^2 t^2$

$\dfrac{\partial y}{\partial r} = \dfrac{dy}{dx}\dfrac{\partial x}{\partial r} = (2x - 7)(19s) = 19s(2x - 7)$

13. $z = (4x + 3y)^3$, $x = r^2 s$, $y = r - 2s$, $r = 0$, $s = 1$

$\dfrac{\partial z}{\partial r} = \dfrac{\partial z}{\partial x}\dfrac{\partial x}{\partial r} + \dfrac{\partial r}{\partial y}\dfrac{\partial y}{\partial r}$

$= 12(4x + 3y)^2(2rs) + 9(4x + 3y)^2(1)$

$= 3(4x + 3y)^2(8rs + 3)$

When $r = 0$, $s = 1$, then $x = 0$, $y = -2$, and $\dfrac{\partial z}{\partial r} = 324$.

15. $w = e^{3x-y}\left(x^2 + 4z^3\right), x = rs, y = 2s - r, z = r + s, r = 1, s = -1$

$$\frac{\partial w}{\partial s} = \frac{\partial w}{\partial x}\frac{\partial x}{\partial s} + \frac{\partial w}{\partial y}\frac{\partial y}{\partial s} + \frac{\partial w}{\partial z}\frac{\partial z}{\partial s}$$

$$= \left[e^{3x-y}(2x) + \left(x^2 + 4z^3\right)e^{3x-y}(3)\right](r) + \left[e^{3x-y}(-1)\left(x^2 + 4z^3\right)\right](2) + \left[e^{3x-y}\left(12z^2\right)\right](1)$$

$$= e^{3x-y}\left[\left(3x^2 + 2x + 12z^3\right)r - 2\left(x^2 + 4z^3\right) + 12z^2\right]$$

When $r = 1$ and $s = -1$, then $x = -1, y = -3, z = 0$, and $\dfrac{\partial w}{\partial s} = -1$.

17. $\dfrac{\partial c}{\partial p_A} = \dfrac{\partial c}{\partial q_A}\dfrac{\partial q_A}{\partial p_A} + \dfrac{\partial c}{\partial q_B}\dfrac{\partial q_B}{\partial p_A}$

$$= \left[\frac{1}{3}\left(3q_A^2 + q_B^3 + 4\right)^{-\frac{2}{3}}(6q_A)\right](-1) + \left[\frac{1}{3}\left(3q_A^2 + q_B^3 + 4\right)^{-\frac{2}{3}}\left(3q_B^2\right)\right](1)$$

$$= \left(3q_A^2 + q_B^3 + 4\right)^{-\frac{2}{3}}\left(-2q_A + q_B^2\right)$$

$$\frac{\partial c}{\partial p_B} = \frac{\partial c}{\partial q_A}\frac{\partial q_A}{\partial p_B} + \frac{\partial c}{\partial q_B}\frac{\partial q_B}{\partial p_B}$$

$$= \left[\frac{1}{3}\left(3q_A^2 + q_B^3 + 4\right)^{-\frac{2}{3}}(6q_A)\right](2p_B) + \left[\frac{1}{3}\left(3q_A^2 + q_B^3 + 4\right)^{-\frac{2}{3}}\left(3q_B^2\right)\right](-11)$$

$$= \left(3q_A^2 + q_B^3 + 4\right)^{-\frac{2}{3}}\left(4q_A p_B - 11q_B^2\right)$$

When $p_A = 25$ and $p_B = 4$, then $q_A = 10 - 25 + 16 = 1$, $q_B = 20 + 25 - 44 = 1$,

and $\dfrac{\partial c}{\partial p_A} = (8)^{-\frac{2}{3}}(-1) = -\dfrac{1}{4}$ and $\dfrac{\partial c}{\partial p_B} = (8)^{-\frac{2}{3}}(5) = \dfrac{5}{4}$.

19. a. $\dfrac{\partial w}{\partial s} = \dfrac{\partial w}{\partial x}\dfrac{\partial x}{\partial s} + \dfrac{\partial w}{\partial y}\dfrac{\partial y}{\partial s}$

b. $\dfrac{\partial w}{\partial s} = \left[3x^2 \cdot \dfrac{1}{x - 2y}(1) + \ln(x - 2y)[6x]\right]\left(\sqrt{t - 2}\right) + \left[3x^2 \cdot \dfrac{1}{x - 2y}(-2)\right]\left[-3e^{1-s}(-1)\right]$

$$= \left[\frac{3x^2}{x - 2y} + 6x\ln(x - 2y)\right]\sqrt{t - 2} - \frac{18x^2 e^{1-s}}{x - 2y}$$

Setting $s = 1$ and $t = 3$ gives $x = 1, y = 0$, and $\dfrac{\partial w}{\partial s} = [3 + 0](1) - \dfrac{18}{1} = -15$

Exercise 19.7

1. $f(x, y) = x^2 + y^2 - 5x + 4y + xy$

$$\begin{cases} f_x(x, y) = 2x + y - 5 = 0 \\ f_y(x, y) = x + 2y + 4 = 0 \end{cases}$$

Solving the system gives the critical point $\left(\dfrac{14}{3}, -\dfrac{13}{3}\right)$.

3. $f(x, y) = 2x^3 + y^3 - 3x^2 + 1.5y^2 - 12x - 90y$

$$\begin{cases} f_x(x, y) = 6x^2 - 6x - 12 = 0 \\ f_y(x, y) = 3y^2 + 3y - 90 = 0 \end{cases}$$

Both equations are easily solved by factoring. The critical points are $(2, 5)$, $(2, -6)$, $(-1, 5)$, $(-1, -6)$.

5. $f(x, y, z) = 2x^2 + xy + y^2 + 100 - z(x + y - 200)$

$$\begin{cases} f_x(x, y, z) = 4x + y - z = 0 \\ f_y(x, y, z) = x + 2y - z = 0 \\ f_z(x, y, z) = -x - y + 200 = 0 \end{cases}$$

Solving gives the critical point $(50, 150, 350)$.

7. $f(x, y) = x^2 + 3y^2 + 4x - 9y + 3$

$$\begin{cases} f_x(x, y) = 2x + 4 = 0 \\ f_y(x, y) = 6y - 9 = 0 \end{cases}$$

Critical point $\left(-2, \frac{3}{2}\right)$

Second-Derivative Test

$f_{xx}(x, y) = 2$, $f_{yy}(x, y) = 6$,

$f_{xy}(x, y) = 0$. At $\left(-2, \frac{3}{2}\right)$,

$D = (2)(6) - 0^2 = 12 > 0$ and

$f_{xx}(x, y) = 2 > 0$. Thus at $\left(-2, \frac{3}{2}\right)$ there is a relative minimum.

9. $f(x, y) = y - y^2 - 3x - 6x^2$

$$\begin{cases} f_x(x, y) = -3 - 12x = 0 \\ f_y(x, y) = 1 - 2y = 0 \end{cases}$$

Critical point $\left(-\frac{1}{4}, \frac{1}{2}\right)$

Second-Derivative Test

$f_{xx}(x, y) = -12$, $f_{yy}(x, y) = -2$,

$f_{xy}(x, y) = 0$

At $\left(-\frac{1}{4}, \frac{1}{2}\right)$, $D = (-12)(-2) - 0^2 = 24 > 0$

and $f_{xx}(x, y) = -12 < 0$. Thus at $\left(-\frac{1}{4}, \frac{1}{2}\right)$

there is a relative maximum.

11. $f(x, y) = x^3 - 3xy + y^2 + y - 5$

$$\begin{cases} f_x(x, y) = 3x^2 - 3y = 0 \\ f_y(x, y) = -3x + 2y + 1 = 0 \end{cases}$$

Critical point: $(1, 1)$, $\left(\frac{1}{2}, \frac{1}{4}\right)$

Second-Derivative Test

$f_{xx}(x, y) = 6x$, $f_{yy}(x, y) = 2$,

$f_{xy}(x, y) = -3$

At $(1, 1)$, $D = (6)(2) - (-3)^2 = 3 > 0$ and

$f_{xx}(x, y) = 6 > 0$; thus there is a relative

minimum at $(1, 1)$. At $\left(\frac{1}{2}, \frac{1}{4}\right)$,

$D = (3)(2) - (-3)^2 = -3 < 0$; thus there is

no relative extremum at $\left(\frac{1}{2}, \frac{1}{4}\right)$.

13. $f(x, y) = \frac{1}{3}\left(x^3 + 8y^3\right) - 2\left(x^2 + y^2\right) + 1$

$$\begin{cases} f_x(x, y) = x^2 - 4x = 0 \\ f_y(x, y) = 8y^2 - 4y = 0 \end{cases}$$

Critical points: $(0, 0)$, $\left(4, \frac{1}{2}\right)$, $\left(0, \frac{1}{2}\right)$, $(4, 0)$

Second-Derivative Test

$f_{xx}(x, y) = 2x - 4$, $f_{yy}(x, y) = 16y - 4$,

$f_{xy}(x, y) = 0$. At $(0, 0)$,

$D = (-4)(-4) - 0^2 = 16 > 0$ and

$f_{xx}(x, y) = -4 < 0$; thus a relative

maximum.

At $\left(4, \frac{1}{2}\right)$, $D = (4)(4) - 0^2 = 16 > 0$ and $f_{xx}(x, y) = 4 > 0$; thus a relative minimum.

At $\left(0, \frac{1}{2}\right)$, $D = (-4)(4) - 0^2 = -16 > 0$; thus neither.

At $(4, 0)$, $D = (4)(-4) - 0^2 = -16 < 0$, thus neither.

15. $f(l, k) = 2lk - l^2 + 264k - 10l - 2k^2$
$$\begin{cases} f_l(l, k) = 2k - 2l - 10 = 0 \\ f_k(l, k) = -4k + 2l + 264 = 0 \end{cases}$$
Critical point: $(122, 127)$
Second-Derivative Test
$f_{ll}(l, k) = -2$, $f_{kk}(l, k) = -4$, $f_{lk}(l, k) = 2$
At $(122, 127)$, $D = (-2)(-4) - 2^2 = 4 > 0$ and $f_{ll}(l, k) = -2 < 0$; thus there is a relative maximum at $(122, 127)$.

17. $f(p, q) = pq - \dfrac{1}{p} - \dfrac{1}{q}$
$$\begin{cases} f_p(p, q) = q + \dfrac{1}{p^2} = 0 \\ f_q(p, q) = p + \dfrac{1}{q^2} = 0 \end{cases}$$
Critical point: $(-1, -1)$
Second-Derivative Test
$f_{pp}(p, q) = -\dfrac{2}{p^3}$, $f_{qq}(p, q) = -\dfrac{2}{q^3}$, $f_{pq}(p, q) = 1$. At $(-1, -1)$,
$D = (2)(2) - 1^2 = 3 > 0$ and $f_{pp}(p, q) = 2 > 0$; thus there is a relative minimum at $(-1, -1)$.

19. $f(x, y) = \left(y^2 - 4\right)\left(e^x - 1\right)$
$$\begin{cases} f_x(x, y) = e^x\left(y^2 - 4\right) = 0 & (1) \\ f_y(x, y) = 2y\left(e^x - 1\right) = 0 & (2) \end{cases}$$
From (1), $y = \pm 2$. From (2), $x = 0$, $y = 0$. The only critical points are $(0, -2)$ and $(0, 2)$. [$y = 0$ does not give rise to a common solution of (1) and (2).]
Second-Derivative Test
$f_{xx}(x, y) = e^x\left(y^2 - 4\right)$,
$f_{yy}(x, y) = 2\left(e^x - 1\right)$, $f_{xy}(x, y) = 2ye^x$. At $(0, -2)$, $D = (0)(0) - (-4)^2 = -16 < 0$; thus neither. At $(0, 2)$,
$D = (0)(0) - (4)^2 = -16 < 0$; thus neither.

21. $P = f(l, k)$
$= 1.08l^2 - 0.03l^3 + 1.68k^2 - 0.08k^3$
$$\begin{cases} P_l = 2.16l - 0.09l^2 = 0 \\ P_k = 3.36k - 0.24k^2 = 0 \end{cases}$$
Critical points: $(0, 0)$, $(0, 14)$, $(24, 0)$, $(24, 14)$
Second-Derivative Test
$P_{ll} = 2.16 - 0.18l$, $P_{kk} = 3.36 - 0.48k$, $P_{lk} = 0$. At $(0, 0)$,
$D = (2.16)(3.36) - 0^2 > 0$ and $P_{ll} = 2.16 > 0$; thus relative minimum.
At $(0, 14)$, $D = (2.16)(-3.36) - 0^2 < 0$; thus no extremum. At $(24, 0)$,
$D = (-2.16)(3.36) - 0^2 < 0$; thus no extremum. At $(24, 14)$,
$D = (-2.16)(-3.36) - 0^2 > 0$ and $P_{ll} = -2.16 < 0$, so relative maximum Thus $l = 24$, $k = 14$ gives a relative maximum.

23. Profit per lb for $A = p_A - 60$.

Profit per lb for $B = p_B - 70$.

Total Profit $= P = (p_A - 60)q_A + (p_B - 70)q_B$

$P = (p_A - 60)[5(p_B - p_A)] + (p_B - 70)[500 + 5(p_A - 2p_B)]$

Thus

$\begin{cases} \dfrac{\partial P}{\partial p_A} = -10(p_A - p_B + 5) = 0 \\ \dfrac{\partial P}{\partial p_B} = 10(p_A - 2p_B + 90) = 0 \end{cases}$

Critical point: $p_A = 80$, $p_B = 85$

Second-Derivative Test

$\dfrac{\partial^2 P}{\partial p_A^2} = -10$, $\dfrac{\partial^2 P}{\partial p_B^2} = -20$, $\dfrac{\partial^2 P}{\partial p_B \partial p_A} = 10$. When $p_A = 80$ and $p_B = 85$, then

$D = (-10)(-20) - (10)^2 = 100 > 0$ and $\dfrac{\partial^2 P}{\partial p_A^2} = -10 < 0$; thus relative maximum at $p_A = 80$, $p_B = 85$.

25. $p_A = 100 - q_A$, $p_B = 84 - q_B$, $c = 600 + 4(q_A + q_B)$.

Revenue from market $A = r_A = p_A q_A = (100 - q_A)q_A$.

Revenue from market $B = r_B = p_B q_B = (84 - q_B)q_B$.

Total Profit = Total Revenue − Total Cost

$P = (100 - q_A)q_A + (84 - q_B)q_B - [600 + 4(q_A + q_B)]$

$\begin{cases} \dfrac{\partial P}{\partial q_A} = 96 - 2q_A = 0 \\ \dfrac{\partial P}{\partial q_B} = 80 - 2q_B = 0 \end{cases}$

Critical point: $q_A = 48$, $q_B = 40$

$\dfrac{\partial^2 P}{\partial q_A^2} = -2$, $\dfrac{\partial^2 P}{\partial q_B^2} = -2$, $\dfrac{\partial^2 P}{\partial q_B \partial q_A} = 0$.

At $q_A = 48$ and $q_B = 40$, then $D = (-2)(-2) - 0^2 = 4 > 0$ and $\dfrac{\partial^2 P}{\partial q_A^2} = -2 < 0$; thus relative maximum at

$q_A = 48$, $q_B = 40$. When $q_A = 48$ and $q_B = 40$, then selling prices are $p_A = 52$, $p_B = 44$, and profit = 3304.

27. $c = 1.5q_A^2 + 4.5q_B^2$, $p_A = 36 - q_A^2$, $p_B = 30 - q_B^2$

Total Profit = Total Revenue – Total Cost

$$P = (p_A q_A + p_B q_B) - c$$

$$P = 36q_A - q_A^3 + 30q_B - q_B^3 - (1.5q_A^2 + 4.5q_B^2)$$

$$\begin{cases} \dfrac{\partial P}{\partial q_A} = 36 - 3q_A - 3q_A^2 = 3(4 + q_A)(3 - q_A) \\ \dfrac{\partial P}{\partial q_B} = 30 - 9q_B - 3q_B^2 = 3(5 + q_B)(2 - q_B) \end{cases}$$

Since we want $q_A \geq 0$ and $q_B \geq 0$, the Critical point occurs when $q_A = 3$ and $q_B = 2$.

$\dfrac{\partial^2 P}{\partial q_A^2} = -3 - 6q_A$, $\dfrac{\partial^2 P}{\partial q_B^2} = -9 - 6q_B$, $\dfrac{\partial^2 P}{\partial q_B \partial_A} = 0$. When $q_A = 3$ and $q_B = 2$, then

$D = (-21)(-21) - 0^2 > 0$ and $\dfrac{\partial^2 P}{\partial q_A^2} = -21 < 0$; thus relative maximum at $q_A = 3$, $q_B = 2$.

29. Refer to the diagram in the text.

$xyz = 6$

$C = 3xy + 2[1(xz)] + 2[0.5(yz)]$

Note that $z = \dfrac{6}{xy}$. Thus

$$C = 3xy + 2xz + yz = 3xy + 2x\left(\dfrac{6}{xy}\right) + y\left(\dfrac{6}{xy}\right)$$

$$= 3xy + \dfrac{12}{y} + \dfrac{6}{x}$$

$$\begin{cases} \dfrac{\partial C}{\partial x} = 3y - \dfrac{6}{x^2} = 0 \\ \dfrac{dC}{dy} = 3x - \dfrac{12}{y^2} = 0 \end{cases}$$

A critical point occurs at $x = 1$ and $y = 2$.
Thus $z = 3$.

$\dfrac{\partial^2 C}{\partial x^2} = \dfrac{12}{x^3}$, $\dfrac{\partial^2 C}{\partial y^2} = \dfrac{24}{y^3}$, $\dfrac{\partial^2 C}{\partial x \partial y} = 3$.

When $x = 1$ and $y = 2$, then

$d = (12)(3) - (3)^2 = 27 > 0$ and

$\dfrac{\partial^2 C}{\partial x^2} = 12 > 0$. Thus we have a minimum.

The dimensions should be
1 ft by 2 ft by 3 ft.

31. $y = \dfrac{3x - 7}{2}$

$$f(x, y) = -2x^2 + 5\left(\dfrac{3x - 7}{2}\right)^2 + 7$$

Setting the derivative equal to 0 gives

$-4x + 5(2)\left(\dfrac{3x-7}{2}\right)\left(\dfrac{3}{2}\right) = 0$,

$-4x + \dfrac{15}{2}(3x - 7) = 0$,

$-8x + 15(3x - 7) = 0$, $37x = 105$, or

$x = \dfrac{105}{37}$. The second-derivative is $\dfrac{37}{2} > 0$,

so we have a relative minimum. If $x = \dfrac{105}{37}$,

then $y = \dfrac{28}{37}$. Thus there is a relative

minimum at $\left(\dfrac{105}{37}, \dfrac{28}{37}\right)$.

33. $c = q_A^2 + 3q_B^2 + 2q_A q_B + aq_A + bq_B + d$

We are given that $(q_A, q_B) = (3, 1)$ is a critical point.

$$\begin{cases} \dfrac{\partial c}{\partial q_A} = 2q_A + 2q_B + a = 0 \\ \dfrac{\partial c}{\partial q_B} = 6q_B + 2q_A + b = 0 \end{cases}$$

Substituting the given values for q_A and q_B into both equations gives $a = -8$ and $b = -12$. Since $c = 15$ when $q_A = 3$ and $q_B = 1$, from the joint-cost function we have

$15 = 3^2 + 3(1^2) + 2(3)(1) + (-8)(3) + (-12) + d,$

$15 = -18 + d$, $33 = d$. Thus $a = -8$, $b = -12$, $d = 33$.

35. a. Profit = Total Revenue − Total Cost

$P = p_A q_A + p_B q_B - $ total cost

$$= \left(35 - 2q_A^2 + q_B\right)q_A + \left(20 - q_B + q_A\right)q_B - \left(-8 - 2q_A^3 + 3q_A q_B + 30q_A + 12q_B + \frac{1}{2}q_A^2\right)$$

$P = 5q_A - \dfrac{1}{2}q_A^2 - q_A q_B + 8q_B - q_B^2 + 8$

$$\begin{cases} \dfrac{\partial P}{\partial q_A} = 5 - q_A - q_B = 0 \\ \dfrac{\partial P}{\partial q_B} = -q_A + 8 - 2q_B = 0 \end{cases}$$

Critical point: $q_A = 2$, $q_B = 3$

$\dfrac{\partial^2 P}{\partial q_A^2} = -1$, $\dfrac{\partial^2 P}{\partial q_B^2} = -2$, $\dfrac{\partial^2 P}{\partial q_B \partial q_A} = -1$

At $q_A = 2$ and $q_B = 3$, then $D = (-1)(-2) - (-1)^2 = 1 > 0$ and $\dfrac{\partial^2 P}{\partial q_A^2} = -1 < 0$;

thus there is a relative maximum profit for 2 units of A and 3 units of B.

b. Substituting $q_A = 2$ and $q_B = 3$ into the formulas for p_A, p_B, and P gives a selling price for A of 30, a selling price for B of 19, and a relative maximum profit of 25.

37. a. $P = 5T\left(1 - e^{-x}\right) - 20x - 0.1T^2$

b. $\dfrac{\partial P}{\partial T} = 5\left(1 - e^{-x}\right) - 0.2T$

$\dfrac{\partial P}{\partial x} = 5Te^{-x} - 20$

At the point $(T, x) = (20, \ln 5)$,

$\dfrac{\partial P}{\partial T} = 5\left(1 - e^{-\ln 5}\right) - 0.2(20) = 5\left(1 - \dfrac{1}{5}\right) - 4 = 0$

$\dfrac{\partial P}{\partial x} = 5(20)e^{-\ln 5} - 20 = 100\left(\dfrac{1}{5}\right) - 20 = 0$

Thus $(20, \ln 5)$ is a critical point. In a similar fashion we verify that $\left(5, \ln\dfrac{5}{4}\right)$ is a critical point.

c. $\dfrac{\partial^2 P}{\partial T^2} = -0.2$, $\dfrac{\partial^2 P}{\partial x^2} = -5Te^{-x}$,

$\dfrac{\partial^2 P}{\partial T \partial x} = 5e^{-x}$

At (20, ln 5),

$D = (-0.2)\left[-5(20)e^{-\ln 5}\right] - \left(5e^{-\ln 5}\right)^2$

$= 20\left(\dfrac{1}{5}\right) - \left[5\left(\dfrac{1}{5}\right)\right]^2 = 3 > 0$,

and $\dfrac{\partial^2 P}{\partial T^2} = -0.2 < 0$. Thus we get a

relative maximum at (20, ln 5).

At $\left(5, \ln\dfrac{5}{4}\right)$,

$D = (-0.2)\left[-5(5)e^{-\ln\left(\frac{5}{4}\right)}\right] - \left[5e^{-\ln\left(\frac{5}{4}\right)}\right]^2$

$= 5\left(\dfrac{4}{5}\right) - \left[5\left(\dfrac{4}{5}\right)\right]^2 = -12 < 0$, so there is

no relative extremum at $\left(5, \ln\dfrac{5}{4}\right)$.

Exercise 19.8

1. $f(x, y) = x^2 + 4y^2 + 6$, $2x - 8y = 20$

$F(x, y, \lambda) = x^2 + 4y^2 + 6 - \lambda(2x - 8y - 20)$

$\begin{cases} F_x = 2x - 2\lambda = 0 & (1) \\ F_y = 8y + 8\lambda = 0 & (2) \\ F_\lambda = -2x + 8y + 20 = 0 & (3) \end{cases}$

From (1), $x = \lambda$; from (2), $y = -\lambda$.
Substituting $x = \lambda$ and $y = -\lambda$ into (3)
gives $-2\lambda - 8\lambda + 20 = 0$, $-10\lambda = -20$, so
$\lambda = 2$. Thus $x = 2$ and $y = -2$. Critical point
of F: (2, –2, 2). Critical point of f: (2, –2).

3. $f(x, y, z) = x^2 + y^2 + z^2$, $2x + y - z = 9$

$F(x, y, z, \lambda) = x^2 + y^2 + z^2 - \lambda(2x + y - z - 9)$

$\begin{cases} F_x = 2x - 2\lambda = 0 & (1) \\ F_y = 2y - \lambda = 0 & (2) \\ F_z = 2z + \lambda = 0 & (3) \\ F_\lambda = -2x - y + z + 9 = 0 & (4) \end{cases}$

From (1), $x = \lambda$; from (2), $y = \dfrac{\lambda}{2}$; from (3),

$z = -\dfrac{\lambda}{2}$. Substituting into (4) gives

$-2\lambda - \dfrac{\lambda}{2} + \left(\dfrac{-\lambda}{2}\right) + 9 = 0$, $-6\lambda + 18 = 0$, so

$\lambda = 3$. Thus $x = 3$, $y = \dfrac{3}{2}$, $z = -\dfrac{3}{2}$.

Critical point of F: $\left(3, \dfrac{3}{2}, -\dfrac{3}{2}, 3\right)$.

Critical point of f: $\left(3, \dfrac{3}{2}, -\dfrac{3}{2}\right)$.

5. $f(x, y, z) = x^2 + xy + 2y^2 + z^2$, $x - 3y - 4z$
$= 16$

$F(x, y, z, \lambda)$
$= x^2 + xy + 2y^2 + z^2 - \lambda(x - 3y - 4z - 16)$

$\begin{cases} F_x = 2x + y - \lambda = 0 & (1) \\ F_y = x + 4y + 3\lambda = 0 & (2) \\ F_z = 2z + 4\lambda = 0 & (3) \\ F_\lambda = -x + 3y + 4z + 16 = 0 & (4) \end{cases}$

Eliminating x from (1) and (2) yields $y = -\lambda$.
Substituting $y = -\lambda$ into (2) yields $x = \lambda$.
From (3), $z = -2\lambda$. Substituting $x = \lambda$,
$y = -\lambda$, and $z = -2\lambda$ into (4) yields $\lambda = \dfrac{4}{3}$.

Critical point of F: $\left(\dfrac{4}{3}, -\dfrac{4}{3}, -\dfrac{8}{3}, \dfrac{4}{3}\right)$.

Critical point of f: $\left(\dfrac{4}{3}, -\dfrac{4}{3}, -\dfrac{8}{3}\right)$.

7. $f(x, y, z) = xyz$, $x + 2y + 3z = 18$ $(xyz \neq 0)$
$f(x, y, z, \lambda) = xyz - \lambda(x + 2y + 3z - 18)$

$\begin{cases} F_x = yz - \lambda = 0 & (1) \\ F_y = xz - 2\lambda = 0 & (2) \\ F_z = xy - 3\lambda = 0 & (3) \\ F_\lambda = -x - 2y - 3z + 18 = 0 & (4) \end{cases}$

From (1) and (2), $y = \dfrac{x}{2}$. From (1) and (3),

$z = \dfrac{x}{3}$. Hence from (4), $x = 6$, so $y = 3$ and

$z = 2$. Critical point of f is (6, 3, 2). Note that
it is not necessary to determine λ.

9. $f(x, y, z) = x^2 + 2y - z^2, 2x - y = 0, y + z = 0$

Since there are two constraints, two Lagrange multipliers are used.

$F(x, y, z, \lambda_1, \lambda_2) = x^2 + 2y - z^2 - \lambda_1(2x - y) - \lambda_2(y + z)$

$\begin{cases} F_x = 2x - 2\lambda_1 = 0 & (1) \\ F_y = 2 + \lambda_1 - \lambda_2 = 0 & (2) \\ F_z = -2z - \lambda_2 = 0 & (3) \\ F_{\lambda_1} = -2x + y = 0 & (4) \\ F_{\lambda_2} = -y - z = 0 & (5) \end{cases}$

From (1), $x = \lambda_1$. From (3), $z = -\dfrac{\lambda_2}{2}$. From (4) and (5), $2x = -z$, so $\lambda_1 = \dfrac{\lambda_2}{4}$. Substituting $\lambda_1 = \dfrac{\lambda_2}{4}$ into (2) yields $\lambda_2 = \dfrac{8}{3}$. Thus $\lambda_1 = \dfrac{2}{3}$, $x = \dfrac{2}{3}$, and $z = -\dfrac{4}{3}$. From (5), $y = -z$ and hence $y = \dfrac{4}{3}$. Critical point of f: $\left(\dfrac{2}{3}, \dfrac{4}{3}, -\dfrac{4}{3}\right)$

11. $f(x, y, z) = xyz, x + y + z = 12, x + y - z = 0 \ (xyz \neq 0)$

Since there are two constraints, we use two Lagrange multipliers.

$F(x, y, z, \lambda_1, \lambda_2) = xyz - \lambda_1(x + y + z - 12) - \lambda_2(x + y - z)$

$\begin{cases} F_x = yz - \lambda_1 - \lambda_2 = 0 & (1) \\ F_y = xz - \lambda_1 - \lambda_2 = 0 & (2) \\ F_z = xy - \lambda_1 + \lambda_2 = 0 & (3) \\ F_{\lambda_1} = -x - y - z + 12 = 0 & (4) \\ F_{\lambda_2} = -x - y + z = 0 & (5) \end{cases}$

Subtracting (2) from (1) gives $yz - xz = 0$, so $y = x$. Subtracting (5) from (4) gives $-2z + 12 = 0$, so $z = 6$. Substituting $y = x$ and $z = 6$ in (5) gives $-2x + 6 = 0$, so $x = 3$. Thus $y = 3$. Critical point of f: (3, 3, 6).

13. We minimize $c = f(q_1, q_2) = 0.1q_1^2 + 7q_1 + 15q_2 + 1000$ subject to the constraint $q_1 + q_2 = 100$.

$F(q_1, q_2, \lambda) = 0.1q_1^2 + 7q_1 + 15q_2 + 1000 - \lambda(q_1 + q_2 - 100)$

$\begin{cases} F_{q_1} = 0.2q_1 + 7 - \lambda = 0 & (1) \\ F_{q_2} = 15 - \lambda = 0 & (2) \\ F_\lambda = -q_1 - q_2 + 100 = 0 & (3) \end{cases}$

From (2), $\lambda = 15$. Substituting $\lambda = 15$ into (1) gives $0.2q_1 + 7 - 15 = 0$, so $q_1 = 40$. Substituting $q_1 = 40$ into (3) gives $-40 - q_2 + 100 = 0$, so $q_2 = 60$. Thus $\lambda = 15$, $q_1 = 40$ and $q = 60$. Thus plant 1 should produce 40 units and plant 2 should produce 60 units.

15. We maximize $f(l, k) = 12l + 20k - l^2 - 2k^2$ subject to the constraint $4l + 8k = 88$.

$F(l, k, \lambda) = 12l + 20k - l^2 - 2k^2 - \lambda(4l + 8k - 88)$

$$\begin{cases} F_l = 12 - 2l - 4\lambda = 0 & (1) \\ F_k = 20 - 4k - 8\lambda = 0 & (2) \\ F_\lambda = -4l - 8k + 88 = 0 & (3) \end{cases}$$

Eliminating λ from (1) and (2) yields $k = l - 1$. Substituting $k = l - 1$ into (3) yields $l = 8$, so $k = 7$. Therefore the greatest output is $f(8, 7) = 74$ units (when $l = 8, k = 7$).

17. We maximize $P(x, y) = 9x^{\frac{1}{4}}y^{\frac{3}{4}} - x - y$ subject to the constraint $x + y = 60,000$.

$F(x, y, \lambda) = 9x^{\frac{1}{4}}y^{\frac{3}{4}} - x - y - \lambda(x + y - 60,000)$

$$\begin{cases} F_x = \dfrac{9}{4}x^{-\frac{3}{4}}y^{\frac{3}{4}} - 1 - \lambda = 0 & (1) \\ F_y = \dfrac{27}{4}x^{\frac{1}{4}}y^{-\frac{1}{4}} - 1 - \lambda = 0 & (2) \\ F_\lambda = -x - y + 60,000 = 0 & (3) \end{cases}$$

Solving (2) for λ and substituting in (1) gives $\dfrac{9}{4}x^{-\frac{3}{4}}y^{\frac{3}{4}} - \dfrac{27}{4}x^{\frac{1}{4}}y^{-\frac{1}{4}} = 0$, $\dfrac{9}{4}x^{-\frac{3}{4}}y^{\frac{3}{4}} = \dfrac{27}{4}x^{\frac{1}{4}}y^{-\frac{1}{4}}$, $y = 3x$.

Substituting for y in (3) $\Rightarrow -4x - 60,000 = 0$, so $x = 15,000$, from which $y = 45,000$. Thus each month $\$15,000$ should be spent on newspaper advertising and $\$45,000$ on TV advertising.

19. We minimize $B(x, y, z) = x^2 + y^2 + 2z^2$ subject to $x + y = 20$ and $y + z = 20$.

Since there are two constraints, we use two Lagrange multipliers.

$F(x, y, z, \lambda_1, \lambda_2) = x^2 + y^2 + 2z^2 - \lambda_1(x + y - 20) - \lambda_2(y + z - 20)$

$$\begin{cases} F_x = 2x - \lambda_1 = 0 & (1) \\ F_y = 2y - \lambda_1 - \lambda_2 = 0 & (2) \\ F_z = 4z - \lambda_2 = 0 & (3) \\ F_{\lambda_1} = -x - y + 20 = 0 & (4) \\ F_{\lambda_2} = -y - z + 20 = 0 & (5) \end{cases}$$

Eliminating y from (4) and (5) gives $x = z$. From (1) and (3), $\lambda_1 = 2x$ and $\lambda_2 = 4z$. Substituting in (2) we have $2y - 2x - 4z = 0$, $2y - 2x - 4x = 0$, $2y - 6x = 0$, $y = 3x$. Substituting in (5) gives $-(3x) - x + 20 = 0$, so $x = 5$. Thus $z = 5$ and $y = 15$. Therefore, $x = 5, y = 15, z = 5$.

21. $U = x^3 y^3$, $p_x = 2$, $p_y = 3$,

$I = 48 \left(x^3 y^3 \neq 0 \right)$

We want to maximize $U = x^3 y^3$ subject to $2x + 3y = 48$.

$F(x, y, \lambda) = x^3 y^3 - \lambda(2x + 3y - 48)$

$$\begin{cases} F_x = 3x^2 y^3 - 2\lambda = 0 & (1) \\ F_y = 3x^3 y^2 - 3\lambda = 0 & (2) \\ F_\lambda = -2x - 3y + 48 = 0 & (3) \end{cases}$$

From (1), $\lambda = \dfrac{3}{2} x^2 y^3$ and from (2),

$\lambda = x^3 y^2$. Thus $\dfrac{3}{2} x^2 y^3 = x^3 y^2$, so $x = \dfrac{3}{2} y$.

Substituting this expression for x into (3)

yields $y = 8$. Hence $x = \left(\dfrac{3}{2} \right) 8 = 12$.

23. $U = f(x, y, z) = xyz$
$p_x = 2$, $p_y = 1$, $p_z = 4$, $I = 60$

$(xyz \neq 0)$

$F(x, y, z, \lambda) = xyz - \lambda(2x + y + 4z - 60)$

$$\begin{cases} F_x = yz - 2\lambda = 0 & (1) \\ F_y = xz - \lambda = 0 & (2) \\ F_z = xy - 4\lambda = 0 & (3) \\ F_\lambda = -2x - y - 4z + 60 = 0 & (4) \end{cases}$$

From (1) and (2), $\dfrac{1}{2} yz = xz$, so $y = 2x$.

Similarly, from (1) and (3), $z = \dfrac{x}{2}$.

Substituting $y = 2x$ and $z = \dfrac{x}{2}$ into (4) yields $x = 10$. Thus $y = 20$ and $z = 5$.

Exercise 19.9

1. $n = 6$, $\Sigma x_i = 21$, $\Sigma y_i = 18.6$, $\Sigma x_i y_i = 75.7$,
$\Sigma x_i^2 = 91$.

$$\hat{a} = \frac{\left(\Sigma x_i^2 \right)\left(\Sigma y_i \right) - \left(\Sigma x_i \right)\left(\Sigma x_i y_i \right)}{n \Sigma x_i^2 - \left(\Sigma x_i \right)^2}$$

$$= \frac{91(18.6) - 21(75.7)}{6(91) - (21)^2} = 0.98$$

$$\hat{b} = \frac{n \Sigma x_i y_i - \left(\Sigma x_i \right)\left(\Sigma y_i \right)}{n \Sigma x_i^2 - \left(\Sigma x_i \right)^2}$$

$$= \frac{6(75.7) - 21(18.6)}{6(91) - (21)^2} = 0.61$$

Thus $\hat{y} = 0.98 + 0.61x$. When $x = 3.5$, then
$\hat{y} = 3.12$.

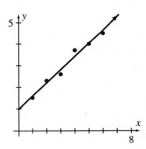

3. $n = 5$, $\Sigma x_i = 22$, $\Sigma y_i = 37$, $\Sigma x_i y_i = 189$,
$\Sigma x_i^2 = 112.5$. $\hat{a} = 0.057$, $\hat{b} = 1.67$. Thus
$\hat{y} = 0.057 + 1.67x$. When $x = 3.5$, then
$\hat{y} = 5.90$.

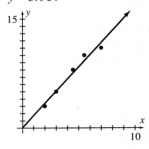

5. $n = 6$,

$\Sigma p_i = 260$, $\Sigma q_i = 329$, $\Sigma p_i q_i = 12,760$,

$\Sigma p_i^2 = 13,600$.

$$\hat{a} = \frac{\left(\Sigma p_i^2\right)\left(\Sigma q_i\right) - \left(\Sigma p_i\right)\left(\Sigma p_i q_i\right)}{n\Sigma p_i^2 - \left(\Sigma p_i\right)^2}$$

$$= \frac{(13,600)(329) - (260)(12,760)}{6(13,600) - (260)^2} = 82.6$$

$$\hat{b} = \frac{n\Sigma p_i q_i - \left(\Sigma p_i\right)\left(\Sigma q_i\right)}{n\Sigma p_i^2 - \left(\Sigma p_i\right)^2}$$

$$= \frac{6(12,760) - (260)(329)}{6(13,600) - (260)^2} = -0.641$$

Thus $\hat{q} = 82.6 - 0.641p$.

7. $n = 4$,

$\Sigma x_i = 160$, $\Sigma y_i = 420.8$, $\Sigma x_i y_i = 16,915.2$,

$\Sigma x_i^2 = 7040$. $\hat{a} = 100$, $\hat{b} = 0.13$. Thus

$\hat{y} = 100 + 0.13x$. When $x = 40$, then

$\hat{y} = 105.2$.

9.

Year (x)	1	2	3	4	5
Production (y)	10	15	16	18	21

$n = 5$,

$\Sigma x_i = 15$, $\Sigma y_i = 80$, $\Sigma x_i y_i = 265$, $\Sigma x_i^2 = 55$.

$$\hat{a} = \frac{\left(\Sigma x_i^2\right)\left(\Sigma y_i\right) - \left(\Sigma x_i\right)\left(\Sigma x_i y_i\right)}{n\Sigma x_i^2 - \left(\Sigma x_i\right)^2}$$

$$= \frac{55(80) - 15(265)}{5(55) - (15)^2} = 8.5$$

$$\hat{b} = \frac{n\Sigma x_i y_i - \left(\Sigma x_i\right)\left(\Sigma y_i\right)}{n\Sigma x_i^2 - \left(\Sigma x_i\right)^2}$$

$$= \frac{5(265) - 15(80)}{5(55) - (15)^2} = 2.5$$

Thus $\hat{y} = 8.5 + 2.5x$

11. a.

Year (x)	1	2	3	4	5
Quantity (y)	35	31	26	24	26

$n = 5$, $\Sigma x_i = 15$, $\Sigma y_i = 142$, $\Sigma x_i y_i = 401$, $\Sigma x_i^2 = 55$. $\hat{a} = 35.9$, $\hat{b} = -2.5$. Thus $\hat{y} = 35.9 - 2.5x$.

b.

Year (x)	−2	−1	0	1	2
Quantity (y)	35	31	26	24	26

$n = 5$, $\Sigma x_i = 0$, $\Sigma y_i = 142$, $\Sigma x_i y_i = -25$, $\Sigma x_i^2 = 10$. $\hat{a} = \dfrac{\Sigma y_i}{n} = 28.4$ and $\hat{b} = \dfrac{\Sigma x_i y_i}{\Sigma x_i^2} = -2.5$.

Thus $\hat{y} = 28.4 - 2.5x$.

Exercise 19.11

1. $\displaystyle\int_0^3\int_0^4 x\,dy\,dx = \int_0^3 xy\Big|_0^4\,dx = \int_0^3 4x\,dx = 2x^2\Big|_0^3 = 18$

3. $\displaystyle\int_0^1\int_0^1 xy\,dx\,dy = \int_0^1 \frac{x^2 y}{2}\Big|_0^1\,dy = \int_0^1 \frac{y}{2}\,dy = \frac{y^2}{4}\Big|_0^1 = \frac{1}{4}$

5. $\displaystyle\int_1^3\int_1^2\left(x^2-y\right)dx\,dy=\int_1^3\left(\frac{x^3}{3}-xy\right)\Big|_1^2 dy$

$\displaystyle=\int_1^3\left[\left(\frac{8}{3}-2y\right)-\left(\frac{1}{3}-y\right)\right]dy=\int_1^3\left(\frac{7}{3}-y\right)dy$

$\displaystyle=\left(\frac{7}{3}y-\frac{y^2}{2}\right)\Big|_1^3=\left(7-\frac{9}{2}\right)-\left(\frac{7}{3}-\frac{1}{2}\right)=\frac{2}{3}$

7. $\displaystyle\int_0^1\int_0^2(x+y)dy\,dx=\int_0^1\left(xy+\frac{y^2}{2}\right)\Big|_0^2 dx$

$\displaystyle=\int_0^1(2x+2)dx=\left(x^2+2x\right)\Big|_0^1=3$

9. $\displaystyle\int_0^6\int_0^{3x}y\,dy\,dx=\int_0^6\frac{y^2}{2}\Big|_0^{3x}dx$

$\displaystyle=\int_0^6\frac{9x^2}{2}dx=\frac{3x^3}{2}\Big|_0^6=324$

11. $\displaystyle\int_0^1\int_{3x}^{x^2}14x^2y\,dy\,dx=\int_0^1\left(7x^2y^2\right)\Big|_{3x}^{x^2}dx$

$\displaystyle=\int_0^1\left(7x^6-63x^4\right)dx=\left(x^7-\frac{63x^5}{5}\right)\Big|_0^1$

$\displaystyle=-\frac{58}{5}$

13. $\displaystyle\int_0^2\int_0^{\sqrt{4-y^2}}x\,dx\,dy=\int_0^2\frac{x^2}{2}\Big|_0^{\sqrt{4-y^2}}dy$

$\displaystyle=\int_0^2\frac{4-y^2}{2}dy$

$\displaystyle=\int_0^2\left(2-\frac{y^2}{2}\right)dy=\left(2y-\frac{y^3}{6}\right)\Big|_0^2$

$\displaystyle=\left(4-\frac{4}{3}\right)-0=\frac{8}{3}$

15. $\displaystyle\int_{-1}^1\int_x^{1-x}3(x+y)dy\,dx$

$\displaystyle=\int_{-1}^1 3\left(xy+\frac{y^2}{2}\right)\Big|_x^{1-x}dx$

$\displaystyle=\int_{-1}^1 3\left[x(1-x)+\frac{(1-x)^2}{2}-\left(x^2+\frac{x^2}{2}\right)\right]dx$

$\displaystyle=\int_{-1}^1 3\left[x-\frac{5x^2}{2}+\frac{(1-x)^2}{2}\right]dx$

$\displaystyle=3\left[\frac{x^2}{2}-\frac{5x^3}{6}-\frac{(1-x)^3}{6}\right]_{-1}^1$

$\displaystyle=3\left[\frac{1}{2}-\frac{5}{6}-0\right]-3\left[\frac{1}{2}+\frac{5}{6}-\frac{4}{3}\right]=-1$

17. $\displaystyle\int_0^1\int_0^y e^{x+y}dx\,dy=\int_0^1 e^{x+y}\Big|_0^y dy$

$\displaystyle=\int_0^1\left(e^{2y}-e^y\right)dy$

$\displaystyle=\left[\frac{e^{2y}}{2}-e^y\right]_0^1=\frac{e^2}{2}-e-\left(\frac{1}{2}-1\right)$

$\displaystyle=\frac{e^2}{2}-e+\frac{1}{2}$

19. $\displaystyle\int_{-1}^0\int_{-1}^2\int_1^2 6xy^2z^3\,dx\,dy\,dz$

$\displaystyle=\int_{-1}^0\int_{-1}^2 3x^2y^2z^3\Big|_1^2 dy\,dz$

$\displaystyle=\int_{-1}^0\int_{-1}^2 9y^2z^3\,dy\,dz=\int_{-1}^0 3y^3z^3\Big|_{-1}^2 dz$

$\displaystyle=\int_{-1}^0 27z^3\,dz=\frac{27z^4}{4}\Big|_{-1}^0=-\frac{27}{4}$

21. $\int_0^1 \int_{x^2}^x \int_0^{xy} dz\, dy\, dx = \int_0^1 \int_{x^2}^x z\Big|_0^{xy} dy\, dx$

$= \int_0^1 \int_{x^2}^x xy\, dy\, dx = \int_0^1 \frac{xy^2}{2}\Big|_{x^2}^x dx$

$= \int_0^1 \left[\frac{x^3}{2} - \frac{x^5}{2}\right] dx = \left[\frac{x^4}{8} - \frac{x^6}{12}\right]_0^1 = \frac{1}{24}$

23. $P(0 \le x \le 2,\ 1 \le y \le 2) = \int_1^2 \int_0^2 e^{-(x+y)} dx\, dy$

$= \int_1^2 -e^{-(x+y)}\Big|_0^2 dy = \int_1^2 \left[-e^{-(2+y)} + e^{-y}\right] dy$

$= \left[e^{-(2+y)} - e^{-y}\right]_1^2 = e^{-4} - e^{-2} - e^{-3} + e^{-1}$

25. $P(x \ge 1,\ y \ge 2) = \int_2^4 \int_1^2 \frac{x}{8} dx\, dy = \int_2^4 \frac{x^2}{16}\Big|_1^2 dy$

$= \int_2^4 \left(\frac{4}{16} - \frac{1}{16}\right) dy = \int_2^4 \frac{3}{16} dy = \frac{3y}{16}\Big|_2^4$

$= \frac{12}{16} - \frac{6}{16} = \frac{3}{8}$

Chapter 19 Review Problems

1. $2x + 3y + z = 9$ can be put in the form $Ax + By + Cz + D = 0$, so the graph is a plane. The intercepts are $\left(\frac{9}{2}, 0, 0\right)$, $(0, 3, 0)$, and $(0, 0, 9)$.

3. $z = y^2$. The y, z-trace is $z = y^2$, which is a parabola. For any fixed value of x, we obtain the parabola $z = y^2$.

5. $f_x(x, y) = 4(2x) + 6(1)y + 0 - 0 = 8x + 6y$
$f_y(x, y) = 0 + 6x(1) + 2y - 0 = 6x + 2y$

7. $\dfrac{\partial z}{\partial x} = \dfrac{(x+y)(1) - x(1)}{(x+y)^2} = \dfrac{y}{(x+y)^2}$

Because $z = x(x+y)^{-1}$,

$\dfrac{\partial z}{\partial y} = x\left[(-1)(x+y)^{-2}(1)\right] = -\dfrac{x}{(x+y)^2}$.

9. $f(x, y) = \ln\sqrt{x^2 + y^2} = \frac{1}{2}\ln\left(x^2 + y^2\right)$

$\dfrac{\partial}{\partial y}[f(x, y)] = \frac{1}{2} \cdot \dfrac{1}{x^2 + y^2}(2y) = \dfrac{y}{x^2 + y^2}$

11. $w_x(x, y, z) = 2xyze^{x^2yz}$

$w_{xy}(x, y, z) = 2xz\left[y\left(e^{x^2yz} \cdot x^2z\right) + e^{x^2yz} \cdot 1\right]$

$= 2xze^{x^2yz}\left(x^2yz + 1\right)$

13. $\dfrac{\partial}{\partial z}[f(x, y, z)] = (x+y)[2z]$

$\dfrac{\partial^2}{\partial z^2}[f(x, y, z)] = (x+y)[2] = 2(x+y)$

15. $\dfrac{\partial w}{\partial y} = (x\ln z)\left[e^{yz} \cdot z\right] = xze^{yz}\ln z$

$\dfrac{\partial w}{\partial z} = x\left[e^{yz} \cdot \frac{1}{z} + (\ln z)\left(e^{yz} \cdot y\right)\right]$

$= xe^{yz}\left[\frac{1}{z} + y\ln z\right]$

$\dfrac{\partial^2 w}{\partial x\partial z} = e^{yz}\left[\frac{1}{z} + y\ln z\right]$

17. $f(x, y, z) = \dfrac{x + y}{xz} = \dfrac{1}{z} + \dfrac{y}{xz}$

$f_x(x, y, z) = -\dfrac{y}{x^2 z}$

$f_{xy}(x, y, z) = -\dfrac{1}{x^2 z}$

$f_{xyz}(x, y, z) = \dfrac{1}{x^2 z^2}$

$f_{xyz}(2, 7, 4) = \dfrac{1}{2^2 \cdot 4^2} = \dfrac{1}{64}$

19. $\dfrac{\partial w}{\partial r} = \dfrac{\partial w}{\partial x}\dfrac{\partial x}{\partial r} + \dfrac{\partial w}{\partial y}\dfrac{\partial y}{\partial r}$

$\quad = (2x + 2y)\left(e^r\right) + (2x + 6y)\left(\dfrac{1}{r + s}\right)$

$\quad = 2(x + y)e^r + \dfrac{2(x + 3y)}{r + s}$

$\dfrac{\partial w}{\partial s} = \dfrac{\partial w}{\partial x}\dfrac{\partial x}{\partial s} + \dfrac{\partial w}{\partial y}\dfrac{\partial y}{\partial s}$

$\quad = (2x + 2y)(0) + (2x + 6y)\left(\dfrac{1}{r + s}\right)$

$\quad = \dfrac{2(x + 3y)}{r + s}$

21. $2x + 2y - 4z\dfrac{\partial z}{\partial x} + \left[x\dfrac{\partial z}{\partial x} + z(1)\right] + 0 = 0$

$(-4z + x)\dfrac{\partial z}{\partial x} = -(2x + 2y + z)$

$\dfrac{\partial z}{\partial x} = \dfrac{-(2x + 2y + z)}{-4z + x} = \dfrac{2x + 2y + z}{4z - x}$

23. $P = 20l^{0.7}k^{0.3}$. Marginal productivity functions are given by

$\dfrac{\partial P}{\partial l} = 20(0.7)l^{-0.3}k^{0.3}$ and

$\dfrac{\partial P}{\partial k} = 20(0.3)l^{0.7}k^{-0.7}$. Thus

$\dfrac{\partial P}{\partial l} = 14l^{-0.3}k^{0.3}$ and $\dfrac{\partial P}{\partial k} = 6l^{0.7}k^{-0.7}$.

25. $q_A = 200 - 3p_A + p_B$, $q_B = 50 - 5p_B + p_A$.

Since $\dfrac{\partial q_A}{\partial p_B} = 1 > 0$ and $\dfrac{\partial q_B}{\partial p_A} = 1 > 0$, A and

B are competitive products.

27. $f(x, y) = x^2 + 2y^2 - 2xy - 4y + 3$

$\begin{cases} f_x(x, y) = 2x - 2y = 0 \\ f_y(x, y) = 4y - 2x - 4 = 0 \end{cases}$

Critical point: $(2, 2)$

$f_{xx}(x, y) = 2$, $f_{yy}(x, y) = 4$, $f_{xy}(x, y) = -2$

At $(2, 2)$, $D = (2)(4) - (-2)^2 = 4 > 0$ and $f_{xx}(x, y) = 2 > 0$; thus relative minimum at $(2, 2)$.

29.

$xyz = 32$. Let S be the amount of cardboard used.

$S = xy + 2yz + 2xz$

$= xy + 2y\left[\dfrac{32}{xy}\right] + 2x\left[\dfrac{32}{xy}\right]$

$= xy + \dfrac{64}{x} + \dfrac{64}{y}$

$\dfrac{\partial S}{\partial x} = y - \dfrac{64}{x^2}$, $\dfrac{\partial S}{\partial y} = x - \dfrac{64}{y^2}$

The critical point occurs when $x = 4$, $y = 4$, and $z = 2$, which gives a minimum.
The dimensions are 4 ft by 4 ft by 2 ft.

31. Profit $= P = (p_A - 50)q_A + (p_B - 60)q_B$

$P = (p_A - 50)\big[250(p_B - p_A)\big] + (p_B - 60)\big[32,000 + 250(p_A - 2p_B)\big]$.

$\dfrac{\partial P}{\partial p_A} = (p_A - 50)(-250) + \big[250(p_B - p_A)\big](1) + 250(p_B - 60)$

$= -500p_A + 500p_B - 250(10) = 500(-p_A + p_B - 5)$

Also, $\dfrac{\partial P}{\partial p_B} = (p_A - 50)(250) + (p_B - 60)(-500) + \big[32,000 + 250(p_A - 2p_B)\big]$

$= 500p_A - 1000p_B + 49,500 = 500(p_A - 2p_B + 99)$

Setting $\dfrac{\partial P}{\partial p_A} = 0$ and $\dfrac{\partial P}{\partial p_B} = 0$ gives

$-p_A + p_B - 5 = 0$ (1)

and

$p_A - 2p_B + 99 = 0$ (2)

Adding Equations (1) and (2) gives $-p_B + 94 = 0$. So $p_B = 94$. From Equation (1), $p_A = p_B - 5$, so

$p_A = 94 - 5 = 89$. At $p_A = 89$ and $p_B = 94$, $D = \dfrac{\partial^2 P}{\partial p_A^2}\dfrac{\partial^2 P}{\partial p_B^2} - \dfrac{\partial^2 P}{\partial p_B \partial p_A} = (-500)(-1000) - (500)^2 > 0$

and $\dfrac{\partial^2 P}{\partial p_A^2} = -500 < 0$.

Thus there is a relative maximum profit when A is 89 cents per pound and B is 94 cents per pound.

33. $f(x, y, z) = x^2 + y^2 + z^2$, $3x + 2y + z = 14$

$F(x, y, z, \lambda) = x^2 + y^2 + z^2 - \lambda(3x + 2y + z - 14)$

$$\begin{cases} F_x = 2x - 3\lambda = 0 & (1) \\ F_y = 2y - 2\lambda = 0 & (2) \\ F_z = 2z - \lambda = 0 & (3) \\ F_\lambda = -3x - 2y - z + 14 = 0 & (4) \end{cases}$$

From (1), $x = \frac{3\lambda}{2}$; from (2), $y = \lambda$, from (3), $z = \frac{\lambda}{2}$. Substituting into (4) gives

$-3\left(\frac{3\lambda}{2}\right) - 2\lambda - \frac{\lambda}{2} + 14 = 0$, from which $\lambda = 2$. Thus $x = 3$, $y = 2$, and $z = 1$.

Critical point of F: (3, 2, 1, 2), so the critical point of f: (3, 2, 1).

35.

Year (x)	1	2	3	4	5	6
Expenditures (y)	15	22	21	26	27	34

$n = 6$, $\Sigma x_i = 21$, $\Sigma y_i = 145$, $\Sigma x_i y_i = 565$, $\Sigma x_i^2 = 91$

$$\hat{a} = \frac{\left(\Sigma x_i^2\right)\left(\Sigma y_i\right) - \left(\Sigma x_i\right)\left(\Sigma x_i y_i\right)}{n\Sigma x_i^2 - \left(\Sigma x_i\right)^2} = 12.67$$

$$\hat{b} = \frac{n\Sigma x_i y_i - \left(\Sigma x_i\right)\left(\Sigma y_i\right)}{n\Sigma x_i^2 - \left(\Sigma x_i\right)^2} = 3.29$$

Thus $\hat{y} = 12.67 + 3.29x$

37. $\displaystyle\int_0^4\int_{y/2}^2 xy\, dx\, dy = \int_0^4 \frac{x^2 y}{2}\Big|_{y/2}^2 dy = \int_0^4\left(2y - \frac{y^3}{8}\right)dy = \left(y^2 - \frac{y^4}{32}\right)\Big|_0^4 = (16 - 8) - 0 = 8$

39. $\displaystyle\int_0^1\int_{\sqrt{x}}^{x^2} 7\left(x^2 + 2xy - 3y^2\right)dy\, dx = 7\int_0^1\left(x^2 y + xy^2 - y^3\right)\Big|_{\sqrt{x}}^{x^2} dx = 7\int_0^1\left[\left(x^4 + x^5 - x^6\right) - \left(x^{\frac{5}{2}} + x^2 - x^{\frac{3}{2}}\right)\right]dx$

$= 7\left[\frac{x^5}{5} + \frac{x^6}{6} - \frac{x^7}{7} - \frac{2x^{\frac{7}{2}}}{7} - \frac{x^3}{3} + \frac{2x^{\frac{5}{2}}}{5}\right]_0^1 = 7\left[\frac{1}{5} + \frac{1}{6} - \frac{1}{7} - \frac{2}{7} - \frac{1}{3} + \frac{2}{5}\right] - 0 = \frac{1}{30}$

Mathematical Snapshot Chapter 19

1.

$y = Ce^{ax} + 5$, $y - 5 = Ce^{ax}$, $\ln(y - 5) = ax + \ln C$

x	y	$y-5$	$\ln(y-5)$
0	15	10	2.30259
1	12	7	1.94591
4	9	4	1.38629
7	7	2	0.69315
10	6	1	0.00000

$n = 5$, $\Sigma x_i = 22$, $\Sigma \ln(y_i - 5) = 6.32794$, $\Sigma[x_i \ln(y_i - 5)] = 12.34312$, $\Sigma x_i^2 = 166$

$$a = \frac{n\Sigma[x_i \ln(y_i - 5)] - (\Sigma x_i)[\Sigma \ln(y_i - 5)]}{n(\Sigma x_i^2) - (\Sigma x_i)^2}$$

$$= \frac{5(12.34312) - 22(6.32794)}{5(166) - (22)^2} \approx -0.22399$$

$$\ln C = \frac{(\Sigma x_i^2)[\Sigma \ln(y_i - 5)] - (\Sigma x_i)\{\Sigma[x_i \ln(y_i - 5)]\}}{n(\Sigma x_i^2) - (\Sigma x_i)^2}$$

$$= \frac{166(6.32794) - 22(12.34312)}{5(166) - (22)^2} \approx 2.25112$$

$C \approx e^{2.25112} \approx 9.50$

Thus $y = 9.50e^{-0.22399x} + 5$.

3. Newton's law of cooling: $\frac{dT}{dt} = k(T - a)$, where $a = 45$. Thus $\frac{dT}{dt} = k(T - 45)$, $\frac{dT}{T - 45} = k\,dt$,

$\int \frac{dT}{T - 45} = \int k\,dt$, $\ln|T - 45| = kt + C$. Because $T - 45 > 0$, $\ln(T - 45) = kt + C$. Thus $T - 45 = e^{kt+C}$, or

$T = e^{kt+C} + 45 = e^C e^{kt} + 45 = C_1 e^{kt} + 45$, where $C_1 = e^C$. So $T = C_1 e^{kt} + 45$. When $t = 0$, then $T = 124$.

Hence $124 = C_1 + 45$, or $C_1 = 79$. Thus $T = 79e^{kt} + 45$. When $t = 128$, then $T = 64$, so

$64 = 79e^{128k} + 45$, $19 = 79e^{128k}$, $e^{128k} = \frac{19}{79}$, $128k = \ln\frac{19}{79}$, $k = \frac{\ln\left(\frac{19}{79}\right)}{128} \approx -0.01113$. Thus

$T = 79e^{-0.01113t} + 45$.

Appendix A

Exercise A.1

1.

3.

5. Let t represent the number of years after 1996, and P represent the population.

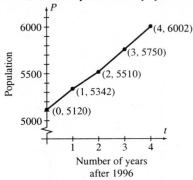

Number of years
after 1996

7. The data point directly above 1990 on the horizontal axis lies at 75 on the vertical axis. The total number of freshmen enrolled in calculus in 1990 was 75.

9. The line segments are going up from left to right, indicating an increase in enrollment, between 1990 and 1993, 1995 and 1998, and again between 1999 and 2000. Since the line graph is rising from left to right, the slope of the line graph is positive during these time periods.

11. The line segment is horizontal between 1994 and 1995, indicating no change in enrollment. Since the line segment is horizontal, the slope of the line graph is zero during this time period.

13. The steepest downward-slanting line segment corresponds to the period between 1993 and 1994, so this is the period when the enrollment decreased most rapidly.

15. The lowest point on the graph is for the year 1990 and corresponds to the lowest enrollment, which was 75 students.

17. a. A possible graph is shown, where t represents the number of days after Monday, and P represents the price per share.

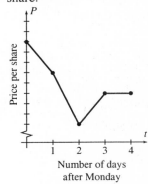

Number of days
after Monday

b. The lowest point on the graph is for Wednesday, indicating the lowest value of the stock for the given week.

19. a.

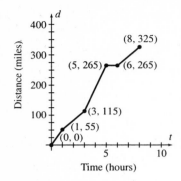

b. No plotted data point corresponds to 2 hours. However, as indicated by the line segment connecting (1, 55) and (3, 115), we will assume a constant driving rate per hour during this time period. On the segment, the point directly above 2 hours lines up with 85 miles. After 2 hours, the drivers had traveled approximately 85 miles.

c. Since the distance traveled remains constant between 5 and 6 hours, we will assume the drivers took a break during this time period. Since the line segment is horizontal, between 5 and 6 hours, its slope is 0.

d. The steepest upward-slanting line segment corresponds to the time period between 3 and 5 hours, so this is the period when the drivers traveled the fastest. The slope of the line graph during this time interval is greater than the slope of the line graph during the remaining intervals, as indicated by the steepest upward-slanting line segment.

21. a.

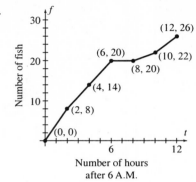

b. The steepest upward-slanting line segment corresponds to the time period between 6:00 A.M. ($t = 0$) and 8:00 A.M. ($t = 2$), so this is the time period when the greatest number of fish were caught.

c. The number of fish caught remained constant between 12:00 P.M. ($t = 6$) and 2:00 P.M. ($t = 8$) as indicated by a horizontal line segment. Since the line segment is horizontal, between 12:00 P.M. and 2:00 P.M., its slope is 0.

d. The slope of the line graph between 8:00 A.M. ($t = 2$) and 12:00 P.M. ($t = 6$) remains the same, indicating that the number of fish caught per hour remained constant over this 4-hour time period.

Exercise A.2

1. Let A = the area of the trapezoid, h = its height, and b_1, b_2 be the lengths of its bases. Then, $A = \dfrac{1}{2}h(b_1 + b_2)$.

3. The equation is of the form $y = mx + b$. We need to determine the slope and y-intercept of the line.

$$m = \frac{y_2 - y_1}{x_2 - x_1} = \frac{4 - 2}{-3 - 1} = \frac{2}{-4} = -\frac{1}{2}$$

$$y = -\frac{1}{2}x + b$$

$$2 = -\frac{1}{2}(1) + b$$

$$2 = -\frac{1}{2} + b$$

$$\frac{5}{2} = b$$

Therefore, $y = -\frac{1}{2}x + \frac{5}{2}$ is the desired equation.

5. Since the percent change remains constant, an exponential function of the form $y = ab^x$ can be used to model this situation. Since $y = 15{,}525$ when

$x = 0$, $15{,}525 = ab^0 = a \cdot 1 = a$.
Hence, $y = 15{,}525b^x$.
To find b, use the fact that the car is worth 91% of its original value after 1 year.
That is, $y = (0.91)(15{,}525)$ when $x = 1$.
$(0.91)(15{,}525)$ when $x = 1$.

$$(0.91)(15{,}525) = 15{,}525b^1$$

$$0.91 = b$$

Therefore, $y = 15{,}525(0.91)^x$ is the desired equation.

7. Let P represent the probability and E and F be the events. Then,
$P(E \cup F) = P(E) + P(F)$.

9.

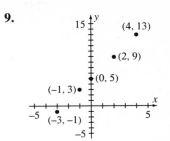

Based on the graph, the data appear linear. Thus, the model is of the form $y = mx + b$. From the graph we see that $b = 5$. We will use $(0, 5)$ and $(2, 9)$ to determine m.

$$m = \frac{9 - 5}{2 - 0} = \frac{4}{2} = 2$$

Therefore, $y = 2x + 5$ is the desired equation.

11.

Based on the graph, the data appear to be exponential. Thus, the model is of the form $y = ab^x$. Since $b = 1$ when $x = 0$, we have

$$1 = ab^0 = a \cdot 1 = a.$$

Hence, $y = b^x$. To find b, we will use the point $(1, 3)$.

$$3 = b^1$$

$$3 = b$$

Therefore, $y = 3^x$ is the desired equation.

13.

Based on the graph, the data appear to be quadratic. Since $x = 1$ is the axis of symmetry, $(1, 3)$ is the vertex. Thus, we will use the model

$$f(x) = a\left(x + \frac{b}{2a}\right)^2 + c - \frac{b^2}{4a}, \text{ where}$$

$\left(-\dfrac{b}{2a},\ c - \dfrac{b^2}{4a}\right)$ is the vertex of the parabola.

Hence, $f(x) = a(x-1)^2 + 3$.

To find a, we will use the point $(0, 5)$.

$5 = a(0-1)^2 + 3$

$5 = a + 3$

$2 = a$

Therefore, $f(x) = 2(x-1)^2 + 3$ or

$f(x) = 2x^2 - 4x + 5$ is the desired equation.

15.

Based on the graph, the data appear to be logarithmic. Thus, the model is of the form $y = a \log_b x$. Since

$2^1 = 2,\ 2^3 = 8,$ and $2^5 = 32$, we can see that the desired logarithmic equation is

$y = \log_2 x.$

17.

Based on the graph, the majority of the data seem to fit a linear model.

19.

Based on the graph, the majority of the data seem to fit a quadratic model.

21.

Based on the graph, the majority of the data seem to fit an exponential model.

23. a. With a fixed cost of $100 per month and a variable cost of $40 per reel, we have $C = 100 + 40r$.

  b. $C = 100 + 40(10)$
$$= 100 + 400$$
$$= 500.$$
It will cost $500 to produce 10 reels per month.

  c. $1000 = 100 + 40r$
$$900 = 40r$$
$$22.5 = r.$$
The company can produce 22 reels if they can afford costs of $1000 per month.

25. a. Use the given points, $(0, 0)$, $(1, 64)$, and $(3, 96)$, to find the values of a, b, and c. Since $h = 0$ when $t = 0$, we have $c = 0$. We obtain the following system:
$$\begin{cases} 64 = a + b \\ 96 = 9a + 3b \end{cases}.$$
Multiply the first equation by -3 and add the result to the second equation.
$$-192 = -3a - 3b$$
$$\underline{\quad 96 = 9a + 3b \quad}$$
$$-96 = 6a$$
Thus, $a = -16$. Substituting -16 into the equation $64 = a + b$ for a, we find that $b = 80$. Therefore, $h = -16t^2 + 80t$ is the desired equation.

  b. The time at which the rocket reaches its maximum height and the maximum height are given by the vertex of the parabola. The vertex is given by
$$\left(-\frac{b}{2a}, \; h\left(-\frac{b}{2a} \right) \right).$$
$$-\frac{b}{2a} = -\frac{80}{2(-16)} = \frac{-80}{-32} = 2.5$$
$$h(2.5) = -16(2.5)^2 + 80(2.5) = 100$$
The rocket reaches its maximum height, 100 feet, 2.5 seconds after being shot upward.

27. a. Let N represent the number of bacteria present at the end of t days. Increasing each days population by 200% gives the following data table.

t	0	1	2	3	4	5
N	2000	6000	18,000	54,000	162,000	486,000

  b. Since the percent change remains constant, an exponential function of the form $N = ab^t$ can be used to model this situation. Since $N = 2000$ when $t = 0$, we have $2000 = ab^0 = a \cdot 1 = a$. Hence, $N = 2000b^t$. To find b, we use the point $(1, 6000)$.
$$6000 = 2000b^1$$
$$3 = b$$
Therefore, $N = 2000(3)^t$ is the desired equation.

  c. Substituting 10 for t in $N = 2000(3)^t$, we obtain
$$N = 2000(3)^{10} = 118,098,000$$
118,098,000 bacteria are present at the end of 10 days.

29. a. The two points which are least likely to fit the model are (2, 1.3) and (6.5, 34.1).

   b. Answers may vary, but should be close to $y = 3.1x + 1.5$.

   c. Answers may vary, but should be close to $y = 44.9$.

Exercise A.3

1. Average rate of change from (0, 4) to (1, 1):
$$\frac{1-4}{1-0} = \frac{-3}{1} = -3$$
Average rate of change from (1, 1) to (2, –2):
$$\frac{-2-1}{2-1} = \frac{-3}{1} = -3$$
Average rate of change from (2, –2) to (3, –5):
$$\frac{-5-(-2)}{3-2} = \frac{-3}{1} = -3$$
Average rate of change from (3, –5) to (4, –8):
$$\frac{-8-(-5)}{4-3} = -3$$
Since the average rate of change remains constant, the relationship is linear over the given domain.

3. Average rate of change from (0, 0) to (1, 1):
$$\frac{1-0}{1-0} = \frac{1}{1} = 1$$
Average rate of change from (1, 1) to (2, 8):
$$\frac{8-1}{2-1} = \frac{7}{1} = 7$$
There is no need to go further. Since the average rate of change does not remain constant, the relationship is nonlinear over the given domain.

5.

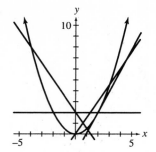

   a. The average rate of change is
$$\frac{f(3)-f(0)}{3-0} = \frac{0.5(3)^2 - 0.5(0)^2}{3}$$
$$= \frac{4.5}{3}$$
$$= 1.5$$

   b. The average rate of change is
$$\frac{f(1)-f(-4)}{1-(-4)} = \frac{0.5(1)^2 - 0.5(-4)^2}{5}$$
$$= \frac{0.5-8}{5}$$
$$= -1.5$$

   c. The average rate of change is
$$\frac{f(2)-f(-2)}{2-(-2)} = \frac{0.5(2)^2 - 0.5(-2)^2}{4}$$
$$= \frac{2-2}{4}$$
$$= 0$$

   d. The average rate of change is
$$\frac{f(2.01)-f(2)}{2.01-2} = \frac{0.5(2.01)^2 - 0.5(2)^2}{0.01}$$
$$= \frac{2.02005 - 2}{0.01}$$
$$= \frac{0.02005}{0.01}$$
$$= 2.005$$

7.

a. The average rate of change is

$$\frac{g(3) - g(1)}{3 - 1} = \frac{3^3 + 3(3) - [1^3 + 3(1)]}{2}$$

$$= \frac{36 - 4}{2}$$

$$= \frac{32}{2}$$

$$= 16$$

b. The average rate of change is

$$\frac{g(2) - g(-2)}{2 - (-2)} = \frac{2^3 + 3(2) - [(-2)^3 + 3(-2)]}{4}$$

$$= \frac{14 - (-14)}{4}$$

$$= \frac{28}{4}$$

$$= 7$$

c. The average rate of change is

$$\frac{g(1) - g(0)}{1 - 0} = \frac{1^3 + 3(1) - [(0)^3 + 3(0)]}{1}$$

$$= \frac{4 - 0}{1}$$

$$= 4$$

d. The average rate of change is

$$\frac{g(0.1) - g(0)}{0.1 - 0} = \frac{(0.1)^3 + 3(0.1) - [(0)^3 + 3(0)]}{0.1}$$

$$= \frac{0.301}{0.1}$$

$$= 3.01$$

9. Her average rate of growth was

$$\frac{60 - 42}{12 - 8} = \frac{18}{4} = 4.5 \text{ inches per year.}$$

11. The average rate of change is

$$\frac{128 - 65}{2 - 0.5} = \frac{63}{1.5} = \$42 \text{ per hour.}$$

13. a. The average rate of change is
$$\frac{70-49}{14-8}=\frac{21}{6}$$
$$= 3.5 \text{ degrees per day}$$

b. The average rate of change is
$$\frac{65-70}{18-14}=\frac{-5}{4}$$
$$= -1.25 \text{ degrees per day}$$

c. The average rate of change is
$$\frac{73-57}{21-5}=\frac{16}{16}$$
$$= 1 \text{ degree per day}$$

d. The average rate of change is
$$\frac{79-63}{30-3}=\frac{16}{27}$$
$$\approx 0.59 \text{ degree per day}$$

15. a. The average rate of change is
$$\frac{g(4)-g(1)}{4-1}=\frac{5-5}{3}$$
$$= \frac{0}{3}$$
$$= 0$$

b. The average rate of change is
$$\frac{g(2)-g(-1)}{2-(-1)}=\frac{5-5}{3}$$
$$= \frac{0}{3}$$
$$= 0$$

c. The average rate of change is
$$\frac{g(4+h)-g(4)}{4+h-4}=\frac{5-5}{h}$$
$$= \frac{0}{h}$$
$$= 0$$

d. The average rate of change is
$$\frac{g(x_0+h)-g(x_0)}{x_0+h+x_0}=\frac{5-5}{h}$$
$$= \frac{0}{h}$$
$$= 0$$

17. a. The average rate of change is
$$\frac{f(5)-f(0)}{5-0}=\frac{5^2+2(5)-5-[0^2+2(0)-5]}{5}$$
$$= \frac{30+5}{5}$$
$$= \frac{35}{5}$$
$$= 7$$

b. The average rate of change is
$$\frac{f(8)-f(3)}{8-3}=\frac{8^2+2(8)-5-[3^2+2(3)-5]}{5}$$
$$= \frac{75-10}{5}$$
$$= \frac{65}{5}$$
$$= 13$$

c. The average rate of change is

$$\frac{f(3+h)-f(3)}{3+h-3} = \frac{(3+h)^2 + 2(3+h) - 5 - [3^2 + 2(3) - 5]}{h}$$

$$= \frac{9 + 6h + h^2 + 6 + 2h - 5 - 10}{h}$$

$$= \frac{h^2 + 8h}{h}$$

$$= h + 8$$

d. The average rate of change is

$$\frac{f(x_0+h)-f(x_0)}{x_0+h-x_0} = \frac{(x_0+h)^2 + 2(x_0+h) - 5 - (x_0^2 + 2x_0 - 5)}{h}$$

$$= \frac{x_0^2 + 2x_0 h + h^2 + 2x_0 + 2h - 5 - x_0^2 - 2x_0 + 5}{h}$$

$$= \frac{2x_0 h + h^2 + 2h}{h}$$

$$= 2x_0 + h + 2$$

19. a. Slope $= \dfrac{g(x_0+h)-g(x_0)}{x_0+h-x_0}$

$$= \frac{-2(x_0+h) - 6 - (-2x_0 - 6)}{h}$$

$$= \frac{-2x_0 - 2h - 6 + 2x_0 + 6}{h}$$

$$= \frac{-2h}{h}$$

$$= -2$$

b. Slope $= \dfrac{g(3+0.1)-g(3)}{3+0.1-3}$

$$= \frac{g(3.1) - g(3)}{0.1}$$

$$= \frac{-2(3.1) - 6 - [-2(3) - 6]}{0.1}$$

$$= \frac{-12.2 + 12}{0.1}$$

$$= \frac{-0.2}{0.1}$$

$$= -2$$

c. Slope $= \dfrac{g(3+0.01)-g(3)}{3+0.01-3}$

$$= \frac{g(3.01) - g(3)}{0.01}$$

$$= \frac{-2(3.01) - 6 - [-2(3) - 6]}{0.01}$$

$$= \frac{-12.02 + 12}{0.01}$$

$$= -\frac{0.02}{0.01}$$

$$= -2$$

d. Slope $= \dfrac{g(3+0.001)-g(3)}{3+0.001-3}$

$$= \frac{g(3.001) - g(3)}{0.001}$$

$$= \frac{-2(3.001) - 6 - [-2(3) - 6]}{0.001}$$

$$= \frac{-12.002 + 12}{0.001}$$

$$= \frac{-0.002}{0.001}$$

$$= -2$$

e. Since $g(x)$ is linear, the average rate of change between any two points is constant.

21. $x(t)$ is linear since its average rate of change is constant. We are given that $m = 2$ and $x = 5$ when $t = 1$.

$$x(t) = mt + b$$
$$5 = 2(1) + b$$
$$3 = b$$

Thus, $x(t) = 2t + 3$.

23. Possible graph:

25. The average rate of change over the interval $[x_0, x_0 + h]$ represents the average cost per unit for this interval.

Exercise A.4

1. A typist's rate is calculated by counting the number of words typed during a timed typing session and dividing by the length of the session in minutes. Thus, the 70 words per minute is an average rate of change.

3. The tachometer indicates how fast a car's engine is running at the moment. Thus, the 5000 revolutions per minute is an instantaneous rate of change.

5.
$$\frac{f(-4 + h) - f(-4)}{h} = \frac{(-4 + h)^2 - (-4)^2}{h}$$
$$= \frac{16 - 8h + h^2 - 16}{h}$$
$$= \frac{-8h + h^2}{h}$$
$$= -8 + h$$

As h approaches 0, $-8 + h$ approaches -8. Therefore, the slope is -8.

7.
$$\frac{f(3 + h) - f(3)}{h} = \frac{\frac{1}{3 + h} - \frac{1}{3}}{h}$$
$$= \frac{3 - (3 + h)}{h[3(3 + h)]}$$
$$= \frac{-h}{3h(3 + h)}$$
$$= \frac{-1}{3(3 + h)}$$

As h approaches 0, $\dfrac{-1}{3(3 + h)}$ approaches $\dfrac{-1}{3(3)} = -\dfrac{1}{9}$. Therefore, the slope is $-\dfrac{1}{9}$.

9.
$$\frac{f(1 + h) - f(1)}{h} = \frac{[(1 + h)^2 - (1 - h)] - (1^2 - 1)}{h}$$
$$= \frac{1 + 2h + h^2 - 1 - h - 0}{h}$$
$$= \frac{h + h^2}{h}$$
$$= 1 + h$$

As h approaches 0, $1 + h$ approaches 1. Therefore, the slope is 1.

11. In Problem 9, we found that the slope of the graph of $f(x) = x^2 - x$ at $x = 1$ is 1. Therefore, the slope of the tangent line to the graph of f at $(1, 0)$ is 1. Use the point-slope formula to write the equation of the line through $(1, 0)$ with slope 1.
$$y - 0 = 1(x - 1)$$
$$y = x - 1$$
The equation of the tangent line is $y = x - 1$.

13. First find the slope of the graph of $f(x) = \sqrt{x}$ at $x = 1$.
$$\frac{f(1+h) - f(1)}{h} = \frac{\sqrt{1+h} - \sqrt{1}}{h}$$
$$= \frac{\sqrt{1+h} - 1}{h} \cdot \frac{\sqrt{1+h} + 1}{\sqrt{1+h} + 1}$$
$$= \frac{(1+h) - 1}{h(\sqrt{1+h} + 1)}$$
$$= \frac{h}{h(\sqrt{1+h} + 1)}$$
$$= \frac{1}{\sqrt{1+h} + 1}$$
As h approaches 0, $\dfrac{1}{\sqrt{1+h} + 1}$ approaches

$\dfrac{1}{\sqrt{1} + 1} = \dfrac{1}{1+1} = \dfrac{1}{2}$. Therefore, the slope of the tangent line to the graph of f at $(1, 1)$ is $\dfrac{1}{2}$. Use the point-slope formula to write the equation of the line through $(1, 1)$ with slope $\dfrac{1}{2}$.

$$y - 1 = \frac{1}{2}(x - 1)$$
$$y = \frac{1}{2}x - \frac{1}{2} + 1$$
$$y = \frac{1}{2}x + \frac{1}{2}$$
The equation of the tangent line is
$$y = \frac{1}{2}x + \frac{1}{2}.$$

15. $\dfrac{f(x+h) - f(x)}{h} = \dfrac{11 - 11}{h} = \dfrac{0}{h} = 0$

As h approaches 0, $0 = 0$, thus $\dfrac{dy}{dx} = 0$.

17. $\dfrac{f(x+h) - f(x)}{h} = \dfrac{5(x+h) + 11 - (5x + 11)}{h}$
$$= \frac{5x + 5h + 11 - 5x - 11}{h} = \frac{5h}{5} = 5$$

As h approaches 0, $5 = 5$, thus $\dfrac{dy}{dx} = 5$.

19. $\dfrac{f(x+h) - f(x)}{h}$
$$= \frac{10(x+h)^2 + 11 - (10x^2 + 11)}{h}$$
$$= \frac{10x^2 + 20xh + 10h^2 + 11 - 10x^2 - 11}{h}$$
$$= \frac{20xh + 10h^2}{h} = 20x + 10h$$
As h approaches 0, $20x + 10h$ approaches $20x$, thus $\dfrac{dy}{dx} = 20x$.

21. $\dfrac{f(x+h)-f(x)}{h} = \dfrac{\frac{1}{5(x+h)+11} - \frac{1}{5x+11}}{h}$

$= \dfrac{\frac{1}{5x+5h+11} - \frac{1}{5x+11}}{h} \cdot \dfrac{(5x+5h+11)(5x+11)}{(5x+5h+11)(5x+11)}$

$= \dfrac{5x+11-(5x+5h+11)}{h(5x+5h+11)(5x+11)}$

$= \dfrac{-5h}{h(5x+5h+11)(5x+11)}$

$= \dfrac{-5}{(5x+5h+11)(5x+11)}$

As h approaches 0, $\dfrac{-5}{(5x+5h+11)(5x+11)}$ approaches $-\dfrac{5}{(5x+11)^2}$, thus $\dfrac{dy}{dx} = -\dfrac{5}{(5x+11)^2}$.

23. $\dfrac{f(x+h)-f(x)}{h} = \dfrac{\frac{3}{12-5(x+h)} - \frac{3}{12-5x}}{h}$

$= \dfrac{\frac{3}{12-5x-5h} - \frac{3}{12-5x}}{h} \cdot \dfrac{(12-5x-5h)(12-5x)}{(12-5x-5h)(12-5x)}$

$= \dfrac{3(12-5x) - 3(12-5x-5h)}{h(12-5x-5h)(12-5x)}$

$= \dfrac{15h}{h(12-5x-5h)(12-5x)}$

$= \dfrac{15}{(12-5x-5h)(12-5x)}$

As h approaches 0, $\dfrac{15}{(12-5x-5h)(12-5x)}$ approaches $\dfrac{15}{(12-5x)^2}$, thus $\dfrac{dy}{dx} = \dfrac{15}{(12-5x)^2}$.

25. $\dfrac{f(x+h)-f(x)}{h} = \dfrac{\sqrt{5(x+h)-11} - \sqrt{5x-11}}{h}$

$= \dfrac{\sqrt{5x+5h-11} - \sqrt{5x-11}}{h} \cdot \dfrac{\sqrt{5x+5h-11} + \sqrt{5x-11}}{\sqrt{5x+5h-11} + \sqrt{5x-11}}$

$= \dfrac{5x+5h-11-(5x-11)}{h\left(\sqrt{5x+5h-11} + \sqrt{5x-11}\right)} = \dfrac{5h}{h\left(\sqrt{5x+5h-11} + \sqrt{5x-11}\right)}$

$= \dfrac{5}{\sqrt{5x+5h-11} + \sqrt{5x-11}}$

As h approaches 0, $\dfrac{5}{\sqrt{5x+5h-11} + \sqrt{5x-11}}$ approaches $\dfrac{5}{2\sqrt{5x-11}}$, thus, $\dfrac{dy}{dx} = \dfrac{5}{2\sqrt{5x-11}}$.

27.
$$\frac{f(x+h)-f(x)}{h} = \frac{\sqrt{12-5(x+h)}+10(x+h)^2+11-\left(\sqrt{12-5x}+10x^2+11\right)}{h}$$

$$= \frac{\sqrt{12-5x-5h}+10x^2+20xh+10h^2+11-\sqrt{12-5x}-10x^2-11}{h}$$

$$= \frac{\sqrt{12-5x-5h}+20xh+10h^2-\sqrt{12-5x}}{h}$$

$$= \frac{\sqrt{12-5x-5h}-\sqrt{12-5x}}{h}\cdot\frac{\sqrt{12-5x-5h}+\sqrt{12-5x}}{\sqrt{12-5x-5h}+\sqrt{12-5x}}+20x+10h$$

$$= \frac{12-5x-5h-(12-5x)}{h\left(\sqrt{12-5x-5h}+\sqrt{12-5x}\right)}+20x+10h$$

$$= -\frac{5}{\sqrt{12-5x-5h}+\sqrt{12-5x}}+20x+10h$$

As h approaches 0, $-\dfrac{5}{\sqrt{12-5x-5h}+\sqrt{12-5x}}+20x+10h$ approaches $-\dfrac{5}{2\sqrt{12-5x}}+20x$, thus

$$\frac{dy}{dx} = -\frac{5}{2\sqrt{12-5x}}+20x.$$

29.
$$\frac{c(q+h)-c(q)}{h} = \frac{[0.05(q+h)^2+28(q+h)+5000]-(0.05q^2+28q+5000)}{h}$$

$$= \frac{0.05q^2+0.1qh+0.05h^2+28q+28h+5000-0.05q^2-28q-5000}{h}$$

$$= \frac{0.1qh+0.05h^2+28h}{h} = 0.1q+0.05h+28$$

As h approaches 0, $0.1q+0.05h+28$ approaches $0.1q+28$. Thus $\dfrac{dc}{dq}=0.1q+28$. When $q=75$,

$\dfrac{dc}{dq}=0.1(75)+28=35.5$. When 75 rugs are produced, the marginal cost is \$35.50 per rug.

31. The avoid confusion, we will use k instead of h.

$$\frac{h(t+k)-h(t)}{k} = \frac{[-16(t+k)^2+32(t+k)]-(16t^2+32t)}{k}$$

$$= \frac{-16t^2-32kt-16k^2+32t+32k+16t^2-32t}{k}$$

$$= \frac{-32kt-16k^2+32k}{k}$$

$$= -32t-16k+32$$

As k approaches 0, $-32t-16k+32$ approaches $-32t+32$. Thus, $\dfrac{dh}{dt}=-32t+32$.

a. When $t = 0$, $\dfrac{dh}{dt} = -32(0) + 32 = 32$. Thus, after 0 seconds, the ball's velocity is 32 ft/sec.

b. When $t = 2$, $\dfrac{dh}{dt} = -32(2) + 32 = -32$. Thus, after 2 seconds, the ball's velocity is -32 ft/sec.

c. When $t = 3$, $\dfrac{dh}{dt} = -32(3) + 32 = -64$. Thus, after 3 seconds, the ball's velocity is -64 ft/sec.

Exercise A.5

1. The first region is a triangle with base = 2 and height = 2. Area $= \dfrac{1}{2}bh = \dfrac{1}{2}(2)(2) = 2$ square units.

The second region is a triangle with base = 1 and height = 1.

Area $= \dfrac{1}{2}bh = \dfrac{1}{2}(1)(1) = \dfrac{1}{2}$ square unit.

The third region is a rectangle with base = 2 and height = 1.
Area $= bh = 2(1) = 2$ square units.
The fourth region is a quarter circle with radius = 1.

Area $= \dfrac{1}{4}\pi r^2 = \dfrac{1}{4}\pi(1)^2 = \dfrac{\pi}{4}$ square units.

Total area $= 2 + \dfrac{1}{2} + 2 + \dfrac{\pi}{4} = \left(4\dfrac{1}{2} + \dfrac{\pi}{4}\right)$ square units.

3. Find the area of the region by summing the areas of the rectangles.

Area $= 2(2) + 2(9) + 2(6)$
$= 4 + 18 + 12$
$= 34$ square units

5. Find the area of the region by summing the areas of the rectangles.

Area $= 1(2) + 1(3) + 1(5) + 1(7) + 1(6) + 1(4) + 1(1)$
$= 2 + 3 + 5 + 7 + 6 + 4 + 1$
$= 28$ square units

7. a. The exact area of the region is the area of 2 trapezoids, one from $x = 0$ to $x = 3$, and the other from $x = 3$ to $x = 8$.

Area of trapezoid 1 is $\dfrac{1}{2}h(b_1 + b_2) = \dfrac{1}{2}(3)(6 + 3) = 13.5$

Area of trapezoid 2 is $\dfrac{1}{2}h(b_1 + b_2) = \dfrac{1}{2}(5)(3 + 8) = 27.5$

Total area $= 13.5 + 27.5 = 41$ square units

b. Divide the interval $[0, 8]$ into 4 subintervals of equal width. Each rectangle has width $\dfrac{8}{4} = 2$.

Evaluate the function at the right endpoint of each subinterval to get the height of each rectangle.

x	$3 + |x - 3|$
2	4
4	4
6	6
8	8

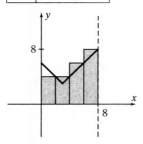

Area of rectangle $1 = bh = 2(4) = 8$
Area of rectangle $2 = bh = 2(4) = 8$
Area of rectangle $3 = bh = 2(6) = 12$
Area of rectangle $4 = bh = 2(8) = 16$
The total approximate area is $8 + 8 + 12 + 16 = 44$ square units.

c. Divide the interval [0, 8] into 8 subintervals of equal width. Each rectangle has width $\frac{8}{8} = 1$.

Evaluate the function at the right endpoint of each subinterval to get the height of each rectangle.

x	$3 + \lvert x - 3 \rvert$
1	5
2	4
3	3
4	4
5	5
6	6
7	7
8	8

Since the width of each rectangle is 1, the area of each rectangle is its height.
The total approximated area is $5 + 4 + 3 + 4 + 5 + 6 + 7 + 8 = 42$ square units.

d. Divide the interval [0, 8] into 4 subintervals of equal width. Each trapezoid has height $\frac{8}{4} = 2$.

Evaluate the function at the left and right endpoints of each subinterval to get the lengths of the bases of each trapezoid.

x	$3 + \lvert x - 3 \rvert$
0	6
2	4
4	4
6	6
8	8

Area of trapezoid $1 = \dfrac{1}{2}h(b_1 + b_2) = \dfrac{1}{2}(2)(6+4) = 10$

Area of trapezoid $2 = \dfrac{1}{2}h(b_1 + b_2) = \dfrac{1}{2}(2)(4+4) = \ 8$

Area of trapezoid $3 = \dfrac{1}{2}h(b_1 + b_2) = \dfrac{1}{2}(2)(4+6) = 10$

Area of trapezoid $4 = \dfrac{1}{2}h(b_1 + b_2) = \dfrac{1}{2}(2)(6+8) = 14$

The total approximated area is $10 + 8 + 10 + 14 = 42$ square units.

e. The estimations in parts (c) and (d) give the best approximation to the actual area.

9. a. The region between the curve and the x-axis is one quarter of a circle with radius 4.

Area $= \dfrac{1}{4}\pi r^2 = \dfrac{1}{4}\pi(4)^2 = 4\pi \approx 12.57$ square units

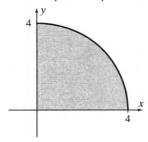

b. Divide the interval $[0, 4]$ into 4 subintervals of equal width. Each rectangle has width $\dfrac{4}{4} = 1$.

Evaluate the function at the right endpoint of each subinterval to get the height of each rectangle.

x	$\sqrt{16 - x^2}$
1	≈ 3.87
2	≈ 3.46
3	≈ 2.65
4	0

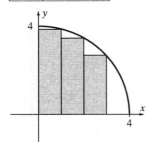

Area of rectangle $1 = bh \approx 1(3.87) \approx 3.87$
Area of rectangle $2 = bh \approx 1(3.46) \approx 3.46$
Area of rectangle $3 = bh \approx 1(2.65) \approx 2.65$
Area of rectangle $4 = bh = 1(0) = 0$
The total approximated area is $3.87 + 3.46 + 2.65 + 0 \approx 9.98$ square units.

c.   Divide the interval $[0, 4]$ into 8 subintervals of equal width. Each rectangle has width $\dfrac{4}{8} = \dfrac{1}{2}$.

Evaluate the function at the right endpoint of each subinterval to get the height of each rectangle.

x	$\sqrt{16 - x^2}$
$\dfrac{1}{2}$	≈ 3.97
1	≈ 3.87
$\dfrac{3}{2}$	≈ 3.71
2	≈ 3.46
$\dfrac{5}{2}$	≈ 3.12
3	≈ 2.65
$\dfrac{7}{2}$	≈ 1.94
4	0

Area of rectangle $1 = bh \approx \frac{1}{2}(3.97) \approx 1.985$

Area of rectangle $2 = bh \approx \frac{1}{2}(3.87) \approx 1.935$

Area of rectangle $3 = bh \approx \frac{1}{2}(3.71) \approx 1.855$

Area of rectangle $4 = bh \approx \frac{1}{2}(3.46) \approx 1.73$

Area of rectangle $5 = bh \approx \frac{1}{2}(3.12) \approx 1.56$

Area of rectangle $6 = bh \approx \frac{1}{2}(2.65) \approx 1.325$

Area of rectangle $7 = bh \approx \frac{1}{2}(1.94) \approx 0.97$

Area of rectangle $8 = bh = \frac{1}{2}(0) = 0$

The total approximated area is $1.985 + 1.935 + 1.855 + 1.73 + 1.56 + 1.325 + 0.97 + 0$
≈ 11.36 square units.

d. Divide the interval $[0, 4]$ into 4 subintervals of equal width. Each trapezoid has height $\frac{4}{4} = 1$.

Evaluate the function at the left and right endpoints of each subinterval to get the lengths of the bases of each trapezoid.

x	$\sqrt{16 - x^2}$
0	4
1	≈ 3.87
2	≈ 3.46
3	≈ 2.65
4	0

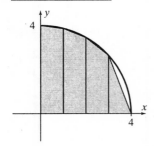

Area of trapezoid $1 = \frac{1}{2}h(b_1 + b_2) \approx \frac{1}{2}(1)(4 + 3.87) \approx 3.935$

Area of trapezoid $2 = \frac{1}{2}h(b_1 + b_2) \approx \frac{1}{2}(1)(3.87 + 3.46) \approx 3.665$

Area of trapezoid $3 = \frac{1}{2}h(b_1 + b_2) \approx \frac{1}{2}(1)(3.46 + 2.65) \approx 3.055$

Area of trapezoid $4 = \frac{1}{2}h(b_1 + b_2) = \frac{1}{2}(1)(2.65 + 0) = 1.325$

The total approximated area is $3.935 + 3.665 + 3.055 + 1.325 \approx 11.98$ square units.

    e.   The estimation from part (d) using 4 trapezoids gives the best approximation to the actual area.

11. The region between $f(x) = x^2$ and the x-axis for x values in the interval $[1, 5]$. The width of the rectangles and the height of the trapezoids are both 1 unit. Evaluate $f(x)$ at the right endpoint of each subinterval for the rectangle approximation, and at both endpoints of each subinterval for the trapezoid approximation.

x	$f(x) = x^2$
1	1
2	4
3	9
4	16
5	25

    a.   Area of rectangle $1 = bh = 1(4) = 4$
          Area of rectangle $2 = bh = 1(9) = 9$
          Area of rectangle $3 = bh = 1(16) = 16$
          Area of rectangle $4 = bh = 1(25) = 25$
          The total approximate area is $4 + 9 + 16 + 25 = 54$ square units.

    b.   Area of trapezoid $1 = \frac{1}{2}h(b_1 + b_2) = \frac{1}{2}(1)(1 + 4) = 2.5$

Area of trapezoid $2 = \frac{1}{2}h(b_1 + b_2) = \frac{1}{2}(1)(4 + 9) = 6.5$

Area of trapezoid $3 = \frac{1}{2}h(b_1 + b_2) = \frac{1}{2}(1)(9 + 16) = 12.5$

Area of trapezoid $4 = \frac{1}{2}h(b_1 + b_2) = \frac{1}{2}(1)(16 + 25) = 20.5$

The total approximate area is $2.5 + 6.5 + 12.5 + 20.5 = 42$ square units.

    c.   The trapezoid estimation is the best approximation to the actual area.

13. The region between $h(x) = x^2 + x$ and the x-axis, for x values in the interval $[2, 6]$. The width of the rectangles and the height of the trapezoids are both 1 unit. Evaluate $h(x)$ at the right endpoint of each subinterval for the rectangle approximation, and at both endpoints of each subinterval for the trapezoid approximation.

x	$h(x) = x^2 + x$
2	6
3	12
4	20
5	30
6	42

a.   Area of rectangle $1 = bh = 1(12) = 12$
Area of rectangle $2 = bh = 1(20) = 20$
Area of rectangle $3 = bh = 1(30) = 30$
Area of rectangle $4 = bh = 1(42) = 42$
The total approximate area is $12 + 20 + 30 + 42 = 104$ square units.

b.   Area of trapezoid $1 = \dfrac{1}{2}h(b_1 + b_2) = \dfrac{1}{2}(1)(6 + 12) = 9$

Area of trapezoid $2 = \dfrac{1}{2}h(b_1 + b_2) = \dfrac{1}{2}(1)(12 + 20) = 16$

Area of trapezoid $3 = \dfrac{1}{2}h(b_1 + b_2) = \dfrac{1}{2}(1)(20 + 30) = 25$

Area of trapezoid $4 = \dfrac{1}{2}h(b_1 + b_2) = \dfrac{1}{2}(1)(30 + 42) = 36$

The total approximate area is $9 + 16 + 25 + 36 = 86$ square units.

c.   The trapezoid estimation is the best approximation to the actual area.

15. $f(x) = -x^2 + 3x + 4$, $g(x) = -x^2 + 3x$

The area under $f(x)$ can be divided into 2 sections (see graph). The top section is equivalent to the area under $g(x)$, so they have that area in common. The bottom section is a rectangle that the area under $g(x)$ does not include.

Exercise A.6

1. The lower limit of summation is 12, upper limit of summation is 17, and the index of summation is t.

3. $\displaystyle\sum_{i=1}^{7} 6i = 6\sum_{i=1}^{7} i = 6 \cdot \frac{7(7+1)}{2} = 6 \cdot 28 = 168$

5. $\displaystyle\sum_{k=3}^{9} (10k + 16) = \sum_{k=3}^{9} 10k + \sum_{k=3}^{9} 16 = 10\sum_{k=3}^{9} k + \sum_{k=3}^{9} 16 = 10\sum_{i=1}^{7} (i+2) + 7(16) = 10\sum_{i=1}^{7} i + 10\sum_{i=1}^{7} 2 + 112$

$\displaystyle = \frac{10(7)(8)}{2} + 10(7)(2) + 112 = 280 + 140 + 112 = 532$

7. $\displaystyle 36 + 37 + 38 + 39 + \cdots + 60 = \sum_{i=36}^{60} i$

9. $\displaystyle 5^3 + 5^4 + 5^5 + 5^6 + 5^7 + 5^8 = \sum_{j=3}^{8} 5^i$

11. $\displaystyle 2 + 4 + 8 + 16 + 32 + 64 + 128 + 256 = \sum_{i=1}^{8} 2^i$

13. $\displaystyle\sum_{k=1}^{52} 10 = 10\sum_{k=1}^{52} 1 = 10(52) = 520$

15. $\displaystyle\sum_{k=1}^{n} \left(5 \cdot \frac{1}{n}\right) = \left(5 \cdot \frac{1}{n}\right)\sum_{k=1}^{n} 1 = \left(5 \cdot \frac{1}{n}\right)(n) = 5$

17. $\displaystyle\sum_{k=51}^{100} 10k = 10\sum_{i=1}^{50} (i+50)$

$\displaystyle = 10\sum_{i=1}^{50} i + (10)(50)\sum_{i=1}^{50} 1$

$\displaystyle = 10 \cdot \frac{50(51)}{2} + 500(50) = 12,750 + 25,000$

$\displaystyle = 37,750$

19. $\displaystyle\sum_{k=1}^{20} (5k^2 + 3k) = 5\sum_{k=1}^{20} k^2 + 3\sum_{k=1}^{20} k$

$\displaystyle = 5 \cdot \frac{20(21)(41)}{6} + 3\frac{20(21)}{2}$

$\displaystyle = 5(2870) + 3(210) = 14,980$

21. $\displaystyle\sum_{k=51}^{100} k^2 = \sum_{i=1}^{50} (i+50)^2 = \sum_{i=1}^{50} (i^2 + 100i + 2500)$

$\displaystyle = \sum_{i=1}^{50} i^2 + 100\sum_{i=1}^{50} i + 2500\sum_{i=1}^{50} 1$

$\displaystyle = \frac{50(51)(101)}{6} + 100\frac{50(51)}{2} + 2500(50)$

$\displaystyle = 42,925 + 127,500 + 125,000 = 295,425$

23. $\displaystyle\sum_{k=1}^{10}\left\{\left[4-\left(\frac{2k}{10}\right)^2\right]\left(\frac{2}{10}\right)\right\} = \frac{1}{5}\sum_{k=1}^{10}\left(4-\frac{1}{25}k^2\right) = \frac{1}{5}(4)\sum_{k=1}^{10}1 - \frac{1}{5}\left(\frac{1}{25}\right)\sum_{k=1}^{10}k^2 = \frac{4}{5}(10) - \frac{1}{125}\cdot\frac{10(11)(21)}{6}$

$\displaystyle = 8 - \frac{1}{125}\cdot 385 = 8 - \frac{77}{25} = \frac{123}{25} = 4\frac{23}{25}$

25. $\displaystyle\sum_{k=1}^{n}\left\{\left[4-\left(\frac{2}{n}\cdot k\right)^2\right]\left(\frac{2}{n}\right)\right\} = \frac{2}{n}\sum_{k=1}^{n}\left(4-\frac{4}{n^2}k^2\right) = \frac{2}{n}(4)\sum_{k=1}^{n}1 - \frac{2}{n}\left(\frac{4}{n^2}\right)\sum_{k=1}^{n}k^2 = \frac{8}{n}(n) - \frac{8}{n^3}\cdot\frac{n(n+1)(2n+1)}{6}$

$\displaystyle = 8 - \frac{4(n+1)(2n+1)}{3n^2}$

27. $f(x) = -x^2 + 3x$ over $[0, 3]$; $\Delta x = 0.05$

Since the length of a subinterval is 0.05, the number of subintervals is $N = \dfrac{3}{\Delta x} = \dfrac{3}{0.05} = 60$.

The subintervals are $[0, 0.05]$, $[0.05, 0.10]$, and so on. Using the midpoint rule, evaluate $f(x)$ at 0.025, 0.075, and so on. Therefore, $x_k = 0.05k - 0.025$. The sum is

$\displaystyle\text{Area} \approx \Delta x \sum_{k=1}^{N} f(x_k) = 0.05\sum_{k=1}^{60} f(0.05k - 0.025)$

$\displaystyle = 0.05\sum_{k=1}^{60}[-(0.05k - 0.025)^2 + 3(0.05k - 0.025)]$

$\displaystyle = 0.05\sum_{k=1}^{60}(-0.0025k^2 + 0.0025k - 0.000625 + 0.15k - 0.075)$

$\displaystyle = 0.05\sum_{k=1}^{60}(-0.0025k^2 + 0.1525k - 0.075625)$

$\displaystyle = 0.05(-0.0025)\sum_{k=1}^{60}k^2 + 0.05(0.1525)\sum_{k=1}^{60}k - 0.05(0.075625)\sum_{k=1}^{60}1$

$\displaystyle = -0.000125\frac{(60)(61)(121)}{6} + 0.007625\frac{(60)(61)}{2} - 0.00378125(60)$

$\displaystyle = -9.22625 + 13.95375 - 0.226875$

$\displaystyle = 4.500625 \text{ square units}$

Exercise A.7

1. $f(x) = x + 4; [-1, 3]$

$$\text{Area} = \sum_{i=1}^{n}\left[-1 + i\left(\frac{4}{n}\right) + 4\right]\left(\frac{4}{n}\right)$$

$$= \sum_{i=1}^{n}\left(\frac{4i}{n} + 3\right)\left(\frac{4}{n}\right)$$

$$= \sum_{i=1}^{n}\left(\frac{16i}{n^2} + \frac{12}{n}\right)$$

$$= \frac{16}{n^2}\sum_{i=1}^{n}i + \frac{12}{n}\sum_{i=1}^{n}1$$

$$= \frac{16}{n^2}\cdot\frac{n(n+1)}{2} + \frac{12}{n}\cdot n$$

$$= 8\left(\frac{n+1}{n}\right) + 12$$

As *n* increases without bound, $\dfrac{n+1}{n}$ gets closer to 1.

$$\lim_{n\to\infty}\left[8\left(\frac{n+1}{n}\right) + 12\right] = 8 + 12 = 20$$

3. $f(x) = 8; [4, 9]$

$$\int_a^b f(x)\, dx = \int_4^9 8\, dx$$

5. $f(x) = x^2 + x + 2; [-2, 5]$

$$\int_a^b f(x)\, dx = \int_{-2}^5 (x^2 + x + 2)\, dx$$

7. $f(x) = 3^x + 5; [-5, 5]$

$$\int_a^b f(x)\, dx = \int_{-5}^5 (3^x + 5)\, dx$$

9. $\int_0^6 4\, dx$

Since the area is all above the *x*-axis, it represents a positive number.

11. $\int_{-2}^4 (x^2 - 3)\, dx$

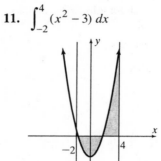

There appears to be more of the area above the *x*-axis than below, so it represents a positive number.

13. $\int_0^3 2^x\, dx$

Since the area is all above the *x*-axis, it represents a positive number.

15. a. Since $f(x) = 7$ is a constant function (horizontal line), the area under the curve is the area of a rectangle with width 7 and length b.
Area $= w \cdot l = 7b$

So $\int_0^b 7 \, dx = 7b$

b. $\int_0^{10} 7 \, dx = 7(10) = 70$

17. a. $f(x) = 3x + 2$ is a linear function which crosses the y-axis at 2. The area under f is the area of a trapezoid with height b and bases with lengths $f(0) = 2$ and $f(b) = 3b + 2$.

$$\text{Area} = \frac{1}{2} h(b_1 + b_2) = \frac{1}{2} b(2 + 3b + 2)$$

$$= \frac{1}{2} b(3b + 4)$$

$$= \frac{3}{2} b^2 + 2b$$

So, $\int_0^b (3x + 2) \, dx = \frac{3}{2} b^2 + 2b$

b. $\int_0^{10} (3x + 2) \, dx = \frac{3}{2}(10)^2 + 2(10)$

$$= \frac{3}{2}(100) + 20$$

$$= 170$$

19. a. $\int_{-3}^4 f(x) \, dx = F(4) - F(-3)$

$$= 2(4) - 2(-3)$$

$$= 8 + 6$$

$$= 14$$

b. Another antiderivative has the form
$G(x) = 2x + b$
Choose any real number b, say 2.
$G(x) = 2x + 2$

c. $\int_{-3}^4 f(x) \, dx = G(4) - G(-3)$

$$= 2(4) + 2 - [2(-3) + 2]$$

$$= 10 - (-4)$$

$$= 14$$

21. $\int_0^6 5 \, dx = F(6) - F(0)$, where $F(x) = 5x + b$
Choose $b = 0$.

$\int_0^6 5 \, dx = 5(6) - 5(0) = 30$

23. $\int_3^{10} -2 \, dx = F(10) - F(3)$, where
$F(x) = -2x + b$
Choose $b = 0$.

$\int_3^{10} -2 \, dx = -2(10) - [-2(3)]$

$$= -20 + 6$$

$$= -14$$

25. $f(x) = 3x^2 - x + 1$, $F(x) = x^3 - \frac{1}{2} x^2 + x$

$\int_0^3 f(x) \, dx = F(3) - F(0)$

$$= 3^3 - \frac{1}{2}(3)^2 + 3 - \left[0^3 - \frac{1}{2}(0)^2 + 0 \right]$$

$$= 27 - \frac{9}{2} + 3$$

$$= 25 \frac{1}{2}$$

27. $f(x) = e^x$, $F(x) = e^x$

$$\int_0^3 f(x)\,dx = F(3) - F(0)$$

$$= e^3 - e^0$$

$$= e^3 - 1$$

$$\approx 19.09$$

Exercise A.8

1. For a particular value of t, the function $C(t)$ tells us the cost of maintaining an automobile in that year. Since we want the cumulative cost for several years, we need the integral $\int_{1990}^{2000} 100e^{0.03t}\,dt$.

3. For a particular value of t, the function $h(t)$ tells us the height of the ball at that time. We want to know the time when the ball hits the ground; that is, we want to know t when $h(t) = 0$. We need to use the function itself to write the equation $-16t^2 + 128t + 3 = 0$ and then solve for t.

5. The function $v(t)$ describes the velocity of the particle at time t. Since acceleration is the rate of change of velocity, we need to find the derivative $v'(t)$ to determine the acceleration of the particle when $t = 2$.

7. The function $v(t)$ describes the velocity of the particle at time t. Thus, to find how fast the particle is moving when $t = 2$, we use the function itself to find $v(2)$.

9. $C(x) = 20 + 0.60x$

    a. $C(50) = 20 + 0.60(50) = 20 + 30 = 50$
The cost of the rental is $50.00 when you drive the truck 50 miles.

    b. $\dfrac{C(x+h) - C(x)}{h} = \dfrac{[20 + 0.60(x+h) - (20 + 0.60x)}{h}$

$$= \frac{20 + 0.60x + 0.60h - 20 - 0.60x}{h} = \frac{0.60h}{h} = 0.60$$

As h approaches 0, 0.60 is constantly 0.60. Thus, $C'(x) = 0.60$ for all x in the domain of C, so $C'(50) = 0.60$. When you have driven the truck 50 miles, the cost is increasing at the rate of $0.60 per mile.

11. **a.**   Since an employee receives $300 for each year with the company, we multiply the number of years t by $300 to find the amount of the bonus. Thus, $b(t) = 300t$.

    b. $\dfrac{300(t+h) - 300t}{h} = \dfrac{300t + 300h - 300t}{h} = \dfrac{300h}{h} = 300$

As h approaches 0, 300 is constantly 300. Thus, $b'(t) = 300$.
The employee's bonus increases at the rate of $300 per year.

    c.   The integral $\int_0^{10} b(t)\,dt$ approximates the sum of an employee's annual bonuses during the first ten years with the company.

13. $r(t) = 10 \ln t$

   a.   The year 2000 corresponds to $t = 10$. The value $r(10) = 10 \ln 10 \approx 23.03$ approximates the number of books Xul read in 2000. Thus, Xul read about 23 books in 2000.

   b. $r'(5) = \dfrac{10}{5} = 2$

       $t = 5$ corresponds to the year 1995. Thus, in 1995, the number of books Xul reads annually was increasing at the rate of about 2 books per year.

   c. $\displaystyle\int_1^{10} r(t)\, dt = R(10) - R(1) = 10(10)(-1 + \ln 10) - 10(1)(-1 + \ln 1) \approx 140.26$

       Between 1991 and 2000, Xul read about 140 books.

15. a. $b_l(5) = 1.6(5) = 8$

       $b_e(5) = 6.67 \ln(1 + 5) \approx 11.95$

       $t = 5$ corresponds to the year 2006. Thus, in 2006, the program's budget would be \$8 billion with model b_l and \$11.95 billion with model b_e.

   b. $b_l{}'(5) = 1.6$

       $b_e{}'(5) = \dfrac{6.67}{1 + 5} \approx 1.11$

       In 2006, the program's budget is increasing at the rate of \$1.6 billion per year with model b_l and about \$1.11 billion per year with b_e.

   c. $\displaystyle\int_0^5 b_l(t)\, dt = B_l(5) - B_l(0) = 0.8(5)^2 - 0.8(0)^2 = 20$

       $\displaystyle\int_0^5 b_e(t)\, dt = B_e(5) - B_e(0) = 6.67(1 + 5)[-1 + \ln(1 + 5)] - 6.67(1 + 0)[-1 + \ln(1 + 0)] \approx 38.36$

       In the first five years of the program, the cumulative budget would be about \$20 billion with model b_l and about \$38.36 billion with b_e.

   d.   Referring to part (a), we see that the bigger budget in 2006 is \$11.95 billion with model b_e.

   e.   Referring to part (b), we see that the greater rate of growth in 2006 is \$1.6 billion per year with model b_l.

   f.   Referring to part (c), we see that the bigger cumulative budget is \$38.36 billion with model b_e.

17. a.   Since $v(t)$ represents the velocity, we find $v(6) = \dfrac{7}{3600}(6) = \dfrac{7}{600}$. After 6 seconds, the car is moving

       at a rate of $\dfrac{7}{600} \approx 0.012$ miles per second.

   b. $v'(t) = \dfrac{7}{3600}$ represents change in velocity, so we find $v(6) = \dfrac{7}{3600}$. The speed of the car is

       increasing at a rate of $\dfrac{7}{3600} \approx 0.002$ miles per second per second.

c. $\int v(t)\,dt$ represents the position of the car, so we find

$$\int_0^6 v(t)\,dt = V(6) - V(0) = \frac{7}{7200}(6)^2 - \frac{7}{7200}(0)^2 = \frac{252}{7200} = \frac{7}{200}.$$ In the six seconds, the car travels

$\dfrac{7}{200} = 0.035$ mile.

Review Problems

1. Let t represent the number of months after October and A represent the amount of money spent on groceries.

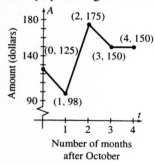

3. The steepest downward-slanting line segment corresponds to the period between October $(t = 0)$ and November $(t = 1)$, so this is the period when the price spent per month decreased most rapidly.

5. Let C = the cost of producing x units. Then $C = 550 + 22.50x$.

7. a.

Based on the graph, the data appear to be quadratic.

b. Since the model is of the form $h = at^2 + bt + c$, we will use three points to find the values of a, b, and c. Since the rocket is shot upward from the ground, $h = 0$ when $t = 0$ and $c = 0$. We obtain the following system using $h = 84$ when $t = 1$ and $h = 136$ when $t = 2$.

$$\begin{cases} 84 = a + b \\ 136 = 4a + 2b. \end{cases}$$

Multiply the first equation by -2 and add the result to the second equation.
$$-168 = -2a - 2b$$
$$\underline{136 = 4a + 2b}$$
$$-32 = 2a$$

Thus, $a = -16$. Substituting -16 into the equation $84 = a + b$ for a, we find that $b = 100$. Therefore, $h = -16t^2 + 100t$ is the desired equation.

c. Substitute 6 for t.
$$h = -16(6)^2 + 100(6) = 24$$
The height of the rocket is 24 feet after 6 seconds.

d. The rocket returns to the ground when $h = 0$.
$$0 = -16t^2 + 100t$$
$$0 = -4t(4t - 25)$$
$$0 = -4t \quad \text{or} \quad 0 = 4t - 25$$
$$0 = t \qquad\qquad 25 = 4t$$
$$\qquad\qquad\qquad 6.25 = t$$
The rocket returns to the ground 6.25 seconds after being shot upward.

9. a. Average rate of change from (0, 4) to (1, 1):

$$\frac{1-4}{1-0} = \frac{-3}{1} = -3$$

Average rate of change from (1, 1) to (2, –2):

$$\frac{-2-1}{2-1} = \frac{-3}{1} = -3$$

Average rate of change from (2, –2) to (3, –5):

$$\frac{-5-(-2)}{3-2} = \frac{-3}{1} = -3$$

Average rate of change from (3, –5) to (4, –8):

$$\frac{-8-(-5)}{4-3} = \frac{-3}{1} = -3$$

Since the average rate of change remains constant, the relationship is linear over the given domain.

b. Average rate of change from (0, 0) to (1, 1):

$$\frac{1-0}{1-0} = \frac{1}{1} = 1$$

Average rate of change from (1, 1) to (2, 4):

$$\frac{4-1}{2-1} = \frac{3}{1} = 3$$

There is no need to go further. Since the average rate of change does not remain constant, the relationship is nonlinear over the given domain.

11. a. The original size of the document is 300 kilobytes.

b. Convert minutes to seconds and calculate the percentage of 300 kilobytes that has been downloaded, to obtain the following table:

time	302 sec	204 sec	130 sec	20 sec
size	3 K	126 K	213 K	297 K

c. Average rate of change from (302, 3) to (204, 126):

$$\frac{126-3}{204-302} = \frac{123}{-98}$$

$$\approx -1.26 \text{ kilobytes per second}$$

Average rate of change from (204, 126) to (130, 213):

$$\frac{213-126}{130-204} = \frac{87}{-74}$$

$$\approx -1.18 \text{ kilobytes per second.}$$

Average rate of change from (130, 213) to (20, 297):

$$\frac{297-213}{20-130} = \frac{84}{-110}$$

$$\approx -0.76 \text{ kilobytes per second.}$$

d. The negative sign indicates that as the amount of time left decreases, the amount of the document which has been downloaded increases.

e. The period where the size of the document is changing the fastest is from 302 seconds to 204 seconds, where it is changing at a rate of 1.26 kilobytes per second.

13. $x(t)$ is linear since its average rate of change is constant. We are given that $m = 4$ and $x = 3$ when $t = 1$.

$$x(t) = mt + b$$
$$3 = 4(1) + b$$
$$-1 = b$$

Thus, $x(t) = 4t - 1$.

15. First we find the slope of the graph of $f(x) = \sqrt{x+2}$ at $x = 2$.

$$\frac{f(2+h) - f(2)}{h} = \frac{\sqrt{(2+h)+2} - \sqrt{2+2}}{h} = \frac{\sqrt{h+4} - 2}{h} \cdot \frac{\sqrt{h+4} + 2}{\sqrt{h+4} + 2} = \frac{(h+4) - 4}{h(\sqrt{h+4} + 2)} = \frac{h}{h(\sqrt{h+4} + 2)}$$

$$= \frac{1}{\sqrt{h+4} + 2}$$

As h approaches 0, $\dfrac{1}{\sqrt{h+4} + 2}$ approaches $\dfrac{1}{\sqrt{4} + 2} = \dfrac{1}{2+2} = \dfrac{1}{4}$. Therefore, the slope of the tangent

line is $\dfrac{1}{4}$. Use the point-slope formula to write the equation of the line through $(2, 2)$ with slope $\dfrac{1}{4}$.

$$y - 2 = \frac{1}{4}(x - 2)$$

$$y = \frac{1}{4}x - \frac{1}{2} + 2$$

$$y = \frac{1}{4}x + \frac{3}{2}$$

The equation of the tangent line is $y = \dfrac{1}{4}x + \dfrac{3}{2}$.

17. $\dfrac{f(x+h) - f(x)}{h} = \dfrac{\frac{1}{3-(x+h)} - \frac{1}{3-x}}{h} = \dfrac{(3-x) - [3 - (x+h)]}{h(3-x)[3-(x+h)]} = \dfrac{3 - x - 3 + x + h}{h(3-x)[3-(x+h)]}$

$$= \frac{h}{h(3-x)[3-(x+h)]} = \frac{1}{(3-x)[3-(x+h)]}$$

As h approaches 0, $\dfrac{1}{(3-x)[3-(x+h)]}$ approaches $\dfrac{1}{(3-x)(3-x)} = \dfrac{1}{(3-x)^2}$.

Thus, $\dfrac{dy}{dx} = \dfrac{1}{(3-x)^2}$.

19. Find the area of the region by summing the areas of the trapezoids.

$$\text{Area} = \frac{1}{2}(1)(0 + 1) + \frac{1}{2}(1)(1 + 3) + \frac{1}{2}(1)(3 + 5) + \frac{1}{2}(1)(5 + 8) + \frac{1}{2}(1)(8 + 9) + \frac{1}{2}(1)(9 + 3) + \frac{1}{2}(1)(3 + 0)$$

$$= \frac{1}{2} + 2 + 4 + 6\frac{1}{2} + 8\frac{1}{2} + 6 + 1\frac{1}{2}$$

$$= 29 \text{ square units}$$

21. a. The region between the curve and the *x*-axis, to the right of the *y*-axis, is one quarter of a circle with radius 3.

$$\text{Area} = \frac{1}{4}\pi r^2 = \frac{1}{4}\pi(3)^2 = \frac{9}{4}\pi \approx 7.07 \text{ square units}$$

b. Divide the interval [0, 3] into 3 subintervals of equal width. Each rectangle has width $\frac{3}{3} = 1$.

Evaluate the function at the right endp oint of each subinterval to get the height of each rectangle.

x	$\sqrt{9-x^2}$
1	≈ 2.83
2	≈ 2.24
3	0

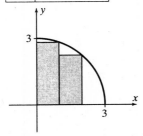

Since the width of each rectangle is 1, the area of each rectangle is its height.
The total approximated area is $2.83 + 2.24 + 0 \approx 5.07$ square units.

c. Divide the interval [0, 3] into 6 subintervals of each width. Each rectangle has width $\frac{3}{6} = 0.5$.

Evaluate the function at the right endpoint of each subinterval to get the height of each rectangle.

x	$\sqrt{9-x^2}$
0.5	≈ 2.96
1	≈ 2.83
1.5	≈ 2.60
2	≈ 2.24
2.5	≈ 1.66
3	0

Area of rectangle 1 = $bh \approx 0.5(2.96) \approx 1.48$
Area of rectangle 2 = $bh \approx 0.5(2.83) \approx 1.415$
Area of rectangle 3 = $bh \approx 0.5(2.60) \approx 1.30$
Area of rectangle 4 = $bh \approx 0.5(2.24) \approx 1.12$
Area of rectangle 5 = $bh \approx 0.5(1.66) \approx 0.83$
Area of rectangle 6 = $bh \approx 0.5(0) \approx 0$
The total approximated area is $1.48 + 1.415 + 1.30 + 1.12 + 0.83 + 0 \approx 6.145$ square units.

d. Divide the interval $[0, 3]$ into 3 subintervals of equal width. Each trapezoid has height $\dfrac{3}{3} = 1$.

Evaluate the function at the left and right endpoints of each subinterval to get the lengths of the bases of each trapezoid.

x	$\sqrt{9 - x^2}$
0	3
1	≈ 2.83
2	≈ 2.24
3	0

Area of trapezoid 1 = $\dfrac{1}{2} h(b_1 + b_2) \approx \dfrac{1}{2}(1)(3 + 2.83) \approx 2.915$

Area of trapezoid 2 = $\dfrac{1}{2} h(b_1 + b_2) \approx \dfrac{1}{2}(1)(2.83 + 2.24) \approx 2.535$

Area of trapezoid 3 = $\dfrac{1}{2} h(b_1 + b_2) \approx \dfrac{1}{2}(1)(2.24 + 0) \approx 1.120$

The total approximated area is $2.915 + 2.535 + 1.120 \approx 6.57$ square units.

e. The estimation from part (d) using 3 trapezoids gives the best approximation to the actual area.

23. The region bounded by $f(x) = -\dfrac{x^3}{5} + 6x$ and the x-axis on $[0, 5]$. The width of the rectangles and the height of the trapezoids are both 1 unit. Evaluate $f(x)$ at the right endpoint of each subinterval for the rectangle approximation, and at both endpoints of each subinterval for the trapezoid approximation.

x	$f(x) = -\dfrac{x^3}{5} + 6x$
0	0
1	5.8
2	10.4
3	12.6
4	11.2
5	5

a.   Area of rectangle $1 = bh = 1(5.8) = 5.8$
Area of rectangle $2 = bh = 1(10.4) = 10.4$
Area of rectangle $3 = bh = 1(12.6) = 12.6$
Area of rectangle $4 = bh = 1(11.2) = 11.2$
Area of rectangle $5 = bh = 1(5.0) = 5$
The total approximated area is $5.8 + 10.4 + 12.6 + 11.2 + 5 = 45$ square units.

b.   Area of trapezoid $1 = \dfrac{1}{2}h(b_1 + b_2) = \dfrac{1}{2}(1)(0 + 5.8) = 2.9$

Area of trapezoid $2 = \dfrac{1}{2}h(b_1 + b_2) = \dfrac{1}{2}(1)(5.8 + 10.4) = 8.1$

Area of trapezoid $3 = \dfrac{1}{2}h(b_1 + b_2) = \dfrac{1}{2}(1)(10.4 + 12.6) = 11.5$

Area of trapezoid $4 = \dfrac{1}{2}h(b_1 + b_2) = \dfrac{1}{2}(1)(12.6 + 11.2) = 11.9$

Area of trapezoid $5 = \dfrac{1}{2}h(b_1 + b_2) = \dfrac{1}{2}(1)(11.2 + 5) = 8.1$

The total approximated area is $2.9 + 8.1 + 11.5 + 11.9 + 8.1 = 42.5$ square units

c.   The rectangle approximation is $1\dfrac{1}{4}$ square units greater than the actual area, while, the trapezoid approximation is $1\dfrac{1}{4}$ square units less than the actual area. Both estimates are equally valid.

25. $\displaystyle\sum_{n=8}^{16} (5n - 3) = \sum_{n=8}^{16} 5n - \sum_{n=8}^{16} 3 = 5\sum_{n=8}^{16} n - \sum_{i=1}^{9} 3 = 5\sum_{i=1}^{9}(n + 7) - 9(3)$

$$= 5\sum_{i=1}^{9} n + 5\sum_{i=1}^{9} 7 - 27 = \frac{5(9)(10)}{2} + 5(9)(7) - 27$$

$$= 225 + 315 - 27 = 513$$

27. $\displaystyle\sum_{k=1}^{n}\frac{k^3}{n(n+1)^2}=\frac{1}{n(n+1)^2}\sum_{k=1}^{n}k^3$

$$=\frac{1}{n(n+1)^2}\left[\frac{n^2(n+1)^2}{4}\right]=\frac{n}{4}$$

29. $f(x)=x^2-4x+4$ over [0, 3]; $\Delta x=0.01$

Since the length of a subinterval is 0.01, the number of subintervals is $N=\dfrac{3}{\Delta x}=\dfrac{3}{0.01}=300$. The

subintervals are [0, 0.01], [0.01, 0.02], and so on. Using the midpoint rule, evaluate $f(x)$ at 0.005, 0.015,
and so on. Therefore,
$x_k=0.01k-0.005$. The sum is:

$\displaystyle\text{Area}\approx\Delta x\sum_{k=1}^{N}f(x_k)=0.01\sum_{k=1}^{300}f(0.01k-0.005)$

$\displaystyle=0.01\sum_{k=1}^{300}[(0.01k-0.005)^2-4(0.01k-0.005)+4]$

$\displaystyle=0.01\sum_{k=1}^{300}(0.0001k^2-0.0001k+0.000025-0.04k+0.02+4)$

$\displaystyle=0.01\sum_{k=1}^{300}(0.0001k^2-0.0401k+4.020025)$

$\displaystyle=0.01\left(0.0001\sum_{k=1}^{300}k^2-0.0401\sum_{k=1}^{300}k+4.020025\sum_{k=1}^{300}1\right)$

$\displaystyle=0.01\left[\frac{0.0001(300)(301)(601)}{6}-\frac{0.0401(300)(301)}{2}+4.020025(300)\right]$

$=0.01(904.505-1810.515+1206.0075)$

$=0.01(299.9975)$

$=2.999975$ square units

31. $f(x)=-x^2-x+2$; [−1, 1]

$\displaystyle\int_{a}^{b}f(x)\,dx=\int_{-1}^{1}(-x^2-x+2)\,dx$

33. $f(x)=4\log x$; [1, 100]

$\displaystyle\int_{a}^{b}f(x)\,dx=\int_{1}^{100}\log x\,dx$

35. $\displaystyle\int_{1}^{4}(2x+3)\,dx$

37. $\int_{-3}^{2} \left[\left(\frac{1}{2} \right)^x - 3 \right] dx$

39. a. $f(x) = x + 3$ is a linear function which crosses the y-axis at 3. The area under f is the area of a trapezoid with height b and bases $f(0) = 3$ and $f(b) = b + 3$.

$$\text{Area} = \frac{1}{2} h(b_1 + b_2) = \frac{1}{2} b(3 + b + 3)$$
$$= \frac{1}{2} b(b + 6)$$
$$= \frac{1}{2} b^2 + 3b$$

So, $\int_0^b (x + 3) \, dx = \frac{1}{2} b^2 + 3b$

b. $\int_0^{10} (x + 3) \, dx = \frac{1}{2}(10)^2 + 3(10) = 80$

41. $\int_{80}^{100} 5000 \, dx = F(100) - F(80)$, where
$F(x) = 5000x + b$
Choose $b = 0$.
$$\int_{80}^{100} 5000 \, dx = 5000(100) - 5000(80)$$
$$= 500,000 - 400,000$$
$$= 100,000$$

43. $f(x) = 6x^2 - 2x - 3$, $F(x) = 2x^3 - x^2 - 3x$

$\int_0^3 f(x) \, dx = F(3) - F(0)$
$$= 2(3)^3 - (3)^2 - 3(3) - [2(0)^3 - (0)^2 - 3(0)]$$
$$= 54 - 9 - 9 - 0$$
$$= 36$$

45. a. $E(31) = 830e^{0.03(31)} \approx 2103.64$
$t = 31$ corresponds to the year 2001. Thus, the energy costs for a 1900 square-foot home were about $2103.64 in 2001.

b. $E'(31) = 24.9e^{0.03(31)} \approx 63.11$
In 2001, the energy costs for a 1900 square-foot home were increasing at a rate of about $63.11 per year.

c. $\int_0^{31} E(t) \, dt = F(31) - F(0) = 27,667e^{0.03(31)} - 27,667e^{0.03(0)} \approx 42,455.27$
The cumulative energy costs for a 1900 square-foot home between 1970 and 2001 were about $42,455.27.

47. a. Since $v(t)$ represents velocity, we find $v(6) = \dfrac{1}{2400}(6)^2 = \dfrac{36}{2400} = \dfrac{3}{200}$. Thus, 6 seconds after liftoff

the shuttle is moving at a rate of $\dfrac{3}{200} = 0.015$ miles per second.

b. $v'(t)$ represents change in velocity, so we find $v'(6) = \dfrac{1}{1200}(6) = \dfrac{1}{200}$. Thus, 6 seconds after lift off

the speed of the shuttle is increasing at a rate of $\dfrac{1}{200} = 0.005$ miles per second per second.

c. $\displaystyle\int v(t)\,dt$ represents the position of the shuttle, so we find

$\displaystyle\int_0^6 v(t)\,dt = V(6) - V(0) = \dfrac{1}{7200}(6)^3 - \dfrac{1}{7200}(0)^3 = \dfrac{216}{7200} = \dfrac{3}{100}$. In the first 6 seconds, the shuttle

travels $\dfrac{3}{100} = 0.03$ mile.

Explorations in Finite Mathematics Software

This software enhances the understanding and visualization of many of the topics covered in the textbook. The self-documented software consists of two programs called FINITE1 and FINITE2.

Part 1 (Execute by entering FINITE1)

Part 1 covers finite math topics involving linear equations, linear inequalities, and matrices. In particular, it contains routines to perform Gaussian elimination, matrix operations, matrix inversion, simplex method, graphical solution of linear programming problems, the method of least-squares, and regular and absorbing Markov chains. The software follows the conventions of the text.

Part 2 (Execute by entering FINITE2)

Part 2 contains routines for Venn diagrams, Venn diagram counting problems, Venn diagram probability problems, computation of combinations, permutations, and factorials, statistical analysis of data, Galton board, binomial distribution, areas under normal curve, simple interest, compound interest, loan analysis, annuity analysis, and finance tables.

Requirements

The software runs on *any* IBM compatible computer having at least 384 K of memory

Technical Support

If you have questions about the software, contact David I. Schneider by e-mail at dis@math.umd.edu.

To Invoke Explorations in Finite Mathematics from Windows 95 (or later version)

1. Place the diskette in a drive, say drive A.
2. With Windows 95 and Windows 98, click the Start button, point to Programs, and click MS-DOS Prompt. With Windows 2000, click the Start button, point to Programs, point to Accessories, and click Command Prompt.
3. If the DOS or Command window does not fill the screen, hold down the Alt key and press the Enter key to enlarge the window.
4. Type A: and press the Enter key.
5. Type CD \FINITE and press the Enter key.
6. Type FINITE1 or FINITE2 and press the Enter key.

To Invoke Explorations in Finite Mathematics from Windows 3.1

1. Place the diskette in a drive, say drive A.
2. From Program Manager, double-click on the DOS icon in the Main program group. Or, exit Windows.
3. Type A: and press the Enter key.
4. Type CD \FINITE and press the Enter key.
5. Type FINITE1 or FINITE2 and press the Enter key.

To Invoke Explorations in Finite Mathematics from DOS on a computers that does not use the Windows operating system.

1. Place the diskette in a drive, say drive A.
2. Type A: and press the Enter key.
3. Type CD \FINITE and press the Enter key.
4. Type FINITE1 or FINITE2 and press the Enter key.

Matrices and Systems of Inequalities On Diskette

Matrices and systems of inequalities appearing in examples from the text have been saved on the diskette with either suggestive names or names of the form CxSxEx. For instance, the matrix appearing in Chapter 6, Section 4, Example 2 has the name C6S4E2. The list of saved matrices appropriate to the current routine is displayed on the screen whenever you request "Load a matrix saved on disk."

Windows 3.1, 95, 98, or 2000 can be used to capture the entire screen into a picture that can be printed from Paint or inserted into a word processing document, such as Word.

To capture the contents of the screen and print it from Paint:
1. Press the Print Screen key.
2. Return to Windows and invoke Paint from the Accessories program group.
3. Press Ctrl+V to place a copy of the screen in the window. (Note: That is, hold down the Ctrl key and press the V key.)
4. Press Ctrl+I to invert the colors on the screen. (Otherwise, your printout will appear as white-on-black.)
5. Make sure your printer is turned on and ready to print.
6. Press Ctrl+P to print the contents of the Paint window.

To capture the contents of the screen and paste it into a Word document:
1. Carry out steps 1 through 5 above.
2. Press Ctrl+C to place a copy of the screen into the clipboard.
3. Invoke Word, open the document into which the picture is to be inserted, and move the cursor to the desired location for the picture.
4. Press Ctrl+V to insert the picture.
5. Alter the size of the picture by clicking on it and dragging one of its handles.

Visual Calculus

The Visual Calculus software enhances the visualization and therefore the understanding of the *ideas* behind the calculus. Visual Calculus can be run on any IBM compatible computer.

To Invoke Visual Calculus from Windows 95 (or later version):
1. Place the Visual Calculus diskette in a drive, say drive A.
2. With Windows 95 and Windows 98, click the Start button, point to Programs, and click MS-DOS Prompt. With Windows 2000, click the Start button, point to Programs, point to Accessories, and click Command Prompt.
3. If the DOS or Command window does not fill the screen, hold down the Alt key and press the Enter key to enlarge the window.
4. Type A: and press the Enter key.
5. Type CD \VC and press the Enter key.
6. Type VC and press the Enter key.

To Invoke Visual Calculus from Windows 3.1:
1. Place the diskette in a drive, say drive A.
2. From Program Manager, double-click on the DOS icon in the Main program group. Or, exit Windows.
3. Type A: and press the Enter key.
4. Type CD \VC and press the Enter key.
5. Type VC and press the Enter key.

To Invoke Visual Calculus from a computer not containing Windows:
1. Place the diskette in a drive, say drive A.
2. Type A: and press the Enter key.
3. Type CD \VC and press the Enter key.
4. Type VC and press the Enter key.

Note: If you are using a slow computer, first copy the files from the diskette into a subdirectory of your hard drive and run VC from that subdirectory. Otherwise, there will be some noticeable delays in the execution of the program.

To select a routine from a menu, do one of the following:
a) Press the first letter of the routine.
b) Press the down-arrow and up-arrow keys to highlight the routine, and press Enter.
c) Double-click the routine with a mouse.

To manage a screen used to display functions:

a) Use the right- and left-arrow keys to move the crosshairs around the graph – or click on a new point with the mouse. (Notice information about the point at the crosshairs is displayed in the upper-left part of the screen.) Use the down- and up-arrow keys to decrease or increase the distance that the crosshairs moves.

b) To invoke a bracketed command found in the left column, either press the key surrounded by <>, or click on the command with the mouse.

To manage a screen used to input functions:

a) Use Tab (or Shift+Tab) to move forward (or backwards) from region to region.

b) Buttons are activated by pressing Alt+*highlighted letter* or by moving to the button and pressing the Enter key.

c) With a mouse, you can move to a box (or activate a button) by clicking on the box (or button).

d) Whenever a function is requested, the user can either type in a function or press F4 to select from lists of functions in the textbook. To select an item from a list, highlight the item by either cursoring down to it, clicking on it, or pressing the first digit of the item one or more times, and then press Enter. (Alternatively, double-click on the item.) To remove the lists without making a selection, press F4 again.

e) A caret (^) must be used for exponentiation. (For example, $x^5 \sin x$ is written x^5sin x.) The following functions can appear in expressions: log (common log), ln (natural log), sin, cos, tan, cot, csc, sec, arcsin, arccos, arctan, arcsec, arccsc, arccot, exp (same as e^x, but more efficient), sqr (square root), fact (factorial), int, sgn. In the routine "Graphs of Functions", the expression for $g(x)$ can involve $f(x)$, e.g. $f(x-2)$, and the expression for $h(x)$ can involve $f(x)$ and/or $g(x)$, e.g. $f(g(x))$.

f) Press P to display the pi symbol and press I to display the infinity symbol. In a numeric input box press S to display the square root symbol.

To print the graph of a function

The graphing routines have a "Print graph(s)" command that works with most dot-matrix or laser printers and prints a smooth curve. If the command does not work with your printer, you can produce a printout of the screen with one of the following two methods.

Method A: (For computers that have Windows)
1. Press the Print Screen key.
2. Return to Windows and invoke Paint from the Accessories program group.
3. Press Ctrl+V to place a copy of the graphics screen in the window.
4. Press Ctrl+I to invert the colors on the screen. (Otherwise, your printout will appear as white-on-black.)
5. Make sure your printer is turned on and ready to print.
6. Press Ctrl+P to print the contents of the Paint window.

Method B: (Requires DOS only or Windows 3.1)
1. To prepare for graphics screen dumps, you must enter the command GRAPHICS from DOS before invoking Visual Calculus.
2. In Visual Calculus, press Shift+PrintScreen at any time to produce a printout of the screen.

To enter functions:

Mathematical Expression	Computer Expression	Mathematical Expression	Computer Expression
x^2	x^2	e^x	exp(x) or e^x
$x^{1/2}$	sqr(x) or x^(1/2)	$x^{1/3}$	cbr(x) or x^(1/3)
$\log_e x$	ln x or ln(x)	$\log_{10} x$	log x or log(x)
$\ln 3x$	ln(3x)	$x^2 \ln x$	x^2ln x
$x!$	fact(x)	$[x]$	int(x)

Summary of Operation for Input Screen

\<Tab\>	move around input screen
Shift+\<Tab\>	move around input screen in reverse order
Alt+*highlighted letter*	push button marked with the letter
Click Mouse	move to input box or activate button
F4	obtain list of appropriate functions from textbook (must be used in a function input box)
P	obtain the pi symbol
S	obtain the square root symbol (cannot be used in input box or a function)
I	obtain the infinity symbol (used only in Limits and Series)

To copy a function from one input box to another:

1. Place the cursor at the beginning of the function.
2. Hold down a shift key and press \<End\>. (The function is now highlighted.)
3. Press Ctrl+Ins or Ctrl+C. (The function is now saved in the clipboard.)
4. Move to another function input box either in the same routine or in another routine.
5. Press Shift+Ins or Ctrl+V.

Invocation options

When Visual Calculus invoked with the command VC, bw and/or cga can be added to affect the operation of the program. For instance, to obtain the bw option, enter VC bw.

Option	Effect
bw	All graphics will appear in blue and white. This option should be invoked if you are doing screen dumps. (It isn't needed when using the Print command.) This option might be helpful when projecting images onto a large screen or when using a monochrome monitor.
cga	Emulates Color Graphics Adapter. In graphics mode, graphs and text will be thicker. This option might be helpful in a classroom when projecting images onto a large screen.

Main Routines

Analyze a Function and its Derivatives displays the graphs of one or more of f, f', f'' and displays the values of these functions at any point. A Solve command finds zeros, relative extreme points, and inflection points. A Tangent Line command draws a tangent line to $f(x)$ or $f'(x)$ at the crosshairs.

Examine Solutions of Differential Equations graphs the solution of a differential equation of the form $y' = g(t, y)$ with an initial value and determines the coordinates of points on the graph. Graphs with different initial values can be superimposed. Successive Euler approximations may be displayed.

Function Evaluator (1 and 2 variables) displays the value of a function and its derivatives. [1 variable: $f(x)$, $f'(x)$, and $f''(x)$ are displayed. 2 variables: $f(x, y)$ and its two first partial derivatives are displayed.] A single push of a button increases the value of x (and/or y) by an amount input by the user and recomputes the function values.

Graphs of Functions sketches the graphs of 1, 2, or 3 functions. The coordinates of points can be found by moving crosshairs with the arrow keys or clicking on the point with a mouse. A Solve command finds the zeros of a function or the intersection points of two functions. A Zoom command enlarges a rectangular region.

Integrals, Definite calculates the definite integral of a function. Also, the routine illustrates five numerical methods.

Least Squares calculates the line of best fit and also allows the user to move a line around the screen to find the best fit.

Observe Limit of f(x) as x approaches a evaluates $f(a + h)$ and $f(a - h)$ for $h = .1$, $.01$, $.001$, ... and guesses the limit. Can have a = infinity.

Series and Partial Sums evaluates finite and infinite sums.

Demonstration Routines

Ball Thrown Straight Up shows the connection between the motion of a ball and the graph of its height function

Car in Motion moves a car across the screen with its position, and hence velocity, determined by a function input by the user.

Garden Fencing Problem shows the connection between a function to be optimized and the corresponding physical problem.

Plot Cosine and Sine Functions traces out the graphs of the sine and cosine functions as a point moves around the unit circle.

Secant Line Approaching Tangent Line moves a secant line closer and closer to a tangent line.

Tangent Line Approaching Curve illustrates the fact that locally a curve looks like its tangent line.